Australia & the Pacific

IAN HOSKINS has worked as an academic and public historian in Sydney for 30 years. His book *Sydney Harbour: A history* won the Queensland Premier's Literary Prize for History in 2010 and *Coast*, his history of the New South Wales coast, won the New South Wales Premier's Prize for Community and Regional History in 2014. He was the CH Currey Fellow at the State Library of NSW in 2019 exploring the Library's extensive Pacific collections.

*To Lisa who first suggested a Pacific trip and made the arrangements.
It was a wonderful journey, thanks for everything.*

'A captivating general history of Australia viewed in a Pacific context … Hoskins's meticulously researched and well-crafted account of Australia's place in the Pacific certainly deserves a wide readership.'
ROSS FITZGERALD

≋

'Ian Hoskins has written a major book. It is a fundamentally important subject, and is timely, original, fair-minded and accessible … a fascinating history that shows how Australia's relationships with the Pacific have shaped and informed each of our worlds. He reveals the major underlying historiographical and political disputes with subtlety, clarity and power, while always displaying a remarkable fairness of judgement.'
IAIN MCCALMAN

≋

'It is possibly no secret that I have been a passionate campaigner for Australia – and especially the Australian media – to pay more attention to the island nations to Australia's North and East. Therefore, I am more than happy to see the publication of Ian Hoskins's *Australia & the Pacific*. I spent the majority of my career as a journalist visiting and reporting on these island nations and I believe that today it is even more crucial for us to understand exactly what is going on in our region.'
SEAN DORNEY

Australia & the Pacific

A history
Ian Hoskins

NEWSOUTH

A NewSouth book

Published by
NewSouth Publishing
University of New South Wales Press Ltd
University of New South Wales
Sydney NSW 2052
AUSTRALIA
newsouthpublishing.com

© Ian Hoskins 2021
First published 2021

10 9 8 7 6 5 4 3 2 1

This book is copyright. Apart from any fair dealing for the purpose of private study, research, criticism or review, as permitted under the *Copyright Act*, no part of this book may be reproduced by any process without written permission. Inquiries should be addressed to the publisher.

A catalogue record for this book is available from the National Library of Australia

ISBN: 9781742235691 (paperback)
       9781742245317 (ebook)
       9781742249872 (ePDF)

Design Josephine Pajor-Markus
Cover design Peter Long
Cover image Shutterstock / Nejron Photo
Printer Griffin Press, part of Ovato

All reasonable efforts were taken to obtain permission to use copyright material reproduced in this book, but in some cases copyright could not be traced. The author welcomes information in this regard.

This book is printed on paper using fibre supplied from plantation or sustainably managed forests.

Contents

Introduction *1*

1 Shifting continents *20*
2 First peoples *41*
3 Converging on Australia *56*
4 In the wake of Spain *72*
5 A Pacific colony *88*
6 An ocean of opportunity *114*
7 Miners and mutineers *141*
8 Saving souls and taking slaves *160*
9 Australia's Pacific *189*
10 A White Australia *203*
11 World War One and its aftermath *215*
12 World War Two *230*
13 Governing Papua and New Guinea *261*
14 Learning from the Pacific *280*
15 Post-war Australia meets the Cold War Pacific *308*
16 Confronting communism and decoupling a colony *324*
17 The end of White Australia, refugees and reassessments *343*
18 Pacific solutions *358*
19 Pacific Islanders in Australia *384*
20 Climate change *402*

Afterword: Mammon or millennial Eden? *422*

Acknowledgments *427*

Bibliography *429*

Notes *447*

Index *477*

Introduction

'Our repressed Oceanic memories'

The Pacific Ocean has washed, scoured and thumped Australia's east coast for more than five million years. The continent had, by then, nearly reached its present position on the ocean's edge, having parted company with Gondwana some 40 million years beforehand. During that time the Pacific's waters rose and fell repeatedly and the continent was shaped and reshaped accordingly. With each exposure and inundation, reefs and marine ecologies have come and gone and been rebuilt. The climate, too, was affected and, with that, the ocean influenced the land.

The last great sea level rise ended just 6000 years ago. Aboriginal people have lived along that ever-changing coast for much longer, adapting to successive environmental conditions. They have been people of rivers, salt marshes, mangroves, forests, dunes and beaches. In 1770 the Pacific delivered James Cook and the company of the naval bark *Endeavour* from Tahiti and New Zealand to the far south of Australia and up to its tropical tip. There the Englishman claimed everything he had seen for his king, George III. As a consequence 11 ships arrived unannounced and uninvited in Sydney Harbour in 1788. Thousands followed that First Fleet carrying passengers, sailors, stock and seed – the willing, the dragooned, the pioneering species of new ecologies. Their arrival led directly to dramatic environmental change and the dispossession of the first harbour people. Ultimately, first Australians up and down the Pacific coast and across the continent lost their land. Australia's deep past and its modern history is intrinsically connected to the Pacific.

Some of those early migrants and mariners lie in the first European burial ground on Sydney Harbour's northern shore, high up in a suburb appropriately named after a ship's lookout, Crows Nest. It is a place I know well as the area's local historian. St Thomas's Cemetery is now a small park but all the human remains and many of the monuments are still there. Graves are normally associated with quietude, but they can speak loudly of local, national and international stories if one spends time studying the stones and making connections. The tall Celtic cross of Commodore James Goodenough is one of the more 'audible' monuments. From 1873 to 1875 he was commander of the flotilla that comprised the Australia Station, Britain's west Pacific fleet based in Sydney Harbour. In that capacity Goodenough played a part in projecting British power into the world's largest ocean. He assisted with the annexation of Fiji in 1874 and policing islands where British subjects, including Australian colonists, operated as traders, planters and missionaries. Australia Station vessels helped to regulate the trade in Pacific island labour which many, including Goodenough, regarded as kidnapping and enslavement. Blackbirding was the vernacular expression. In August 1875 Goodenough sailed on the flagship HMS *Pearl* to Santa Cruz Island in the Solomon group, where the unwelcome activities of the blackbirders had created ill-will. As he moved through a village the Commodore was hit by an arrow. His condition worsened over several days aboard ship and he died before landfall in Sydney. In accordance with his wishes, Goodenough's body – and those of two sailors similarly wounded – were returned for interment at St Thomas's Cemetery. Steam power hastened the *Pearl*'s return.

The farewell of James Goodenough was a particularly reverential moment in colonial New South Wales. Thousands watched the casket being rowed from the *Pearl* to Milsons Point then trundled from harbourside to gravesite where the man, whose name seemed to epitomise the esteem in which he was held, was finally laid to rest. Goodenough was the Victorian-era officer and Christian gentleman *par excellence*. Indeed, having forbad the taking of life in retribution for his impending death, he was declared a 'Christian hero'. Goodenough's passing, in the words of one report, 'produced a deep sensation in the metropolis'.[1] The *Sydney Mail* made explicit the connection of place and deed: 'he now sleeps in our midst, beneath Australian skies, and on shores washed by those Pacific waves he sought to redeem from the taint of slavery'.[2]

That so many turned out for the Commodore suggests that the connection between Australia and the Pacific was keenly felt in 1875. White Australia sat nervously and expectantly on the edge of an ocean that contained at once the threat of invasion or sudden death for those who ventured there, and the potential for personal wealth and colonial influence for the intrepid. By the last quarter of the 19th century, just as the Commodore was felled, the belief that Australia's 'star' was rising over the Pacific was becoming commonplace. The *Sydney Mail*'s reference to slavery is evidence, too, of the moral arguments that accompanied that increasing ambition and power.

Although St Thomas's was not a formal naval burial ground, there are many mariners buried there. It was a custom which seems to have begun in 1850 with the interment of Captain Owen Stanley, who in HMS *Rattlesnake*, charted the east coast of Australia and the islands of the Torres Strait. The Owen Stanley Range, which divides Papua New Guinea, is named after him. Some local residents may be aware of the park's maritime and Pacific association. Many, I know, are not. Though we live in an island nation, Australians do not generally acknowledge their historical connections to the ocean – at least beyond sand and surf.[3] 'Our land is girt by sea' as the national anthem tells us, but Australia's sense of self has been indelibly formed by a plethora of stories from the interior and some from overseas. The World War One battles on the Gallipoli Peninsula in far-away Turkey still loom large in the collective consciousness, as any observer of Anzac Day will testify.

Once revered and now obscure, James Goodenough is just one example of what historian Warwick Anderson has called 'our repressed

Oceanic memories'.[4] Just how national narratives are formed and fixed is an intriguing question. The national amnesia with regard to the Pacific is not for want of good writing. The literature on Australia and the Pacific is rich and I have relied upon it heavily and appreciatively. The scholarship ranges across history, and the natural and social sciences. Yet so formative was the nationalism which emerged a century after colonisation that our collective consciousness still inhabits an imagined bush. Farmers 'battling' fires, droughts, floods – struggles with the very land itself – remain a touchstone for defining the Australian character. That the continent is so huge means there is an endless array of rural narratives with which to distinguish us from other peoples. The abundance of space has allowed another revered national typology to emerge: the suburban dweller. That 'battler' balances work and family and works hard to pay the bills.

Australia's historical and demographic connections to Europe are also enduring, so that the national gaze frequently looks beyond the Pacific horizon. That dichotomy between 'geography and history' was evoked by the long-serving conservative prime minister John Howard during his time in office in the late 1990s and early 2000s. Ironically, to my mind, he did so out of concern that Australians were denying their British origins and agonising too much about their place in the region, Asia particularly. His political and rhetorical sparring partner, Paul Keating, argued the opposite. Of Irish heritage, the Labor prime minister was never nostalgic about Australia's imperial links. The nation, he maintained, needed to engage with the Asia-Pacific region and leave the British past behind. Such engagement was possible for a nation which had discarded its race-based self-identification and immigration policy, once supported by both major parties. 'Ideas that Australia is a western outpost which drifted by mistake to the wrong part of the globe ... are certainly futile ... they are wrong.'[5] With ethnically defined immigration – the policies of White Australia – a receding memory, Keating could emphasise the significance of geography. Howard struggled with the transition.

Introduction

Australia's Anglo-Celtic cultural foundation remains dominant despite the migration from Vietnam, Hong Kong and China which has organically transformed our sense of self and consequently broadened our focus somewhat. Perhaps also because there has been no comparable stream of newcomers from Papua New Guinea, Vanuatu, Kiribati and elsewhere, the 'Pacific' half of Australia's Asia-Pacific region is so often neglected.

That neglect belies the depth of the personal links between Australians and the region, the South-West Pacific particularly. While the number of those who claim Pacific heritage is relatively low, particularly when compared to New Zealand, countless thousands have lived there or worked there. Many Australians were born in the islands as the children of administrators, missionaries, aid workers and volunteers. Tens of thousands have relatives who fought in New Guinea or nearby in the 1940s. Yet even the potential of war to forge national mythology is unrealised in Australia's Pacific story. While the Kokoda Track is a place of pilgrimage for those whose forefathers halted the Japanese advance near the end of its tortuous route, there is much greater emphasis on Australia's far-flung efforts in World War One than those in the second great conflict when Australian territory – New Guinea and Papua – was invaded. In 2015, many millions of dollars were spent on commemorating the 100th anniversary of the landing at Gallipoli in April, while the 70th Victory in the Pacific Day on 15 August passed with barely a hurrah. It rarely rates more than a mention.

≋

'We are one but we are many'

My own curiosity about Australia's Pacific ties was piqued while writing histories of Sydney Harbour and the New South Wales coast; and while pondering the graves of Owen Stanley, Commodore Goodenough and other men of the Australia Station. I also hoped writing a book on the subject might help to mend the national amnesia about the Pacific. The story takes in the ocean to its vast rim – north, south, east and west – but the focus, unsurprisingly, is on those places with which Australia has had most pronounced interaction. It begins with the movement of continents which formed the ocean and the migration of animals and people into that watery expanse millions of years later. The wider Pacific diaspora took place thousands of years after the arrival of people in Australia. The cultures that emerged on the ancient continent, from at least 65 000 years ago, were quite different from those which developed later in the islands; places that themselves were much younger and smaller. With the exception of some cultural exchange around the Torres Strait, it seems Aboriginal cultures were unaffected by the migration which created the regions we call Melanesia, Micronesia and Polynesia. The last great movement of those of Polynesian descent stopped short on Norfolk Island, after colonising New Zealand.

Different though the islands were and are from the neighbouring 'great south land', it was an Islander from the Torres Strait who overturned modern Australia's creation myth that this was a land belonging to no one before James Cook took it for Britain. Eddie Mabo's attempt to secure title to his garden plot on the island of Mer led to the recognition of native title across the continent in 1992. That is one of the most profound of Australia's Pacific impacts.

Japan and the United States (US) feature, not least because Australia fought a war against the former and looked to the latter as a protector – a successor to Great Britain. When a US fleet sailed into Sydney Harbour in 1908, many Australians expressed relief that they shared the Pacific with such a great 'white cousin'. The US remains Australia's most important partner and the transformation of the Pacific into an 'American Lake' after 1945 afforded considerable security to Australia, though many craved more as the long-held concern of invasion from a crowded Asia merged with the perceived threat of communism from that same region.

Introduction

Sitting on the ocean's north-western boundary, China had generated fear and loathing since the 1850s. That huge and consequential country was not far away, even in the age of sail. Australian colonies got their tea and ceramics from there and its first entrepreneurs made fortunes selling seal skins and sandalwood into the Chinese market. But trade did little to break down the sense of humanity's fundamental differences. And that only hardened with the influx of Chinese gold seekers from the 1850s. Though they were sojourners rather than immigrants, the presence of the 'Celestials' helped coalesce the racial definition of the colonies. And while Australia had no direct role in the Opium Wars which signalled the end of China's international power and the beginning of that nation's 'century of humiliation', and was barely involved in quelling the Boxer Rebellion that confirmed its impotence, colonial politicians and writers frequently and openly expressed contempt for the country and its people. Memory of these humiliations at the hands of Europeans fuels an aggressive nationalism in the new Asian superpower, whose leaders frequently threaten to 'punish' those who defy its view of the world.

From the turn of the 21st century China became the world's factory. Its ability to produce all manner of goods cheaply by virtue of a vast workforce labouring to pull themselves out of poverty had a dramatic impact upon Australia's own manufacturing base, given a modern footing after World War Two but struggling 40 years later with overseas competition. China's efficiency and its demand for natural resources returned Australia to a reliance on primary production, the export of mineral wealth and agricultural commodities. China has made Australia wealthy as never before but in doing so increased its dependence upon the Asian superpower, which brings with it economic and strategic vulnerabilities. That reliance upon primary production has also made Australia's transition from a carbon-based economy highly political.

It was in the islands of the South-West Pacific that European Australia first projected its influence and power; trading pork with

Tahiti in the earliest years of a founding settlement, and then taking sandalwood from Fiji as that convict colony was putting down commercial roots. Economies established, and convictism ended, colonists looked to Vanuatu, the Solomon Islands and New Guinea to provide cheap labour for a sugar industry in the continent's far north. It was that trade in people and the rancour it created which led to the demise of Commodore Goodenough. By the end of the 19th century, the South-West Pacific was seen as a natural sphere of influence for the white colonies. Queensland annexed islands in the Torres Strait in the 1870s and then joined with the other colonies in exhorting Britain to follow suit in Papua, so that the Germans might be kept at bay. It did so, somewhat reluctantly, in 1887. Papua was passed on to the new Australian Commonwealth as a colony in 1906 and New Guinea – an artificial creation of European politicians and cartographers – was made an Australian territory after the rival Germans were ousted in the initial weeks of World War One.

The people who lived there would not be displaced by a 'settler society' and therefore were not generally dismissed as the doomed representatives of a primitive race, as were Australia's Indigenous people. That distinction, informed by context as much as anything, was one of many human 'differences' considered by Europeans as they encountered the Pacific through the 18th and 19th centuries. Motivated by the Enlightenment's zeal for discovery, description, variation and understanding, British and French explorers documented what they found in words and pictures and sweeping collections of artefacts. The interlopers variously compared those cultures to their own, sometimes favourably as in the case of Polynesia, but usually not so. In the process, perceived difference helped the explorers and colonisers define themselves. The vast Pacific shaped the Europeans' mindsets not least because their gradual intellectual grasp of the world created a global view – quite literally – not shared by the myriad Indigenous people who had lived beside and within its expanse for thousands of years previously. The Australian historian Bernard Smith explored that transformation in a work which revolutionised the writing of history, *European Vision and the South Pacific*, first published in 1960. That wonderful book has influenced my writing very much. In particular, it prompted me to consider how the Pacific has shaped modern Australia.

Self-definition was one of the goals of the anthropology which emerged alongside discovery and colonisation through to the early 20th century. For Bronislaw Malinowski, who undertook fieldwork in the Trobriand Islands of New Guinea, using Australia as a springboard, 'savage humanity' provided clues about 'the origin of human customs, beliefs and institutions'. A believer in cultural evolution, Malinowski knew the world's people to be of one origin. In the previous century, anthropology had challenged the biblically based belief in monogenesis, which held to the belief that there is only one humanity, with theories of polygenesis or different human species. While monogenesis became scientific orthodoxy, that did not preclude the widespread acceptance of eugenics, one of the hardhearted offshoots of Charles Darwin's thesis of species origins, and its terrible campaigns of sterilisation and genocide in pursuit of 'racial purity'.

But in the 50 years following Malinowski, there also emerged a relativistic approach to the study of human society, one which eschewed moral judgments, hierarchies and the use of the term 'savage'. Modern anthropology might be seen to celebrate the diversity within the single human species. The long development of that discipline and the empathy it encouraged mirrored and assisted the development of modern human rights. 'All human beings are born free and equal in dignity and rights', was the assertion of Article One of the Declaration of Human Rights in 1948, following the devastating war against genocidal fascism in Europe.

Throughout the century and a half in which anthropology explored cultures and wrestled with obvious differences between peoples, Christianity held firm to the notion of a single humanity, albeit with many gradations of good and evil. This hierarchy, of course, was used to justify awful cruelties. In America, white Christian slave owners degraded and abused black people, apparently safe in the knowledge that equality under their god only applied in heaven. In contrast, white Christians in Australia were among the most vocal critics of blackbirding – hence the veneration of James Goodenough. For all its hypocrisies, Christianity has played a significant role in the development of modern human rights, not least by turning the figure of an executed political criminal into a god worthy of worship. To empathise with the victim went against the tenets of many ancient and traditional beliefs. Humility existed as a philosophical virtue before Jesus was crucified but thereafter it sat like a moral burr under the saddles of the mighty who professed their faith in the Christian god.

Through the delivery of people and ideas, the impact of European philosophy and religion upon the Pacific has been fundamental and paradoxical. It has unified and devastated, liberated and disempowered. But I believe that the elevation of human dignity over honour-based social systems, and the challenge to practices based upon violence, prejudice and racism, is one of the great gifts to the world of the Enlightenment and Christianity – at least in its kinder manifestations. The concomitant idea of a common humanity runs throughout this book.

Yet universalism has existed in constant tension with difference. The degree to which commonality has been accepted or denied is central, I believe, to understanding modern Australia's ambiguous relationship to the Pacific. That, too, is a theme which I explore. The very real tension between geography and history referred to by John Howard has meant that European Australians have variously considered themselves to be integrated with and apart from the Pacific. Prime Minister Scott Morrison spoke of Australia's Pacific 'family' yet prioritised his perception of the national interest, in particular the need to keep mining coal despite its effect upon sea levels in the Pacific, over the common interest.

Introduction

Paradoxically, perhaps, the path to 'oneness' has come as a result of a general acceptance of heterogeneity or what is more commonly called 'diversity'. When I sailed into Sydney Harbour as a young immigrant in 1966, the White Australia policy was in just the first stages of dissolution and Australia was anything but diverse in its demographic make-up. My parents had the right to vote by virtue of their Britishness rather than any oath of citizenship. There has been, then, a dramatic shift in less than a lifetime. This country's proximity to the Pacific has played an under-appreciated but significant role in that shift.

As the British cultural theorist Robert Young pointed out 25 years ago, diversity is 'the self-conscious identity' of most, if not all, Western democracies.[6] The dualisms of the previous centuries – black/white, man/woman, primitive/advanced – are questioned and reconfigured now more than ever.[7] That there is no longer a single Australian identity but many is axiomatic. Diversity is embedded within myriad corporate mission statements. 'We are one but we are many' is the refrain in the rousing anthem played often by the Australian Broadcasting Corporation (ABC). Respecting the ever-splintering constituency makes the job of securing power very difficult for progressive parties. Those on the right are generally less accommodating of so-called 'identity politics'. Since Young's writing, however, a populist nationalism has emerged in many countries, in reaction to the acceptance of diversity. Identity is no less important for this type of nationalism. Since the 1990s Coalition governments have successfully put forward archetypes of commonsense farmers, suburban 'mums and dads', miners, small business owners as their constituency – the 'lifters' as opposed to the 'leaners' from the other side. Significantly that image of the nation starkly differentiates Australia from its close Pacific neighbours. I explore that more fully in later chapters.

AUSTRALIA & THE PACIFIC

≋

'Big states are rude and nasty'

This book was written in interesting times. Several events occurred during its production which influenced the outcome, both explicitly and implicitly. The impact of Donald Trump's presidency from 2016 to 2020 cannot be overestimated. He was, as foreign policy expert Hugh White suggested in a diplomatic understatement, the 'embodiment' of a nation 'ill-at-ease with itself and with the image of its place in the world'.[8] That is significant for Australia because we widely regard the alliance with the United States as the lynchpin of the nation's security in the Asia-Pacific region. Further, for more than 150 years, that country has sat on the far side of the Pacific as a comparative model for modern Australia – prompting visions of possible futures. Ethnicity has played an important part in that familiarity. For much of the time the US was recognised as a 'white' nation by white Australians. Americans of European descent were kin. Islanders and Asian peoples of the western Pacific were different. More recently the affinity has been ideological. The Australia–US alliance is not just a relationship of strategic convenience but one that is maintained by shared values, as we are regularly reminded from both sides of the Pacific. The thousands of Australians and Americans killed in New Guinea fighting Japan's fascistic militarism is compelling evidence of that. Leaders of both countries played pivotal roles in the creation of the United Nations, which emerged in the aftermath of that conflict.

The chaos that unfolded from 2016 was a sobering corrective to any notion that democracy once secured, however imperfectly, is assured. Trump was an Orwellian and narcissistic demagogue who debased the very epistemological and ethical foundation of truth. The secular and religious humanism that coalesced after the Enlightenment was threatened in the US as it had been trashed in Germany in the 1930s. Unprecedented and polarising though he may have been, America's

Introduction

45th president merely amplified long-term trends and divisions extending back to the nation's Civil War and beyond into history. The political power of white supremacy will continue to divide the 'United States' for many years.

Trump's messages and tactics resonated locally. Throughout his term, many of those on Australia's political right seemed quite unconcerned by his contempt for democratic institutions and simple decency. Rather Trump was an amusing, even useful, disrupter who destabilised and upset the greater enemy – what the veteran foreign affairs commentator Greg Sheridan disdainfully labelled 'the left liberal establishment'.[9] For the right in Australia and the US, Trump's brand of populism, his support for 'the people' against an amorphous elite, outweighed his shortcomings. Indeed, it made him something of a defender of democracy.

Australia has also been riven by division. In the past decade sitting prime ministers have been deposed four times by colleagues as their parties tried to gauge the mercurial moods and interests of a diversifying electorate. Australia's culture wars mirror those across the Pacific, not least because they are prosecuted on behalf of the right in both countries by the highly partisan media outlets owned by Australian-turned-American 'mogul' Rupert Murdoch, for whom Sheridan writes. Once willing to support social democrats in Australia, the immensely wealthy Murdoch seems driven by a desire to disrupt and influence as much as by any ideology. On both continents, his commentators wield great power. Coalition prime minister Malcolm Turnbull saw the hand of the media conglomerate in his second dismissal. It operated, he reflected, 'like a political party'.[10] Former Labor leader Kevin Rudd, who was also twice dismissed, has a similar view. The Murdoch media typically mounts a populist defence of 'ordinary' people who, they claim, are ridiculed when they are not being ignored by 'the elite'. Where that media stirs the political pot in the US and Australia, sowing seeds of cynicism and doubt, a range of conspiracy theories about climate science, deep states and the displacement of white people cascade across the internet.

AUSTRALIA & THE PACIFIC

The Australian Prime Minister Scott Morrison, who assumed office in the most recent parliamentary 'coup' in 2019, mirrored Trump's populism. Morrison shared his counterpart's fondness for coal, his disregard for climate science and his preference for wearing caps – the instantly recognisable accoutrement of the common man. The dramatic shift in attitude to climate change which followed the commencement of Joe Biden's presidency in early 2021, left Australia isolated and the Coalition government scrambling to catch up while maintaining its long-held belief in the viable future of fossil-based fuels. Meanwhile Pacific Island states continue to regard Australia's politicised arguments about climate change and coal mining with anxiety and bewilderment. Rising seas and altered weather will render many islands and atolls uninhabitable. Fortunately for Australia, the two men differed in their responses to the Covid-19 pandemic, which affected both countries from March 2020. Hundreds of thousands died under Trump's inept ego-driven leadership. Morrison's populist instincts at the outbreak of the crisis were overridden by his pragmatism so that the crisis in Australia was not politicised to the degree it was in the US and thousands of lives were saved.

More generally Australians' confidence in the US was shaken during Donald Trump's presidency, evidence of the cultural difference between the two nations.[11] Trust in China has plummeted. Reports of espionage, the imprisonment of Australian nationals, intimidation of the local Australian–Chinese community, a politicised trade policy and hectoring rhetoric on the part of the Chinese Communist Party (CCP) have all played a part in that heightened suspicion. Australia's largest trading partner is also seen as its greatest threat. The nation's leaders and experts agonise over how best to plot a path between obsequious reliance on a US clearly capable of capriciousness, and acquiescence towards our main trading partner, with whom Australia shares fewer values.

Our own history with China has not helped to clarify the issues. Australia feared that country for all the wrong reasons for more than a century from the 1850s. Now, however, legitimate concerns at covert operations in the cyber space and the real world are all too easily dismissed by reference to the latent 'xenophobia' of those raising alarms. The legacy of White Australia and its related Cold War framework still colours and curtails useful debate.

The issue of human rights is particularly vexed. Many Australians – Chinese–Australians among them – feel their government should speak out against the oppression of Hong Kong citizens, or ethnic minorities such as the Uyghur people, who are corralled by the hundreds of thousands in 're-education centres' that appear to be little more than prisons. In 2021 the British Foreign Minister accused the CCP of presiding over 'internment camps, arbitrary detention, political re-education, forced labour, torture, forced sterilisation ... on an industrial scale'. It is, he added, 'Barbarism we all hoped was lost to another era'.[12] Australia's great advocate of Asian engagement, Paul Keating had earlier dismissed such reports with characteristic bluntness. On matters of human rights, Australia's liberal media was guilty of 'pious belchings'; on China's regional assertiveness, the nation's national security agencies were channelling 'phobic' preconceptions rooted in the Cold War.[13] The former prime minister is the supreme realist for whom values-based diplomacy is ineffective, even counterproductive. 'Big states are rude and nasty', he pointed out; the US no less than China.

Keating's unsentimental realism has a long tradition in Australia, not least in the foreign policy of Billy Hughes, who interpreted the national interest primarily through the lens of race and who regarded the nearby islands as little more than a defensive rampart against Asia. With that looking glass shattered by the 1970s, prime minister Gough Whitlam readily embraced Communist China – despite the horrors of the Cultural Revolution. A social democrat in his own country, Whitlam had little time for the messianism which justified American interventions across the world. He may well have agreed with the British sinologist Martin Jacques' recent analysis of the contemporary problem of confronting a rising China: 'the Western paradigm [holds] that we are universal; that everyone should be, one day will be, is required to be like us. That there is only one modernity in the world, it's our modernity. Frankly this is not a sustainable position'.[14] But where does that leave the issue of universal human rights and the belief in a common cause with minorities and political activists? How does Australia do business with a nation that engages in 'industrial scale' slavery? Might not Australian concern at their plight be seen as a laudable defence of a common humanity after so many years of emphasising difference?

China's spreading influence in the western Pacific has led directly to Australia's so-called Pacific 'Step Up', an obvious instance of self-interested cause and effect which prompted the veteran Pacific reporter Sean Dorney to remark sardonically, 'Thank God for China'.[15] Dorney is one of many who have decried Australia's declining interest in the local region over recent decades. As Chinese companies take up construction contracts throughout the islands and reports occasionally circulate of the possibility of a permanent Chinese naval presence there, the Australian Government has, indeed, become more attentive. There is increased aid and plans for a two-billion-dollar infrastructure bank. Bemused critics of governmental neglect point to the soft power efficacy squandered by cuts to the ABC's Pacific services in 2014. Dorney, with his wealth of local knowledge and earned trust, was jettisoned in that process. The ABC is a pillar of the 'left liberal establishment' for those on the right, and the budget cuts it suffered under conservative prime minister Tony Abbott were widely interpreted as one of many fronts in Australia's culture war. If that was the motivation, Pacific relations were collateral damage.

In 2017 news of China and Donald Trump was displaced for a time by the referendum to allow same-sex marriage. Australians voted overwhelmingly to overturn the long-held binary belief that marriage is between a man and a woman. That shift in opinion came remarkably quickly, just a generation after the widespread and often murderous persecution of gay men. For those on the conservative right, the outcome was evidence of the power of the liberal elite. Supporters

Introduction

saw a triumph for diversity. The debates which ensued revolved around discrimination, religious freedom and the difference between hateful and free speech.

That discussion became a shouting match when a young, devout Christian footballer of Pacific heritage called Israel Folau warned his fellow Australians of the awful wrath his one true god had in store for homosexuals and other 'sinners'. There were contradictions, even hypocrisy, expressed on all sides in response. Predictably, but no less interestingly, the Murdoch press embraced Folau as a 'quiet Australian' exercising his right to speak his truth to the power of the all-dominating cultural elites.[16] I was equally intrigued by this echo from our Pacific past. Folau's fundamentalism was an expression, one generation removed, of the religiosity introduced to the islands by missionaries from Australia and elsewhere over 200 years. Expressed in a pluralistic and largely secular Australia which has moved on from its founding faith – in what I would call the spirit of the Enlightenment – the message of a vengeful god was jarring to many, but clearly not all. Modern Australia is, after all, the creation of the dialectal interplay of Enlightenment and Christian beliefs.

In November 2019 Folau's belief in divine intervention led him to draw a direct connection between Australia's godlessness and the bushfires which were then beginning their sweep across the continent. His quoting of the biblical Book of Isaiah, with its reference to the fiery consequences of broken covenants, was not defended with quite as much passion by commentators who had supported religious freedom during the marriage debate. They attributed the fires to arsonists and over-abundant trees, rather than God's wrath or a warming world. Yet that year was the hottest on record for Australia and the bushfires reignited a debate about climate change that seemed to have been extinguished by the 2019 re-election of the conservative Coalition government under Scott Morrison. Before and during the campaign, he and his ministers had proudly expounded the benefits of mining and burning coal despite the consequences for the climate and the world.

The similarity to nationalist positions overseas, most obviously in the US and Brazil, is not coincidental. As the Israeli historian Yuval Harari has observed, the new nationalism's fundamental inability to deal with the global problems such as climate change makes denial an attractive political option.[17]

Significantly it was images of infernos and beaches glowing in the red light of the apocalypse which changed the national narrative where years of scientific warnings had failed to do so. Equally ineffective had been the decade of pleading by Pacific Islanders concerned by their own impending apocalypse – sea level rise. 'Big states are rude and nasty' as Paul Keating observed, so it took a domestic disaster to focus Australia's attention. It is with the issue of climate change and the expediency of Australia's responsibilities to its 'Pacific family' that I end the book.

≋

'like a torn scrap of paper, like an unread message ...'

There are, of course, many ways to present a history of Australia and its Pacific neighbourhood, though there have been remarkably few attempts to do so. Had I worked as a reporter, administrator, aid worker or entrepreneur my insights would be very different. So, too, if I were a missionary or the son of the same. Instead, I am an historian trying to make sense of what I have read and observed in research and travels. What follows could be termed a thematic survey. It proceeds chronologically from the shifting of continents and ends with contemporary climate controversies. Its breadth might thereby satisfy historian Fernand Braudel's definition of the *longue durée*; that is, history covering an extended timeframe and which is cognisant of the significance of geography, landscape and the movement of living things. The timing of geological events and the ancient movement of peoples are under constant revision and contestation by geologists and archaeologists. I have presented generally agreed dates but encourage

Introduction

readers to investigate the literature further if they wish. Within this book, there are many characters well known to readers of Australian history and some who are probably not. I hope all have been cast in an interesting new context. The challenge has been to balance detail and narrative, to produce both a work of reference and a compelling account of Australia's place in the Pacific; one that meanders and tacks but only as much as is necessary. In the interest of accuracy I have retained some terms in direct quotes, particularly those pertaining to 'race', that may be considered offensive today.

It has been an astonishing odyssey guided both by the rich secondary literature, referred to earlier and throughout this work, and primary sources; those writings which are contemporary with their time and which make Australia's relationship with the Pacific so immediate. Some of that work came from the pen of the great Australian poet and commentator James McAuley, whose own intellectual path took a dramatic turn in New Guinea, which he visited many times; first as a serviceman, then as a researcher, teacher and administrator. These words from his 1961 essay 'My New Guinea' still speak to Australia's wider relationship with its Pacific region:

> There the great island lies with its archaic bird-reptile shape. The smoking mountains speak low thunder, the earth shakes lightly, the sun glares down on the impenetrable dark green mantle of forest with its baroque folds, the cloud-shadows pass over the green, a white cockatoo rises off the tree tops like a torn scrap of paper, like an unread message ...[18]

CHAPTER 1

Shifting continents

'... how the continents are made'

On a new winter's morning in 2015 I unfolded a *Sydney Morning Herald* to take in news of the city, region and world in what was still a breakfast ritual of longstanding in the harbour city. The *Herald* is Australia's oldest surviving newspaper and has reported under its 'morning' banner since 1842. In earlier decades the near Pacific loomed large for readers with news of island trade, the activities of colonial rivals and the apparent oddities of local cultures. More recently, reportage has tended to focus on refugee internments, social unrest, strategic rivalry and extreme weather events. But on that June day in 2015 we learned of the sudden appearance of a new Pacific neighbour – indeed 'the newest island on earth'. A patch of land had emerged from the sea some 65 kilometres north-west of Tonga's capital, Nuku'alofa. Its creation occurred with near-Biblical speed. Following a volcanic eruption in November 2014, the island was there by the new year. When reporter Peter Munro and photographer Edwina Pickles crunched up the beach some months after that there was already a crater lake and a fine black soil that supported life. Plants sprouted, crabs scuttled, and roosting seabirds were turning the dark rock white with their droppings. As vulcanologist Jocelyn McPhie remarked, 'This is essentially how the continents are made'.[1] That may have been an overstatement but the emergence was a real-time insight into the processes which had populated the vast Pacific for millennia.

The island was subsequently named Hunga Tonga-Hunga Ha'apai. Just how long it will remain part of the Tongan archipelago remains to be seen. If the place does not stabilise it may disappear back into the sea with the entropic effect of rain, wind and waves. Existence in the deceptively named Pacific Ocean can be precarious.

The quick birth and uncertain future of tiny Hunga Tonga-Hunga Ha'apai could hardly contrast more with the vast ancient island I call home. Elements of the landmass that became Australia were formed as continents moved around the globe in jigsaw-like rearrangements of tectonic plates, over thousands of millions of years. One theory has a supercontinent called Nuna – not even the oldest configuration at 2000 million years – being assembled with pieces of the planet called cratons whose existence extends back close to the creation of Earth itself. Zircon dated to more than four billion years has been found in Australia's west, suggesting that some pieces of the continent are nearly as old as the planet itself.

Nuna was followed by an arrangement called Rodinia around 1000 million years ago. This broke up some 200–250 million years later. Pangaea was formed by the conglomeration of Laurasia and Gondwana, which comprised the future Australia and lands that became India, Antarctica, Africa and South America. By 500 million years ago, the Australian part of this landmass straddled the equator. Three hundred and fifty million years later it had joined present-day Antarctica.[2]

The formation and splitting of supercontinents defined the oceans. The Panthalassic Sea appeared after the break-up of Rodinia. Pangaea divided that body of water to create the Tethys Ocean to its east. The disintegration of Pangaea led to the formation of the Atlantic Ocean around 180 million years ago and the Pacific some 10 million years later. Gondwana separated from Pangaea around 160 million years ago and was itself splitting up some 60 million years after that. As Gondwana broke apart, the landmass that became Australia acquired a Pacific coast.[3]

The separation of Australia from Gondwana began around 80 million years ago and was completed 40 to 50 million years later.[4] The new continent headed north-west, then north-east, carried on the Indo-Australian Plate, sometimes referred to simply as the Australian

Plate. It arrived within one of two degrees of latitude of its current position at the south-west rim of the Pacific some five million years ago.[5]

The eastern side of ancient Australia, including much of its present-day Pacific coast, was the last part to be formed. Earth scientists refer to the Tasman Line, a dog-leg delineation extending from the far north Queensland coast down to north-eastern South Australia, back into New South Wales and curving again into South Australia, east of Adelaide. The basement rocks to the west of this line are Precambrian, or older than 545 million years. Those to the east, including almost all the present-day Pacific coast, are younger.[6] Some rock, such as Sydney's signature coastal sandstone, was laid down around 220 million years ago as the compressed sediment of rivers that had once flowed over Gondwana.

Even after the slow passage to the Pacific rim, Australia's shape was not immutable. Sea level variations changed the coastline landmass many times as the continental shelf was exposed and submerged. The cause was the freezing and melting of ice caps, particularly around the south pole, where the landmass we call Antarctica was turned into a frozen continent by the rearrangement of lands and the redirection of warm ocean currents that followed the break-up of Gondwana. The departure of Australia, and Tasmania specifically, was particularly influential in this climate change.[7] At the sea's most recent low point, perhaps 21 000 years ago, the traversable landmass stretched from New Guinea to Tasmania. That place is known to geologists and archaeologists as Sahul or Greater Australia; zoologists refer sometimes to Meganesia. Sea levels rose again around 10 000 years ago and low-lying land to the north and south were inundated to create the now-familiar outline of continental Australia, separated from New Guinea and Tasmania.

Shifting continents

≋

'It does not shake or shiver like New Zealand or Japan'

Those names – Nuna, Rodinia, Pangaea, Gondwana, Sahul and Meganesia – sound like the otherworldly creations of fantasists rather than scientists. They are seldom referred to in the country whose deep history extends back through their epochs. The exception is Gondwana, a place long discussed in Australia and, in recent decades, one which has gained a popular currency as an almost mystical precursor to present-day Australia; a land of unspoiled, unpeopled rainforests from which the 'Australian ark' separated to nurture what became its unique flora and fauna in splendid isolation.

The name, in fact, derives from a region in India. The existence of a lost land of Gondwana was proposed by the Vienna-based geologist Eduard Suess in his major work, *Das Antlitz der Erde* (*The Face of the Earth*), published in three volumes between 1885 and 1909. Suess saw correlations between the geology of disconnected continents and fossil evidence across disparate lands in the form of ancient plants from the genus *Glossopteris*. This and other peatland plants formed the Permian-era coal deposits common to the Gondwanan landmasses. For him the disappearance of Gondwana was explained by dynamic sea levels and continental collapse. Long-gone land bridges once connected the existing continents, explaining common geology and allowing the spread of flora throughout the lands that would become India, South America, South Africa and Australia. Much as it introduced its readers to a new Pacific island in 2015, the *Sydney Morning Herald* offered up the latest geological news in 1906, probably in the wake of the publication that year of the translated second volume of Suess's opus, which included discussion of Australia and the Pacific.[8] The newly founded Australian Commonwealth, 'girt by sea' as one patriotic anthem put it, was once a province of a much larger place.

Another small, rather cryptic article appeared six years later headed 'Some lost lands'. Then the *Herald* reiterated the existence of

'Gondwanaland' and referred to Suess by surname only, as if he was already familiar to the readership. But among a series of barely explained geological details was the startling revelation that some 'land masses have undergone considerable redistribution'.[9] This was not the work of Eduard Suess but German meteorologist and geophysicist Alfred Wegener, who in January 1912 had delivered a paper in Frankfurt airing his controversial theory of continental drift. The *Herald*'s March report, it seems, was conflating old news with ideas that were very recent.

Wegener suggested that the continents drifted 'like pieces of a cracked ice floe in water'.[10] Gondwana had not collapsed in parts, it had split apart. Like others before him, Wegener was intrigued by the obvious puzzle-like fit of continents – something made quite apparent in the 19th century, with the ever more accurate mapping that both followed and guided European colonisation. Drift explained that in a way collapse could not. Wegener's consolidated work *Die Entstehung der Kontinente und Ozeane (The Origins of Continents and Oceans)* appeared in print in 1915 and again in 1920, 1922 and 1929.[11] The Australian press renewed its interest in the subject with each edition. In Adelaide the *Mail* carried a long article on Wegener's theory of 'Floating Continents' in 1923. News of drifting landmasses was picked up in regional papers. The *Wikepin Argus*, which served a tiny railway town some 200 kilometres east of Perth, reprinted a witty summary of Wegener's thesis in 1925: 'Australia seems to us a very stable, solid, well-balanced part of the Earth's surface. It does not shake or shiver like New Zealand or Japan, and its volcanoes have been dead for ages. Now scientists assert that the whole continent is drifting slowly northward ... One theorist thinks that Tasmania is a bit that has lagged behind. This, of course, would account for many things'.[12]

That the *Argus* article also made humorous comparisons to Jonathan Swift's flying island of Laputa is evidence of the ongoing novelty of the idea and perhaps the incredulity of the Australian public. Continental movement over deep time was confronting, even if it had followed a suite of ideas that had transformed received wisdom about the appearance of humans on earth. Wegener's theory was being advanced within living memory of the publication of Charles Darwin's paradigm-shifting theory of organic evolution over unimaginable timeframes and the consequent connection of all living things. Before *On the Origin of Species* appeared in 1859, there were relatively few Europeans or their colonial cousins who questioned the Biblical truth of an earth created 6000 years previously by an all-powerful god for the singular benefit of humans. Just one year before that milestone, human remains were found alongside those of extinct animals in a cave in Devon, England, putting in doubt the accepted longevity of human existence itself. Despite this, there were many who remained hostile to the scientific challenge to religious orthodoxy for decades after.

The Suessian idea of ancient lands which had sunk Atlantis-like held sway through the 1920s and 1930s. Possibly the appeal of that classical antecedent explains its durability. Wegener's drift theory was still not orthodoxy when South African geologist Alexander Du Toit dedicated his provocatively named book *Our Wandering Continents* to the German geologist in 1937.[13] Two decades later again it had not apparently convinced the Australian geologist, explorer and author Charles Laseron when he took up the task of educating his fellow Australians about the ancientness of their land. 'Nature is a tireless sculptor', he suggested. The argument was for the creative primacy of wind, water and vulcanism over vast time, rather than lateral movement. For Laseron 'Gondwanaland' was a place of certain existence but uncertain location: 'Where exactly it lay we know not, whether it joined Australia with South America across Antarctica, or whether it lay across the Indian Ocean to South Africa'. The greater part of that 'mysterious continent', of which western Tasmania may have been a relic, 'sank under the waves'.[14]

There was great ferment in the Earth sciences in the decade after Laseron's death in 1959, the results of which would help explain the mystery of Gondwanaland and indeed the origins of continents. But in the shorter term some reconsidered an older idea and the origins of the Pacific Ocean itself. In the late 19th century, George Darwin, son of Charles, had suggested that a piece of the Earth was thrown into space by the centrifugal force of rotation to form the Moon. The Pacific Ocean filled the vast basin thereby created. Fifty years later Rachel Carson suggested that 'the moon is the child of the earth' in the book that launched her reputation as a nature writer, *The Sea Around Us*. 'There is to this day a great scar on the surface of the globe' where crust was thrown off: 'This scar or depression holds the Pacific Ocean'.[15] Writing in *New Scientist* in 1963, British Petroleum staff scientist Tom Gaskell suggested that the departure of a large piece of the Earth itself prompted the rearrangement of lands. 'If the moon was ejected from the Pacific, leaving a single continent on the opposite hemisphere', he wrote, 'the present distribution of land masses is readily explained by the subsequent continental drift ...'[16]

The theory remained current in popular atlases until the end of the decade when analysis of moon rocks brought to Earth by Apollo 11 helped dispel the idea. However, it was still unclear what propelled the continents that Wegener imagined had moved across the Earth's crust like ice floes on water. The idea that huge thick tectonic plates lay beneath continents and oceans and were driven by expanding sea floors was clarified gradually by oceanic surveys of the Pacific after World War Two. In 1962 American naval commander Harry Hess, who had conducted many of those studies, published a paper called 'The History of Ocean Basins' in which he suggested that continents were carried along on larger plates by the movement of an ocean floor continuously created by magma rising from deep sea ridges. The 'conveyor belt' concept was further explained by the notion of subduction zones – evident as trenches – in which the expanding floor disappeared back down beneath an adjoining plate and into the asthenosphere. This is the layer of melted rock below the crust and the Earth's outer shell – its upper mantle or lithosphere.

Just as conflict had initiated research on the geomorphology of the ocean floor in the 1940s, nuclear testing during the Cold War motivated advances in seismographic sensors so that the location of ocean earthquakes around ridges and trenches, rather than volcanoes, was confirmed. That work, in turn, helped to determine the location of plate fault lines. In 1967 the American geophysicist W Jason Morgan explained how plates of a fixed size comprised the lithosphere and could move around on a spherical earth. Soon after, his findings were independently echoed by that of two other geophysicists working in partnership, Dan McKenzie and Robert Parker. They based their proposal on research undertaken in the North Pacific. They called it the 'paving stone theory of world tectonics' and were confident it would apply to other regions. It did and was widely accepted as 'plate tectonics'.[17]

The names Hess, Morgan, McKenzie and Parker are well known to those interested in geophysics. Less acknowledged is the part played by the Australian geologist Sam Carey, who was an early supporter of the idea of continental drift. His doctoral thesis, completed in 1939, was called *Tectonic Evolution of New Guinea and Melanesia*. In 1956, one year before Charles Laseron excited readers with his evocation of a collapsing Gondwanaland, Carey organised the Continental Drift Symposium at the University of Tasmania, where he held a professorship. It attracted international participation despite the relative remoteness of the venue, and the work it generated was an important step in the gradual acceptance of plate tectonics. But in the 1950s this was still contentious. Carey believed he was not offered fellowship to the Australian Academy of Science when it was established in 1954 because he supported the continental drift theory. The rejection was not forgotten. Carey stayed on in Tasmania, even after the general acceptance of plate tectonic theory and opportunities to teach elsewhere. He remained a 'loner', in the suggestion of one biography, who preferred independence in far-flung Tasmania to more prestigious institutions with their histories of adherence to orthodoxy.[18]

'the form of an island is gradually assumed'

Tectonic maps now show the Indo-Australian Plate moving up to meet the skull-shaped Pacific Plate, defining the 'back' of that vast cranial-like piece of lithosphere as it figuratively faces the Americas. The continent of Australia sits well back from the eastern edge of the plate that bears its name. It consequently shares this vast mobile piece of the Earth with some Pacific islands with which it has no other apparent connection. Lord Howe and Norfolk islands, the archipelagos of Vanuatu, New Caledonia, New Guinea and New Zealand are all 'continental' islands.[19] The Society Islands, by contrast, are truly 'oceanic' sitting, as they do, near the middle of the Pacific Plate some 5800 kilometres from Australia. They are the most distant from any continent of the ocean's myriad of islands.[20] The location of New Guinea and New Zealand near the colliding edge of the Australian Plate resulted in uplift. In the case of New Guinea this was the central spine of highlands we know as the Owen Stanley Range. New Zealand acquired its Southern Alps in a similar way.

Those islands, called Aotearoa by their first people, had split from Gondwana as a single mass, 'Zealandia', around 85 million years ago; well before Australia departed from the same. Ninety per cent of Zealandia exists underwater as spreading plateaus, ridges and rises. Lord Howe and Norfolk islands, which lie approximately 600 and 1400 kilometres off the New South Wales coast respectively, are part of this submerged 'continent', as is New Caledonia at its northern extremity. The deep Tasman Sea basin separates Australia from extended Zealandia.[21]

The meeting of the Pacific Plate with the various plates that surround it has created volatility as well as uplift. Earthquakes and volcanic activity are still a feature of life in these places, so that the great arc from New Zealand around to New Guinea, Japan, the Aleutian Islands and North America is called the Ring of Fire. Hunga Tonga-

Hunga Ha'apai is on the Australian Plate but close to its line of contact with the Pacific Plate. Australia itself sits well back, relatively stable and flat. It tends not to 'shake or shiver'. Nonetheless those lands that share continental origins with Australia, or have emerged from the complex geological processes at the edge of plate boundaries, tend also to contain mineral resources created over deep time. New Zealand has coal, gas and gold. New Guinea has copper, oil, gas and gold. New Caledonia has nickel in abundance. Bougainville and the Solomon Islands, created near the boundaries of the Australian, Pacific and other minor plates, have copper and gold.

None, however, compare with the mineral wealth of vast Australia. Some of the richest land is in that continent's west, also its oldest region. Rocks in the Pilbara of north-western Australia contain the fossils of methane-producing and methane-consuming micro-organisms that are nearly 3.5 billion years old.[22] The Australian landmass holds the remains of some of the oldest known life on Earth.

That region also contains some of the world's largest iron ore deposits, created around 2.5 billion years ago. Discovered in the 1950s, iron ore was earning Australia more export dollars than any other commodity by the end of that century. The mineral wealth that helped to create modern Australia also contributed to the post-war resurgence of other Pacific rim nations: resource-poor Japan and the insatiable Chinese economy that emerged from the ruinous years of the dictator Mao.

Australia has oil but is much richer in gas. This hydrocarbon wealth was created at different times from as early as 300 million to 10 million years ago and is evidence of the abundant plant life which existed on the Australian landmass before and after its split from Gondwana. The plant communities of countless forests and swamps were compressed to create hydrocarbons. As with gas and oil so, too, with high-grade coke and thermal coal, formed 299 to 252 million years ago in the Permian period. It was the first of the continent's fossil fuels to be systematically exploited. Coal was found on the New South Wales coast north and south of Sydney barely a decade after convicts and their gaolers first disembarked.

As the sons of industrialising Britain, the colonial authorities were well aware of the potential of the black chunks and named the first site of coal extraction, Newcastle, after the regional English coal-mining town. They had their reluctant wards digging the fuel out of the Pacific cliffs at the mouth of 'Coal River' – later called the Hunter – from 1801. Two centuries later Australia's Newcastle was the biggest coal-exporting port in the world.

And so it is mineral wealth, as well as age, which distinguishes Australia from the oceanic islands on the Pacific Plate. Those lands have been formed variously by volcanic activity and the industriousness of coral polyps. Some, such as Hawaii – the 'Big Island' – and little Hunga Tonga-Hunga Ha'apai, are volcanoes that have risen from cracks in the sea bed. Islands can also be created by the growth of coral and the accumulation of other material around a volcanic peak which has subsequently subsided, leaving an atoll and lagoon, an idea Charles Darwin posited following his Pacific crossing in HMS *Beagle*: the voyage which changed human understanding of life on Earth. Exposed reefs are transformed into places that sustain life by sediment within which plants might sprout from seeds blown in, floated to or deposited by the birds that criss-cross the ocean. It is a phenomenon beautifully described upon first-hand observation by the great circumnavigator of Australia, Matthew Flinders, who worked his way carefully along the Great Barrier Reef in 1802:

> the coral, sand, and other broken remnants thrown up by the sea adhere to the rock, and form a solid mass with it, as high as the common tides reach. That elevation surpassed, the future remnants, being rarely covered, lose their adhesive property, and, remaining in a loose state, form what is usually called a key upon the top of the reef. The new bank is not long in being visited by sea-birds; plants take root upon it; a cocoanut, or the drupe of a pandanus is thrown on shore; land-birds visit it and deposit the seeds of shrubs and trees; every high tide, and still more every gale, adds something to

the bank; the form of an island is gradually assumed; and last of all comes man to take possession.[23]

That sequence of events was ecologically accurate but it also spoke much of the prevailing European world view: all was there for 'man', by divine dictate or scientific logic.

≋

'so far it flew'

In contrast to the Australian continent, resources of worth to humans on oceanic Pacific islands have come from the flora and fauna that live on and around them rather than the rock beneath. Nauru would seem to be an exception, but it is not. The coral atoll sits approximately 3000 kilometres north-east of Australia's northernmost point, Cape York. Some hundreds of millions of years ago, it emerged from the ocean as a mound of limestone. The exposed rock weathered into dramatic pinnacles, the valleys between which were subsequently filled with up to 24 metres of phosphate – the mineralised result of leached bird droppings deposited over millennia between 220 000 and 80 000 years ago.[24] A soil was formed over this which supported coconut palms and other shrubs; enough cover, it seems, to warrant the name 'Pleasant Island' being bestowed by the first Europeans to see the place in 1798. Nauruans made the most of the flora and fauna, but a century after Pleasant Island was so named, Europeans began mining the organically derived mineral wealth for use as fertiliser for crops grown in Australia's depleted soils. Thereby began the tragic entanglement in the economic and security concerns of Australia, which saw Pleasant Island transformed into a dysfunctional gulag in the 21st century. We shall return to that story later.

Historical and current accounts of Nauru's avian life indicate which birds might have filled the limestone crevices with guano. The island is still home to the White Tern, and the Brown and Black Noddy, which breed there. It is also a staging post for several migratory species; the Ruddy Turnstone, Pacific Plover, and Bar-tailed Godwit among them.[25] These migrants are embodiments of the wonder of natural adaptation, for they have learned and evolved to fly extraordinary distances across the Pacific Ocean from northern hemisphere breeding grounds in Siberia, the Aleutian Islands and Japan, to take advantage of the warmer weather and food in Australia. With this continuous cycle of flight they strive to live in an endless summer.

Their arrivals and departures were surely observed by Australia's first peoples and taken as indicators of seasonal change. The extent of the marathon has more recently been understood. Writing in 1929, Australian naturalist Michael Sharland described the Golden Plover as a 'globe trotter'. Because of the work of ornithologists such as the Englishman Henry Seebohm, Sharland knew the birds had come from Siberia. In the years before the acceptance of continental drift and tectonic shift, it was relatively easy to explain how the plover knew what lay at the end of its sea passage; they were following 'a route set by ancestors over mountain ranges or along shorelines which have since disappeared with subsidence'.[26] The term 'globe trotter' made more sense in this imagined scenario.

Subsequent understanding of continental movement and the evolution of birds has made the phenomenon of migration even more astonishing. The Pacific Ocean had long separated Siberia and Australia when shorebirds such as the plover evolved with other modern species some 66 million years ago. This was after the asteroid strike which led to mass extinction and created new niches for other species, mammals included. The present flyways of the Golden Plover, the Arctic Skua, Shearwaters and others from the northern Pacific to Australia somehow developed over this time; generational adaptation over millennia which accommodated 'ice ages' and thaws along with varying sea levels, climates and food supplies that accompanied them.

Birds have adapted physiologically and behaviourally alongside the rhythms of weather and currents. In attempting to understand the impulse and ability to migrate, ornithologists refer to endogenous factors which relate the internal functioning of the animals – nervous system, hormones and so forth – and exogenous triggers such as light, temperature, air pressure and food supply. Birds can navigate variously using the magnetic field of the Earth, the position of stars and even smell. Topography, which may help European species, is of little assistance for Pacific flyovers. Learned behaviour is important but this does not explain the migration of immature birds unaccompanied by adults. The factors, summed up perhaps in common parlance as 'instinct', are varied and complex. The navigational abilities of the Bar-tailed Godwit, which flies the Pacific to Australia's northern and eastern shores, are still mysterious. The physiological transformation they undergo in order to make the trip, however, is well recorded but no less astonishing. Having bred and fed in the north, the Godwit's body weight doubles, its heart and muscles expand, and the bird's blood becomes viscous to better store oxygen. It can fly up to 1000 kilometres in a day for more than a week without food or water; though some, it seems, touch down at Nauru.[27] The Latin name *Limosa lapponica* reflects a long-held scientific association with northern climes, namely Lapland. The origin of the name Godwit is less certain but, for Australian poet and bird lover Dame Mary Gilmore, it suggested a divine wisdom manifest in the little creature: 'Godwit indeed art thou!' Evoking the Christianity that lay at the heart of her radical sense of social justice, Gilmore tried to fathom the Godwit's 'fortitude' and 'power to know':

> So far it flew
> Upon the distant verge of sight,
> I saw (and scarcely knew
> I saw so small dimensions ran),
> A bird that looked no larger than
> A mote, and yet it held in view
> Immeasurable flight![28]

Where the Godwit breeds in the north and 'winters' in Australia, the Short-tailed Shearwater does the opposite. It nests on islands in the south-east of Australia, particularly on and around Tasmania, and migrates to the north-east Pacific to take advantage of plankton-rich seas in the northern summer, 'flying' underwater to feed much as penguins do. The birds' breeding and migration patterns were investigated in the late 1940s by government scientist Dominic Serventy in response to the commercial harvesting of birds and eggs on Tasmania's offshore islands. The route of the Shearwater's journey, it transpired, was a vast figure '8' up through the Tasman Sea around the second larger loop in north.[29] The Short-tailed Shearwater shares this range with its sooty cousin. New Zealand–born, Sydney-based writer Olaf Ruhen was as captivated with the capacity of the Sooty Shearwater as Gilmore was with the Godwit. Both were part of a small group of writers – Michael Sharland, Alec Chisholm, Allen Keast and Judith Wright among them – who expressed and encouraged the growing fascination among non-Indigenous Australians with the ecologies which surrounded them, thereby seeding the modern conservation movement. Twenty years later Ruhen described the Shearwaters' return to Australia: 'the remorseless flow of air-borne bodies was an awe-inspiring phenomenon never to be overlooked or disregarded. There was a majesty in the birds' obedience to the will of their tribe, to the strict and never-changing discipline, to the seasonal call of the breeding-places'. Where Gilmore saw the hand of God, Ruhen evoked tribal loyalty and discipline. Scientific answers to their endurance and drive have only enhanced the wonder of bird-lovers. The decline of Shearwater numbers in recent years, in turn, points to the hand of 'man' in determining the migration by our transformation of climate and ocean ecologies. It also emphasises the global connection of those ecologies. Mass bird die-offs in the north-east Pacific due to food shortages, the probable result of warming waters and over-fishing, has tempered the 'remorseless flow' of Shearwaters back to their Australian homes.[30]

The presence of Australian species in neighbouring New Zealand is often less mysterious than the global migration of birds. They have ridden the westerly wind by accident or with intent. The arrival of some of these birds can be dated with a degree of certainty. Tiny Australian Silvereyes, which somehow survived the elements over 4000 kilometres, began appearing in New Zealand in the 1800s. Their novelty was evidenced by the name given them by Māori: *tauhou* or stranger. There are many other birds and insects which have crossed the Tasman, not as seasonal migrants but colonists remaining within ecological niches produced, perhaps, by human-induced landscape change in the 19th century. Because of the predominant wind, the traffic of permanent settlers is mainly one way: from Australia to the east.[31]

Not surprisingly the avian traffic to and from Australia and other parts of the Pacific has had flow-on effects for the ecosystem of the island continent. 'By what they have carried, birds have left their mark everywhere' is the recent observation of biologist Tim Low, who continues the work of Sharland and the nature writers of the previous century. He refers to 'seed highways' across the oceans and suggests that Japanese Snipe, which fly non-stop from the northern Pacific islands after which they are named, have been responsible for at least some of the plant species Australia shares with Japan, sedges and rushes in particular. Because the Snipe and others are migratory, the transfer is two-way. Asia has probably acquired Australian Fringed Lilies in this way.[32]

This image of biological permeability, independent of human intervention, is something of a corrective to the popular notion of Australia as an isolated ark carrying its marvellous menagerie of unique species. A similarly contestable notion of ecological exceptionalism underpins some New Zealanders' sense of self. It is telling that the people of those islands are often called 'Kiwis' after the small flightless birds found nowhere else. Their island home is sometimes named 'moa's ark'; a reference to the extinct giant flightless bird – the moa – for which the place is also famous. Yet recent advances in genetics have challenged the idea that New Zealand's flora and fauna represent a 'time capsule' fragment of Gondwana. Kiwis are quite closely related to emus and cassowaries and probably did not evolve on New Zealand alone. Much else has come across from Australia. Indeed, Tim Low maintains that Australia has biologically dominated the Pacific, primarily because of its adventurous birds.[33]

The connection with New Guinea to the north is so strong that Low refers to it as 'Australia's northern province'. That there are shared birds should not be surprising given the proximity, just 150 kilometres across the Torres Strait which separates both mainlands. The Torresian Imperial Pigeon is one of many birds that frequents both lands. The four birds of paradise that can be found in Australia are, along with the 39 species in New Guinea, evidence of a shared biota that goes back to Gondwanan times. So, too, is the monotreme long-beaked echidna and the marsupial tree kangaroo. The presence of those tree dwellers has permitted the survival of the fruit-eating birds of paradise. Had there not been a deep-water divide between the fauna of Asia and Greater Australia – the so-called Wallace Line – monkeys may have dominated the New Guinea rainforest, putting an end to the splendidly plumed birds.

As New Guinea crumpled with the collision between the Australian and Pacific plates, mountains with their own micro-climates were formed, which allowed the perpetuation of the type of rainforest that once had flourished in Gondwana and the Australian mainland after its split and before its drying from 23 million years ago. There is more of the ancient supercontinent represented in New Guinea's lush flora than in the rainforests of Australia, where Asian 'latecomers', such as figs and fan palms, define even the much-touted 'Gondwanan Wet Tropics' of Queensland's Daintree.

New Guinea is, in this biological formulation, 'an Australian refuge'.[34] The poet Mark O'Connor evoked the same connection in the 1980s:

> These were our islands of legend
> where the barren Continent turns lush,
> and our wisps of cloud-forest
> become solid counties, mists weighted with orchid spores.[35]

Shared ecology is just one element among many in Australia's complex and vastly underappreciated relationship with its northern neighbour.

≋

'... the reefs have grown upwards'

By contrast the Great Barrier Reef is Australia's alone. Indeed, it peters out in the Torres Strait, where fresh water and sediment from New Guinea's Fly River disgorge into the Pacific. Tiny Bramble Cay, home to many seabirds, sits as the Reef's most northerly outcrop, some 50 kilometres from the mouth of the Fly and marking the extent of Australia's maritime zone and the most northerly piece of terrestrial Australia.

The Great Barrier Reef extends for 2300 kilometres along Australia's east coast. As its name suggests, it protects more than half of the continent from the Pacific waves which pound beaches and rock platforms further south. The line of coral can be seen from space. In its present form it has existed for 8000 to 10 000 years, for that is when the present sea level stabilised after the last great glacial melt. But reefs have lined this continental shelf for as long as 18 million years, growing and dying as the sea level has risen and receded. When the sea was at its most recent low, exposing the greater Australian continent Sahul, the platform which now supports the Reef was probably forested. Its present extent reflects the range of the warm water, which can support vast accumulations of coral, the calcium carbonate skeletons of many species of polyps. Some regard the Reef as the world's largest single organism.

It was first charted by James Cook, who fell afoul of its coral labyrinth in 1770. Cooktown and the Endeavour River commemorate the place where his epoch-making voyage nearly ended. Shortly after resuming his journey, the great navigator claimed possession of the entire coast with its reef and near islands for his king, George III. It was Cook's countryman and admirer, Matthew Flinders, who named the complex of coral and rock 'the Great Barrier Reefs' in the process of consolidating knowledge of the British acquisition. Though Flinders used the plural in recognition of the series of coral formations which comprised the whole, his 1814 account of an 1802 voyage was, in the words of historian Iain McCalman, the 'modern Reef's foundation document'.[36]

Flinders was followed in 1818 by Phillip Parker King, the governor's son and Australia's first colonial-born navigator of renown. The work of both men was acknowledged by Charles Darwin in his 1842 work *On the Structure and Distribution of Coral Reefs*, which anticipated in several ways the more famous *On the Origin of Species* published in 1859. Not least the earlier work described the gradual development – the evolution – of ecosystems over time, a concept that differed clearly from Biblical creationism in which all life was perfectly made by God in seven days. It also challenged the 'catastrophism' theories of sudden change expounded by others who were struggling to explain the evidence of apparently displaced rocks, and the fossil remains of creatures long gone, that accorded with Christian precepts. Since Cook's encounter with Australia's huge Pacific reef, the nature of coral and its role in the creation of islands exercised the minds of European scientists. Darwin's theory, arrived at by deduction rather than observation, held that such islands were formed as coral grew up to remain within its viable depth around an existing piece of land – often a volcano – as it gradually submerged with the subsidence of the sea floor.

Darwin's first real-life encounter with a tropical reef in Tahiti seemed to confirm his thesis. In its final stages in 1836, that epochal voyage aboard HMS *Beagle* brought him to Sydney's well-established harbour, from where he set out to find examples of the continent's famously strange fauna. The first observations of a platypus and other creatures in this western Pacific land would influence the coming theory of evolution, as did the many and varied finches and mockingbirds shot on the Galapagos Islands at the ocean's eastern edge.

Darwin did not venture north to the 'Great Barrier Reefs', which had 'excited much attention' by his own admission. Had he done so and continued around to the Huon Peninsula on the northern coast of present-day Papua New Guinea, the Englishman would have seen terraces of coral extending 140 metres above the ocean, the result of both tectonic uplift and many rises and falls in sea level. Instead, the *Beagle* headed west to the Cocos Islands in the Indian Ocean. Darwin included Australia's reef in his general theory of coral construction: 'The barrier-reefs of Australia and of New Caledonia ... [in structure and form] resemble those encircling many of the smaller islands of the Pacific Ocean'. Both barrier reefs and atolls, he concluded, were the result of subsiding foundations upon which coral are attached, 'and that during this downward movement, the reefs have grown upwards'.[37]

However, what may have held for the islands of the Pacific did not necessarily apply to the Great Barrier Reef. With its foundation on a continental shelf, sea level change was the main catalyst for the Reef's coral formation, something Darwin did not seem to consider in that instance. His theory of creation and subsidence had some people imagining tracts of collapsed land, well before Eduard Suess wrote *The Face of the Earth*. Darwin's great influencer, Charles Lyell, admitted to thinking of nothing but the 'tops of submerged continents' for days after hearing his coral thesis in 1837. This was not Darwin's intention. The disappearance of continents beneath the sea sounded rather like 'catastrophism', the belief in the primacy of abrupt change. Such thinking, of course, contradicted the great theory that was taking shape in Darwin's mind – the gradual evolution of isolated populations into different species. 'I should require the weightiest evidence', he wrote to Lyell in 1856, 'to make me believe in such immense changes within the period of living organisms in our oceans'.[38]

Although *On the Structure and Distribution of Coral Reefs* was written without first-hand observation of the Great Barrier Reef, it stimulated further investigation of that formation by some who supported Darwin's thesis and, in the case of Alexander Agassiz, one who was vehemently opposed to it. The US-based and independently wealthy Agassiz sailed from San Francisco to Brisbane and travelled north to the Reef in a chartered steamer. There, as he wrote later, the 'superb' coral reefs 'opened my eyes' to reef formation. There had been no subsidence, rather uplift and 'erosion and denudation' were the creative forces. Darwin's theory of atoll formation was given credence by the work of the Welsh–Australian geologist TW Edgeworth David, whose expeditions to the Ellice Islands in the late 1890s – present-day Tuvalu – revealed basalt beneath 340 metres of coral.

As it transpired, another theory, overlooked by both Darwin and Agassiz, held the key to understanding the formation of continental reefs. That sea level change might relate to climate and the water sequestered in glaciers had been suggested by the Scotsman Charles Maclaren as early as 1841 following pioneering work on glaciers, strangely enough, by Agassiz's father Louis. He coined the term *Eiszeit* – or 'ice age' – in 1837.

The significance of sea level fluctuation finally became apparent in studies undertaken in 1913 on the island of Mer, part of the Murray Island group at the far northern end of the Reef. British and colonial men had dominated the investigation of the Reef in the 19th century and early 1900s, but the 1913 team was led by North Americans. Alfred Mayor, a Harvard-trained acolyte of Alexander Agassiz, and another Harvard academic, Reginald Daly, put together more pieces of the coral reef jigsaw. These included the rise and fall of oceans in time with glaciation, the importance of water temperature – both hot and cold – for the survival of corals and the lethality of sediment. They had chosen Mer because of its pristine waters after the beds of Thursday Island were covered with silt.[39] All this would come to the fore a century later as the health of the Reef was compromised by a perfect storm of sea level rise, warming water, ocean acidification and mainland run-off. The changes then were rapid and caused by human rather than geological action.

CHAPTER 2

First peoples

'I use nature for my book'

Mer sits inside the ribbon of reefs that extends beyond the tip of Cape York. To the west is the Torres Strait and to the east is the deepening blue of the Pacific. Mer faces the ocean from behind the coral barrier. Mer was annexed by the colony of Queensland along with Bramble Cay and the other islands of Torres Strait between 1872 and 1879. All consequently became Australian territory and, just as Bramble Cay marks the northern extent of that possession, Mer sits at its eastern edge. As with many Australian places, the island has two names: that by which it is known among its first people and a second, given in the process of colonisation. Indigenous Mer became the colonial landmark Murray Island when Captain Edwards of HMS *Pandora* saw it in 1791, having searched the Pacific for the mutineers who had famously seized the *Bounty* and set its captain, William Bligh, adrift in a long boat. *Pandora* was wrecked on the reef shortly after, but Edwards survived and the name Murray Island persisted.

The island is the peak of a sea mount, well to the east of the forested plain stretching from present-day Australia to New Guinea in ancient Sahul. It has existed in its present water-bound form for perhaps 6000 years, but when the sea was lower the island would have been larger. Archaeological evidence suggests that it has only been inhabited by humans for perhaps 2500 to 3500 years.[1] Over that time, the Meriam people of Mer, Dauar and Waier, a trio sometimes collectively called the Murray Islands, developed a complex social structure and set of origin stories. This was not an isolated spot in the sea but rather a place existing within a network of lands joined, not separated, by water.

Trade was one manifestation of this and was apparently second nature to the Islanders. The extraordinary appearance of Flinders and HMS *Investigator* in 1802 triggered the launching of several waves of canoes of up to 100 local men wanting to swap, not fight, with the sudden arrivals.

Remarkably, this was not the mariner's first encounter with the people of the Torres Strait. He had sailed by in 1792 with the indefatigable and irascible William Bligh, back in His Majesty's service after the *Bounty* mutiny and then in command of HMS *Providence*. The reception was much the same then, as later. The urge to trade, motivated by an apparent knowledge of iron and desire for its unparalleled strength, was evident on both occasions. Unable to make the metal with the resources available on their Pacific island, the Meriam offered coconuts and plantains – things they grew.

The journal entry of 30 October 1802 provides a detailed description of the appearance, demeanour and material culture of the pre-colonial Islanders. The men were 'active', 'tolerably muscular' with 'countenances expressive of a quick apprehension'. They wore ornaments of shell and their water craft were double outriggers with woven mat sails. On shore there were settlements with huts surrounded by palisades. Flinders made a quick calculation of the population based upon the 200 men who met his vessel. The 'three small isles', he estimated, supported 600 men, women and children. It was, in relative terms, 'a large population'.[2]

Exchange linked the Meriam to the people of the two continents between which they lived. To the north was New Guinea – *Op Deudai* – from where canoes and ornaments were procured. *Waki* was the Meriam trade word for the Papuan Hornbill. Red ochre, and the feathers and long leg bones of emus were obtained from the Australian mainland to the south – *Keo Deudai*. Language and origin stories connected the Meriam culturally to New Guinea, the other islands and, to a lesser extent, mainland Australia. But over the millennia of occupation, these few hundred people developed a distinctive and complex culture. That the Meriam were remarkable in the richness of their cultural expression in such a condensed setting was commented upon by Europeans who followed Flinders. The cultures of Mer, Dauar and Waier might be seen, to use Claude Levi-Strauss's beautifully appropriate term, as very 'foliated'.[3] Many aspects of this complexity survived the upset which came in the wake of *Investigator*. For a variety of reasons, not least the ability to incorporate change into a traditional world view, the Meriam retained what the anthropologist Nonie Sharp could still describe in 1993 as their 'integral quality'.[4] But though there is exceptionalism suggested here, the people of the Murray Islands also provide an insight into adaptation, cultural expression and the attachment to place that manifested in a myriad of ways as humans moved towards Pacific shores from Asia.

The Meriam's god Bomai came from the big island to the north, in present-day West Irian. He took on many forms: a whale, dugong and octopus among them. The latter embodied the cohering idea of 'many into one', so that the eight clans of the islands correlated with the eight tentacles of the mythic cephalopod. A second god called Malo followed Bomai. It was Malo who brought the law which mediated all relationships on the islands. This included the idea of *wauri tebud*, 'shell friends', whereby the gifting of the cone shell, the *wauri*, became a form of establishing friendship. The reach of *wauri tebud* extended all the way to the Lockhart River on the Great Barrier Reef coast of *Keo Deudai*.[5] Malo's Law, as it has subsequently been called, is a strict code of rules guarding against theft and trespass. The Law also justifies the imposition of taboo on certain foods, typically plants, in the interest of conservation and preservation of food supplies.

Bomai brought forth the fertility of Mer so that the Meriam could trade their garden produce for turtle and dugong caught on other islands. Planetary movements, winds and tides guided the planting. 'Use new moon to plant vegetables that bear fruit on the surface and full moon for plants that grow down', was the advice handed to one senior Meriam man in the first half of the 20th century. 'I use nature for my book' was his summation of this knowledge.⁶ Life was, and still is, a cycle of renewal, decay and renewal, as is so often the case with people who live intimately with nature.

The Meriam are gardeners but they are also sea people. Some clans are horticulturalists, others are fishers. Their double outriggers are stable 'blue water' craft. Nonie Sharp expresses it thus: 'an Islander's canoe, itself like a living thing, an extension of its owner, sails in matched union with the sea, following the patterns of its movement'. The people draw meaning from the animals with whom they share the sea. Their totemic system of internal differentiation includes identification with the tern, the Tiger shark, Green turtle, whale, dolphin and mackerel. The Torresian Imperial pigeon has a special place, for its migrations to and from *Op Deudai* and *Keo Deudai* 'joins the continents' and encompasses the world of the Meriam.⁷

≈

'I never saw the slightest attempt at gardening'

Europeans aside, the people of Mer, Dauar and Waier were among the more recent arrivals in the Pacific world. The date of the first human movement to the ocean's rim has been progressively moved back by archaeologists. In 2017, evidence of occupation in Arnhem Land, in the present-day Northern Territory, was dated at 65 000 years. The first people arrived on craft probably built from Asian bamboo or coconut wood and ventured relatively short distances at times of low sea levels, pushed by need and possibly imaginations sparked by plumes of smoke from burning forest over the horizon. Paradoxically these migrants may also have ventured forth when the sea level was high, for that was when occupied territory had been inundated and population pressure was greatest. They subsequently moved down the east coast to distant present-day Tasmania and colonised the top end of Sahul – present-day New Guinea.

In the early 1960s the prevailing archaeological theories led the Australian historian Manning Clark to begin his monumental history of Australia with an account of Negrito people being displaced by Murrayians who were, in turn, forced southward by another group called Carpentarians.[8] By the 1970s Australian archaeologist Alan Thorne was suggesting that the human remains he had recovered at Kow Swamp in south-east Australia were descended from *Homo erectus*. Bones analysed at Lake Mungo, however, were of *Homo sapiens*. As late as the 1980s Thorne maintained it was 'beyond doubt' that archaic and modern humans came together and eventually produced the modern 'Aboriginal Australian'.[9] This theory of a synthesised population formed after many waves was based upon the physical examination of bones. It is now accepted that Australia was settled by *Homo sapiens* alone. Recent analysis using genomic testing lends support to a single migration to Sahul.[10] The northern and southern inhabitants of that continent diverged genetically from each other between 25 000 and 40 000 years ago, well before Australia and New Guinea were divided by water. Possibly land separated populations as effectively as sea.[11]

Genetic diversion was followed by cultural differentiation. Perhaps 9000 years ago, at a place called Kuk in the Wahgi Valley of New Guinea's Western Highlands, people began creating a drainage system for horticulture. People had lived there for more than 30 000 years.[12] Bananas, yams and taro, all native to the island, were grown there.[13] Sugar cane was cultivated on the lowlands. From around 6000 years ago a different wave of people, called Austronesians by anthropologists and linguists, moved across from Asia to the now separate islands of New Guinea. They brought with them other vegetables and fruits for cultivation as well as domesticated pigs, fowls and dogs. These plants and animals found their way by trade to the highlands where their usefulness was incorporated into receptive cultures.

Whatever the origins of the first inhabitants of greater Australia, it is generally accepted that the Austronesians came from China through Taiwan and the Philippines to northern New Guinea. They were the people who would begin the great Pacific island migrations to New Caledonia and Samoa. The travellers took with them animals and plants and a patterned pottery called Lapita ware. Maps showing the extent of Lapita culture resemble a great net cast from the north coast of New Guinea to encompass the Solomons, Vanuatu, Fiji, Tonga and Samoa – but not Australia or New Zealand.[14]

The difference between the cultures of the Torres Strait, New Guinea, and beyond, and those of the Australian mainland has been a matter of debate in anthropological circles for decades. The emphasis in more recent times has been on cultural exchange and therefore connection. The difference, nonetheless, was marked in both material culture and practice. Headhunting was customary in the Torres Strait and New Guinea but not in Australia. Aboriginal Australians used spears and boomerangs where Melanesians and Islanders had bows and arrows. Animals domesticated for consumption were a feature of life in New Guinea and many islands but not the Australian continent. Aboriginal Australians did not engage in pottery-making whereas Melanesians did – at least some of them. When the missionary James Chalmers took Motuan cooking pots to Kiwai Island in New Guinea's Fly River in the 1890s, upon the assumption he was sharing something useful, they were spurned. The Kiwai Islanders liked their food roasted not boiled.[15] Long-established tastes, rituals and needs may have similarly militated against the Aboriginal people's adoption of pottery or metallurgy, without which boiling water is difficult. When the botanist John MacGillivray sailed aboard HMS *Rattlesnake* from Sydney to south-east New Guinea in 1849, making notes of the people he encountered on the mainland and in the Torres Strait, he saw that Islanders dried turtle meat for use while sailing, while Aboriginal people ate it 'fresh' – that is, roasted.[16]

Architecture, too, was different. Where woven pandanus and thatching was used in the islands for the walls and roofing of permanent dwellings, bark was the primary cladding throughout Australia for temporary and permanent habitations. At up to 9 metres in diameter, the domed huts of the forest-dwelling Dyirbaingan people of north-east Queensland were among the larger mainland houses but these were seasonal habitations and smaller than the permanent bamboo-framed domes of the Meriam people. The difference with the pitched roof structures of Melanesia, Micronesia, Polynesia and New Zealand is even more marked. The last traditional longhouse of the Kiwai people of New Guinea's Fly River delta was 100 metres long and 22 metres wide when measured in the 1970s.[17] Ecology, culture and the preferences these established must have played a major part in the origins of these distinctions, as with others.

Europeans also noted the difference between island and mainland traditions of plant husbandry. The distinction made an impression upon MacGillivray, who wrote that 'on Murray and Darnley and other thickly peopled and fertile islands a considerable extent of the land in small patches has been brought under cultivation ... On the mainland again I never saw the slightest attempt at gardening'.[18] In northern Australia pieces of yam were replaced or planted for later harvest but this was unlike tending defined gardens. For the gardeners of Kiwai Island, for instance, fencing was necessary to keep out wild pigs, a problem not encountered on the continent before Europeans introduced these animals.[19] In the 1930s Australian government anthropologist FE Williams described the trellis horticulture and yam gardens of the Keraki people – 'little affected by European contact' – around the Morehead River, which flowed into the Torres Strait just over 200 kilometres away from Cape York. Poles up to 2 metres high were set in place and 'as the weather changes and the tubers ripen, the green leaves gradually turn colour and the Keraki garden becomes a sunlit fairyland of pale green and yellow'.[20] In contrast, a contemporary account of the Wik people of the Archer River region on the west coast of Cape York described a community which knew where to find yams, arrowroot and water lily roots beyond the campsites that shifted with the seasons: 'For hours they [the women] gather, dig and hunt and as they wander through the bush they keep their eyes open for anything that can be of service to their arts and crafts'.[21]

Viewing the world in terms of hierarchy – as was the way with dominating civilisations since ancient times – Europeans ranked horticulture higher than 'hunting and gathering' on the scale of social progress. In 1897 Torres Strait Islanders were exempted from the first Queensland *Aborigines Protection Act* in part because of their mode of gardening. Unsurprisingly, such judgments rankle contemporary Aboriginal writers and researchers. So much so that author Bruce Pascoe has rejected the term 'hunter-gatherer' as one akin to primitivism while emphasising Aboriginal agricultural practices – broadly defined – in his revisionist and frequently cited account of traditional culture, *Dark Emu*. In 2020 researchers at the Australian National University presented evidence of ancient banana cultivation in the Torres Strait as proof of Indigenous Australian agriculture.[22]

It is, but only in so much as the Islanders became 'first Australians' when their lands were annexed by the colony of Queensland in the 1870s. Expurgation of 'hunter-gatherer' diminishes very real differences between Torres Strait and Melanesian cultures, on the one hand, and Australian mainland cultures on the other. Mobility, for instance, was a feature of the latter where it was not of the former, which were often bound by the limits of an island or highland valley. This, in turn, affected architecture. Anthropologist Paul Memmott, who has documented Aboriginal dwellings more than most, has written: 'The mobile hunter-gatherer lifestyle often resulted in relatively impermanent architecture.'[23]

Simply discarding 'hunter-gatherer' in favour of agriculturalist also obscures the remarkable diversity of cultures among Aboriginal peoples, who occupied environments as disparate as rainforest, desert and coast. Many groups shaped environments through burning regimes – so-called 'firestick farming'. Others did not. Some engaged in what can be termed agricultural practices, others lived primarily off the bounty of the sea or the forest. Those in arid zones moved frequently in search of food and water. Consequently, some Aboriginal groups constructed large permanent habitations such as stone huts, though these were not necessarily always occupied. Others, who were more mobile, made temporary shelters. Where geology provided ready-made rock shelters, those were used.

Few, if any, within Australian academic and professional circles would share Pascoe's anachronistic association of hunting and gathering with primitivism, although it has gone largely unchallenged in the enthusiastic reception of his thesis.[24] As the Australian archaeologist Harry Lourandos made clear 30 years ago, gathering and hunting was not a passive response to environment.[25] It was neither a simple mode of living nor a way of life that negated attachment to place. Rather the reverse was true. It is now widely acknowledged that hunting and gathering often produced a better diet and lifestyle than agriculture. As historian David Christian has noted, early farmers may well have been 'pushed' towards agriculture by adverse circumstances rather 'than pulled by its advantages'.[26] Aboriginal Australians seem to have left well enough alone. Paradoxically Pascoe's characterisation of hunter-gatherers as 'primitive', 'nomadic' people without 'agricultural methods' seems to accept the hierarchical distinctions which caused offence in the first instance.

Torres Strait Islander Eddie Mabo emphasised the difference between island and mainland planting and harvesting practices as he began his campaign to regain title over land on his island home of Mer in the 1980s. In Mabo's understanding, Aboriginal people ranged over land communally held as hunters and gatherers, while Islanders tended specific plots. That distinction, 'explained to lawyers and anyone willing to listen' in the 1980s, gave Mabo hope that his appeal might win within a British-based legal system of land tenure.[27] Ultimately it did. But in 1992 the High Court of Australia also saw fit to apply the concept of unextinguished relationship to land to the whole of the mainland, hunter-gatherer lifestyles notwithstanding. A Pacific mode of horticulture thereby helped to unpick white Australia's creation myth of *terra nullius*.

≋

'from some unknown land across the sea'

There has been much interest in recent decades in the contact between Macassans from the Indonesian archipelago and Aboriginal people of the northern Australian coast. Dugout canoes which replaced local bark vessels were an important cultural exchange which accompanied the trade in trepang, tortoise and pearl shell. The Macassans, however, rarely ventured east of the country of the Yanyuwa people, whose territory was centred on the Sir Edward Pellew Group of Islands and adjacent coast on the western side of the Gulf of Carpentaria. This was Asian not Pacific contact, yet several centuries of interaction between these visitors and the Yanyuwa influenced the later reception of Europeans in a most interesting way. The arrival of pale strangers was 'not the extraordinary event' it was for most other Aboriginal groups, in the words of archaeologist and historian Richard Baker.[28] Consequently, the Yanyuwa did not greet Europeans as ancestors returned. They were simply another set of visitors. This difference suggests that foreign visitation on the Pacific coast, where Europeans were received as kin returned from the dead, was rare if not non-existent before colonisation.

Farther to the east, Melanesian double outrigger canoes were adopted by Aboriginal people even if their gardening practices were not. These vessels and their use reached around in a great arc from the southern shores of New Guinea to some 400 kilometres down the Great Barrier Reef. The Meriam lived in the middle of this region of graduating cultural flow. It was down at the southern end of the distribution of the canoe that their myth of Bomai-Malo was joined with the local stories of crocodile and Rainbow Serpent creators.[29]

The double outrigger was suitable for Torres Strait and coastal waters. Open ocean journeying was another matter. Having occupied the continent, Aboriginal people went no further. The arrival of

Austronesians in New Guinea and the surrounding islands, conversely, precipitated a movement east to New Caledonia, Fiji, Samoa and Tahiti over the course of a millennia from 3200 years ago. Tahiti and its satellites became the centre of a culture that came to be called Polynesian. From there the Austronesians undertook further journeys of exploration and colonisation; north to Hawaii and south-west to New Zealand, between 1200 and 800 years ago. It is probable that Easter Island in the far eastern Pacific was peopled during this timeframe. Single outrigger craft were designed to give greater open ocean stability and the possibility of on-board living quarters and storage pens. As with the first Australians 60 000 years earlier, these travellers went where no humans – archaic or modern – had ventured before. With the Americas inhabited by 14 000 years ago, and possibly earlier, this spread from New Guinea and the Solomons into the vast expanse of the Pacific was the last stage in the human colonisation of the habitable earth. These ocean travellers took with them the technology to make pottery, which was gradually abandoned. Other tools and techniques and domestic food sources, such as pigs, chickens, breadfruit and taro, endured to varying extents throughout the diaspora, thereby transforming islands which had formerly been the preserve of migrating and windblown animals, or those carried by the currents. The occupation of the Polynesian islands east of the Fijian archipelago was assisted by a 1000-year span of favourable weather.[30]

Historians, anthropologists and archaeologists generally agree that this Polynesian expansion stopped at New Zealand, so that the westerly curve of Pacific migration was not joined as a circle and Australia remained, it seems, a very early but largely separate stepping stone in the human diaspora. Having studied the possible motivations, strategies and maritime means of migration, archaeologist Geoffrey Irwin concludes that Australia and a handful of other islands remained outside the Polynesian arc 'because people chose not to sail in their direction'.[31] The pushes and pulls of that remarkable human movement had petered out.

There are, nonetheless, tantalising elements in Australia's first Pacific coast cultures that suggest some contact with others from over the horizon. The spread of shell fish hook technology along the extent of that east coast in pre-colonial times was broken for a considerable distance of 1000 kilometres between the lower Great Barrier Reef and Point Plomer, near present-day Port Macquarie in New South Wales. The gap raises questions about the dispersal of technology, the effect of environment upon take-up and the possibility of an independent interaction between peoples of the Pacific and the south-east Australian coast. The northern hooks relate to Melanesian design, while those to the south of Point Plomer more resemble Māori types. Shell hook technology was evident in Polynesian cultures before it was adopted by Aboriginal people south of Point Plomer. Hooks appeared there around the time a temporary Polynesian foothold was established on Norfolk Island 1400 kilometres off New South Wales, around 600 years ago.[32]

Furthermore, oral tradition has some coastal Aboriginal people looking to the sea – the Pacific – for their origin stories. The Wodi Wodi people of the region some 130 kilometres south of Sydney regarded the sacred mountain Kulunghutti, or Coolangatta, to be the point of departure for souls returning across the sea whence they came. In one account related to anthropologist RH Mathews by an Aboriginal elder towards the end of the 19th century, Kulunghutti was connected by the 'very long stem of a cabbage tree, imperceptible to human vision, [which] reached from some unknown land across the sea'. The souls of the departed 'walked away along it to the sea coast and onwards across the expanse of water'.[33] When Europeans began appearing at places along that coast from 1788 onwards, they were often regarded as ancestors returned without apparent colour; as one American seaman noted in 1842, 'having passed through so much water in their posthumous trip through the ocean'.[34] In 1961 another anthropologist, JH Bell, spoke to members of a southern Sydney Aboriginal community, many of whom had familial links to the

Wodi Wodi and others further south. He heard one 'widely known' story that 'Aborigines came to the South Coast in canoes from across the Pacific Ocean'.³⁵

≈

'... from "time immemorial"...'

There is currently no genomic evidence to support a Pacific origin for Aboriginal people.³⁶ However, descendants of the 'First Australians' do not necessarily feel the need to reconcile scientific finding and traditional knowledge. The landmark 'Uluru Statement from the Heart', delivered after Indigenous discussion about Constitutional reform and recognition of First Peoples in 2017, began with a straightforward declaration of Indigenous sovereignty and possession which extended back, 'according to common law from "time immemorial", and according to science more than 60 000 years ago'.

The desire to determine a scientific basis and a timeframe for the peopling of Australia and the Pacific is only as old as the European colonisation of the continent, for both were the result of Enlightenment-era enquiry. The ability to encounter and compare cultures in the age of Europe's great commercial, military, philosophical and scientific expansion was unprecedented. Accordingly, on board the *Endeavour*, Joseph Banks pondered the possibility of a common origin for the Māori of New Zealand and the people of Tahiti. In the century and a half after those musings, the upheaval generated by the theories of Darwin, Suess and Wegener created an intellectual space to be filled by all manner of conjecture about people and places. Flux begat flux. Some wrote of a lost land called Lemuria, named after the lemurs of the supposed vestigial land bridge island of Madagascar; a connection between Australia and Gondwana. Darwinian ideas of natural selection were applied to humans and these ancient landscapes were consequently populated by a hierarchical panoply of people. Culture and physiology were investigated in order to arrive at answers. So, too, were geographic origins.

At one end of the intellectual spectrum were pulp novels that fantasised about advanced civilisations which had occupied so-called Lemuria – ancient Australia – before the tenure of the 'stone-age' Aboriginal people. Those writings, which emerged in the 1890s during the lead-up to the Federation of Australia's colonies and the white nationalism that accompanied the union, suggested European Australians were the rightful inheritors of a civilised deep past.[37] At the other end was Herbert Basedow, one of the first Australian-born anthropologists, who took a far more compassionate but no less hierarchical view of the impact of geographical history upon the human present. Speaking to the Royal Society of South Australia in 1914 of work which would inform his 1925 book *The Australian Aborigine*, Basedow presented the first 'Australians' as the occupants of an arcadia separated from the rest of the world by the disappearance of Lemuria and the link to Gondwana. The Aboriginal people lived, thereafter, 'hermetically sealed' from the influences which affected human development in other parts of the world. That was an overstatement. The adoption of Malo's Law in some parts of Cape York, the use of outrigger canoes in the north and the possibility of fish hook introduction in the south-east, are clear examples to the contrary.

Debates about the degree of 'diffusion' from external influences are longstanding and ongoing in Australian archaeology. As the consensus around a single migration to the continent firms, so too arguments for internally generated cultural changes have coalesced. In 2006 archaeologist Ian McNiven suggested that perhaps the biggest influence from the Pacific *throughout* Australia was ecological not directly cultural (the emphasis is mine).[38] The introduction of the dingo from Melanesia – rather than South-East Asia – around 3500 years ago led to the extinction and depletion of other mainland species, including the thylacine, while giving Aboriginal people across the continent a hunting partner, totem and camp companion. It is the case, nonetheless, that whatever technologies and thoughts permeated from peoples beyond the coast, they were transformed by Aboriginal people into something definably of the mainland, not the Pacific.

Basedow's picture of a people completely cut off nonetheless permitted him to present an entirely cultural, rather than biological, basis for difference. It was only through 'good fortune' – historical accident – that cosmopolitan Europeans had been given the 'opportunity to blossom forth into all the splendour of civilisation'.[39] That was an acknowledgment of a connection which others had questioned. And Basedow allowed for the possibility of an ancient Aboriginal occupation and respect for the profundity of Indigenous voice and knowledge on the part of anthropologists such as Ted Strehlow and WEH Stanner; something that would become hugely significant in later decades. In this respect it was one important Australian step in an already old intellectual and emotional journey; what the historian of Pacific encounters, John Gascoigne, has called the acceptance of a 'shared humanity'. That realisation had been particularly stimulated by the 'increasing convergence of human beings' in the Pacific – the last great region to be occupied by people and the last to be caught up in the incremental acquisition of lands by Europeans.[40] This movement, of course, would lead to the colonisation of Australia.

CHAPTER 3

Converging on Australia

'change the date'

Writing in 1895, George Collingridge was less concerned with the Aboriginal origins of Australia than its European past. In mid-winter that year, tucked away among ancient trees to the north of the port of Sydney, he penned the final touches of his great work *The Discovery of Australia*; being *'A Critical Documentary and Historic Investigation Concerning the Priority of Discovery of Australasia by Europeans'*. Collingridge was not completely secluded. From Hornsby Junction, the professional artist and amateur historian could travel to town with its libraries, learned societies, clubs and conversations aboard a steam train that snaked through native bush, then orchards, cow pasture, and subdivisions before arriving at the North Shore Ferry Company terminal at Milsons Point opposite the docks of the busy Pacific harbour in Circular Quay and Darling Harbour. The train ride itself was a temporal trip through a century of colonial history from forest to ferries, and it is not inconceivable that Collingridge regarded it as such. Within a decade his 'upper north shore' would be a place for wealthy commuters, distinguished by large villas which housed bankers, merchants, architects and the occasional artist. The dwellings often featured half-timbered gables which hinted at a medieval heritage and high-pitched roofs to disperse non-existent snowfalls, some tiled with Welsh slate. They were manifestations of the cultural affinity with Britain that persisted alongside the nationalist sentiment which had accompanied the establishment of the Australian Commonwealth in 1901.

Even when he was in central Sydney, Collingridge was at the edge of Britain's empire and far removed from the great collections of the imperial centre and the continent. Nonetheless, the multi-lingual artist managed to assemble documentary evidence of the European presence around Australian waters before James Cook – generally recognised as the first to encounter the east coast in 1770. The Dutchman Willem Janssen (Janszoon), was yet to be acknowledged as the first occidental to make landfall anywhere on the continent in March 1606 after he sailed from Java to the Gulf of Carpentaria.

George Collingridge was convinced that the Portuguese knew of the existence of Australia more than a century before the Dutch. His book included an illustration of the bottom half of a wooden globe bearing a Latin inscription which translated as: 'southern land was recently discovered in 1499 but is not yet fully known'. Charts copied in France from lost Portuguese originals – the so-called Dieppe Maps – showed a coastline not unlike that of northern Queensland, thereby casting into question Cook's standing as the 'discoverer' of the continent's Pacific coast.

It was all rather contentious in a set of colonies with strong links to Albion; particularly so in the first colony, New South Wales, which had enthusiastically celebrated the centenary of British colonisation in 1888. At the time Sir Henry Parkes spoke of the 'crimson thread of kinship' which tied the colonial offspring to mother Britannia, as he opened Sydney's spacious Centennial Park, created for 'the people' to mark the occasion. In 1879 a statue of the great navigator Cook had been unveiled in Hyde Park in the centre of Sydney, before 60 000 people. The Englishman stood on top of an inscribed stone plinth which informed the curious that he 'Discovered This Territory 1770'. A likeness of Arthur Phillip, the first governor, was being planned for the Botanic Gardens as Collingridge wrote his preface. Collective and personal connections to Britain had long been inscribed on the landscape itself, from the naming of the colonies of Victoria and Queensland in honour of the revered monarch, to the countless houses, hotels and streets christened Albion, George, Nelson and so forth.

Not wanting to march to that drum beat, Collingridge chose 'Jave-la-Grande' as the name for his new dwelling at Hornsby Junction, which he had built of the sandstone that so characterised the Sydney region. The moniker was taken from the map upon which Collingridge based much of his conjecture; Java la Grande or Java Major was the land that spread out below Java Minor, the East Indies. It was essentially the Terra Australis of the 1499 discovery. It was in 'Jave-la-Grande' that the revisionist completed his new history of Australia.

Somewhat optimistically Collingridge hoped that his book might turn public opinion enough so that 1899 would see a commemoration of the 400th anniversary of the European discovery of Australia, much as the US had just done with their Columbian Exhibition of 1893; a celebration of modern American civilisation dressed in the white finery of the classical age whence it had ostensibly emerged. It was not the first time a colonial Australian had looked across the Pacific to that other New World for encouraging comparison or succour, and it would not be the last.

But identification with rising America seemed not to be Collingridge's motivation for placing so much faith in his claim for a Portuguese discovery. A lukewarm attachment to the England of his birth assisted the construction of the counter-narrative, as did a profound dislike of the Dutch. Collingridge's Catholicism, of continental rather than English persuasion, was another factor. Remarkably, 30 years earlier, he had fought bravely with the internationalist Zouave unit helping to defend the Papal States against Giuseppe Garibaldi's republicans during the final stages of Italian unification.

But even Catholic devotion did not completely determine his reading of the evidence. Collingridge disagreed, for instance, with Cardinal Patrick Moran who was then making his own attempts at rewriting the origin story of his adopted colonial homeland. Moran sided with the Spanish and argued that Pedro de Quiros, a Portuguese-born navigator in the service of Spain, had planted a cross on the Queensland coast, part of his 'New Jerusalem', which he called Australia del Espiritu Santo in 1606 – perhaps pre-empting the Protestant Dutchman Janssen.

Collingridge had included in his own work an account of this landfall by Luis Vaez de Torres, who sailed with Quiros. Both those men wrote of the pigs and chickens which inhabited the new land and the bows and arrows of the local people, neither of which accord with the natural or cultural history of Queensland. Determined to make his own mark as an historian, Collingridge argued against Moran's claim that Quiros had found Australia.

Such were the sectarian divisions within Australian society when all were supposed to be united within the new Commonwealth, that Moran's version of history informed the Catholic school syllabus, while state schools and non-Catholic faith-based institutions emphasised the revelatory role of James Cook. Collingridge's account was critiqued upon publication but it was attacked more roundly in 1917 by the Professor of History at the University of Sydney, George Arnold Wood. Such was the detail contained in Collingridge's work it took Wood, an expert in maritime history himself, that long to dismiss the maps which showed Java la Grande. They were, in the professor's opinion, nothing more than 'brilliant geographical romances'.[1]

Wood's emphatic debunking of the possibility of a Portuguese knowledge of Australia was, in turn, repudiated by OHK (Oskar) Spate in 1957 in his capacity as the Foundation Professor of Geography in the Research School of Pacific Studies at the Australian National University, then just over a decade old and indicative of the nation's expanding intellectual interest in its region. It was not good enough to dismiss the maps because the fantastical detail did not so much as include a 'wallaby', for that was the nature of maps of the time, some were credible despite the artistic licence. Collingridge's contentions were not endorsed but neither was the matter settled; there was a 'need for a new survey'.[2] By the time Spate himself set about that project in the 1960s and 1970s, nothing more had come to light to confirm or refute the claim for Portugal. The 'Portuguese may well have sighted much of the continent', Spate concluded, '... but this was not on the record'.[3]

The debate was joined at various times subsequently by academics, amateurs and antiquarians. In 2014 a document from 16th-century Portugal was advertised by a rare book dealer in New York as fresh evidence of pre-Dutch knowledge. It was an illuminated 'processional' with music and text for a religious ceremony, and interest was piqued by a creature nestled within a letter 'D' which resembled a kangaroo, or Spate's missing wallaby, nibbling a shrub. Dated between 1580 and 1620, the document was 'proof' that the artist had travelled to Australia or at least seen specimens or drawings of its fauna.[4] Unsurprisingly the processional found its way into an Australian collection, for local interest in the arcane matter of first footfalls was greater there than elsewhere. Even then the debate had only been carried on among non-Indigenous Australians, whether they were Anglophiles, Catholics or contrarians such as George Collingridge.

For Indigenous people, the details surrounding the arrival of the Portuguese, Dutch or British were neither here nor there when Aboriginal presence extended back beyond 60 000 years. The point was made starkly in 2017 when a supporter of the formal recognition of Australia's First People took issue with the sentiment footnoting Cook's likeness in Hyde Park and sprayed over the reference to his 'discovery' in 1770 with the words 'Change the Date'.

≋

'a vast religious imperialism'

The curiously illuminated Portuguese processional may also, of course, have been inspired by the European discovery of New Guinea, which shared marsupial fauna with Australia. The island was named after its African counterpart in 1545 by Iñigo Ortíz de Retes sailing under the command of the Spanish navigator Ruy López de Villalobos. It had been sighted by the Portuguese in 1511, who then coined the name 'Papua' in 1526, using a Malay word for frizzy hair.[5] Some three decades after Villalobos's voyage, a map was produced showing 'Nova Guinea' with a large un-named green mass beneath it, which is sometimes regarded as the first depiction of Australia.[6] Inhabiting this mysterious country is a hunter, uncharacteristically armed with a bow and arrow, confronting an angry griffin, which is even more unlikely. A lion flees the scene. These embellishments obviously suggest that the map was not a record of an actual encounter with the land below New Guinea, despite the depiction of a galleon sailing north close to its Pacific shore. The document belongs to the era of European expansion in which conjecture and fantasy infused reality. Accordingly, marine monsters share the ocean with a mermaid and her consort.

Intriguingly, the map did show that the southern landmass was separated from New Guinea by a strait before Luis Vaez de Torres proved as much after parting company with Quiros and sailing through the strait that would bear his name in October 1606. In the process, Torres may have glimpsed the northernmost point of Australia perhaps six months after Janssen landed on its western side.[7] Torres kept his discovery a secret in the interests of his king and country. It remained so until 1762 when the British occupied Spain's main Pacific port, Manila, and found out about the existence of 'Torres Strait', just in time for James Cook's own momentous Pacific voyage of discovery in 1769.

The map which showed 'Nova Guinea' also accurately placed the 'Islas de Salamon', or the Solomon Islands, to the east of the larger island. These had been encountered and so-named by the Spaniard Alvaro de Mendaña in 1567 in the belief, or at least hope, they were the land of Ophir; home to the legendary gold mines of King Solomon. That, at least, puts an earliest possible date on the document. It was this voyage which prompted a second voyage by Mendaña in 1595, when he was accompanied by Pedro de Quiros, and during which they named one of the Solomon Islands 'Santa Cruz' or Holy Cross. Their attempt at settlement failed. Quiros survived, returning to name Espiritu Santo in 1606 and, according to Cardinal Moran, installed a Catholic cross on Australia's Pacific coast.

The names Solomon Islands, Santa Cruz and Espiritu Santo – which means Holy Spirit – evince two of the motivations for Spanish imperialism in the Pacific: the quest for gold and the quest for souls. A third imperative was the search for a route to the Spice Islands of South-East Asia, where exotic condiments, as precious as anything that glittered, could be traded. One of Quiros's first commands at Espiritu Santo, after his men fired upon the local people, was to have a church built of plantain bows. There was no contradiction between worshipping God and seeking mammon, despite what the Bible might say in some of its many parts, for gold would pay for the salvation of those who would otherwise be damned for eternity. It might also be considered reward for the effort. Oskar Spate described Mendaña and Quiros's quest as 'a vast religious imperialism in the South Sea'.[8] That territory could be taken in the name of the Spanish king was similarly reconciled. Philip II was immortalised in 1544 by his loyal explorer Villalobos when he christened the Philippines, in honour of the crown prince and king-in-waiting.

That western Pacific archipelago had been brought into the Spanish world by Ferdinand Magellan, the man who is credited with naming the Pacific Ocean itself in 1520, shortly after he navigated from the labyrinthine strait that now bears his name and that connects the Atlantic with the biggest ocean on the globe. The vast expanse of blue could scarcely have contrasted more with the fractured south-western coastline of South America with its myriad islands and dead ends and through which Magellan methodically wound his way.

There was European knowledge of the ocean's existence even before Magellan emerged from his labyrinth. Men from the Iberian Peninsula at the mouth of the Mediterranean had been plundering, conquering and converting the peoples of the Americas since Christopher Columbus arrived in the Caribbean in 1492. He sailed for the King of Castile; literally the land of castles, which with neighbouring Aragon was effectively Spain. Vasco de Balboa crossed the Panamanian isthmus from east to west in 1513 and, with those who accompanied him, made the first European sighting of the 'South Sea' – Magellan's Pacific. In keeping with the spirit of the age, Balboa claimed the ocean and all its imagined islands, also for the King of Castile. Three years later with the ascendancy of Charles I over both Castile and Aragon, navigators such as Magellan, Quiros and Torres would sail in the service of the King of Spain.

Souls and gold were significant but Magellan's fleet of five ships was called the Armada de Molucca, for its purpose was to find a passage to the Moluccas, the Spice Islands. Before scurvy took hold, the expedition's chronicler Antonio Pigafetta communicated with a Tehuelche man who had been kidnapped on the east coast of South America in the region they subsequently called Patagonia, a name probably derived from the Spanish for 'dog with large paws', itself a reference to the size of the people who lived there. Kidnapping indigenous people would become a frequent occurrence in the explorations that followed. Sometimes it was enacted as retribution, sometimes in the process of hostage-based negotiation. Occasionally the captive was the 'beneficiary' of the urge to save heathen souls. Torres's messianism was strong enough to prompt the kidnapping of 20 Papuans during the navigation of the passage between New Guinea and Australia in 1606.[9]

Pigafetta compiled a word list and developed a rapport with the captive which recorded, among other things, the Tehuelche words for head, nose, ears and mouth. It was an important moment in Europe's encounter with 'the other', for Pigafetta showed genuine interest in understanding the man.[10] This was different from the contempt for religious diversity that generally characterised Christian Europe and the Spanish in particular; such that Columbus could equate peace and well-being with freedom from 'heresy and evil'.[11] The conversations between Pigafetta and the 'Patagonian' foreshadowed the ethnological and anthropological interests of a later age. More immediately they can be understood in the spirit of inquiry rather than inquisition. As it was, the man was converted to Christianity. He died at sea, while holding a crucifix, from an un-named sickness probably contracted from his captors. The last weeks of that life spent aboard Magellan's ship were profound on many levels.

Having left the coast of South America on 18 December 1520, the Europeans made landfall in Micronesia on the island of Guam on 6 March of the following year. Not knowing how to find the Spice Islands, Magellan instead arrived in the Philippines. The hierarchical society Magellan found in Cebu was far more familiar than those he encountered in Patagonia or Micronesia. The European established such a rapport with Rajah Humabon that he converted the man to Christianity and interceded militarily on his behalf. That was a mistake and Magellan was killed at the Battle of Mactan. Power play was no less opaque in Cebu than elsewhere, particularly for outsiders. The Rajah subsequently turned on his new foreign allies and the Spanish fled. They returned to Europe by the Indian Ocean, thereby completing the first circumnavigation of the globe, which is often credited to Magellan, though his dismembered remains stayed in Cebu.

≋

'Terre Australe'

As it turned out, and despite Magellan's fatal odyssey, the Spanish were compelled to concede that the Spice Islands were legitimately Portugal's under the 1494 Treaty of Tordesillas, in which the Pope had divided the world in two, allocating one part each to the Portuguese and the Spanish. But the navigator's legacy was greater than any market in nutmeg. Almost immediately a sense of the magnitude of the ocean crossed, and the arrangement of land around it, began appearing in representations of the world. A 1523 globe by Johannes Schöner attempted to combine Magellan's discoveries with Claudius Ptolemy's much older but newly revived theories, which imagined a large southern landmass balancing the known lands of Europe and Asia. Ptolemy's resurrection and Magellan's journey were early manifestations of Europe's Renaissance, which most importantly facilitated an intellectual and physical embrace of the world beyond its continental borders.

The name 'Pacific Ocean' was not universally adopted. Influenced by Schöner's globe, French cartographer Oronce Fine's 1532 map showed the world from north and south poles as if each might be wrapped around a sphere. Fine called the Pacific 'Mare magellanicum' or Magellan's Sea. Brabantian cartographer Abraham Ortelius's 'New World Map' of 1564 referred to it variously as 'Magellan's Sea', 'The Pacific' and 'South Sea'. The latter term would persist into the 18th century to evolve into 'South Seas' by the 1890s. Then it generally referred to the south-west Pacific, the area of greatest relevance to rising Australia. That Ortelius had flying fish leaping from his well-illustrated ocean is evidence of a familiarity with Pigafetta's account of Magellan's journey.

Both Fine and Ortelius depicted a vast south land. Fine's top and bottom views allowed him to easily identify the 'Antarctic Circle' which lay in the middle of 'Terra Australis', a place he claimed had been 'recently discovered but not yet fully known'. The discovery referred to here, in fact, was Tierra del Fuego, which Magellan saw on the south side of his strait and Fine took to be the tip of the southern continent rather than an island. The inscription sounded very much like that on Collingridge's 1499 chart, which he thought was evidence of a Portuguese discovery on the western side of the Pacific. Such was the desire to find the elusive Terra Australis, which all were certain existed.

The Flemish geographer Gerard Mercator's 1569 world map was particularly significant in the history of European cartography for the criss-crossed navigation and latitudinal lines he superimposed on the oceans. Indeed, it was intended as an aid to navigation – hence the encouraging number of galleons shown sailing the various seas. Mercator referred to Magellan's sea in Spanish, 'El Mar Pacifico', but acknowledged the navigator by name in one of various scroll-like cartouches explaining maritime discoveries for the benefit of those who would follow.

By the time Mercator drafted his helpful chart, others had already sailed in Magellan's wake from Spain's American possessions, also called New Spain. Manila became the centre of Spanish power in 1571. The trans-Pacific traffic that ensued entailed exchanging Central American gold and silver for Asian luxuries in Manila, which were then shipped to Acapulco to be transported across the Panamanian isthmus to Europe. It was the realisation of the busy ocean foreshadowed in Mercator's map. This was the 'Spanish Lake' that Oskar Spate explored so thoroughly in his 1979 study.

By then the Treaty of Tordesillas had long been redrawn in the Treaty of Zaragoza of 1529.[12] The new line of division between the Portuguese and Spanish worlds ran down the middle of the yet uncharted continent of Australia. It cut through the territories of at least 17 Aboriginal groups who occupied the continent's monsoonal north and dry interior. These were homelands which had probably existed for thousands of years; a reality of little relevance to the Europeans, had they even known of the existence of the ancient land and its people.

That 135° meridian persisted on maps of the continent after the Dutch began filling in its western coastline in the 17th century, discoveries that stemmed somewhat incidentally from their displacement of the Portuguese in the Spice Islands at the beginning of the 17th century. Janssen's first landfall in 1606 was one of these. Accordingly, it distinguished New Holland in the west from unknown tracts in the east on Melchisédech Thévenot's famous 1663 Map of New Holland. Having effectively removed the Portuguese, the Dutch inherited the western side of the 135° meridian by right of discovery. The French cartographer and polymath did not venture to plot a Pacific coastline on that territory. Interestingly, however, Thévenot called the uncharted expanse to the east 'Terre Australe' and claimed that it had been discovered in 1644. This clearly contradicted the earlier assertions of Ortelius, Quiros and others but, by then, the Spanish were a spent force and had not documented let alone occupied the land that fell within the bifurcated Catholic world of old. Thévenot was referring to two short lengths of coast which had just been mapped by the Dutchman Abel Tasman; the bottom of so-called Van Diemen's Land and part of 'Zeelandia', or New Zealand. Having set aside New Holland as a potential Dutch possession, Thévenot was suggesting that the territory on the other side of the meridian was available as a possession – perhaps for his own beloved France.[13]

There was clearly still much conjecture and implicit politicking in the 'science' of cartography. Accuracy was paramount for one of the pre-eminent successors to Thévenot in the French world of map making, Guillaume de l'Isle. His *Atlas Nouveau* of 1730 featured a map of the world in two hemispheres.[14] While de l'Isle could not resist including emotive embellishments on the margin of his map – there was a mermaid and what may have been Neptune blowing a conch – he did restore 'Terre Australe' to its former position at the bottom of the world, well below New Holland, which was still without a Pacific coast. The half-drawn continent was shown connected to New Guinea because Torres's 1606 discovery of the strait that separated the two lands was still a Spanish secret.

In the end, of course, it was James Cook who drew in the missing Pacific coast and added another name to the continent: New South Wales. That was in 1770. Accordingly, some 18 years later, it was the British rather than the French who colonised Thévenot's 'Terre Australe'. Arthur Phillip, the colony's first governor, set its western boundary along the 135° meridian – the Tordesillas line redrawn after Magellan's Pacific trip. Such were the long-lasting ripples from that extraordinary voyage. The continent remained a bifurcated entity – New Holland facing the Indian Ocean and New South Wales bordering the Pacific – until well after Matthew Flinders sailed around it at the beginning of the 19th century and then suggested another version of 'Terre Australe' for the whole: Australia. But it was not until after Britain claimed the entire continent in 1828 that New Holland and New South Wales were unified under that single name. Australia was not the south land that navigators and cartographers had variously wished into existence for more than 300 years. Rather its colonisation and naming were the unforeseen outcome of that quest.

≈

'Prosperity comes riding in boats'

That Magellan and the other early European explorers of the western Pacific did not sail into un-politicised seas is clear from the fate that befell the navigator on Cebu. It is unsurprising, therefore, that the trade the Spanish established in the Philippines was built upon pre-existing networks which had linked the peoples of the Asia-Pacific regions for centuries. History did not begin with the arrival of the Portuguese, the Spanish or the English, as the likes of George Collingridge sometimes implied. This was the region from where the Pacific itself had been colonised by Austronesians from around 6000 years before present.

Pre-European developments in and around the Asian seas which bordered the Pacific were extraordinarily complex; often peaceful and lucrative, sometimes very violent, usually in flux. In the 9th century, for instance, Koreans played a significant role in trade between China and Japan before their gradual 'withdrawal from the sea' in the words of historian Lincoln Paine; one part in a pattern of maritime ebb and flow that seemed to characterise relations in this part of Asia defined by islands, long coastlines and competing interests.

Japanese contact with China extended back at least to the first century of the common era. They, like maritime people elsewhere, developed superstitions and rituals to offset the danger that accompanied ocean sea travel in vessels driven by currents, wind and muscle. In the third century, the Chinese remarked upon the curious Japanese practice of sailing with a 'keeper of taboos', one who did not wash or groom and whose role was to keep misfortune at bay. If the keeper failed, he was killed. If successful, he was handsomely rewarded.[15] The Koreans, Japanese and Chinese often fought each other and others. There was small-scale piracy and raiding but also large-scale naval battles. In 663 a Chinese fleet of 170 vessels destroyed 400 Japanese ships. In the 10th century, Chinese ships were destroyed in the estuary of the Red River by Vietnamese defenders who had filled one branch of the river with sharpened poles which pierced the hulls of the invaders. And so it continued.

In the 15th and 16th centuries, the Japanese warred among themselves and so retreated from the sea, as the Koreans had earlier done. It was not until the early 1600s, as the Spanish were consolidating their power in the Philippines, that they emerged from civil strife to enter the long period of political stability often referred to as the Tokugawa era, in which a shogun ruled with the sanction of the emperor. Trade and diplomacy were resumed among near neighbours, including Siam (Thailand), Korea, the Philippines and the Ryūkyū Islands, later called Okinawa. Indeed, trade was encouraged as a means of strengthening the central power of the shotgun over the various military lords, the *daimyō*, whose power struggles had driven two centuries of war. There was trade with the Spanish and other Europeans until Christian proselytising led to the exclusion of all except the Dutch, whose single-minded pursuit of commerce was tolerated.

Evangelising, that very European style of destabilisation and interference, led also to the third shogun restricting Japanese travel in the 1630s, so that voyaging west of Korea and south of the Ryūkyū Islands except for diplomacy and sanctioned trade was banned. There had, nonetheless, been 350 Japanese merchant ships plying the border seas of the western Pacific during the previous three decades. Though the travel ban foreshadowed the more complete seclusion with which the Tokugawa era is most often associated, Japanese self-identification with isolation did not take hold until the 1790s.[16] The Tokugawa's early openness to Asian relations did not extend to China. The tribute and subservience demanded by the Chinese Emperor was anathema to a shotgunate establishing its power among the *daimyō*. Internal stability was paramount to both power structures.

The Chinese had dominated trade in the border seas down to the Spice Islands since the Tang Dynasty in the 7th century. They also ventured west to India and Africa. 'Prosperity comes riding in boats' was one line in a verse celebrating the accomplishments of the 9th-century Chinese ruler of Vietnam, Goa Pian.[17] And then came another reversal. Faced with threats along land borders, the Ming Dynasty rulers withdrew from the sea. An oft-quoted edict declaring that 'not even a little plank is allowed to drift to the sea' has been dated to 1371, which pre-dates the seven extraordinary tribute voyages under the command of Ming admiral Zheng He between 1405 and 1433.[18] These were vast fleets of treasure ships larger than anything built in Europe. The primary intention was neither commercial nor military but rather to impress and secure tribute from 'barbarian' nations, thereby confirming, to the Chinese at least, their supremacy as the 'Middle Kingdom'. From 1433 China's interest in blue-water navigation 'came to an abrupt end'.[19]

The voyages took the Chinese as far west as Aden. In 2002, the best-selling and iconoclastic author Gavin Menzies argued that two of these huge tribute fleets also travelled to Australia between 1421 and 1423; one from the west across the Indian Ocean, the other over the Pacific from the east. The suggestion has been dismissed by experts with even more disdain than Wood's rejection of Collingridge's Portuguese thesis.[20] There is general agreement, however, that the Chinese abruptly discontinued their interest in the sea in 1433, a consequence again of internal problems and a desire for stability. This termination of maritime enterprise was so emphatic that records of the tribute voyages, and the construction plans for the great vessels which undertook them, were destroyed leaving the archival gap that Menzies attempted to fill six centuries later. Maritime trade was not resumed until 1567, just before the Spanish established their pre-eminence in Manila in 1571. But so significant was the release of the entrepreneurial diaspora, particularly from Fujian, that Manila's Chinese population outgrew the Spanish and creoles by more than ten to one within 15 years. By 1750 it had increased to 40 000 despite official and popular attempts to curtail migration through legislation and violence. Both presaged the experiences of Chinese people in Australia and across the Pacific to the United States in the 19th century. They were integral to the economy yet culturally distinct and persecuted. The Chinese ability to tolerate social subordination while remaining industrious and peaceful led the Englishman Edmund Scott in 1606 to equate them with Europe's Jews, and in doing so reveal the resentment and prejudice that such resilience could engender: 'crouching under' the local elite, they 'rob them of their wealth and send it to China'.[21]

China, itself, was central to Spain's commercial interest in the western Pacific. Europe's demand for silk, porcelain and other luxuries from the Middle Kingdom was large and growing. Conversely, Chinese interest in anything the Spanish had to offer by way of goods was negligible. So South American silver and gold was shipped across the Pacific to pay for the beautiful things that Ming Dynasty China offered to Europe. Officially only one annual round trip was permitted between 1593 and 1815. In practice there were more. Most tellingly, the wealth that flowed to China from South America helped to fund the construction of the Great Wall to keep out the Mongols to the north.[22] The proud culture that sought protection behind a wall, and with little interest in the offerings of others except as tribute, stood in stark contrast to the avarice, arrogance and genuine curiosity that was fuelling Europe global expansion.

CHAPTER 4

In the wake of Spain

'... Cursed be that I did so'

One thing led to another. Spanish treasure ships attracted the English, shark-like, to the Pacific – thereby beginning their interest in the South Sea. Sir Francis Drake left the Tudor kingdom of Elizabeth I and a young William Shakespeare to sail around the tip of South America and up the west coasts of both continents in 1577. He captured two Spanish galleons and named an area somewhere along present-day northern California 'New Albion', in the apparent belief that the people he encountered there wanted him as their king; something Drake agreed to on behalf of 'her most excellent majesty'.[1]

Drake's success attracted others over the course of a century. Some were simply pirates, others were privateers whose queen had given them licence to attack England's enemy, though they were not formally naval officers. The extraordinary William Dampier was one of those. His first Pacific voyage was in 1679–80. A second from 1685 took him across the ocean to the Philippines, China and Siam (Thailand) and then by chance to the north-west coast of Australia – which Dampier knew as New Holland. His 1688 landing was the first recorded English encounter with the continent. After surviving storms, sickness and capture in Sumatra, Dampier returned to England to write up two accounts of his experiences. As a result, he was given charge of an expedition to further investigate New Holland, New Guinea and the still mysterious Terra Australis in 1699.[2] The privateer turned explorer was also an assiduous observer of 'the wonderful Works of God in different Parts of the World'. But in his diligent 'Search and Inquiry' into 'the true Nature and State of Things', Dampier was a product of the

Enlightenment and a forerunner of James Cook and his companions.[3]

The explorer had hoped to approach from the Pacific Ocean rather than across the Indian, but could not round Cape Horn 'by Reason of the Time of Year ... [it being] in the Depth of Winter there'.[4] Had he done so, we might be crediting Dampier with 'discovering' Australia's east coast, and his first negative impression may have been balanced by views of more fertile territories. In the end the Englishman came from the Cape of Good Hope in the west fully expectant of finding the coast he had touched a decade earlier: 'keeping an E.S.E. [east, south east] Course, the better to make my way for New Holland'. He made landfall at a place he called Shark's Bay for the number of those fish there. Dampier described wallabies, turtles, a dugong and oysters 'both of the common kind for Eating, and of the Pearl kind'.[5] That was near Broome, where he also saw the 'smokes' of the local people. There followed a violent encounter which resulted in the first Aboriginal casualty at the hands of the British. After five weeks 'ranging off and on the Coast of New Holland', Dampier sailed on to Timor in need of fresh water.

On this voyage, the names 'New Holland' and 'Terra Australis' were used interchangeably in accord with Thévenot's 1644 map. Having stopped at Timor, Dampier continued north of New Guinea intending 'to come around by the South of Terra Australis in my Return back'; that is, to sail down the continent's Pacific coast. He failed in that but did manage to navigate around a large island to the east of New Guinea. In contrast to New Holland, it made a good impression. There was abundant water, berries, coconuts, 'hogs and dogs' and 'strong well-limb'd Negroes'. Dampier used the word 'pleasant' several times in his description of the place, which he thought 'may afford as many rich commodities as any in the World'. The local people, he suggested, 'may be easily brought to Commerce'. Obviously enamoured, the Englishman called the island 'Nova Britannia [New Britain]', a counterpart to Drake's New Albion on the Pacific's opposite shore and evidence of an expanding sense of the great ocean.[6] The name 'New Britain' survived because no-one challenged the British claim to it for another two centuries. By contrast, 'New Albion' in the Americas was erased.

William Dampier's accounts were widely read. His careful descriptions of New Holland and New Guinea appeared in print in 1702 as *A Voyage to New Holland*. It was his third book. Dampier's first and second works, *A New Voyage Round the World* and *Voyages and Descriptions* were published in 1697 and 1699. A fourth book, *A Continuation of a Voyage to New Holland*, was printed in 1709. The popularity of Dampier's writings was due in part to a public appetite for the real and imagined exotic adventures of pirates and privateers raiding the 'Spanish Main', the route taken by that empire's treasure ships from the 'New World'. The appearance of these stories in literature and theatre did, of course, reflect actual English predation upon its maritime rival in the Caribbean, the Indian Ocean and the Pacific. Men like Dampier and his one-time commander Woodes Rogers, who circumnavigated the globe with Dampier and also wrote about it, were the heroes and forerunners of an incipient British empire. The pirate Henry Morgan, who raided Spanish possessions on both sides of the Panamanian isthmus in the late 1660s and early 1670s, was knighted for his efforts. Others such as Edward Teach, the infamous Blackbeard, became anti-heroes as a result of their murder and theft along Britain's own maritime routes, particularly those connecting the rising power to its North American possessions in the mid-18th century.

Daniel Defoe made much of the coincidence of English piracy with a new form of story-telling – the novel.[7] He may have been the anonymous author of the *King of Pirates*, which elaborated upon the real-life adventures of Richard Avery. Defoe was certainly the creator of the completely fictional *The Life, Adventures, and Pyracies of the Famous Captain Singleton* published in the same year, 1720. Both followed his most famous work, *Robinson Crusoe*, a narrative in which pirates play a part in the uneven fortunes of the hero, who is shipwrecked on an island of enslaving 'savages'. Crusoe saves one of their victims, whom he names Friday. It is generally accepted that Defoe based his story upon the experiences of Alexander Selkirk, abandoned on an east Pacific island called Juan Fernandez and rescued by William Dampier and Woodes Rogers during their circumnavigation in 1709. Remarkably Selkirk and Dampier had been comrades on an earlier raiding voyage up South America's Pacific coast in 1703, during which Selkirk chose to be left behind after falling out with the captain.[8]

The idea of the desert island and the marooned man resonated down the decades to Robert Louis Stevenson's description of his fictional pirate, Ben Gunn, in the serialisation of *Treasure Island* in 1881; dressed, as he was originally, in the goatskin of Selkirk and Crusoe.[9] His reputation made, Stevenson would end his days in the early 1890s on the Samoan islands, not as a man abandoned, but an artist in paradise who occasionally sojourned in 'civilisation', the port of Sydney included.

John Gascoigne has argued that *Robinson Crusoe* 'did more to stimulate interest in the South Seas than any factual voyage account', among the British at least.[10] The relationship between the characters, Crusoe and Friday, has subsequently been seen as prototypical of the inequitable encounters that followed with systematic colonisation: Crusoe saved Man Friday; the Englishman would convert the dark-skinned man to Christianity; Crusoe wanted to be called 'master'. However, Defoe also used the fictional cross-cultural encounter to explore and critique the beliefs of his own people. Accordingly, in the process of his education, Man Friday questioned the omnipotence of the Christian god and the nature of faith and logical enquiry. In doing so, Gascoigne has suggested, 'The Pacific, in the voice of Man Friday, was beginning to speak back'.[11]

Of course, this was a conversation within the collective European mind, rather than an actual dialogue between colonisers and colonised. But it is a remarkable idea to consider given that Britain's colonial enterprises, driven by certainty, destiny, curiosity and greed, had barely begun. The cultural historian Lynn Hunt argues that 18th-century novels such as *Robinson Crusoe* allowed readers to 'extend their purview of empathy... across traditional social boundaries'.[12] She refers specifically to boundaries of class and gender but readers might also traverse lines of ethnicity – 'race' – and nationality through these books, coming to recognise the diverse peoples of the shrinking world as human beings like oneself. It was an imaginative development which led ultimately to the foundation of modern human rights in that century and would extend to modern relativist anthropology 200 years after.

The back chat within the English mind had, in fact, already begun. Well before Defoe created Man Friday, the challenge of other perspectives, which empathy courted, emerged from the mouth of Caliban in Shakespeare's play *The Tempest*, written in 1610–1611. Like the relationship between Friday and Crusoe, that of Caliban and Prospero – who had been exiled to the former's island – is more complex than the simple dichotomy of master and slavish brute suggests. One passage from the ostensible 'savage' seems to clearly anticipate the future grievances of the colonised and the coloniser's duplicity:

> This island's mine, by Sycorax my mother
> Which though tak'st from me. When though cam'st first,
> Thou strok'st me and made much of me, wouldst give me
> Water with berries in't, and teach me how
> To name the bigger light, and how the less,
> That burn by day and night; and then I loved thee,
> And showed thee all the qualities o'th isle, ...
> Cursed be that I did so.[13]

Caliban's god, Setebos, has the same name as the Patagonian deity noted by Magellan; and it has long been thought that Shakespeare's character was based, in part at least, on the Patagonian man with whom Antonio Pigafetta conversed during the first European Pacific crossing in 1520. As the literary historian Stephen Greenblatt has remarked, *The Tempest* threw up many questions about power and difference, not least: 'Who is the civilised man and who is the barbarian?'[14] For all the arrogance and hubris that accompanied Britain's growing power, there was uncertainty and self-reflection as well.

Perhaps the most extraordinary of these early veiled critiques came from Jonathan Swift who, in 1726, presented an account of 'travels into several remote nations of the world' under the pen name Lemuel Gulliver. Two of those nations were close to Australia, still unknown but skirted by actual navigators. The island of the wondrous Houyhnhnms was south of Nuyts Land, the name given to Australia's southern coast after the Dutch explorer Pieter Nuyts mapped it in 1627. Lilliput, inhabited by tiny people, sat somewhere between Van Diemen's Land, partially charted in 1642, and Sumatra. That placed it in present-day South Australia.[15]

The book was *Gulliver's Travels*. Just two decades after Dampier's assiduous accounts, and contemporaneous with Defoe's works of fact and fiction, Swift was playing very provocatively with the idea of truth and the purpose of exploration. In his summary chapter Gulliver claimed to have presented his 'gentle reader' with 'a faithful history' of his travels when, by then, it would have been clear to any educated or canny reader that the previous accounts of giants and diminutive peoples were fantastical. Swift then suggests that it is the 'chief aim' of the traveller to 'make men wiser and better, and to improve their minds by the bad as well as the good example of what they deliver concerning foreign places'. It may have been that he had done exactly that, despite the fact that the good and bad people and places he described were concoctions.

More challenging still was his characterisation of the prevailing imperialism, described in a scenario whereby 'a crew of pirates' encounter a land by chance and 'go ashore to rob and plunder'. They see a 'harmless people' and murder them despite their 'kindness'. The pirates take 'formal possession' of the land for the king, 'set up a rotten plank or a stone for a memorial', change the name of the land and return home to be rewarded for their efforts. They subsequently establish a 'modern colony' to 'convert and civilize an idolatrous and barbarous people'.[16]

Swift's account might at first be taken as a critique of Spanish methods. Indeed, he went on to explain that his description did not apply to the British nation, which was 'an example to the world for the wisdom, care and justice in planting colonies'. It is difficult, however, to interpret this disclaimer as anything other disingenuous, in keeping with the book's satirical tone. Little wonder then that *Gulliver's Travels* and its author had fallen from favour by the end of the century as Britain was consolidating its empire in a way that sometimes echoed Swift's apocryphal pirates. In 1814 Sir Walter Scott described the book as 'severe, unjust and degrading'.[17]

≋

'So where then is his great land?'

Amidst the Pacific busyness, Australia sat in a slipstream created both by historical accident and the natural forces of current and wind, so that European contact along its east coast was denied; possibly just as Polynesian landfall had been forestalled in previous centuries. If the Portuguese had arrived in the 15th century, as George Collingridge claimed, their secrecy and the unhelpfulness of the strange maps that followed did not assist others. Torres came very close to touching the continent when he passed through his strait from the Pacific in 1606. Janssen, of course, arrived from the other direction, reaching the west coast of Cape York. But he went back the way he came. Dampier's intention to arrive from the eastern Pacific was foiled by the seasons so he managed only to explore Australia's north-west coast and the shores of New Guinea and New Britain.

There had been other glances and glimpses. Two of those, Nuyts Land and 'Dimens Land', gave Jonathan Swift actual fragmentary coastlines near which to position his fanciful 'nations'. The Dutch had explored without serious imperialistic intent, though the names they proclaimed, New Holland, and the lands of Arnhem, Nuyt and

Van Diemen held the possibility of territorial claims by right of first discovery. Driven by strong westerlies, the Dutch explorer Dirk Hartog made landfall on the Indian Ocean coast in 1616 and left an inscribed pewter plate nailed to a post as evidence; much like Swift's rotten plank. His countryman Abel Tasman's two voyages took him along the south and north of the continent in 1642 and 1644 respectively. On the second trip, when he encountered the bottom of Van Diemen's Land, Tasman mapped a possible continental east coast he called New Zealand.

The pervading mystery of the Pacific side of New Holland, or *Terra Australis* in Dampier's conflation of the two lands, was abundantly evident in the maps produced, which consistently showed an incomplete continent with an absent or clearly conjectural eastern edge. Didier Robert de Vaugondy's Reduced Map of Australasia, printed in 1756, had a distorted Pacific coast extending from the southern and eastern sides of Van Diemen's Land up to Espiritu Santo. That was based upon Quiros's belief that he had found the coast of *Terra Australis* back in 1605. Curiously, however, de Vaugondy named the entire landmass 'Nouvelle Holland'.

The Frenchman Louis Bougainville had a copy of this document when he led an expedition of two ships, *Boudeuse* and *Étoile*, across the Pacific in the wake of Magellan and Quiros in 1768. He found Espiritu Santo but the vast continent which was supposed to lie behind it proved illusory, as the navigator suspected it would. Claiming that island for France, Bougainville asked, 'So where then is his great land?'[18] Sailing south-west with caution, Bougainville and his crew met breakers and sand spits. It was the Great Barrier Reef. The outer ring was consequently named after him: Bougainville Reef. The low land that some thought they saw beyond was, in the opinion of the commander of the *Étoile*, the coast of New Holland. Bougainville was not prepared to risk all to put an east coast on New Holland or any coast on Terra Australis. The Frenchman justified his momentous decision in his journal: 'The encounter with these succession of breakers does not allow me to continue to seek here Quiros's southern continent'.[19] And so Pacific Australia remained *incognita* to Europe.

Bougainville's voyage was an attempt to regain some national honour following France's defeat by the British and their allies in the Seven Years War five years earlier. That was a conflict fought globally, on oceans and lands near and far from Europe. It resulted in the French losing Canada. Bougainville's orders were commensurately expansive: to 'examine the Pacific Ocean as many as possible and as best he can the lands lying between the Indies and the western shores of America' with a view to drawing up 'Acts of Possession in the name of the Majesty' where the islands offered 'items useful to [France's] trade and her navigation'.[20]

With Britain's maritime ascendancy and the lingering ambitions of the French, Spain's power waned. It remained a presence on both sides of the Pacific, despite Manila having been taken by the British during the seven-year conflict. That was the occupation which revealed the secret of Torres's strait. But the Spanish had done little to take the islands in between, Quiros's makeshift church on Espiritu Santo notwithstanding. In the second half of the 18th century, the Spanish Lake was a void to be filled.

≋

'what would you think?'

Tahiti sat near the middle of that expanse. On 6 April 1768 Louis Bougainville dropped anchor off the island and met its people. Europe's encounter with this tiny place had huge cultural and political consequences. Here was an apparent manifestation of ideal nature and humanity as depicted by Renaissance artists and imagined by Enlightenment philosophers, for whom the classical world was a source of inspiration. Bougainville likened one young woman to Venus – the Roman Goddess of Love. The Frenchman called the island New

Cythera, after the Mediterranean island which accommodated one of three major temples to Aphrodite, the Greek model for Venus. In accord with his task of furthering the reach of France, Bougainville took possession of his New Cythera and the islands that surrounded it for Louis XV.

Inquiry stimulated fancy but it also generated searing self-critique. Bougainville's acquisitive Pacific voyage prompted the French thinker Denis Diderot to question outright the presumption that underpinned these colonial additions. Toying with fiction and fact in the manner of Defoe and Swift, Diderot penned a 'Supplement to Bougainville's *Voyage*', the navigator's published account of his exploration. In a series of invented conversations and narratives he took Bougainville's representation of Tahiti as an unsullied paradise and used that to attack his own country for despoiling and stealing it. One old man addresses the French navigator: 'We are innocent, we are happy, and you can only harm our happiness. We follow the pure instinct of nature, and you have tried to erase its trace from our souls'. Then the Tahitian questions the act of possession: 'This country yours! Why? Because you set foot in it? If one day a Tahitian were to land on your shores and carve on one of your stones, or the bark of one of your trees, "*This country belongs to Tahiti*", what would you think?' [italics in original].[21] Diderot's remarkable critique embodied both the problematic idealisation of 'otherness' and worthy self-reflection that would echo down the years in Western thought.

In fact, Bougainville's Tahitian encounter had been pre-empted by the British. In 1767 the explorer Samuel Wallis and his naval crew made landfall there while circumnavigating the globe in yet another search for the south land. It is a point of minor disagreement among historians whether the beginning of Europe's emotional embrace of the Pacific should be traced to British or French origins. Though his was the first European expedition to find the island, Wallis named it rather prosaically after his sovereign, George III, and claimed it for his king and country before the French did the same. 'New Cythera' suggests that the French were more enamoured with the philosophical, or at least poetic, significance of the place.

Nonetheless, Wallis's encounter had implications that were as much a product of Enlightenment reason and inquiry as Diderot's excoriating critique. Oddly enough, where the *philosophe* saw Tahiti as the home of Venus, Wallis's accurate mapping revealed that the island was an ideal site from which to observe the transit of the planet Venus across the sun. The navigator fixed it firmly on the map with latitudinal and longitudinal coordinates so that further calculation could occur, to solve what the Astronomer Royal called, 'the noblest problem in astronomy' – the distance of the Earth to the Sun and thereby size of the solar system.[22] It would also assist Britain's expansion around the globe by placing a friendly archipelago in the middle of the ocean's charts. The resulting expedition to Tahiti was, of course, the enterprise that brought James Cook and the complement of HMS *Endeavour* to the Pacific in 1768–1770.

Compared to Bougainville's breathless evocations of female and natural beauty, Cook's account of the 10-week stay on Tahiti was punctilious in the extreme. He noted that the women of the island were 'very liberal with their favours' and was at pains to determine whether the sexually transmitted infection that was evident had been introduced by those under his command or was rightly called the 'French disease'. He decided, with partial relief, that it was the legacy of Wallis's visit – but there was no rumination on the corruption of paradise in the manner of Diderot. Meanwhile, his men were desperately pulling the iron nails from their own ship's timbers so that they might trade this rare resource for sexual favours.

The island's classical resonance was not lost on the young gentleman Joseph Banks, who had happily paid a phenomenal £10 000 for his passage, such was his wealth and desire for curiosities both natural and cultural. He amused himself by naming various Tahitians after figures from ancient times based upon their characteristics and appearance. There was Lycurgus, so-called for his pursuit of 'justice' following the theft of valuables by Islanders, and Hercules 'from the large size of his body'. Banks did, however, determine the indigenous name for the island, '*Otahite*', and resolved to refer to it as such rather than King George Island, New Cythera or any other European invention.[23] In time, 'Otahite' became Tahiti. Banks argued that the Tahitian priest and navigator Tupaia be allowed to travel with the *Endeavour*, against Cook's procedural caution. It was not the first time a local person had been taken by visiting Europeans but Tupaia went willingly; evidence of the confidence with which the Polynesian man contemplated ocean voyaging and by extension the nautical character of his culture. It also indicates the confidence with which the Tahitian encountered 'otherness'. Revealing his countenance – wilful gentleman, collector and incipient ethnologist – Banks wrote: 'I have therefore resolvd to take him ... thank heaven I have a sufficiency and I do not know why I may not keep him as a curiosity, as well as some of my neighbours do lions and tygers ... the amusement I shall have in his future conversation and the benefit he will be of to this ship ... will I think fully repay me'.[24] As it turned out Tupaia and another Islander died in Batavia en route to England.

Despite their very different backgrounds and outlooks, both Cook and Banks were products of the Enlightenment. Cook was the careful observer and calculator, able to produce accurate charts and surveys of coastlines. He also benefitted from a meritocracy that cut across birthright and recognised individual potential; so that a labourer's son, schooled in a village and apprenticed in a shop, could rise through the ranks of the navy and ultimately become a national hero. Banks was born to new wealth, rather than ancient title, and that gave him access to science and allowed him to indulge his interest in many things. Botany was foremost but the diversity of human cultures was also a source of fascination. He, too, was an observer but he was also a collector and taxonomist. Both were men of the world – one in the service of his king and country, the other in service to science and himself.

Having assisted with resolving astronomy's problem and taken leave of Tahiti and its neighbouring islands, Cook opened 'Secret Instructions' which ordered him to address the Admiralty's enduring question: the existence or otherwise of the south land. If possible, the navigator was to 'fall in with the Eastern side of the Land discover'd by Tasman and now called New Zeland'. All discoveries would, he was assured, 'redound greatly to the Honour of this Nation as a Maritime Power, as well as to the Dignity of the Crown of Great Britain'.[25]

Cook circumnavigated New Zealand and consequently it took shape on naval charts as two large islands. The decision then confronting Cook was whether or not to continue further south in search of the elusive landmass, the very existence of which he doubted. With the condition of the *Endeavour* 'not thought sufficient' for the high latitudes, the commander and his officers determined to fall in with the 'East Coast of New Holland'. That certainty was based upon a familiarity with de Vaugondy's map. The explorer was clearly distinguishing between the mysterious *Terra Australis* and the continent already partially charted. Having given up on the former, he anticipated the latter. On 19 April 1770, the expedition's botanical artist, Sydney Parkinson, noted tellingly, 'we discovered the land of New Holland'. Over the course of five months, Cook charted the continent's Pacific coast, thereby completing its essential outline.

That voyage also made clear differences between the place that would become Australia and the Pacific from where the Europeans had travelled. While the *Endeavour*'s Polynesian passenger could converse with the Māori of New Zealand, Banks noted that when the Gweagal people of Botany Bay called to the newcomers, 'neither us or Tupaia understood a word'. Far to the north inside the Reef, upon which the *Endeavour* was holed by coral, the Polynesian prevailed upon the local Guugu Yimithirr people to sit and communicate, but in gestures not shared words. The ever-observant Banks thought that the local language was 'totally different from that of the Islanders; it sounded more like English in its degree of harshness'. He often heard the word 'Chircau', which he took to be an expression of wonderment.[26]

Banks pondered Pacific connections. A coconut, found washed up and 'full of barnacles', had him wondering whether it had floated from Espiritu Santo. The Englishman commented upon the similarity of the outrigger canoes of the far north to those of the islands. They were very different from the folded and tied bark watercraft seen around Botany Bay, but also distinct from the larger, heavily decorated ocean-going vessels he had seen in Tahiti.

At Waalumbaal Birri, which the British subsequently called Endeavour River, the enforced stay for repairs to the ship's damaged hull allowed exchange and communication. But it was not trade as had occurred in Tahiti. The Europeans gave fish and baubles to the local people, who took them without reciprocating. As there were no domestic pigs or chickens to barter for, the Europeans gathered and hunted their own food as best they could. Banks particularly enjoyed the green turtle that was caught in abundance. The company shot and ate the large leaping macropod which both nourished and intrigued, for they had not seen its like in Europe, the Pacific or anywhere else. Cook described it as a mix of deer, hare and greyhound. The Europeans learned the local name, 'kangaroo', which they would eventually apply to various species of the genus across the continent.

James Cook would famously reflect upon the encounters with the Gweagal and Guugu Yimithirr: 'They live in a Tranquillity which is not disturbed by the Inequality of Condition: the Earth and Sea of their own accord furnishes them with all things necessary for life ... In short they seemed to set no Value upon any thing we gave them ... they think themselves provided with all the necessarys of Life and they have no superfluities'.[27] If the local people expressed wonderment, they did not apparently accompany it with a longing to possess. Though Cook did not make the connection explicit, there was a clear echo here of Robinson Crusoe, whose self-sufficient exile had cured him of any covetousness; having all he needed, there was 'no room for desire'.[28] Cook's reflection could also be interpreted as a reiteration of Diderot's imagined 'noble savage'. Indeed, the navigator's great

20th-century biographer, JC Beaglehole, dismissed this pondering as uncharacteristic 'nonsense', reflective of a familiarity with French thought, but not a fundamental affinity.[29]

It might also be taken as a considered statement of fact based upon careful observation and significant encounter – as an anthropological expression imbued with empathy. Historian Bernard Smith made the case for Cook becoming 'the official philanthropist of the Enlightenment' over the course of his three Pacific voyages – trying to 'raise' the people of the ocean with the best that Europe brought so that they might be better able to resist the worst. Creating a market for European-style trade was a strategy employed on Tonga during the third voyage in 1777.[30] But in Polynesia there was at least a desire for some things that the newcomers brought, iron in particular. On Australia's Pacific coast, there was apparently none.

The recognition of different peoples, along with their world views and their natural rights, was affecting the development of international law. Might was not necessarily right. Cook's 'Secret Instructions' accordingly carried with them the stipulation that any territorial gain required 'the Consent of the Natives'. Even more prescient were the 'hints' written by Lord Morton for the consideration of Cook, Banks and others. The need for consensual occupation was there with the further assertion that conquest did not equate with title to land. But so, too, was the affirmation that the peoples encountered were the equals of Europeans, for all were 'the work of the same Omnipotent Author'.[31]

And yet, on 22 August 1770, not three weeks after leaving Waalumbaal Birri, Cook 'hoisted English coulers' on a small island off the long northern tip of the continent and 'took possession of the whole Eastern Coast ... together with all the Bays, Harbours Rivers and Islands situate upon the said coast' in the name of King George III.[32] The tension between Indigenous right and European might had clearly not been resolved – even in the mind of someone as reflective as James Cook. One is reminded of the question posed by Diderot's dispossessed

In the wake of Spain

Tahitian. If Cook's homeland had been so taken by Aboriginal people, what would he have thought? Empathy clearly came second to duty, king and country.

CHAPTER 5

A Pacific colony

'... the discoveries we have made, tho' not great ...'

James Cook and his crew arrived back in England in early July 1771. In the home waters anchorage called The Downs, the commander wrote two letters to the Secretary of the Admiralty, Philip Stephens, announcing his return and briefly outlining aspects of the voyage. The correspondence was characteristically modest and customarily deferential, but the mariner's understatement is still remarkable. 'I flatter myself', he wrote, that the journals, charts, plans and drawings created during the voyage 'will be found sufficient to convey a tolerable knowledge of the places they are intended to illustrate, and that the discoveries we have made, tho' not great, will apologize for the length of the journey'.[1] Cook had circumnavigated New Zealand, charted a Pacific coast for New Holland, and given it a British name, New South Wales. He had named a potential port after Secretary Stephens himself, one among several places that honoured Englishmen thereafter. Port Jackson, Cape Byron and Moreton Bay were others. Cook added that coastline to the growing list of British possessions.

That done, the *Endeavour* travelled west through the Torres Strait guided by the Spanish knowledge gleaned during the British occupation of Manila in 1762, and Cook's own ability to read the sea. He thereby took 'no small satisfaction ... by being able to prove that New-Holland and New-Guinea are two Separate Lands or Islands', something that was still 'a doubtful point with Geographers'.[2] Letters written, the navigator sailed the last leg of that momentous trip to Woolwich on the River Thames from where he had started out on 20 July 1869 – three years earlier to the day.

Press reports of the *Endeavour*'s return epitomised the excited mix of fact and fiction that typically followed voyages of discovery. One wrongly equated Tahiti with the 'Southern Continent'. Another described the 'copper' coloured residents of that 'earthly paradise' as 'hospitable, ingenious and civil'. It was an expression of shared humanity that suggested that those who lived in distant seas might be just like 'us'.

New Holland, on the other hand, was mentioned in passing as a place of mishap and 'troublesome savages'. It would take many years for the name 'New South Wales' to gain currency among the people for whom Cook had acquired it.

≋

'[a] most desirable and beautiful union'

Cook returned to the Pacific in 1772, in large part to continue the search for the southern continent. That three-year journey took the navigator on an extraordinary course, meandering and backtracking and on three occasions entering the Southern Ocean close to Antarctica. There was no great continent filled with riches of the type which had excited imaginations for centuries.

Cook's vessel HMS *Resolution* was separated from its second, HMS *Adventure*, which made landfall on Van Diemen's Land. Its commander, Tobias Furneaux, was well aware he was following in the wake of Abel Tasman but it is unlikely he knew that the French had recently passed that way in 1772, pulled by their own curiosity about what lay to the south of New Holland and pushed by the dutiful return of a Tahitian man, Aotourou, who had travelled with Bougainville to France in 1769 as the embodiment of the enthralling Pacific. Aotourou died on his way home but the expedition, under the command of Marc-Joseph Marion Dufresne, continued. Accordingly, they became the first Europeans to encounter Tasmanians, ending the 10 000-year-old isolation of those people. One officer compared the 'Diemenlanders' to 'the inhabitants of New Holland of whom Dampier speaks' and the French supposed that this place was part of the greater landmass.[3] The Islanders were amazed by the Frenchmen's mirrors and their pale skin, purposefully exposed to convey their humanity. Conversely, the French wondered at the others' nakedness in such cold climes. A Palawa person was killed after a misunderstanding. Many more would follow, one, two and three generations in the future. So many, in fact, that the term 'genocide' is now often applied to the treatment of the first Tasmanians. The French left, largely unimpressed with what they had seen. They continued on to New Zealand where they buried a bottle containing their country's claim to that land, 'France australe'. The acts of possession kept layering upon each other.[4]

The *Adventure* and the *Resolution* were reunited then separated, again, in October 1773. Furneaux returned to England, leaving Cook on his Pacific voyage. On board the *Adventure* was another Polynesian: Mai, or Omai. He became the first of his people to arrive in England, where he was feted as the personification of natural virtue and the counterpoint to European 'decadence'. Mai was also one of the first Pacific people to recognise the power of the newcomers and its potential to change traditional politics and warfare. He endured the journey to England to secure weapons and support to fight the men of Bora Bora who had attacked his home of Ra'iatea. Tahiti was a collection of competing peoples on its spread of islands as well as a paradise.

In the same month Mai disembarked in London, October 1774, Cook encountered a small island north of New Zealand, and closer to those islands than Australia: 'We found the Island uninhabited and near a kin to New Zealand', he wrote, 'the Flax plant, many other Plants and Trees common to that country was found here but the chief produce of the isle is Spruce Pines which grow here in vast abundance and to a vast size, from two to three feet diameter and upwards, it is of a different sort to those in New Caledonia and also to those in New Zealand and for Masts, Yards &ca superior to both'. He named the place 'Norfolk Isle, in honour of that noble family', and the tree that impressed thereby became the Norfolk Island Pine. Cook added the place to his growing list of imperial acquisitions as he 'had done all the others ... discovered'.[5]

It was one thing to declare possession of a land but quite another to secure that through occupation. The newcomers made speeches, planted flags and buried bottles like so many seeds on foreign shores in the hope that empires might grow there, but it was more than a decade after Cook claimed the Pacific coast of 'New Holland' that people in England began discussing plans for establishing colonies in the 'South-Seas'. In August 1783, as the British were considering peace terms with their seceding North American possessions, the American-born loyalist James Mario Matra drafted and presented 'A Proposal for Establishing a Settlement in New South Wales' to the coalition government of Charles Fox and Foreign Secretary Lord North, the man many had blamed for losing Virginia, New York, Massachusetts and the others. Having cast his lot with the losing side, the ambitious Matra needed a position with prospects. His plan was a way to curry favour and advancement.[6]

The man had social connections, at least. He knew Joseph Banks from Cook's first Pacific voyage. Though a low ranked officer on the *Endeavour*, the American felt confident enough to write to Banks in July 1783 referring to 'a rumour of two plans' for Pacific settlements, one of which involved New South Wales and Banks himself. The gentleman scientist was, by then, a baronet and had already given evidence to a House of Commons committee suggesting that New South Wales might serve Britain well as a penal colony. That was in 1779, three years after the Americans had declared independence, putting an end to convict transportation to those colonies. New South Wales rated only unflattering mentions in the first accounts of the *Endeavour*'s voyage, but those in power now imagined it as a place with potential.

Matra was encouraged enough to write up a plan in some 2500 words and present it to Banks within a month of their meeting. He opened his appeal thus: of all the recently discovered lands 'which know no sovereign', there were none 'more inviting than New South Wales'. Indeed, by virtue of the 'mere animal existence' of its human inhabitants, the place was there for the taking. That 'rudest state of society' was sustained by fishing alone, which, as the English philosopher John Locke had argued in 1690, afforded no more right of tenure to humans than it did to a bear or a bird, despite what others thought.[7] Defoe reiterated that position in 1719, so his character Robinson Crusoe mixed his labour with nature's resources to make the island on which he found himself his 'own mere property ... [with] undoubted right of dominion'.[8] Cook might have internalised that belief so thoroughly it allowed him to claim New Holland's Pacific coast so soon after acknowledging the tranquillity of the people who lived there.

The resources of the New South Wales coast had grown happily in the memories of both Matra and Banks, so they fitted well the needs of their nation, and themselves. Where the former sought personal security, the latter wanted to indulge his all-consuming interest in science and collecting. Accordingly, they emphasised those products the British wanted from other parts of the globe: sugar, cotton, tobacco and tea. Proximity to the flax plants of New Zealand promised enough quality sailcloth for a fleet of warships. That land's pine trees were also 'eminently useful' to a naval power. Each one was a ready-made mast. Conveniently enough, they grew right down to the water's edge, making for easy export to New South Wales and from there to the 'King's yards' at Deptford on the Thames.

Adding to the economic and military advantages that nature provided was the strategic benefit of establishing a colony in such a 'large tract of country'. From there Britain might 'annoy' both Dutch possessions in the East Indies and Spain's South American colonies. Warships from New South Wales could intercept the Manila ships laden with silver and gold heading west for the Chinese market or the produce that was returning to the Americas. In Matra's all-encompassing plan the Pacific Ocean seemed a mere pond. A colony on its south-western rim could help offset the trade imbalance with China by sourcing furs from the ocean's north-eastern shores in order to entice Chinese buyers, who wanted little from the foreigners other than silver and gold.

And who would populate this place? Matra's colony was to be remarkably cosmopolitan. The 'mother country' would provide some whom, he added reassuringly, would remain filial to their place of origin. There would be displaced American loyalists, prompting Matra to describe his colony as a place of 'asylum' for those of 'broken fortunes', whom Britain was duty-bound to protect. Yet other settlers might be sourced from the Pacific itself; he mentioned New Caledonia and Tahiti specifically. Somewhat disingenuously Matra imagined that whole families would willingly leave their island homes for a future in a British colony. And, with the assurance that accompanies patriarchal thinking, he added that 'as many women as may serve for the men' of the colony could also be 'procured'. There was even the possibility of Chinese immigration, an idea he claims to have shared with Joseph Banks. Matra did not discuss the social hierarchies that such a mixing of peoples might entail, possibly because he assumed those of European heritage would dominate. It was clear, however, that this New South Wales would be a multi-racial Pacific colony.[9]

There was no mention of convicts but a subsequent discussion with Lord Sydney changed that. And so began a shift in emphasis from free to penal colony. New South Wales, Matra agreed, 'would be a very proper region for the reception of criminals'. Convicts would not be sold in servitude, or left to languish, but given an opportunity to reform through hard work and the possession of land; they would be given a stake in the place from which they could not return. The benefits were twofold: 'economy to the publick' through avoiding the cost of incarceration at home, and 'humanity to the individual' through the provision of a new beginning. It was, Matra wrote, a 'most desirable and beautiful union'.[10]

The distinguished naval officer Sir George Young presented the elements of this scheme to the succeeding Pitt administration in 1784, thereby keeping the idea alive in government minds. Young's brother-in-law Sir John Call offered yet another suggestion, one which held open the possibility of colonising New Zealand, instead of New South

Wales, and referred specifically to the advantages of procuring the naval resources available on unoccupied Norfolk Island.

Two years later Lord Sydney himself addressed the Lords Commissioners of the Treasury on the problem of emptying Britain's 'crowded' gaols, thereby reducing the dangers of escape and 'infectious distempers'. A place of exile in Africa had been considered and rejected, which left the coast of New South Wales 'as a place likely to answer the above purposes'. Royal agreement had already been granted for vessels to be fitted and supplied to convey 750 convicts to Botany Bay. Gone was mention of American loyalists and Chinese emigrants, although the island women remained. Their role was now made as explicit as decorous communication would permit. Women would rectify the gender imbalance, thereby saving the settlement 'from gross irregularities and disorders' – homosexual unions.[11] A colony that comprised men alone could hardly thrive, morally or numerically.

The accompanying plan itemised and costed the tools needed for the venture, down to individual allocations. Among these were 40 crosscut saws, 100 broadaxes, 12 ploughs and 40 iron hand mills. The list of agricultural and building materials totalled £1100. The last item was £100 worth of fishing lines, hooks and nets. This was to be a colony of farmers rather than fishers, mixing labour with the earth to secure property rights in contrast to the 'animal existence' of the existing inhabitants. The possibility of cultivating flax and harvesting the New Zealand timber which grew 'close to the water's edge', as Matra had described, remained in Sydney's plan, evidence of the aspirational American's residual influence. But the list did not include skilled flax or timber workers – just guards for the prisoners. The matter was consequently decided. On 25 April 1787 Arthur Phillip duly received his instructions as Captain-General and Governor-in-Chief of New South Wales. The fleet sailed on 13 May 1787 and arrived in Botany Bay eight months later. First-hand assessment soon undermined the flattering descriptions of that place, so that Phillip quickly determined to try the unexplored harbour to the north, Port Jackson. That is where, on 26 January 1788, the First Fleet dropped anchor at what would soon be named Sydney Cove, in honour of the man who championed the endeavour.

≋

'... on a deep basis of imagination'

James Matra's role in establishing Britain's first Pacific colony has barely entered the popular historical consciousness despite an attempt in 1925 to have him christened as 'The Father of Australia'.[12] And despite George Collingridge's eagerness to write the Portuguese into Australia's origin story, Cook and Phillip have remained the country's 'founding fathers'; 1888, 1938, 1970 and 1988 all saw elaborate anniversary celebrations of the British arrivals, in New South Wales at least.

Similarly, Australia's colonisation as a response to overflowing British gaols has been popularly accepted, if not always celebrated, since the first histories of the colony were written in the 19th century. It was apparently confirmed with the 1893 publication of Australia's foundation documents, including Matra's 1783 proposal and Lord Sydney's 'Heads of a Plan', in a remarkable project of public education the New South Wales government undertook. Thousands of plans, reports, letters and journal extracts were reprinted in seven volumes as the *Historical Records of New South Wales*. The series covered 30 years and has remained an essential source of primary information ever since. In 1987, just in time for the bicentenary of colonisation, expatriate writer Robert Hughes could still characterise the place as a brutal prison camp: 'In Australia, England drew the sketch for our own century's vaster and more terrible fresco of repression, the Gulag'.[13] The study that unfolded thereafter was far more nuanced than that introduction suggested. But *The Fatal Shore* has remained an enduring and definitive popular history in Australia and overseas, confirming the imperative role of penology and the place of brutality in the nation's beginnings.

Nonetheless, there has been debate about imperial intent. One of the earliest revisions came in 1966 with Geoffrey Blainey's *The Tyranny of Distance*, an innovative work that has been acknowledged as a classic of Australian history despite its failure to dislodge the convict narrative. Blainey sought to understand the origin story thematically – in this case the significance of distance and isolation – rather than simply as a sequence of heroic and tragic events which ultimately proved the supremacy of British civilisation. For him the more convincing answer to the question of why the king and his ministers decided upon such a costly venture, that of sending 11 ships of convicts to the other side of the world, lay 'hidden' in the documents so often cited. It was the strategic advantage of flax and timber, touted by Matra in 1783 and carried through to Sydney's plan, that made the scheme viable. More specifically it was the flax and pine of Norfolk Island, which had so impressed Cook in 1774, that was the key to the project. The island, not the continent, was 'the main attraction'. It would provide the stock for cultivation on the mainland: 'Norfolk Island was the plant nursery; Australia was to be the market garden and flax farm surrounded by gaol walls'.[14]

One major problem with Blainey's argument was the lack of attention given to the island in the very documents he examined. Call's plan referred to the island, and Phillip was instructed to 'send a small establishment thither'. He was also requested, rather vaguely, to investigate the advantages of the flax found 'in the islands not far distant from the intended settlement'. But any consequent cultivation was of an explorative nature and then for producing 'clothing for convicts' as much as sailcloth. New Zealand was the stated source of flax and timber in all the other plans.

Just as problematic is the absence of expertise and equipment allocated for an enterprise that was supposedly at the core of the argument for colonisation. Blainey dismissed the subsequent failure to cultivate useful flax or harvest Norfolk's timber for naval use, choosing instead to emphasise their 'initial promise'.[15] Possibly because of his emphatic argument, the island's strategic significance remained to varying degrees in histories that followed *The Tyranny of Distance*.

The historian Alan Frost combed archives more extensively to find evidence that corroborated the strategic rather than penal imperative for colonisation. It was unrealistic, he suggested, to think the British government was willing to bear the cost of the scheme simply to be rid of convicts; there must have been other motives. Securing naval materials in a time of threatened Baltic supplies was one, as Blainey had suggested. Establishing a 'base for ships following the eastern route into the Pacific Ocean' was another. Denying French occupation by making tangible Cook's claim of possession was a third.[16]

Others have sweepingly suggested that the purpose of the convict colony was to provide one part of a 'network' of commercial ports 'from the Pacific and Indian Ocean to China and beyond', part of a grand imperial plan in the service of profit.[17] Yet for all these possibilities, it is striking how little strategic intent is reflected in the initial plans and how little the King and his ministers did to make any such Pacific base a reality, either by instructing Phillip, or providing supplies and personnel on the First Fleet. Neither did they send assistance in the fleets that followed, despite the governor's pleas for even a serviceable permanent vessel when others had departed, been wrecked or rotted away. His government expressly forbad Phillip from allowing 'every sort of intercourse' between the colony and the possessions of the East India Company, which held a monopoly of trade in the region by Royal Charter; China or any port established by another European power. It also forbad him to construct vessels that might undertake such intercourse. It was as if the colony was to be self-sustaining and removed from the world. Peopling New South Wales made tangible Britain's claim for the Pacific half of the continent but there was little else to further strategy or commerce.

That said, the colony's administrative reach was vast. Phillip's territory extended from Cape York in the north (10° 37') to 'South Cape' (43° 39') on the tip of Van Diemen's Land, which was considered part of British New South Wales. The separation of that island from the mainland was not determined for another decade. He drew a western boundary where Cook had deferred that decision, so that the eastern half of the continent was New South Wales and the other remained New Holland should the Dutch choose to occupy what was potentially theirs by right of discovery. Less defined was the colony's oceanic reach. Phillip had authority over 'all the islands adjacent in the Pacific Ocean' between the latitudes of the two capes. No eastern boundary was placed upon this domain, and no definition of the word 'adjacent', so it conceivably extended to Tahiti. It did not take in New Guinea, which lay to the north of Cape York, but it did include the New Hebrides (Vanuatu) and Fiji. Oddly enough the stricture resulting from this equating of continental and oceanic territories meant that Phillip's purview only included the top third of New Zealand's south island. Just how the governor was to administer this Pacific expanse, and to what end, was unclear.

More certain was the importance of proximity to China for offsetting the cost of transportation. Phillip had clear instructions to disembark people and stores as quickly as possible so that the privately owned, publicly chartered transports could be 'engaged by the East India Company' to return via Canton with 'cargoes of tea and other merchandize'. Britons were already addicted to the tea that grew in the cool Chinese hills and were enthralled by the Chinese ceramics with which to consume it – delicately patterned teacups and pots. Indeed, whole dinner services in porcelain were being imported to fill fashionable Georgian dining rooms. The Orient had entered British homes and consciousness in the 18th century via the powerful medium of taste given rein with expanding affluence. It would never leave. Possibly, by making a round trip to Australia economically viable, the acquired taste for tea and Chinoiserie influenced the decision to head to Botany Bay more than naval strategy or the vegetation of Norfolk Island.

There is another explanation for the venture. New South Wales was 'built', historian Alan Atkinson has proposed, 'on a deep basis of imagination' rather than materialist concerns of empire or commerce. It was conceived after, and because of, a century of extraordinary intellectual ferment. Long-established beliefs in the rights of Englishmen to reject tyranny, which had inspired the American Revolution, joined with newer Enlightenment thoughts of liberty and equality to reframe the problem of disposing of convicts. Rather than simply establishing a gulag, as Robert Hughes described, Lord Sydney sought to create an isolated British commonwealth with the humanitarian vision of liberty and land for term-served miscreants, rather than lifelong misery. The template for such an audacious idea lay in a work of fiction, *Robinson Crusoe*, written as that century of ideas unfolded and set, no less, on another Pacific island. After his lonely ordeal, the protagonist is happy to see his island settled by a multicultural group of settlers which had benefitted by Crusoe's survival advice and whose new leader had 'divided Things so justly'.[18] The optimism was echoed in Matra's plan: 'Give them a few acres of ground ... [and] it is probable they will be moral subjects of society'. And it was carried through with Sydney's drafted instructions for Phillip: 'To every [emancipated] male shall be granted 30 acres of land, and in the case he shall be married, 20 acres more; and for every child who may be with them ... a further quantity of 10 acres ...'.[19] Sydney's intent, in Atkinson's subtle understanding, was to create a colony in which 'the convicts would be peasants in a country of their own'.[20]

≋

'where the settlers possess the advantage of a luxurious soil'

The First Fleet surgeon George Worgan clearly had Crusoe in mind when he ruminated on a day spent tagging along with naval officers at the entrance to Port Jackson on 28 May 1788: 'While the Gentlemen were Astronomizing, to get the Latitude, I & my Man Friday were rambling about, to shoot a few Birds'. Worgan embraced his days in

Lord Sydney's convict commonwealth with an easy humour and sense of the absurd, which set him apart from most others. That trait allowed the surgeon to see humour in the Aboriginal people he encountered; 'merry', 'happy' and 'unoffending' were among the adjectives he applied to those upon whose territory he had arrived uninvited. That demeanour dissipated quickly. By the end of 1788 Phillip reported that 'The natives now avoid us more than they did when we first landed'. Theft of their fishing equipment was one cause. Their realisation that the newcomers were there to stay was undoubtedly another. Then disease devastated the harbour clans. The waterway was never empty of Indigenous people, but the colony changed traditional social structures forever and the population dramatically depleted in those first two years. The balance of power around its shores swung decisively in favour of the colonists.

Those were bewildering months for the newcomers, whether they were forced arrivals or volunteers. George Worgan brought a piano with him, presumably expecting suitable accommodation in which to play it. Like his 1400 or more fellows, the surgeon thought he was going to Botany Bay, and was surprised to be inhabiting the larger harbour of Port Jackson. A note to his brother Richard, Worgan's first letter home, began with a jocular caution against consulting a gazetteer to locate 'Sydney Cove', for the place was yet to be introduced to European cartographers.

Another letter, from a convict, was smuggled out on a returning transport in November 1788. The anonymous author was a woman who wrote on behalf of her sisters, a minority of the overall number but among whom there was the added burden of male predation, childbirth and abandonment in parenthood. She described their condition and the settlement itself – 'two streets' and 'four rows of the most miserable huts' in 'this solitary waste of the creation', then included a note of fortitude: 'We are comforted with the hopes of a supply of tea from China ... [and] ... flattered with getting riches when the settlement is complete and the hemp which the place produces is brought to perfection'. The convicts had clearly been informed of hopes for harvesting flax. The knowing tone in the correspondence offsets any sense of optimism. Flattery is not always truthful.

In fact hopelessness spread, in large part because fresh food was in such short supply. The bulk of rations consisted of salted meat. The cattle that came with the people escaped soon after disembarking. Occasionally those who possessed guns shot and ate an emu or kangaroo. The harbour and sea beyond the heads provided some relief in the warmer months but the absence of experienced fishers, the unfamiliar ecology and the real dearth of fish thwarted the sanguine assumption in the governor's instructions that the fruit of the sea would 'most likely' supplement food stores. Even more misplaced was the optimism that the seeds brought from Britain and the Cape Colony would produce vegetables and grain. There was little evidence of the fertility described by Matra. Instead, plants withered without expert gardeners in the foreign environment.

The convict letter ended on a note of despair. 'The separation of several of us to an uninhabited island', she wrote, 'was like a second transportation'. The island was Norfolk and that second transportation had occurred within three weeks of the arrival at Sydney Cove, coinciding with a bout of scurvy in the fledgling settlement. Phillip was fulfilling his instructions to occupy the place and so sent Lieutenant Philip Gidley King with a party of 21 to do so. There were nine male and six female convicts. The others were administrative, military and medical men. Two 'pretended to have some knowledge of flax-dressing', in the words of the colony's first-hand historian and judge advocate, David Collins. Possibly they exaggerated their credentials to escape the misery on the mainland. King later 'lamented their ignorance'.[21]

In September of that first year, Phillip wrote enthusiastically to Lord Sydney of the 'excellent timber' and luxuriant flax on Norfolk Island, albeit with a request for 'proper persons' to be sent out to dress the plant after the pretenders had failed. Indeed, Phillip described an island paradise with rich soil, fresh water, and a surrounding sea abundant in fish and turtle. The place was the antithesis of Sydney Cove. Phillip's embellishment may have been motivated by a personal need to express hope in the face of hardship or the desire to relate at least some good news to his mentor and the colony's champion. Possibly it was both.

It took so long to travel to and from London that the governor's despatch of September was answered by Sydney's successor as home secretary, William Grenville, in June 1789. It arrived on Phillip's desk a year later. Remarkably Grenville expressed regret that Norfolk, 'where the settlers possess the advantage of a luxurious soil', had not been the 'principal settlement' given its advantages and the difficulties encountered at Sydney Cove.[22] As it was, Britain had spent so much money and effort upon the latter that a complete relocation was impossible. Nonetheless, Grenville recommended increasing the size of the Norfolk settlement.

Phillip had already done that. In March, the governor relieved Lieutenant King of his post on the island and sent his own second-in-command, Major Robert Ross, with two companies of marines, some free persons along with 184 convicts and 27 children – 418 people in all. That was almost half the population of Sydney.[23] In recognition of the size of the offshoot colony, Ross was made Lieutenant Governor. King had enjoyed the lesser rank of commandant. David Collins wrote of the sense of desertion in the harbour; the 'little society that was in place was broken up, and every man seemed left to brood in solitary silence over the dreary prospect before him'.[24] The impetus was not timber-getting or flax cultivation – the wood was unsuitable for masts and spars and no one knew how to process flax – but relieving the strain on resources in Sydney, and Collins made that point clearly. The tiny Pacific island of Norfolk had been a secondary settlement and now, in many ways, it was an alternative one. That parallel reality was reflected in the name of the place where the settlement was 'fixed', Sydney Bay. In 1796 there were 887 people living there, a combination of men, women and children, who were variously administrators, military, free settlers and convicts.[25]

A Pacific colony

≈

'a desire of settling for life'

The place the transportees inhabited was very different from the one they left. The soil covering the ancient sandstone of Port Jackson was barren compared to the 'luxurious' younger loam on Norfolk. But where Sydney had a huge, safe waterway, the island offered only perilously exposed bays. The former was made over millennia as three waterways cut through the old stone and created a valley which filled with sea water after the last glacial melt. Norfolk Island was the peak of a volcanic mount. There were small coral reefs but the place was either too young or too far south for a protective ring of coral like those surrounding the Tahitian and other Pacific islands.

Norfolk supported a jungle of rainforest and pine, 'choked up with underwood', and thickets of the flax Cook described.[26] Islands are ideal incubators for species variation, as Charles Darwin later discovered on the Galapagos group. Consequently, the Norfolk Island pine was different from that which grew on other Pacific islands. The palm *Rhopalostylis baueri* occurred only there and on one of the Kermadec Islands. The flax plant, *Phormium tenax*, grew also in New Zealand but not in Australia. Botanists debate over whether or not it is native to Norfolk. It may have been delivered by birds or by the Polynesians who arrived hundreds of years earlier.[27]

There was a sub-species of Boobook owl, related to that on New Zealand, and a petrel, possibly a sub-species of *Pterodroma solandri*.[28] That bird, about the size of a large pigeon, came to nest in burrows on the island's highest peak – which the colonists named Mount Pitt – each March. The petrels ranged across the entire north Pacific from Japan to the Aleutian Islands, tucking their webbed feet beneath their tails and soaring like Shearwaters just above the sea. They could alight on the waves, 'pattering' in a manner that gave them their name, petrel – after St Peter, the apostle who walked on water.[29] Legs suited to ocean landings and take-offs were less useful on land, where the birds were barely able to support their own weight. So, the petrels of Norfolk crash-landed and did their best to crawl to a burrow, lay an egg and nurture their single chick. John Hunter described a mountain so riddled with holes that walking up it was difficult. The petrels' feeding range was great but they only bred on the safely uninhabited Norfolk and nearby Lord Howe islands. Consequently, they came in the hundreds of thousands to a sanctuary without predators except, perhaps, the Pacific rat.

The balanced cycle which had developed over millennia ended in 1789 when the breeding season coincided with the arrival of the colonists. The sudden presence of so many birds, vulnerable on their land legs and unused to predation, was a boon to settlers who had yet to harvest their first crops. The birds' misfortune was the colonists' good luck and the slaughter for food began almost immediately. Such was its rapacity that Ralph Clark, one of the officers, was moved to keep a tally in his daily journal. The numbers kept climbing in the journal's margin. By mid-July 1790 Clark had counted 172 184 birds killed. The actual figure was undoubtedly much higher as not all kills were reported. Added to this was egg gathering and habitat destruction so that there was no chance of population renewal. The last Norfolk petrel was probably dead by 1800.

Just as they can nurture diversity by virtue of their isolation, island environments are quickly destroyed with sudden impacts such as the arrival of predators, both human and non-human. Then they turn from sanctuary to abattoir. The petrel may not have been the island's first extinction. A 'ground dove', which John Hunter painted around 1790, was never recorded again. This may have been the 'pigeon' which Hunter noted in 1788 was 'so tame that we knocked them down with sticks'. On his second visit in 1791 Hunter found that the local cabbage palm had already been 'almost destroyed' by clearing, presumably with dire consequences for the parrots that depended upon its fruit.[30] The last of a local species of kaka, related to two others on New Zealand, reportedly died in a cage in London in 1851. The great ornithologist and illustrator John Gould saw one of these parrots, tame and uncaged, hopping about a Sydney house in 1838.[31] He did not draw or paint it so its features are known only through brief descriptions.

The colonists called the petrel the 'Mount Pitt Bird', after its breeding site, and the 'Bird of Providence' for the role it played in sustaining them. Given Norfolk's important part in alleviating conditions in Sydney, both by lessening the burden and eventually providing food for the mainland, it might be argued that the petrel rescued the larger colony. It was perhaps the first of innumerable and terrible ecological costs paid so that the Britain's Pacific outpost might survive and prosper. The seals of Bass Strait, the Pacific Ocean's Southern Right and Sperm whales and Fiji's sandalwood would all follow soon enough.

Such was the wholesale destruction of birds and habitat that Major Ross introduced laws to prevent over-harvesting. Ross's impulse was to both preserve a valuable resource and prevent unnecessary cruelty. Live birds were being eviscerated to extract their single egg, which some Islanders enjoyed more than their flesh, then left to die. Upon discovering this, Ross amended the law to forbid killing birds 'Cruely and Wantenly'.

His sentiment, shared by other officers, reflected the rise in empathy for living things which, in 18th-century Britain, paralleled that for fellow human beings. In the mid-1700s poets and philosophers began challenging the long-held disregard for animal suffering – the 'cruelty of indifference' as described in Keith Thomas's pioneering study.[32] This was one of the lessons of Samuel Taylor Coleridge's 1798 poem *The Rime of the Ancient Mariner* in which the pointless slaying of an albatross leads to the becalming of a ship in the Pacific and the subsequent loss of the entire company bar the mariner. That Coleridge had earlier addressed an ass as his 'brother' in verse is further evidence of the changing mindset. Laws would follow poetic revelations more gradually in the 19th century. But, as the historian Tim Bonyhady has argued, Ross's legal moves against indifferent cruelty on Norfolk pre-dated legal measures in England, which itself led Europe in animal welfare.[33] On that small Pacific island, where the environmental impacts of humans were immediately obvious, the connection between 'man and the natural world' – again a quote from Thomas – was clear enough to warrant codifying a conservation and humanitarian ethic.

The fate of the Norfolk petrel, however, suggests Ross's regulation was largely ignored. That in itself is interesting, for this was a penal colony – part of Robert Hughes's dreadful gulag. One might assume a lieutenant governor's will was easily enforced by the threat and delivery of punishment. Clearly there were many transgressions; convicts were hunting birds and collecting eggs to easily fill an empty stomach or simply because they preferred the taste of the tender fish-flavoured flesh and yolk to other meals on offer. The comparison with the bleak reality of salt pork rations in Port Jackson could not be starker.

Ross's island regime was noteworthy for other reasons. He represented, in the words of Alan Atkinson, 'the other way for European Australia, the alternative to Phillip's way'.[34] At Port Jackson the governor had instituted a strict, though not arbitrary or simply sadistic, hierarchy. He was a benign despot who took seriously the instructions that stipulated everything produced by convict labour was to be considered public property. Phillip was sparing in his allocation of land. He did not make the first grants until February 1792, just months before he left. Confronted immediately by an unsuitable site at Botany Bay, and an ongoing food crisis at Port Jackson, Phillip's priority was survival. The governor did not act beyond the authority granted him but Ralph Clark, the man who later tallied the bird kill on Norfolk, was surprised when the commission was read out before everyone at Sydney Cove: 'I never herd of any one Single Person having So great a Power in Vested in him as the Governor ...'[35]

That private remark is a glimpse into the popular understanding of power and authority and the willingness to question it. It was a faint echo perhaps of the debates that had led to the American colonists parting company with the 'tyrannical' King George, who they felt had trampled their established rights and freedoms 14 years earlier.

Robert Ross governed differently. Though often portrayed as a difficult man, Clark described him warmly and in terms of a friend.

Ross certainly accommodated the frailties of his junior officer, both before and during their shared experience on Norfolk Island. In his close reading of the colonial power plays, Atkinson has called Ross a 'talker' rather than an administrator, someone who sought personal confidence and returned good will and obedience with trust. But his was a personal exercise of power so that perceptions of betrayal were also taken badly.

The different approach to governing was displayed as soon as the company of colonists landed on Norfolk, after HMS *Sirius* had been wrecked delivering them to the rocky wave-swept coast there. Amidst this catastrophe Ross declared martial law. Knowing this exceeded his powers, he sought the compliance of both free people and convicts with 'voluntary oaths' of obedience beneath the king's colours. As Atkinson has noted, it was the only time that an 'entire community' in Australia would take part in 'a fundamental act of government' before the passage of universal suffrage in the colony of South Australia more than a century later.[36] The paradox of martial law introduced by consensus has perhaps served to disguise the novelty of the action. Ross followed this by allocating land to groups of convicts to farm as if it were their own. The intent was to instil a sense that all had a stake in the success of the venture – to 'cultivate', in his own words, 'a desire of settling for life'.[37] The echoes here of Robinson Crusoe and his successor on that fictional Pacific island are clear.

The experiment came to an end in November 1791 when Ross was relieved of his command by the man he had replaced, Philip Gidley King – returned to Norfolk as lieutenant governor, having spent three months in England. A 'protégé' of Phillip, King was an administrator of lists and central control. In Atkinson's words, he had 'aimed to prune' the 'spirit of commonwealth' seeded by Ross.[38] On Norfolk he closed a newly opened theatre because of an incident of violence. He reduced the membership of the Settlers and Landholders Society, which the Islanders themselves had established in 1793 with a view to regulating prices and providing mutual benefit.[39] King found the levelling spirit of the age 'insidious'.[40]

Yet faced with a population that was growing naturally and through migration from the mainland, the lieutenant governor also encouraged individual self-reliance by allocating land to convicts to work in their own time. They built schools, and by 1796, 75 children were in attendance. The younger ones knew only the island as their home.

In 1793 King also attempted to revive the production of flax by funding the kidnapping of two Māori men from New Zealand so that they might share their knowledge. Flax had long been used to make clothing on those islands but, unbeknown to the lieutenant governor, its preparation was the work of women. The captured men, called in various accounts Hoo-doo/Wookee/Huru and Too-gee/Tookee/Tuki, had little to offer and they were returned after six months. Nonetheless, during that time King himself learned as much as he could of their language and customs. Despite their coercive recruitment, the two men seem to have befriended their captors, so much so that King returned them personally to their homeland. Their time on Norfolk left King hopeful that 'a good understanding may with common prudence and precaution be cultivated' between the two peoples.[41] Indeed he seeded a colonial outpost, quite literally, in the Bay of Islands by giving the two Māori potatoes to grow and farm. In 1805, as governor of New South Wales, he proudly reported to Earl Camden that British whaling vessels were calling in for fresh supplies there. The Māori were 'a very tractable people', King wrote, eager to assist with producing the whale oil and, it transpired, flax for rope. To secure the relationship he ordered that 'sows and other stock' be sent from Norfolk Island to the Bay of Islands.[42]

For while flax processing struggled on Norfolk, pig production had flourished. Thousands of pounds of salted pork were sent to the mainland. Grain, too, was sometimes in surplus. Yet, when local people wanted to build their own trading vessel, Governor John Hunter, who had accompanied Phillip on the first fleet and returned to preside over the colony in 1795, forbad such a liberty. A sloop was built on the island, but for government use. Called the *Norfolk* and made of island pine, it was used for surveying more than transporting produce. It was this vessel which Matthew Flinders and George Bass sailed to confirm the existence of Bass Strait.

Hunter frequently wrote to the Duke of Portland of the difficulties of encouraging efficient farming around Sydney without 'capable and industrious people' – a problem that Phillip had raised as early as 1792.[43] Clearly Lord Sydney's agricultural commonwealth of yeoman emancipists had manifested in Norfolk Island but not taken root on the mainland, possibly for lack of skill or effective encouragement. Neither was fishing an option for sustaining the colony, despite proximity to harbour and coast. The narrow continental shelf and the temperate waters did not support teeming schools of cod, and confounded efforts to establish a significant fishery. In any case, a fleet of fishing boats would only encourage escape attempts.

Hunter was confronted with the near-impossible task of administering a growing penal colony which nearly doubled in size during his administration from just over 3000 to some 6000 non-Indigenous people. Conversely the proportion of convicts halved due, in part, to the number of children being born.[44] The governor was confounded by struggling farmers; the demands of settlers; the restriction on boatbuilding; and the impact of the barely understood environment, which made farming and fishing difficult even for those with some skill. And then there was the trade monopoly of the East India Company, which fettered commerce and the availability of currency and the opportunistic dealing of officers under his command. The governor had to ensure his wards neither revolted nor died from want of provisions. All that while keeping expenses to a minimum, for Britain had been at war with revolutionary France since 1793 and there was now little patience, or even concern, in Whitehall with the needs of the far-flung Pacific possession, which still required support a decade after establishment. John Hunter was a fine naval officer whose intelligence extended to an interest in natural history. He painted the plants, fish and birds he saw and collected. It was Hunter who left to posterity the only known image of the Norfolk Island dove. Yet to Portland, he was forced to admit that the responsibilities for 'the whole of the intricate concerns of this colony' were 'extremely arduous and fatiguing'.[45]

In 1800 the hapless Hunter was replaced by Philip Gidley King, whose reputation had been enhanced by his administration of Norfolk Island. Then, in June 1803, Secretary of State Lord Hobart wrote to King instructing him to evacuate the island and send the inhabitants to Port Dalrymple in northern Tasmania. The reasons given were expense, the difficulty of communication with the mainland and the lack of a good harbour on Norfolk. Possibly the failure of the harvest in 1802, the island's first, was influential. But as Hobart was drafting his order on the other side of the world, Governor King was penning a report which indicated that grain production was healthy and more than 18 500 pounds of salted pork had been sent to Sydney.[46] King disagreed with the decision to evacuate the island. His first two major commands were on Norfolk and his son Phillip had been born and raised to boyhood there. But his arguments against abandonment were rational as well as emotional. The island's fertility had allowed self-sufficiency since 1794 and could support three times its population of 1023, the equivalent of the number of people living in Sydney and surrounds in 1804. Norfolk 'has been of greatest assistance to this Colony', he suggested, and leaving it would be a 'great loss'. The people of the island had sent more than 55 000 pounds of prepared pork, representing around 500 pigs, in 1803–1804. The vast majority of this was produced on settler, as opposed to government, farms. There had been just 44 pigs in 1790, most government-owned.[47] Norfolk, as it turned out, became the colony's market garden, rather than the flax nursery of Geoffrey Blainey's imagined colonisation plan.

But there was another 'political' reason for the evacuation, one that negated all advantages of staying – the need to secure the recently discovered Bass Strait from the French. Reflecting to Joseph Banks in 1804, King thought this strategic imperative the decisive one, given reports of 'the intention of the French to settle Van Diemen's Land'.[48]

The analogy with a giant chess game is obvious, as the lords moved their pawns to block an opponent on the imperial fringe.

Most Islanders were removed between 1807 and 1808. Many went willingly upon the promise of replacement acreage and the safe transportation of their accumulated possessions. Others, however, were reluctant to leave the life they had established over a decade or more in a salubrious place with relatively self-sufficient freedom. It was a new governor, William Bligh, who presided over the move and he reputedly gave the order to shoot any recalcitrant Islanders who fled to the woods.[49]

Islands have a particular effect upon their human societies just as they do their faunal and floral communities. That was at the basis of the possibilities suggested in *Robinson Crusoe* and the fantasies of *Gulliver's Travels*. Islands are sanctuaries which can foster affinity, or they can be places of exile, discontent and disconnection. In either case they create communities that are 'eccentric', to use Tasmanian-born writer Peter Conrad's description.[50] Through the 1790s and early 1800s, Norfolk Island fostered another type of penal colony with a set of possibilities and challenges that distinguished it from Sydney. Ross and King each fostered a distinctive community, the one communal, the other more centralised but still with some freedom for convicts and the acknowledgment that free men had the right to consult their 'benign despot'. Under the harsher regime of the third administrator, Joseph Foveaux, there was a plot to unseat the ruler. This act of apparent disorder suggests, in itself, an established understanding of rights and freedoms. The planned uprising involved both convicts and disgruntled soldiers. Under the genial John Piper, who replaced Foveaux, the sense of injustice subsided. The rebels who were not hanged immediately upon discovery of the plot, expressed their 'Thanks for the Humane and Indulgent Treatment' Piper gave them.[51]

And importantly Norfolk was settled without dispossession, so that ownership was never contested or questioned. Fear of attack by aggrieved First People was never a concern. That was not the case on the other island where the Norfolk settlers were sent, Tasmania. Black and white fought a brutal war into the early 1830s, followed by forced removal of the Indigenous people. A few people stayed on Norfolk but it was no longer important. In April 1810 another governor, Lachlan Macquarie, would completely write off its usefulness: 'I am decidedly of the opinion that the settlement ought to be entirely withdrawn ... It is a place of no use whatsoever to the mother country or to this colony in either a political or a commercial point of view'.[52]

The early settlement on Norfolk Island, it could be argued, accorded more with the model of the reformative agricultural commonwealth first imagined in London than any other of Australia's early colonial settlements. Certainly, the practical significance of this near Pacific island to the mainland has been overlooked in the historical record. Not so the period from 1825 to 1840, when Norfolk was again populated and turned into a prison for offenders deemed too bad even for the other isolated settlements beyond Sydney: Newcastle, Port Macquarie and Moreton Bay. It became a notorious place of exile and brutality in the ocean away from scrutiny and with no hope of escape. The regime that was enforced there was indeed akin to Robert Hughes's gulag. By their deeds, wrote Governor Brisbane, the 'Felons on Norfolk Island have forfeited all claim to protection of the law'.[53] It was as if the 'rights of Englishman' cherished by Lord Sydney had never existed, and the ideas of equality that emerged from the Enlightenment ferment had no relevance – except perhaps in the minds of those so stripped. Faced with a sentence of 100 lashes for breaking a flagstone, and probably more for being outspoken, Laurence Frayne challenged the Commandant James Morisset: 'I tell you in stark naked blunt English that you are as great a tyrant as Nero ever was'.[54]

The flogging went on until the arrival of Alexander Maconochie in 1840. He believed, not unlike Lord Sydney, that convicts had rights that should be respected and hopes that might be encouraged. Maconochie's radical 'experiment' in reform rather than terror was tolerated for just five years, after which he was sent home to England and Norfolk was gradually emptied by 1855. This was just one of several dramatic shifts which evinced the peculiar role of this and other islands as social and ecological laboratories.

CHAPTER 6

An ocean of opportunity

'... a governor would be forgiven almost anything except heavy expenditures'

The Sydney that greeted Lachlan Macquarie at the end of 1809 was a very different place from that which had exhausted Hunter more than a decade earlier. Though still an open-air prison for receiving convicts, it was also a town, with many former felons and some settlers who had arrived willingly. The merchant Robert Campbell, for example, came to Sydney Cove from India to set up a permanent business in 1800. There he competed with Mary Reibey, James Underwood and Simeon Lord, one-time convicts who had established enterprises through cleverness and good fortune. The formerly struggling penal outpost had developed an economic momentum of its own, fuelled by the hopes and avarice of those who wanted to build futures very different from the destinies that confronted them on the other side of the world.

The new realities and opportunities available in this Pacific port were reported in the *Sydney Gazette*, the establishment of which in 1803 was itself evidence of a maturing society. The shipping news announced the availability of tea, ceramics and fabrics from China, recruiting calls for 'South Sea' whalers, losses at sea and sometimes the rescue of those shipwrecked. China and the Philippines in the north-west Pacific were regularly mentioned but reports from the south-western Pacific, New Zealand, 'Oteheite' and 'Feejee' were as numerous as any news from Asia and even Europe.

Sydney had, of course, been part of a Pacific trade network from its establishment. Those vessels that delivered convicts as transports continued on to China, sometimes via Norfolk Island, to collect tea and other goods for the British market. Some roamed the Pacific in search of whales. Some whalers came out carrying goods for the Sydney market before carrying on to kill whales. The whaling magnates Samuel Enderby and Alexander Champion argued successfully that this did not damage the prospects of the all-powerful and favoured East India Company, because American whalers were already doing just that as they came across the Pacific from the east. The company retained its China monopoly until 1833, but local traders attempted to do business in the Pacific well before then. In 1805 Simeon Lord set imperial affinity aside when he partnered an American called Peter Chase in taking a load of valuable sandalwood from Fiji to China and delivering Chinese goods to Sydney in return. In dutiful defence of the company, Governor King refused to allow the cargo to be landed and it was shipped across the Pacific to the US, where Lord still made an extraordinary profit of US$30 000.[1]

King's adherence to the rules of commerce were not always so strict. He allowed the Sydney firm of Kable and Underwood to build a 186-ton ship which contravened the prohibition on constructing large vessels. It was named *King George*, an expression of loyalty that may have salved the transgression. King needed to keep private commerce alive to reduce the cost of running a colony or, better still, make it self-sufficient. He 'turned a blind eye to colonial shipbuilding', in the words of the historians Graeme Aplin and George Parsons, 'realising that a governor would be forgiven almost anything except heavy expenditures'.[2]

King's leniency was both practical and ideologically based. He looked favourably upon individual effort, whether that came from farmers on Norfolk Island or former convicts in Sydney Cove whose eye was firmly fixed on trade. That was much less the case with his successor Governor Bligh, whose regime, from August 1806 to January 1808, attempted both to tighten central control on a settlement of assertive individuals and discourage maritime commerce in favour of agriculture. And yet the tactfully christened 100-ton schooner *Governor Bligh* was slipped in 1807 followed by the appropriately named brig *Perseverance* which, at 136 tons, was capable of trips to the Pacific and China. There was flexibility and opportunism even in Bligh's penal colony.

Supplementing locally built vessels were the 'prizes', ships captured by British subjects in time of war. The Napoleonic War of the early 19th century had succeeded the Revolutionary Wars of the 1790s and Spain was an ally of the enemy France in both periods. It still had considerable Pacific possessions. The Spanish prize *Pegasus*, for example, was taken by HMS *Cornwallis* and sold for the colonial sealing trade in 1808. Spanish vessels were also seized in sanctioned acts of privateering – as in the days of Drake. In 1806 the whaling ship *Walter* called in at Norfolk Island laden with both Sperm whale oil and Spanish cargo seized off the coast of Peru – some of which was probably traded for fresh produce. In that year also the 240-ton *Santa Anna* was taken by the *Port au Prince*, described as a 'private ship of war', on the Mexican coast. The Admiralty pronounced its capture legal, and within six months the vessel was sold to Simeon Lord in Sydney for a considerable £3200. Sometimes ships were renamed, often with a view to currying the favour of governors or firming friendships. The *Hunter*, taken in 1797, was an early example. The *Santa Anna* kept 'her' Spanish name, making no secret of foreign origins and reminding colonists that their far-flung colony was part of a world at war.

Prizes allowed some circumvention of the company's complex monopoly. Goods could be transported from Sydney and sold in China along with the vessel, so that traders did not undertake an illegal or unprofitable return voyage. However, governors might grant permission for such a round trip if circumstances necessitated it. Lord had bought the *Santa Anna* on the understanding that Bligh would permit him to send it to China and return with cargo. Either the governor reneged or there was a misunderstanding, for Robert Campbell received the trade permit instead. The Sydney traders negotiated many such difficulties in the volatile political and commercial environment of a penal colony that was shifting to become a commercial centre. These were compounded by the ever-present risk of shipwreck. Having lost his Chinese chance, the resourceful Lord sent the *Santa Anna* down to the Bass Strait sealing grounds. In 1810 the vessel sailed to England with 20 000 skins worth as much as £10 000, and sold somehow despite the monopoly. It was just a fraction of the 218 000 skins he had sent since 1805, and Lord was only one of several traders.[3] The seal population of Bass Strait and the Southern Ocean had collapsed by the 1820s.

In the decades before Aboriginal land was secured for the vast flocks of sheep with which Australia would come to be most closely associated, traders looked to the sea and the islands for things to harvest and sell into the Chinese market in return for tea, ceramics and fabric. As DR Hainsworth, the great economic historian of early Sydney, has suggested, it was not wool which created the colony of New South Wales, but rather the commercial community that developed in the first two decades of the 19th century, building the conditions for the wool industry. That community of traders, in turn, honed their skills and built their fortunes in the colony's oceanic region, the Pacific.

The seal skins and oil, which Governor King hoped might be profitable exports, disappointed. Sandalwood did better. That tree grew naturally in India and the western Pacific. The Chinese had used its oil in scenting incense for centuries. The dense, fine-grained timber was also ideal for making beautiful objects. As he was experimenting with sheep breeds, so successfully that he would be remembered as the 'father' of the Australian wool industry, John Macarthur was also thinking of Pacific sandalwood. One plan, thought out in 1807, had Sydney placed in a four-part network that linked it with Fiji, Canton and Calcutta. Sydney-based men would cut and transport sandalwood in Fiji, take it to Canton and trade it directly or indirectly for goods there, which would then be forwarded to Calcutta to be 'cleared' of East India Company claims through a trading house and shipped to Sydney.

That circle scheme never came about but it exemplifies the commercial and geographic vision of colonial merchants. Macarthur's investment in a cargo of Canton-bound sandalwood, and the Sydney-bound produce which it had financed, put him at odds with Governor

Bligh. It helped precipitate the governor's deposition. It was not convicts who led Sydney's only colonial coup, but merchants, soldiers and, in the case of Macarthur, an entrepreneur.[4] Bligh was accused of tyranny and acting arbitrarily. Those who removed him said they were defending 'the laws of the British nation, and the rights and liberties of Englishmen'.[5] Here are more echoes, this time of Lord Sydney. But they were sounding in a port town where capitalistic urges were in the ascendancy – urges that dovetailed easily with the 'ancient' right to own and keep property but which did not sit well with centralised authority in a penal colony or a benign vision for a commonwealth of yeomen and families. Macarthur took immediate advantage of Bligh's arrest by sending his vessel *Elizabeth* – named after his redoubtable wife – to Fiji to gather 120 tons (108 tonnes) of sandalwood, return it to Sydney and then ship it to Canton, in breach of the rules of commerce.[6] A fraction of the Pacific sandalwood taken to China ended up back in Sydney as the sticks and guards of delicately painted Oriental fans.

≋

'... Pacific-minded'

As early as 1810 Macarthur was admitting that the 'immense quantities' of sandalwood being taken had produced a glut in the Chinese market.[7] The Pacific environment was increasingly seen as a cornucopia of commodities. But like all unregulated wild harvests centred on islands, whether of flora or fauna, the exploitation of sandalwood was unsustainable. Stands of Fijian sandalwood were effectively depleted by 1816 and the trade there ended. The market responded to scarcity accordingly and prices rose again, prompting the discovery of other trees on other archipelagos. However, as Hainsworth has argued, it was the 'lure' of the Fijian trees that 'took the colonists to the Islands [and] made them Pacific-minded'.[8]

Nonetheless, it would be inaccurate to regard the sandalwood trade as the beginning of the colony's economic or cultural relationship with the great ocean. There was, as we have seen, Norfolk Island, which drew many back and forth over 15 years and, in the process, turned a considerable proportion of the early colonial population into Pacific Islanders. Memories no doubt faded over the generations dispersed in Tasmania and elsewhere but one enduring legacy of this first connection was the love of Norfolk Island Pines, which became a favourite garden and park planting in Sydney in the 1800s.

Connections beyond Norfolk also pre-dated the first throes of the sandalwood trade for, such was the frequency of voyaging with whalers, sealers and patrolling naval vessels, and the attendant cross-fertilisation of crews and intelligence, that the 'South Sea' islands were better known than even the near interior of the Australian continent in the first decades of the 19th century. The colony's territory extended administratively to 'all the islands adjacent in the Pacific Ocean' in the opposite direction, so that the East India Company's monopoly did not affect what was effectively internal colonial commerce. With the increasing demand for animal protein in the form of salted pork to feed convicts on the government books and on private farms, Philip Gidley King could look beyond Norfolk Island to Tahiti without the complications of protected interests.

Pork soaked in brine and packed tightly between layers of salt in wooden casks kept for months in cooler climates – and weeks, at least, in the warmer Pacific. Desiccated, it might last years before being rehydrated and cooked. Europeans had known of salt's preserving qualities since ancient times. Salted pork accompanied the spread of Britain's empire. It added nutrition and flavour to broths and stews. It was versatile; the dense fat could be used like oil – for cooking and water-proofing. Salted pork was a winter staple in the North American colonies and an important source of protein for sailors criss-crossing the globe. Mariners could easily procure it when they called in at Pacific islands, where pigs had been reared since the first human migrations. Indeed, the presence of 'hogs' was one of several aspects of Polynesian life that Europeans found familiar, in contrast to the edible animals of the Australian continent, none of which were domesticated. Islands suited omnivorous pigs in a way they did not sheep or cattle. Where the latter depended upon pasture, pigs could be fed all manner of scraps or left to forage. By the 18th century the Tahitian islands were sustaining substantial numbers of the animals for consumption and sacrifice. During his visit in 1770, Joseph Banks counted more than 50 large pig skulls on one *marae*, or ceremonial platform, alone.

In 1801, with 2365 people to feed on full rations, Governor King sent a government ship to procure Tahitian pork to add to that reared on Norfolk Island. The *Porpoise* returned with 31 000 pounds of meat which had been salted and packed on site by colonists. The *Norfolk* – the second colonial vessel to bear that name – delivered another 35 000 pounds three months later. George Bass, the irrepressible surgeon, explorer and entrepreneur, was contracted to procure another ton, excluding 'heads, feet and flays'.[9] Representing at least 500 animals, those first cargoes took most, if not all, the available animals and within six months most of them had been consumed. After the Tahitian pig population recovered, more vessels arrived from Sydney, including the appropriately named *Venus* owned by John Macarthur, ever ready to capitalise. An estimated three million pounds of pork, the product of perhaps 25 000 butchered pigs, were imported from Tahiti up to 1830.[10]

The new pork market, based entirely upon the need to feed dependent Britons in New South Wales, required a dramatic economic and social reform in the islands, which was only possible with centralised authority. Fortunately for Governor King, that existed in the newly established Pomare dynasty. In August 1801 King Pomare I wrote to the governor, thanking him for the gifts that arrived with the *Porpoise* and assuring him that he would 'Endeavour in the procuring of many [hogs]' and not restrict anyone from 'Bartering' with the British.[11] Indeed there followed royal decrees which restricted the domestic use of pigs so that more would be available for the colonial market.

Pomare wrote his letter from his seat in Matavai Bay where Cook had fortuitously anchored and set up his observatory in 1770. That, and the navigator's subsequent visits, coincided with power contests in the islands and a longer-term shift in religious practice which involved the elevation in status of Oro, the god of war and fertility. Cook's immediate assumption that Pomare was the king of all the islands helped, in fact, to bring about that very ascension. Where power had once been balanced, it became concentrated and the traditional right to banish or even kill an oppressive ruler waned. James Cook himself was feted as a high priest of the cult of Oro, and Pomare used a Union Jack the Englishman had given him as his own ensign. That bond made William Bligh's 1788 quest for breadfruit much easier, for he was feted as Cook's son.[12] The voyage of HMS *Bounty* would, of course, see Bligh cast adrift by his own men along with a handful of loyalists; such were the paradoxes of authority and power on colonial peripheries.

Unintentional assistance to the Pomare family became alliance and active aid so that a well-established relationship existed for the newly appointed Governor King to maintain. He did so by participating in the customary Tahitian exchange of gifts called *taio*. Pomare sent King a 'very handsome dress and war-dress' and received a cloak of prestigious red cloth. The Tahitian also got muskets with which to shore up his power.[13]

≈

'... be ever guarded against surprise and treachery ...'

The term 'Pacific-minded' barely conveys the complexity of the relationships, the opportunities and risks that flowed from the remarkable oceanic reach of the colony established within two decades of Sydney's founding. With the trade in salt pork and then sandalwood, as well as pearl shell, came encounters whereby cultures collided and accommodated each other. The experiences of the Scottish surgeon turned entrepreneur, Alexander Berry, give some insight into that emerging Pacific world and the expanding colonial orbit. After Berry arrived in Sydney with a speculative cargo from the Cape of Good Hope in January 1808, Bligh's removal threw his plans into disarray. He was quick to capitalise, however, on the evacuation of Norfolk Island by transporting some of those settlers to Tasmania. In 1809, the Scotsman sailed in charge of the *City of Edinburgh* to collect a cargo of ship's timbers, called spars, in New Zealand where the maritime timber industry had established after its failure on Norfolk. There he took advantage of a maturing trade relationship between Māori and Europeans. Berry then sought the prized sandalwood. Such was Sydney's growing cosmopolitanism that he was able to engage a Fijian man, 'Jimmy', for firsthand intelligence of the islands. His crew included a Chinese blacksmith, a Chinese carpenter, and an 'Indian Portuguese' man-servant. At Taveuni in Fiji, Jimmy cautioned Berry about the integrity of the local chief – rightly, as it transpired, for the Scotsman was assaulted and detained. There followed a complex interaction between the European trader and his captor, one which revolved around the opaque communication of authority and demonstrations of physical prowess; Berry's ability to defend himself, it seems, impressed the chief. In the end he traded his freedom and that of his men by giving the chief the tooth of a Sperm whale, called 'toombooa' by the Fijians and which was clearly an object of some social significance.

On Bau, near Vatulele, Berry found the sandalwood he had sought. He discovered also 'a number of runaway sailors and convicts' living with the local people.[14] Just from where these people had fled is unclear but it is not inconceivable some had come from New South Wales. The Pacific was already a place of refuge for Europeans escaping their circumstances in a manner not possible in the 'Old World' – be those penal incarceration, the involuntary labour of the press-ganged mariner or simply the injustice of social hierarchy. In later decades these voluntary castaways would be called beachcombers.

The *City of Edinburgh* returned to New Zealand, where the crew repelled a Māori attack and gathered intelligence about the fate of another vessel, the *Boyd*. Proceeding to Whangaroa near the Bay of Islands, the company found the *Boyd* burned to the water line and 'the bones of the crew lying over the beach'.[15] The vessel had called in to collect spars on its way from Sydney to the Cape of Good Hope when it was attacked by local people, apparently in response to the harsh treatment of a young Māori man of noble birth aboard. Many of the *Boyd*'s company of more than 60 were eaten. Berry rescued the survivors – a man, two women and an infant girl – and proceeded on to South America to sell his cargo. One of those who escaped, Betsey Broughton, returned to Sydney and married the inheritor of Throsby Park, one of the finest sheep farms in New South Wales. The canny and formidable Berry returned to Sydney within a decade to become a legislator and one of the wealthiest men in the colony.

The destruction of the *Boyd* and the massacre of its company was a brutal and shocking event, and formed a turning point in Pacific relationships. Governor King had described the Māori as a 'tractable' or compliant people. For those of an Enlightenment frame of mind they were 'noble savages', impressive in stature and virtuous because of their separation from European vice. With the *Boyd* killings, the Māori were more widely regarded simply as 'savages'. The *Sydney Gazette* carried the following warning: 'commanders and crews of vessels traversing these seas will temper friendship and harmony towards the uncivilised Islanders with prudence and caution and be ever guarded against surprise and treachery'.[16] The Pacific world seemed no more knowable for all the Pacific-mindedness that was accruing.[17]

≋

'the Geographical limits of this Territory'

Reports of the *Boyd* massacre came just six weeks after Lachlan Macquarie took up office as the fifth governor of New South Wales in January 1810. The new man duly reported the 'melancholy' event in a despatch to Lord Castlereagh, the Secretary for War and the Colonies, unaware that he had resigned from that office the previous year. Such was the delay in news from what most still regarded as 'home'. Intelligence from the near Pacific was fresh and therefore reliable, something that must have assisted others to accept the South Seas colony as a new home. Macquarie also reported that seven missionaries from Tahiti had fled an insurrection there and found sanctuary in Sydney, the nearest British outpost. The uprising against King Pomare II, son of the man who had first traded pork with the colonists, began in 1808. His subjects, it seems, were tired of high-handedness and resorted to their traditional right to exile a despot. The ongoing depletion of the local pig population, and the social upheaval which accompanied that, surely played a part. Macquarie called it 'a most serious ... rebellion against a reigning prince'.[18] The governor might have had in mind the fate of his predecessor, William Bligh, in the colony's own rebellion. Justifications for both could be found in English and French writings on tyranny and freedom. These were tumultuous times.

The new governor received his Pacific news from mariners and traders such as Alexander Berry, who were criss-crossing the ocean with increasing frequency. Information came also from missionaries, including those who asked for refuge in Sydney. British men and women from the London Missionary Society (LMS) had arrived in Tahiti in 1797 to spread the word of their god quite independently of the settlement at New South Wales. The LMS was founded in 1795 and the Pacific venture was their first attempt to evangelise to 'heathens' in other lands. The mission had had a difficult start and the 1810 refugees were not the first to seek sanctuary in the colony because of violence; 11 Christians arrived in Sydney in 1798, just 14 months after disembarking at Tahiti. Those people knew nothing about the place to which they had taken themselves. A decade later the evangelists were hardly neutral parties. Missionaries had been instrumental in facilitating relations between New South Wales and the Pomare family, thereby shoring up the power of the disrespected king. The Christians returned to Tahiti in 1812 and

Pomare II was baptised the following year. Just as devotion to Oro had helped his father, so this monarch consolidated his power by godly association.

The word of Jesus spread quickly due, in large part, to the population's growing literacy. This remarkable development occurred not through suppressing the local language and elevating the English tongue, as would happen elsewhere, not least the British Isles, but through the reiteration of the vernacular into text. Polynesian words were systematically written down for the first time. The revolution in communication began with spelling books produced in London and delivered to the islands in 1811. These were quickly followed by translations of the Old and New Testaments printed in Sydney, just a decade after the town got its first local newspaper. Returning refugee missionaries took them to Tahiti so that the Islanders could hear and read the Christian gospel. The stabilisation of Pomare's power was a welcome secondary result, for turmoil made the task of evangelising all the more difficult. A Polynesian Bible was published on Tahiti itself in 1818.[19] 'Oteheite' thereby became the crucible of Christianity in the Pacific, more than two centuries after Quiros and Mendaña attempted to create the same in the Solomons. It was a very different form of the religion, however, for the English evangelists emphasised the personal relationship with their god through the written word rather than the mediating influence of Catholic priests and sacred objects. Nothing, however, was simple or straightforward in the transfer of culture. As Tracey Banivanua-Mar has argued, Indigenous people in Australia and the Pacific learned that 'literacy was a tool of empire whose power was coded' and that access to those secrets allowed one to better 'navigate' the change which was underway.[20]

In the year that Tahitians first saw their own language in text, Macquarie appointed the pioneering missionary William Henry as a magistrate to live among them and help maintain law and order. The move was significant for several reasons. It clearly confirmed the evangelists' colonial role. It also demonstrated Macquarie's concerns about the conduct of European sailors and traders in the Pacific. He referred to 'plunder', the meaning of which was clear enough, and 'wanton insults' upon island women, which may have covered a range of abuses including rape.[21] Further, placing a magistrate on Tahiti suggests the particular importance of that place as a mid-Pacific stop for supplies, rest and recreation. Pomare himself had encouraged these visits with promises of hospitality as part of a strategy of consolidating favour with those who could provide legitimacy through association and firepower.

To deal with abuses beyond Polynesia, Macquarie brought down a proclamation which required that the master of every vessel clearing out to New Zealand or any island in the 'South Pacific Ocean' pay a bond of £1000. It is a remarkable document, not just for the penalty it threatened but for recognising that the behaviour of Europeans was a large part of the problem, in wake of the New Zealand massacre no less. The long list of grievances which could lead to forfeiture is equally significant for the awareness it demonstrates of indigenous culture and attachment to place, albeit in the interest of protecting trade between the colony and its Pacific region. Macquarie prohibited 'trespass' upon 'Plantations, Gardens, Lands, Habitations, Burial Grounds, Tombs or Properties of the Natives of the said islands' so that the inhabitants might also enjoy their 'Religious Ceremonies, Rites or Observances' without interruption or disturbance.[22]

Such cultural sensitivity might be evidence of Enlightenment influences. And it probably was. Yet colonial reverend Samuel Marsden, whom few would associate with any form of tolerance, supported the spirit, if not the detail, of the order. Marsden is remembered as the 'flogging parson'; one of the coterie of brutal authority figures who peopled Robert Hughes's *Fatal Shore*. He was described therein as having 'the face of a petulant ox'.[23] Marsden was a man who sanctioned, and indeed ordered, extreme violence in the cause of righteousness. The flogging of the Irishman Paddy Galvin during the convict insurrection of 1804, 'in hopes of making him inform', was nothing less than torture.[24]

Yet Marsden was not simply a sadistic zealot. For all his harshness and religious bigotry, he regarded all humans as equals in the eyes of his god, much as Lord Morton did when counselling James Cook against taking the lands of 'natives' without their consent. The reverend was an acolyte of William Wilberforce, remembered respectfully for his campaign against slavery rather than his own pious zealotry. It was their shared moral rectitude that led Wilberforce to support Marsden's appointment as the assistant to colonial Reverend Richard Johnson, whom Wilberforce had also recommended seven years earlier. The goal, at that time, was not to convert 'savages' but to save convict souls.

One of the most tangible expressions of Marsden's even-handedness was that he paid equal wages to Polynesian and European sailors in his employ, for which, in the reverend's words, 'they were astonished and much gratified', such was the discrimination already in play within the Pacific's emerging multicultural workforce.[25] And recognising that all people were capable of depravity, the reverend condemned the behaviour of European mariners as forcefully as any sins of the 'heathen' whom they abused. Remarkably he regarded the attack on the *Boyd* as a response to provocation, rather than treachery. A young Māori crewman whom the captain had abused and flogged was the son of the chief responsible for the slaughter. The massacre could thereby be explained as revenge and restitution rather than mindless violence. That Marsden, who condoned flogging in his own constituency, condemned the use of the whip by another adds another element of paradox to his character.

Macquarie clearly thought he had some legal authority over Tahiti. In explaining the appointment of magistrate Henry to Earl Bathurst, the governor reiterated that the island sat within 'the Geographical limits of this Territory'.[26] It was, in his understanding, part of New South Wales – for that was what Governor Phillip's instructions had stipulated. Accordingly, Macquarie also expressed his support for establishing a 'settlement' on New Zealand's north island, a proposal that came from the merchant Simeon Lord and associates who intended to buy flax from the local people. The colonial governor felt able to promise a 14-year monopoly to the traders upon the approval of 'His Majesty's Ministers'.[27]

That expansive definition of New South Wales was altered in 1817 with the passage of the *Act for the more effectual Punishment of Murders and Manslaughters Committed in Places not within His Majesty's Dominions*. The legislation was initiated by both violence in Honduras and ongoing abuses 'in the South Pacific Ocean' including New Zealand and Tahiti. Macquarie's proclamation of 1814 had done little, it seems, to quell the mistreatment of Pacific Islanders. It was the well-connected Samuel Marsden who helped to bring about the legal redrawing of the colony, though that may not have been his intent. The reverend had raised his concerns from afar, writing to colleagues in the London Missionary Society in 1816 urging them to lobby politicians to specifically outlaw predations in the Pacific. The Act which followed ruled that Tahiti, New Zealand and other Pacific islands fell outside His Majesty's dominions such as New South Wales. Abuses enacted there were, by definition, now offences committed on the 'high seas'.[28]

≋

*'the noblest specimens of "savages"
that I have ever met with'*

The 1817 Act restricted the governor's horizon of authority but it did not put an end to interactions between New South Wales colonists and the islands. New Zealand, in particular, was a land of opportunity. There was the perennial promise of flax, of course. Lord's enterprise and other early endeavours came to little but by the 1830s the industry was well established and profitable. It relied on the labour and skill of Māori women scraping the plant with mussel shells; they produced excellent fibre, in contrast to early colonial attempts, until competition from mechanical production led to a decline in the 1840s.

The fortunes of the flax trade were likely connected to the rise and fall of sealing, for the long-anticipated success of the fibre manufacture followed immediately upon the decline of the seal slaughter.[29] Flax filled the economic hole left by the end of sealing. There was also whaling, particularly around the north island. Deep-sea hunts for Sperm whales brought crews to shore for supplies, rest and recreation. Local men might be recruited to work as crew. Whaling for the Singing humpbacks led to the establishment of shore stations. The ships were American, British and sometimes Australian. Archibald Mosman, who would be immortalised in the name of a Sydney bay and the salubrious suburb surrounding it, operated a facility at Cloudy Bay. There were 104 ships visiting the Bay of Islands annually from 1836 to 1840. Sydney was less important, with fewer than 40 visits per year.

As with the seal business, there was little thought of sustainability here, for either it did not occur to the hunters or their employers that the bountiful ocean might one day be emptied, or their only goal was fast profit. In any case they killed calves alongside their mothers, who then became easy targets as they remained with their dead offspring. It was the brutality of the industry, the motivations of the multi-ethnic crews who prosecuted it and the multifarious meanings of whales to humanity that Herman Melville explored in his great and complex novel *Moby Dick*.[30] The eroticised pleasure of butchering whales brings men together regardless of 'race' or religion, in this case the young New Yorker Ishmael and the tattooed cannibal Queequeg, whose character was based on the Māori man Tupai Cupa described in George Lillie Craik's 1830 work *The New Zealanders*. By the time Melville's book was published in 1851, cannon was replacing hand-held harpoons and the slaughter was shifting to the northern Pacific, following the depleted prey.[31]

Such was the mobility of the Pacific workforce, and the complexity of the colonial economy which employed it, that some of the Māori men who pulled the oars of the whale boats found related work across the Tasman in Sydney. Rowing similar craft from the pilot station near the heads of Port Jackson, they were among the first people newcomers encountered and made an obvious impression upon English artist and writer Louisa Anne Meredith when she arrived in 1839: 'The crew of the harbour-master's boat were New Zealanders, fine intelligent-looking, copper coloured fellows, clad in an odd composite style, their national dress and some British articles of apparel ... much the noblest specimens of "savages" that I have ever met with'.[32] By then Māori were a very visible presence in Sydney. In one of the many picturesque accounts of the colony that accompanied the widening arc of imperial travel, the naval surgeon Peter Cunningham described hearing the 'horrific whoop' that accompanied their war dance, the *haka*, carrying across the water from one of several anchored vessels. In the 1820s the streets of the town were made more interesting by the Pacific peoples coming ashore before sailing off again – 'Chinese, Otaheitians, South Sea Islanders, Zealanders etc'.[33]

Samuel Marsden had done much to foster the cross-Tasman and trans-Pacific visitation. His primary purpose, of course, was to save 'savage' souls. This was best conducted in civilised surrounds, or as near to those as Sydney could provide, for he thought Tahitians had 'a very superior idea of their own Wisdom'. Exposure to the ways of Marsden's world, habitations and tools no less than behaviour, would 'convince them we are much wiser, if not better than them'.[34] The same strategy of instilling a sense of the 'inadequacy of their own material culture', in the words of Marsden's biographer, applied to the New Zealanders. He thereby engaged in an incipient anthropological comparison between different ways of life with the goal of winning minds. For while the cleric recognised that people had equal potential, he clearly believed that British culture, at its best, most closely approximated the ideal of the Christian god. Accordingly, Marsden saw the raising of the Union Jack in New Zealand 'as the signal and dawn of civilisation, liberty and religion' in a 'dark and benighted land'.[35]

An early and poignant response to this cultural crusade came from the Māori warrior and chief Hongi Hika, who lived with Marsden at his Parramatta rectory for three months during 1814. A fine craftsman,

Hongi turned a fence post from the reverend's sheep farm into a carved likeness of himself with such intricate detail of his facial tattoos that it is likely he used a mirror. If so, it was a landmark moment of self-representation in Māori art.

The New South Wales reverend was no theorising administrator; he was practical, multi-skilled and willing to meet 'heathens' on their own terms. Marsden, no less than John Macarthur, was responsible for founding the Australian wool industry and could subsidise his Pacific work with money made from his successful sheep farm. This included the purchase of a brig, *Active*, for travel between New South Wales and New Zealand, and crewed by the Polynesians who enjoyed equal pay. The reverend therein transported cattle and horses to New Zealand on his first trip and personally rode after one terrified beast just landed on a beach in the Bay of Islands – to the wonderment of the local people, who had never seen such animals, let alone a man able to control them. During this three-month stay Marsden caught and cured fish to trade for Māori flax, which he planned to sell in Sydney to offset costs. He sat, talked and walked with Māori, apparently unfazed by their cannibalism and body art. The reverend willingly slept naked in a hut on the banks of the Waikati River which he shared with the Māori, having discarded his soaked clothes.[36] When he returned in March 1815 Marsden had with him eight sons of Māori chiefs who were, he hoped, beginning their journey of spiritual enlightenment. The *Active* sailed poorly and their first landfall was Port Stephens, well to the north of Sydney. There, according to Marsden's colleague John Nicholas, the local Aboriginal people responded fearfully to the tattooed Māori, never having seen their likes before.[37]

Whether they were of military, commercial, scientific or religious bent, the wide-ranging Europeans could not resist describing, classifying, comparing and contrasting the many people they encountered in their ever-expanding expeditions. Nicholas, who was a dabbling traveller with no particular interest in evangelising, thought that Australia's Indigenous people were 'not one common race' with the

Māori. Instead he detected links with Polynesia and possible origins in China.[38] Nicholas used the term 'race' to refer to distinct peoples in a manner based upon appearance. Marsden pondered behaviour. The two emphases anticipated the nature/nurture divide in anthropology. Likely influenced by Biblical stories too, Marsden suggested that the Māori were 'sprung from some dispersed Jews' because of their predilection for trade.[39]

It was this willingness to swap and sell, along with their hierarchical and patriarchal social structure, that helped to convince Marsden that the Māori were more tractable than the Gadigal, Burramuttagal and other Indigenous people he encountered around Sydney. It was in New Zealand that the colonial reverend held out his highest hopes for evangelism, and to there he directed his greatest efforts. Whereas the convicts and Aboriginal people of New South Wales seemed immune to his ministering, Marsden became, in the words of New Zealand historian Paul Moon, 'the founding father of Christianity' across the Tasman. So much so that many questioned the reverend's commitment to the colonial 'flock' that surrounded him in New South Wales.

Marsden's affection and respect for the New Zealanders, and his regard for their impressive physicality, was sincere and shared by the British artist Augustus Earle, who visited the islands after travelling to and through New South Wales in 1826 and 1827. Earle was the first to paint a full-length portrait of an Aboriginal person – in this case Bungaree, who had sailed around the continent with Matthew Flinders 25 years earlier – in oils. That very act carried with it a degree of respect. Yet after his New Zealand sojourn, the artist began depicting Aboriginal people as dissolute. Both men's attitudes are examples of what Bernard Smith characterised as 'hard primitivism' in his pioneering study of European first impressions of Pacific peoples. That was a version of 'savage nobility' which saw virtue in the character of the hunter and warrior. It perhaps explains Marsden's accommodation of cannibalism. The 'soft primitivism' of Tahitians, by contrast, had captivated Bougainville but was less attractive to those who frowned upon its associated indolence. James Cook's impression of the self-reliant Australian Indigenous people, who wanted nothing he offered, was an example of 'hard primitivism'. This nobility was reflected in the classically inspired artwork of Gweagal warriors challenging the British at Botany Bay in 1770. But with the onset of disease, displacement and, importantly, Aboriginal resistance and reluctance to worship and work in white ways, even remarkable individuals such as Bungaree stopped being 'noble savages' and were compared poorly to the majestic Māori as described by Marsden and depicted by Earle.

It gave Marsden great satisfaction to see the alacrity with which the Māori embraced European agriculture. In 1814 he inspected a field of wheat sown with seed he had sent across earlier to the north island. The reverend was not just the father of Christianity but a pioneer of New Zealand agriculture. Ruatara, a chief from the Bay of Islands, was one of Marsden's early converts to cropping, as was Hongi, who had spent time at the Parramatta rectory. His people grew potatoes with such success that they could afford to buy muskets in Sydney to expand their power, which also involved taking slaves. This period of upheaval is sometimes called the 'musket wars'. Estimates of the casualties of Māori-on-Māori violence range as high as 80 000. Some 30 000 people may have been displaced. These are extraordinary figures given the population was probably between 150 000 and 200 000. There began a trade in the dried heads of Māori to satisfy curious Europeans in Sydney and Britain. Such were the forces unwittingly unleashed in 'traditional' societies by outsiders who had imagined other ends.

It has been argued that Ruatara regarded missionaries such as Marsden as 'his Pakeha', that is 'his Europeans'. They enabled his personal and tribal power rather than being paternal authority figures guiding a pliable 'native'. Further, the result of such a strategic and proprietorial relationship for northern chiefs such as Ruatara and Hongi was that Christianity was confined to the north. Hongi died in 1828 and thereafter Christianity spread to the south. It was in large part an organic movement led by Māori missionaries and converts. Some of these were freed slaves for whom notions of equality and universal love under the Christian god were an attractive alternative to war and servitude.[40]

There were many other changes in New Zealand directly related to the activities of New South Wales colonists in the decade after Hongi's death. The flax trade rose to a profitable peak. Timber was cut and loaded in increasing amounts. Sheep were introduced and wheat was grown with such success that, in 1836, the *Sydney Gazette* anticipated that New Zealand would become 'the perfect granary for New South Wales'.[41] There was similarity here to earlier hopes for Norfolk Island.

And just as with that smaller Pacific island, the colonists of New South Wales and a few from Van Diemen's Land began to migrate across the sea. In 1831 there were perhaps just 330 Europeans. In 1839 there were as many as 2000. The creation of the New Zealand Association – later the New Zealand Company – heightened interest in Australia's close neighbour, as it began offering land to Britons and colonists. But where those who went to Norfolk Island did so largely under the direction of the governor trying to manage a penal colony of uncertain sustainability, the New Zealand émigrés went of their own volition as fortune seekers pulled by the promise of more-fertile land and pushed by drought and poor wool prices in the older colony.

To report upon the effects of this unofficial colonisation – and in some way mitigate its worst effects – the one-time New South Wales resident James Busby was appointed as British 'Resident' in New Zealand. He arrived at the Bay of Islands from Britain via Sydney in 1833. In the belief that trade was a good counter to violence, and an effective agent of British civilisation, Busby negotiated the entry of Māori-operated vessels into Port Jackson under a flag of the local chiefs' choosing. It became a symbol of sovereignty for those people and 52 tribal leaders, called *rangatira*, signed a Declaration of the Independence of New Zealand as a result of the shared identity it fostered. Busby co-signed the document in recognition of its claim. But his accounts of increasing disorder and 'permanent anarchy' raised concerns in London.[42] Similarly Marsden described the Bay of Islands settlement of Kororareka as a place where 'Satan maintains his dominion'. Characteristically for the reverend, he identified those committing the evils as 'runaway Convicts, and Sailors, and Publicans' rather than 'savages'.[43] Neither Busby's nor Marsden's accounts accurately represented the situation in New Zealand as a whole but both men favoured British intervention. 'Some civilised Government must take New Zealand under its Protection', urged the reverend in 1837.

Marsden penned those words on his last trip across the Tasman Sea. He died the following year. Much criticised during his life for his neglect of Aboriginal people, Marsden was also mourned by peers as the 'Father of the Mission' in New Zealand where his 'brightest trophies' – Māori converts to Christianity – were won. The 'flogging parson' of New South Wales remained critical of predatory Europeans and protective of his Pacific wards to the end.

Marsden did not, therefore, live to pass judgment on the Treaty of Waitangi, or *Te Tiriti o Waitangi*, drafted and signed in 1840 to counter settlers' and private companies' chaotic dismembering of the territories, which Busby was powerless to forestall. It was the document that allowed Britain to annex New Zealand that year. In fact, there were several treaties if one considers the copy in English, another in Māori and still further translations made by missionaries. The British thought they were gaining sovereignty over both islands with acknowledgment of some Māori land title rights, while the *rangatira* intended only the cessation of governorship. British law, they imagined, would end tribal conflict and curb the rapacity of white land seekers, much as was intended with the Declaration of 1835. Consequently, the 'discrepant texts', some have argued, 'inscribed a cultural abyss which could not be bridged'.[44] What might have been an extraordinary and inclusive foundation compact out of which a shared heritage was forged became one which would heighten Māori identity against the Pakeha, who were seen to wilfully ignore the sovereignty and good will of the first people. Indeed, violence followed soon after in what is sometimes called the First Māori War.

In 1845, British soldiers of the 58th Regiment were transferred from their garrison duty in New South Wales to fight tribes in the Wanganui region.

It is unsurprising that the *rangatira* signed the treaty with varying degrees of understanding despite the literacy and the newly devised Māori text, encouraged by Marsden and other missionaries. But unfamiliarity with European legalism was not the same as gullibility. For the chief Taonui, who was aware of outcomes for Aboriginal people across the Tasman, acceptance of the compact was accompanied by worldly caution: 'How do the Pakehas behave to the black fellows of Port Jackson? They treat them like dogs!'[45]

For all its faults, the treaty highlighted the difference between the colonisation of New Zealand and Australia. Where native title rights were recognised in accordance with international law and the self-evident occupation by indigenous people in the former, they had been pointedly ignored or rejected in the latter ever since Cook's remarkable annexation of the east coast in 1770, when all evidence of occupation seemed to amount to nothing. The significant exception was the colony of South Australia, where Letters Patent, laying out how the place was to be established in 1836, recognised Aboriginal title. The 1834 *South Australian Constitution Act*, however, did not. The earlier document prevailed and the Letters Patent, along with their acknowledgment of Indigenous ownership, were ultimately 'brushed aside as a strange but unimportant anomaly' in the words of historian Henry Reynolds.[46] The real anomaly was that Australia would remain *terra nullius* in legal terms for more than 150 years.

The Treaty of Waitangi was timely for those who hoped British power would consolidate in the south-west Pacific. The agreement of 1840 pre-empted by six months the arrival of the French on the South Island of New Zealand, with similar hopes of acquisition. They established a foothold at the so-named French Bay but the settlement never grew beyond cottages and vineyards. Britain's imperial rivals were more successful in Tahiti two years later when the French established a protectorate in which local sovereignty was recognised. The catalyst had been the expulsion of French Catholic priests in 1837 in favour of English missionaries, and ensuing demands by the French Government for reparation and special favour for their traders and settlers. Queen Pomare – the grand-daughter of Pomare II – joined with other Tahitian chiefs in pleading for British protection: 'Don't let these good seeds perish ... take us under your protection, let your Flag cover us and your Lion defend us'. Secretary of State Palmerston demurred, noting that the expulsion of French in favour of English missionaries was an 'unjustifiable act of violence' and accepting the advice of the Colonial Office that the existing costs and difficulties in administering the 'vast territorial extent' of dominions in the Pacific, including the extension of 'sovereignty' over New Zealand, made it 'dangerous and impolitic to contract similar obligations' towards Tahiti. Empire evidently had its limits even for the world's pre-eminent naval power.[47]

And so, as New Zealand became part of Britain's Pacific empire, with ever-strengthening ties to New South Wales, the island that was once notionally part of its territory and had sustained the fledgling settlement with its exports of pork, left that colonial orbit to be absorbed by the great imperial rival. France annexed Tahiti in 1880, following the abdication of Pomare V.

≋

'... that far-off country ...'

By the 1850s shipping, with the people, produce and news accompanying it, was moving regularly back and forth between New Zealand and Australia, as the whole continent was now called. The name 'New Holland' faded away after the creation of the Swan Colony in the west in 1829, for everything was now unambiguously British. South Australia was established in 1836. In the east, New South Wales was spawning colonial offspring through subdivision rather than annexation. Van

Diemen's Land became a separate colony in 1825. Victoria divided from New South Wales in 1851 and Queensland separated in 1859. The 'great circle' route took vessels from Britain down to the Indian Ocean, sometimes to Fremantle but always along Australia's southern coast to Adelaide, Melbourne and Sydney. There ships proceeded to New Zealand and eastward across the Pacific to return to Britain around Cape Horn.

That was the path the Englishman John Askew followed after he was gripped by a desire to see 'that far-off country in the southern hemisphere, called Australia' in late 1851.[48] Travel for adventure and self-improvement, once the preserve of Britain's wealthy on their European Grand Tours, could now be imagined and realised by the middle classes. Apparently possessing the means to travel without working, albeit in the cheapest steerage class, Askew committed his own neighbourhood to memory as if 'daguerreotyped' and set off from Brigham in Cumberland to the other side of the world.

He was as interested in people as in places. Like many, if not most, other educated Englishmen, Askew observed humanity through the lens of race. In the years before Charles Darwin's revolutionary work on evolution, scientific orthodoxy held with a Christian-inspired monogenism; that is, a belief in a single human species divided by types. Accordingly, when John Askew arrived in the New South Wales port town of Newcastle, at the end of his Australian tour, he recalled Johann Blumenbach's influential 1795 classification of humans into five types: the Caucasian, the Mongolian, the (native) American, the Malay, and the Ethiopian or Negroid. The traveller concluded that all but the American were present in Newcastle and consequently mused there was much material for the ethnologist there. Māori sailors represented Blumenbach's 'Malay'. Eleven of them crewed the barque *William Hyde*, within which Askew had opportunely secured a berth to take him to New Zealand on the last leg of his tour.[49] There were Aboriginal mariners, too, whom Askew took to be part of the Negroid race. British colonists and Chinese 'coolies' made up the other two types of humanity.

1 Grave of Commodore James Goodenough, in the former St Thomas's Cemetery, Crows Nest, Sydney, 2021.

Ian Hoskins

2 Young Chinese Australians gather on the steps of the Mitchell Library in Sydney to protest the suppression of democracy in Hong Kong and intimidation in Australia by the Chinese Communist Party, November 2019.

Ian Hoskins

3 A heifer wanders through fire-ravaged grazing land north of Armidale, New South Wales, November 2019. That nationwide catastrophe helped focus attention on climate change where the plight of Pacific island nations had not.

Ian Hoskins

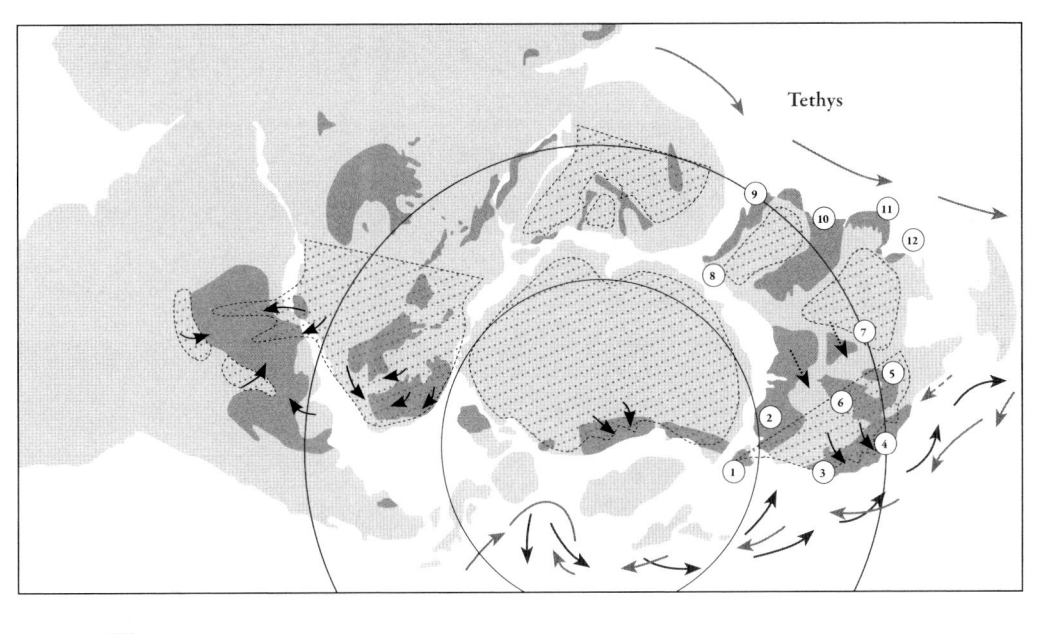

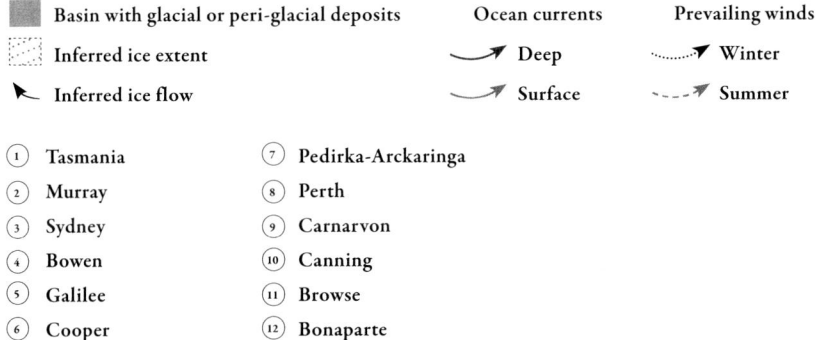

	Basin with glacial or peri-glacial deposits		Ocean currents		Prevailing winds
	Inferred ice extent	→	Deep	⋯▸	Winter
▶	Inferred ice flow	→	Surface	---▸	Summer

① Tasmania
② Murray
③ Sydney
④ Bowen
⑤ Galilee
⑥ Cooper
⑦ Pedirka-Arckaringa
⑧ Perth
⑨ Carnarvon
⑩ Canning
⑪ Browse
⑫ Bonaparte

4 This is a reconstruction of the supercontinent Gondwana from around 300 million years ago, showing Australia, Antarctica, India, Africa and South America. This part of the larger Pangaea supercontinent separated from the other, Laurasia, around 160 million years ago. The division of the Tethys Ocean has yet to produce the Pacific and other oceans. Some of Australia's major coal and coal seam gas deposits, numbered here, were formed at this time.

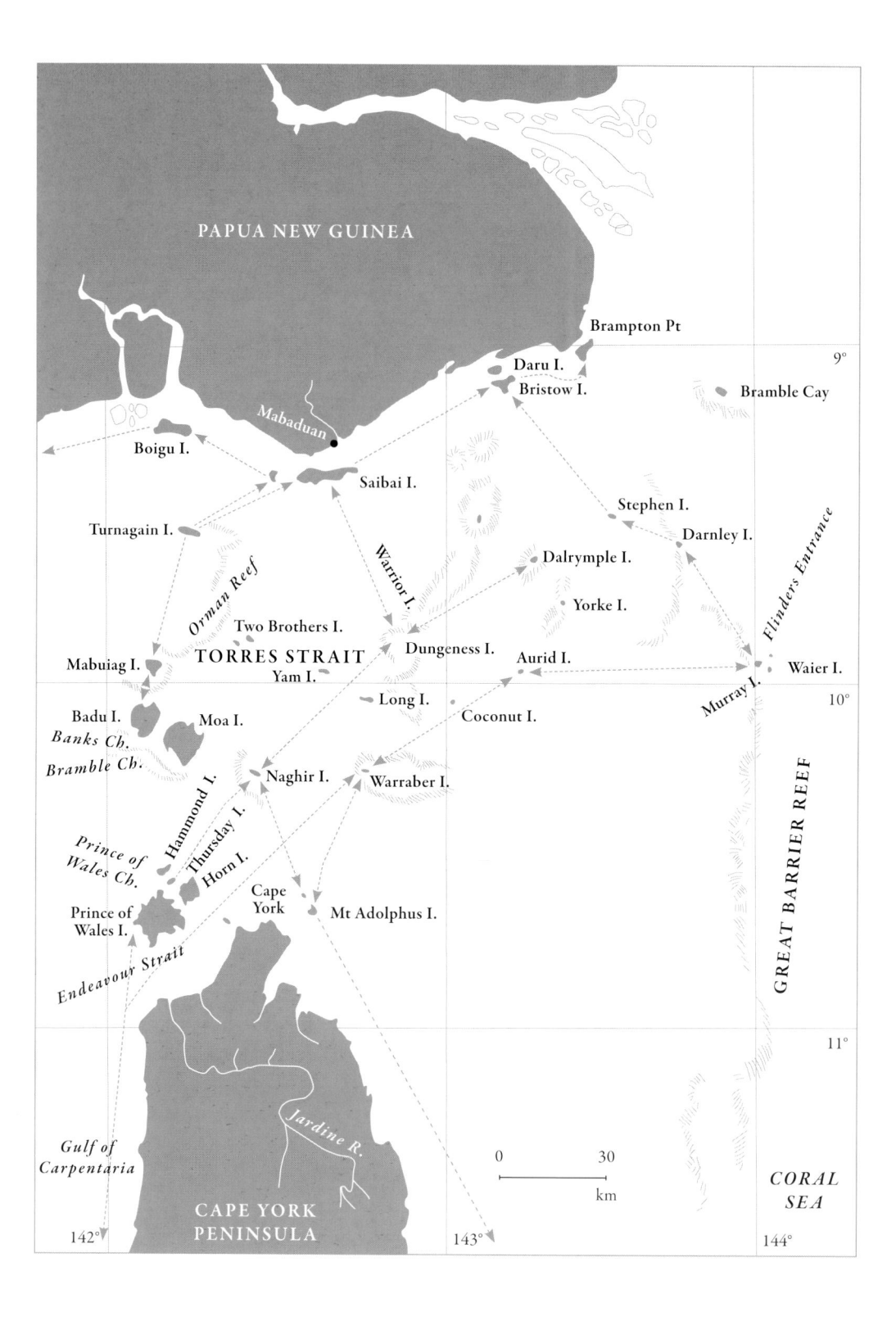

5 Pre-colonial trade routes between Australia, the Torres Strait Islands and New Guinea. Mer is referred to as Murray Island.

6 *Canoe Darnley Island December 1849.* The outriggers of the eastern Torres Strait were highly decorated like other Pacific island vessels. Australian Aboriginal watercraft were less embellished. The publication of this lithograph coincided with Owen Stanley's voyage north to the Strait and nearby islands.

National Library of Australia

A MAP of the NEW DISCOVERIES in the SOU

7 A Map of the New Discoveries in the South Seas with the Tracks of the Navigators (1784) was published in 1785 by G&T Wilkes of London. The paths would be even more complex if earlier Spanish, Portuguese and English voyages had been included.

National Library of Australia

8 'A Young Mount Pitt Bird' by an unknown artist c.1792. This is possibly the only image of the Norfolk Island petrel in existence. A contemporary watercolour by John Hunter, so named, probably depicts a species of shearwater.

State Library of New South Wales

9 A 'South Pacific' colony. This 1792 map published by Robert Wilkinson in London shows Norfolk Island, already occupied, as an insert in New South Wales. Mount Pitt, with its colony of petrels, is visible in the north-west – an easy walk from the 'new settlement' in the south-east.

State Library of New South Wales

10 *Trading with the natives, Coral Haven, June 1849*, watercolour by Oswald Brierly. On-water trade in the Louisiade Archipelago, during the survey visit of HMS *Rattlesnake* shown here, mirrored the earlier experience of Europeans in the Torres Strait.

State Library of New South Wales

11 Māori chief Hongi Hika carved this likeness of himself while staying with Reverend Marsden west of Sydney in 1814.

Photographer David James, courtesy Macleay Collections, Chau Chak Wing Museum

12 This undated chromolithograph shows Chinese miners on an Australian goldfield washing tailings for remaining gold. The thoroughness of the Chinese was a source of irritation to European miners.

National Library of Australia

New Hebrides.— Native recruits on board Malakula.

13 *New Hebrides – Native recruits on board Malakula.* Islanders were employed on the vessels that transported labourers in the 'blackbirding' trade. Presumably those carrying guns in this photograph from around 1890 were crew members.

State Library of Queensland

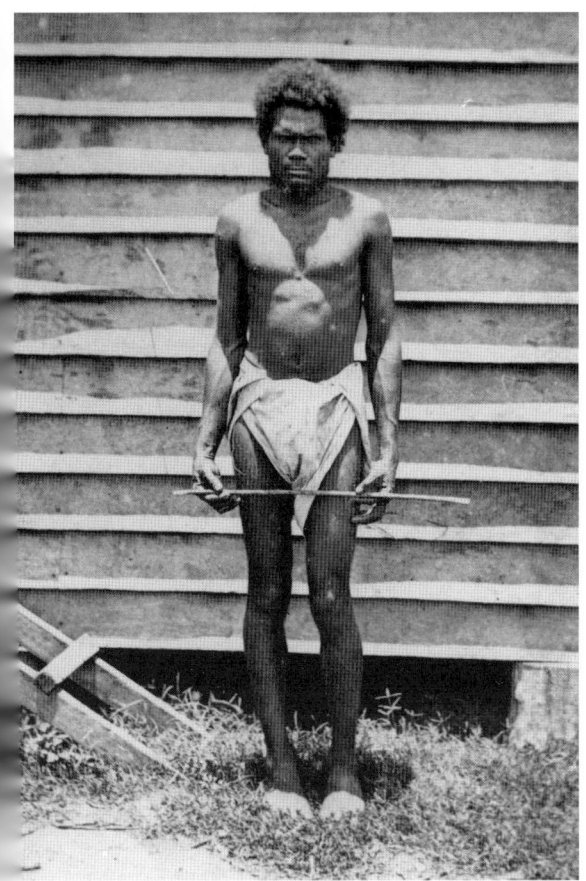

14 & 15 Two sides of the 'blackbirding' experience in Australia. One photograph, left, taken near Foulden Queensland around 1880, shows an islander man in a form of traditional clothing looking uncertainly at the camera. The other, above, taken perhaps 15 years later near Mackay Queensland, shows a wedding group. These South Sea Islanders are wearing European attire for what was almost certainly a Christian wedding.

State Library of Queensland

NEW GUINEA GARDEN.

16 *New Guinea Garden* from Burns Philp's 1886 publication *British New Guinea*. The shipping firm's book was at once a celebration of Britain's declaration of a protectorate two years earlier, and an inducement to travel with Burns Philp to the territory that would be called Papua. This image presents a reassuringly cultivated landscape – the garden.

State Library of New South Wales

17 Japanese people were employed in Australia's pearling industry from the late 19th century. This photograph shows a Japanese man in modern diving gear and basic rope safety line in 1933. The man in the jacket is Queensland Governor Sir Leslie Orme Wilson.

State Library of Queensland

18 *Dining Hall, St Barnabas, Norfolk Island*. Islanders and white missionaries dine together at the Melanesian Mission on Norfolk Island 1906.

National Library of Australia

19 In 1901, 50 years after the beginning of the gold rush, Melbourne's Chinese community built this arch to welcome the Duke and Duchess of Cornwall and York and demonstrate their affiliation with Australia – despite the new Commonwealth's avowed rejection of non-whites.

National Library of Australia

The account that followed presents a rare insight into the minutiae of the Australia–New Zealand livestock trade, which had begun in earnest with the depression of the 1840s and the consequent need to sell off the already-vast Australian flocks of sheep. The *William Hyde* had been converted into a live sheep transport with pens constructed on deck for 730 animals. One hundred and forty cattle were put below, having been brutally hoisted aboard with a rope around the neck and a front leg forced through the 'nooze' to avoid strangulation. Fifty horses were loaded more gently with a canvas stay beneath their bellies. The entire 'living cargo' came from one district near Singleton. Although the ship's captain, John Applethwaite, was highly experienced, the *William Hyde* was at the mercy of the weather, like every other sailing vessel. A strong headwind slowed the voyage. The sheep died in large numbers. It fell to Mrs Applethwaite to nurse them 'as carefully as ever Miss Nightingale nursed the wounded soldiers at Scutari' in the Crimean War. The *William Hyde* put into Auckland rather than the intended port of Wellington.

The redoubtable Lucy Applethwaite was a small woman in her early twenties, already a seasoned 'captain's wife' and the mother of two children, whom she raised aboard ship. John Applethwaite had captained the barque on its trip from Plymouth to Adelaide in 1849 and married the 16-year-old Lucy shortly after in Sydney. They spent much of the next decade together in the shipping business on board the *William Hyde*. The financial implications of the death of so many animals is unclear but the loss did not end the Applethwaites' time afloat. The *William Hyde* kept working the Australia–New Zealand run with refits for other cargo. In September 1852 the vessel transported 107 passengers from Auckland to Sydney.

For his part Askew took his leave of the Applethwaites in Auckland and went ashore to explore. There he saw Māori cutting large logs of Kauri pine and constructing European-style boats for their chiefs while dressed like British workmen. Others wore the traditional woven flax mats which the Englishman likened to the garb of Roman soldiers.

Askew found them 'noble' and thought their faces bore a 'Jewish cast', an interesting echo of Samuel Marsden's thoughts.[50] He then boarded another vessel to take him home.

Askew's adventures were published in London in 1857 under the title *A Voyage to Australia and New Zealand*. His book joined an ever-expanding library of travel accounts of the colonies. Askew had intended to write up his experiences and to make his journal a guide for prospective immigrants, as it was replete with travel tips and costings. He was well aware before leaving that gold had just been discovered in Australia.

CHAPTER 7

Miners and mutineers

'Men meet on apparently equal terms'

Gold had helped to turn the Pacific into the Spanish Lake in the 16th century, establishing the sea routes between America and Asia. Three centuries later the precious metal lured people from Asia to America. The first gold rush was in California on the west coast of North America. The discovery that caused the delirium occurred in 1848 but the rush did not begin in earnest until the following year, hence the term '49ers' for those who streamed to the territory which the Americans had just secured from Mexico after the war of 1846–1848. The port town of San Francisco had a population of 800 when gold was discovered. This grew to 40 000 by 1851. California went from a territory of 15 000 non-Indigenous inhabitants to a population of nearly 100 000. It joined the US in September 1850.[1] The flood of humanity caused chaos but also created business opportunities across the Pacific. In June 1852 someone in Tasmania decided that the potential profit in selling apples, onions and potatoes in San Francisco warranted the risk of a four-month journey of nearly 13 000 kilometres. The brig *Exchange* was duly loaded up in Hobart to begin a voyage from the Pacific south-west to the north-east. After a rough Tasman Sea crossing the vessel stopped for repairs on New Zealand's South Cape and continued on to America.[2] The rush also created a sudden market for fuel. Steam engines on shore and at sea needed coal to power them. In 1850, 14 colliers left Newcastle, bound for San Francisco.

As many as 8000 people sailed from Australia to California seeking fortune or new beginnings, hoping for luck as much as the fruits of hard work. Some turned around as soon as they could, such was the difficulty. 'When you get ashore there is neither house nor place to go. At present you would see thousands walking along the beaches starving', said one man, newly disembarked from Sydney in February 1850.[3] There were those who had staked everything and could not return, and others who chose to put down roots in the new territory. That was literally the case of Mary Strack, newly married to a young Irishman in Victoria, who established a profitable market garden outside San Francisco. The couple were set up for their new life by Mary's anxious father, who gave them £150, his 'new London revolving rifle' and twelve dozen bottles of champagne to sell upon arrival.[4]

The Stracks left Australia in September 1850. Circumstance had forced them to depart from Sydney, where most of the San Francisco–bound voyages began between 1849 and 1850, some 101 of them. Tasmanians farewelled 59 vessels, large and small. Only a handful of craft departed from the small settlements of Melbourne and Adelaide.

The ebb tide turned into a return flow the following year when gold was discovered in New South Wales and then Victoria. Between 1851 and 1861 the population of Australia increased three-fold from 400 000 to nearly 1 200 000. The nuggets found early near Sofala, 238 kilometres west of Sydney, were bigger than any discovered in California but the Victorian rush which followed outstripped that in the first colony. By 1863 Melbourne had transformed from a small river port in a fledgling colony to the largest of the colonial cities with as many as 140 000 residents, 40 per cent more than Sydney. Many came across the Pacific from the depleted Californian goldfields, both returning colonists and new arrivals.

The man who began the Australian rush had himself been part of the 'madness' in California. Edward Hargraves left Sydney in July 1849 and returned in 1851. Shortly after, he followed up reports of finds over the Blue Mountains. He was not, therefore, the first to discover gold in Australia, as is often supposed. Indeed, there had been a small rush in Victoria in 1849 which, extraordinarily enough, was quelled by authorities who feared the potential for instability. Nor was it true that Hargraves' Californian experience had sharpened his eye for gold-bearing country. However, the Australian returned from America determined to find gold at home and by doing so became a causal link between the Californian rush and the Australian experience that followed so soon after. Explaining the false starts of the preceding colonial discoveries, Alan Atkinson has noted that 'California made the world aware of the way riches might be gathered, as if by magic, in remote spots'.[5] Following that shift in collective consciousness, Hargraves' timing was perfect.

The Australian was not interested in monopolising any claims or making a fortune as a miner. Hargraves was a huge man and prolonged labour exhausted him. Rather, he cleverly managed news of his own discoveries so that the rush which ensued could not be thwarted by officialdom and, in fact, benefitted him by way of a government appointment and rewards.[6] The Victorian government paid for his advice the following year. The colonial authorities were also guided by the American experience in that they did not want a repeat of the chaos that followed unregulated 'gold seeking' in California. Accepting the inevitable, they introduced a system of gold licences, both to stem the tide as much as possible and pay for the regulation of the masses who would inevitably come.

The presence of authority on Australian goldfields contrasted with the unbridled adventurism in California. It was a legacy of Australia's penal origins and a result of proximity to established population centres. However, as the historian David Goodman has observed of the upheaval on both sides of the Pacific: 'Gold rush society raised deep questions for those who observed it'.[7] The fear of instability and the upset to the established social order was evident in Australia and America as men deserted ships, left jobs and abandoned families for the goldfields. Wealth suddenly obtained by those who might never have otherwise enjoyed it worried others who preferred the existing hierarchies. 'The marvel of gold', as writer Eric Rolls put it, 'was that the working man had the advantage'.[8]

The remarkable coincidence of successive rushes led to comparisons between the societies they affected and created. Some pointed out differences, others highlighted similarities. When Australians fell foul of San Francisco's vigilante committees, they were condemned as 'convicts'. Some were hanged. However, in 1853 the *San Francisco Whig* expressed the more usual belief in shared New World destinies when it predicted that 'Australia will become free, as she of right ought to be. That the achievement of her liberty is possible, our history is sufficient proof'.[9] Within many of the comparisons were elements of national identity, well formed already in the US and just taking shape in Australia. The American gold rush was seen to throw up examples of that nation's rugged individualism, for better or worse, while the colonial goldfields helped to shape the egalitarianism that characterised the Australian mindset. 'Here there are no conventionalities; no touching of hats. Men meet on apparently equal terms' observed Reverend Arthur Polehampton of the Victorian diggings.[10]

No fewer than 143 American vessels anchored in Hobsons Bay near Melbourne in 1853. There were, consequently, many trans-Pacific fertilisations. American miners took part in the celebrated Eureka Stockade uprising against licences and other grievances near Ballarat in Victoria. The language of rights and incipient democracy which accompanied the American split from Britain – 'no taxation without representation' – was reiterated there and elsewhere. The very word 'eureka', derived from the ancient Greek exclamation of discovery, had been transplanted from the Californian fields. In 1854 four American men established the American Telegraph Line of Coaches in Melbourne. It would become Cobb and Co, the Australian equivalent to the iconic Wells Fargo stage coach company of the American west. Miners on the Australian diggings emulated the flamboyant dress and swagger of the 'Yankees'. Enough colonial men chose the American 'goatee' over the full English beard, while affecting a 'twang' in their speech, to attract comment in popular song.[11]

It would not, of course, be the last time that American style influenced white Australians. But neither was it the first colonial exposure to 'Yankees'. They had been visiting Sydney from the 1790s as traders, contravening the East India Company monopoly and compromising security in the penal port in the process. Americans fought colonists over the sealing grounds of Bass Strait in the early 1800s. But it was as whalers that they began to turn the Pacific into an American lake, and they did that, astonishingly, from ports on the east coast rather than the west. Audacity and avarice in the Pacific anticipated the 'Manifest Destiny', which some Americans used to justify taking California from Mexico. So frequent were their island stops by the time they took California, that Tongans had invented a name for the black Americans who came ashore, one derived from their typical occupation in the ship's kitchen – 'Kuke'.[12]

≋

'Englishmen are ever ready to receive foreigners with open arms'

Another Pacific people was also motivated to move across the ocean by the discovery of gold. The Chinese headed east in their thousands to the 'Gold Mountain' of California. Some 20 000 arrived in San Francisco in 1852. Then, as news of Australian gold filtered north, there was a second exodus for the 'New Gold Mountain'. Five hundred came in 1852 and 1853. Two thousand left for Melbourne in 1854. By 1860 there were 45 000 in Victoria and nearly 13 000 scattered throughout the New South Wales fields.

Those bound both for America and Australia typically came from the areas around Canton and departed primarily from the south – Hong Kong and places on the Pearl River. Some, about a third, could afford to pay for the passage. The others borrowed from family, friends, money lenders or merchants willing to risk the outlay of a loan to a traveller for the interest it would return. There was little doubt in anyone's mind that the gold seekers would return; they were 'sojourners' not emigrants.

The aim was to make money and go home to buy land, extend holdings or pay off debts. A trade in humanity developed. A great many Chinese men did go back but thousands stayed. Some, indeed, went back and forth between lives and families left behind and new relationships established in the Australian colonies.

The China they left was in turmoil. The internal strife that followed population booms and the incursions of Western merchants and governments was 'dissolving' the Mandate of Heaven, which had emphasised the value of stability and rationalised the power of the emperor since the time of Confucius, centuries before the birth of Christianity.[13] The Great Wall, which had been funded in part by Spanish silver, could do little to keep out 'barbarians' who arrived by sea. Its naval force had not advanced since the 15th century. At least 20 million, and probably many more, people died in the Taiping Revolt in the south from 1850 to 1864.

China had been exporting tea and ceramics for decades but its reciprocal demand for British goods was still small. Opium was a product that had long had buyers in China but, as it was a drug of addiction, that market could be easily expanded. And so it was when the East India Company traded opium for Chinese silver it then used to buy tea. Attempts to stop the business because of the social and economic disruption it caused were circumvented by smuggling. This continued through the 1820s and 1830s, often with the collusion of corrupt officials. Tension rose, and there were hostile incidents which culminated with the Chinese threatening British ships and subjects, regardless of any connection to opium, so that the resident community were forced to take refuge on merchant vessels off Hong Kong. Britain sent the Royal Navy to support them, shots were fired and the result was the so-called Opium War of 1840.

Remarkably, the Australian press reported the outbreak of war with little or no jingoistic outrage. Rather it reprinted accounts from the British press. Some were neutral, others sympathetic to Britain's actions in defending its honour, the safety of its subjects, the right of its merchants to trade. The *Spectator*, by contrast, was critical in the extreme. The analysis which appeared in the *Sydney Gazette* on 19 September 1840 condemned the British decision to go to war and supported the Chinese right to decide the nature of trade in their own country. It labelled the conflict for posterity: 'the *Opium War* is the name by which history will hand it down'.[14]

Whether fought for opium, free trade or honour, the war vastly improved Britain's position in the Far East and began China's long descent into national dishonour. A punitive peace treaty ended the war, and Hong Kong was ceded to the British empire in 1842. In 1898, after the British negotiated expansion on to the mainland, that perpetual possession became a 99-year leasehold. The concessions the British won created opportunities for other nations. The Americans were particularly keen to enter the door opened by the British, having established a commercial horizon on the Pacific's western edge.

Former US president John Quincy Adams had supported Britain's decision for war. It was the 'arrogant and unsupportable pretensions of China', he said, that precipitated conflict. The demand that emissaries 'kowtow' to the emperor was an affront to him as indeed it was to Viscount Palmerston, who pressed the war for Britain as foreign secretary. Adams shared Palmerston's view that free trade – 'equal reciprocity' – was akin to a human right and one which justified war: 'The fundamental principle of the Chinese Empire is anti-commercial. It utterly denies the equality of other nations.'[15] China would be dragged into the modern age whether the emperor – its 'despotic chief' – wanted it or not. For William Seward, the American consul general in Shanghai in the 1860s and 1870s, there was a duty to transform China, and presumably everywhere else in the world that needed telegraph lines, railroads and never-ending change. 'I should think less of western civilisation and of western manhood if it were not pushing and aggressive in China ... the average American or Englishman ... would be unworthy of the Anglo-Saxon blood which runs through his veins if should teach himself the Chinese habit of thought ... that whatever is is best'.[16]

For all its claims to equality, free trade benefitted established strength. When the war began Britain was the world's pre-eminent economic and maritime nation. Palmerston and others were embracing open markets as the means of increasing national and commercial power, and abandoning the closed mercantilism of the 18th century in the process. Accordingly, the monopoly of the East India Company ended in 1834. The Navigation Laws, which had limited commerce between Britain's colonies and places and firms beyond the empire, would be repealed in 1849.

Both those developments aided the passage of Chinese gold seekers to Australia from 1851, for they liberated commerce and shipping from the restrictions which had so affected New South Wales' interactions with China since the colony's foundation; and against which colonial sandalwood and seal skin traders had chafed. The would-be miners could now arrive in ships owned by Britons, Americans and Europeans, often carrying Chinese cargo bound for the colonies. The Australian ship's captain and businessman Robert Towns pursued profit wherever he could find it and added mass transit to his tea importation interests. In 1852 he treated those aboard his ship *Spartan*, which sailed from the British treaty port of Amoy – another 'Opium War' concession – so badly they mutinied and took over the vessel.[17]

Ships might navigate any of five routes from China to Australia, depending upon the port of departure, destination and winds. Some rounded New Britain to its east and came down through the Coral Sea. Those that arrived via Manila or Singapore sailed east through the Torres Strait. Others came through the East Indies and around the Australian western and southern coasts. The Australasian Steam Navigation Company (ASNC), established when the Australian gold rush began, would transport Chinese men, and possibly some women, between Australian destinations as prospectors discovered more goldfields. Two hundred squeezed onto the ASNC steamer *Victoria* to disembark at Cooktown bound for the Palmer River goldfields in northern Queensland in 1875, and two drowned as they were hustled from one vessel to another. Chinese entrepreneurs got involved in the shipping boom that followed from the ongoing discoveries. The firm of Hop Kee delivered somewhere between 5000 and 20 000 people from Singapore and Hong Kong in the year to May 1875.[18]

There was a difference between the initial reception of the Chinese in colonial Australia and that in America, where concepts of racial hierarchy had long been used to justify a brutal but legal system of slavery. The accompanying belief in white supremacy adversely affected Asians, Mexicans and Native Americans. Britain, by contrast, had officially abolished slavery in 1833 after decades of debate emphasising common human dignity. That was Wilberforce's great struggle. The violence against Chinese miners in California made Australia a more attractive destination: there was at least some protection under the law. Quite a few colonial women found the quiet ways of the Chinese men more appealing than the aggressive masculinity of their European counterparts, for there were far more cross-cultural marriages in Australia than America: 50 in five years in Victoria and more in New South Wales.[19]

Although stirrings of anti-Chinese feeling were growing in Australia, some continued to champion universal principles of justice and liberty. Two decades after Britain abolished slavery, the New South Wales newspaper *Empire* held out the promise of liberty to all who arrived in the colony: 'Is the Negro forbidden to put foot on British ground? Is he not rather by that very act emancipated from the darkness, the dread and the chains of slavery? Is not this Continent open to every being, Negro, Chinaman, and every other who would land thereon with a character free from culpable taint?'[20]

The parallels between 'Anglo-Saxons' across the Pacific are unmistakeable, nonetheless. In 1852, miners in the newly created State of California urged their legislators to 'impede and obstruct' the immigration of the 'motly races' from 'Asia, Polynesia and South America'.[21] A discriminatory tax was duly levied on non-white miners. In 1855 Victoria passed an immigration restriction act aimed specifically at Chinese people, one which limited the number of Asians carried depending on the weight of the vessel. South Australia, where many were landing to head overland to Victoria, followed in 1857. New South Wales introduced restrictions in 1858. These measures contravened the spirit, if not the letter, of the Treaty of Nanking of 1842, in which Britain had accompanied its enforcement of free trade with insisting on the reciprocal freedom of movement for Chinese and British citizens. It was against this attack on the principle of open doors that the *Empire* and other commentators spoke.

White colonists were being challenged by another people like never before. While there was much about the sojourners that conformed to British precepts of worth – qualities such as thrift, ingenuity, hard-working resilience and sobriety – the emphasis was on difference. Competition for gold was clearly at the root of much of the aggression but colonists used Chinese behaviour, culture and appearance to justify their persecution and exclusion. Their food smelled unpleasantly, they were 'clannish', unhygienic, un-Christian, slavish and immoral in ways rarely specified. Voices that held to a 'common humanity' faded so that even the *Empire* came to present a case against their presence: 'the existence of a degraded class in any community is fatal to its peace and destructive of its liberties'.[22] It was, of course, a self-fulfilling argument; the degradation of the Chinese in the press, parliamentary speech and common discourse further fuelled ill-will and the cycle continued. Victoria repealed its immigration restrictions after tensions eased on the goldfields once that first rush diminished in the late 1860s. But the language and mindset of a competitive racial difference – one which rested upon vilifying non-whites – had been fixed; a direct result of the gold rush and the trans-Pacific migrations that ensued. It would endure through the rest of the century and underpin the new Australian Commonwealth's *Immigration Restriction Act* of 1901 – the centrepiece of the White Australia Policy.

'... strictly brought up in the protestant faith ...'

As people criss-crossed the Pacific in hope of finding gold, a snippet of shipping news in Sydney's *Shipping Gazette* on 11 December 1852 noted the arrival, three months earlier, of Rear-Admiral Moresby in HMS *Portland* at Valparaiso, '32-days from Tahiti' via Pitcairn Island. Moresby was commander of the Royal Navy's Pacific Station, established at Valparaiso on the Chilean coast in 1837 to project British power throughout the ocean and defend missionaries, merchants and other subjects of the Crown. Oddly its reach did not extend to Australia which, at that time, fell under the responsibility of the navy's distant India Station. The long-delayed construction of Fort Denison in the middle of Port Jackson in 1857 demonstrated the colonists' nervousness, sitting on the edge of the Pacific with no permanent naval presence, a hostile power in Russia on the ocean's northern rim and newly found wealth from gold. The relevant powers in London acknowledged that colonial anxiety shortly after – along with the strategic and economic worth of the Australian colonies. Accordingly, also, the Australia Station was established near the fort in 1859 to host a permanent British naval presence. The latitude was nearly identical to the Pacific Station at Valparaiso.

Tiny Pitcairn Island is closer to South America than Australia; 'a little speck ... in the vast Pacific', as Moresby's son and shipborne secretary, Fortescue, put it.[23] But it was a safe port of call, for the only inhabitants were British – the descendants of the mutineers who had taken the *Bounty* from William Bligh in 1789 near Tahiti and set him afloat in an open boat with 18 others, the first of two momentous rebellions which that pugnacious and righteous officer faced. The other, of course, was in Sydney when Bligh was the colonial governor. The mutiny on the *Bounty* would pass into international consciousness as possibly the most famous naval rebellion of all time. The colonial mutiny has maintained a peculiar resonance in Australia's self-conscious history writing as an example of incipient anti-authoritarianism. Both are examples of how precarious power can be even in times and places of apparent absolute authority. 'Politics are destructive of discipline', as the historian Greg Dening has observed of the *Bounty*'s dramatic seizure. Bligh's ship was riven with tensions and the captain's injudicious use of 'bad language', of all things, in what Dening described as 'violent tornados of temper' made his discipline appear 'personal' rather than institutional. Those who served under Bligh could thereby cast him as a tyrant in the confined 'wooden world' of naval service.[24]

The remarkable feat of navigation and endurance over nearly seven weeks of soaking misery took Bligh and his loyalists to the north coast of Queensland then to Timor. The vessel sent to reclaim the *Bounty* and capture its 'piratical' crew, HMS *Pandora*, arrived in Matavai Bay in March 1791. Fourteen of the 25 mutineers were duly seized, but the *Bounty* had left in September 1789 with a company of mutineers and Polynesian men and women, under the command of Fletcher Christian, who led the revolt. There ensued a four-month search which took *Pandora* and its furious captain, Edward Edwards, on a westward route not unlike that the usurped captain had taken. But where Bligh's open boat successfully negotiated the coral of the Great Barrier Reef, Edwards' 500-ton frigate was wrecked with the loss of 31 crew and four prisoners. The 99 survivors then set off on their own desperate open boat voyages to Timor, from where a safe return to Britain was possible.

For a nation whose power depended upon its navy and merchant fleets, mutiny was an offence not far removed from regicide in degrees of seriousness. Hence the effort and expense undertaken to capture offenders who might be anywhere in the Pacific Ocean, half a world away. Three of the mutineers were duly hanged. The gallows repentance of one of the condemned spoke of that seriousness and, obliquely, of Bligh's verbal provocation and the lesson not to take discipline personally: 'You see before you 3 lusty young fellows about to suffer a shameful death for the dreadful crime of mutiny and desertion. Take warning by our example never to desert your officers and, should they behave ill to you, remember it is not their cause, it is the cause of your country that you are bound to support'.[25] Transparent justice and mercy were also important and four were found not guilty, two given royal pardons and one acquitted on a legal technicality.

The small library left aboard the *Bounty* had a profound impact upon the fate of the vessel and its crew. One book by John Hawkesworth, *An Account of the Voyages Undertaken by the Order of His Present Majesty for Making Discoveries in the Southern Hemisphere* published in 1773, included the story of Philip Carteret's discovery of Pitcairn Island as he tried to re-establish contact with his commander Samuel Wallis and vessel HMS *Dolphin* in 1767. By the time Carteret sighted Pitcairn, Wallis had made landfall at Tahiti, setting in train the events that would lead to Cook's arrival there and the 'discovery' and colonisation of Australia. Fletcher Christian decided to find Pitcairn, which Carteret had said was uninhabited, and make it his refuge. And eventually he did, despite errors in the recorded position. Along the way, after backtracking north, south, west and east, Fletcher and his company reached the Cook Islands, where stories of the visit of 'Cookies' – James Cook – to Tahiti had already been incorporated into local legend, establishing hope and expectation of an appearance. The *Bounty*, it seemed, was that manifestation.[26] The encounter did not go well and an Islander was shot dead amidst the muddled understandings. The *Bounty* sailed on to eventually make landfall at Pitcairn.

Various works of religious teaching complemented Hawkesworth's book, including Philip Doddridge's 'Sermons on Regeneration', which emphasised the importance of 'public devotion' for instilling trust between 'men'.[27] The poignancy of this text is apparent after one considers the Pitcairn settlement's drunken, brutal beginning. The Europeans discriminated against the Polynesians, whom they referred to as 'Blacks', in the allocation of land. They mistreated the men and took the women as wives in a social sorting that probably had more to do with masculinity and power, than racial prejudice. The abused murdered their abusers as they tended their respective plots, Fletcher Christian among them. The Polynesian men were themselves killed.

Eventually only one white man was left, John Adams. He survived with nine Polynesian women and a girl, and 23 children born on Pitcairn. Having partaken in the brutality and murder, Adams converted himself into a pious patriarch and began a regeneration through the public devotion put forth by Doddridge. The women did not forsake all they had known on Tahiti, for they dug up the skulls of those with whom they had lived and cared for the bones as their culture had taught them to do.

In time there were further ructions and dramatic power plays of the sort which might have occurred in the imagined island societies of Daniel Defoe or Jonathan Swift. The independent arrival of John Buffett in 1823, and then an adventuring navy veteran and privateer called George Hunn Nobbs in 1828, introduced two new potential patriarchs in the last years of Adams' life. They were rivals for the leadership of an already devout community among whom there were aspirants such as Edward Quintal, the son of a murdered mutineer. It was Nobbs who gained the confidence of the Pitcairners, until he too was challenged by yet another stranger, the 'imposter' Joshua Hill.[28] Hill became a zealous and cruel despot. He deposed Nobbs and was himself toppled in a democratic majority vote of Islanders backed by the authority of a visiting Royal Navy captain. That was 1837. Stability established, the Pitcairners settled down to a life of fishing, farming and worship. Nobbs became preacher, doctor and law maker.

Despite their unauthorised occupation of Pitcairn and their mixed English and Polynesian heritage, the members of this pious community identified as British and were regarded as such by visiting naval men who, impressed by their religiosity, sanctioned Nobbs' authority and the form of government which had evolved. Their extraordinary presence in the eastern Pacific became widely known. It was an invitation to visit from one of Nobbs' own daughters that brought Rear-Admiral Moresby and the *Portland* to Pitcairn in August 1852. His son, Fortescue, was particularly struck by one lingering manifestation of Polynesian culture, wave riding:

> Boys and girls can swim through the largest surf, and play about amid the broken water, by the rocks, that we looked upon with terror. One of their greatest amusements is to have a 'slide', as they termed it; that is to take a piece of wood, about three feet long, shaped like a canoe, but having a small keel – called a surf-board – hold this before them, dive under the first heavy sea, and come up on the other side. They then swim out a little way, until they meet a rapid, heavy sea coming rolling in – the higher the better – when they rest their breasts upon the surfboard, and are carried along upon the very apex of the roller at a prodigious rate right upon the rocks.[29]

It was a very early use of the term 'surf-board' and anticipated by 50 years the revolution in 'surf-bathing' that swept the New South Wales coast and gradually shifted Australia's identity from a 'bush' to a 'beach' people. The ease with which the young Pitcairners negotiated the waves could only have been transmitted by the Polynesian women who survived the earlier butchery that killed all but John Adams. That such a sensual pleasure existed alongside Christian devotion is evidence, perhaps, of the enduring power of Polynesian ways on Pitcairn. Elsewhere in the Pacific, missionaries would suppress the practice.

For his part Rear-Admiral Moresby was impressed by the people's piety and expressed as much in a despatch to London: 'It is impossible to do justice to the spirit of order and decency that animates the whole community, whose number amounts to 170, strictly brought up in the protestant faith'.[30] Moresby became a patron and George Nobbs was subsequently taken to London and ordained.

The island's leader was already getting the attention of one of the most powerful men in Britain. In 1848, a letter requesting relocation from the drought-prone island that could not sustain its expanding community had been presented to Viscount Palmerston. He agreed that it was desirable that the 'surplus population' of Pitcairn Island be removed elsewhere in the Pacific 'where their Industry and good conduct may contribute to the wellbeing of such islands'.[31]

There had been an abortive attempt at relocation to Tahiti in the early 1830s. This experience, coupled with their sense of independent community, led the Pitcairners to desire only an uninhabited island – as theirs had been when they arrived. To live among an established people, to amalgamate and change, was not attractive. After the options were considered it was decided that Norfolk Island would do. There were already plans to remove the prison, thus leaving a pleasant and bounteous place fit for pilgrims. The account of the resident reverend, FS Batchelor, was difficult to resist. Norfolk supported 'pine-apples, figs, guavas, lemons, pomegranates, Cape gooseberries, bananas, cabbages, peas and beans', he wrote. 'Cinnamon and other spices abound, while tobacco, arrowroot, red pepper, and sweet potatoes, can be cultivated to any extent.'[32] A vote in September 1855, which remarkably included women and children, confirmed that 153 out of 187 residents wanted to leave. It was an extraordinary democratic moment that pre-dated the provision of universal male suffrage in South Australia in 1856, the first of its kind in the Australian colonies, while giving an unprecedented voice to women and children.

All the Pitcairn Islanders landed on Norfolk on 8 June 1856 after 12 days at sea. The prevalence of certain surnames – Christian, Quintal, Adams, Buffett and Nobbs among them – was evidence of a close-knit community. In time some found Norfolk was not the earthly paradise they had been promised. Others missed the solitary autonomy of Pitcairn. Sixteen returned there in 1859 and another four families went back in 1864. By 1937 there were 233 living on the far eastern island. A century later it remained Britain's only Pacific colony.[33]

The colonial status of Norfolk Island itself was thrown into question by the immigration. It had been Nobbs' understanding, shared by his fellow Islanders, that the Crown had given them Norfolk outright. It had not. The misapprehension was a result of inflated expectation, miscommunication and the already convoluted history of Norfolk's colonial status. In 1843, the island had passed from the control of New South Wales, where convict transportation had recently ended, to that of Van Diemen's Land, which continued to receive Britain's convicts until 1853. When transportation duly ended there, the incoming New South Wales governor, Sir William Denison, suggested that the island be placed back under his colony's control. Instead, Norfolk was effectively cut loose from the established Australian colonies and made a separate British possession with Denison as its separate governor. This was the novel semi-autonomous administrative arrangement in which the Islanders found themselves in 1856. It was, in Denison's own words, 'an experiment' which had as its purpose 'the happiness and prosperity' of a 'very interesting people'.[34]

As the Pitcairners knew better than most, intimate island communities can harbour despots, intensify enmities or foster trust and cohesiveness. Having endured their share of despotism and ill-will, the Islanders seem to have arrived at equality between the sexes well before other Western societies embraced democracy among men. Recalling his first visit to Norfolk in 1857, Governor Denison noted this aspect of the 'experiment' while essentially dismissing it as a facet of a simple and 'primitive people':

> I left untouched the rule which gave the women, as well as the men, a vote in the annual election of the Chief Magistrate. I hope, however, that this experiment on a small scale, will not be assumed as a precedent in the favour of the claims now made on the part of our 'better halves', to have their say in the government of the country, for I doubt very much whether, even among the primitive people of Norfolk Island, it would be found to answer if pushed at all beyond its present limit. I should most certainly not have proposed even this small amount of petticoat government, had I not found it already in existence.[35]

A contemporary visitor remarked upon the island women's 'easy manners'. That they were 'without any appearance of timidity', may explain why the island retained its 'petticoat government'.[36]

The term 'primitive' generally denoted a state of simple cultural development, but Denison may well have been referring to the Islanders' mixed heritage – a combination of Malay and Caucasian in Blumenbach's taxonomy of humankind. The same visitor who remarked upon the confident women of Norfolk also commented upon the appearance of the men: 'they were not English – too dark coloured ... the men are darker than Italians; as dark as some of the lighter coloured Māories, occasionally; but no shade of black – it is more of the bright copper tint'.

The new Norfolk Islanders were dark-skinned at a time when whiteness was becoming all-important to the definition of Australianness. Ostracism might have followed in such a climate but this 'very interesting' community had piety and history on their side. In 1884 the New South Wales judge Alfred McFarland took it upon himself to record their story and place them firmly as heroes in the Australian narrative. He wrote *Mutiny in the 'Bounty!' and Story of the Pitcairn Islanders* in Crows Nest House, the old seat of Pacific trader turned colonial legislator Alexander Berry; such were the inter-connections of Sydney's elite. It was a thorough history but one presented also as 'a tale of bold enterprises, and terrible sufferings; of the impelling motives, acts, and fortunes, of Fletcher Christian, and his mates, on waters and isles of the Southern Pacific'. William Bligh, the victim of the mutiny, was cast as their 'savage villifier'. McFarland concluded his account with a virtual embrace of the 'Children of the mutineers'. It was much 'to know, and feel', he wrote, 'that they are now citizens of New South Wales – the parent Australian State'.[37]

The intent undoubtedly was to foster interest and support for the tiny community, who continued to survive on barely more than they could catch or grow. But it was, nonetheless, a strange note to end on – for the Islanders were not colonial citizens at all. Norfolk was still a possession governed by a shared governor with a set of laws quite different from those operating on the mainland. Indeed, the elected government of New South Wales had little interest in regaining control and responsibility for the place. In 1888, a century after Arthur Phillip followed instructions to occupy the Pacific island, having secured his mainland settlement, the Premier Sir Henry Parkes dismissed a British offer to transfer control back to New South Wales. Norfolk was 'a white elephant' for which there was no obvious use.[38] For their part, the Islanders were content to be left on their own.

There were others, however, who thought the experiment had run its course. They included Secretary of State for the Colonies, Joseph Chamberlain. Great Britain pressed for the transfer to New South Wales, even rejecting New Zealand's claim to the island.[39] Accordingly, in 1896, island laws which had operated since 1857 were repealed and brought into line with those of New South Wales. As a consequence, Norfolk's easy-mannered women lost their right to vote for the council that administered their island. Transfer was delayed because of the impending creation of the Commonwealth of Australia in 1901. Finally, in the *Norfolk Island Act* of 1913, the king was 'pleased to place Norfolk Island under the authority of the Commonwealth'. At the transfer ceremony on 1 July 1914, Charles Nobbs, the grandson of George, pronounced somewhat dutifully, 'We have everything to gain and nothing to lose'.[40] A month later war enveloped the Islanders' new nation and their old empire. Norfolk men joined up and the women provided comforts for the front. In 1918 Gunner George Fletcher Nobbs, whose name spoke so clearly of island origins to those who knew the Pitcairn–Norfolk story, gave his life for king and country.

Optimistic speeches and patriotism aside, accepting destinies decided by those beyond their shores had been hard for an independent and proud island people. It would remain so for the following century. In 2015 there was soul-searching and angst when the federal government ended the self-government finally granted in 1979. For many the benefits of fuller integration with the wealthy Australian Commonwealth did not justify the potential loss of identity and community. In the words of one defiant local: 'We're Islanders, we're descendants from Tahiti and 17th-century Englishmen, we're not from Australia'.[41]

CHAPTER 8

Saving souls and taking slaves

'... a mission field at their doors'

The Pitcairners' arrival was just one chapter in the remarkably compressed human history of Norfolk Island. In the end it was stories of hellish exile and the mutineers' 'exotic' offspring which would most define the history of the island. But there was another, seldom discussed, instalment in the story. In 1853, the bishop of New Zealand arrived on the island to investigate its suitability for his Melanesian mission, established in 1849 as a school for making Pacific people into Christian missionaries. George Augustus Selwyn had with him his friend Sir George Grey, the New Zealand governor. Both thought the place was suitable though it was still under the control of Van Diemen's Land, soon to be renamed Tasmania. For his part Grey was keen on anything that might consolidate the British presence in the Pacific, and planting a cross might well be followed by raising a flag.[1] The bishop simply thought Norfolk was rightfully his for, as he would later argue, he had been given 'charge all islands adjacent to New Zealand' including Norfolk when the new Anglican diocese of New Zealand was formed as a separate entity to the Australian church in 1841. Selwyn acknowledged that the place had been transferred to 'the ecclesiastical jurisdiction' of the Tasmanian bishop in 1842 but, with the end of Norfolk's convict system, he could see 'no reason why the spiritual oversight should not revert to the Bishop of New Zealand' and then an intended bishop of Melanesia, 'for which purpose it is admirably adapted'.[2]

Selwyn's confidence was grounded on an administrative mistake. The Letters Patent which had established his diocese made reference to a latitudinal boundary of 34° north rather than south. New Zealand's new bishop thereby theoretically assumed the pastoral care of every Pacific island to the north of Hawaii. Clerical errors meant little when the Archbishop of Canterbury then confirmed this diocesan reach by declaring that New Zealand had become 'a fountain diffusing the streams of salvation over the islands and coasts of the Pacific'.[3] In this assessment, New Zealand took pre-eminence over Australia in Anglican missionary work.

The idea was to bring converted Melanesians to Norfolk and train them as missionaries so that they might spread Christianity to their communities and other islands. Selwyn's plans for Norfolk, however, were delayed by the relocation of the Pitcairners. They now had to be won over to the idea of sharing their island with a different church as well as Melanesian Islanders. George Nobbs, their religious leader, resisted but Selwyn's chaplain John Coleridge Patteson convinced him. George's biographer and descendant, Raymond Nobbs, has suggested a degree of coercion was involved. Having learned of community disquiet and the pastor's related 'lapses from temperance', Patteson insinuated that he could 'choose to make public what [he knew] about him and the people'. Nobbs was duly supportive.[4]

Selwyn also needed the New South Wales governor, who then legally controlled the island, to acquiesce. Denison was not impressed with the idea and neither was his successor, Sir John Young, who wrote: 'I cannot conceive anything more likely to demoralize the population and turn it from the higher type of race it now assumes back to that of mere South Sea savages ... [than] the introduction of a number of half-savage youths at the period of life when their passions are least under control'.[5] It was the corruption of morals rather than morale that the governor feared. But the reference to uncontrolled 'passions' suggests that Young also harboured racist fears of inter-breeding and biological 'descent'.

Young was swayed, nonetheless, just as Nobbs had been. The mission's purchase of land helped, as did the return of some of the Pitcairners to their old home – an act which suggested ingratitude. By the end of August 1867, the Melanesian Mission controlled 1000 acres (405 hectares) of land on Norfolk, most of it bought, some granted. A stone chapel was built along with a large timber dining hall in which people ate side by side at long tables regardless of colour or gender. The hall appeared to be a blend of European Gothic and traditional Pacific architecture. Such commingling was novel enough for Europeans. It must have been extraordinary for the Melanesians, who were communing with people they would never otherwise have met, other Islanders included, and speaking the learned and shared languages of English and New Guinean Motu.

Patteson's approach to evangelising stressed a common humanity and the universality of Christian ethics. One of his acolytes summed it up in 1902: 'The differences that look so tremendous are really superficial ... To treat them [Melanesians] as fellow human beings, not a separate caste, is the great secret'.[6] As the religious historian Sara H Sohmer has argued, these beliefs belie the typical characterisation of the Victorian-era missionary as someone imbued with 'aggressiveness', 'paternalism' and cultural superiority.[7] None embodied the antithesis to that stereotype more than Patteson's colleague, the anthropologist and linguist Reverend Robert Codrington, who used his time on Norfolk and his Pacific journeys to both minister to Melanesians and study their cultures with a genuine fascination for human diversity. The result was *The Melanesian Languages*, published in 1885, and *The Melanesians: Studies in their Anthropology and Folk-lore*, published in 1891. Codrington acknowledged the 'valuable assistance' of the distinguished 'native' missionary, Reverend George Sarawia, who shared his youthful memories of Banks Island before Europeans arrived. Like many missionaries, Codrington regretted the impact of that contact but he expressed it with unusual sensitivity: 'iron, tobacco, calico, a wider knowledge of the world, have not compensated native people for new diseases and the weakening of social bonds'. His introduction also contained an astonishing degree of self-reflection while making the link between anthropology and religious mission. It was an argument for the value of empathy which drew upon Christian and Enlightenment precepts:

> this book, though written by a missionary, with his full share of the prejudices and predilections belonging to missionaries, is not meant to have what is generally understood to be a missionary character; but the writer is persuaded that one of the first duties of a missionary is to try and understand the people among whom he works, and to this end he hopes that he may have contributed something that may help.[8]

Codrington's writings contrast markedly with those of John Gibson Paton, a Scottish Presbyterian rector who travelled to the New Hebrides, present-day Vanuatu, to convert the local people in 1858. His memoirs are replete with references to 'heathen' people and the 'sin-darkened but sun-lit Southern Isles' which they inhabited.[9] Paton's unwavering faith and stark sense of good and evil helped him overcome enormous personal trials. He married his wife and companion, Mary, two weeks before leaving Greenock, Scotland, for the New Hebrides via Melbourne. She died just three months after landing at Aneityum and only days after giving birth, in February 1859. Their infant son died a month later. Paton carried on, finding solace in his god and working 'for the salvation of [the] savage Islanders'. Rarely, if ever, did he equate his own belief in prayer to an all-knowing and omnipotent god with the 'superstitions' of the 'heathen' which held that magic was the source of ill-fortune and that observing custom, including cannibalism, was a way to maintain existential balance.[10] In contrast to Codrington, Paton found little, if anything, of worth in the cultures he was trying to change. There was kindness but little empathy in his paternalism.

Pious Protestants of the Victorian era were driven to use every moment in the service of their religion. The sermonising words of Sydney's bishop William Broughton, 'If time be wasted eternity is lost', applied as much to non-conformists as they did to Anglicans.[11] For

John Paton time was sacred. In 1862 he returned to Australia to help raise funds for a mission vessel and to inspire more missionaries. The Scotsman travelled through Tasmania, South Australia, Victoria and New South Wales addressing local missionary societies and calling at outback stations unannounced. He was often, but not always, welcomed. In the end Paton amassed more than the £3000 needed to construct a ship. The *Dayspring* was slipped in Nova Scotia in 1863, and sailed to Sydney before conveying missionaries around the islands for a decade. The ship's funding was, in Paton's estimation, the endeavour which cohered the Presbyterian Pacific mission in Australia. 'It was God's own wise Providence, and not my zeal', he wrote with proper humility and faith, '... that matured these arrangements, and gave the Australian Presbyterian Churches a Mission Ship of their own, and a Mission field at their doors'.[12] The *Dayspring* was wrecked on Tanna in 1873, such were the mysterious ways in which the Christian god worked.

Australia had been a part of Europe's religious mission in the Pacific since the 1800s. In the second half of the century it was a staging post from where British and occasionally French missionaries might proceed to the South Seas. Funds and recruits could be raised there, and people might recuperate or retire in the southern colonies away from the heat, disease and threat of violence which accompanied Pacific postings. John Paton did just that after 50 years in his island mission. He and his second wife, Maggie, died peacefully at their home in Victoria in the early 1900s. Together they had reputedly converted the entire island of Aniwa to Christianity. John Paton's handsome books, with their stories of dark-hearted heathens and determined missionaries, remained in print for many years to influence perceptions of both in Australia and Britain.

But while all apparently worked for the 'one true God', there was rivalry between Presbyterians, Wesleyans and Anglicans. Few of these British churches, in turn, trusted the Catholics, who were usually French clerics in Polynesia and Germans in New Guinea. Local people were warned about the 'wickedness' and 'wooden gods' of these papists by British reformed church Christians who had little tolerance for the ritual and material culture of Catholicism: statuary, gleaming monstrances and thuribles fuming with scented smoke.[13] Protestants sought to divine their god's will directly through prayer and the Bible. Possibly the emphasis on ceremony and sacred things was an advantage among people who placed such store on ritual and objects. Where the Catholics saw Protestant sabotage, Paton accused the 'Popish Missionaries' of working to 'pollute and to destroy' all his mission did.[14]

≋

'I am so happy here ...'

Most European missionaries were ordained men. Many, however, were supported by wives, such as Maggie Paton, who ministered in an unofficial capacity to island women, conducted sewing classes and provided medical aid. When Jane Tinney arrived on the small island of Dobu, part of the D'Entrecasteaux group, she believed herself the 'first missionary sister to land in New Guinea'.[15] That was 1892, 19 years after the London Missionary Society's Reverend Samuel McFarlane established a mission in Papua with the help of eight pastors from the Loyalty Islands.[16] Where John Paton's autobiography was published many times over, Tinney kept an intimate and detailed diary which sometimes read like a series of letters. The identity of the imagined reader is not clear; it may simply have been Jane's conversation with herself.

The journal keeping was certainly prompted by the adventure ahead, for it began with Tinney's three-hour train trip from the country town of Moss Vale to Sydney on 10 April 1892. In the port capital she met possibly her first Islanders – 'six Samoan and New Britain natives' – at the Central Methodist Mission Hall. She then accompanied 'about 40 native men and women and about half a dozen children (two or three of them strapped to their mothers' backs) walking from the Centenary

Hall in the middle of the city to Government House'.[17] Polynesians had walked the streets of Sydney since the early 1800s but this group must have attracted special attention and comment. There followed song, war dances, traditional gift giving of taro, yams and woven goods, and speeches in various languages in front of the New South Wales governor and his wife, Lady Jersey. The activities were surely significant for those who performed them, as their cultures placed great store on exchange and ritual. It is unlikely, however, the Earl of Jersey was overly impressed. Social occasions such as this led to his resignation just six months later and less than two years after arriving in the colony. He cited business matters in Britain, where he owned a vast estate. Boredom was also a factor; the earl had imagined a more 'serious' role for himself in the colony.[18]

For her part Tinney was excited. She left shortly after on a sailing vessel with a complement of passengers and crew that reflected Sydney's location on the edge of the Pacific and the many peoples who routinely encountered each other there. In Tinney's words, there were 'a little of all sorts on board ... English, Colonial, Samoan and Fijian passengers, English Captain, crew of Swedes, Norwegians and Solomon Islanders'.[19] Her destination, Dobu, sat amidst other islands off south-eastern New Guinea. It would become well known, in anthropological circles at least, three decades later through the work of Bronislaw Malinowski and Reo Fortune.

Tinney's memoir over the next two years is peppered with earnest remarks about doing 'God's work'. There was something of John Paton's simple distinction between good and evil, the latter including traditional customs from self-decoration to the 'incantations' performed to overcome sickness. The missionaries applied local understanding of forbidden practice to end the body art: 'The designs are generally well done and look very picturesque, though it is one of the things we taboo as being a sign of their heathenism'. Teeth blackening was 'another custom which must go'.[20]

Tinney described a European wedding, the first on the island, which was celebrated in the new church 'in the presence of a large assemblage in full native dress ... The bride was attired in a crème cashmere dress trimmed with silk, and wore a wreath of orange blossom in her hair'. That was followed by the first 'native' wedding with the bride in full local dress. The missionary noted there was trouble getting both bride and groom to say 'I do'. And having done so each left by different doorways, apparently in accord with local custom regarding partnering. Just how long that union lasted is unclear, for Tinney also observed that Dobuan marriage and divorce laws were 'slack'. Even the women were permitted to end a formal relationship, something that was difficult and shameful in 'respectable' colonial society.[21]

The missionary knew the transformation of Dobu culture prompted fears among some of the older people. They worried, she noted, 'that we will draw the young people away from their old customs'.[22] Established patterns were being redrawn, but the new ways were being adopted with reference to the old, as the marriage ceremony suggests. A hybrid culture was emerging.

And there was something more. Tinney herself was transformed by the freedom which distance from her own social codes permitted. Unchaperoned and single in a place which had seen fewer than five white women, the missionary was clearly having the time of her life. She said as much early on after an island boy taught her how to make bread. Later she exclaimed 'I am so happy here'. On her 25th birthday, just months into the posting, she wrote: 'My Birthday! The first I have spent away from home, but I would rather be here working for Christ than be at home. I cannot help but look back over the past year. What a year of change it has been!' Over the following two years, Tinney presided over religious services and climbed a mountain with her friend and fellow missionary, referred to most properly as 'Miss Walker', along with a group of island women. She learned to paddle a dugout canoe and nearly drowned in a fast-running river while doing so. On that occasion the absurdity of clinging to an upturned boat while holding an open umbrella prompted laughter rather than screams. In Miss Walker's company, Tinney bathed at the beach in broad daylight, something impossible in respectable Australia before the growth of modern beach culture. The locals were amused at the Australians' unfamiliarity with the elements, for they themselves could 'swim and dive as easily as they walk', as Tinney mused.[23] Contrary to concerns for her well-being expressed by the Administrator of Papua, Sir William MacGregor, Tinney gained weight, stayed in 'excellent health' and was not at all homesick.

The missionary also brought with her an attitude to human life that clearly differed from the Dobuans'. Tinney intervened to prevent an elderly woman from being buried alive, possibly because she was thought to be near death or burdensome. Her encounters with infanticide forced her to question universal values: 'I always thought a Mother's love was a natural thing'.[24] She was told of cannibalism, recently practised, whereby victims were roasted alive, to the self-confessed glee of the perpetrators. Yet confronting practices such as these did not evoke a sense of outrage, disgust or dismissal, but rather one of compassion: 'May God hasten the time when, not only in Dobu, but all over New Guinea cannibalism will be a thing of the past'.[25] It was a humane hope. Indeed, it may well have been shared by some Papuans and Torres Strait Islanders, who for years had lived in fear of raids from neighbouring groups.

In January 1895 Tinney heard Papuans had killed a white man, one of a group of 10 miners. 'So far, I think more men have found their graves than have found their fortunes in N.G', she wrote, without obviously condemning the killers. 'We get a number of callers here now', Tinney continued, 'Far more than we used to. Last Monday there were three cutters and a steamer, all belonging to traders anchored here at once'. World markets were finally, perhaps inevitably, bringing the intrepid and the desperate, the hard and the practical to tiny Dobu searching for commodities rather than souls.[26] There is a clear sense that Jane Tinney's newfound world was changing too.

'... in their natural state ...'

The traders turning up at Dobu were part of a second wave of Australian commercial expansion into the Pacific, if those seeking Tahitian pork, Fijian sandalwood and whales in the first three decades of the 19th century are considered the first. The man who 'discovered' the Melanesian sandalwood that fuelled the renewed incursion was the astonishing explorer–trader–mariner Peter Dillon. Standing nearly two metres tall, he was known throughout the oceanic south-west, with respectful familiarity, simply as 'Peter'.

Born in England in the year New South Wales was colonised, Dillon was soon serving in the Royal Navy like so many boys of his generation. And, like other mariners, he found his way to a Pacific that was opening slowly to European opportunity and adventure. He arrived in Fiji as a 20-year-old in 1808 and was employed in the first wave of the sandalwood trade. In Sydney, Dillon captained Samuel Marsden's missionary vessel *Active* for a time and worked with the emancipist trader Thomas Reibey securing salt pork in Pomare's Tahiti. In the 1820s Dillon's exploits and reports were regularly printed in the Sydney press. One such occasion was the wreck of his vessel *Calder* in Valparaiso in 1825. Then the *Sydney Gazette* referred to him as 'our respected and unfortunate friend'.[27] He survived that setback and was enterprising enough to secure another ship for the return trip. It was Dillon who, in 1826, learned of the fate of the French expedition under La Perouse and for that intelligence was awarded the title of Chevalier in the Foreign Legion by the French government.

It was Dillon, too, who discovered fresh stands of Melanesian sandalwood on Eromanga in the New Hebrides. He chose not to publicise his find widely, either desiring to manage the harvest to his own advantage or out of respect for the hitherto isolated Islanders whose world, he knew only too well, would be transformed by the rush that would follow. Possibly it was simply caution, for the Eromangans had wanted nothing to do with the objects he tried to trade. Word got out nonetheless and sandalwood began trickling to China on some colonial vessels whose owners and captains were willing to take the risk of a long route to the source of tea and ceramics.[28]

Two events exacerbated the rush that did indeed overtake the islands of the south-west Pacific. The first was the end of the East India Company monopoly over the China trade which had so hindered colonial commerce. That was 1833. The second was the location of more large stands of sandalwood near New Caledonia in 1841. Such was the secrecy that accompanied those potentially lucrative discoveries that vessels leaving Sydney for the Isle of Pines, the Loyalty Islands, New Caledonia or the New Hebrides typically declared false destinations; 'clearing for Guam' became a euphemism for simply heading somewhere in the close Pacific.[29] Of the seven vessels that left Sydney in the second half of 1841 probably bound for the islands, five put out for 'Guam' and one was headed for the equally unlikely destination of New Guinea, then barely known by colonists. The barque *Jean* returned from 'Guam' in March 1842 with 320 tons of sandalwood. That year 16 more vessels left Sydney and two went from Hobart, all almost certainly destined for the Pacific. In 1847, 29 vessels left Sydney and Hobart for the islands. Four were lost but the remainder were loaded with at least 1500 tons of sandalwood intended for the Chinese market.[30]

The early expeditions were speculative and risky. The very real possibility of being wrecked threatened all wind-powered maritime ventures but resource extraction in the Melanesian region brought with it the added danger of being clubbed to death and eaten. Although cannibalism would become the quintessential manifestation of 'savagery' in the colonial age, with distortions and misrepresentations that permeated Western popular culture into the 20th century, the practice did exist. Eating the flesh of enemies or those captured in raids was a widespread means of cultural fulfilment in many Pacific societies and, in some places, a way to procure much-needed protein. As one Hebridean chief told the Presbyterian missionary John Inglis in the 1850s: 'It is very well for white men to talk in this way [of ending cannibalism]; they have plenty of Bull-ama-cow (beef); we have none; and unless we eat human flesh, we have nothing else'.[31]

Australian colonists had been attempting to come to terms with cannibalism at least since the massacre and consumption of the *Boyd*'s passengers and crew in 1810. Even then there were mixed views, with some talking of treacherous heathens and others, such as Samuel Marsden, finding cause in the misdeeds of Europeans. Similarly, the widely reported death of John Williams of the London Missionary Society at the hands of cannibals on Eromanga in 1839 brought forth a message of forgiveness and understanding in the colonial press: 'In the meantime let no bitter thoughts come against the murderous savages, the white man taught them their treachery and blood ... gunpowder and Christianity are not found in the same book'.[32] In 1842 the Sydney press reported that the captain of the Sydney-based sandalwood brig *Martha* had been eaten on the New Caledonian island of Maré, prompting distress but little demand for retribution. Instead, an expedition was sent to Mare to determine the circumstances. The findings were inconclusive and there was no retaliation. Rather the lengthy description of possible scenarios was followed by an equally long letter of advice from two other sandalwood getters, Edward Foxall and a man called White, who had just spent three harrowing months on the Isle of Pines in New Caledonia cutting wood among people whom they barely understood. There was 'no hostile feeling towards Europeans', they emphasised, but it was 'folly', to go to the islands 'for the purpose of trade' without an interpreter. The local people were of a 'very excitable nature', did not tolerate indignity towards their chief, and were quick to take offence. Actions, therefore, had repercussions and situations could escalate rapidly.

Although Foxall and White described the Islanders they worked among as being 'in their natural state' only one step removed from 'the beasts of the field' and with 'utter ignorance of right from wrong', they also acknowledged their humanity and intellect. Common ground could be found and trade conducted. But Europeans who went to the South Seas for gain, they argued, had to deal with Islanders on local terms.[33] Power resided with the cannibals, not the interlopers.

Traditional Melanesian morality, which gave paramount loyalty to chief, clan and tribe, was very different from that which was emerging in the European mind as Christianity melded with Enlightenment humanism in defence of universal human dignity and the right to life – much as Jane Tinney would confront 50 years later. For Foxall and White, as for many colonists, the opacity of Melanesian cultures was confounding. The 'excitability' which brought with it the possibility of sudden and extreme violence was taken as evidence of people existing in a philosophical and literal state of nature – the 'natural state' Foxall and White referred to – whereby each group was at war with another. It was the opposite of the 'noble savagery' of Polynesia, the perfect natural state described by Jean-Jacques Rousseau, which had captivated the Frenchman Bougainville and to some extent the Englishman Banks. Melanesians epitomised what Bernard Smith called 'ignoble savagery', that other European 'preconception' which provided a framework for understanding human difference. The hard and soft primitivisms Smith described were subsets of the generally approving preconception of 'noble savagery'. By the 1840s ignobility had largely displaced this concept in European minds, whether they were missionaries or traders. Indeed, Melanesians seemed patently to live in the 'brutish' state of nature posited by Thomas Hobbes, whose philosophy presented a 'natural law' of human self-interest and hostility – a distinct counterpoint to Rousseau's pre-civilised innocence. Colonists increasingly comprehended the examples of human existence around them as evidence of evolution, social if not scientific. Realists such as Foxall and White attempted to work with that state of affairs. Others such as John Paton sought to change it.

'... through motives of cupidity ...'

Where the early sandalwood getters came and went as quickly as they could with caution and some trepidation, James Paddon set up a permanent station just off Aneityum in 1844 – four years before Protestant missionaries came to stay and 15 years before John Paton arrived with his Bible and pregnant wife, Mary. Both Paddon and Paton were men of fortitude. The trader provisioned his station with supplies sent from Sydney and then used it to diversify his business, advertising the opportunity for resupply to whaling captains in the colonial press. The economic connection to Australia and, by extension, the colonial influence upon its region was palpable. Having established himself thus through the Pacific possessions of his own country, the Englishman could take advantage of French expansion. When the latter annexed New Caledonia in 1853, Paddon assisted French migration, provisioned the émigrés and began a flourishing cattle industry to sustain them. The French government subsequently granted him 4000 hectares of land on the island. Paddon was a man for whom borders meant little in the face of commercial opportunity. He was a businessman foremost and the epitome of the Pacific pragmatist. For this reason, too, he was respected for his ability to negotiate with local people, who reputedly remembered him fondly after his death in 1864. Fairness, forthrightness and the willingness to follow up dishonoured agreements with consequence, it seems, was at the heart of mutual understanding in the very masculine world of island warriors and traders. Dorothy Shineberg, the pioneering historian of the sandalwood trade, summarised Paddon's reputation thus: 'No one wronged him with impunity ... and his courage was equal to every situation.'[34]

James Paddon's great competitor was Robert Towns, the man who looked at the Pacific as a place of endless opportunity for profit, whether that meant killing its creatures, cutting its trees or transporting its people. Like Peter Dillon, and probably Paddon, Towns had been an English boy sailor. Generationally he sat between the two, born in Northumberland in 1794 and arriving in Sydney in 1827 after learning maritime trade in the Mediterranean, some 16 years before Paddon began his Pacific business. By that time Towns had left the sea and settled in Sydney to orchestrate the voyages of others in his service. The man's interests were diverse and his pockets deep, the result initially of shipping immigrants to the colonies and harvesting whales in the ocean around them. Where Paddon directed business from his well-appointed island stations – he established a public library of sorts on Inyeuc off Aneityum – Towns kept tight control on his captains from Sydney Harbour, where his wharf and warehouses became landmarks. That he could do so via mail shows the extent of the traffic which had developed between the colonies and the islands. Between 1855 and 1860 Towns had as many as eight vessels involved in the sandalwood trade, to Paddon's nine, in a business that employed at least 31.[35]

As the visits became more frequent, Melanesians were brought within the transformational logic and demands of an international market in which Australian colonists participated significantly. The trade goods which Peter Dillon had offered in vain in the 1820s became currency in the 1840s. Accordingly the value of initial barter items such as fish hooks, nails and glass bottles diminished as they became commonplace, to be replaced by finished tools such as axes, stimulants like tobacco and ultimately firearms. Obsolete traditional tools and weapons were set aside to be subsequently traded as ethnological curios with the Europeans.

Labour, too, became a commodity. Island men worked as timber getters, seamen and servants. Their worlds expanded as they moved around neighbouring islands they might not otherwise have visited, meeting some who were long-time enemies and others of whose existence they had been unaware. Some came to Sydney. Robert Towns' Melanesian sailors saw the wharves of Port Jackson as early as 1842, but the man generally acknowledged as the first to bring Islanders to Australia to work in agriculture was Ben Boyd, the flamboyant entrepreneur, banker and landowner who operated vast sheep runs in the south of New South Wales and a whaling station on the adjacent coast at Twofold Bay. Boyd's personal yacht, *Wanderer*, and his fleet of steamers elicited gasps of wonder from Sydneysiders when they arrived in the harbour in 1841 and 1842. They helped to establish his reputation in the minds of some as a man of vision and daring – just what was needed to move New South Wales along. For Boyd's enterprises began in the midst of a depression and just after the end of convict transportation to that colony in 1840. He confronted, therefore, a sluggish economy in the final stages of transition from relying on unfree labourers to wage workers who might even negotiate their remuneration and conditions. His solution to the problem of securing 'cheap labour' was bringing as many as 200 men from the New Hebrides and Loyalty Islands to work as shepherds in 1847.

The scheme was clearly something of a novelty, one which raised concerns about the precedent it set. The *Sydney Chronicle* suggested there were considerations other than 'mere economy' in importing non-white labour. Uppermost was the well-being of the community when those arriving were 'a distinct race' whose 'code of morality', the *Chronicle* speculated, was utterly different from that operating in the colony; what would happen if 'heathens' ran amok?[36]

Initially, no concurrent concern was expressed for the transplanted Islanders. However, it is obvious they were unprepared for the experience from the description by one colonist who witnessed their arrival in Sydney: 'all were naked ... they crowded round, looking at us with utmost surprise, and feeling the texture of our clothes with their fingers'. Some who were taken to Boyd's sheep runs rebelled and walked nearly 650 kilometres back to Sydney, itself an astonishing feat of fortitude that the *Sydney Morning Herald* described with unveiled sarcasm directed at Boyd: 'back through all the dreary waste, in defiance of heat and cold, hunger and thirst, toil and travel, back have the silly miscreants wandered ... .'[37] It may have been one of these men who was subsequently found dead, having swum out to the vessel *Portenia*, which had previously delivered Islanders to Australia, in an attempt to depart the colony. He was denied access and drowned. A blue shirt in a bundle – likely a shepherd's kit – was found nearby.[38]

Boyd's colonial ventures foundered spectacularly, leaving many debts unpaid and an unknowable legacy in the islands from where his shepherds came. But the Pacific was ever an ocean of opportunity, particularly for those who could set regret or responsibility aside. In 1849 Boyd took himself off to California in the *Wanderer* to seek fortune on the goldfields. He reportedly transported 14 New Hebrideans to work his claim, but without success.[39] Returning west again in 1851, Boyd disembarked on Guadalcanal in the Solomons, having instructed one of 'his favourite natives' not to allow any Islanders to board.[40] Shots were heard and Boyd's crew never saw him again. The 'melancholy' news of his 'murder' was widely reported in the colonial press. One Sydney resident, Thomas Fennell, was moved to write an 'Epigram' defending the man against those who impugned him in death: 'Let not thy spirit then, poor Benjamin/Wince at the stings of those poor wasps …'[41] For its part the strongly Catholic newspaper, *Freeman's Journal*, hinted that divine justice had had a part in the violent death of a man who so mistreated his brethren, namely the 'haggard' and 'hungry' Islanders who had arrived in Sydney from faraway sheep runs with bleeding feet: 'We presume not to say that the Lord of Heaven and the Creator of these men has punished the individual who through motives of cupidity imported those miserable creatures to Australia'.[42]

≋

*'they would sing and chant and talk
to the people back in the islands'*

As 'the incarnation of the puritan virtues of thrift, sobriety, [and] industry', Robert Towns was quite unlike Benjamin Boyd.[43] But for both men the Pacific was an oyster to be shucked. Undeterred by Boyd's experience with bewildered Islanders and the criticism it attracted, Towns imported 73 more 'natives' in 1863, as field workers for his newly established cotton plantations on the Logan River near Brisbane and Cleveland Bay some 1300 kilometres north. The enterprises took advantage of Queensland's *Alienation of Crown Lands Act*, passed in 1860, which offered a land bonus for each bale of 'good, clean Sea Island cotton grown and exported to Great Britain'.[44] Growing cotton became even more promising when the US Civil War curtailed production there. Towns persevered until 1868 without turning a profit and then gave cotton growing away. By then African-Americans were toiling again in the cotton fields of Alabama, Georgia and Mississippi, albeit as freed people, and prices had fallen.

Plantation cropping using cheap 'coloured' labour, however, was still appealing and Towns and others turned their attention and capital to growing sugar in this manner in Queensland's sub-tropical north. The region was the equivalent distance south of the equator as the Caribbean islands were to the north of that great divide. The 18th-century sugar fortunes made in the British West Indies were legendary and it was soon apparent that sugar could also be a great success in Queensland. By 1869, 28 sugar mills were operating in the colony and, in 1872, 20 per cent of the 25 000 hectares then under cultivation was given over to sugar.[45] Problems with 'rust' disease were overcome by experimentation with cane varieties and locations. Sugar growing was abandoned at Cleveland Bay, but only after that settlement was renamed Townsville in honour of Robert Towns in 1865. It was Mackay, some 400 kilometres to the south, that became known as 'Sugaropolis'. By 1874 the area was producing one-third of Queensland's cane.[46] Accordingly, Mackay became the centre of Pacific island plantation labour. It was 'home' to roughly one-third of the approximately 10 000 Islanders working in Queensland over the 20 years to 1900. One in ten were women.

Official reports such as census counts often referred to these people as 'Polynesians', although they largely originated from New Guinea to New Caledonia, and the name 'Melanesian' was concurrently used for that part of the Pacific. Selwyn's Melanesian Mission, for instance, was well established by the time Islanders were arriving in numbers in Australia. Possibly the significance attached to Polynesia in the early years of colonisation had planted that name so firmly in colonial minds that it served as a catch-all for the western Pacific. Islanders were also called Kanakas. That word seems to have at least two origins; 'Kanaka' referred to someone from Hawaii, while 'Kanak' was also a New Caledonian native. By the 1860s, Kanaka was understood as 'a general name applied to all natives of the South Sea Islands'. Thereafter, it referred more specifically to those indentured for labour in Australia.[47] Lists created at the time of recruitment were more assiduous in detailing island origins, and personal names were grouped together next to 'Tanna', 'Torres Group' and so forth. The Islanders undoubtedly identified themselves more specifically by their name and kin, their village and possibly their island. In time descendants would come to call themselves collectively South Sea Islanders.

But before inter-marriage, shared experience and time itself helped to create cohesive communities, there was rivalry and hostility between groups whose animosity and feuds extended back generations and who now found themselves working together or near to each other. The transition from a traditional island life to one on an Australian plantation, albeit remote, must have been confronting. Physical violence was one manifestation of this; use of magic or sorcery to attack or defend against wrong-doing was another. For while many Islanders had converted to Christianity, they brought aspects of their traditional spirituality with them to Queensland. Faith and community provided the link to Christianity. These were strongly animistic belief systems with a holistic connection between humans and the natural world, and a concomitant store placed upon magic and sorcery to summon natural forces. What emerged on the Queensland plantations was a 'syncretic' culture which held strongly to the power of magic, knowledge, ritual and objects alongside an adherence to Christian belief in supernatural power and the significance of ritual. The distinction between religion and magic so important to Europeans did not apply. Traditional religion infused everyday life including gardening, doctoring and courtship. Unsurprisingly, cultural retention was particularly strong in the Mackay district, where many Islanders lived together or near each other. There, a form of transplanted ceremonial building called a Tarunga hut was erected for purposes of ritual and magic, and to maintain a system of community authority which remained in place through to the 20th century. One old Mackay resident, interviewed in the 1970s, recalled: 'When I was a boy I saw the tribal elders going there [the Tarunga hut] ... they would sing and chant and talk to the people back in the islands ... The elders could pass sentence on you for anything you had done wrong'.[48]

≋

'... thud came the arrow into my left side ...'

The South Sea labour trade, as it became known, not only founded one of Queensland's most enduring and significant industries – sugar cane production – it was central to profound debates about the place of the colonies within the British Empire. It affected matters of security which, in turn, prompted some to suggest that Great Britain and its Australasian possessions might indeed have divergent interests – a century after colonisation, and as those possessions sought to find common cause and discuss creating an Australian Commonwealth. So began the articulation of a national rather than an imperial interest. But, just as importantly, the business, which one colonial public servant would describe in hindsight as 'the disgraceful traffic in human beings', triggered fundamental arguments about morality and humanity in the colonies.[49]

Robert Towns was more than sanguine about his business ethics at the beginning of that traffic. In 1863 he challenged missionaries to find fault with his endeavour in an open letter: 'I with my cotton emigration ... will do more towards civilising the natives in one year than you can possibly do in ten'.[50] Towns' intended readership included John Paton, with whom he had had disagreements in Sydney over transport costs in the islands. Paton certainly recalled Towns and his boast when writing his autobiography three decades later. Referring to the businessman as 'Captain T—', Paton described him as the founder of 'the shocking Kanaka labour-traffic to the Colonies'. Far from civilising, Paton accused Towns and others of spreading 'disease and vice, misery and death'. The missionary went further, calling the business 'Colonial slavery'. Many agreed.[51]

The Islanders who were taken to Queensland to work were not chattel, or legal property, to be bought and sold for the duration of their lives as slaves in the US had been. Rather they were indentured workers who came for a defined period, typically three years, before returning to the islands. Some were recruited under written contract and were protected in Queensland by the *Masters and Servants Act* of 1861. However, in the absence of regulation, many Islanders left their homes without formal agreements. This led to misrepresentation, coercion and violence on the recruiters' part, and misunderstanding and resentment on the Islanders'. Lingering ill-will in the islands frequently resulted in retribution being meted out to other Europeans whether or not they were connected with the labour trade; for what the Christian Bible called 'eye for an eye', the Islanders generally saw as justified payback. The term 'blackbirding' was coined, carrying with it the strong connotation of enslavement. Robert Towns' recruiter Captain Ross Lewin gained notoriety for his brutal methods – he reportedly confined a chief with hands and feet bound inside a 500-gallon tank for two weeks – but there were others.[52]

Moral outrage and pragmatic concern at the ensuing mayhem led to the passage of Queensland's *Polynesian Labourers Act* of 1868, aimed at regulating and controlling 'the introduction and treatment' of Pacific Islanders. The Act established mandatory labour contracts and the licensing of recruiters. Registers of those recruited and their place of origins were to be kept. It introduced minimum standards of conditions for those recruited both during their passage and their term of employment, and promised fines for dishonest dealings and the forfeiture of a bond of £500 if the law was breached. So that these regulations could be enforced, 12 different forms were drafted and a tax of £20 per labourer levied upon the recruiter or captain to pay for the resulting administration.

Missing, however, were government agents on board the vessels to ensure adherence to the law. Pressure for this amendment came from London, where Queensland's labour business had been monitored with increasing concern. There was some profundity in these arguments about slavery and regulation. Australia had been colonised in the same year as the first Act to regulate slavery in the Empire – the 1788 'Dolben Act' – and William Wilberforce's active entry into the abolitionist cause. The British slave trade had been abolished in 1807 and imperial slavery itself effectively abolished by 1840. The commodity which had justified Britain's significant role in the system was sugar. That, too, was the crop which motivated 'blackbirding' in Australia. There were those in Britain's parliament in the 1860s and 1870s, not least members of the Aborigines Protection, London Missionary and Church Missionary Societies, who were heirs to the abolitionist campaigns of Wilberforce and others. The debate they started in the House of Commons was successful although the amendments were only reluctantly introduced by the newly installed Queensland government of Arthur Palmer, a forthright, wealthy and well-born pastoralist whom one Colonial Office clerk nonetheless described as 'one who appears to have recently learned writing and not to have learned manners at all'.[53]

Neither the 1868 Act, nor its amendment, were enough to ameliorate the worst aspects of the trade, which often involved intercolonial vessels and destinations other than Queensland. One of the most shocking incidents occurred in early 1872 when the crew of the recruiting vessel *Carl* shot most of the Islanders, bound for Fijian plantations and secured in the hold, after they protested against their conditions. Fifty were thrown overboard. The owner James Murray a 'monster in human shape', reportedly led the atrocity, singing the Civil War tune 'Marching through Georgia' while killing his victims in an apparent state of derangement.[54]

However, it was the earlier trial of the master of the *Daphne* in Sydney in 1869 which revealed the inadequacy of existing laws and led to the British parliament's further intervention. The *Daphne* was supposed to have delivered Islanders to Queensland, but instead the recruiter Ross Lewin took them to Fiji because of a 'better market' for their employment. There, Commander George Palmer of HMS *Rosario* inspected the schooner and found 100 naked Islanders in the hold. With the consequent discrepancies in documentation Palmer detained the *Daphne* and charged its master with slave dealing under the imperial *Slave Trade Act* of 1824. The case was dismissed in Sydney's Water Police Court because they were not being taken to a place where slavery was permitted, *ipso facto* there could be no slavery.[55]

The result was the passage in Britain of the *Pacific Islanders' Protection Act* of 1872, to prevent and punish 'Criminal Outrages upon Natives of the Islands in the Pacific Ocean'. The Act acknowledged that South Seas recruiting was not enslavement as had been practised earlier in the empire but rather the removal of people without their consent; the legislation was thereby generally known as the 'Kidnapping Act.' Significantly, too, the Act recognised the Islanders' morality by making allowances to consider their evidence, notwithstanding differences in language and religion. It 'shall be the duty of the court or commissioner, or officer administering the same,' the legislation stipulated, 'to ascertain, as far as possible, in what form such oath will be binding upon the conscience of such witness or deponent'. It was a significant departure from the mindset of Edward Foxall and first mate White who, back in 1842, wondered if these Islanders had any conscience at all.

The incident which had finally ensured passage of the 'Kidnapping Act', in the face of ongoing reluctance from an expenditure-conscious imperial Treasury, was the killing of Bishop Patteson of the Melanesian Mission in September 1871. The clergyman was unlucky enough to go ashore on Nukapu in the Santa Cruz Islands after the unwelcome visit of labour recruiters. There he was beaten to death by an aggrieved relative of a recently kidnapped Islander. Amidst many appalling events, it was Patteson's killing which highlighted most clearly in London and Australia the violence the labour trade unleashed. Few could argue that the head of the Melanesian Mission had not been a friend to the Islanders.

But perhaps even more illustrative of the cycle of violence and retribution which kept spinning in the Pacific are the actions of HMS *Rosario*, then under the command of Albert Markham, to determine the circumstances of the bishop's death. It was this voyage that incidentally led to the seizure of the *Carl* and the revelations of the grisly details of the murder of its human cargo. Markham later wrote of his shame that such 'horrible and revolting transactions actually occurred on board a ship owned and manned by Englishmen, and sailing under the British flag'.[56] Yet as he patrolled the Solomons and New Hebrides, Commander Markham himself felt compelled to fire upon Islanders in retaliation for attacks and perceived wrongs. On one of these occasions, on Varsalai in the Santa Cruz Islands, Markham extracted an admission of sorts, with interpreter at hand, that the Islanders had killed crew members of the recruiting vessel *Wild Duck*. It was punishment in the Islanders' minds for kidnapping a chief and other villagers. Markham levied a fine of several pigs, which implied that the Islanders were wrong to retaliate despite the Europeans' initial offence. When the reparation was not delivered within the agreed period and the Islanders fled into the bush, Markham himself retaliated by ordering his men to burn the village to the ground and destroy as many canoes as they could find. In the wake of the *Rosario*'s destructive cruise, Commodore Frederick Stirling of the Australia Station expressed unease that such 'indiscriminate' punishment might as easily harm the innocent as the guilty. There was indeed some irony in the self-professed agents of 'civilisation' delivering justice in the form of a collective payback, which more resembled tribal law than British notions of individual guilt and punishment. As historian Tracey Banivanua-Mar has suggested, Markham was, in effect, 'going native'.[57]

The violent cycle touched the navy's highest level. In August 1875 James Goodenough, who had taken over from Stirling as Commodore of the Australia Station, was hit in the ribs by an arrow on one of the Santa Cruz Islands while personally investigating an attack upon the squadron's schooner HMS *Sandfly*. An extended letter, begun before Goodenough landed and continued as he lay wounded in his cabin, illustrates with some drama the opacity which confronted those charged with keeping peace in a region of clashing cultures. That task was doubly confounding for Goodenough, who was a devout Anglican as well as a man of war:

> (Thursday August 12th) I am going on shore to the spot where the Sandfly was last year to see if I can make friends with the unfortunates, who seem most friendly and anxious to be civil ... (Tuesday August 17th) But I was disappointed ... As we drew in to the shore canoes came about us, eager, vociferous and friendly, and with a rather villainous look ... one man came up with a present of a yam, and I gave him some calico, with which he seemed pleased ... [Harrison] was bargaining for some arrows with a tall man ... Casting my eye to the left I saw a man with a gleaming pair of black eyes fitting an arrow to a string, and in an instant just as I thought it was a sham menace, and stared him in the face, *thud* came the arrow into my left side ...

The letter concluded with a poignantly ambiguous half-finished thought: 'I don't feel ...'

Tetanus set in over the following days and knowing that he was dying, Goodenough addressed his crew, as a Christian and a commanding officer. To those who were tempted to desert when on shore – and in Sydney the temptation was great – he urged that they 'think of the love of God'. He spoke without acrimony of the 'poor natives' who attacked him for 'they couldn't know right from wrong'.[58]

Goodenough was buried in the small cemetery of St Thomas's Anglican Church on land the resourceful and pragmatic one-time Pacific trader Alexander Berry had given to the north shore parish. Thousands lined the road from Sydney Harbour to pay their respects as the gun carriage and casket made its way up the ridge to 'Crows Nest'. In St Thomas's Cemetery they passed the extraordinary Egyptian-style pyramid Berry had built for his wife and himself, and beneath which the old merchant had been laid to rest just two years earlier. Such was the cosmopolitan nature of imperial culture. Goodenough, the model of a Victorian officer and gentleman, was 44 years old. Two sailors, killed in the same encounter and buried beside him, were both just 18. The Commodore's last public act in Sydney before that Pacific cruise had been to unveil a statue of Captain Cook at Randwick. The revered navigator had, of course, been killed in Hawaii in 1779, having unwittingly transgressed local custom. The similarity between the men's fates was not lost on those who reported the Commodore's funeral.[59] It might also be imagined that one man led the way for the other.

≋

'I cannot but look upon annexation as a positive duty'

HMS *Rosario* was a 'screw sloop', an example of the transition from the age of wood and wind in which Europe discovered the Pacific to that of iron, steam and coal when it started to possess it. Built on the Thames in 1860, the *Rosario* was an all-timber vessel – one of the last of its kind in this regard – and was powered both by the breeze that filled its sails, and steam which drove its single propeller. *Rosario* took its name by descent from a Spanish galleon captured by the English in 1588, a small lesson in the history of Britain's imperial ascent. When it commenced its eventful Pacific cruise in October 1871, HMS *Rosario* was one of seven vessels of the Australia Station located at Garden Island in Sydney

Harbour. From 1859 the station shared the Pacific with the Royal Navy base at Valparaiso. Governor King had recommended, unsuccessfully, the permanent posting of two sloops as early as 1805. Then the disruptive activities of Europeans around Tahiti, Americans particularly, were the concern. By the middle of the century colonists were most worried about the threat of Russian attack from the north Pacific port of Kamchatka. The Admiralty's instructions given to Captain Fremantle stationed in Sydney in 1854 outline the role of security, power projection and maintenance of order in a region inhabited by many and varied British subjects:

> You are to protect British interests in the colonies of New South Wales, New Zealand and the Islands adjacent and also to visit or detach a ship to visit the Feejee, Navigators and Friendly Islands, and it will be your object to give to the natives an impression of the power and of the friendly disposition of the British nation and whilst giving due weight to the representatives of the British consuls and missionaries and to strengthen their hands for good, you will repress any tendency to undue interference or encroachments on the rights of the chiefs and natives.[60]

Recognising the rights of Islanders while giving 'an impression of power' was the judicial balancing act that would confront the likes of Commander Markham and Commodore Goodenough.

The Sydney-based squadron was substantially strengthened for patrol work after the 1872 Act with the construction of five schooners in 1873. They were slipped just three coves away from Garden Island in John Cuthbert's Darling Harbour shipyard, and so were ready for immediate service without the delay of sailing time from Britain. By the end of the year the Australia Station was 10 vessels strong, half of them new. HMS *Sandfly* was one of the harbour-built schooners. The station flagship was the 21-gun screw corvette HMS *Pearl*, the vessel on which Commodore Goodenough died in 1875.

The labour trade, and the problems it generated for the officers of the Australia Station, involved much more than Queensland's sugar industry. By the 1870s British subjects, colonials included, were to be found throughout the Pacific islands living as traders, planters or 'beachcombers' – those runaways and deserters who, in the words of one observer, had taken 'leave for ever of their own race, and cast their lot in with the natives'.[61] Well over 1000 British subjects were living in Fiji alone by 1870. Despite being represented by a consul who dealt with Cakobau, declared King of Fiji in 1867, their security was precarious not least because of exploitative labour practices.

Britain's empire was expanding. The extension of Crown rule over India in 1858 alone added more than 300 million people and a landmass half the size of the Australian continent to that global balance. However, expansion was not always sought or welcomed by politicians and administrators at the imperial centre. The reluctance of the Colonial Office to assume control over the Pacific islands after the annexation of New Zealand in 1840 remains a powerful corrective to simplistic characterisations of ever-eager imperialists. The British who had settled in the Fijian islands were a particular problem. When, in 1859, the ascendant Fijian chief Cakobau had offered to cede his territory to the British government if they would pay his debt to an American trader, the British declined. They were cautiously cognisant of Cakobau's questionable authority. Instead, the Melbourne-based Polynesia Company took on the outstanding amount in exchange for 200 000 acres of land in 1869. The combined request from the Australian colonies that Britain declare a protectorate in Fiji to quell the disorder there in 1870 was refused and countered with the suggestion from the Secretary of State for the Colonies, Lord Kimberley, that New South Wales assume responsibility for the islands. The colony declined that offer, much as it would the pass on the opportunity of controlling Norfolk Island in 1888. Cost and bother were ever-present entries in the tally sheet of imperialism.

But so too were security, order, national honour and morality. All these motivations moved the British MP William McArthur, Christian and member of the Aborigines Protection Society, to form the Fiji Committee and press for annexation. His pressure resulted in the newly appointed Commodore Goodenough being sent to Fiji from Sydney to report first-hand on the situation in 1873. With the British consul there he recommended taking possession as the only solution to balancing the need for order with the interests of the white community, Fijians and indentured workers. Britain had a responsibility as an imperial power and the original home, direct and indirect, of most of those who had caused the problems: 'I cannot but look upon annexation as a positive duty', he wrote in April 1874.[62] Back in London there was popular agreement. The *Spectator* was typically droll:

> Some two thousand or so of our countrymen, blundering after their manner about the world in search of some profitable work to do, have settled upon a group of islands in the South Pacific ... We may not be bound, as Lord Kimberley says, to follow British subjects everywhere, and compel them to behave decently, but we certainly have the right to do it when the general interests of mankind require each action; and when the Britons demand protection, and especially armed protection, the right becomes a duty.[63]

Fiji became a British colony on 10 October 1874, after Commodore Goodenough had conveyed the New South Wales governor, Hercules Robinson, on HMS *Pearl* to finally accept the offer of cessation from King Cakobau on behalf of the British government. Robinson thereby became the first governor of Fiji, a position he held concurrently with his gubernatorial duties in New South Wales. Such were the ties that linked the Pacific colonies of a hesitant imperialist.

CHAPTER 9

Australia's Pacific

'There must be some mistake somewhere'

In the 1870s, Islanders were being transported south, east and west in the interests of traders and planters. The patrols of Australia Station vessels were accordingly widespread. It was on one naval cruise through the Torres Strait that Captain John Moresby came upon a useful harbour which could be entered through a reef and named it Port Moresby, after his father, who had commanded the Pacific Station at Valparaiso. That discovery aside, the captain seized several vessels in Torres Strait, including some operating in the pearl shell and *beche de mer* or trepang fishery. Prosecution there was difficult, for the Islanders employed were neither crew nor kidnapped passengers, but 'divers'. The law seemed always to be playing catch-up with conditions of employment in a Pacific world where opportunities to make money were only limited by one's imagination and daring.

Historian Regina Ganter has likened the men behind these schemes to 'resource raiders', exhausting a commodity in one area then moving to another.[1] Sandalwood was the perfect example. Unsurprisingly, then, traders such as James Paddon and Robert Towns were among those who established interests in Torres Strait *beche de mer* and pearl shell in the 1860s. Macassan fishers had long obtained the former for the Chinese market. In the late 19th century there were enough Chinese people in Australia to create local demand but most of the marine creatures were exported to Hong Kong and China. The trade was worth £13 000 a year by 1880. The business north of Townsville employed 40 vessels but the pearl shell fishery supplying button manufacturers in the US and

Europe was even more lucrative. Five luggers in 1870 became 109 in 1877. Exports of unprocessed shells brought in as much as £100 000 in the 1880s.[2]

The presence of Europeans introduced all the tensions that had characterised contact in Melanesia: violence, rivalry between missionaries and traders, modification of tradition, adaptation, and incorporation into larger wholes. The eminent anthropologist AC Haddon described the impact on Mabuiag Island, directly north of Cape York and halfway to New Guinea, in 1898:

> The advent of the white man has upset former economic conditions ... The men now spend all their time 'swimming diving' as it is called, that is, they go in parties in sailing boats, and dive by swimming for pearl-shell in shallow water ... Thus it comes about that agriculture, as well as fishing, is greatly neglected, and a considerable portion ... of their food has to be bought from the stores.[3]

But there was something else. The Torres Strait Islands' proximity to the Queensland colony invited annexation, both to protect the newcomers from attack by local people and to secure the *beche de mer* and pearl shell trade from covetous foreigners. In two stages, 1872 and 1879, the Torres Strait Islands were taken for Queensland – first those within 60 miles (97 kilometres) then right up to the coastline of New Guinea. The colony thereby became a coloniser. The Queensland government established an administrative centre at Somerset on Cape York, then on Thursday Island amidst the archipelago, which petered out north to New Guinea. The first Queensland *Aborigines Protection Act* in 1897 exempted Torres Strait Islanders on account of 'their marked mental superiority over the mainland native'.[4] The Government Resident on Thursday Island, John Douglas, made this assessment based upon the Islanders' apparent willingness to work in the new economy and their tradition of gardening.

For a time, then, they had the rights of other British citizens. They lost these after Douglas died in 1904 and Torres Strait Islanders joined their Aboriginal neighbours as non-citizens subject to the control of the Chief Protector of Aborigines. However, unlike so many of their counterparts on the mainland, the people of Mer and elsewhere remained on their island homes. Neither did they suffer the frontier violence that characterised colonisation on the mainland. In 1884, for instance, some 200 Kalkadoon warriors had been killed in a set-piece battle with whites and Aboriginal Native Police, who were employed in an effective strategy of divide and conquer. The bloodshed took place far inland from Townsville but not far from the Combo Waterhole, which poet Banjo Paterson would immortalise as the billabong in the ballad 'Waltzing Matilda', one of the most popular songs in a white Australia starting to find its heart and soul in great inland expanses rather than its Pacific hinterland.

The administrative outpost at Thursday Island was also an ideal forward station from which to extend Queensland's control all the way into New Guinea itself. In April 1883 the Queensland premier Thomas McIlwraith did just that when he sent the island's magistrate to Port Moresby to run a Union Jack up the London Missionary Society's flagpole and take possession of the island's eastern half, ostensibly to forestall the presence of any non-British power so close to Queensland's recently declared maritime territories. Germany was the source of concern on this occasion. The resident missionary William Lawes was bewildered and unimpressed: 'that an Australian colony should be allowed to take this step is to us most surprising. Here is the largest island in the world ... annexed by a Police Magistrate who comes in a little tub of a cutter! There must be some mistake somewhere'. Writing on behalf of his mission, and perhaps the local people he felt he represented, Lawes continued: 'We would much rather not be annexed by anybody, but if there was any probability of a foreign power taking possession of New Guinea, then let us have British rule: but as a Crown colony, not as an appendage to Queensland'. The reason for his concern was clear; Queensland 'having basely and cruelly treated' its own Aboriginal population, what fate awaited New Guinea's people if they were 'handed over to the tender mercies' of the colonists?[5]

There was just as much surprise and bewilderment in London. McIlwraith was not strictly 'allowed' to do any such thing. As the Colonial Secretary Lord Derby subsequently told the premier, ignoring the 'constitutional principle' of colonies acting within their authority could only lead to serious 'difficulties and complications'.[6] Those of a humanitarian mindset also suspected McIlwraith's motivations. The opinions of missionaries reinforced their concerns, as did those of Sir Arthur Gordon, the High Commissioner for the Western Pacific based in Fiji since 1875, who was known for his sympathy towards 'coloured' people. The flag raising was, they surmised, less about fear of foreigners and more reflective of avarice. James Chalmers and William Wyatt Gill of the London Missionary Society, who had both worked in New Guinea, would put it bluntly: 'It is to be hoped the country is not to become part of the Australian colonies – a labour land, and a land where loose money in the hands of a few capitalists is to enter in and make enormous fortunes, sacrificing the natives and everything else'.[7] Where Lawes found Queensland's domestic record worrying, these people were perturbed by the trade which had furnished sugar workers for over a decade. Conveniently located, New Guinea was now in the purview of labour recruiters after 10 years of missionary activity and peripheral exploration.

Lawes had touched on another matter – New Guinea's place in defending Australia. That the large island to the continent's north represented a security threat while it remained 'un-owned' was not new. Writing in the mid-1870s, in one of the first locally published books to discuss Australasia and its 'Oceanic region', William Brackley Wildey suggested 'at New Guinea an army and navy could be assembled without hindrance, and might remain *in terrorem* over us; and in the event of war, hostile vessels could sally out and capture our gold-laden argosies; and possibly Australia'.[8]

While some believed McIlwraith's unilateralism was motivated by 'loose money', it was also catalytic, placing the issue of New Guinea and security uppermost in colonists' minds. And though few outside Queensland supported a colonial administration there, many wanted a British presence. In June 1883 Victorian premier James Service emphasised the security disadvantages that imperial ties entailed to the governor of his colony: 'Australia is in this respect fettered in her actions by forming part of the British Empire. She cannot take the course which her truest interest dictates without the authority of the Crown'.[9] It was a remarkable expression of colonial unity and separate interest. So strong were the security concerns that the colonies also pressed for extending that control to the Solomons and New Hebrides. There was soon talk of establishing an Australasian 'Monroe Doctrine' in the western Pacific, a direct reference to President Monroe's 1823 declaration, which had warned Europe off interfering in the western hemisphere. As international law expert Cait Storr has suggested, the first resolution of the first convention held to discuss federating the Australian colonies in Sydney in November and December 1883 'mimicked' in 'intent and tone' the American declaration: 'further acquisition of dominion by any Foreign Power in any of the islands of the Western Pacific, would be highly detrimental to the future safety and well-being of the British possessions in Australasia, as well as injurious to the interests of the whole Empire'.[10] The name of that extended meeting, the 'Australasian Convention on the Annexation of Adjacent Islands and the Federation of Australasia', leaves little doubt about how significant collective security was in the movement towards unity.

Missionaries joined the colonial debate, John Paton among them. Fiji had set a welcome precedent, he argued, and extending British rule would suppress the worst aspects of the labour trade from those islands to New Guinea. Following on a proud history of freeing slaves elsewhere, it would go a long way to expunging the 'stain on our British glory and Australasian honour' recruiting had caused. There need be no imposition upon local people, for the 'natives' of the New Hebrides were only too willing to be brought within the Empire's benevolent embrace. They 'hate the French', Paton added – as perhaps did he.[11]

The first order of business for the Australasian Geographical Society, after its foundation in Sydney in April 1883, was to comment upon the past and future of New Guinea and propose an exploratory expedition there following 'the action of the Queensland Government'. Its honorary secretary, Edmond Marin La Meslée, spoke in June of the difference between New Guinea and Australia, granting to the former the status of 'rough civilisation' because of the 'neatly fenced gardens', agricultural pursuits and settlements. Aboriginal people, he suggested with a broad, misleading sweep, were 'nomads' who by implication had little attachment to place. New Guinea needed a different approach, therefore, one based upon sound knowledge and some respect for tenure. For 'it was no use trying to put a stop to colonising enterprises with a race whose genius itself lies in that direction'. Anglo-Saxons, he contended with resignation, pursued 'money' and 'gold' wherever it was to be found. That apparent law of nature did not mean, however, that they should set aside the well-being of others. 'Humanity has its rights', he declared, whether reprising Lord Moreton or Diderot, and it was incumbent upon the occupying power to protect those.[12]

For his part McIlwraith defended his pre-emption by arguing that he was acting on the colonies' behalf, indeed bringing them together in common cause. Writing in July 1883, in the lead-up to the Federal Convention, he observed: 'In the last century similar timely acts of annexation won large portions of America for the Anglo-Saxon race. Why then should not Queensland be permitted, with the sanction of Her Majesty's Government, to assist in carrying out this national and beneficial policy?'

Lord Derby's several responses were consistent both in rejecting annexation and in their tenor of tested patience. Samoa and Tonga were independent states, the peer pointed out, therefore they could not simply be taken without a 'violation of international law'. The other islands in the western Pacific, namely New Britain, New Ireland, the Solomons and Santa Cruz, were 'a considerable distance from

Australia, and are for the most part of great size, and inhabited by warlike and cannibal tribes'. Had the colonies, therefore, 'sufficiently considered the extent of the responsibilities which the annexation or protectorate would involve …?' Neither was there evidence that 'some foreign power' was about to establish itself on the shores of New Guinea. He also observed wryly that that country contained 'several millions of savage inhabitants' of whom one thing was certain: 'they have given no sign of a desire that their land should be occupied by white men'.[13]

In the swirl of ideas and anxieties that followed the flag-raising in Port Moresby, there was, then, acknowledgment of the wishes, even the 'rights', of local people. McIlwraith promoted the contrasting view. His approving reference to the Anglo-Saxons of North America sweeping away Native Americans and Mexicans carried with it the implicit question, 'Why can't we do that?' Therein, too, lay a call for colonial union that clearly suggested Australian and imperial interests might diverge. McIlwraith looked to America as a model and regarded racial supremacy as the imperative. These would remain awkward themes in Australia's political thought, notably its immigration and foreign policy, for many years to come.

But another narrative countered such simmering talk of independence and nationalism: global Britishness. Charles Dilke advanced it in *Greater Britain*, published in 1868, as did Sir John Seeley in *Expansion of England*, which followed in 1883, just as the colonial governments were making their forthright appeals to the 'Mother Country' to annex islands and assuage their fears. Seeley's work created, in the words of historian Neville Meaney, 'an image of a global Great Britain in which all those of British race and culture were united as one people'.[14] It was a potent form of global nationalism, for which race was both a scientific and cultural category. Other whites, such as Germans, could thereby be excluded. It was New South Wales politician Sir Henry Parkes who did most to follow up McIlwraith's call for 'federation' and blend it with Seeley's vision of a greater England. Where in 1883 McIlwraith wrote provocatively that Britain's refusal to annex New Guinea raised 'very serious questions intimately connected with the future interests of the Australasian Colonies', Parkes spoke reassuringly of the possibility of union, and thereby greater defence, 'without breaking the ties' that bound the colonies to the 'mother country'. That speech, at a banquet in the New South Wales rural town of Tenterfield in the spring of 1889, is widely acknowledged as foundational in the campaign to unify the colonies. The following year Parkes spoke of the 'crimson thread of kinship' which bound the Australian colonies to Britain. That remained the dominant form of patriotism, finding practical expression in the military support for the Boxer Rebellion in China, the Boer War in South Africa, and most terribly World War One.

The matter of New Guinea's annexation was decided in 1884. The formation of the German New Guinea Company in May of that year forced Britain's hand, along with the German government's stated intention to annex the north-eastern section of the island for the firm. A British protectorate was declared over the corresponding south-eastern section in November when the flagship of the Australia Station delivered Commodore James Erskine to raise the Union Jack. But, in what might seem a rebuke to colonial hectoring, the naval officer explained the action not in terms of defending the colonies but rather the 'lives and properties of the native inhabitants' from those who would deliver 'injustice, strife and bloodshed'.[15] The territory was formally annexed in 1887. Queensland had hoped for a role in its administration but the Colonial Office decided otherwise. The first administrator, Dr William MacGregor, quickly put an end to the labour trade.[16]

≋

'... in Queensland plenty of everything to be got.'

Two more events occurred as the debate over annexing New Guinea was reaching its resolution; both emphasised the bloodiness and injustice of Queensland's labour trade. The first was a crime, the second an enquiry of the highest order.

The sugar industry had recruited some 2600 people from New Guinea in the 18 months from the beginning of 1883. In June 1884 the crew of the *Hopeful* murdered two of them. The vessel belonged to the newly incorporated Townsville shipping firm Burns Philp. It was a bad start to a sideline that James Burns had referred to as 'nigger hunting', as he tried to dissuade his partner Robert Philp from proceeding down that path to profit.[17] The company's reputation was damaged but its income was not. Within 30 years the name Burns Philp was synonymous with Australian shipping and trading in the Pacific.

Burns was concerned with appearances rather than ethics. But this itself indicated the opprobrium which had attached to the trade. White Queenslanders, however, were divided on the issue. The death sentence passed on the *Hopeful* murderers prompted such angry protestations that the colony's governor Sir Anthony Musgrave was moved to write to Lord Derby: 'I had not believed it possible that now in any part of the Queen's dominions it should be openly contended that the life of a black human being is not as sacred as that of a white man'.[18] The remark is all the more astonishing coming from one who was born in the former slave colony of Antigua and had just served as governor of Jamaica, where the hierarchies of plantation society were still evident.

By then McIlwraith, who supported 'coloured' labour on large plantations, had been replaced in the premiership by Samuel Griffith, who held to an opposing ideal of small-scale landholdings operated by colonists of British descent – Anglo-Saxons. These were, broadly speaking, the two visions which had emerged for Australia's tropical north. Those who saw the economic need for cheap workers generally thought labourers of colour were physiologically suited to the tropics; McIlwraith also proposed importing 'coolies' from India. There were many others, however, who viewed the issue through the lens of industrial relations and race. Islanders undercut wages to the advantage of exploitative capitalists. The pen-and-ink artists of the *Bulletin*,

Worker and *Boomerang* produced excoriating caricatures variously depicting Queensland as a place of whip-wielding plantation owners dominating cowering black men, or of sharply dressed, leering Islanders overstepping their social station. The imagery drew both on the antebellum American south, with its awful slave system, and the post-bellum north populated by cocky urban 'negroes'. There was some sympathy for Pacific people while they remained in the islands but the lesson was becoming clear; there was no place for cheap 'coloured labour' in Australia. It was a defining issue for northern Queensland, so that cartoons or photographs of black fieldworkers came to represent the region, while reliance on those workers helped to coalesce a separatist sentiment which would continue well after the question was decided. North Queensland, with its long Cape York protruding into the tropical Pacific, was palpably different from the south.

Griffith was a humanitarian as well as a supporter of small-scale white farmers. The Royal Commission he called into the labour trade from New Guinea and elsewhere in late 1884 was motivated by genuine concern at Islanders' welfare. Its conclusions condemned recruiters more than plantation owners. The commissioners found that interpreters and the mandatory government agents were frequently absent, so that recruited Islanders 'had little conception of the real purpose for which they were invited on board or engaged to go in the ship to Queensland'.[19] It did not help that timeframes were measured in 'moons' and 'yams', presumably relating to the horticultural cycle of that well-known staple.

White people who worked in the industry had often challenged the impression of hapless and duped Islanders, particularly after the 1868 Act and further regulation in 1880. William Wawn's refutation of this and other criticisms of the trade was detailed, articulate and handsomely presented by Swan Sonnenschein, the London publisher that specialised in Pacific literature. Wawn's dedication left little doubt as to the argument that followed: 'to the Sugar Planters of Queensland' and 'Those Bold Pioneers who have opened up the Rich Agricultural Districts along the coast ... and who have done more towards the

Practical Civilisation of the Cannibal and the Savage than all the Well-intentioned but Narrow-minded Enthusiasts of the Southern Pacific'.[20] By 'Enthusiasts' Wawn undoubtedly meant missionaries such as John Paton. It sounded a lot like Robert Towns.

Wawn's most interesting observation, in this respect, challenged the 'guileless' representation of the 'South Sea Islander as a grown-up child'. He described a practice that had evolved from early, regrettable abusiveness into 'a regular institution', particularly for those from the New Hebrides and Solomon Islands who saw that it worked 'much for their own benefit as for ours'. Far from slavery, recruiting was a considered transaction; 'they lose a few warriors out of each village, but an extra musket in the tribe makes up for that deficiency'. Having spent three years in Queensland, the Islander was returned while 'still a young man, in the prime of life, strengthened and set up by his late labour, possessed of knowledge and experience of the world'. Then in another poke at self-interested moralists, Wawn suggested that the worldliness gained in Australia made Islanders less 'pliable' in the hands of the missionary. Therein lay the missionaries' motivation for opposing the trade in labour.[21]

Wawn had a point. After 20 years of contact with recruiters, some communities had adapted to the practice. Islanders were capable of assessing advantage and disadvantage, and expressing their displeasure, sometimes very violently. Historian Deryck Scarr is not alone in acknowledging that 'labour ships and plantation work became an accepted part of the Islanders' lives'.[22] A century after the trade, the son of one of those who went willingly as a recruit recalled his father's explanation of a young man's motivations to leave his island home on Aoba more than once, and then stay away: 'Oh when you get a bit of Queensland, you sort of get it in your blood. When you see them schooners out at sea in full sail coming in, oh, it gives you the urge. You want to go again ...'.[23] Islanders, too, had an urge to see the world, just as their migrating ancestors did.

For all that, the royal commissioners also emphasised that the people who worked Queensland's sugar plantations felt attached to the place. 'The love of home of these Islanders amounts to a passion', they wrote in 1885.[24] Leaving was wrenching. It was a remarkable investigation not least because it gave voice to Pacific Islanders themselves, rather than missionaries, politicians or defensive recruiters. The commissioners travelled to plantations to talk to as many as 500 workers, taking care to record the testimony with the aid of interpreters. Having assessed what they heard, they repudiated in the strongest terms 'the suggestion that the truth is not to be found in natives of the islands of the Western Pacific'. The people they interviewed 'were anxious to tell the actual facts of the incidents on which they were questioned, and that their story is to be accepted'.[25] It was a rejection of the widespread belief that Pacific Islanders were incapable of telling or understanding the truth either through moral failure or ignorance.

A man called Awenuri was one of those who took the opportunity to speak his truth. He recalled that Captain Wawn had told him he was going to Queensland for three years, but only after he was on the boat. 'If you had known would you have come?' asked a commissioner. 'No', he replied. 'I did not wish to come', he continued, 'but boat's crew say that in Queensland plenty of everything to be got'.[26] There was coercion and coaxing, push and pull.

≈

'Such conduct cannot escape the censure
of the civilised world – nor should it.'

The Royal Commission led to the end of labour recruiting, for a time. Importing Islanders stopped in 1890 but started again in 1892, such was the dependency upon cheap plantation labour in the deep north. Working conditions improved greatly. It was not until 1901, when the colonies had finally come together as the Commonwealth of Australia, that the issue was decided once and for all. Then it was the ideal of race purity which trumped pragmatism and profit, although mechanisation also promised to ease the need for Islanders. The 1901 *Immigration Restriction Act* which surreptitiously permitted authorities to exclude people of colour via a dictation test was joined by the *Pacific Island Labourers Act*, which explicitly barred 'natives not of European extraction' from any Pacific island except New Zealand. None of these people were permitted to enter Australia after March 1904 and from 1907, when the last round of three-year contracts expired, people were liable to be deported. Those who had arrived before 1880, owned freehold land or married outside their 'race' were allowed to stay. One of those who was not exempt protested on the eve of his deportation: 'White fellow no more want black man, use him altogether, chase him away, plenty kanaka no money, go back poor'.[27] To help the planters in their transition from depending on cheap labour, the government placed a duty upon imported sugar.

Race was now an idea used both culturally and biologically to explain why black people, white people and Asians could not co-exist happily. The common humanity John Paton championed, or indeed that the hard-nosed William Wawn suggested, seemed irrelevant in the scheme of nation building. Australia's first prime minister Edmund Barton explained the logic behind deporting Islanders: 'The difference in intellectual level and the difference in knowledge of the ways of the world between the white man and the Pacific Islander, is one which cannot be bridged by acts or regulations'.[28] There was bipartisan agreement. The Labor Party's first national leader, John Christian Watson, supported the policies 'because of the possibility and probability of racial contamination'.[29]

Those exempt from deportation survived as best they could in a country where religion, respectability and work ethic apparently meant less than skin colour. Race-conscious trade unions made finding fieldwork difficult. In the memory of one son of a Solomon Islander, born in Queensland in 1929: 'We helped one another, man. We had to do it otherwise we would be dead'.[30]

But there had been some in the European community who disagreed with the policy, particularly when the reality of deportations became evident and sugar workers were sent back to hostile villages or the wrong island altogether. Queenslanders, many of strong Christian faith, put some of the hardest questions. 'At whose door will the murders lie?' queried the *Johnstone River Advocate*, after the killing of deportees in the Solomons was reported.[31] The feeling may well have been heightened by personal connections. Some 589 of the 2484 people baptised on local plantations by the Queensland Kanaka Mission came from the Solomons, and the island of Malaita, from where many of that group originated, was awash with guns as a result of the labour trade.[32] 'Under what law or sense of justice can a person born, registered, reared and schooled in the State, be deported?' asked the *Darling Downs Gazette* in 1907. 'Such conduct cannot escape the censure of the civilised world – nor should it.'[33]

CHAPTER 10

A White Australia

'... the British representative came at the tail'

The Australian Commonwealth came into being on the first day of January 1901 when it swore in a British lord as the new nation's first governor-general, the Queen's representative. Sir Henry Parkes, who died in 1896, did not live to see the Federation he had championed. But it was entirely fitting that the Earl of Hopetoun took his oath of office in Sydney's Centennial Park, the huge green amphitheatre Parkes created to celebrate 100 years of colonisation in 1888. When he opened 'the people's park', Sir Henry referred to the 'great line of kinship' between Australia and Britain. That became the 'crimson thread' at the 1890 Federation Conference. The reference to blood made clear that kinship was a biological relationship.

The park was a perfect ceremonial space, for it allowed thousands to assemble and, the organisers hoped, be motivated by civic spectacle. The focal point in 1901 was a domed pavilion in the florid, classicist Beaux Arts style which had been particularly popular in the US, where it gave form to the wondrous and dream-like 'White City' during the Chicago World Exposition in 1896. The pavilion spoke unambiguously of high culture, civic spirit and the classical foundations of Western civilisation. That both Chicago's model city and Sydney's pavilion were gleaming white was no coincidence, for that hue was intrinsic to notions of cultural and racial beauty and purity in both countries.

In fact, Sydney's assembled masses crowded all the way from the city to the park, lining streets along which a very long parade moved towards the climactic ceremony. Those thoroughfares were decorated with symbolic arches. Three of these, the wool, wheat and coal arches, formed literal manifestations of the exports by which Australia was defining itself as a land of natural wealth. Three others were Beaux Arts designs: the American Arch the US had paid for in a gesture of solidarity; the self-explanatory Commonwealth Arch, which bore the words of the newly commissioned prime minister, Edmund Barton, 'A Continent for a Nation and a Nation for a Continent'; and the Military Arch inscribed with two dedications: 'Welcome to our Comrades from the Southern Seas' and 'Welcome to our Comrades from Across the Seas'. The former referred to khaki-clad colonial troops returning from the Boer War and the latter to other, more colourful imperial units: the red-coated English, kilted Scots, and even turbaned Indians. Remarkably, in light of the anxiety over New Guinea in the 1880s, there was also a German arch which declared 'United Germany hails United Australia', although the crowning figure of a rampant eagle might have undermined that sentiment of amity from the rival Pacific power.

The military made up the largest part of the parade, a display of both the empire's breadth and might. The soldiers were preceded by civilian floats and carriages representing organised labour, Christian denominations, the legal profession, politicians, fire brigades and the press corps, whose special presence was evidence of the vibrancy of colonial publishing and reportage. At the rear was the governor-general in waiting. For historian Russel Ward the presence of mounted shearers at the head of the procession, 13 years before the cataclysm of World War One, suggested that the 'symbolic exemplar of national character was apparently still the bushman rather than the soldier'.[1] But, in fact, the official order of precedence was least to most, something not lost on the nationalistic and republican *Bulletin*, which noted wryly that 'in the order of Australia the nation, the British representative came at the tail because he was the least necessary'.[2] Absent entirely were any Pacific or Asian faces, for they had no accepted place in the new national order.

In the various invitations designed for the rolling events, Australia was depicted as a young white maiden looking across to the matriarch Britannia, who bore a strong resemblance to warrior queen Boudica.

Women would be permitted to vote in the new Commonwealth, and were among the first in the world to enjoy that right. Australia was a social laboratory in this respect, but one where rights were reserved for white people. The franchise was not stripped from the relatively few people of colour who already enjoyed it but neither would it be granted to those who did not, men or women.

There were more arches and another procession in Melbourne in May celebrating Federation and the visit of the Duke and Duchess of Cornwall and York, come to open the first Australian parliament. By then Queen Victoria, who had defined an age of imperial expansion, had died. She was honoured with her own edifice, as was her successor Edward VII. German 'citizens' paid for an arch, somewhat less menacing than the German government's structure in Sydney. And on Swanston Street stood an astonishing, temple-like gateway of silk. It was funded by the local Chinese community, now well established since the first gold seekers arrived in 1851. The arch was not located on the royal route, but that it existed at all, no less inscribed with the term 'Welcome by the Chinese Citizens', was a remarkable claim of legitimacy and belonging by this marginalised and denigrated group.

≈

'... the tribulations of democracy ...'

Henry Parkes would not have been impressed. As premier of New South Wales, he had done all he could to stop Chinese people from arriving, despite acknowledging that they were a 'sober and industrious people'. Asians and Europeans simply could not live together without rivalry, disharmony and ultimately inequality, he thought. Assimilation was impossible, either through cultural exchange or biological union, even if that entailed love between individuals. It mattered little that marriages between Chinese men and 'white' women were often harmonious. Playing up to a gathering of cheering, laughing constituents in his harbourside seat of St Leonards in Sydney in 1888, Parkes had claimed to speak for all the colonies when declaring that there should be no 'admixture of Asian blood'. It was 'a sacred obligation on every citizen to preserve the British type in the nation'.[3] The nationalists of the *Bulletin* would have disagreed with the emphasis on imperial filiality but concurred with the general sentiment. The slogan 'Australia for the white man', had appeared below the journal's masthead since 1886.

The British–Australian progressive intellectual and politician CH Pearson presented the most nuanced position on race patriotism in his work *National Life and Character*, which attracted commendation while causing disquiet in the colonies, the US and Britain. Published in 1893, it both provided a detached commentary and defended the ideal of a 'white Australia', which itself was a bulwark of 'higher Civilisation'. By that he meant the egalitarian experiment unfolding on the 'remote continent' where there was universal male and some female suffrage, where wages were higher than for British working men and red meat rather than offal was a staple. 'The fear of Chinese immigration which the Australian democracy cherishes, and which Englishmen at home find hard to understand' was, he wrote, 'the instinct of self-preservation, quickened by experience'. But China's rise was inevitable, Pearson conceded, as was that of other non-European people. Indeed, it would be enabled by the very social forces which had facilitated European dominance: 'It is now more than probable that our science, our civilisation, our great and real advance in the practice of government are bringing us nearer to the day when the lower races will predominate in the world, when the higher races will lose their noblest elements, when we shall ask nothing from the day but to live, nor from the future but that we may not deteriorate'. It was a bleak prophecy for those who expected never-ending white supremacy and Pearson hoped he would not live to see it fulfilled. The paradox of colonisation was that the conquerors were creating the conditions for their own displacement: 'It has been our work to organise and create, to carry peace and law and order over the world, that others may enter in and enjoy'. The genie of progress, once released from the lamp, was impossible to restrain. The 'solitary consolation' was that the changes were 'inevitable'.[4]

Pearson's defence of race patriotism was easy for readers to accept but his prediction of a non-white future ran counter to the 'victory of civilised nations' over 'barbarians' Charles Darwin had described in *The Descent of Man* in 1871, published just over a decade after his theory on the evolution of species. Where Darwin expressed a cautious perplexity at the reasons behind these conquests, Herbert Spencer and others simply saw such replacement as a natural law of the evolutionary imperative Darwin had outlined for animals and plants.[5] European civilisation, whether carried forward by the British, Americans or Germans was self-evidently fitter, stronger and better than anything it encountered. Cathedrals were superior to thatched huts. Democracy was more dynamic and enlightened than Oriental despotism. Those who understood Pearson's counter-narrative proposing the consequential rise of non-white peoples hoped, at least, to forestall that future or quarantine Australia from it.

By 1901 it was Japan rather than China that Australia feared most. The threat from the latter had been demographic rather than military; teeming millions escaping poverty and 'swarming' down from the north-west Pacific into an under-populated Australia in the wake of the first gold seekers. China itself was beset by scrambling European powers able to dictate their own terms of diplomacy and trade. The US, too, was there to open China's door. The quashing of the Boxer Rebellion – 'the first explosion of twentieth-century Chinese nationalism' – in 1900–1901 by a multinational force which included Australians confirmed the decline of Chinese authority, which had begun in the Opium Wars.[6] The proud Asian nation was halfway into its 'century of humiliation'. By contrast the other 'hermit kingdom', Japan, had developed remarkably since American gunboat diplomacy compelled its interaction with the West in 1854. The consequent reinstatement of imperial rule, the Meiji Restoration in 1868 permitted rapid social reform. The seeds that the West had sown sprouted with remarkable speed, bearing out

Pearson's prediction. Balancing tradition and modernisation, Japan was a formidable Asian power by 1901.

At that time the Japanese made up a small fraction of the 1.25 per cent of people of Asian birth living in Australia. By contrast those of European descent were at least 97 per cent of the 3 773 801 people counted at the 1901 census. But on Thursday Island where they worked as divers and shipbuilders, the Japanese outnumbered Europeans. These north Pacific migrants had been recruited in their hundreds during the 1890s, working alongside, and often replacing, 'South Sea' Islanders. They had commercial as well as physical skills so that the threat of business competition joined the perceived threat to security. One Japanese visitor in 1893 was moved to remark: 'The whites are beset by fears that they cannot put aside'.[7] The pen-and-ink artist at the *Worker*, Monty Scott, accordingly depicted 'The March of the Jap' with kimono-clad men dancing down from Cape York on their geta clogs.

Such was the mentality of the transplanted European community in the 'Southern Seas'. The historian David Walker aptly labelled it 'the anxious nation'. Newspapers and journals portrayed Asian men, particularly, as rapists, drug dealers, job thieves, gamblers and lepers. Novelists and even playwrights eventually joined politicians, cartoonists and commentators of the press and soapbox in doing so. Throughout this very masculine conversation, white women were held up as symbols of national purity, like the radiant Centennial Pavilion.

The novelist Rosa Campbell Praed thought the paranoia and manly pride ridiculous. Her novel *Madame Izan: A tourist story* placed a wealthy white woman in Japan as a tourist seeking a cure for blindness while a Queensland grazier chaperoned her. She subsequently rejects her consort in favour of a Japanese man. The woman's blindness is an obvious metaphor for Praed's ideal attitude to race. In David Walker's words, she 'conceived emptiness not in geographic and population terms but as a failure to develop the mind and spirit of the nation'.[8]

Praed was one dissenting voice in a time when racial difference, defined in both cultural and biological terms, had become a foundational assumption drowning out notions of universal humanity, whether these were grounded in Christian or Enlightenment thought. Bernard O'Dowd was another. The poet and editor of the journal *Tocsin* also wrote of the need to be 'nobly colour-blind' while keeping alive the welcoming sentiment expressed in the *Empire* during the gold rush: 'Whatever his colour be we must take our fellow man in Africa, in Asia and in Europe by the hand as a man and a brother', charged O'Dowd. Rejecting such all-embracing solidarity would mean that 'the tribulations of democracy and the Labour movement will be the tribulations for many long and bloody centuries'.[9] That O'Dowd linked democracy with colour-blind egalitarianism was profound. It also evidenced the latency of Christian and Enlightenment ideals. The articulation of universal human rights which followed the logical denouement of racist thinking – Nazism, Fascism, the Holocaust and World War Two – would revive these.

The *Immigration Restriction Act* was the first Australian parliament's prioritised attempt to fulfil Parkes' 'sacred obligation' to guard against the 'admixture of Asian blood'. The use of a dictation test, rather than an overt colour bar, allowed officials to set discretionary and intentionally impossible language exams for unwelcome people. It thereby sidestepped British concerns about racial exclusion stemming from the 1896 Anglo-Japanese Commercial Treaty, which established reciprocal rights of entry between Japan and Britain, including its colonies. But it also contradicted any sense of imperial solidarity and equality, which held that everyone from the Shetland Islands through India and on to Fiji were subjects of the Crown regardless of skin colour. As Pearson had noted, 'Englishmen at home' found it hard to understand such distinctions. If Pacific security created the first fissure in the bedrock of shared Australian and British interest, race created the second.

AUSTRALIA & THE PACIFIC

≋

*'... conscious of the pride of ownership
as we watched that thin grey line ...'*

Both came together in the 1902 when Britain signed a military pact with Japan. As the ascendant Asian power had already constructed a significant navy, the alliance's purpose was both to offset Russian naval strength in the north-west Pacific and allow Britain to concentrate on supremacy in European waters, where Germany's battleships were challenging 'Britannia's' rule over the waves for the first time since it had defeated the French at Trafalgar. The agreement did nothing to calm local nervousness. British strategic priorities – imperial and naval – had concerned colonists for decades; hence the long-held desire for a direct role in naval defence. The 1865 *Colonial Naval Defence Act* gave the Australasian colonies, including New Zealand, the right to raise their own flotillas for self-defence. Colonial ships would be accorded the 'status and rights' of British men-of-war. The *Australasian Naval Defence Act* of 1887 allowed the colony to fund an 'Auxiliary Squadron' to supplement the Australia Station. In 1891 five cruisers and two torpedo boats entered Sydney Harbour to do just that. While the colonies gained some control over the movement of these auxiliary vessels, the Admiralty resisted any notion of separate navies for fear of a divided command.

In 1901 the Australian Commonwealth inherited the various colonial military units and assumed responsibility for collective defence. But within the empire, Australia was still a self-governing colony, one which could make laws with respect to 'External Affairs' but not conclude treaties with foreign powers. The nation had only one diplomatic post, in London. It still depended upon Britain for matters of strategy and security. Indeed, when the new Commonwealth and the Imperial Government renegotiated naval matters in 1902–1903, they reaffirmed the centralisation of naval control. The Admiralty's First Lord, the Earl of Selborne, put the case for the prevailing 'Blue

Water' strategy, and against the localisation of naval forces, as clearly as possible to the 1902 Colonial Conference in London: 'The sea is all one and the British Navy, therefore must be all one'.[10] The colonial Auxiliary Squadron was scrapped.

Three years later the Imperial Japanese Navy defeated the Russian Far Eastern Fleet, fighting the Battle of Tsushima in the north-west Pacific with steel warships using radio communications. Japan was now a modern industrial nation. Australia's prime minister, Alfred Deakin, who as Edmund Barton's attorney-general had shepherded the *Immigration Restriction Act* through the House of Representatives, expressed his alarm in a manner that the new majority who populated Australia's cities and towns could understand: 'Japan at her headquarters is, so to speak, next door, while the Mother Country is many streets away, and connected by long lines of communications'.[11] New naval technology added to what seemed like a perennial British disregard for Australia's interest. Ships were faster and their range greater. For Deakin the 'comfortable outlook' relative isolation afforded had 'passed away'.[12]

In 1907 Britain gave Australia the power to negotiate commercial treaties as a 'dominion' rather than a colony. But at the same Colonial Conference which granted that concession – the last meeting of imperial entities to be so-named – Deakin's request for greater Australian involvement in imperial foreign policy was refused. He returned from London intent on building an Australian naval force, nonetheless. The following year, without consulting the British, the prime minister invited the US Navy's 'Great White Fleet' to visit Australia during its world cruise – to display that country's naval might to Japan as much as any other nation. The 16 white battleships which sailed across the Pacific also made manifest the idea that the ocean was now an 'American Mediterranean', much as it had once been a Spanish lake. They operated upon thinking the American strategist Alfred T Mahan set down in 1890 which emphasised the centrality of sea power for national security in commerce and war. America's navy allowed it to project power across the Pacific. After it declared war on Spain in April 1898, ostensibly to end Spain's colonial rule in Cuba, the US destroyed the Spanish Navy in Manila in August and Spain ceded the Philippines to the US. In the meantime, the US annexed Hawaii in July 1898 with a view to ending hostility between white planters and indigenous people, and establishing an ideal blue-water naval base in the eastern Pacific.

London did not welcome Deakin's unilateral invitation to this foreign Pacific power but it was hugely popular in Australia. The first port of call was Sydney Harbour – home to the Royal Navy's Australia Station. Hundreds of thousands lined the shores and thousands more crowded small boats to wonder at American naval might, and perhaps ponder the local weakness of the British.

The Catholic cardinal Patrick Moran took the opportunity to praise the US as an example for Australia; for, being of Irish birth, he had no particular love of the empire. In this regard he may have spoken for as much as a quarter of the population. It was Moran who likened the Pacific to an 'American Mediterranean' and followed that by suggesting it should also be Australia's 'Mediterranean', such was the nearby islands' potential. 'Australia holds the key of the Pacific Ocean', the cardinal declared somewhat optimistically.[13]

Moran had opposed anti-Chinese legislation as un-Christian and was vilified in the *Bulletin* for doing so. His embrace of the Americans was not obviously motivated by racial affection. Many others, however, looked to this rising Anglo-Saxon power as a bulwark against Asia. The term 'crimson thread of kinship' was now applied to new friends from across the Pacific: 'In the harbour of our seas ... / You found a brother of the blood, to / Welcome your White Fleet, / To strengthen crimson kinship ties, / And o'er seas kinsmen greet ...'[14] The battleships were white, both literally and symbolically. The cartoon which occupied the front page of the journal *Clarion*, edited by the xenophobic writer, later politician, Randolph Bedford, showed a young Australia greeting a bearded Uncle Sam stepping out of the rolling breakers. 'I've been waiting for you, shake!' says the boy. 'We're the only White Men in the Pacific, shake!' answers the American.

The American visit was followed in 1909 by Britain's 'Dreadnought crisis', a panic about the threat of Germany's rapid production of capital ships. Some in Australia even started a fund to construct a Dreadnought to give the Royal Navy. Soon after, however, the Admiralty itself suggested that Australia acquire a 'fleet unit' which would operate with Australian crews as one part of a Pacific fleet. Having resisted colonial desires for a dedicated naval force for so long, the proposal was more a realistic reappraisal of the strategic environment in the Pacific than a respectful concession to Australian defence concerns. The Royal Navy was no longer supreme in every ocean.

The fleet unit was to comprise a battle cruiser, three light cruisers, six destroyers and two submarines. The heavy vessels and submarines would be built in the UK but in April 1911 then prime minister, Labor's Andrew Fisher, proudly announced the 'launch of the first Australian built ship of the Australian navy' when the destroyer *Warrego* was slipped at Cockatoo Island in Sydney Harbour. The still incomplete force formally became the Royal Australian Navy (RAN) two months later. In 1913 the Royal Navy transferred its Australian establishments, including Garden Island, to the Commonwealth. On 4 October the extant elements of the RAN steamed into Sydney Harbour to replace the vessels of the Australia Station. The *Sydney Morning Herald* inevitably compared the occasion to the Americans' arrival five years earlier and christened it a 'Great Grey Fleet':

> [It was] a smaller but a greater thing to us than the warships of the United States. We were conscious of the pride of ownership as we watched that thin grey line over the water come creeping on from the east and growing larger and larger as it came.[15]

Bands played and people sang. Randolph Bedford's newly penned anthem, 'Australia: My Beloved Land' was among the rousing tunes performed. Australia, the revellers intoned, should 'keep ever pure from alien stain' for its riches were 'only for the white'.[16]

CHAPTER 11

World War One and its aftermath

'a very pleasant little picnic'

The 'two ocean dilemma' – how to defend both the Atlantic and the Pacific – was largely intractable in FW Eggleston's estimation. Despite his belief in the empire, the progressive intellectual and politician predicted a divergence of interest between Britain and Australia as the Admiralty necessarily concentrated naval strength to defend home waters. The situation would be dire if Germany and Japan ever allied with each other. Written in 1912, this was, as historian Stuart Ward has observed, a 'remarkably prescient critique' of the notion of common interest.[1]

The compact with Japan remained in place so that when war came on 4 August 1914 it was between Britain and Germany and its European allies. As a dominion without an independent foreign policy, Australia was automatically involved. The telegram relaying as much arrived in Melbourne on 5 August. When Japan entered the war on Britain's side on 23 August, Australia and its feared Pacific neighbour became unlikely partners. In November the Japanese cruiser *Ibuki* helped to escort the 38 ships carrying Australian and New Zealand volunteers to the northern hemisphere to defend their king and empire, but suspicions of the Asian ally did not recede.

The Australian government had initially offered 20 000 men, the strength of an army division. At least that many left in the vast summer convoy. By the end of 1914 more than 50 000 men had volunteered. They consequently became the Australian Imperial Force or AIF. With their colleagues across the Tasman the force was officially called the Australian and New Zealand Army Corps or ANZAC, a name that quickly melded with the nation's sense of self. It was an identity combining both a common-held Britishness and Australian exceptionalism. Under British command in Egypt, the Australians distinguished themselves with bad behaviour towards the locals they called 'Gyppos'. They nonetheless impressed the English poet John Masefield, serving there with the British Army: 'For physical beauty and nobility of bearing they surpassed any men I had ever seen'.[2] A legend was being made. The muscularity of the Australians was due, in large part, to their remarkable diet of animal protein; beef and mutton made cheap by the grazing of many millions of hectares of pasture. The days of importing Tahitian pork were long gone.

Genuine though Masefield's response undoubtedly was, the famous first AIF also comprised men somewhat shorter than the magical '6-foot'. Five foot six inches was the minimum for acceptance, and it reduced as the carnage continued. Furthermore, the soldiers for the First Battalion of the First Division came from the dusty streets of Sydney, not the backblocks of rural Australia; for the population was, by then, largely an urban and suburban one despite the cultural prominence of 'the bush' in word and image.

However, the first soldiers sent to fight, kill and die were not ANZACs at all but men of the Australian Naval and Military Expeditionary Force (AN&MEF). That was the unit quickly raised in August in answer to the British request to neutralise German forces in New Guinea. A further 500 men had eagerly volunteered and signed up on Thursday Island but were dismissed shortly after as they were ill-equipped, untrained, and 'physically unfit for tropical campaigning'.[3] Australia had, in fact, shared a land border with the imperial rival since 1906 when the new Commonwealth assumed control of the colony of Papua. It was a dream come true for those who longed for Australian Pacific pre-eminence and island buffers. The AN&MEF took New Britain and that island was brought into the empire 200 years after William Dampier christened it 'Nova Britannia'. Protected by the might of the new Royal Australian Navy (RAN), they landed several kilometres south of Rabaul, the administrative centre. The 2000 Australians faced a potential German force of around 300 men, most of whom were 'native soldiers'. The British rear admiral who commanded the Australian fleet, George Patey, wrote a polite but firm letter to the German governor, advising him that resistance was futile in the face of overwhelming force. In the hours it took to deliver the letter and receive a reply, six Australians were killed or mortally wounded, the first of the 60 000 who would die over the next four years. One of those, the doctor Brian Antill Pockley, had written to his parents just before the action predicting 'a very pleasant little picnic'.[4] The Germans lost at least 31 men, all but one of them 'natives'. A further 35 Australians died when the submarine AE1 sank off Rabaul on 14 September, the first loss for the new navy.

Five days earlier, on 9 September, HMAS *Melbourne* landed men to destroy the wireless station on Nauru, which had been a German possession since 1886 when Britain and Germany divided eastern New Guinea between them. In 1914 Nauru was both a strategic and an economic prize. The British-owned Pacific Phosphate Company was mining high-grade phosphate for fertiliser there under licence from the Germans, up to 800 tons a day by the outbreak of war. Some of it was making its way to Australia's nutrient-poor soils. In November the company's steamer *Messina* took more Australian troops to Nauru to occupy the island, where 30 Germans lived beside 40 British managers, 500 Chinese labourers and 1700 Islanders, who had been watching colonisers export large parts of their island since 1907. The soldiers arrested and interned the Germans, and officials ceremonially lowered the German flag and raised its British equivalent to impress the new regime upon the population.

Nauru sat south of the equator. The Australians also expected to occupy German territory to the north of that line. On 14 November Defence Minister George Pearce instructed his newly appointed Australian Commissioner for the Pacific, Brigadier-General Sir Samuel

Pethebridge, to visit Germany's 'various islands and possessions' and 'place such troops in occupation as may be available, thus relieving any members of the Japanese forces who may be now temporarily in occupation'.[5] But to the Japanese, there was nothing temporary about their presence on the Palau and Caroline groups. They had obviously relayed that understanding to the British, for London subsequently contacted the Australians advising them that 'it would be discourteous and disadvantageous to the Japanese if we turned them out of Angaur [in the Palau Group] when they are helping us in every way with their Fleet throughout the Pacific'.[6] The message became more explicit on 3 December with another telegram telling the Australians to stay away from the Mariana, Caroline and Marshall islands also. Once again British interests overruled those of their Pacific dominion.

'If we ever become a nation of mongrels ...'

The submarine AE1 went down through misadventure rather than enemy action. There were no heroic encounters between Australian and German ships in the great Pacific as some had predicted and possibly hoped. After escorting the island campaigns the formidable HMAS *Australia* steamed eastward in search of the German Pacific Squadron but the Royal Navy sank most of those ships in the Atlantic to where they had retreated. The *Australia* was ordered to Britain in December 1914 and remained in the northern hemisphere for the remainder of the war. Other RAN warships followed the flagship there.

In 1917 the German raider *Wolf* was thereby free to roam the western Pacific, laying mines, capturing and sinking prizes, and taking hundreds of prisoners in the process. It targeted Australia's east coast and, in July, crippled the steamer *Cumberland* with a mine near Gabo Island off Victoria. The following month, it seized and sank the Burns Philp steamer SS *Matunga* on its way to New Britain from Brisbane, after its full complement of crew and passengers transferred to the German vessel. There were already more than 200 prisoners on board the *Wolf*, among them the American John Cameron, his child and Australian-born wife Mamie. Cameron's sailing vessel *Beluga* was carrying benzine to Australia from San Francisco when it was attacked, and sunk after most of its cargo was taken.

Conditions below were unpleasant but the Germans treated the family humanely. The *Wolf*'s commander had assured them: 'Tell your wife and little girl that they have nothing to fear, that we are not the Huns you probably think we are'.[7] It was a reference to the vitriolic propaganda common throughout the Allied nations, Australia included. Where once Asians and black people were the targets of pen-and-ink artists in the *Bulletin* and other publications, now the able hand of Norman Lindsay depicted Germans as sub-human monsters – expediently ejected from the ranks of whiteness. 'The modern German is proved out of place in the Aryan family', declared the *Bulletin* in July 1915.[8]

Cameron's boat was destroyed because it was an enemy vessel, for the US had recently entered the war on the Allied side. With a population of more than 100 million, it quickly raised a million-man army – called the American Expeditionary Forces (AEF) – through conscription. Australia fielded more than 300 000 volunteers drawn from a total population of only 4 000 000. By 1918 the AIF had a reputation as outstanding frontline soldiers while the Americans were still coming to terms with the horror of the Western Front. In July four companies of American soldiers fought beside Australians for the first time at the battle of Hamel, commanded successfully by the AIF's General John Monash. That was also the first offensive action by AEF units. The Americans referred to Australians by the nickname 'Digger', earned on the rocky slopes of Gallipoli. Australians called their new allies 'Sammy', a reference to Uncle Sam and a more affectionate term than 'Yank'. The press and historians of both nations would subsequently ponder who made the most difference at the end of the unprecedented slaughter; the huge tide of fresh American men and materials which helped thwart Germany's last offensive or the dogged determination of the ANZACs pushing the Germans back after Hamel. The killing ended in November.

The frontline camaraderie between Australians and Americans contrasted with the enmity their respective leaders felt during the ensuing peace negotiations. Prime Minister William 'Billy' Hughes and President Woodrow Wilson loathed each other. The men exemplified the two dominant strains of foreign policy motivation in the 20th century: old-fashioned realpolitik and a modern values-based diplomacy.

Hughes was a race patriot, a Welsh immigrant to colonial New South Wales who wanted the Commonwealth that emerged shortly after to be a bastion of Britishness. Such was his belief in Britain and its empire that he tried twice to introduce conscription to the country he led. Both attempts failed. But while Germany had been the enemy at hand, and Hughes hoped to curtail its capacity to challenge Britain again through punitive peace terms, Japan remained the long-term threat. Wartime alliances and convoy escorts had not changed that. Hughes was what subsequent historians and foreign policy analysts would call a 'realist', one who believed in a world of competing hostile interests, where power and its balance was the only way to ensure national survival. Australia's best chance was to remain within a strong empire. Japan was a threat because it was a rising power intent on asserting its interests and becoming the regional hegemon.

Woodrow Wilson was an idealist and an internationalist. As Margaret Macmillan, the eminent historian of the peace, has put it, his was 'a liberal and a Christian vision'.[9] Drawing on both the Enlightenment's elevation of individual rights and his religiously based belief in human dignity, America's 28th president was the first leader of a major power to put forward the defence of universal values as a legitimate reason for declaring war. 'The world must be made safe for democracy', he argued before Congress in April 1917. 'Self-governed nations' did not go to war against their neighbours as autocratic states did, therefore fostering democracy was the world's best hope if it was to avoid another catastrophic conflict. America was compelled to enter the war, not to avenge the loss of American lives to German U-boats but because German militarism threatened basic norms. 'Our motive ... [is] only the vindication of right, of human right, of which we are only a single champion' declared the president.[10]

The ambiguity of that last phrase is a clue to the motivation, or at least rationalisation, of American foreign policy as the turmoil of the 20th century unfolded with a second world war and then an ideologically charged cold war. America would be the defender of universal values while itself being exceptional as its 'single champion'. Infused with Wilsonian idealism, America's sense of 'Manifest Destiny' – which had earlier allowed it to brush aside Native Americans, Mexicans and Spaniards and enlarge its continental and global possessions – started to evolve into something altogether more altruistic, in theory if not always in practice. America was on the way to becoming what Franklin Roosevelt would later call 'the Arsenal of Democracy'.

Australians too had their ideals. 'Freedom and honor [sic]' were the words that appeared on the bronze plaques given to the families of those killed in action. But the freedom evoked here referred to an absence of subjugation which was very ethnically specific; 'Britons shall never be slaves as long as Britannia rules the waves', as the 18th-century poem and song went. Neither that, nor honour, necessarily spoke to the universal human dignity embodied in the Christianised democracy Wilson championed.

The president also believed in collective security, embodied in the League of Nations. Against this aspect of internationalism, Hughes preferred the security of the empire or, at the very least, Anglo-Saxon unity. He placed faith in the benefits of the Four Power Treaty between Britain, France, the US and Japan, calling it a 'magnificent achievement' for peace in the Pacific because the British and American navies more than counterbalanced the power of Japan's force if ever the Japanese decided to assert themselves.[11] But Hughes went along with Wilson's league in any case.

Through lecture tours, meetings, and his involvement with the peace treaty, Billy Hughes also put Australia on the world diplomatic stage, despite the fact that the nation he led still did not have the authority to formulate its own foreign policy. For, in recognition of the blood and treasure they had expended in the service of empire, Britain had permitted its dominions a place at the negotiating table. Hughes made the most of the opportunity. Sixty thousand war dead, he famously said to Wilson, gave him the right to make demands on behalf of his modestly populated nation's interest, in the face of the 1 200 000 000 others the peace conference represented.

That national interest was located firmly in the Pacific. Consequently, Hughes argued fiercely for the right to annex Germany's possessions in New Guinea and surrounding islands. His case essentially reiterated that which the colonies put to Britain in the 1880s: that Australia could not give up the line of islands to the north and northeast to any foreign power without compromising its security. He used the term 'Monroe Doctrine' often in full knowledge that Wilson would not concede his own country's right to the regional security it defined in 1823. But Hughes was arguing for Australian, not British possession of New Guinea. Wilson's anti-colonial liberalism could not abide that. The compromise was a League of Nations C-class mandate which allowed Australia full power to administer and legislate. New Guinea thereby became a territory within the Commonwealth, not a colony as Papua remained.

Hughes wanted the mandate extended to Nauru but it was British self-interest rather than American moralism which thwarted that. After the loyalty Australia had shown in four years of slaughter, the denial left a bitter taste. 'Britain has no more claim to this island than to any of the others', Hughes told Britain's colonial secretary, Lord Milner, in May 1919. Australia's interest in this tiny Pacific speck was both economic and strategic. With its wealth of phosphate – the bounty provided by countless seabirds over millennia – Nauru produced a profit which could offset the cost of governing the other mandate territories. But more than that, Australia's very viability depended upon cheap Nauruan fertiliser: 'Without a sure and reasonably cheap supply of phosphate our agriculture must languish and instead of peopling our vast unoccupied interior population will continue to hug the seaboard where they will be comparatively easy prey to any predatory power'.[12] It was an overstatement but the missive displays the degree to which Australia regarded its Pacific position as both entitled and ever vulnerable, integrated and apart. In the end the phosphate was divided three ways: 42 per cent each to Australia and Britain, with New Zealand receiving the remaining 16 per cent. The mandate was Britain's but Australia administered the territory.

In its own fully mandated territory Australia committed to prohibiting 'the slave trade' and 'forced labour' except for essential works and then with 'adequate remuneration'. Australia was to 'promote to the utmost the material and moral-being and the social progress of the inhabitants'.[13] Hughes, however, was hardly interested in spreading British civilisation to the 'natives'. When asked about permitting ongoing missionary work he answered with his typical irreverent humour: 'Of course … I understand that these poor people are very short of food, and for some time past they have not had enough missionaries'.[14] Wilson was unamused but Article 5 of the mandate accordingly ensured 'freedom of conscience and the free exercise of all forms of worship' along with entry and residency rights to 'all missionaries'.

The same article permitted nationals of any League of Nations member including Japan to enter the mandated territory, a concession which Hughes would have preferred to avoid. He also objected to the condition in Article 4 which forbad establishing military bases in the territory. The upside was that this restriction also applied to the Japanese-controlled territories north of the equator, the former German possessions in Palau and the Caroline and Marshall Islands. Hughes wanted to keep Japan as far away as possible. The military exclusion was better than nothing. But it contradicted Hughes's repeated characterisation of the mandated islands as 'ramparts' for defending Australia. Unfortified New Britain and the other islands were hardly more than obstacles.

Hughes would not back down on the issue of racial equality. The Japanese delegation to the conference determining the covenant of the League of Nations insisted that discrimination on the grounds of race be explicitly forbidden, given that 'equality of nations' was a 'basic principle' of the league. Hughes saw this as a fundamental threat to his own nation's basic principle of preserving a White Australia. The prime minister's single-minded determination, won the day for racial discrimination and exclusivity even against the better judgment of an American president whose own country was riven with discrimination, both legal and customary. The Japanese backed down on their threats to walk away from membership. In September 1919, Hughes explained his position to a sympathetic audience in Australia's parliament as he sought approval of the peace treaty.

> Honourable members who have travelled in the East or in Europe will be able to understand with what difficulty this world assemblage of men, gathered from all corners of the world [to discuss the League] ... were able to appreciate this ideal of those 5 000 000 people who dared to say, not only that this great continent was theirs, but that none should enter in except such as they chose.

That last phrase would echo through the decades when debates about asylum seekers flared up in a nation that had long officially dispensed with White Australia. In 1919 Hughes's summation to his colleagues was a profoundly proud declaration of Australian exceptionalism. His was a nation unique in its ethnic homogeneity: 'We are more British than the people of Great Britain'. It was his generation's 'great destiny' to 'hold this vast continent in trust for those of our race who come after us, and who stand with us in the battle of freedom'.[15]

Racial exclusivity, Hughes argued, underpinned Australian liberty and equality. As he explained to the Japanese, it was not superiority or enmity which necessitated this restriction but simply difference. The two cultures could not mix without ill effect for both people. Hughes presented a rather different rationale to his North Sydney constituency in a widely reported speech in 1922, just a kilometre from where Henry Parkes had cautioned his electors against the 'admixture of Asian blood' in 1888. 'The White Australia principle is a part of the very warp and wool of our national life. We are pure ... If we ever become a nation of mongrels our virtue and our strength will flow from us'.[16]

≈

'the romantic nationalism of the warrior'

All the Australians who fought and died had volunteered for service. Their motivations were many and varied: patriotism, national honour, personal honour, adventure, escape, limited options among them. Two Aboriginal men, friends from western Victoria, joined up to defend a country that had already been taken from their people. Both William Rawlings and Harry Thorpe won the Military Medal for valour. Both died on the same day in August 1918. Queensland-born William Woof nearly made it through the maelstrom from beginning to end. He joined the expedition to New Guinea on 16 August 1914, and was discharged in March 1915 just in time to join the 20th Battalion AIF and serve in Gallipoli. From there he went to the Western Front. Woof was reported killed in action in October 1918. He had been missing since April. He saw the breadth of the conflict from the Pacific to Europe. His death was one tiny part of the narrative of national birth which formed around the war. Australia became a nation proper, it was said, on the battlefields of Gallipoli and the Western Front. Just what his wife, Ada, thought of it all is uncertain.

Thomas Aloysius Jenkins also joined the Australian Naval and Military Expeditionary Force but he remained in the tropics. Jenkins returned to help his wife in their grocery shop in Hughes's North Sydney electorate. That stretch of Alfred Street, Milsons Point, was a short distance from Sydney Harbour and the great barrel-roofed ferry wharf which linked north and south shores and had provided George Collingridge access to the city when he was writing his history of Australia's discovery in the 1890s. In 1924 work began on the huge bridge which would span the harbour. Four years later most of the buildings on the Jenkins' side of the street had been demolished to make way for the structure. The ferry wharf went too. The Jenkins home and shop remained like a single tooth in a gaping mouth. Jenkins refused to move and was only persuaded to do so when he was given a job working on the great arch, ensuring support for his family.

The Sydney Harbour Bridge was completed in 1932, the worst year of the Great Depression. It was a symbol of Australia's maturation after the 'baptism of fire' in war. But the bridge's opening also highlighted the divisions within Australian society. The social democratic Labor premier Jack Lang had decided to cut the ribbon himself rather than defer to the king's representative. That stand and Lang's leftist policies were enough to prompt a former British Army veteran, Francis de Groot, to don a military uniform, mount a horse and slash the ceremonial ribbon with a sword before the premier could cut it with bejewelled scissors.

De Groot was a member of the New Guard, an extreme right-wing group of disaffected citizens, men for the most part, who thought Australia was in danger of communist take-over. The leafy and semi-rural suburbs along the winding train line which extended north from the harbour, well away from the city's industrial precincts, were fertile recruiting grounds for New Guard believers. Many were ex-soldiers ready to take up rifles to defend their country against an enemy within, for the world was in disarray in the 1930s. The Depression was only one part of a terrible mix of circumstances. Nazism became the state ideology in Germany, feeding off the lasting effects of the crippling war and its punitive peace. Josef Stalin was beginning his purges of political enemies and the ethnicities he distrusted. Millions were out of work in Britain and America. Demagogues railed for and against democracy and those they blamed for the world's ills: Jews, capitalists, communists. Nationalism challenged international ideals such as universal 'brotherhood' and collective security.

Historian Neville Meaney identified a safety valve within Australia's disaffected right which defused the totalitarianism urge. Liberal democracy was strongly embedded in the culture due in large part to loyalty to empire and the 'constitution under the Crown'. The 'romantic nationalism of the warrior', Meaney argued, did not evolve into fascism while identification with white Britishness remained strong. Indeed, links were firmed further when Australia promoted an empire trading bloc in the midst of the Depression. Cheap Japanese textiles were subjected to import duties to protect still-dominant British businesses.[17]

In Japan, too, there was upheaval. The impact of the Depression was less severe than in the US and Britain but was nonetheless amplified by the intensity of social strains in a culture which had catapulted itself into modernity while trying to maintain meaning in tradition. Homburgs, fedoras and flat caps were nearly as common as kimonos on the streets of Tokyo. The British monarchy had been a model for Japan's own fragile imperial democracy. The British navy was an example for the Japanese fleet. The nation's alliance with the world's pre-eminent naval power was a source of pride. Workers and feminists used the new ideas to challenge a deep-rooted patriarchy and hierarchy.

There was deep-rooted racism too, despite Japanese protestations at the defeat of the league's racial equality clause. Indeed, the insult which that caused related more to Japan's desire to be accepted in the first tier of Western nations than any general crusade for Asian dignity. After Japan annexed Korea in 1910 migration from that country increased markedly. As was often the case with despised minorities, the characterisations were wide-ranging and often contradictory. Koreans 'took jobs' but were also 'lazy'. They were 'stupid' but clever enough to conspire with socialists in the wake of the 1923 Kantō earthquake in the hope of fostering social change. As many as 6000 Koreans were killed in the paranoid reprisal.[18]

At the end of the war James Murdoch, Japanese specialist and Australia's first Professor of Oriental Studies at the University of Sydney, reported with some confidence to the Director of Military Intelligence EL Piesse that 'German militarism is now being held up as a terrible example'. Scottish-born Murdoch had lived and taught in Japan and was writing a multi-volume history of the country. He would criticise Hughes's intransigent stand on racial equality, predicting that the 'agitation' it caused could be 'dangerous'.[19] Piesse agreed but Hughes was unmoved. If Germany's defeat initially weakened the militarist sentiment, this and other slights subsequently strengthened it. The army had been a crucible for extreme nationalism for decades. In 1931 junior field officers concocted reasons to invade Manchuria. The unauthorised act gave licence to others in Tokyo to contemplate dispensing altogether with democracy and the decadent capitalism with which it seemed twinned. The Manchurian Incident created popular solidarity where there had been division. It blew a 'divine wind', in the Justice Ministry's words. Manchuria's new rulers renamed it Manchukuo in 1932. That year the prime minister, Inukai Tsuyoshi, was assassinated by navy officers and Admiral Saitō Makoto appointed in his place. It was the beginning of the end of parliamentary democracy.

Japan's education manifesto 'The Cardinal Principles of the National Polity', published in 1937, exemplified the rejection of Western liberal thought, placing the emperor's supremacy at the core of a national life supported by militarism and patriarchy. It did not reject all Western ideas, however. Workplaces were reformed along the lines of Nazi Germany's 1934 Law for the Organisation of National Labour.[20] The fascistic nationalism which followed shared with Germany, Spain and Italy a belief in redemptive violence in the service of the state, but it did so by drawing upon Japanese myths and traditions, most obviously the code of the *Bushi* or warrior.

World War One and its aftermath

The invasion of Manchuria can be seen as the first act of the Pacific War. When the League of Nations condemned it in 1933, Japan responded by leaving the organisation. It invaded China in July 1937. In December that year Japanese troops murdered, raped and maimed as many as 300 000 Chinese people in the city of Nanjing over several weeks of unrestrained rampaging. Those atrocities anticipated the brutality that would characterise Japanese conduct towards the vanquished throughout the wider war that followed. The US opposed the occupation of China by imposing crippling trade embargoes. After diplomacy by a succession of prime ministers failed to resolve the impasses, General Tōjō Hideki assumed power in October 1941. Faced with the choice of retreat and national humiliation or attacking the rival Pacific power, Tōjō chose war. Japan bombed Pearl Harbor in December.

CHAPTER 12

World War Two

'We do not live in Utopia'

Australia was unprepared for war despite Hughes's bleak warnings. He was something of a political outsider in the 1930s though no less opinionated for that. 'We do not live in Utopia', he observed when Australia's powerful new navy arrived in 1913.[1] Twenty years later, after Japan refused to leave China and departed the League of Nations instead, Hughes wrote: '[the] East, roused from its age-old slumbers, has awakened'.[2] But what might appear in hindsight as an inexorable, and possibly obvious, descent into war was not so clearly framed at the time. Faced with awful possibilities, hope is an understandable motivation. Few, if any, in Australia welcomed the thought of another conflict so soon after the cataclysm of World War One. Some thought Japan should be allowed to remain in China, a concession to its understandable urge to expand as a rising power and one which could curb the urge to spread further. Chinese suffering might prevent similar misfortune elsewhere. Australia was selling pig iron to Japan as late as 1939 in the interests of the local economy, earning Prime Minister Robert Menzies the name 'Pig Iron Bob' from those on the left who opposed such dealings with fascistic militarism.

And Japanese aggression had become most apparent as Australia struggled to deal with the Great Depression. It was a bad time to rebuild a military which had just been dismantled. The AIF no longer existed as it was a voluntary force. As a British dominion Australia's navy was subject to the disarmament treaty arrived at in Washington in 1921–22, helping to offset the total tonnage the Royal Navy sent to the bottom. HMAS *Australia*, the RAN's first flagship, was scuttled outside Sydney

Heads in 1924. The destruction of a huge warship barely more than 10 years old prompted some questions: 'One wonders what kind of fools we had looking after our interests at the Washington Conference', asked the Adelaide *Advertiser*.[3] HMAS *Sydney* and *Melbourne* were scrapped in 1929.

There was some renewal when the government commissioned two new heavy cruisers, the second *Australia* and HMAS *Hobart* in 1928, both designed to accommodate the earlier disarmament agreement. A rebuild began slowly after the Manchurian Incident. Two armed sloops were laid down at Cockatoo Island. The navy bought a light cruiser from the British before it was slipped in 1934. That became the second HMAS *Sydney*. It purchased that vessel's 'sister-ships', HMAS *Hobart* and HMAS *Perth*, in 1938 and 1939 respectively. The aging HMAS *Adelaide*, which had been placed in reserve in 1928, was refitted in 1938. After war broke out in Europe in September 1939 the need for ships became more urgent.

Just as Australians wished that Japan might be satisfied with its limited expansion, they also hoped that Britain's post-war Pacific strategy would finally provide Australia with the naval protection it had sought since the 19th century. The fortification of Singapore as a home for an eastern fleet was much vaunted. In 1923 those who argued for a fleet base on Australia's east coast were attacked as myopic and overly obsessed with perceived threats from Japan. 'If certain critics wanted war with Japan they could hardly be more provocative', argued the *Sydney Morning Herald*, '... Britain must construct a base of her own in the most central strategic position'.[4] As ever, the line between provocation and due caution in diplomacy was not easily settled, for history rarely provides the clear lessons claimed for it.

That was how the Labor leader John Curtin expressed his uncertainty about Britain's commitment to its dominion as early as 1936. In parliament his questioning of the 'competence' and 'readiness' of British statesmen to come to Australia's 'aid' prompted the government bench response, 'Great Britain has never failed us'.

To this Curtin retorted, 'History has no experience of the situation I am visualizing'. That scenario involved a Royal Navy base in Singapore incapable of defending Australia because of geographical constraints and the simple fact that the Japanese would outgun it.[5]

In the end the eastern fleet did not even steam to the new forward base. Two months after the declaration of war against Germany in 1939, and a full two years before Japan attacked American and British possessions in the Pacific, Australia's High Commissioner in London noted his suspicion of Britain's commitment to its Pacific dominion. Prime Minister Winston Churchill's 'real conception of the strategy of the war', Stanley Melbourne Bruce conjectured after a ministerial meeting, 'is to win the European theatre with a full concentration of our forces and not dissipate them by trying to deal with the situation in the Far East at the same time'.[6] By the late 1930s his fears were widely shared. Even the empire loyalist Prime Minister Robert Menzies was forced to acknowledge the divergent interests geography created: 'What Great Britain calls the Far East is to us the near north'.[7] Aiding Britain first was both loyal and possibly rational if it were characterised as forward defence. But it necessitated exposing the continent to attack. That was, in the words of historian Peter Cochrane, Australia's 'perpetual dilemma'.[8]

≈

'Everyone seemed dazed'

Possibly the threat of fascism raised the stakes higher than ever, beyond national or even imperial interest. The Melbourne *Herald* sounded positively Wilsonian in its editorial upon the outbreak in September 1939: 'It is Britain's war and our war because it is a war to save for the world those principles of justice and freedom upon which our civilisation has been built'.[9] Australia responded to Britain's peril with all the enthusiasm mustered in the earlier crisis. Despite misgivings about imperial priorities, Menzies informed the country of the emergency, employing the simple logic of loyalty and emphasising the country's dominion status; Britain had declared war on Germany and 'as a result' Australia was also at war. A target of 20 000 men, as in the first war, was met and the 6th Division 2nd AIF was formed; the previous five divisions having served in the 1st AIF. They were necessarily volunteers because Australia's regular army and militia could not serve overseas. By the first half of 1940, 100 000 men had enlisted, so the AIF had three divisions: the 6th, 7th and 8th. Later in 1940 additional brigades formed another division, the 9th, in Britain. The core of the Royal Australian Air Force (RAAF) went to Britain and several navy vessels to the Mediterranean. HMAS *Perth* escorted troops to the Middle East. The 8th Division stayed home with the militia brigades and a few aeroplanes. HMAS *Australia* and *Canberra* patrolled in Australian waters for German raiders.

The tragic story of the 8th Division was played out in and near the Pacific. Held back in the event of Japanese aggression, two brigades were sent to Malaya in 1941, two battalions to the East Indies and one to the mandated territory's capital, Rabaul. That deployment occurred even though the League of Nations had ruled against militarising such territories; a belated realisation of Billy Hughes's description of the islands as 'ramparts' for defending the Australian continent. Having left the league in 1933, the Japanese did not hesitate to use their mandated territories as forward bases.

Japan coordinated its attack on Malaya with the surprise bombing of the American naval base at Pearl Harbor in the Hawaiian Islands on 7 December 1941. The planes in that 'infamous' action were delivered by aircraft carrier, a new possibility in naval warfare. Three days later Japan attacked two British battleships, the old HMS *Repulse* and the new HMS *Prince of Wales*, by air and sank them. They had belatedly reached Singapore and then steamed out in vain to intercept the Japanese. It was an Australian, Charles Kingsford Smith, who had inadvertently revealed the paradoxical significance of aircraft in a region dominated by water when he made the first pan-Pacific flight in 1928. But it was the Japanese who paid the most attention to the strategic importance of carriers and a naval air force.

The 8th Division engaged the, as yet, unchallenged Japanese on 14 January 1942 as they pushed down through Malaya. That day Churchill wrote to the new Australian prime minister, John Curtin, saying he thought the peninsula was doomed. The 8th was pushed back to Singapore with elements of the British and Indian armies, which had survived the Japanese attack. The island's fortifications had only been completed in 1939 but there was little to defend its northern approach and the base was now without a fleet. After he was told that the British were considering abandoning Singapore, Curtin cabled Churchill: 'After all the assurances we have been given, the evacuation of Singapore would be regarded here and elsewhere as an inexcusable betrayal. Singapore is a central fortress in the system of Empire and local defence'.[10] That was 25 January 1942. The island fell to the Japanese on 15 February. The empire lost 130 000 men in the worst defeat in its history. Some 15 000 were Australians, most of them from the 8th Division. Hundreds would die in Changi Prison and well over 4000 perished in the horrific 'Sandakan Death March' on Borneo and along the Thai–Burma railway they were forced to construct. It was not quite the betrayal Curtin had feared, but the lack of preparation after so many sanguine assurances shook Australian confidence in Britain yet again. Tactics and strategy were dreadfully wanting; Japanese aeroplanes sank battleships, a naval base had fallen to soldiers. The Australians blamed British commanders. For his part the British General Archibald Wavell, who commanded this theatre of war known as ABDA (American, British, Dutch, Australian), accused Australian soldiers of cowardice and disobedience, among other things.[11]

The edifice of imperial loyalty was not crumbling, for the existential threat to all within the empire was unifying in its profundity, but there were more cracks. On 27 December 1941, well before Singapore fell, Curtin had made the most important appeal to the US since Deakin's invitation to the Great White Fleet in 1908. It is widely regarded as a pivotal moment in Australian foreign policy, the switch from one 'great and powerful friend' to another. 'Australia looks to America, free of any pangs as to our traditional ties or kinship with the United Kingdom', he wrote in a New Year's message to the people printed in the Melbourne *Herald*. Furthermore, the war in Europe and that in the Pacific were quite distinct; so that 'Australia can go and Britain can still hold on'. It was an extraordinary acknowledgment that the offspring's survival was not essential to the parent. 'We are, therefore, determined that Australia shall not go, and we shall exert all our energies towards the shaping of a plan, with the United States as its keystone.'[12] Of vital importance too was the return of the 6th, 7th and 9th Divisions to Australia for the Pacific campaign. The arguments which ensued between Churchill and Curtin, supported by his senior officers, over where Australian troops should fight, further evinced the divided interest. 'We feel a primary obligation to save Australia' was Curtin's exasperated response to Churchill when the latter diverted the returning 7th Division to Burma without consultation.[13] The soldiers began arriving home in March. The other two divisions were back by the end of the year. The Australians' fate in Singapore exacerbated Curtin's anger. Ten days before his cablegram to Churchill insisting on the return of the 7th, the 8th Division had simply ceased to exist.

In addition to the more than 15 000 killed and taken prisoner in Malaya and Singapore, most of the 1000 men of the 2/22nd Battalion sent to defend Rabaul in early 1941 had been killed or captured. In fact, the Australian chiefs of staff and the government knew they and the other defence personnel stationed there were doomed in December, when they made the decision to maintain the force as a 'forward air observation line' and to 'make the enemy fight for this line' though it was 'beyond the capacity of the small garrison' to withstand the probable attack from the Japanese mandated islands.[14] The enemy arrived in force on 23 January and the Australians were overwhelmed. Several defenders tried to escape to the south and reached a plantation called Tol. There they were surprised and captured. On 3 February men were roped together in groups of nine or ten and led off into the plantation to be shot or bayonetted. The cruelty had a tactical purpose, as a contemporary document titled 'Notes for Unit Commanders' indicates in graphic fashion: 'To eradicate the sense of fear in raw soldiers carnivals of bloodshed [and/or] human sacrifices to the war god are most effective. Killings with bayonets should be carried out whenever the opportunity occurs'.[15] As many as 160 were executed in the worst single atrocity to befall Australians at Japanese hands. Six men survived that slaughter and managed to find their way back to Australia, where they related news of the massacre to authorities. It was written up for Chief of the General Staff Vernon Sturdee, on 28 April in a note marked 'Most Secret'.[16] News of the massacre was nonetheless reported widely in April 1942.

Over 400 men from Lark Force escaped New Britain after the Japanese invasion. Many civilians, women and children particularly, had already been evacuated from Rabaul in December 1941. Those families living on surrounding plantations found their way to the harbour to embark for Australia on whatever vessels were available. Planter Jock MacLean sailed to town on 22 December two days after getting news of the order to evacuate: 'On arrival ... I immediately went to Burns Philp and Co to book passages for my wife, son Donald and daughter Isabel. Many people were about, rushing from one place to another. Everyone seemed dazed'. Having bade them farewell, he wrote: 'Rabaul looked gloomy and deserted as the life and charm had sailed away the previous day to Australia. God protect them!'[17] The remarkable Jock MacLean made his way to Buna on the north coast of Papua, and across the Owen Stanley Range to Port Moresby, unwittingly anticipating the path of the Japanese invasion that would follow in July, and arriving just in time for a Japanese air raid. He was reunited with his family in Brisbane on 4 June. The final leg of MacLean's odyssey was almost comically mundane. He caught a train to Sandgate and a bus to 'Stop 14a' at Redcliffe. Everyday life continued, often as normal, despite the fighting to the north.

Marjorie Manson, her *de facto* husband, Ted Harvey, and her 11-year-old son, Dickie, remained on a plantation appropriated from the Germans in the early 1920s. They were not so fortunate. Harvey was an unofficial 'coastwatcher', keen to send information to Australia from behind the lines. His radio transmitter was discovered and all three – Ted, Marjorie and Dickie, who had struck a Japanese soldier in his mother's defence – were consequently shot as spies on the outskirts of the town. The tragedy of Rabaul was made even more awful by the despatch of 842 prisoners of war and 208 captured civilians aboard the *Montevideo Maru*. Bound for a prison camp off China in an unmarked prison ship, the vessel was torpedoed by an American submarine on 1 July 1942, and all the Australians on board died.

'... soaked with petrol and burnt to ashes'

With a deep-water sheltered harbour created by a collapsed volcano, Rabaul became the main Japanese base in the south-west Pacific. It was 'the nest', in the words of the commander of Australian naval forces Rear-Admiral John Crace.[18] Japan installed dozens of anti-aircraft guns and greatly improved the airfield from where Australian Wirraway fighters had flown their hopeless sorties, as well as building others. Indian and Chinese prisoners were forced to dig tunnels into volcanic and coral rock for storing supplies, establishing secure hospitals, and creating a refuge from anticipated air attack. They planted gardens, built roads and installed radar. Twenty-three diesel power stations were built where before a single Australian plant had partially powered the town. More than 600 barracks, messes and other structures were erected using local timber and newly constructed sawmills. Local people were pressed to labour for the invaders. They, too, were brutalised.

From Rabaul Japan launched other attacks. Troops landed at Lae and Salamaua on the north coast of New Guinea in March. It assembled a much larger landing and support force destined for Port Moresby in the harbour the following month. The Japanese military had considered invading Australia but quickly discounted the idea because of the huge logistical cost. Instead, by April they intended to cut Australia off from aid across the Pacific. With the continent neutralised as an American base, they could take New Guinea, Nauru and the Solomons, followed by Samoa and Fiji. The first moves began in early May with a landing at Tulagi in the Solomon Islands. Eleven transports left Rabaul shortly after bound for Port Moresby. Alerted by intercepted intelligence, American and Australian naval forces moved to stop the convoy.

The several actions which followed from 4 to 8 May have become known as the Battle of the Coral Sea. It was the first ever naval action in which ships did not engage each other directly. Rather aircraft took off from carriers and Rabaul to bomb, torpedo and strafe their opponent's ships. The first engagements involved HMAS *Australia* and *Hobart*. Both narrowly survived. At one point the former disappeared behind the wall of water thrown up by high-level bombing. Sailors outside the bridge, nearly 20 metres above the waterline, were forced to their knees under the weight of the descending deluge. The heavy carrier USS *Lexington* was destroyed as was the Japanese light carrier, the *Shōhō*. While the loss of the *Lexington* might have been a tactical victory for Japan, their intended invasion was thwarted. It was the Allies' first strategic triumph in the Pacific theatre. The outcome of the Battle of Midway, exactly one month later, was less ambiguous. Japan's plan to decisively destroy American naval power in the western Pacific had the opposite outcome. The Japanese lost four heavy carriers and over 3000 sailors and air crew. The Japanese government kept the news of the devastating defeat from its people and, indeed, many in the Japanese military.

The reversal of Japanese plans to take Port Moresby by sea in early May had profound effects for Australia's Pacific War. Submarines to be used in that action instead headed down the east coast of the continent. Three midget vessels released from these larger craft infiltrated Sydney

Harbour on 29 May. The attack on the nation's largest city, and its main naval base for nearly a century, brought the war 'home' to Australians, perhaps even more than the Japanese bombing of Darwin in February.

More significant than the Sydney raid were the ramifications of the alternative plan for taking Port Moresby. On 21 July 1942, the Japanese landed at Gona near Buna, where there was an Australian Anglican mission. This was Papua and, therefore, Australian soil. A week later they captured the small town of Kokoda, 100 or so kilometres inland. The missionaries fled but two women, Mavis Parkinson and May Hayman, were found and executed. An officer beheaded a six-year-old boy with his sword.[19] The untested and poorly trained 'Maroubra Force', men from the Papuan Infantry Battalion and the 39th Battalion, opposed the Japanese. These were militia conscripts of the Australian Military Force (AMF) which special legislation passed before the war had permitted to serve beyond the continent. The battalions were pushed back to Isurava. By late August the remnants of the 39th were reinforced by the raw recruits of 53rd Battalion AMF and elements of the 7th Division AIF who, though veterans, had no jungle experience. They wore khaki uniforms intended for desert fighting, not merging into the jungle green. The Japanese covered themselves in foliage. Indeed they were so invisible that the militia and AIF troops would remark they rarely saw a live 'Jap'. The Australians numbered fewer than 2000. They faced 3000 Japanese of the South Sea Detachment, the forward force of 13 000 troops, many of whom had fought in China and Rabaul. Some 1000 New Britain people were forced to work as carriers. Many would die in the jungle and be left to rot where they fell.

The fighting over the following three months is known simply as Kokoda, a reference to the trail or track which connected Port Moresby to the northern village of that name, and along which the respective advances and retreats occurred. The Japanese captured Kokoda village on 29 July and the Australians took it back on 2 November. In between soldiers had climbed and descended the precipitous Owen Stanley Range twice. The turning point was Imita Ridge just 60 kilometres from Port Moresby. In the third week of September, the defenders were a depleted band suffering from exhaustion, trauma, dysentery, malaria and malnutrition. The diseased Japanese, at the end of their very long line of supply, were sustained by just eight tablespoons of rice a day, their loyalty to the emperor and a resurrected warrior code. When their commander ordered a retreat back to Buna, they broke. 'Neither history nor education had any meaning to them now', wrote one Japanese war correspondent. 'Discipline was completely forgotten.'[20] On the track back north they ate Australian dead. Elsewhere they would eat each other.

In the meantime, the Australians had successfully repelled a Japanese landing at Milne Bay to the south-east. After the Kokoda campaign the AIF and the AMF fought the Japanese at Gona and Sanananda and the Americans landed nearby to take Buna. These battles were far bloodier than either nation's commanders expected. The 7th Division was 'bled white' in the words of historian Peter Brune.[21] The Japanese suffered greater casualties. When the returned 9th Division joined the 7th to take Lae on 16 September 1943, Australia had effectively regained its Papuan colony. War correspondent Kenneth Slessor, who was there at the liberation of the wrecked and reeking town, described the clean-up in the aftermath: 'Japanese corpses were collected in craters, soaked with petrol and burnt to ashes. The warrens of holes, dugouts and trench-systems, choked with a filthy jumble of dirty clothes, bloodstained rags, decayed food and nauseating refuse, were drenched with petrol and fired in the same way'.[22]

Australians and Americans again fought together at Saidor on the mandated mainland territory in February 1944. That battle was part of a larger campaign, Cartwheel, intended to isolate Rabaul. So, too, was the fighting on Bougainville, where Australians relieved US soldiers at the end of that year. Where the Kokoda campaign was a walking war, with lines of men trudging through the jungle advancing, retreating, or simply lost, the war on Bougainville came to resemble future Asian Pacific conflicts. Infantry could summon aircraft strikes. Napalm was used to destroy gardens, thereby depriving the Japanese of food supplies. Bulldozers ploughed through the forest followed by jeeps.[23] By that time, the strategic threat to Australia was over.

≋

'All that a man takes to this war he must carry on his back'

The nation's official war correspondents, photographers and artists presented the conflict in the near Pacific to Australians in words and images. Kenneth Slessor reported from New Guinea and Papua from June 1943 to February 1944, having sent despatches from Britain, Greece and the Middle East since 1940. An established journalist and admired poet, his pieces were carefully composed and compelling. He was well qualified to compare the war in the desert to that in the jungle: 'Here are no easy roads or open spaces ... there can be none of that quicksilver switching of men and material, from pressure point to pressure point along the battleline, which distinguished the struggle in North Africa ... All that a man takes to this war he must carry on his back'.[24]

His writing on the air war was full of admiration. Slessor was particularly enthralled with the Beaufighter, a beautifully designed aircraft with two barrel-like rotary engines that sat on forward wings like bulging biceps. By the end of 1942 the 'Beau' was one of the most effective weapons in the RAAF's arsenal; so dramatically different from the ponderous planes used in the war's first 12 months. The Japanese reputedly called it 'Whispering Death'. It symbolised the turning tide. Several hundred would be built beside the Yarra River in Melbourne as part of the government's move towards defence self-sufficiency and the extraordinary boost the existential emergency of the Pacific War gave to Australian manufacturing. Slessor was taken on a sortie and, enthralled by the machine's speed at low level, shared that experience in an article printed in the Melbourne *Argus*:

> Come with me on a barge-sweep, an ordinary unspectacular all-in-the-day's-work barge-sweep over New Britain in one of these Australian-manned Beaufighters ... There is a green rush of jungle below ... so close that we seem to be sliding from bough to bough. Seeing the earth so near, you feel that you are actually driving a car at a mad rate over the treetops.[25]

It was a rare moment of exhilaration for the journalist, who found it difficult to work within the confines of officialdom. Slessor resigned as a correspondent in February 1944, a month after publishing his Beaufighter piece, in response to accusations of inaccurate reporting from within the military.

George Johnston also brought literary skill to his war reporting. His experience in New Guinea in 1942 coalesced an already well-established belief that, in the words of his biographer, 'the full status of Australian manhood was somehow tied to the dark forces of blood sacrifice'.[26] It was a union begun in World War One and now continued at Kokoda. Indeed, Johnston predicted that 'the name of the Kokoda Trail is going to live in the minds of Australians for generations, just as another name, Gallipoli, lives on freshly today'.[27] He published this, and other insights, in 1943 as *New Guinea Diary*. It was replete with vignettes of Australian mateship, endurance and humour gained first-hand and through interviews in Port Moresby. The experience was formative and obviously influenced the writer's enduring study of Australian masculinity, the novel *My Brother Jack* published in 1964. The book also detailed the 'magnificent' fighting done by the 'all-native' Papuan Infantry Battalion. Among them was the formidable and apparently fearless Sergeant Katue who waged an especially lethal war against the Japanese with a small force of local men recruited as he moved from village to village.[28] It was an acknowledgment that went beyond the typical descriptions of 'native' stretcher bearers.

Johnston also went to China and from there presented Australians with a perspective on the Pacific War's wider impact. Nationalist and communist forces had been fighting the Japanese, as well as each other, since 1936 and in doing so had prevented tens of thousands of soldiers engaging the Australians and Americans. Johnston was shocked by what he saw. Conscious of white Australia's long-held antipathies to Asians of any nationality, he wrote to foster empathy among readers of the *Argus*: 'Imagine the entire population of Melbourne abandoning their homes and taking to the roads in flight from the city ... Already [on the road south from Liuchow] thousands of refugees have died by the sides of the road, where the bodies of old men and women, cripples and children are rotting in the hot sun'.[29]

Where in New Guinea Johnston had largely gleaned information at briefings in Port Moresby and from men returned from fighting to get a 'big picture' of the war, newspaper journalist Osmar White and ABC radio broadcaster Chester Wilmot walked with the soldiers as they retreated along the Kokoda Track. Newspapers from Adelaide to North Queensland carried White's reports. His accounts were remarkably frank. 'We could not see them. They could see us and we could not see them', he wrote, quoting one soldier: 'In other words, the Japanese knew more jungle warfare than we did'.[30] That must have been an unsettling admission in the midst of an existential crisis and after 80 years of an ascending sense of racial supremacy, albeit one always tinged with fear. The book he published in early 1945, *Green Armour*, was no less frank. 'I have always been annoyed by the prevailing belief that the Australian troops rallied magnificently and, beating the Jap at his own game, fought their way inch by inch to Kokoda', declared White. It was geography that beat the Japanese and 'a barrier of unpeopled sea and jungle [which] saved Australia'. That said, the writer remained in awe of the men with whom he marched: 'I was convinced for all time of the dignity and nobility of common men. I was convinced for all time that common men have a pure and shining courage when they fight for what they believe to be a just cause'.[31]

That emphasis on dignity rather than honour is significant. The one elevated life, the other so often destroyed it. White believed the

Japanese incapable of respecting the former. They were, in his mind, 'primitives'. It was one of the many lessons he grappled with during his nine months in New Guinea. He thought it was the greatest conundrum of all. Perhaps for that reason his ruminations were occasionally unclear. 'The primitive warrior always has the edge on the civilized if he can contrive equality of arms and the wilds for a battlefield'. 'Primitives' used the landscape to their advantage, employing surprise to overcome technological advantage. That sounded like guerrilla warfare. There was no definite racial element in White's idea of primitivism for, alongside the historical examples of Native Americans, he also referred to the colonial forces that fought the British for American independence in the late 18th century. Conversely, the respect for life seemed to stem from material well-being, a philosophical or ethical luxury afforded, perhaps, by the 'civilisation' of the West – although he did not use that term.

He put it most clearly as follows: 'in a war with nations that have not for generations possessed the good things, a code that sets a higher value upon individual human life and comfort than upon any material product of society may be perilous, if enviable'.[32] It was a peculiar misreading of the very non-material motivation of Japanese soldiers prepared to do anything for their divine emperor and the warrior code, but one which demonstrated the bewilderment Australians felt when confronted by atrocities and Japanese fighters' desire to die rather than be taken captive. Honour which fortified the will mattered more than the dignity and lives of others. The converse was articulated by one Australian of the 8th Division who survived the brutal incarceration on Singapore: 'Mateship was the simple recognition of the importance of another human being's experience'.[33]

White and Wilmot walked the Kokoda Track with the cinematographer and photographer Damien Parer. Where White, Wilmot, Slessor and Johnston used words to create images in their readers' minds, Parer literally presented moving pictures. His footage of the New Guinea war was groundbreaking. The renowned filmmaker Ken

G Hall produced *Kokoda Front Line!* for Cinesound and it opened in Sydney in September 1942, just as the tide turned on the Kokoda Track. People queued to watch it, though the newsreel ran for less than 10 minutes. Osmar White thought Parer was a genius. He was also a devout Catholic, praying every night.[34] That may have influenced his craft, for the footage towards the end of *Kokoda Front Line!* contained sequences of suffering and redemption in equal measure. Parer's sense of spirituality and dignity was enhanced by cinematographic technology; there was none of the strange jerkiness that characterised moving pictures of World War One. Men slipped, staggered and stumbled here as they did in real time. Some brief moments of action were in fact re-enactments, but the scenes of soldiers interacting and lost in thought were unrehearsed and authentic.[35]

Australia's reporters and photographers struggled to get their material through the censors. A critical report by Chester Wilmot on the destruction of Allied aircraft at Port Moresby, inadequately protected on the ground during a Japanese raid in August, was one of many 'not passed'. The Australian commander Thomas Blamey withdrew Wilmot's accreditation in November 1942. Perhaps ironically, when Kenneth Slessor resigned over criticism of his coverage, that confrontation was widely reported in the papers. The comparison with censorship in the US is striking. In Australia, George Silk's photographs of war dead were withheld from publication, yet *Life* magazine printed a visceral image of three dead Americans on the beach at Buna accompanying a moving elegiac article. Brutal footage of US marines invading Tarawa Island was shown in American cinemas at the president's insistence. It made the re-enacted snippets of fighting in *Kokoda Front Line!* appear a little anodyne. In this time of emergency there was a tension between the democratic responsibility to inform and the autocratic urge to withhold. Australian authorities felt the latter strongly.

Australians also experienced propaganda courtesy of the artist Norman Lindsay, whose work was published in the *Bulletin* in the second war just as it had been in the first. In 1942 the Department of

Information presented vilifying caricatures in a series of broadcasts on Australian Broadcasting Commission (ABC) radio, which purported to describe 'The Jap As He Really Is'. That included the observation that the Japanese were 'a bespectacled ape-like race that lent colour to the theory of evolution'. There was a negative response to this approach from many individuals, church leaders and community groups but the notion had currency whether it was intended as a slur or a biological fact. General Blamey described the Japanese as 'a cross between human being and ape' when addressing survivors of the Kokoda campaign in 1942.[36]

For all the crudeness of their radio broadcasts, Australian authorities also appointed official war artists – rather than propagandists – to record events. These documenters were less constrained by censorship, possibly because their work was less immediately available. The work created by the painter Ivor Hele was quite unlike that produced by totalitarian regimes, whereby soldiers and the much-vaunted 'people' were resolute and triumphant in the nation's service against a caricatured enemy. Like Slessor and Parer, Hele had come to New Guinea from the Middle East. Throughout he focussed on the male body, an interest honed by study in Paris and Munich before the war. His desert drawings in red charcoal and pencil resembled Renaissance studies of muscle and bone. The anatomical detail was composed and perfect. He drew sketches in pencil, and pen and ink, in the heat of the battle or its immediate aftermath, the line work conveying immediacy and movement, then created oil paintings back in his South Australian studio.

The Middle East scenes were studies in impressionistic realism. In New Guinea, however, his paintings of men with gaunt, haunted faces were reminiscent of El Greco's depiction of Christ. Suffering and perhaps redemption were present, but never triumphalism. Whatever religiosity might be read into the works is at least matched by a secular sensuality. The darkness of the jungle presented an opportunity for chiaroscuro, so that the muscular torsos of naked commandoes bathing and resting were highlighted against the gloom; as was the distended belly of an emaciated Japanese corpse, arm severed and presumably eaten by a starving comrade. In *Grenade Throwing, Bobdubi Ridge* (1944), the bodies are barely distinguishable from the muddy darkness across which they crawl. In *Walking Wounded, Missim Trail* (1944) and *Stretcher Case Awaiting Bearers, Old Vickers Position* (1944), Australians are shown in the green fatigues which had finally replaced sandy khaki. So-coloured, and draped in rain sheets with slouch hats made flaccid by the wet, they are almost part of the jungle foliage, merged with the terrain which was as much an enemy as the Japanese. The suggestion was that the battle-hardened Australians had attained their own invisibility; they and the forest in which they fought were finally one.

As a commando fighting in the Salamaua and Lae area in mid-June 1942, Stephen Murray-Smith lived the experience Hele depicted. In a lengthy unpublished memoir, he remembered smearing his entire body in mud before action. 'WE NEVER SAW THE SUN', he reminded himself, 'and lived in a damp, perpetual gloom' (emphasis in original).[37]

The Australian War Memorial collection bought many of Hele's works in 1944. Such were the exigencies on the home front that picture frames were unavailable for a planned show that year. However, a successful touring exhibition through cities and regional areas followed in 1945 featuring *Grenade Throwing, Bobdubi Ridge* and *Stretcher Case Awaiting Bearers*. The reviewer for the *Adelaide News* commended the works for their 'humanity and sympathy'.[38]

≋

'... lost on the Kokoda Trail.'

Service personnel themselves had an opportunity to publish their thoughts and experiences in the journal *Salt*, which the Australian Army Education Service produced throughout the war. The tenor of that writing was heroic and humorous. By contrast, the abuse suffered by Australian prisoners of war at the hands of the Japanese was detailed for all to read as early as 1946. Rohan Rivett's *Behind Bamboo* sold more than 100 000 copies through eight reprints. An official multi-volumed history of World War Two appeared in the 1950s, a scholarly companion to historian CEW Bean's longer, blow-by-blow account of World War One. The fifth volume, dealing with the south-west Pacific, was published in 1959. It was written by Dudley McCarthy, once a journalist and more recently a public servant specialising in Pacific affairs.

Farmer, historian, writer and poet Eric Rolls served as a signaller in New Guinea and Bougainville. His experiences gestated for a quarter of a century before finding expression in a collection of verse called *Green Mosaic: Memories of New Guinea*, which he published in 1977. There were poems about butterflies, birds and bamboo mingled with vignettes of the local people, who were dealing with the disruption of the war and 50 years of colonial change. 'Saki's Tribe' had lost their place as raiders of people, pigs and crops and now wandered hungry on the outskirts of other people's territories: 'Once they seized life/Now they cadge it'.[39] Signaller Rolls had time, it seems, to contemplate life around him, perhaps because war typically comprised long stretches of tedium between times of terror. At Shaggy Ridge, where battles in early 1944 followed the fall of Lae, Rolls stayed behind to report:

> The fighting moved on
> But the station stayed on the vantage point
> To report weather and aircraft movements
> And soon even bullets
> Might have been welcome enough
> To shatter boredom.[40]

Many other memoirs and histories appeared in the 1990s, prompted by the 50th anniversary of battles and the end of the war itself, or the survivors' contemplative old age. These accounts were written to document aspects of a complex conflict that some feared would be lost to the public memory, or to make personal reckonings before it was too late. In 1995 Bob Hall put together a series of stories from Aboriginal and Torres Strait Islanders who fought 'from the fringe', and whose experiences had rarely been publicly acknowledged. Kathleen Ruska, later known as Kath Walker, then Aboriginal writer and activist Oodgeroo Noonuccal, joined the Australian Women's Army Service in 1942 as a wireless operator. She spoke about the contradictions that war brought to a racially charged home front. Black Americans dated white Australian women while serving in a segregated US military. For the young Kathleen the Australian Army granted unprecedented, if temporary, respite from discrimination: 'they didn't give a stuff what colour you were. There was a job to be done ... and all of a sudden the colour line disappeared'.[41] Indigenous Australians served in the Torres Strait where Thursday and Horn islands became major bases. The Japanese bombed the latter's airfields extensively from March 1942 to June 1943.

Torres Strait man Tom Lowah carried less benign memories. White recruiters rounded him up at bayonet point to serve in the Torres Strait Light Infantry Battalion, one of more than 400 local men to do so. They worked loading and unloading stores on Thursday Island, and were paid at one-third the rate of white recruits. After a labour strike, that was raised to two-thirds.[42]

From 1996 Lionel Veale self-published several volumes documenting his time near Wewak and elsewhere as a 'coastwatcher', one of those who spent isolated weeks and months behind enemy lines reporting Japanese movements, often assisted by local people, sometimes fearing betrayal. In 1997 Brian Gomme released the diary he had kept as a gunner in the 7th Division at Gona. The writing had been 'something to do' in quieter moments and kept as a record for his family. Publishing it put his experiences on the public record. In a setting he thought resembled a 'Tarzan' movie, Gunner Gomme used hand grenades to kill fish for his dinner and traded tinned beef rations for fresh fruit with 'natives' whom he considered honest and whose good 'health and physique' he attributed to avoiding 'the vices of civilized people'.[43]

Tod Schacht's frank account of his time on Bougainville in 1944 with the 9th Battalion AMF was published in 1999. By then Kathleen Thurston was already assembling the notes, photographs, films and recordings of her father Ted Fulton, whose pre-war experience in New Guinea as a miner led to his recruitment into the Australian New Guinea Administrative Unit. ANGAU, as it was known, organised local labour for the war effort and provided guides and intelligence for the military. Fulton's tropical war was spent traversing rugged terrain, avoiding Japanese patrols and negotiating with local people who, caught in the middle of a conflict not of their making, often 'did not know who was in control'.[44] Fulton's memoirs were published in 2005.

Despite all the millions of words written about Australia's Pacific War and the pictures taken and painted of it, historian Peter Brune could still lament in 2003 that in 'commemorating the Papuan campaign we have, as a nation, got lost on the Kokoda Trail'.[45] George Johnston was prophetic when he suggested that Kokoda would take its place beside Gallipoli in the national memory. It has, almost. But to many, such as Brune, that came at the expense of an understanding of the broader war.

It is probably unrealistic to hope for a wide knowledge of Australia's Pacific War, even though it was the only time the Commonwealth has been invaded and the continent itself bombed; the colony of Papua in the first instance, and Darwin, Broome and Townsville in the second.[46] Certain aspects of the New Guinea campaign, however, do seem to have lodged in the collective consciousness. One is the camaraderie between Australian troops and local people. In 1946 Queensland-born Eric Feldt, who organised coastwatchers like Lionel Veale, wrote of the support provided to his men on New Britain under threat of Japanese reprisal. The Islanders took orders from the invaders but acted surreptitiously and at great risk to themselves and their kin. The chiefs 'made it plain they would give underground assistance', Feldt recalled. And with the insight of one who had spent many years in New Guinea as a patrol officer he noted, 'Dissimulation is second nature to the native, as it is to most subject peoples'.[47]

Damien Parer's film immortalised the so-called 'fuzzy wuzzy angels', who carried and guided wounded soldiers along the track from Kokoda. The still images of official war photographer, George Silk, complemented his 1942 footage, which showed them in documentary honesty. Silk's 1943 photo of Raphael Oimbari assisting the blinded Private George Whittington towards a field hospital at Dobodura near Gona became iconic. The Department of Information, for whom Silk worked, censored it initially but American *Life* magazine published it. Only then did the photograph appear on the cover of the Australian publication *The War in New Guinea: Official war photographs of the Battle for Australia*. Johnston, too, praised the 'loyal Papuans'.

Unsurprisingly, the story is more complex. Racial difference and colonialism's profound power imbalance were ever present. That is epitomised by the commentary that accompanied the dignifying footage of Papuan carriers in *Kokoda Front Line!*. 'With them [the Australians] the black skinned boys are white', remarked the narrator jauntily. Whatever equality may have operated under the duress of battle did not necessarily apply elsewhere. Local people were not always willing helpers. Tod Schacht noted that ANGAU officers, many of whom were former patrol officers, were nicknamed 'boong bashers' because of their harsh recruiting and management practices. He witnessed them bullying Bougainville men whose job was to build huts, despite one being debilitated with malaria.[48] While Papua New Guineans are generally proud of the service their ancestors gave to Allied forces during the war, Asi Arere's memories of the war were less of noble service than forced labour: 'They [ANGAU officers] did not treat us properly. They were always hitting people and knocking us over'.[49] In New Guinea respect and control sometimes broke down as the balance of power shifted. In January 1942 looting broke out on one of Jock MacLean's plantations after a 'boss boy', or Indigenous overseer, told his co-workers that 'the English and Australian men were not strong because they ran away, and left the natives to the Japanese to look after'. 'I had no more control over my one hundred labourers from then on', wrote MacLean.[50] The 'dissimulation' to which Feldt referred went both ways.

Britain's ineptitude and its disregard for Australia's security is also widely remembered. The impotence of Singapore's guns has come to symbolise both imperial arrogance and decline. Similarly, the AIF's withdrawal from the Middle East to defend Papua and New Guinea, against Churchill's wishes, is regarded as an expression of Australian independence from that empire. In the minds of nationalists such as Paul Keating it was a salutary lesson. As Labor Party prime minister in 1992, he took the opportunity of an otherwise routine Anzac Day anniversary, marking the 77th year since the landing on Gallipoli, to travel to Port Moresby to emphasise the more significant 50th anniversary of the '*two* great dramas' (emphasis in original) that unfolded in New Guinea. One, of course, was the fight against the Japanese. The other was John Curtin's battle against Britain. By 'insisting' on the return of the AIF, 'John Curtin defied those people Australia had never before defied', Keating declared. Furthermore Curtin 'defied those in Australia who criticised him for his defiance'. That was a veiled attack on loyalists such as Robert Menzies, whom Keating, with his Irish roots, equated with the conservatives of his own time. 'John Curtin was right' to defy Churchill. He was also right 'when he declared that in the hour of crisis, after the fall of Singapore, Australia looked to the United States'. Australia's Pacific War, in Keating's formulation, was fought to define a place in the region, not the empire:

> The Australians who served here in Papua New Guinea fought and died, not in the defence of the old world, but the new world. *Their* world [emphasis in original]. They died in defence of Australia and the civilisation and values which had grown up there. That is why it might be said that, for Australians, the battles in Papua New Guinea were the most important ever fought.[51]

'a substantial abrogation of Australian sovereignty'

What were the values Australians were defending? Japan and Germany had been allied since the Tripartite Pact of 1940. Both countries agreed to respect the establishment of 'a new order' in each other's spheres, Europe and East Asia. Those new orders were totalitarian, anti-democratic and violently repressive. Nazi Germany was genocidally racist. Against them were ranged not only the Allied military forces but also a collective of 26 countries, including Australia, called the 'United Nations' – a precursor of sorts to the United Nations (UN), formally established in October 1945. Their Declaration, signed in early 1942, made a commitment to defend 'life, liberty, independence and religious freedom ... human rights and justice'.[52] This was the philosophical basis of Australia's war. That UN values ran through Australian society, notwithstanding the deep vein of racism and exploitative self-interest also to be found there, is evidenced by the belief of the aforementioned un-named soldier in Changi in 'the simple recognition of the importance of another human being's experience'.[53]

John Curtin made mention of the 'United Nations' in an exultant letter to General MacArthur when the latter arrived in Australia on 17 March 1942 to take command of the American forces already assembled there to take the fight to the Japanese. 'This is a momentous occasion for the peoples of the United Nations', the prime minister wrote, ' ... You have come to Australia to lead a crusade the result of which means everything to the future of the world and mankind'. And he continued, 'At the request of a sovereign nation you are being placed in Supreme Command of its Navy, Army and Air Force ...'[54] That referred to the process which would see MacArthur become the Supreme Commander of the Allied forces in Australia and the near Pacific. From 18 April, MacArthur had formal command of some 370 000 Australian combat troops. His theatre of command was subsequently called the South West Pacific Area (SWPA) to distinguish it from the South Pacific Area which included Norfolk Island and New Zealand. Delighted though Curtin was with MacArthur's appointment, the US did not consult Curtin about the demarcation and neither was he pleased with it. The Americans held sway, as did MacArthur.

That was the reality of Curtin's 'look' to America to which Paul Keating referred approvingly in 1992. His speech was intended both to shift the focus of Anzac Day from Gallipoli to New Guinea and make a claim for the mantle of a sovereign foreign policy for the Labor Party. The address was delivered amidst that renewed interest in Australia's New Guinea and Papuan campaign which prompted the memoirs of Ted Fulton and Tod Schacht. There was considerable academic review at this time too. One unifying theme was a critical reassessment of the Australian–US relationship and the role of the divisive figure of General MacArthur, whose counsel Curtin generally accepted over his Australian officers. The conclusions often sat awkwardly with Keating's nationalist and polemical revisionism. Lex McAulay's popular history of the Kokoda campaign, published the year before the prime minister's Anzac address, was forthright but typical. Curtin was 'putty in MacArthur's hands'. The American was an egotist who controlled the media for his own ends. And somewhat more robustly: 'Curtin allowed MacArthur to become virtual dictator of Australia'.[55] Military historian David Horner essentially concurred when he described the command of Australian forces 'by a foreign general', as 'a substantial abrogation of Australian sovereignty'.[56] British generals and admirals had commanded Australian soldiers and sailors in World War One and in the first years of the second great conflagration. The difference was, of course, that being British was not being foreign.

But the war was a catalyst for diplomatic independence. The nation exchanged diplomats for the first time in 1940 when RG Casey went to Washington and Clarence Gauss arrived to represent the US. Whereas Australia's state of war against Nazi Germany was a consequence of Britain's decision, Australia declared war against Japan on its own behalf in 1941. Australia's parliament finally adopted the 1931 *Statute of Westminster*, which had allowed for the end of British authority over the dominion foreign policy, in late 1942.

It was the case, therefore, that the 'abrogation' to which Horner referred came just as Australia was beginning to assert its sovereignty in foreign affairs. At MacArthur's request the Allied War Council, which had been responsible for Australia's strategy at the highest level, was whittled down to two permanent participants – MacArthur and Curtin. It thereby became the Prime Minister's War Conference, to which others came and went. Lieutenant-General Sturdee described the relationships that ensued. The Australian chiefs of staff were regarded 'almost entirely as housekeepers'.[57] At MacArthur's so-called 'Allied Headquarters' almost all senior staff were Americans, despite urgings from the US Army Chief of Staff General George C Marshall to include Australians in view of the partnership and their experience.

Curtin was not stupid or sycophantic. He saw in MacArthur an important ally in opposing Churchill and President Roosevelt's 'Defeat Germany First' strategy. The general shared Curtin's belief that the fight against Japan should be prosecuted as a priority, indeed as a second front. To this end Australia's security was reassuringly vital. But MacArthur's motivations were not necessarily the same as Curtin's. There was a personal desire to retake the Philippines, which had been lost under his command and from where he had fled, albeit under orders. There was also rivalry with the American Admiral Chester Nimitz, who would command the naval-based island-hopping push to Japan's homeland. Nimitz commanded the marines. MacArthur favoured an army-led offensive back up through Rabaul to the Philippines.

MacArthur was a master of rhetoric and image. He carefully prepared the words delivered upon his Australian arrival from the Philippines, with which he would be enduringly associated: 'I came through and I will return'. To Australia he publicly and extravagantly pledged 'the full resources of all the mighty power of my country and all the blood of my countrymen'. MacArthur then stressed the bond between the two countries. 'There is a link which binds our countries together which does not depend upon written protocol, upon treaties of alliance, or upon diplomatic doctrine', he continued. 'It goes deeper than that. It is that indescribable consanguinity of race which causes us to have the same aspirations, the same hopes and desires.'[58] The 'indescribable consanguinity' referred to a biological affinity that came with common ancestry. It was a remarkable evocation, probably unintentional, of the mood of 1908 when Australians had looked to the US as a potential saviour against a rising Japan, and spoken of common blood.

The emphasis, thereby, was on an ethnic partnership, not a broader crusade for the world. There was mention of 'personal liberty' and the struggle against 'perpetual slavery' but not of international crusades for human rights. For a nationalist like MacArthur, that sounded too much like the Democrat Woodrow Wilson, and maybe even the current president, Franklin Roosevelt. It was no coincidence that isolationist Republicans considered MacArthur a presidential contender for the 1944 election.

For all his talk of 'consanguinity', MacArthur was not above criticising Australian soldiers for their failings and downplaying their successes. Even his American biographer noted that the general's press releases routinely referred to American soldiers but rarely Australian troops. They came under the general term 'Allied'.[59] That vanity and lack of generosity is a constant theme in Australian writing about the New Guinea and Papuan campaigns.

MacArthur's criticism of Australian troops during the fighting along the Kokoda Track is particularly resented. On 17 September 1942, after a month of fighting across the Owen Stanley Range and just as the Japanese advance was about to be stopped, the American told Curtin he no longer had 'confidence' in the Australian soldiers. Then, remarkably, he suggested the Australian Commander-in-Chief, General Thomas Blamey, go to Port Moresby to take personal command 'to energise the situation' and 'to save himself' from the recriminations which would follow if Moresby fell. MacArthur, clearly, was not going to take responsibility for such a disaster. For Peter Brune, the unjustified pressure on Curtin and Blamey resulted in the removal of two of the heroes of Kokoda, Lieutenant-General Sydney Rowell and Brigadier Arnold Potts, who personally commanded the fighting withdrawal along the track from Isurava until after the turn-around in September 1942. Brune's outrage is evident in his assessment of Potts' dismissal: 'It is staggering to think that [Potts'] ... near flawless fighting withdrawal' was rewarded with being relieved of command. 'Brigadier Arnold Potts is quite simply an Australian hero ... one that an apathetic nation has still to honour'.[60] MacArthur did not resile from his criticism of Australians even when the American 32nd Division similarly faltered against Japanese resolve at Buna.

The Pacific War, and indeed World War Two, formally ended on 2 September 1945 when Japan signed the terms of surrender. Emperor Hirohito, for whom perhaps three million Japanese people died, had announced his country's surrender on 15 August in a radio message delivered in an arcane form of Japanese that few could understand. The two atomic bombs which precipitated that submission were dropped on 6 and 9 August. Up until then Australians fought Japanese soldiers on and around New Guinea in a series of 'mopping up' campaigns, which even MacArthur acknowledged had little strategic significance. He was apparently open to including Australian forces in the final assault upon Japan but then duplicitously argued for a campaign in Borneo in mid-1945.[61] The Labor government and Thomas Blamey supported the decision to prosecute the war in New Guinea and Bougainville, rather than contain the Japanese and allow them to wither as a threat from hunger and disease while their homeland was assaulted, despite criticism from the press and the opposition. Blamey spoke of Australia's responsibility for 'liberating the natives' from Japanese control in its territories but he could mount no such argument for the Borneo assaults.[62] It is very probable that the campaigns were an attempt to offset domestic concerns that Australia, in the words of one official war historian, Paul Hasluck, 'should end the war not as a fighting ally but as a general providore'.[63] By then thousands of women and military-age men were working to supply the war effort with food and materials. And, most significantly, being an 'active belligerent' gave claim to political influence in the impending aftermath.

Tod Schacht, who helped to relieve the Americans on Bougainville, recalled this tail-end war with bemusement if not bitterness. The 9th Militia Battalion had the 'honour', he wrote, of finishing off 'bewildered Japanese troops who had grave problems with dwindling medical supplies and an acute food shortage'. In the meantime, General MacArthur was free to pursue 'his obsession of returning to the Philippines as a conquering hero', something he did in October 1944.[64] New Britain was invaded and air raids pummelled Rabaul throughout the war, including in many sorties by the Royal New Zealand Air Force operating from Bougainville, but the Allies did not take the town before the end of hostilities.

Such is the mercuriality of collective memory that even the likes of Douglas MacArthur could not control the 'narrative' that emerged to dominate perceptions of America's Pacific War. The role of the marines on islands such as Tarawa and Iwo Jima overshadowed the army with whom Australians fought in what would be called 'the forgotten war of the South Pacific'.[65] A single image can encapsulate a complex story, and so it was with Joe Rosenthal's iconic photograph of marines raising a flag on Iwo Jima in February 1945. That picture was subsequently materialised in the larger-than-life Marine Corp memorial unveiled in 1954 at the nation's war cemetery in Arlington, Virginia. Unlike the *Life* magazine photograph of dead GIs half-buried on a Buna beach, it proclaimed victory.

With the defeat of Japan, the Pacific Ocean was unquestionably an 'American lake'. But talk of 'consanguinity' or common interest meant little in the emerging world of superpower politics, just as it had been easily set aside during the fighting. Those Americans charged with making the new order chose to remember and acknowledge what was expedient. Australia was not invited to contribute to the terms of

Japan's surrender. The nation was not even mentioned as a 'belligerent' on the document as Paul Hasluck, himself a former minister for external affairs, pointedly observed as late as 1970.[66] General Blamey signed the surrender on behalf of his country on 2 September 1945, but then there were signatures also from the Soviet Union, which had only declared war against Japan on 9 August, and the French and Canadians, whose involvement was negligible.

Representation from the Soviet Union symbolised the ironies of international politics, for the US was already aware that old allies were quickly becoming new foes, and former enemies might be useful new friends. Japan was to serve as a buffer to communist expansion in the north-west Pacific. Having spilled so much blood so close to home, Australia would accordingly have less influence over the aftermath than Billy Hughes had won for his country in World War One, which was fought so far away.

At the end of the fighting some 224 000 Australians were serving in the Pacific. More than 17 000 had died since 1941, nearly half of those as prisoners of war. The returned received a service medal, the Pacific Star. It was embossed with a crown and 'GRI VI', which stood for 'George VI King and Emperor'. There was no mention of Australia there either.

Jack Hart was one of the returned. He had escaped the massacre of Australians on New Britain in 1942. Badly injured and cared for by his comrades, Jack recovered in Sydney and went back to fight the Japanese in New Guinea. During the Battle of Sattelberg he came face to face with an enemy soldier at close range. Both were surprised and reached for their guns, but Jack's reflexes were quicker. There had been no time to think, that came later. Jack removed personal effects from the body; a flag and family photograph. That act put a name to the face of the enemy, Kawashita Hirokichi. It also haunted Jack for decades. He died in 1998. By then his son had married a Japanese woman. For many years they tried to locate Kawashita's family but, failing to do so, presented the flag to the Wakayama Peace Museum near the soldier's home town in 2017. It was a small act of 'atonement' for that death but Jack had already made peace with his demons, living, painting and writing for years on an island in another part of the Pacific, the South China Sea.[67]

CHAPTER 13

Governing Papua and New Guinea

'without distinction of any kind'

John Curtin did not see the end of the Pacific War. He died on 5 July 1945, aged just 60. The stress of occupying the highest office in such a prolonged emergency is widely thought to have been a factor. He was 'a war casualty if ever there was one', in the words of historian Geoffrey Searle.[1] Curtin's successor Ben Chifley spoke with plain Christian relief when the Japanese accepted unconditional surrender: 'Fellow citizens, the war is over ... let us offer thanks to God. Let us remember those whose lives were given that we may enjoy this glorious moment ...'[2]

Herbert 'Doc' Evatt had been minister for external affairs under both prime ministers but attempted to shape a postwar foreign policy more than either man. He was furious upon learning of the peace terms the 'Big Three' – Britain, the Soviet Union and the US – delivered to Japan after the Potsdam Conference in late July 1945. 'Australia has shed at least as much blood as Russia or France in winning the war against Japan and should have equal rights with those powers in the settlement.'[3] The comparison with Billy Hughes is obvious but the outcome was quite different. An attempt to use Manus Island, part of the mandated territory of New Guinea which Hughes won, as a bargaining chip to ensure US interest in the western Pacific came to nothing.

The perennial problem of advancing Australia's national interest alongside, or even against, those of more powerful partners had exercised the minister since he took the job in 1941. In 1944, Evatt helped draft the ANZAC Pact with New Zealand in mutual recognition of their particular interests in regional security. That declaration of independence during a wider war annoyed the Americans but had little impact on great power politics. Not only were the terms of Japan's surrender drafted and delivered without consultation but the peace treaty, when eventually concluded in 1951, was nothing like the settlement Evatt wanted – one which would both punish and hobble the country Australians had feared for half a century.

Evatt did negotiate a commanding role for Australia within the British Commonwealth Occupation Force. Twelve thousand Australian troops went to Japan in 1946 and assumed responsibility for the Hiroshima Prefecture, still devastated by the impact of the atomic bomb dropped on 6 August. They were not the first from Australia to see the ruins. Melbourne-born journalist Wilfred Burchett, who sometimes reported as 'Peter Burchett', had scooped everyone, having bluffed his way into the city within two weeks of the surrender in September 1945. 'In this testing ground I have seen the most terrible and frightening desolation of four years of war reporting', he wrote in Sydney's *Daily Telegraph*, '... Hiroshima does not look like a normally bombed city at all'. The destruction was new and so too were the weapon's after-effects. Burchett drew upon established understanding to describe what he was witnessing as bodies not otherwise harmed by the blast started succumbing to sores and organ failure. People were dying of 'atomic plague'.[4]

Australia's control of the Hiroshima Prefecture allowed photographers Allan Cuthbert and Alan Queale to take some of the first pictures of the devastation. Their images of the skeletal dome of the City Commercial Display Building became iconic. Occupiers were forbidden to fraternise with the occupants but as the writer TAG Hungerford, who was part of the Australian force, recalled, they 'learned the elementary but necessary Japanese vocabulary for work, business and love'. There were more than 370 marriages between Australian men and local women. Because of the White Australia policy and still-raw post-war antipathies, Japanese wives were not permitted to join their husbands in Australia until the mid-1950s.[5]

As Evatt was trying to press Australian interests upon the Americans, he was also attempting to build a post-war policy framework in which the voice of small and medium-sized nations would have some sway against the great and powerful. That work began in the San Francisco Conference of April to June 1945, out of which the second United Nations (UN) was born. Evatt helped to strengthen the power of the General Assembly of all member nations in relation to the Security Council with its five permanent big power members: the US, the Soviet Union, Britain, France and China. He argued against giving a veto to any one of the permanent Security Council countries. That was defeated in the face of Soviet intransigence. However, the charter signed by the representatives of 50 nations reaffirmed, among other things, 'the equal rights ... of nations large and small.'

All of this Evatt did because he believed Australia's destiny and security depended upon ensuring its influence in the south-west Pacific. To that end he shared the views and followed the lead of Billy Hughes. There were other similarities; a belief in Australia's role as a 'trustee' for 'British civilization' in the Pacific, and a forthright manner which mightily irritated the Americans and the British.[6] But there were fundamental differences too. Evatt believed in collective security and internationalism, whereas Hughes thought Australia's defence was best assured within the empire. And perhaps most significantly, Evatt was a liberal moralist in the vein of Woodrow Wilson, Hughes's nemesis. He spoke of a 'decent world order' rather than spheres of influence. Evatt advanced the idea of trusteeship over colonisation, whereas Hughes preferred the latter but accepted the former as a compromise in order to secure New Guinea for Australia. Evatt believed absolutely in the UN's potential, while Hughes had regarded the League of Nations with the disdain of a realist dismissive of 'utopias'. The affirmation in the UN Charter of a 'faith in fundamental human rights, in the dignity and worth of the human person, in the equal rights of men and women' reflected Evatt's idealistic world view rather than that of Billy Hughes. Both highlighted Australia's place on the world stage but Evatt's was by far the more enduring and positive contribution. In the contemporary words of Edward Stettinius, the US Secretary of State, 'Dr Evatt has done more than any other person to write the United Nations Charter'.[7]

The charter's noble ideals presaged the Declaration of Human Rights (UNDHR) in 1948, a statement made while Herbert Evatt was president of the General Assembly and that he helped to draft. The Australian and others on the committee considered a wide range of philosophical traditions from Asia and the Middle East as well as the US and Europe, both secular and religious. It enshrined collective, economic and social rights, according with Evatt's social democratic beliefs. The bedrock of civil rights which opened the declaration affirmed his liberalism. Article 1 declared that 'All human beings are born free and equal in dignity and rights. They are endowed with reason and conscience and should act towards one another in a spirit of brotherhood'. Article 2 posited that the rights and freedoms the declaration presented should apply 'without distinction of any kind, such as race, colour, sex, language, religion, political or other opinion, national or social origin, property, birth or other status'.[8] It was a remarkable statement of absolute equality which owed a great deal to Enlightenment and Christian thought in emphasising the dignity and inherent worth of the individual. Saudi Arabia abstained from ratifying it, as did the Soviet Union and several countries in what would be called the Eastern bloc. There was a philosophical disagreement about civil versus economic rights here but perhaps more importantly a worry that non-binding human rights might, to quote political theorist Micheline Ishay, 'challenge the sanctity of domestic jurisdiction guaranteed by the legally binding UN charter'.[9] They would.

≋

'If Australians have learned one lesson from the Pacific war ...'

The contradictions were immediately apparent, not least in those countries with a heritage deeply rooted in both Enlightenment thought and Christianity. In the US, whose former first lady Eleanor Roosevelt had done so much to advance the declaration, a disingenuous arrangement of 'separate but equal' services and facilities allowed the former slave states to sidestep constitutional guarantees to equality. 'Jim Crow' laws codified the segregation, and the threat or reality of vigilante violence enforced these as much as legal repercussion. Such was the customary race-based oppression that had emerged out of that country's long history of sanctioned slavery. In the 1940s vigilantes lynched some African-American soldiers while they were still in uniform. Civil rights workers, black and white, would be beaten and murdered with impunity into the 1960s.

In Australia the 'principle of White Australia' was still unassailable across the political spectrum. Labor's immigration minister, Arthur Calwell, spoke often and passionately about the need to populate a near-empty land lest another Asian country unleash its 'teeming millions' upon Australia as Japan had tried to do. 'If Australians have learned one lesson from the Pacific war', declared Calwell, '... it is surely that we cannot continue to hold our island continent for ourselves and our descendants unless we greatly increase our numbers'.[10] The 'our' in that statement referred to white Australians, the custodians of 'British civilisation'. This sentiment went back past Billy Hughes to the days of Henry Parkes. In the post-war reconstruction, the government assisted British immigrants financially. Displaced Europeans also arrived but as 'aliens' and in numbers and type as could be assimilated into Anglo-Australia. Whatever constituted Britishness was not transferable at all to non-whites. Black people and Asians, therefore, remained unwelcome in any configuration.

However, just as there were voices against anti-Asian sentiment in earlier decades so, too, in the post-war period did some question the race-based sense of identity. The outspoken Anglican bishop of Goulburn, in rural New South Wales, was one. The Right Reverend Ernest Burgmann put the case for regional over traditional or even biological identity. 'We have to remind ourselves that geographically we are Oriental, we are not European', argued Burgmann. 'We are an island just off the south-east coast of Asia, and are part of the Oriental world ... Surely the important thing is culture-making not colour-making?'[11] It was an incipient call for multiculturalism, before that term was coined, one that accorded entirely with the sentiment of the UNDHR. Indeed, Burgmann was a member of the Australian delegation to the UN in 1948. But in 1940s Australia, that was still a fringe viewpoint.

If some were articulating a rational and humane alternative to race-based identity, what was the basis for continuing to exclude so many others? And, why after a war against an ideology based upon the cruellest expression of racism, was race-based policy allowed to remain? It is perhaps ironic, but hardly surprising, that the recent terrible war with Germany's ally Japan helped to perpetuate Australia's deep-seated fears of Asia and the racism embedded within that. Calwell frequently gave expression to this xenophobia from within government. His outrage at the suggestion that Japanese war brides be allowed to come to Australia is a case in point: 'While relatives remain of men who suffered at the hands of the Japanese, it would be the grossest act of public indecency to permit a Japanese of either sex to pollute Australian shores'.[12] That was 1948. The year before, the immigration minister's widely reported quip, 'two Wongs don't make a white', prompted resentment in Asia. Some in Australia criticised it, but only because it did not help the region understand the reasoning behind White Australia.[13]

For his part, Herbert Evatt tried to explain that reasoning in less offensive terms. He respected the Right Reverend Burgmann and the feeling was mutual, however Evatt could still declare in 1947 – the year before Australia signed the UNDHR – that '"White Australia" was basic to the economy of this country'.[14] His case was about ensuring work for the white working class, of whom he was a defender, rather than racial 'pollution'. Evatt's was essentially the same argument as that mounted by the more moderate labour representatives against importing indentured Pacific Islanders to Queensland's cane fields in the late 1800s. People of colour worked for less money and thereby devalued white labour, leading to inequality for everyone and damaging resentment which helped none but profiteers. In this mindset, black and white labour was incompatible.

That amounted to another version of the case for 'separate but equal'. The difference was that Australia had successfully managed to keep out significant numbers of non-white people and did not face the 'race problems' of the US. Nor was its Indigenous population a majority as in South Africa, where 'separate but equal' was about to be enshrined by apartheid and race laws forbidding intermarriage. Aboriginal Australians worked extensively in the pastoral industry but only for rations, so there was little competition with white people there. Policies of child removal and the biological assimilation of 'mixed race' Aboriginal people would, it was hoped, further ameliorate such 'race problems' as did exist. Evatt, like others on the Labor side of politics, saw the existing immigration policy as the bedrock of a fair social democracy; albeit one for white people.

The Liberal administration which assumed office in 1949 concurred with the apparent incompatibility of 'whites' and 'non-whites'. Calwell's successor as immigration minister, Harold Holt, put Australia's position as innocuously as he could. White Australia was not based upon a theory of 'racial superiority', rather the 'frank and realistic recognition that there were important differences of race, culture and economic standards which make assimilation unlikely'.[15] That denial of superiority came shortly after the United Nations Educational, Scientific and Cultural Organization (UNESCO) issued its Statement on the Nature of Race and Race Difference, which declared that there were 'no scientific grounds whatsoever for the belief that there were pure races or a hierarchy of superior and inferior groups'.[16]

'our position as Europeans is so different'

Both Evatt's and Holt's defence of White Australia rested upon the notion of difference, and therein lay the complex history of European attempts to understand the myriad of peoples they encountered as empires, colonies and markets spread across the globe. The 19th century had seen a remarkable churn of ideas about human origins and relationships. Johann Blumenbach's five types of humanity, which helped John Askew comprehend those he observed in the New South Wales port of Newcastle in the 1850s, was only one of many taxonomies on offer to the literate.

No doubt other personal or vernacular distinctions formed in the minds of men and women who negotiated the amazing array of people now criss-crossing the Pacific. The newly emerging human 'sciences' offered ethnologies and ethnographies. The 'first substantive textbook' of the so-called science of anthropology, Theodor Waitz's *Introduction to Anthropology*, was translated from German into English in 1863.[17] It was contemporary with Charles Darwin's *Origin of Species* and the debates about biological evolution that ensued.

Gradually Herbert Spencer's term 'survival of the fittest' would be applied as a 'natural law' to human interactions, although the notion of the unavoidable displacement of Indigenous people was already widely accepted. Likewise, the suggestion that humankind was not of one origin and biological type was taking hold among scientists. Polygenism was challenging monogenism and displacing Christian belief in a singular humanity under God. It also disrupted the earlier Enlightenment understanding of oneness and, indeed, the injustice of colonisation. A former ethical dilemma was now a matter of regretful inevitability. As early as 1838, one anonymous contributor to the *Phrenological Journal and Magazine of Modern Science* warned against the 'amalgamation' of 'Europeans and Zealanders [Māori]' because, however 'cold and mercenary' it appeared, 'the native race [would] gradually retire before the settlers, and ultimately become extinct'. It was 'the natural course of events'.[18] Clearly the ground had been well prepared for social Darwinism. It was left to Theodor Waitz to present the awful logic of the polygenism he opposed: 'If there be various species of mankind, there must be a natural aristocracy among them ... All wars of extermination, whenever the lower species are in the way of the white man, are not only excusable, but fully justifiable'.[19]

Simple distinctions between Europeans and 'Zealanders', 'Malays', 'Mongoloids' or anyone else implied an existing level of 'racial purity'. That presupposition was complicated, and never resolved, by the matter of hybridity. 'Anglo-Saxon' itself was a term which recognised the amalgamation of two 'races'. British theorists had also to accommodate Celts, who were sometimes characterised as more primitive and child-like than their Saxon usurpers – not unlike the Indigenous peoples being encountered in the Pacific. That they had been absorbed without apparent detriment to the dominant Saxons did little to allay fears of 'mixed-race' unions in the new colonies. Was the self-evident superiority of white people compromised by non-white blood? The answer was increasingly 'yes'. The terms 'degeneration' and 'racial purity' entered the vernacular regardless of the user's knowledge of biology or anthropology. Labor leader John Watson supported deporting cane cutters in the 1900s because of the probability of 'racial contamination'. Often the assumed corruption was biological, sometimes it was cultural. Frequently it was an unexplained mix of both.

The educator and historian James Bonwick, whose transcriptions of colonial records would contribute invaluably to the development of critical history in Australia, wrote in 1870 of the demise of Tasmanian Indigenous people at European hands. For Bonwick the problem of difference was not so much biological as cultural: 'Physically we have relations with them ... but mentally and morally our position as Europeans is so different and our means of studying them so slight, that we are unable to comprehend our identity with them'. It was that 'unbridgeable cultural gap', to use historian George Stocking's words, which modern anthropology attempted to close with its receptiveness to cultural relativity.[20]

It would be a long time before notions of racial decline and extinction fell away in discourse about Aboriginal people. Lecturing in Paris in 1931, the anthropologist Herbert Basedow predicted, with a declaration of shame, that Aboriginal people would become extinct within 12 years. He believed that, having developed in isolation after the Lemurian land bridge to the rest of the world had collapsed, these people could not co-exist with modernity. Basedow was not referring to those of mixed ancestry or the Aboriginal people who lived in or around Australia's many towns and cities and were attempting to adapt to the new discriminatory ways, but those whose way of life was in its 'pristine and uncontaminated condition', as if purity of race was something both cultural and biological. Like other professional and amateur anthropologists, Basedow took it upon himself to document what he could of a people and/or their culture before either or both vanished.[21]

≈

'the fact of fixed propriety rights in the soil'

Despite the generalised notions of white superiority, European perceptions of Melanesian people in the late 19th century differed from their attitudes towards Australian Aboriginal people. What emerged was less a narrative of impending doom than one of responsible tutelage and transition. Among the first distinctions made was between the sedentarism of the former and the apparent nomadism of the latter. Where Indigenous Australians lacked obvious ownership of territory by virtue of their mobility, people in New Guinea had gardens and fixed settlement and habitations. In 1883 Edmond Marin La Meslée, secretary of the new Geographic Society of Australasia, hoped the Anglo-Saxon tendency to rapaciousness might be moderated by recognising this distinction and, most significantly, by the rights of a common humanity, as it had not in Australia.[22]

Nonetheless, with the acquisition of New Guinea, other Australians were keen to fulfil the 'genius' of their kind and, in the process, disprove the axiom that tropical lands were the preserve of 'dark races'. That was the belief that had emerged in professional and popular thought after the apparent physical, mental and moral deterioration of those Europeans who had taken up residence on islands from the British West Indies to the Dutch East Indies and the various lands of the Pacific. A wary British administration, however, made protecting Indigenous land rights a priority. Mindful of what had occurred in Australia, William MacGregor, the administrator and later lieutenant-governor from 1888, introduced several ordinances to prevent dispossession through sale and dislocation by displacement. Remarkably MacGregor recognised that the customary practice of shifting villages, as new gardens were created, maintained the connection to place. People did not relinquish their ownership of previous sites. 'All these mutations', wrote MacGregor, '… only tend to confirm the fact of fixed propriety rights in the soil'.[23]

Having lobbied so loudly to annex New Guinea, Australia moved slowly to formalise Britain's offer of the territory on establishing the Commonwealth in 1901. The *Papua Act* was passed in 1905 and proclaimed the following year. British New Guinea thereby became an Australian colony. The name 'Papua' was applied to distinguish it from German New Guinea on the north side of the mainland and in New Britain. The long reign of the first Australian lieutenant-governor, (Sir) Hubert Murray, began in 1908 though he had resided in Port Moresby since 1904. He took control of a territory which white people had only partially explored and barely understood. His first thoughts were to encourage European settlement. To a royal commission convened in 1906 to investigate future Australian policy in the colony he remarked upon the 'scantiness of white settlement'. There was 'none except by missionaries'.[24] Murray thought there should be more. He had already described the British territory as 'the most unprogressive place you can possibly imagine', in a letter to his half-sister Evelyn. The administration had 'done all they could in a covert way to discourage immigration and have done their best to keep the island as a field for exploration and ethnological study'.[25] British New Guinea was, it seems, a moribund living museum.

That was hardly accurate. Gold mining at Mambare, for example, had proceeded such that the death rate among carriers was 21 per cent in 1903–04.[26] Nonetheless, those who planned the transition to full Australian rule mirrored Murray's views. New ordinances replaced those MacGregor brought in. The land laws were 'probably the most liberal in the tropics' wrote the new director of mines, agriculture and works, Miles Staniforth Smith, with satisfaction. As a Western Australian senator, Smith had been unusually interested in Australia's prospects in New Guinea and drafted one of three reports on its development. Despite his enthusiasm he was passed over as lieutenant-governor in favour of Murray, and as his deputy became a rival.

The schism widened around the issue of settlement and probably attitudes to colour. Smith had been, to quote historian Russel Ward, 'perhaps the most racist member of either House' during the immigration policy debates at Federation. He believed in the separateness of humankind, perhaps even their division into different species. Intermarriage, he warned, produced infertility.[27] While Smith and Murray shared a paternal concern for 'native' welfare, the attitudes of the latter moved increasingly towards a belief in 'the unity of mankind'. 'The idea that a black or brown man is not really a man like ourselves', he would declare, 'is probably responsible for many of the worst outrages which have been committed'. Equally egregious was the related notion that the 'native' was a child.[28] That fallacy undermined cross-cultural understanding and thereby impeded the administration of effective policy and justice, for how was a 'child' to be tried for murder or other crimes? Murray's optimistic anticipation of white settlement, which encouraged plantations on which local people would be employed, gave way to a dual policy which no longer viewed 'natives' as simply the 'hewers of wood and drawers of water for European settlers'. Rather the aim was to create 'a form of civilisation which may appeal to him [the Papuan] more readily'. The local tradition of cultivation could be developed to create market-based 'native plantations' which would operate in tandem with subsistence gardening.[29] With the League of Nations' establishment and the articulation of its liberal ideals on the condition of colonies and mandates, Murray readily declared a watershed moment in colonial administration. Local people could no longer be regarded as 'assets', he wrote in 1925. Neither was a colony to be viewed as a 'business proposition'. Rather it would give primacy to the 'well-being' of Indigenous peoples. They were to be afforded dignity.

Local white people became uneasy with developments in Papua as early as 1911. It was all rather too 'soft-hearted'. 'White pioneers' were not being encouraged enough, was the complaint aired in the local settler mouthpiece the *Papuan Times*. In 1920 the White Citizens Association of Port Moresby met to call for Staniforth Smith to replace Murray. The lieutenant-governor and his administration had 'lost the confidence of the white residents through its hostility to progress, [and] its contempt of the white race'.[30]

≋

'stinking wild man'

Murray was not removed. But neither did Billy Hughes fully endorse his approach. When Australia gained control of German New Guinea in 1919, another royal commission was convened, this one to decide upon the future of the new acquisition, much as happened with Papua. A major question was whether to amalgamate the administrations. Murray headed the enquiry but the two other commissioners overruled his recommendation for unification. They were Atlee Hunt, the secretary to the Department of Home and Territories; and Walter Lucas, islands manager for Burns Philp. Hughes probably knew the preference of these two men for separation prior to appointing them, for he wanted his hard-won war prize to pay for itself in the way that Papua did not. Mandate or not, there would be no soft-heartedness. Civilian rule began in the Australian territory in 1921, after the passage of the *New Guinea Act* in 1920.

Australia appropriated German lands and sold them as freehold to its own settlers. Only the administration was allowed to acquire real estate from local people, following certification from a district officer that the sale was consensual. However, when 'the wider interests of the Territory' demanded it, that approval was set aside.[31] Australia envied the German system, which had created an ordered and profitable colonial economy, and compared it favourably to Papua. Rabaul, on the land of the Tolai people, was a beautiful, well-planned town where Port Moresby was not. However, Germany had often violently enforced the labour relations which created and maintained that physical order. The new regime ameliorated some of this, gradually eliminating flogging, which had been commonplace under the Germans. It steadily increased health spending, surpassing that in Papua.

Nonetheless, it was widely felt that Australian New Guinea was a harsher place for 'natives' than Papua. Certainly, 3000 local people in Rabaul felt aggrieved enough to go on strike in January 1929. It was the first industrial action of its kind in either territory and white people might have viewed it as an interesting adaptation to modern employment methods on the part of the people they were trying to 'civilise'. They did not. Rather, in that moment of unrest, whites openly expressed fear of retribution from disorderly 'kanakas' – an indication itself of existing distrust and unease within the community. Two of the leaders each received three-year gaol sentences. In an ironic re-enactment of Australian colonial history, they and their followers were locked up on a prison hulk anchored in Rabaul's harbour.[32]

Neither did the Australians welcome the presence of Chinese

people, whom the Germans had tolerated as part of their emphasis on economic efficiency. Asians had been excluded from Papua in a curious application of 'White Australia' to a land of black people. But the resident Chinese of the mandated territory were allowed to stay. Rabaul even had its own 'Chinatown', where Australian personnel would go to be fitted out with tailored tropical dress. Sarah Chinnery, whose husband was the territory's anthropologist, described a place of 'fine shops presided over by dignified and courteous Chinese, and dark stores crammed with silks and carvings and Eastern curios'. The customers were the Chinese themselves, for this was a well-established, self-contained community: 'Pretty Chinese girls flit about in silk coats, with collars buttoned up modestly to their ears, and long blue trousers of silk'.[33]

What developed was a basic three-tiered racial hierarchy comprising New Guinean, Asian and European people in that order of ascension. Each had their place and rarely did they cross boundaries. The common language was 'pidgin', a derivation of English that pre-dated the German arrival and which the Germans and their successors adopted.

Chinese people were not expelled but neither were their families allowed to join them from China. It was a method of containment for the race-conscious Australians and a matter of distress to the Chinese. The Australians applied racial epithets such as 'nigger' and 'coon' to the New Guineans, having borrowed these from the US, where they were corruptions of 'Negro' and 'raccoon'. White people of all classes spoke these words in both Papua and New Guinea though not, perhaps, in polite company. 'Kanaka' was widely used, as it had been on the Queensland cane fields, with a degree of deprecation. All local men were 'boys'. The everyday rituals of racial supremacy were particularly pronounced in New Guinea where 'masta' was the common form of address for a white man, 'Misus' for a white woman. Blacks were required to stand up when spoken to. Facilities were racially segregated as they were in the American south. Judy Tudor, who worked in Rabaul and on the mainland, described life in pre-war New Guinea as conforming to a form of 'natural apartheid' where the two peoples met 'at such points as were mutually advantageous – but where we called the tune'.[34] That 'tune' involved strictly mediated interaction to preserve the outward expression of white supremacy, and transgressions could result in the sanction of both 'races'. White people widely understood that to invite familiarity from black people was to open the door to contempt.

New Guineans expressed disrespect, if not contempt, less openly. The anthropologist H Ian Hogbin, who conducted research at Busama near the large town of Lae in the 1940s, became aware that local people applied the name 'bumbum' surreptitiously to whites – himself included. Its literal meaning, 'stinking wild man', was not too distant from the European notion of 'primitive'.[35]

≈

'... He knew us in all our ways ...'

In Papua, Hubert Murray made a point of visiting districts and meeting those he governed, and those with whom he governed, as often as possible. He was for many years the only European law officer in the territory and was, therefore, judge and jury in criminal cases heard in Port Moresby and elsewhere. Murray's endurance in the heat, humidity and difficult terrain is all the more astonishing, for the lieutenant-governor was a large man and already 47 years old when he assumed his office. But then he also found time to write numerous books and papers on the subject of colonial administration. That his wife Sybil had departed shortly after arriving with their children freed Murray from familial duties and gave him time to read and compose. His prose demanded the reader's attention in the manner of much late-19th-century long-form discourse – the era during which he was educated. But it also had wit, self-deprecation and some irreverence. Throughout there was the twisting and turning of a mind that was trying to reconcile a sincere belief in basic equality with the dilemma of governing people whose ways were so different. Murray wrote and spoke of the 'superior race', 'inferior races', 'savage races' and 'primitive races' as if such judgments were clearly quantitative and not qualitative. These people were not distinct species yet there were inherent differences. 'I believe that the best Papuans are superior to the worst Europeans', he observed after 30 years in the job, 'but that Europeans as a whole have an innate superiority over Papuans'.[36] It was as if he imagined a Venn diagram in which the intersecting categories of people were defined by both biology and culture, which worked itself out in individuals to differing degrees. The intersection evinced a common humanity, while the outer rings were evidence of irreconcilable difference.

Murray's declared role was to create a 'civilisation' that would appeal to Papuans. In fact, much of his concern was directed at Papuan men, in part because of the patriarchal preoccupations of his own cultural milieu, but also because so much local male energy was expended in ritual and violence. He recognised that killing, head-taking and cannibalism were an integral part of life for many but he could not, as the representative of a 'civilised nation', allow that to continue. Pacification, which entailed patrolling, law enforcement, communication and education, was thereby one of his most difficult duties. He also understood that killing brought with it purpose, excitement and reward. Once quashed, something meaningful needed to fill that cultural void. It was perhaps a concession to the anthropological functionalism that Murray, as an administrator, disliked. Functionalists believed that in 'primitive' societies all custom was integrated and integral. The destruction of one part threatened the whole. Murray's civilising mission, as he understood it, was to end objectionable practices such as cannibalism. If a replacement could be found, that was well and good; if not, so be it.

Murray also recognised that creating a native proletariat would not do. Paid employment or commercial planting were, in themselves, no substitute for the life that went before. In Papua there was no sanctioned forced labour. Awarding prizes for gardening was one compensation or inducement. Competitive sport was another. Murray favoured Rugby and was keen to introduce it with the help of the missions. He noted its promise in 1929 with a characteristic drollness which barely hid the magnitude of his challenge: 'Football ... must at best seem but a milk and water substitute for a head-hunting raid, and could not go far to satisfy the Papuan's craving for bloodshed. Still it is the best we can do, and, when the old traditions of blazing villages and bleeding heads have at last died out, it is quite likely that the young men will lose the lust for murder which is so curious a feature to-day ...'[37] That the introduction of a recently invented English game was the 'best' that could be done to replace a well-established cultural practice on the other side of the world is perhaps some indication of Murray's dilemma as harbinger of change. Nonetheless, football, in the League variation of the Rugby code, would take hold as a national game in later decades.

Hubert Murray died in office in 1940. By then his approach of cautious paternalism was widely respected, within Papua and more broadly in the empire. He had supporters among the local people too. The interpreter-turned-leader, Ahuia Ova, was one of Murray's closest Papuan allies and spoke with eloquence and conviction at the lieutenant-governor's memorial mass:

> Governor Murray is dead. He worked until he died ... He treated us always as friends. His way towards us was the way of a friend ... The ways of his people were not our ways. But he understood us and made our lives happy ... He came among us and saw our lives ... He knew us in all our ways ... There has been only one Governor in our time. He was the best of men; our children and their children will talk of him.[38]

Writing from the self-critical perspective of late 1960s Australia, then in the throes of considering decolonisation, the journalist Peter Hastings had a less generous assessment, and one which suggested a degree of mutual dependency between the administrator and his wards: 'For the exercise of his talents, Murray needed the brown and primitive man, for whom he felt genuine, if remote, sympathy, but of whose social psychology he was never certain'.[39]

CHAPTER 14

Learning from the Pacific

*'Government snips now and then at a leaf
or two and does nothing to the roots'*

Hubert Murray's uncertainty about the thoughts and behaviour of those he administered was not for want of scholarly enquiry. The lieutenant-governor availed himself of the latest anthropological thinking about 'primitive society'. It was a period of great change in that profession, and both Papua and New Guinea were still social laboratories to where anthropologists travelled to see societies as yet unaffected by contact with modernity. As Bronislaw Malinowski, one of the founders of the new British anthropology, put it in 1922: 'The hope of gaining a new vision of savage humanity through the labours of scientific specialists opens out like a mirage, vanishing almost as soon as perceived'. Malinowski anticipated the disappearance of such cultures in 'a generation or two'.[1] It was a cultural, rather than biological, extinction; something that distinguished Pacific predictions from those made about Australia. Paradoxically it was Murray's job to facilitate that disappearance, albeit by easing rather than forcing 'savage humanity' into the modern era. Therein lay his problem with the anthropologists. But if the administrator could use their insights to better bring about change, he would.

Just as it had been a staging post for missionaries, Australia became a convenient operational centre for those who wanted to study humanity. When Nikolai Miklouho-Maclay arrived in Sydney in 1878 he was feted by the city's scientific elite. The Russian had been living on the north-east coast of New Guinea since 1871, carrying out the first extended field work in the territory. The local people wondered if he was the creator spirit Kilibob.[2] In Sydney Miklouho-Maclay would marry, advocate for the rights of the Islanders he had come to know, and lobby against German annexation of their land. The British anthropologist AC Haddon used Thursday Island as a base in 1888 and 1898 to study Murray Island (Mer) and other Torres Strait communities. As a result, the Australian press reported on his activities and some of his findings. The later Cambridge Expedition, which also visited Borneo and Sarawak, was subsequently called a 'landmark in the history of anthropology', being 'the first time a group of highly trained scientists set out to make a full and careful study of the social, economic and religious life of a native people'.[3]

The Polish-born, London-based Malinowski travelled to Australia for the extended Congress of the British Association for the Advancement of Science in 1914 – in partnership with the Australasian Association for the Advancement of Science (AAAS), founded in 1888 – and stayed for the duration of the war, which broke out during the congress. Like Miklouho-Maclay, he mingled enough in local society to meet and marry an Australian woman, in Malinowski's case the ethnological journalist and photographer Elsie Masson, whose father Professor Orme Masson had initiated the congress. During this time he conducted the research that would form the basis of *Argonauts of the Western Pacific*, an exploration of the trading culture in the islands off the south-eastern tip of the New Guinea mainland, including Dobu Island, where Jane Tinney had stayed and taught in the early 1890s. Published in 1922, it is widely regarded as a pioneering work for the extended field observation it undertook and the complexity of the social structures it described and analysed. By then Malinowski was back in England teaching anthropology. There he would influence some of the new generation of Australian anthropologists, including WEH Stanner.

The congress which brought Malinowski to Australia catalysed the development of academic anthropology in the country and the extension of research relationships across the Pacific to the US. There followed the establishment of the Australian National Research Council

(ANRC) in 1919, and Sydney and Melbourne hosting the Pan-Pacific Science Congress in 1923. The first had been held in Hawaii in 1920 and was dominated by American contributors. The Australian-based congress was altogether more 'Pan-Pacific' and helped form a sense of the region, not least for Australians. It was a most significant and prestigious undertaking for Australia's scientific community, who made up 320 of the 400 delegates.[4] It also forms an example of how cultural cooperation can run as a cross-current in a time of fear and suspicion. Just after Billy Hughes obstructed Japan's calls for racial equality at the League of Nations, that country was participating in an Australian-run forum with its largest ever overseas scientific contingent. Attendees discussed botany, chemistry and geology, with Alfred Wegener's theory of continental drift creating great interest. The AAAS had recognised the discipline of anthropology since its inception. Unsurprisingly, then, it had its own section in the 1923 congress. This in turn assisted the AAAS arguing for a Chair of Anthropology at an Australian university. The congress subsequently resolved that anthropological research in the western Pacific was needed 'urgently' because of 'the loss of most valuable scientific material', the need to fulfil responsibilities under the New Guinea mandate and better assist 'native races' to adapt to the new economies. The collective also pressed the need to research Aboriginal people as 'one of the lowest types of culture available for study', before they and their 'primitive beliefs and customs' disappeared altogether.[5] A Chair was established at the University of Sydney in 1925, with somewhat reluctant support from the Australian government, and more enthusiastic assistance from the Rockefeller Foundation in the US. It was filled by the distinguished British anthropologist Alfred Radcliffe-Brown.

The intention had been to train district officers and make anthropology 'a study having immediate and important bearings on the administration of native peoples' to quote Radcliffe-Brown, and this did happen in time.[6] Kenneth Thomas was one of those who read the latest theory and attempted to apply it to his day-to-day work as a patrol and district officer. He had arrived as a cadet in Rabaul in 1927 and went straight to the Burns Philp store to buy a pith helmet, and Chong Hing the tailor for his requisite tropical whites. Clearly interested in the people among whom he found himself, sometimes as the only 'white man', Thomas started writing up his observations and collecting. In 1929 he completed a diploma in anthropology and came second in the year. He learned that culture is always changing and to read critically the observations of the traders and missionaries who preceded him, for they were 'unskilled' and their interests lay 'elsewhere'.[7] In other words, Thomas and his classmates were being taught to set subjective prejudice aside for objective analysis free from value judgment. After graduating, Thomas drafted a paper titled 'The Fisherfolk of Vanimo' and submitted it to Radcliffe-Brown for comments. It was subsequently published in the journal *Oceania* in 1941 as 'Notes on the natives of the Vanimo Coast, New Guinea'.

Radcliffe-Brown established *Oceania* at the University of Sydney in 1930. Its title used the term coming into vogue to describe the south Pacific as a place of many islands in a vast sea. The journal's stated purpose placed Australia squarely within this region; it was 'devoted to the study of the native peoples of Australia, New Guinea and the islands of the Pacific'. *Oceania* became one of the most successful publications of its kind. The first editorial emphasised applied anthropology: 'Now the administrator and educator amongst native peoples are engaged in modifying a culture. Only when we have a fair understanding of how the culture works as a functioning system can we know how to set about producing any particular modification that may be desired or avoid bringing harm to the people themselves by our interference'.[8] That stated, most of the contributors on Pacific matters were university-educated anthropologists. They included Raymond Firth and H Ian Hogbin. Kenneth Thomas was the exception as a writer with administrative experience in the field. There were a remarkable number of women writing up their Pacific and Australian fieldwork. In rejecting prevailing views about female fragility and dependence, Camilla Wedgwood,

Beatrice Blackwood and Ursula McConnel, among others, travelled down the metaphorical trail blazed by the likes of Jane Tinney.

Hubert Murray was open to anthropological research, provided he could control what was changed and what remained the same. His own appointed 'government anthropologist', South Australian–born FE Williams, was one of the journal's more frequent contributors. By the 1930s he shared Murray's suspicion of functionalism's emphasis on cultural integrity. Culture was, he thought, a 'sorry tangle' and working to identify and end some of its more damaging aspects was part of the colonial administration's work.[9] That had not always been the case. In 1923, a year after his appointment as assistant government anthropologist, Williams completed a book on an extraordinary cultural condition he named 'Vailala Madness', after the village in which he had witnessed the behaviour. Miklouho-Maclay may have encountered an earlier manifestation in the 1870s, but Williams' work was the first extended description of the phenomenon which would become widely known as 'cargo cult', the belief that goods would arrive from elsewhere by ship, or later aeroplane, in response to observing particular practices, often revolving around European artefacts such as flags and uniforms. At Vailala, around where there had been much recent testing for oil, a group of local people came to reject traditional rites and objects in anticipation of a vessel arriving from 'heaven' with returned ancestors – white men – bearing amazing things. The belief was accompanied by a form of mania. Williams interpreted it as evidence of cultural breakdown caused by the supplanting of tradition; in this case Christian doctrine had disrupted magical practices. It was also, most directly, a dramatic response to the sudden encounter with and delivery of 'cargo' – the panoply of Western industrial manufacture – by a people who derived their material culture solely from the flora, fauna and rocks around them. Williams' description of Vailala Madness, and later discussions of other cargo cults such as 'John Frum' in the New Hebrides (Vanuatu), would be discussed for decades thereafter.

The arc of these writings revealed as much about the state of anthropological thought in the West as it did about the practices themselves. Cargo cults were variously interpreted as symptoms of collapse, evidence of childishness, manifestation of the trauma of war, rational responses to European interference, and figments of the colonial imagination. The work of another Australian, Peter Lawrence's *Road Belong Cargo* (1964), became a classic study on the subject. Writing in *Oceania* in 2000, Doug Dalton wondered whether cargo cults were 'a parodic enactment of particularly absurd aspects of Western colonial bourgeois culture and the image of unlimited goods it projects'.[10] That assessment may have accurately captured the nature of the fantasy of endless economic exploitation but it negated the seriousness with which Islanders carried out their cargo rites.

The New Zealand–born anthropologist Reo Fortune was another who wrote often for the newly founded *Oceania*. With the financial assistance of the ANRC, he had travelled to Dobu and nearby Tarawa in Malinowski's wake, researching practices that would inform his book *Sorcerers of Dobu*, published in 1932. As the islands were part of Hubert Murray's colony of Papua, he had to seek permission from the administration in Port Moresby. Having received that in late 1927 or early 1928, it was soon apparent that researcher and administrator did not agree on the role of anthropology. Furthermore, Fortune's project highlighted the ethical dilemmas confronting modern anthropology, whose practitioners changed, by virtue of their presence and documentation, the very practices they had wanted to observe and, in many cases, preserve.

While colonial law tolerated 'garden magic' – ritual used to improve food procurement – it forbad punitive incantations and rites. Fortune's work revealed that people on and around Dobu still practised such 'black magic' extensively and he was concerned that his research might lead to its suppression. 'I will not act as a spy', he wrote to Murray in April 1928, '... my sympathy is with the native, sorcery, burial rites, and all ... Government snips now and then at a leaf or two and does nothing to the roots – and the growth is strong and resistant ...'[11]

Punishing such activities only led to further secrecy, which was bad for the indigenous people and certainly frustrating for the scientist.

The correspondence between Fortune and Murray reveals the conflicting interests colonial administration and anthropological enquiry stirred up, and is no less fascinating for the evidence it entailed of cultural retention despite the government's recent efforts and 40 years of work by missionaries such as Jane Tinney. Before he returned to Sydney in late May 1928, Fortune suggested that the locals should actually rise up against the administration. Confronted by that information and the anthropologist's earlier letter, Hubert Murray decided the New Zealander was himself 'a little mad'. He shared that insight with Radcliffe-Brown in July 1928. For his part, the professor conceded he thought the people of Tarawa would soon be 'extinct' for, in the absence of discernible art or religion, the 'whole of their social system seems to rest upon the basis of sorcery and magic'.[12] To end that, as the administration and the missions were trying to do, was to end a way of life. It was, as historian Geoffrey Gray suggests, a confession that anthropology was powerless to 'alter that fact'.[13] The whole affair threw into question the purpose of anthropology beyond documenting the doomed.

The discipline's application to the needs of European administrators did not end, however. World War Two brought with it a new set of challenges as thousands of young Australian and American men arrived in Papua and New Guinea and the need to understand local people became a strategic imperative. An organisation called the Allied Geographic Section (AGS), South West Pacific Area was created to compile information relating to the landscape and its people. Four volumes of bibliography and maps were printed covering the region from China and the Philippines to the East Indies. Volume Two, published in 1944, dealt with New Guinea, Papua, the Solomons, New Hebrides and Micronesia. It cited nearly 1000 works on anthropology, zoology, botany and geology for New Guinea, Papua and New Britain alone.

FE Williams' studies were among those. He had died the previous year in a plane crash in the Owen Stanley Range. His last work was a set of 100 tips for troops stationed in Papua and New Guinea, published by the AGS in 1943. *You and the Native* was both respectful and patronising, supportive of equality and yet qualified in its egalitarianism. In short, it reflected the often-contradictory mindset of Murray and his anthropologist. Point 6 suggested that 'The native is nearly, if not quite, as good a man as you. Don't underrate his intelligence'. Point 8 contradicted a fundamental premise repeated from the time of the first missions: 'Don't believe it when you are told he has the mentality of a child. That is rubbish. An adult native is an adult'.

His book advised soldiers to respect local ways, to observe from a distance, not to interfere with ceremonies or souvenir objects. It emphasised the significance of pigs, and of village women. Liaisons were, therefore, best avoided. There was the emphatic declaration that non-consensual sex was 'rape', whomever the victim.

The booklet concluded with observations on the accepted superiority of the 'whiteman's' ways. The 'native' was in awe of 'Europeans', was the advice, and that could be used to the soldier's advantage. But with superiority came responsibility both to the local people, who the book acknowledged had not caused the war being fought in their land, and to one's peers: 'Your conduct can raise or lower the general standard. You are therefore a guardian of the white man's prestige'.[14]

≋

'journeys from which there was no return'

The seventh point listed in *You and the Native* was one of the few to unambiguously describe the quality of the local men: 'In New Guinea bushcraft, in hardihood, in mobility, he [the native] leaves you [the European] standing'. Such was the chasm of difference between black and white people – the 'unbridgeable gap' – that even the modern anthropologists rarely spoke of lessons Europeans could learn in anything other than a detached scientific or museological way. That 'they' were 'us' at a different time and place was probably implied by the terms 'savage' and 'primitive', but the connection was so tenuous as to be almost irrelevant. Jim Taylor had come close to making the link without resorting to disparaging adjectives when he wrote to his mother of the wonders of his work as a district officer in New Guinea in the early 1930s: 'It is the human race at its very beginning as it were'.[15]

Taylor's senior officer was EWP Chinnery, the territory's first anthropologist when appointed in 1924 and director of district services and native affairs from 1932. Both men were keen to make contact with people in the 'highlands', the hitherto 'unexplored' mountains which dominated the territory of New Guinea on the mainland. Both maintained their belief in the role of anthropology despite their counterparts' travails in the adjacent colony of Papua. In fact, anthropology was embedded within the New Guinea administration more thoroughly than in Papua. From 1926 patrol officer cadets needed to have university entry qualifications, be single and be aged between 20 and 24. The study which Kenneth Thomas undertook at the University of Sydney was mandatory for his promotion to patrol officer. Competition was nonetheless keen in the Depression of the early 1930s. Only 10 of the 1659 who applied for positions under Chinnery in late 1932 were selected.[16]

Jim Taylor was present at many 'first contacts' in the highlands, those momentous events when a people whose world rarely extended beyond the neighbouring valley were confronted by pale strangers wearing clothes and who were followed by a long line of brown-skinned helpers looking familiar but carrying unimagined things – cameras, shovels, axes, guns. As the historian Bill Gammage has written: 'All these were journeys from which there was no return'.[17] His insights into the nature of this last phase of exploration in New Guinea are best recounted in his own words:

> Explorers intend to discover, move in time and space to do it, and travel permanently expectant. Discovery is first geographical, then intellectual, then belatedly cosmological ... [New Guinean] police and carriers, with no notion of maps, were more vague about where they were, but more familiar with what they saw ... For the people met, discovery was first cosmological.[18]

That cosmological encounter was captured on film for the first time when the Queensland-born gold prospector Mick Leahy and his party travelled into the highlands in 1930. A rush had begun in 1926 following discoveries in the Bulolo Valley in 1922, such that gold came to rival the economic dominance of copra produced from coconut plantations the Germans had established; in the mid-1930s copra was around half of total exports and gold more than one-third.[19] By 1930 smaller holdings had been worked out and the tough and uncompromising Leahy went off in search of new streams in places his competitors had never seen. The villagers whom they met thought the Australians and their porters were variously returned ancestors, people from the sky, or lightning in human form. For many they were spirits. Their response to these first encounters was wide-eyed amazement. If the party passed a second time through a village, the reception was more likely hostile as fear gave way to a sense of territoriality and a desire to kill the strangers and claim their goods. Mick Leahy and his group shot people, including several when a group charged the expedition at the village of Tari, across the border in Papua. Many years later Mick's younger brother Dan, who was also there, justified the killing on the basis of self-defence. Had he and his brother been killed, the many carriers with them would have been massacred.[20] He was almost certainly correct. Violence may not have been inevitable when Europeans passed uninvited through communities who had never seen their like before, but it was highly likely. The Leahys obviously thought the risk to human life, their own and others', worth taking when gold was the prize. Mick, Dan and a third sibling, James, became legendary in this end chapter of European exploration.

Jim Taylor thought it best that first contact come with an official patrol. Whether or not he knew of the toll the 1930 expedition had taken, he invited the redoubtable Mick Leahy to join him in 1933 to 'open' the country from Bena Bena to Mount Hagen. They reconnoitred the area by plane first and so became known as 'sky people' to those they subsequently encountered. Taylor described the 'great emotion' with which they were received as ancestors or spirits. As with the Leahys, this turned to hostility upon their return march. The landscape they walked through was highly cultivated. The 'Bena Bena people' had built villages of up to 100 circular houses and planted 'excellent' gardens of corn, sugar, cucumbers and sweet potato that resembled a 'patchwork quilt'. The Wahgi people lived in oblong-shaped farmhouses surrounded by '"Chessboard" gardens', while around Mount Hagen there were 'beautiful park-like enclosures, planted with ornamental trees and shrubs'.

Many of the highlanders Taylor saw were handsome and healthy. At Mount Hagen the stone axes were finished with a 'high degree of art and skill'. Steel was not known there but neither did the tools carried by the Australians immediately impress: 'I had the greatest difficulty to induce natives to accept tomahawks and steel knives in payment for food'.[21] It sounds like a civilisation, although a very different one.

In 1938 Taylor led the longest ever patrol undertaken in New Guinea, lasting 15 months and travelling 3000 kilometres from Mount Hagen to the headwaters of the Sepik River near the border of Dutch New Guinea and back. After that epic trek, and in spite of all he had seen before, Taylor began imagining social transformation – specifically the introduction of British civilisation – with commercial agriculture which both 'the native' and 'the European' would carry out. A government or cooperative bacon works could repay the former's 'speciality' at raising pigs. 'The savage charm and fascination of pristine New Guinea is not for later generations', he wrote in the annual report. 'This is something to be sorry for, but I believe the advantages to be gained by extending Pax Britannica to these regions will more than make up for that regrettable and irreparable loss.'[22] On other occasions he called it 'Pax Australiana'. They were indeed 'journeys from which there was no return'.

≋

'something quite different, something utterly modern'

Margaret Mead journeyed to Manus Island in the Admiralty group in 1928–1929 with her new husband and anthropological collaborator Reo Fortune. They went via Rabaul and met with the Chinnerys, with whom they would socialise on future visits. Mead and Fortune had first encountered each other as he was preparing for his time on Dobu. They worked together most famously on a study of the Arapesh people on the New Guinea mainland in 1932. The Admiralty Islands to the northwest of that mainland were part of the Australian mandated territory. The Manus project was Mead's alone. She was an American and had studied under Franz Boas. Her approach to culture was thereby vastly different from that of the British-trained researchers. It took as its basis the primary significance of culture over biology and emphasised the significance of psychology. In *The Mind of Primitive Man*, published in 1911, Boas had rejected the relationship between culture and race and, though using the term 'primitive' to distinguish some cultures from the complexity of European societies, also questioned the notion of superior and inferior peoples.

Mead's work was groundbreaking. Her *Coming of Age in Samoa*, first published in 1928, was distinct from other Pacific anthropologies and certainly the plethora of ethnological travel tales in its relativism. In placing culture at the centre of human development it questioned the universality of human values but also held out the possibility of learning from 'primitive' peoples. The Adelaide-based *Observer* newspaper, which reviewed *Coming of Age in Samoa* alongside SGC Knibbs' *The Savage Solomons*, described the work as 'something quite different, something utterly modern'.[23]

The result of Mead's Manus research, *Growing Up in New Guinea*, was similarly 'utterly modern' both in approach and style. It was a beautifully written work in a way many other 'objective' studies were not, free from the moralising or superior sneers of popular writing. The anthropologist chose a small island, Pere, off the southern coast of Manus. It was, she thought, a 'relatively untouched' place but one whose people had some sense of the outside world. 'To the Manus native the world is a great platter, curving upwards on all sides, from his flat lagoon village where the pile houses stand like long-legged birds, placid and unstirred by the changing tides … [Beyond] lies Rabaul the capital of the white man's government of the territory of New Guinea, and far up the outer rim of the world lies Sydney, the farthest point of their knowledge'.[24] Mead spent six months there observing and sharing the local life. The point was to study child rearing, not present an overview of an entire culture. The language was literary and evocative. 'The Manus baby is accustomed to water from the first years of his life. Lying on the slatted floor he watches the sunlight gleam on the surface of the lagoon as the changing tide passes and repasses beneath the house.'[25] The children were brought up in a secure world with few expectations and almost complete freedom. Fathers, not mothers, were the major caregivers. There was so little demand upon the young that they grew up with little respect for tradition, art or even their elders. Yet, upon adulthood, the need to survive and procure closed in and conformity to the culture was the result. Mead came to the conclusion, disturbing no doubt to some, that social change could not be brought about by educating children without also altering adult behaviour. People absorbed their world. Culture, even more than formal education, was all important. Studying 'primitive' societies, that is those that were 'homogenous and simple', made clear this process. But those findings were applicable to more complex cultures, for they showed that human behaviour was due 'not to original nature but to social environment'.[26] It was a universal truth that, paradoxically, challenged universalism. Margaret Mead became the most famous anthropologist of the

20th century, due in large part to the relevance Western cultures so different from those that she studied accorded to her work.

≋

'How brain-tired city men envy their care-free existence ...'

Those who worked in New Guinea or Papua before the Pacific War probably numbered in the low thousands. They were administrators and their families, anthropologists, missionaries, medics, miners, planters, traders, soldiers and sailors. Doris Booth was a nurse who accompanied her husband to the Bulolo goldfield in 1924 and found herself tending injured and sick carriers 'going to and from the field'. She wrote up her experiences in a book titled *Mountains, Gold and Cannibals*, in which she admitted to a fascination with the people she encountered; the 'quiet study of natives often helped to pass a weary day'.[27] Others returned to Australia to share their experiences with friends and families in stories both written and spoken. Walter Calov recounted his time doctoring in New Guinea, Papua and the Solomons during the 1920s in an unpublished memoir circulated among his family. Some of it sounded like a holiday, some of it was hard work. Much was remarkable. In the mandated territory, Dr Calov, as the resident medical officer, was required to attend the whipping of a convicted local man and was appalled by the practice: 'The prisoner stood facing a post with his hands fastened to it, and a native sergeant of police flogged him with a harness strap ... Those who say that such and such a villain should be flogged should see a flogging'.[28]

White Australians thereby came to understand the Pacific in many ways in the half century or so before World War Two. Several of the families involved in transporting and employing South Sea Islanders acquired collections of artefacts, bought or received as gifts. They subsequently sold or donated a considerable number of these to the Queensland Museum, not long after it moved to a purpose-built structure in 1879. The institution itself was established in 1862. The Reverend William Lawes gathered a vast private collection of artefacts during his time in Port Moresby. His expertly taken photographs of drums, jewellery and weapons were made available as prints through Charles Kerry's studio in Sydney. There were a myriad other photographers and collectors of South Sea materials and subjects.

Connections with New Zealand, too, were many and varied and reflected a century of Tasman crossings. The link was particularly strong in Sydney, which was serviced regularly by vessels of Huddart Parker Ltd and the Union Steamship Company. There the transplantation of New Zealand place names suggested the extent of that transmigration. The north shore suburb of Waitara, for instance, was named after a region in New Zealand caught up in the Māori Wars of the 1860s. It was in Waitara, after 25 years as a trade unionist and politician, that Jacob Garrard chose to build and name his house 'Wairere' in the early 1900s, probably after the highest waterfall on the north island. Garrard had migrated to New Zealand as a boy and from there to Sydney. 'Te Waari' sat on a waterfront lot of the subdivided estate of Pacific trader turned politician Alexander Berry, as the home of the Ward family, who had cross-Tasman connections. In suburban streets to the east were houses called 'Waitangi' and 'Rotorua'. Māori words were scattered among the English, Scottish and Aboriginal house names.

There were literal transplantations too. A brisk trade in New Zealand plants catered for Australian colonists' love of ferns and pine trees in the mid-to-late 1800s. Arthur Yates established a branch of his family's Manchester seed business in Auckland in 1883 and another in Sydney in 1887 when he migrated a second time. The company did much to foster the trans-Tasman trade in plants. *Yates Gardening Guide for Australia and New Zealand* became one of the most popular books of its kind from the 1890s.

In 1910 Sydney and Melbourne hosted a 'Māori Village', a commercial exercise in popular anthropology that was the brainchild of Makereti (Maggie) Papakura. She had been born Margaret Thom, the daughter of an Englishman and a Māori woman. Papakura was brought up by her mother's relatives and developed a love of Māori culture and, evidently, a desire to show it to the world. She became something of a minor celebrity as a tourist guide in her own country, and well known to Australian visitors. She had a populated village constructed on the shores of Sydney Harbour in January and in the Exhibition Centre in Melbourne in November. A meeting house and nine decorated 'whares', or dwellings, were built. Performers enacted cultural displays 'to let British people see what the old Māori games, and dances, and customs really were'. Visitors received explanations from the performers themselves, 'fierce looking warriors' and 'attractive Māori girls'.[29] The Māori Village, particularly in its incarnation by the harbour, was thereby different from contemporary ethnological displays in the great expositions and exhibitions of the day, where 'native' peoples appeared in zoo-like situations or were totally absent from arrangements of 'savage' artefacts. In the touring Māori Village they spoke for themselves. Papakura, it seems, was as much applied anthropologist as impresario. Indeed, she completed a bachelor's degree in anthropology at Oxford University just before she died in 1930.

It had long been within the means of adventurous spirits, such as John Askew, to pay for a passage to the other side of the world and back. Papakura's innovation was to bring the 'other' to the curious. But as a tour guide in her home land she was also tapping into a new Pacific tourism trade. In the early 20th century, Australians could simply buy a ticket which took them sightseeing around the islands. As Papakura's Māori Village was being unpacked in Australia, the Burns Philp company – now more than 25 years old and with 12 steamers in its fleet – was well placed to offer package tours of the region. Tourism was thereby integrated into a thriving, diversified business with trading posts in many of the islands serviced by shipping.

Such was the prevalence of overseas sightseeing that the company could market its cruises on the basis of an already accepted touristic ennui: 'The world has been so thoroughly scoured by travellers in search of new sights and new sensations that very few places now remain which have not been "done to death" by the ever-increasing crowds of tourists ... where civilisation has not yet effaced the distinctive aboriginal manners and customs'. European civilisation was erasing the unique and Burns Philp emphasised the need to see that before it vanished. It sounded very similar to the urgency motivating anthropologists. As a marketing strategy it would work remarkably well for the next century, even as the world grew ever smaller. Change quickened but also became a relative thing. The islands of the western Pacific 'are almost in the same primitive condition as when the early navigators cast their wondering eyes upon them', the company's booklet breathlessly promised for the 1913–1914 season. 'Until quite recently the natives lived their own barbaric life, rarely disturbed by the white intruders except traders and adventurers.'

The company offered a 33-day trip around the Papuan coast. The Solomons, too, were an option. In the latter one could enjoy 'a charming series of visits to barbaric islands, giving glimpses of primitive native life and a surfeit of beautiful scenery'. The people were 'bright, happy, brown barbarians, indolently wiling away the time, sunning themselves in chattering, gossiping groups, or employed in pottery making, cooking or other light pursuits'.

Already, then, a vague sense of self-criticism and reflection was emerging in these narratives. Civilisation, much vaunted elsewhere, could be destructive to its inventors as well as to the colonised: 'How brain-tired city men envy their care-free existence ... The contrast from the busy whirl of civilisation is startling'. It was a version of the 'noble savagery' which had characterised the first Pacific encounters, implying, 'Wouldn't you rather be them?' But, of course, that could not be. The movement to 'civilisation' – modernity, capitalism or however that was now defined – was inexorable. It would eventually gather up everyone, presumably in one global culture: 'The picturesque simplicity of the natives is not yet destroyed by the influence of civilisation. That they will rapidly absorb the manners and dress of the white man is incontestable, but, in the meantime, they are almost as interesting as when discovered by the early Spaniards'.

Travel promotion such as this appealed overtly to a popular interest in anthropology, and perhaps history, in that it promised a portal to the past before the future arrived. And so the New Hebrides trip offered 'the student of ethnology ... a varied insight into savage life and customs ... many a peep at heathen temples or relics of cannibal customs not yet entirely abolished'. It is hardly surprising, for Burns Philp had been involved in scientific expeditions for decades. It provided the charter boats for Royal Geographical Society's New Guinea trips in the 1880s. In promoting its cruise to the Solomons, the company reprinted a photograph of a Malaitan canoe which had appeared in CM Woodford's 1909 study of Solomon Island canoes published in the *Journal of the Royal Anthropological Institute of Great Britain and Ireland*. It is quite likely Burns Philp had been involved in that expedition.[30] They were by their own estimation becoming the '"Cook and Son" for all Eastern travel from Australia'.[31]

Tourism transformed those it touched. Two decades later Kenneth Thomas was describing Hanuabada, the stilt village built over the water at Port Moresby, as 'more of a tourist show place, than a normal village'. The inhabitants, he told the audience of a lecture he presented in the 1930s 'play to the gallery, and live, to some extent on the tourist trade in curios'.[32]

Earlier tourists may have prepared for their Pacific adventures by attending anthropological talks, and reading books and papers. The journal of the Royal Australian Historical Society, established in 1901, was replete with discussion of Pacific exploration. There were also the many travelogues published in the late 1800s. Most, such as Basil Thomson's *South Sea Yarns* (1898), were British in origin and tone. Edward Reeves' *Brown Men and Women or The South Sea Islands in 1895 and 1896*, was unusual coming from the pen of a New Zealander. Published in 1898, it was filled with tales of old days and ways and attacks on prurient self-interested missionaries, as was becoming the fashion.

There were surprisingly few Australian travelogues and even less fiction or poetry set in the Pacific. Australia's great interior, with its rivers, deserts, forests and grazing herds, dominated the literary imagination as its colonies unified and a single identity appealed. Louis Becke was the notable exception. Born in the former convict settlement of Port Macquarie in 1855, George Lewis (Louis) Becke ran away to sea as a youth. He met and sailed with the American Bully Hayes, who was one of the more ruthless participants in the Pacific labour trade. Becke himself became a trader of goods before returning to Sydney, selling a small collection of artefacts to the newly established Technological Museum and reflecting his experiences by writing stories, which he also sold. His first collection, *By Reef and Palm*, was published in 1894. It was so popular there were three more print runs before the year's end. Thirty-three more books followed.

Becke was unusual as a writer of fiction rather than memoir or travelogue, but much of what he penned was based upon observation or encounter. His work is interesting, too, for its depiction of a Pacific already in the throes of cultural upheaval rather than the twilight of stasis as the Burns Philp travel guide suggested. Becke described places which had long been affected by American, British, French and Australian colonial trade. Those intending tourists who were familiar with Becke's jaded tales may have considered them simply as rollicking adventures. Possibly they accentuated the desire to see the unspoiled bits of the Pacific. For his stories, to use Nicholas Thomas's term, 'are played out in a zone of interaction and hybridity' rather than cultural purity.[33] That hybridity extended to the people. So Becke's works are populated by 'half castes', moralising missionaries, and dissolute white men. Beachcombers, those European men who had rejected 'civilisation' for an easier life in the islands, were commonplace. Becke's disdain for respectability echoed their disaffection and the writing of many of his male contemporaries. His work may be taken as a vicarious critique of a society apparently emasculated by civility. It is clear, in any case, that Becke thought the result of contact was the ruination of once-proud cultures and the degradation of the white people responsible. In the suggestively titled *The Ebbing of the Tide*, published in 1894, he wrote of the Ellice Islands (Tuvalu):

> they have degenerated from a fierce, hardy, warlike race into white-shirted, black-coated saints, whose ideal of a lovely existence is to have public prayer twice a day on week-days and all day on Sundays.[34]

Possibly Becke saw a version of himself in these hobbled warriors, betwixt and between in a changing world not of his liking. He had had a relationship with an island woman during his trading days on Ellice Island. After a failed marriage in Sydney, a return to the islands and some time in London, he died a heavy drinker, in debt and alone in a Sydney hotel room in 1913.

≈

'I have never seen anything quite so beautiful as a man on a surf board ...'

Australian masculinity received a most significant cultural gift from the Pacific in the 1880s with the introduction of the art of bodysurfing. It apparently came from island men working in Sydney's beachside suburbs. Freddie Williams referred to one Islander he saw bodysurfing at Little Coogee on the city's south side, and called 'Tommy Tanna'. That name was a common moniker for New Hebrideans in Australia, and was synonymous with Kanaka.[35] 'Tommy', who made a living as a gardener in the beachside suburb of Manly, taught Williams in the late 19th century, who subsequently passed on his knowledge. Within a decade, the surf on Australia's Pacific coast became something to embrace rather than fear. It foamed, caressed and carried near-naked bodies at a time when the cultural taboos of the Victorian era still prohibited displays of flesh and sensuality. Women also took up surf bathing, as it came to be called. So that, when daylight bathing bans were lifted in the early 1900s, the beach became an exceptional place where the sexes mingled in a mass spectacle of sensuality. Dripping swimsuits clung to bodies, revealing curves in a manner unthinkable a decade earlier. The discovery of the beach was a cultural revolution worthy of any anthropological study. By the 1930s it had transformed Australia's sense of itself, and the surf bather and life saver were as much models of national manhood as the drover and soldier. The world's first surf magazine, *The Surfer*, was published in Sydney from 1917.

Samoan short boards – similar to the devices used by the Pitcairn Islanders 50 years earlier – were in evidence around Manly as early as 1906. Such was the pan-Pacific network which had emerged that Manly alderman and Tourist Bureau head Charles Paterson was able to acquire a Hawaiian long board. Local man Tommy Walker also secured a board and there followed demonstrations on how to stand, rather than lie, on the waves. Sydneysiders were thereby primed for the much-celebrated visit of Hawaiian swimming champion and board rider, Duke Paoa Kahanamoku in 1914–15.[36] Duke rode and was watched by hundreds. He met a Manly boy called Claude West and left him a board with personal tips on how to ride. West then became a towering figure in the local surfing scene.

The press across the country reported on Kahanamoku's visit, following his swim races, including the 'Kahanamoku Carnival' in Brisbane, more keenly than the surfing. The 'Duke' broke records and was sometimes beaten himself by local swimmers. Those men, in turn, owed something to another islander, Alick Wickham, who introduced the overarm style subsequently called the 'Australian Crawl' to his adopted country. Wickham was born in the Solomons of mixed ancestry. After being credited with 'inventing' the style, he respectfully deferred to the tradition of his homeland: 'The only stroke I ever used before swimming in New South Wales was the crawl stroke – that is the natural stroke of the natives of Rubiana'.[37]

Had the anthropologists of the period been interested in looking at the flow of culture from the Pacific to Australia they might have seen mastery of water for leisure as the first most significant instance of exchange. As it was, they were obsessed with documenting 'primitive' people before they changed; cultural flow was a one-way problem. It has been suggested more recently that Wickham's and Kahanamoku's popularity was due to the long-time allure of 'savagery'; that they were 'nimble savages' – the equivalent of the 'noble savages' of 18th-century fascination.[38] Perhaps, however, the equanimity with which these people of colour were received was another example of a cultural crosscurrent, made possible by masculinity and sporting prowess. They were not some sort of performing 'other', but rather a version of 'us'.

Physicality, both in prowess and beauty, certainly helps to explain the epiphanies of a small group of Australian intellectuals who ventured to Hawaii in the 1920s and 1930s. (Sir) Frederic Eggleston, the liberal internationalist who had been party to Australia's League of Nations negotiations, co-founded a Melbourne branch of the Institute of Pacific Relations in 1926 just a year after its inception and became Australia's first ambassador to China in the 1940s. Where Louis Becke saw racial decay, Eggleston was entranced by the results of the 'mixed up' relations between 'races' in the Polynesian islands he visited. A diary note penned in Hawaii captures the feeling: 'I have never seen anything quite so beautiful as a man on a surf board ...'[39] The historian Stephen Roberts and the anthropologist AP Elkin also found something altogether liberating in the hybrid culture they encountered in that most eastern part of the Polynesian diaspora, which had received Japanese settlers in the late 1800s and many white Americans before and after annexation by the US. Roberts described Hawaii as the 'best example of racial experimentation in the Pacific'.[40] It was in some respects a collective echo of Bougainville, Banks and others' intoxicated musings but the revelations led all three Australians to question the basis of White Australia. In 1948, as Herbert Evatt was walking his moral tightrope, repeating the argument for racial exclusion while supporting 'Universal

Human Rights', Elkin spoke in terms very similar to that other dissenter, the Right Reverend Burgmann: 'What matters in nation-building is not colour – but culture, attitudes, values, and manner of life'.[41]

≋

'I was discussing changing aesthetic conventions and their relation to reality'

Eggleston was one of the many Australian intellectuals and administrators who supported establishing a national university. The idea, long considered, gained impetus from the boom in local research undertaken during the war and planning for reconstruction in its aftermath. The Australian National University (ANU) was established in Canberra in 1946 with the multi-disciplinary Research School of Pacific Studies as one of its founding institutes due, in part, to Eggleston's urging. Its creation reflected the growing sense that Australia needed to know its region as an independent entity within it; although there was an obvious paradox in an oceanic perspective emanating from the nation's 'bush capital', surrounded as it was by sheep paddocks. For more than a decade there was some inconvenience, too, as limited transport options separated Pacific researchers from their region. The renowned geographer Oskar Spate joined the school in 1951. New Zealand–born historian JW Davidson was appointed as its first professor of Pacific history in 1950.

Davidson was then assisting with editing James Cook's journals. His mentor JC Beaglehole, another New Zealander, led that work, and would become the pre-eminent scholar of the Cook voyages. It was suggested to Davidson and Beaglehole that an Australian art historian, then in London, be enlisted to catalogue the drawings and paintings created in association with Cook's expeditions. Bernard Smith was on leave from his position at the National Art Gallery of New South Wales, where he had worked since 1944.[42] The recommendation had come from Charles Mitchell, an historian based at the Warburg Institute, where Smith was studying and immersed in the library of art historian Aby Warburg, the institute's namesake, which had been relocated to London from Germany when the Nazis assumed power in 1933. Stimulated by that resource and other imperial collections, including the colonial art and works of exploration accumulated by New Zealander Rex Nan Kivell, Bernard Smith embarked upon a reimagining of art history.

The resulting article, 'European Vision and the South Pacific', was published in the *Journal of the Warburg and Cortauld Institutes* in 1950. In it, Smith placed the art and writing of the Pacific produced during Cook's voyages of discovery and Australia's consequent colonisation in a historical context, that of European imperialism. But this was not a simple account of the arrival of 'civilisation'. The works that concerned Smith were not merely evidence of an unfolding narrative of who went where and when; they were sources to analyse for what they revealed about the 'European vision', or understanding, of what they encountered. The implication therein was that comprehension was subjective rather than objective. Different people, from the commander Cook to the scientist collector Banks and the exiled convict Thomas Watling, responded variously to the people and landscapes encountered. Smith wrote about images that perpetuated the idea of the 'noble savage' current in British thought since the 17th century and so important to Enlightenment writers such as Diderot as a figure to admire, if not emulate. He charted the transition to 'ignoble savagery', the fallen native who would be supplanted. It was a profoundly different way of writing about the history and art of the Pacific, or anywhere for that matter.

On the basis of that work, and the confidence that much more could be discussed, Smith applied successfully to complete a PhD on the topic at the ANU under Davidson in 1953. The title 'European Vision and the South Pacific, 1820–1850: A study of the impact of Pacific peoples and environment on Europeans in Australasia' made it clear that this was not a work simply about the projection of power, military or cultural, upon subject people. It was quite the opposite. Smith was interested in how the Pacific and its people changed Europeans. The thesis became a book, which Oxford University Press accepted for publication in 1957. There was much discussion by letter of the title, based upon marketing, decorum and fidelity to the content but, in the end, it was agreed to use *European Vision and the South Pacific* – the same as the 1950 article.

Smith hoped that its release would coincide with the centenary of Darwin's *The Origin of Species* in 1959. 'My book does suggest that the opening of the Pacific played a part in the growth of the theory of organic evolution – much of the argument is concerned with this', he explained to the publishers.[43] That deadline was not met and publication followed in 1960. The relationship between 'art and science' in the context of exploration was a major theme, with ethnology one of those sciences. Smith acknowledged the 1936 work of Arthur O Lovejoy and Franz Boas, *Primitivism and Related Ideas in Antiquity*, in particular their discussion of 'hard' and 'soft' primitivism, which he would apply to various depictions of Polynesians, Melanesians and Australian Aboriginal people. He found resonances in the Biblical and classically infused representations of Indigenous people, which were intertwined with 'rational enthusiasm of the Enlightenment'.[44]

As Smith made clear, the Pacific became a crucible for many ideas – evolution, European decadence, arrogance and supremacy among them. In that vessel also could be found the origins of Australian art, something Smith had already explored at length in *Place, Taste and Tradition: A Study of Australian Art Since 1788* published in 1945.

European Vision was generally well received. It won the Ernest Scott Prize for History in 1960, jointly with JC Beaglehole, who admired the work, as did the renowned art historian EH Gombrich. But there were critics. Writer and commentator Max Harris seemed perplexed by the absence of formalistic judgments about what art was good or bad or derivative, the book's lack of 'lucid ideas of aesthetic worth'. To that, Smith responded: 'I do not think these have a place in historical work. Indeed, I was discussing changing aesthetic conventions and their relation to reality. To do this, and at the same time use our own contemporary conventions in judging the works of the past is, to my mind, extremely bad historical technique'.[45]

European Vision was not fully appreciated or properly understood in its time despite the prize and praise it garnered. Harris clearly did not comprehend the idea of historicising artistic production. Even the sympathetic Geoffrey Searle failed to mention the work in his influential history of Australian 'creative spirit', *From Deserts the Prophets Come*, published in 1973; though Smith's other work on Australian art was well referenced. *European Vision* was overshadowed in its first decades by *Fatal Impact*, a book about the awful effects of colonisation in Australia and the Pacific which appeared in 1966. The author was the expatriate Australian Alan Moorehead, who had made an international reputation with his war reporting, primarily in the Middle East and Europe. The bibliography of *Fatal Impact* listed *European Vision* but the books were starkly different. As the title of Moorehead's work suggested, his work focused on the devastation of Indigenous cultures. It was a reiteration of the 'doomed peoples' theory pre-war anthropologists had advanced, albeit with a strong note of sympathy and cultural self-reproach. 'It's all about how white man has ruined the South Pacific', Moorehead explained. The London *Times* praised the book, in tellingly archaic language, as an exploration of 'savage and civilised man in confrontations unresolved to this day'.[46]

Regardless of the delayed impact, it is difficult to overstate the significance of *European Vision* for the breadth of its scholarship, for the art it assembled and made accessible in 171 plates and for the sophistication and complexity of the analysis. Smith's work anticipated the preoccupations of multi-disciplinary cultural studies. The book's influence, in this respect, was felt two decades later when colonial art and colonial ways of seeing became central to some of the country's most innovative historical writing. That a place and its peoples might be constructions of the intellect – of vision – was not a commonplace premise until the 1980s when anthropology, fine art studies, semiology and history came together. *Orientalism*, published in 1978, was one of the foundational texts of the new approach. Edward Said began that widely referenced exploration of European representations of 'the other' by alerting his readers: 'I have begun with the assumption that the Orient is not an inert fact of nature'.[47] It was something Smith had done with the Pacific three decades earlier.

Said briefly acknowledged Smith's work in his subsequent book, *Culture and Imperialism*, describing it as one of two of 'the most extended analysis' of the role of the arts in allowing colonisers to 'see', 'master' and 'hold' the 'non-European world'.[48] But that barely did the book justice. Bernard Smith did not just present art as an instrument of imperialism in a series of unchanging tropes; he explored representations of 'the other', Pacific people and landscapes specifically, in order to better understand the intellectual and emotional framework of the explorers and colonisers. In doing so Smith presented an extended analysis of the impact the Pacific had upon Europeans themselves and ultimately those whose presence in Australia was a direct result of that ocean's exploration. Different people and places were experienced differently. The artist William Westall, for example, differentiated the inspirational qualities of Australia's 'barrin [sic] coast' and the 'richness of the South Sea Islands'.[49] That, in turn, influenced the manner in which he represented the respective places.

Furthermore, 'European experience of the Pacific was one of cultural exchange', as the intellectual historian Peter Beilharz said in an appreciative summary of Smith's work, which appeared well after its worth was fully realised.[50] Among those who followed was Greg Dening, whose career was just beginning as Smith completed *European Vision*. His multi-disciplinary study of the Marquesas, *Islands and Beaches*, was published in 1980 by the University of Hawaii and became a much-referenced work in cultural studies circles. Sydney-born cultural anthropologist Nicholas Thomas extended the critical approach to the history of collecting, material culture and museology. In 1997 he paid respect to Smith's 'brilliant' but belatedly recognised work while noting that many Pacific historians remained 'irritated' at the enduring popularity of Moorehead's 'misguided' and 'superseded' *Fatal Impact*.[51]

Finally, *European Vision* placed Australian history and indeed, the culture seeded on the continent's Pacific shore, firmly within the history of the region. Smith's study ended at the mid-19th century when 'scientific method triumphed in description of both nature and man' and the old framework of vision, Enlightenment, religion, classicism and romanticism, fell away.[52] It is clear, however, that the European understanding of 'the other' did not set aside 'nobility' and 'ignobility'. Far from it; the emotions, empathy, sympathy, admiration, fear and disgust which filled those two categories were perpetuated in complex ways well into the 20th century, concomitant with 'White Australia's' perception of itself.

CHAPTER 15

Post-war Australia meets the Cold War Pacific

*'... the ships of Quiros on their great concerns /
ride in upon the present from the past'*

As Bernard Smith was finalising and submitting his manuscript for *European Vision and the South Pacific*, another Australian intellectual was thinking about the exploration of that ocean in a very different way. The conservative commentator and poet James McAuley took two years to write 'Captain Quiros', an epic poem of 317 stanzas based on the two Pacific voyages of the Portuguese navigator who sailed in the service of Spain in the late 16th and early 17th centuries. It was both a history lesson and a richly allegorical examination of the corruption of religious faith and tradition, first by human greed and pride, and ultimately by the ruinous individualism of modernity. The verse begins with Magellan's 'Four ships upon the calm Pacific fold' and moves quickly to Alvaro de Mendaña's 1567 search for Terra Australis, and then to Quiros's second voyage in 1606 to establish a New Jerusalem in the Pacific. It ends with the French and British voyages leading to Australia's colonisation and a rumination on the state of modern *Terra Australis*.

The poetic device came as a revelation to McAuley after a late night searching for inspiration, something he recounted in another short verse: 'suddenly' by lamp light the idea emerged, '... over the vast / Pacific with the white wake at their sterns, / the ships of Quiros on their great concerns / ride in upon the present from the past'.[1] If that was the manner of his epiphany, the idea had been well and truly seeded by other works.

An expatriate New Zealander, Douglas Stewart, had written 'Terra Australis' in 1952, a poem in which Quiros met the Australian socialist William Lane mid-Pacific on their way to establish utopias on either side of the ocean in the 17th and 19th centuries respectively. McAuley had toyed with the idea of using Pacific exploration to examine the meaning of his homeland in 1946 with 'The True Discovery of Australia', in which he credits Gulliver with finding the land that was first called Lilliput, 'close to Lake Torrens'. That work anticipated Captain Quiros but its nature was less layers of learned symbolism than merciless satire and caricature. 'Lilliput' – that would be Australia – was a place of tiny philistines who arrogantly think themselves the 'Giants of the South Pacific' while despoiling their own land by 'shifting all the soil into the ocean' through over-cropping.[2]

McAuley wrote 'Captain Quiros' to be read aloud, something he estimated might take 'about two hours'.[3] He completed the work in 1960 but did not publish it in its entirety until 1964. It was a time when poetry mattered in a way it would not even 20 years later, usurped possibly by the versifying of serious folk and rock music. McAuley's contemporaries AD Hope, Judith Wright and Douglas Stewart, for instance, used poems to great effect to present very different ideas about the Australian post-war condition. This mid-century period was a time of 'culture wars', no less than the beginning of the next century, when that term was coined. The difference was that McAuley's erudition would have no counterpart in the ranks of the belligerent broadcasters and partisan print commentators who represented conservativism in the new millennium.

The published *Captain Quiros* appeared as a single work in a handsome slim volume, not unlike the first edition of TS Eliot's *The Wasteland* in 1922. McAuley may well have been pleased with the similarity. Eliot had been an enormous influence on him as a 'precocious' school boy and an equally confident university student.[4] Both McAuley and Eliot were, in turn, influenced by James Frazer's momentous comparative work on 'primitive' superstition and religion,

The Golden Bough, published in 1894. It was one of the most influential anthropological books of the first half of the 20th century.

However both Eliot and McAuley moved beyond religious scepticism, grounded in comparative anthropology, to cultural critiques which embraced the significance of faith. The former's *Notes Towards a Definition of Culture* was published in 1948. It made the case for the importance and naturalism of an organic faith-based culture, as opposed to one imposed by dictators of the right and left – or technocrats, however well meaning. The imposition of Western progressive idealism upon other civilisations was doomed to fail both the givers and receivers of that largesse. McAuley had arrived at a similar conclusion by the mid-1950s.

However, the Australian became a combative warrior in the fight against communist totalitarianism and its stalking horse, 'liberalistic' modernity. His certainty came from the first-hand understanding of the impact of colonisation on 'primitive' society he gained as a prolific policy theorist and educator in New Guinea. McAuley had written privately and publicly on the place from his time there during the Pacific War working for the somewhat mysterious Directorate of Research, a defence-related group which included the anthropologists Camilla Wedgwood, H Ian Hogbin and WEH Stanner, and one tasked with exploring post-war options for Australian rule in Papua and New Guinea. Like TS Eliot, McAuley was also a passionate convert to Catholicism. He consummated his discovery of that faith in 1952, following contact with French missionaries in Australia's Pacific possession. New Guinea focussed McAuley's mind and provided the foil against which he measured his own culture.

'Captain Quiros' was at once the apotheosis of the poet's output, the lyrical expression of a social commentator and a critique of colonialism which drew upon McAuley's personal experience of Melanesian culture. In that last respect it differed significantly from Bernard Smith's exploration, which was entirely based upon documentary evidence. Smith's Pacific was a series of texts and images; McAuley's was a real place. The poet used that familiarity to great visceral effect early on in the work when he described a gift from the Solomon Islanders to de Mendaña: 'when naked bowmen, savagely polite, / Offered a boy's cooked arm and fingers, garnished / With taro roots.'

'Captain Quiros' was written in three parts. The first deals with Quiros's voyage with de Mendaña, a quest driven by the lust for gold and riven with dissension. The people they encounter in the Solomons have a unified functioning culture, with their chief Malope acting as its 'central pole'. Their 'island world' was a place: 'Where man conforming to the cosmos proves / His oneness with all beings, and life moves / To the rhythm of profound analogies'.[5] There follows the almost inevitable series of mistaken encounters which accompanied European voyages of discovery: the reception of the newcomers as ancestors returned, the Indigenous people's attempts to understand the origin of such wealth and apparent magic, and then the revelation that the white sailors are just men. Disorientated and venal, the adventurers quarrel among themselves and a massacre occurs within their ranks. The friendly Malope is killed in the ensuing mayhem and the Europeans depart leaving nothing but damage: 'What trace of those who ill paid his trusting / Welcome? An axe, a memory, both rusting / Into oblivion, might at most be found'.[6]

Quiros returns with a nobler objective – to found a New Jerusalem. One might have thought that would please the newly converted McAuley. But unlike the clerics who, 50 years earlier, had celebrated Quiros's naming of Austrialia del Espiritu Santo as evidence of the Catholic discovery of Australia, McAuley presents this as a flawed enterprise. The navigator is trying to recreate Heaven on Earth and in doing so transgresses God's will. The project inevitably fails and an 'ailing' friar aboard Quiros's ship spells out his error: '... Not ours to bring to birth / That final Realm; nor shall our labours build / Out of the rubble of this fallen earth / The New Jerusalem, which will never be / Christ's perfect bride save in eternity'. This was an attack, thinly disguised or otherwise, on attempts to make earthly utopias. In the 1950s that could only mean communism.

The third section is entitled 'The Times of Nations' and is mostly recounted as a vision from the dying Quiros. It is here that Bougainville and Cook follow in the wake of the earlier navigators, discovering Tahiti and seeing there the idealised state of nature: 'But the new wits, who sit at home and plan / The libertine republic of the good, / Hail this the paradise of Natural Man / Distorting what they have not understood'. What follows is duplicity disguised as a 'reign of Innocence', and 'infamy and blood'.[7] Australia is consequently discovered by 'that English Captain', Cook. The nation is founded on 'harsh penal law' with 'natives shot and poisoned from their land'. 'Common law' and 'ordered liberty' are mingled with the continent's resources to promise a 'happier destiny'.

But this would hardly be McAuley if the narrative ended on a positive note. So, the 'new-turned ground' is crowded with the 'cactus of delusion'. Loss of faith undermines everything, including the classical origins of Western civilisation: 'The architecture of the world we knew, / The cosmic temple framed with cross and dome, / And circle, square and column, proportioned true, / Lies empty like a ruined honeycomb'.[8] The dome is most obviously a reference to St Peter's in Rome but the image of it destroyed is also redolent of Allan Cuthbert's and Alan Queale's photographs of Hiroshima and the hollow frame of the City Commercial Display Building. McAuley's present is an epoch of meaningless estrangement: 'Now in a time of loneliness and dearth / The just shall live by faith without the aid / Of custom that bound man to heaven and earth …'[9]

≋

'a life that is more Polynesian than Puritan'

The society that McAuley found so alienating and horrifying was one well down the path of post-war reconstruction. Another conservative, Donald Horne, painted a word picture of anti-intellectual innocence as men and women socialised at suburban sporting clubs pulling at poker machines and enjoying the enviable amenities that the profits of that gambling paid for in a self-funding cycle of collegiality. Horne's description came in his hugely influential book, *The Lucky Country*. That 'luck', as the author was at pains to point out, came from the land, specifically wealth generated by the exports of primary industry and resource extraction rather than the quality of the people themselves. Australians were 'lucky' leisure seekers for whom the bonds of religion were weakening just as their intellectual curiosity was fading. They inhabited a landscape of neat bungalows, gardens and clubs, but not much else. Horne suggested Australia 'may have been the first *suburban* nation' in the world (italics in original).[10] He also admitted 'suburbanism' – whether a place or a mindset – was the source of alienation for most Australian intellectuals, himself included. For the left-liberal writer, Allan Ashbolt, the suburban block had replaced the church. His 1966 critique of modern life's complacent materialism, which equated the 'high decibel drone of the motor mower' with the peal of bells 'calling the faithful to worship', might have been written by McAuley. Nothing more than a brick veneer house and a manicured block of land was necessary for spiritual sustenance in this barren egalitarian utopia.

The affluence that mining, wool and wheat were generating created a mainland culture very different from that which existed in the Australian territory of Papua and New Guinea which McAuley had come to know and respect since the 1940s. The serried rows of houses, shopping strips and newly invented supermarkets that made up suburbia could hardly have been more different from the Melanesian villages of highland and coast. But McAuley, the poet and writer, was always searching for parallels between coloniser and colonised, and lessons that might be learned thereof. The materialism and rationalism which was corroding tradition in advanced Australia was having a similar effect in primitive New Guinea to where it was being exported. In his book *The End of Modernity*, McAuley quoted anthropologist and friend Raymond Firth: 'It is not possible for human society to exist without some forms of symbolic solutions which rest on non-empirical foundations'. To that McAuley added his own insights from home and the field; 'as the sense of traditional order fades, the community becomes confused and distracted by competing interests acknowledging no common rule'.[11] The literary historian Robert Dixon has identified the anthropological connection perceptively: 'For McAuley, the triumph of secularism and consumerism in the west is a social disorder comparable to an outbreak of cargo cult in Melanesia'.[12]

And what of that other cultural connection between the peoples of post-war Australia and the Pacific – surfing? The revolution that began in the late 19th century with Tommy Tanna's bodysurfing lessons, and which Duke Kahanamoku's board-riding displays perpetuated, was a definitive part of Australian culture by the 1960s. The institutionalised weekend, which began in 1949, along with increasing wealth and job security, was creating a Pacific paradise for those lucky enough to live alongside the great ocean. In 1964, the year that both *Captain Quiros* and *The Lucky Country* were published, Australia celebrated its first world surfing champion, Midget Farrelly. His win came at Manly where Tommy Tanna surfbathed when not tending his employer's garden. Farrelly would remain a national folk hero ever after. Donald Horne could not fail to notice the connection between affluent Australia and traditional Pacific:

> When young men strap their Malibu surf boards (cost $70 to $90) to their cars, drive off to the beach and command the breakers all day they seem to move into a life that is more Polynesian than Puritan ... It might be relevant to look at the life of the South Seas to throw some illumination on life in Australia, instead of the almost exclusive comparison with the United Kingdom and parts of Western Europe ... with an occasional glance at the USA.[13]

Surfing culture would become synonymous with hedonism – drinking, drugs and sex. At its most thoughtful it embodied the Romanticism of the counter-culture of the 1960s and 1970s, finding meaning in an individualistic oneness with the ocean. But both were manifestations of the modern libertine malaise that McAuley condemned in 'Captain Quiros'.

≋

'... to unfurl the Red Flag over the Pacific ...'

The spectre of communism lay behind much of what McAuley wrote from the 1950s, whether in verse or prose. By eating away the connective tissue of faith, the liberality and rationalism of modernity opened the door for that most recent form of totalitarian utopianism. McAuley's conversion to Catholicism, the result of his encounters in a land where 'men are shaken by obscure trances', added vehemence to his anti-communism. In 1954 McAuley joined the Catholic Social Studies Movement, an organisation Catholic intellectual BA Santamaria had established with the support of Melbourne's archbishop Daniel Mannix to promote Catholic teaching, democracy and social justice – particularly in the workplace. It equated communism with Satan but also adhered to the political science belief that the ideology was inherently expansionist. One 1951 issue of its *News Weekly* publication read 'The aim of Communism is the military and political take-over of the entire world'. The Soviet Union was prosecuting that domination but Australia was directly threatened because 'Asian communism's part in the master plan is to unfurl the Red Flag over the Pacific and the Indian ocean ....'[14]

The beliefs of Santamaria, Mannix, and the 'Movement' had considerable support within the labour movement and the Labor Party, which had long been the political home for Australia's working-class Catholics. The vehemence of some of these people led to the so-called 'split'. Those who felt that the Labor Party was not doing enough to combat communist influence in the union movement, from which it had emerged in the 1890s, formed the Democratic Labor Party (DLP). James McAuley was involved in the discussions to establish the breakaway party. He chaired the meeting in September 1956 at which the DLP was created.[15] The presence of communists in organised labour had undermined the Labor Party's standing since the 1940s when strikes affected trains, shipping and power supplies. Chifley moved against the strikers, even allowing troops to dig coal in 1949. However, the industrial unrest, coming when Labor attempted to nationalise the banks, allowed the Liberal/Country Party coalition to win an election by characterising its opponents as weak on communism. It followed up its election promises to outlaw the Australian Communist Party within six months. The Labor Party, with many anti-communist members in its rank and file, supported a ban but not the draconian means proposed to enforce it. Herbert Evatt, appearing for the Waterside Workers' Federation, challenged the bill in the High Court and it was declared unconstitutional by a margin of 6–1. The government then took the issue to the people in a referendum where it was only narrowly defeated.

Having campaigned for the 'no' vote, Evatt claimed that as a victory against a creeping form of totalitarianism from the right, something 'utterly non-British and [the] very antithesis of the glorious traditions of our race'.[16] Such a claim was no doubt meant to counter attacks by the staunchly Anglophilic prime minister, Robert Menzies, on a Labor Party he characterised as socialistic and disloyal to empire. But it also reflected Evatt's strong belief in the ethnic origins of his social democratic philosophy. Regardless, communism – the fear it provoked and political opportunities it presented – helped to keep Labor out of power for more than two decades. The referendum's close results revealed a society that was not quite as complacent and unified as the images of post-war suburbia would suggest.

Anti-communism also helps explain some Australians' willingness to volunteer to fight in Korea after the army of the north crossed the 38th parallel dividing it from the non-communist south in June 1950. Denis O'Brien, a teacher from a small wheat belt town in Victoria, joined up after the Menzies government announced on 26 July that it would send ground troops. In the words of Cameron Forbes, who told his story many years later: 'O'Brien was a staunch ALP man and a socialist. He was anti-communist'. He was also a Catholic who went to an Asian country on the north-west Pacific rim, barely known to most Australians despite the nation's historic fear of its northern neighbours, to defend 'Christian civilisation against the new barbarism of secular humanism'.[17] Many things motivate men to take up arms but O'Brien was not alone in his convictions. For his part, World War Two veteran Reg Saunders served as the first Aboriginal man to receive a commission in the Australian Army. In the early 1960s he discussed his reasons for going with journalist Harry Gordon: 'I love Australia but that's got nothing to do with this. And I don't have strong convictions about Communism. Maybe it's just because I like a certain amount of excitement'.[18] Eight hundred and ninety-six men had volunteered within six days of the government's announcement.[19]

K-Force, as they were called, joined men of the 3rd Royal Australian Regiment (3 RAR), stationed in Japan as part of the occupation there. Denis O'Brien and the 4506 other Australians who served in Korea were among the last from their nation to volunteer to fight in a foreign war. The Menzies government introduced conscription for overseas service in 1964, and then for the war against Asian communism in Vietnam.

Denis O'Brien and his comrades fought as part of a UN-sanctioned police action. North Korea was deemed the aggressor, despite the ideological sympathies of the Soviet Union which did not exercise its Security Council veto, possibly to draw the US into a costly war or to test the UN's endurance.[20] Communist China would not replace the Republic of China on the Council until 1971. The peninsula had been divided into two at the 38th parallel in August 1945 after the Soviet Union's belated entry into the Pacific War, six days before the Japanese surrender. The line represented the occupation zones of a Soviet north and an American south, much as Germany was split between east and west. There followed three years of attempts to unify the two parts amidst the emergence of the bi-polar world of the early Cold War. Underlying that international schism was a local brittleness caused by the effects of Japan's harsh occupation since 1910. Brutalised Korean men, dragooned into service from the 1930s, were among the cruellest of the guards who mistreated Australian prisoners of war. The Japanese Imperial Army used Korean women as sex slaves – so-called 'comfort women'. Thirty years of repression followed by the post-war political division destabilised a country that had been unified since the 10th century, with a culture that went back for a thousand years or more.

Herbert Evatt tried to steer a path in between Soviet and US interests in his capacity as Australia's minister for external affairs, and in accord with his belief in the UN's role as an agent of liberal democracy. All came to nothing and the pro-American Republic of Korea was declared on 15 August 1948 with a communist Democratic People's Republic of Korea following on 10 September. The name of the latter indicates the currency which 'democracy', as an incontestable idea, had attained beyond the extreme right. However, that both regimes were repressive also indicates the hollowness of many claims to representativeness. The Democratic People's Republic quickly became a totalitarian state built upon the personality cult of its leader Kim Il-Sung, who would die while still gripping absolute power in 1994. Syngman Rhee headed a corrupt and authoritarian government until removed from office in 1960.[21]

Support for the Republic of Korea came from the UN but Australia's quick decision to add ground troops to its naval and air contribution reflected both the government's anti-communist stance and its keenness to support the US as the obvious post-war Pacific region power. The Australian position accorded with that of the Americans, expressed in National Security Council Paper 68 (NSC 68) of April 1950, that Soviet communism was a 'new fanatic faith antithetical to our own', one which was inherently expansionist and therefore needed to be 'contained' whenever it pushed forward. The Chinese communists' victory in expelling nationalist forces from the mainland in 1949 was apparent evidence. In early 1950 US Secretary of State Dean Acheson spoke of the need for a 'defense perimeter' around the Pacific rim from the Aleutian Islands in the north-east to the Philippines in the west. Japan, occupied and rebuilding, was a vital part of that perimeter.[22] The attack by North Korean troops in June 1950 confirmed America's Cold War assessments. The *New York Times* took a more racialised view of events, one which may have resonated with some in Australia: 'We are facing an army of barbarians in Korea ... they fight as the hordes of Genghis Khan ...'[23]

Containment informed Australia's new strategy of forward rather than continental defence. Sending troops to Korea is better seen in this context rather than as explicit support for the UN, a body which Menzies regarded with far less enthusiasm than did Herbert Evatt. Menzies, at this time, was courting two 'powerful friends': the British, for whom he felt the 'crimson thread of kinship' no less than Henry Parkes, and somewhat more reluctantly the Americans. It was Menzies' minister for external affairs, Percy Spender, who made the case most specifically for currying favour with Americans through a Korean commitment: 'any additional aid we can give to the United States now, small though it may be, will repay us in the future one hundred-fold'.[24] Spender was vehemently anti-communist but his strategy might be interpreted as foreign policy realism rather than crusading messianism. It was Spender, too, who met personally with President Truman and suggested that the US and Australia might arrive at an 'arrangement' in view of the latter's 'vulnerability and isolation ... in the Pacific'. Menzies famously equated Spender's determination to secure a defence partnership with the Americans as attempting to build 'a superstructure on a foundation of jelly'.[25]

The White House conversation between Spender and Truman occurred in September 1950. The resulting Australia, New Zealand and United States (ANZUS) Treaty was signed in February 1951. Menzies conceded the point and toasted his minister's achievement. The signing of ANZUS took some of the bitterness out of Japan's lenient peace terms. In 1957 Australia moved to integrate its weaponry and defence systems with those of the US. The prime minister explained it thus: 'We have decided, both in aircraft, in artillery, and in small arms, to fit ourselves for close cooperation with the United States of America in South East Asia'.[26]

In Korea, however, Australians had operated as part of the 1st Commonwealth Division which included British and New Zealand units. Australia's 77 Squadron first flew Mustangs, the American-made propeller-powered fighters they had operated since September 1945, and then British-made Meteor jets, which were more contemporary but still totally inadequate against the Russian-made MIG jet fighters. There were echoes there of the one-sided fights between Wirraways and Zeroes in the earlier Pacific War. The infantry used British-designed Vickers and Bren machine guns, Lee Enfield rifles, 25-pounder field guns and 3-inch mortars, all of which were standard issue in World War Two. The Vickers and the Lee Enfield would have been familiar to the Australians' ANZAC forefathers, so old was the technology. But even those survivors of the awful 1916 winter on the Western Front would have found the freezing cold of Korea difficult to withstand. Great coats were swapped for quilted jackets and slouch hats for sheepskin caps modelled on a Chinese style which folded down to protect the eyes and ears. The demand for wool during the Korean War sent Australian clip prices skyrocketing. The early 1950s were boom years on Australia's sheep stations.

The police action which was to re-establish the status quo, or contain the communists at the 38th parallel became an exercise in 'roll-back' to force the Korean Peninsula to reunify, when American forces under General MacArthur pushed the North Koreans back to the Chinese border at the Yalu River by November 1950. Emboldened by the success of his landing at Inchon near Seoul in September, MacArthur had told Truman there was 'very little' chance of the Chinese entering the war despite this provocation. That reassurance came in October. The Chinese counter-attacked in force on 27 November and pushed the Americans and their allies back.

MacArthur ordered a scorched-earth policy, where everything before the Chinese advance was destroyed. The destruction of whole villages and their inhabitants with napalm anticipated the tactics employed in Vietnam a decade and a half later. The UN forces retreated south of Seoul. The Chinese in turn were driven back to the 38th parallel, where it all started, due in large part to the leadership of the American general Matthew Ridgway. Foreseeing no end to the conflict Truman considered a negotiated peace but MacArthur's public and private pronouncements on the need to prosecute the war to the end undermined those plans. He criticised the 'Europe-first' approach of Washington as he had done in World War Two. Asia and the Pacific were where the threat lay in 1951 as in 1942.

The general was relieved of his command in April 1951, because of his 'insubordination' and his unreliability in the event of the use of atomic weapons which were being considered.[27] He went unapologetically and with the same reluctance to countenance his own shortcomings that had characterised his command during the earlier Pacific War. In a speech to Congress, MacArthur ruled out a diplomatic solution to the escalating crisis: 'In war there can be no substitute for victory'. And then with a note of self-pity and pathos he uttered his famous farewell: 'Old soldiers never die; they just fade away'.[28]

Denis O'Brien was killed on 5 October 1951 during the Australian assault on a pyramidal hill which the planners numbered 317 but was known also by its local name, Maryang San. The Australians faced Chinese soldiers of 191st Division drawn from the peasantry, as much of the Chinese People's Volunteer Force was. Across the ranks most were illiterate. They may well have had more political indoctrination, as much as two months, than military training. The 19th Army Group, of which the 191st was a part, lost perhaps 50 000 men in one week in the spring of 1951.[29]

The assault on Maryang San was part of a larger operation aimed at pushing the Chinese from advantageous high ground north of the Imjin River. If successful, this larger attack would place the UN forces in a better military position and their negotiators in a stronger position to decide peace terms. The Australians did push the Chinese off the hill, albeit temporarily. The Battle of Maryang San is regarded as one of their finest moments. The Battle of Kapyong, in which O'Brien also fought, was another. That action, in late April, cost 32 Australian lives and 69 wounded. The Americans beside whom they fought awarded 3RAR the Presidential Unit Citation for gallantry.[30]

Five months later Denis O'Brien had a premonition that he was going to die. He told a friend as much while on leave in Japan in September and bought farewell gifts for his family rather than drinking with friends. The Catholic soldier then sought out the unit priest, Father Phillips, to hear his confession. Phillips related those last meditations to O'Brien's family: 'a few days before the fatal attack he called down at my tent ... We had a very long chat. Then he made his peace with God. The next day he was at Mass and Holy Communion. This was surely a most beautiful preparation and anticipation of the invitation that our Divine Lord was so soon to make of him'.[31]

The war ended in a stalemate and a truce was signed on 27 July 1953. Thereafter, Maryang San, which the Australians held for a month, sat north of the divide – in communist Korea. Denis O'Brien was one of 306 Australians killed in action. Another 32 died of disease and accidents and one as a prisoner of war. Up to three million Koreans died in the war. Two million of these were civilians. Just under 37 000 Americans died. As many as 900 000 Chinese soldiers were killed.[32]

War can deliver material benefits as well as great destruction and suffering. Japan, from where the UN forces were supplied, and to where the personnel went for recuperation, did well out of the Korean conflict. The economic fillip supplemented aid provided by the US intended to remake Japan as a modern capitalist, democratic bulwark against Asian communism. Australia, too, benefitted from Japan's miraculous transformation by providing iron ore, coal, sugar, wheat and wool. It signed a trade agreement with the old enemy in 1957. By 1968 Japan was receiving nearly one-quarter of all Australian exports, almost twice the amount sent to Britain. In return, Australia received the output of that manufacturing revival, in particular cheap motor vehicles and electronic goods such as transistor radios, record players and televisions. All was part of the growing consumer boom of the 1960s and 1970s and integral to the development of a new popular culture, different already from that described by Donald Horne in the early 1960s and sitting between the old ties to Britain and the new allure of America. And so the Korean War indirectly played a part in Australia's slow economic and cultural integration into its region.

That role is rarely acknowledged, for the war itself is seldom remarked upon. It is the 'forgotten war', as historians, perhaps paradoxically, often note as they write about it.[33] The Korean crisis is overshadowed in the popular consciousness by the conflict it presaged, the Vietnam War.

CHAPTER 16

Confronting communism and decoupling a colony

'... to achieve such an habitual closeness of relations with the United States...'

In 1955 James McAuley agreed to edit a new conservative journal of politics and culture. *Quadrant* first appeared in the summer of 1956. Its name referred to the so-called four corners of the world and, as McAuley noted in the first editorial, 'it is this quarter of the globe that we are particularly interested in'.[1]

That issue included an article titled 'The Communist Conspiracy in Asia', by the Tasmanian-born journalist Denis Warner, who was then writing for the British *Daily Telegraph*. Warner had been reporting on the threat posed by China since 1949. Then he questioned the role of Australia's occupation force in Japan, when troops might be better stationed in Singapore to help defend against the threat from communism in Malaya. Warner went to Korea in 1950, wrote commentaries upon the war and predicted the difficulties which would follow victory or defeat: 'eight million North Koreans are but a drop in the bucket of 500 million East Asians now under Communist rule'.[2] In 1954 Warner reported from Dien Bien Phu in Vietnam as the French were losing control of their colony to the Viet Minh. The assessment presented in *Quadrant* in 1956 accorded with the Eisenhower administration's 'domino theory' of Asian countries toppling one after another if China and the Soviet Union were left unchecked.

McAuley's focus was on the threat from leftist fellow travellers and the naïve at home. In *Quadrant*'s 1959 summer issue, he characterised modern liberalism as a tepid but no less dangerous precursor to communism.[3] There followed a highly critical review titled 'Australians in Wonderland or How Not to Be Guided' by the American academic Richard L Walker, author of three Australian books on China. Socialist Labor politician and playwright Leslie Haylen's sympathetic account of Mao's revolution, *Chinese Journey*, had just been published. Dymphna Cusack's *Chinese Women Speak* appeared in 1958 and followed the novelist and social activist's trip through China with her communist partner Norman Randolph Freehill. Cusack had been invited to Peking following the production of her play *Pacific Paradise*, written in response to American hydrogen bomb tests on Bikini Atoll. The third was CP FitzGerald's 1958 study *Flood Tide in China*, written after a cultural tour of China in 1956. British-born FitzGerald had been appointed Professor in Far Eastern History at the ANU in 1954. In that year he joined with Bishop Burgmann, Jim Davidson – then Bernard Smith's doctoral supervisor – and the historian Manning Clark in publicly cautioning the Australian government against accepting overtures from US Secretary of State John Foster Dulles to oppose the Viet Minh militarily. The Vietnamese, they argued, were nationalists, not communists.

Walker's critique of the books centred on the respective authors' silence on Mao's repression of his own people and China's recent 'genocidal' invasion of Tibet. All were apologists in some way. Therein lay the polemics of the foreign policy debate as it would unfold in Australia over the following decade. On the one side, conservatives and those on the right recognised the brutality of Chinese, Soviet and Vietnamese communism and loathed the hypocrisy, blindness and naivety of the liberal left who rejected or ignored evidence of repression. Human rights, it seemed, were not defended if abusive regimes were of the left. On the other, American arrogance and ignorance was seen to be increasing tensions needlessly. As the war in Vietnam unfolded in all its awful, well-reported brutality, it was easier to hurl the accusation of 'hypocrisy' at the US.

FitzGerald and his colleagues were trying to sound a note of 'realism' in attempting to distinguish nationalism from ideology in the motivations of Ho Chi Minh's and thereby separating the conflict with the French from any notion of falling dominoes and worldwide conspiracies. Remarkably the Vietnamese Declaration of Independence, which Ho co-authored in 1945, directly quoted its American antecedent of 1776 in making the case for liberation from the French. The four Australian academics were correct in their assessment while Ho Chi Minh retained real power. But the failure to hold national elections after the 1954 partition of Vietnam which followed the French defeat at Dien Bien Phu was an early indication of the corrupt, anti-democratic motivations of those who purported to represent a free Vietnam in the south. In the north the relegation of 'Uncle Ho' to the role of symbolic figurehead, and First Secretary Le Duan's assumption of power from 1959 resulted in a more unrelenting Maoist stance. The north's fight for reunification became ideological and ruthless. It was not, however, necessarily part of a push for world domination orchestrated from either Moscow or Peking.

The imminent defeat of the French in Vietnam nonetheless conjured images of Asian dominoes. President Eisenhower used the analogy in a press conference in April 1954 as the battle of Dien Bien Phu was underway. The inevitability of the process so described militated against any subtlety in policy response. Once the first domino fell there was a 'certainty' that the last 'will go over very quickly'. The implications for America's ANZUS partners were spelled out clearly: when the 'island defensive chain' of Japan, Taiwan and the Philippines is breached or by-passed, communism 'moves in to threaten Australia and New Zealand'.[4] Despite this alarming scenario, Australia did not intervene as Dulles had hoped. The situation in Vietnam in 1954 was clearly hopeless. The Menzies government did, however, sign the anti-communist South East Asian Treaty Organization (SEATO) at the end of that year, along with Britain, France, New Zealand, Pakistan and the US, which facilitated the pact. Despite the grouping's name, only two South-East Asian nations chose to join: the Philippines and Thailand. South Vietnam was a 'protocol state', not entitled to membership as were independent nations but subject to the protection of the other states.

By 1960 southern rebels called the National Liberation Front or Viet Cong were fomenting widespread resistance to the repressive regime in South Vietnam. The US and Australian administrations interpreted this as evidence of northern aggression against the south rather than a civil war within the south. In 1961 Australia considered a military commitment, in answer to American suggestions to that effect. It provided non-combat instructors and transport aircraft in 1962. Menzies justified that deployment as a response to South Vietnamese requests for assistance, something foreign policy academic Coral Bell would diplomatically describe as a 'very distant approximation of the truth'.[5] As the situation deteriorated by mid-1964, the Americans looked both to increase their military commitment, limited then to 'advisors', and secure overt support from its SEATO allies. This was not a UN-sanctioned police action as the Korean intervention had been. The Gulf of Tonkin incident, which involved an altercation between North Vietnamese and US naval vessels in 1964, was the pretext for committing ground troops in 'the defense of freedom' to quote President Johnson the following year.[6] Australia agreed to commit combatants, although its 'instructors' had already been engaged in effective covert operations under the command of the Australian jungle warfare specialist Colonel Francis 'Ted' Serong. In the paraphrased official summary of Australian involvement in Vietnam, tabled in parliament in 1975, it was revealed that the Department of External Affairs recommended a 'prompt and positive response' so as to 'pick up a lot of credit with the United States'.[7]

That was essentially the same argument that Percy Spender made to Robert Menzies regarding the commitment in Korea. 'Our objective should be to achieve such an habitual closeness of relations with the United States and sense of mutual alliance that in our time of need (the possibility of a crisis in relations with Indonesia) the United States would have little option but to respond as we would want.'[8] Whereas, in

1950, Australia was hoping to ensure assistance with unforeseen future threats, in 1964 it was the real concern about the communist Sukarno government in the continent's nearest South-East Asian neighbour that made 'forward defence' in Vietnam strategically appealing. Britain did not commit troops. As Coral Bell has pointed out, 'The Vietnam War was the first military engagement in which Australia was a participant without Britain also being involved'.[9] Prime Minister Menzies again told the public that deploying combat troops was a response to a request for help from the South Vietnamese government and therefore in line with SEATO obligations to the protocol state. It was a justification which belied Australian eagerness and stretched veracity as much as the commitment in 1962. The government wanted to get involved and needed no extra prompting from the Vietnamese or the Americans.

However, that eagerness was driven by a realist rather than idealist assessment of threat and differed accordingly from the American justification for intervention. In his 'Doctrine' of 1947, President Truman had committed the US to defending the freedom of free nations in accord with the UN Charter. In 1965 President Johnson told Americans that after World War Two their nation bore the ongoing responsibility for the defence of freedom. It was Wilsonianism applied to the worldwide threat of communism. In this formulation, creating a liberal democratic order was both moral and in America's national interest. The world would be a better place if remade in America's image. That task was underway in Japan and western Europe.

Australians shared with their US counterparts a belief in the inherent aggressiveness of communism – Menzies called it 'Imperial Communism' – and politicians did occasionally speak of defending 'freedom' in Asia.[10] But the Australian national interest as defined with the Vietnam intervention seemed more a continuation of a long-held fear of Asia than any desire to be part of a global or even regional crusade for humanity. Communist China, expanding now because of its Maoist ideology, was but the latest incarnation of the yellow peril.

The lessons of World War Two suggested that it was prudent to stop an advancing adversary some way from one's doorstep. This would only be possible with American involvement. There were clear links in all this with Billy Hughes's world view and strategy.

The strategy reflected a general mindset. Stephen FitzGerald, who would become Australia's first ambassador to communist China in 1973, recalled attitudes in his native and still very Anglophilic Tasmania in the 1950s and early 1960s: Asia was a 'place to be kept at arm's length'. There was 'paradox' in that parochialism, for many Tasmanians, FitzGerald knew, had been directly involved with Asia and Asians while serving overseas in New Guinea, Korea and Malaya. But this experience had not permeated the 'general community'. The mainland cities and towns were more cosmopolitan but the insularity was near universal: 'Australia was not in any sense Asian …'[11]

The first official combatants – the First Battalion RAR – arrived in Vietnam in May 1965. They were stationed at a former French coastal resort town called Vung Tau on the South China Sea, due west of the Philippines. Australia's commitment increased to 8300 by 1968. Some 60 000 personnel from the army, air force and navy would serve in and around Vietnam between 1962 and 1972. The American commitment rose to nearly 540 000 in 1968. Vung Tau was one of several towns that grew with the war. Some 3000 'bar girls' were employed in the 170 venues in which Australian, American, New Zealand, Thai and Korean soldiers were entertained while on 'rest and recreation' leave. For the Australians this might have been a three-day break after more than two months patrolling and fighting. Many were conscripts.

From 1966 the Australians operated under their own, rather than US, command. They developed a reputation for informality, much as the ANZACs were differentiated from the British Army in World War One. But as in Korea, both Australians and Americans were foreigners intervening in a war between 'one people'. The difficulty of distinguishing friend from foe and, in time, the purpose of the horrific scale of death and destruction unleashed damaged the minds of many who escaped the bullets, mines and shells. Australian tactics differed from those of the Americans. Where the latter depended upon fire power and helicopter support which noisily announced the US presence, the Australians relied on stealth.[12] Their casualties were accordingly proportionally lower; 521 men were killed and more than 3000 wounded.

All nine battalions of the RAR served at some point during the decade of Australia's Vietnam involvement. The numbers were tiny, however, compared to the US commitment. The support was symbolic for both allies. Australia was demonstrating loyalty and the US was receiving legitimacy. More strategically significant was the role Australia played as the location for American bases. The submarine communication station at North West Cape was operational in 1967. The Central Intelligence Agency (CIA) surveillance station at Pine Gap in central Australia was operational in 1970 following a treaty signed in 1966. The satellite early warning facility at Nurrungar followed in 1971. All were critical in prosecuting America's broader 'Cold War'. The activities at Pine Gap were so secretive – mysterious even to Australian politicians and defence personnel – that many would come to regard its presence as an abrogation of Australian sovereignty, the territorial equivalent perhaps of Douglas MacArthur's command in World War Two. It was a small piece of America in the heart of Australia.

When 1 RAR returned to Sydney after a year 'in country' in June 1966, enthusiastic crowds lined George Street to welcome them. These were young men who had served their country maintaining a forward defence line in Asia. Lyndon Johnson received an equally exuberant reception when he visited in October, the first US president to do so. The American expressed his appreciation of Australia. Harold Holt, who had only just assumed the prime ministership following the voluntary retirement of elderly Anglophile Robert Menzies, declared reciprocal loyalty to the US. It was a profound changing of the guard.

Herbert Evatt had resigned from leading the Labor Party after a stroke in 1962, having tried to negotiate the difficult path between foreign policy independence and obsequious acquiescence. His equivocation on the issue of recognising communist China in the face of Coalition accusations of anti-Americanism and weakness exemplified that difficulty. Evatt's successor Arthur Calwell, long a defender of 'White Australia', also had a deep-seated antipathy to conscription and fought the election in November 1966 accordingly. The Coalition won convincingly. The result was seen, unsurprisingly, as an endorsement of the war and the alliance with America.

Such was his respect for his Australian counterpart that President Johnson returned to Australia in December 1967 to attend the prime minister's memorial service. Holt had disappeared, feared drowned, while scuba diving in a foaming sea outside the heads of Port Phillip Bay.

≈

'a messy and uncertain business'

While it may not have won Labor the 1966 election, the issue of conscription rapidly merged with a broader anti-war and anti-nuclear movement to become the pre-eminent focus of protest. Catholic nuns found common cause with the young men who burned their draft papers in public. News of consequent incarcerations and brutalisation garnered further support for the cause. By 1969 the war itself was widely unpopular. A majority of Australians, 55 per cent according to one poll, favoured withdrawing troops from Vietnam. Accordingly, Labor did markedly better in that year's election, having committed to ending Australia's involvement. In 1970, 200 000 people around the country took part in marches demanding an end – a 'moratorium' – to the fighting.

The radicalisation of Australian society was dramatic. It was part of a huge international social shift in which definable youth cultures emerged and enjoyed unprecedented influence. The neo-Romantic 'counter-culture' and the related anti-war movement in the US were inspirations across the world. Paradoxically that also fuelled an unprecedented level of anti-Americanism in many Western societies. Australia was embracing and rejecting its trans-Pacific neighbour in equal measure. On Australian university campuses there emerged a swirling mix of feminism, environmentalism, libertarianism and Marxism; one given expression in music and fashion which bore little resemblance to anything older generations could relate to. Affluence, technology and demographics played a large part in this. But so, too, did the catalysing effect of the Vietnam War.

One apotheosis of this radicalism – there were many – was an article written by the Adelaide-based academic and anti-war activist Brian Medlin in 1972. The piece, written for *Dialectic*, a journal published by the University of Newcastle, countenanced the 'wholesale assassination' of the Australian cabinet. The measure was rejected, not on the grounds of morality or hypocrisy, but because it would 'strengthen the Australian counter-revolution'.[13]

James McAuley looked upon the anti-war movement and the related radicalisation of Australian universities with disgust. He had taken up a position in the English Department at the University of Tasmania in 1961 and from there taught and politicked in the cause of anti-communism with right-wing Catholics such as BA Santamaria. In 1965 McAuley was the founding president of Peace With Freedom (PWF), a group established to counter left-dominated anti-war sentiment in universities. The following year he travelled to Vietnam with PWF colleagues. There McAuley interviewed Prime Minister Nguyen Cao Ky, who had come to power in 1965 amidst the chaos of South Vietnamese politics. Calwell called Ky a 'fascist dictator'. Just eight years later historian Alfred McCoy would expose his links to the opium trade in South-East Asia.[14] McAuley found him charming and likeable. But the Australian was not naïve. He knew Ky was part of the 'messy and uncertain business' of winning a war. Describing the encounter in an article for the *Sydney Morning Herald*, McAuley reminded readers the situation in the south was better than the 'economic wretchedness and unfreedom' in North Vietnam; 'People outside forget that too easily'.[15]

The student unrest in Australia spread across the continent, even reaching McAuley's institution. It was at the University of Tasmania that the young Stephen FitzGerald had been exposed to Asia in that tiny oasis of cosmopolitanism on the banks of the Derwent River. McAuley argued against faculty support for the moratorium movement. He regarded the radicalism of the time as a juvenile pantomime, bereft of intellectual or moral foundations – sillier than its antecedents. Its characters had a 'mania for dressing up in costume, for play-acting' and regarding themselves with 'fantastic self-importance'.[16] McAuley liaised with the Australian Secret Intelligence Organisation (ASIO), which had long monitored the peace and student movements and compiled dossiers on their members, communists and non-communists alike, but his public role had been made harder after financial links between his journal *Quadrant* and the CIA, via the internationally active Congress for Cultural Freedom, were revealed in 1967.

The tide was turning against the anti-communism advocated by the social conservatives. A new, pragmatic American president, Richard Nixon, was losing the will to fight in Vietnam, and indeed provide the unequivocal support promised in the first two decades of the Cold War. The so-called Guam Doctrine, announced on the western Pacific island that had housed US naval forces since the defeat of the Japanese, was interpreted as a retreat from east Asia and a disavowal of interventionism. The announcement threw into doubt the Australian strategy of forward defence and support for US policy as a means of firming the alliance. The Coalition began withdrawing troops from Vietnam in 1970. Nixon travelled to China in February 1972, the first American president to do so.

The election of the Whitlam Labor government in November 1972 was emblematic of the times. Though Gough Whitlam was from the right of the party, he appealed to a widespread 'progressive' sentiment in Australian society. His government embraced a 'new nationalism' which differentiated Australia from both America and Britain. Whitlam declared support for Aboriginal land rights. He appointed a governmental advisor on women's affairs in 1973, the first such position in the world. Within his first week in office, Whitlam announced that the remaining Australian troops would withdraw from Vietnam.

The recognition of the People's Republic of China followed quickly on 21 December 1972. In the words of McAuley's biographer, the diplomatic turn cast the intellectual into a 'deep depression'.[17] Stephen FitzGerald, still only in his thirties, was appointed as Australia's first ambassador to communist China. In Beijing there was some concern that the new diplomat was in fact academic CP FitzGerald. The author of *Flood Tide in China* was by then *persona non grata* in the republic, having written critically of the famine of the early 1960s and more recently of the Cultural Revolution, Mao's 'great experiment in mass psychology'.[18] The Chinese premier in 1972 was Zhou Enlai, who 10 years earlier had declared that doctrinal purity and 'the centre of world revolution' had 'moved from Moscow to Beijing', and ever since tried to negotiate a path of self-preservation amidst the madness Mao had unleashed.[19] At least 30 million died in the famine of the early 1960s which resulted from Mao's policies. Tens of thousands were murdered and tortured during the Cultural Revolution, which he encouraged. Stephen FitzGerald experienced the Maoist terror during a trip to China in 1968 and was himself threatened with execution at the hands of a mob. But that just convinced him of the need to 'engage'.

In fact, there was engagement already – the wheat trade alone between Australia and communist China was worth the equivalent of $100 million a year through the 1960s. Pragmatism was always balanced against principle. Things were 'messy', as McAuley said of the ethical dilemma of supporting South Vietnam. That balancing act was no less evident when Whitlam, as both prime minister and foreign minister, addressed the National Press Club in Washington in July 1973: 'I have been appalled at the damage we of the West have done to ourselves and to other peoples by our Western ideological preoccupations, particularly in Southeast Asia. We are not going to be readily forgiven for throwing away the chance we had for a settlement in Indochina in 1954 ...'[20]

≋

'... deeply rooted in the needs and the aspirations of the people'

In the decade that Australians spent wading through the literal and figurative quagmires of post-colonial Vietnam, the country was attempting to negotiate its own decolonisation process. Papua New Guinea achieved self-government in 1973 and independence in 1975, both under the Whitlam administration. The process which led to that mirrored the timeframe of the war in Vietnam. A United Nations Mission visit to New Guinea in 1962 had urged Australia to make greater progress in higher education for the territory. The report was equally insistent that the time had come, 'for an imaginative advance which would create a truly representative parliament'.[21] It suggested that a general election for 'such a parliament' in April 1964 might be achievable. The UN mission followed the 1960 Declaration of the Granting of Independence to Colonial Countries and Peoples, which opened with the assertion that 'The subjection of peoples of alien subjugation, domination and exploitation constitutes a denial of fundamental human rights'.[22] The declaration and the 1962 report carried with them the strong suggestion that Australia was denying the human rights of Papuans and New Guineans through inaction. Paul Hasluck, then minister for territories, responded defensively, reminding his audience of public servants in Port Moresby that the UN had 'designated Australia "as the sole authority which will exercise the administration of the Territory"'. Furthermore, Papua was 'an Australian possession'. Any action, he declared, 'will be deeply rooted in the needs and the aspirations of the people'.[23]

Australia had acted, albeit cautiously. It established a Legislative Council of appointees in 1951. A decade later seven of the 28 council members were Papuan or New Guinean. Then, in 1964, a House of Assembly representing both colony and territory was elected by universal suffrage, with a majority of Indigenous members. That shift towards a representative governance occurred just 80 years after the British had declared their protectorate over Papua at the urging of Queensland and the other colonies. The creation of a democratic assembly within living memory of that incursion into a territory of disparate peoples was remarkable. The University of Papua New Guinea opened in 1967.

The dilemma facing the Australian government and its administration in Papua and New Guinea was that they needed to gauge the 'needs and aspirations' of the people whom they had governed. They were confronted with the legacy of Australia's perceived self-interest: the need to establish a security buffer in the north, the need to deny the islands to other powers, the desire for resources including labour, the widespread belief that territories inhabited by 'natives' were there for the taking. There was also the messianic urge to bring Christianity and/or civilisation to those 'darker races', an urge to which Rudyard Kipling famously referred in the context of US Pacific expansion as 'the white man's burden' but one rarely regarded as 'self-interest'. But, as it formed such a strong element of the 'white' sense of self, that was what it was.

Robert Tabua from Daru and Simogen Pita from Wewak were among those elected to the 1964 assembly. Just two years earlier they had been part of a 14-person group permitted to travel to Australia on a 'Political Education Tour', an expedition they had initiated but which the Australian administration facilitated willingly. The group comprised public servants, farmers and teachers. One man from Mount Hagen, Kup Ogut, described himself as an 'entrepreneur'. They spent three weeks with a full itinerary in Canberra and its surrounds visiting Federal Parliament, the Australian War Memorial, parts of the Snowy Mountains Hydro-electric Scheme and the regional centre of Queanbeyan.[24] They would have seen the very white, very 'lucky' country Donald Horne described. If that writer's assessment of his fellow Australians was correct, the Melanesians' curiosity would not have been reciprocated. It was an 'accident of geography', rather than a result of abiding widespread concern, that 'such a suburban and unambitious people as the Australians should become one of the last colonial powers'.[25]

It is unlikely too that the visitors saw any other familiar faces. In 1947 there were just 1600 Melanesians living in Australia. That was less than a fifth of the population in 1901, before the *Pacific Island Labourers Act* took effect. Most of that tiny number lived far away from Canberra in north Queensland. Immigration restrictions had not relented despite a world war and the UN Declaration of Universal Human Rights. Remarkably enough Papuans and New Guineans were Australian citizens – they made up nearly a sixth of the wider Commonwealth population – but they could not travel to the mainland or live there without special dispensation.[26]

'Race' and difference was a major part of the barrier for both sides – the white coloniser and the black person who was colonised. Despite all the nuanced work of anthropologists, Australian commentators repeatedly characterised the task before the country as one of dragging 'stone age' people into the modern era – another expression of the 'burden' that came with superiority. Many in the populace, even those with direct experience of the territories, would have agreed. Though no expert himself, Donald Horne condemned Australia's 'almost complete oblivion to the world of Oceania'. In 1964 he saw no alternative to creating 'a Republic of New Guinea'. For while some local people held out hope for the territories becoming a seventh state of Australia and perhaps sharing some of the nation's good fortune, 'nobody' on the mainland took that seriously.[27] So geography, too, was important for understanding the tenuousness of allegiance. The islands were Australian but clearly not part of the 'lucky country'.

Furthermore, the administration barely controlled the whole of the territories. Many people, particularly in the remoter parts of the western highlands, were only lightly affected by decisions made in

Port Moresby, let alone Canberra. Loyalties there were still very local. And yet the impacts of 80 years of contact with Europeans, whether Australian, British, German or French, were being felt across the islands. Some of these were first-hand; many were twice or three times removed as relationships to ceremony, family, work, gardening, trade, status, enemies and friends changed.

In 1964, as the assembly was coming into existence, CD Rowley was writing the first study of colonial impact which addressed the 'native' perspective. It was a profoundly empathetic analysis which drew on the author's direct experiences and the work of anthropologists. Rowley headed the Australian School of Pacific Administration (ASOPA), situated on the heights above Sydney Harbour in bushland near one of the city's most affluent suburbs. The school had been established in 1946 as the brainchild of the mercurial Alf Conlon, head of the wartime Directorate of Research, and the Labor minister for external territories, Eddie Ward. The school became a training college for administrators while anthropological and historical research was conducted at the ANU. Rowley used the 'New Guinea villager' as the focus of his early 1960s study, for the 'village' was 'the basic social unit' in the territories.[28] So much followed from the disruption to that unit. The introduction of a cash economy through growing ground nuts, coffee, copra and so forth weakened bonds to the garden. 'Slash and burn' agricultural methods created sustainable gardens when the land owned by a group was adequate for such rotation. It was not suitable for intensive cropping. Not all the changes resulted from exploitative intentions. 'Pacification' was intended to eliminate the violence that seemed to be a constant part of life for many Papuans and New Guineans. The life of a pig was substituted for that of a human in some areas where taking a head was a rite of passage. As Rowley noted dispassionately, before colonisation 'the New Guinean village had to maintain itself in a world without imposed order or protection from state power' or, indeed, a universal religion.[29] Revenge and retaliation created an endless dynamic that seemed to sustain just as it destroyed.

The imposition of state power and the reduction of violence transformed villages. They got bigger or they moved to formerly unsafe places. New alliances and relationships were formed. *Wantoks*, or 'one talks' – linguistic networks which bonded those of a very local language or dialect group – grew to link people from a wider region. The horizon expanded for many, but the idea of a nation state called Papua New Guinea was still an extraordinary and difficult concept to realise.

There was movement to the larger centres such as Port Moresby and Lae and Mount Hagen. It was a form of urbanisation radically different from village life. Australian anthropologist Murray Groves had written of the impact of this upon the Motu of Port Moresby in a doctoral thesis he completed at Oxford University before moving to the ANU and the Pacific School in 1956. He summarised his conclusions in an article for *Quadrant* the following year. Groves presented a bleak picture of a people cut off from their culture in a setting that trammelled tradition while fostering a desire for change and newness. 'There is no integrating spiritual tradition at the centre of urban Motu life', he wrote, 'no truth to symbolize, and therefore no symbols. The people have abandoned their past. They shrink from a future they cannot foresee. They live entirely in the present'.[30]

It was an assessment which James McAuley, as the journal's editor, must have found compelling. McAuley worked at ASOPA from its establishment in 1946 until he departed for the University of Tasmania in 1961. He was a senior lecturer, sometime acting principal and regular contributor to its journal *South Pacific*, which he also came to edit. Despite the left-leaning idealism which launched the school, McAuley was soon critical of the goal of introducing 'liberal capitalism' to Papua and New Guinea, preferring instead some form of social development which better sustained tradition rather than endless disruptive change. In an essay published in 1953 McAuley explored 'Australia's future in New Guinea' and made the radical suggestion that incorporating the Melanesian territory completely into the Commonwealth, rather than creating a poverty-stricken republic on Australia's border, was the best option for all involved. It could only work, of course, if the local people could travel and work freely in Australia, most likely Queensland, and thereby realise their aspirations to the higher living standards that would accompany absorption. He did not explain how they might achieve the laudable goal of economic equality without undermining long-held social structures. And incorporation, of course, required the end of 'White Australia', of which McAuley was no supporter. If New Guinea were to follow such a path, he argued, it should take it sooner rather than later before a nationalist sentiment emerged infused with the 'bitterness' that would be the inevitable result of decades of insult to the 'sense of personal being and self-respect of a people' at the hands of white expatriates.[31]

That guarded optimism dissolved into frustration and cynicism in the face of the challenge of providing development in the absence of some greater goal. The 'Mekeo Litany', which McAuley hand-wrote in 1951 presumably for his own cathartic amusement, listed a set of problems besetting local people in an area which had been the focus of intensive rice production. It was clearly a prayer of sorts, with the refrain 'Good Lord deliver them [from]' and 'Litany' used as a play on 'Liturgy'. Among the evils requiring deliverance were 'broken promises', the technocratic mentality of the administrators, 'the notion of Plasticine Man ... and the Meccano Mentality' and the 'idolatry of tractors and ploughs and headers and harvesters'. Of the evils confronting 'us', the administrators, McAuley listed 'ineptitude', bureaucracy and 'confusion'.[32]

Modernity, whether pursued by free market capitalism or centralised socialism, was the problem. It drove people into cities, ate away the sinews of community and eroded the basis of meaning in both developing and developed societies. In a lecture called 'The Clash of Cultures', which McAuley presented at Christian Social Week in May 1956, he spoke of how the ever-changing adaptive civilisation of Europe rose at the expense of stable cultures: 'The modern west is unique. It stands over against [sic] not only its own past but all other civilisations and cultures; as far as the west is concerned they are archaic ...' It was a case, he suggested of "The West against the Rest".[33]

That catch-cry sounded quite a lot like Gough Whitlam's admonition of the US and Australia for the outcome in Vietnam in 1973. 'We of the West' had caused that debacle. Each *mea culpa* came from quite different political traditions, the one social and religious conservatism, the other social and secular progressivism. James McAuley never publicly resiled from his support of the war in Asia. That was, he believed, a case of good against evil.

He wrote his last major piece on the territories, called 'My New Guinea', in 1961 as he prepared to depart for Tasmania and before his anti-communism became all-consuming. In that summation of nearly 20 years of engagement, McAuley described the effect of witnessing 'the great drama of the disintegration of traditional cultures' and 'intellectual crisis' that had created for him as he grappled with 'every question about the nature of man and society'. He also asked 'What kind of New Guinea are we making?' and maintained that Australia must 'bear a great deal of the responsibility' for the outcome regardless of the decisions local people took. Decolonisation was coming too quickly yet it was impossible to forestall. 'New Guinea', he concluded, is 'a test of our quality as a people.'[34]

It was Gough Whitlam who forced the issue as much as anyone. He had visited the territory as opposition leader in December 1969 and January 1971 and made it clear, with characteristic confidence, that self-government and independence would occur within his first term, 'no matter what PNG might want', in the words of James Griffin, who had been one of the first Australian lecturers to teach at the University of Papua New Guinea.[35] For Whitlam it was not in Australia's interest to delay the matter despite the fact that many local people did not want self-government quite so soon. A decade or more later seemed more realistic. Nonetheless when Independence came and Whitlam took the stage in Port Moresby next to the first Prime Minister of Papua New Guinea, Michael Somare, he was regarded as a 'liberator'. The country's first governor-general, Sir John Guise, was gracious as the Australian flag descended: 'We are lowering it not tearing it down'.[36] It was poignant that Guise was the grandchild of an English trader and Papuan woman.

≋

'There was nothing left to remind me that we had ever lived there'

Australian-born Judith Hollinshed went to the Western Highlands in 1956 and became a pioneer of the coffee-growing industry. She raised a family there. In time the community of friends, mainly other expatriates with some local people, recreated something of Australia's suburban culture as they installed pools around airy homes and barbecues became regular events. In 1975 Hollinshed witnessed the lowering of the Australian flag and the raising of the new flag of Papua New Guinea at the growing town of Mount Hagen. Many Australians, she recalled 30 years later, thought 'the country was not ready'. There were cheers and tears as the flags were swapped, emotions that depended largely upon skin colour.

Hollinshed left in 1980, one of thousands of expatriates to do so after Independence. She returned in 2000, to bury the ashes of her husband on the coffee plantation they had run at Alimp near Mount Hagen. The occasion prompted 'a jumble of emotions'. Local people greeted Hollinshed and her sons so warmly, and were themselves so familiar in their habits, that the Australian wondered whether she had 'too easily' cut them from their lives. Yet the streets of Mount Hagen were now lined with rubbish and razor wire extended above high walls. Traditional and colonial orders were changing and, indeed, breaking down. After interring her husband, Hollinshed walked up their old driveway and mused: 'There was nothing left to remind me that we had ever lived there'.[37] James McAuley, who died in 1976, would not have been surprised.

CHAPTER 17

The end of White Australia, refugees and reassessments

"'G'day mate", he shouted, "Welcome to Australia!"'

Papua New Guineans could not enter Australia without an 'Australian guarantor' as late as 1970, although Harold Holt had begun dismantling the White Australia policy in 1966.[1] Māori fared better, but New Zealanders with origins in the islands were kept out until 1973. Nonetheless, trans-Tasman exchange boomed in the early 1970s. The influx of 'Kiwis' – Māori included – doubled, so that the famous beachside Sydney suburb of Bondi gained a reputation as a 'little New Zealand'.[2]

Complete repudiation of the policy of race-based immigration came only after the Whitlam government was elected in 1972. Restrictions on non-European New Zealanders ended the following year. The *Australian Citizenship Act* of 1973 removed the historical privileges given to white British citizens residing in Australia. In 1975 the government passed the *Racial Discrimination Act*, which ratified the 1969 UN Convention on the Elimination of All Forms of Racial Discrimination and outlawed discrimination on the basis of ethnicity.[3]

Fiji's first Indigenous leader, Ratu Mara, had challenged the previous Coalition government on the issue of Islander exclusion in 1972, just months before Whitlam's election. He came to power with Fijian independence in 1970, itself part of the post-war move to decolonisation across the Pacific and the world. Tonga achieved that status in the same year. Western Samoa became independent in 1962. The Cook Islands were self-governing from 1965. Nauru gained independence in 1968.

As the world's smallest republic, it could be accommodated 40 times over in Australia's sprawling suburban capital, Canberra. Tiny though it was, the island had 12 tribes, each represented by a point on the star that graced the nation's new flag.

Australia had been a trustee of Nauru, alongside Great Britain and New Zealand, since the defeat of the Germans in World War One. There was an interlude of three years during the Japanese occupation of the island from 1942, after which Australia's role as the primary administrator resumed. While the UN Trusteeship Council supported Nauruan aspirations, the Menzies government argued against self-government for the island in the early 1950s on the basis that the Islanders were an 'indolent' people who had taken little interest in mining the phosphate built up over thousands of years as birds deposited their droppings on the limestone.[4] Nauru played a disproportionate role in making 'the lucky country' described by Donald Horne. Australia imported 70 per cent of the island's phosphate to fertilise its own nutrient-poor soils. Superphosphate, the product of processed phosphate, made up 90 per cent of all artificial fertiliser for grazing pasture and cropping used in Australia.[5] Ocean and Christmas Islands in present-day Kiribati were also mined. In 1964 annual exports from Nauru to Australia alone were 1 000 000 tons, where they had totalled 300 000 to all buyers in 1927. With that rate of extraction, supplies would only last until 1996, so Nauruans pressed for independence and ownership of the rapidly depleting resource, despite Australian objections.[6] The consequent royalties made the Islanders notionally very rich but phosphate mining had also devastated the environment and fundamentally disrupted Nauruan society. Much of the money was squandered as a result of corruption and inexperience. In 1989, as exhaustion of the phosphate supplies was becoming apparent, Nauru filed a case against Australia in the International Court of Justice. The island republic contended that Australia had breached its trusteeship obligations and was legally responsible for environmental remediation. Australia made preliminary objections, then came to an out-of-court settlement in 1993 paying $73 000 000.

Anticipating the need for other revenue, Nauru had hosted the 1982 Parties to the Nauru Agreement between various Pacific island states, including itself, New Guinea, Tuvalu and Kiribati, which took advantage of the United Nations Convention on the Law of the Sea – adopted in that same year – to collectively manage and conserve tuna stocks within the islands' extended economic zones. But the income from the largest tuna fishery in the world only partially offset the loss of phosphate revenue. In 2006 Nauru resumed mining, this time tapping deeper 'secondary' layers of the mineral, producing 84 000 tonnes in that year.[7] Another revenue stream, from Australia's offshore detention regime, had begun in 2001. I deal with the so-called Pacific Solution in the following chapter.

Australia had prioritised 'political development' in the region alongside welfare in the 1944 ANZAC Treaty with New Zealand. Article 28 referred specifically to 'applying the principles of the Atlantic Charter to the Pacific', a reflection of HV Evatt's influence.[8] The result was the establishment of the South Pacific Commission in 1948. However, as it developed, the commission was a conference of colonial nations, Great Britain, France and the US, alongside New Zealand and Australia. The other powers had little interest in fostering 'political development' in an increasingly complex Cold War world and, after the Coalition's election to government in 1949, Australia did not press the issue. As a former secretary general of the commission reflected, somewhat diplomatically, in 1968: 'Australia has not always played ... the positive and leading role' in the organisation or the region that some had expected of it.[9]

Unsurprisingly the growth of Pacific independence brought with it many changes. Among them was the creation of the South Pacific Forum, later the Pacific Islands Forum, in 1971. Australia attended the first meeting, but was the only nation not to send its head of state. It was at the second meeting in Canberra in early 1972 that Ratu Mara voiced his disapproval of Australia's discriminatory immigration policy. At the third meeting, in 1973, the Whitlam government pressed to include Papua New Guinea to foster that territory's as yet unrealised independence and include it on the Pacific community of nations. The Polynesian members were reluctant, fearing that Australia might use a territorial proxy in its own self-interest. By way of compromise, self-governing Papua New Guinea became an observer. After its independence it joined as the largest 'island' state. Australia's membership was perhaps paradoxical. The forum was the realisation of a collective desire for self-determination in a decolonising world while, before 1975, Australia was still a colonial power. But such was its economic might, it could hardly have been shunned.

The political development that came despite the earlier concerns of commission members brought with it an increase in Australian government foreign aid. In the year of Nauru's independence, 1968, the total was AU$533 000. Small though that was, it represented a 13-fold increase on assistance at the beginning of the decade. The total leapt during Whitlam's years in office to well over AU$4 000 000 in 1974. Even that was modest compared to New Zealand's contribution of $7 300 000.[10]

The disparity reflected the reality that New Zealand was more politically and socially integrated into the south-west Pacific than Australia. That country had discouraged Asian migration, as Australia had, from the 1880s. A 'White New Zealand' policy was enacted in 1920. But the Indigenous people of New Zealand traced their heritage to Polynesia, and Pacific Islanders were not systematically deported as they had been in Australia. From the 1950s, migration from the islands increased with the post-war demand for labour.

Australia's economic integration in the south-west Pacific was another matter. The activities of the shipping and trading firm Burns Philp was emblematic of that connection, until its demise in the 1990s after rapid and ultimately disastrous diversification. So, too, was the widely sold Ox and Palm brand of corned beef, first marketed in 1936 to fill the need for tinned food in the islands. That was one of many products entrepreneurial Australians were shipping specifically to the

20 A 'white Australian' girl meets her Māori counterparts at the 'Māori Village' constructed on the shores of Sydney Harbour in 1910. A commercial exercise in popular anthropology, the display was the brainchild of New Zealander Makereti [Maggie] Papakura.

State Library of New South Wales

21 The Pacific's great gift to Australia. The modern Australian love of surfing and surf bathing was inspired by Islanders. The well-promoted surfing demonstrations by Hawaiian man Duke Paoa Kahanamoku in 1914–1915 further fuelled the passion.

State Library of New South Wales

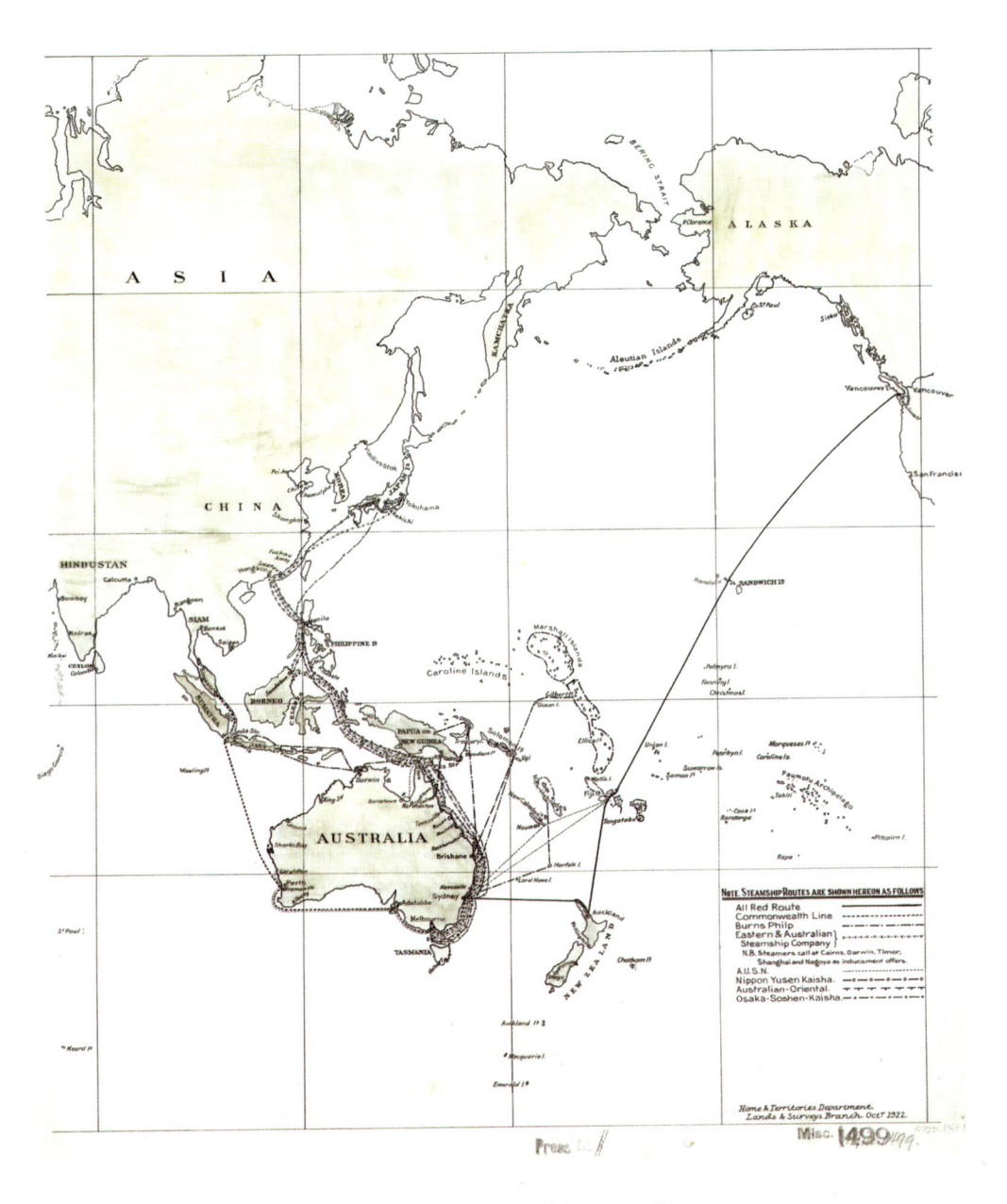

22 Australia's Pacific. This Home and Territories Department map shows steamship routes to and from Australia and Pacific destinations. Interestingly, China and Japan appear to be well serviced.

National Library of Australia

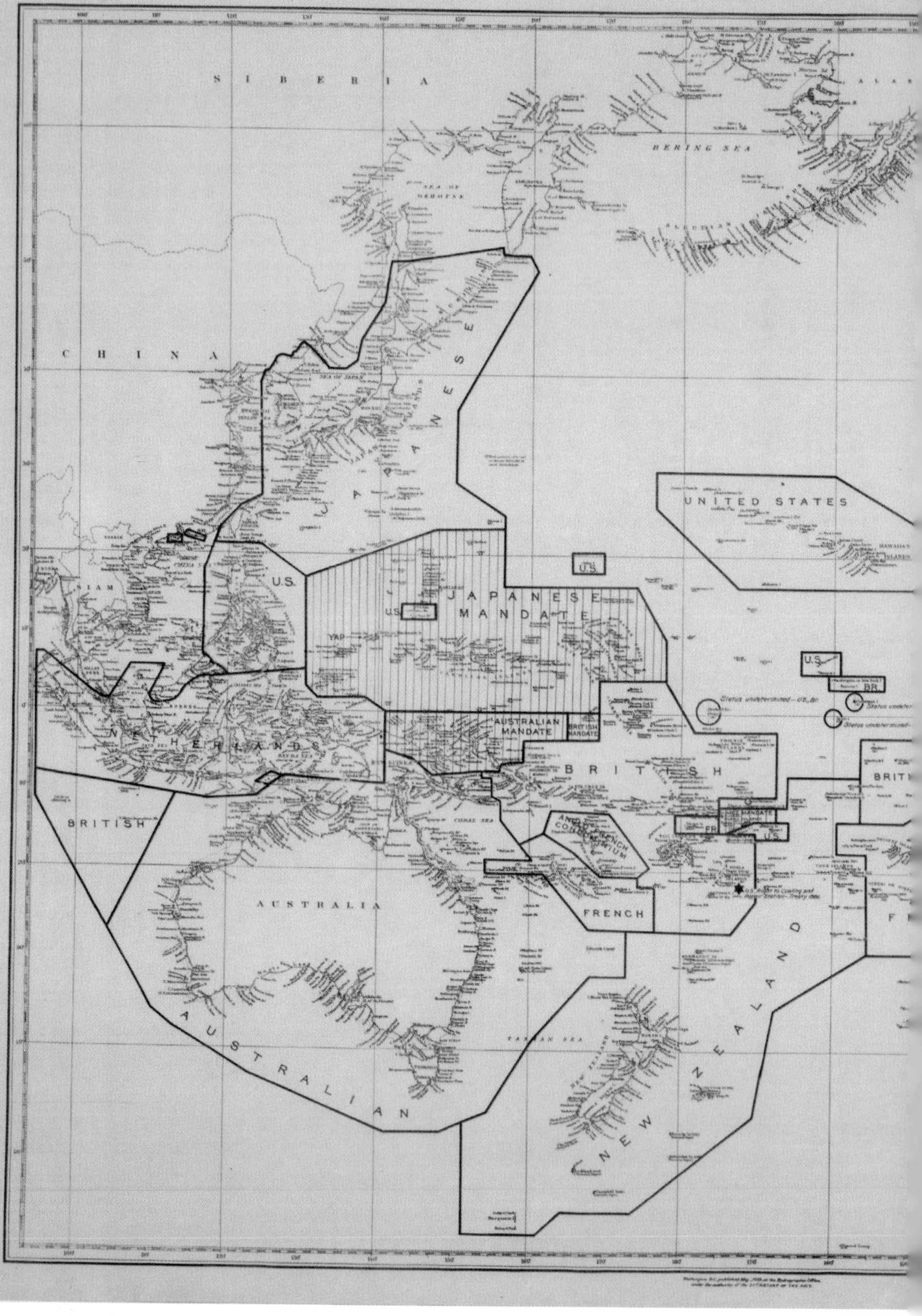

SIBERIA
BERING SEA
SEA OF OKHOTSK
CHINA
SEA OF JAPAN
JAPANESE
UNITED STATES
HAWAIIAN ISLANDS
U.S.
SIAM
U.S.
JAPANESE MANDATE
U.S.
YAP
U.S.
BR.
Status undetermined—U.S., Br.
Status undeter
Status undetermined
NETHERLANDS
AUSTRALIAN MANDATE
BRITISH MANDATE
BRITISH
MANDATE
FR.
U.S.
BRIT
BRITISH
CORAL SEA
ANGLO-FRENCH CONDOMINIUM
AUSTRALIA
FRENCH
F
TASMAN SEA
AUSTRALIAN
NEW ZEALAND

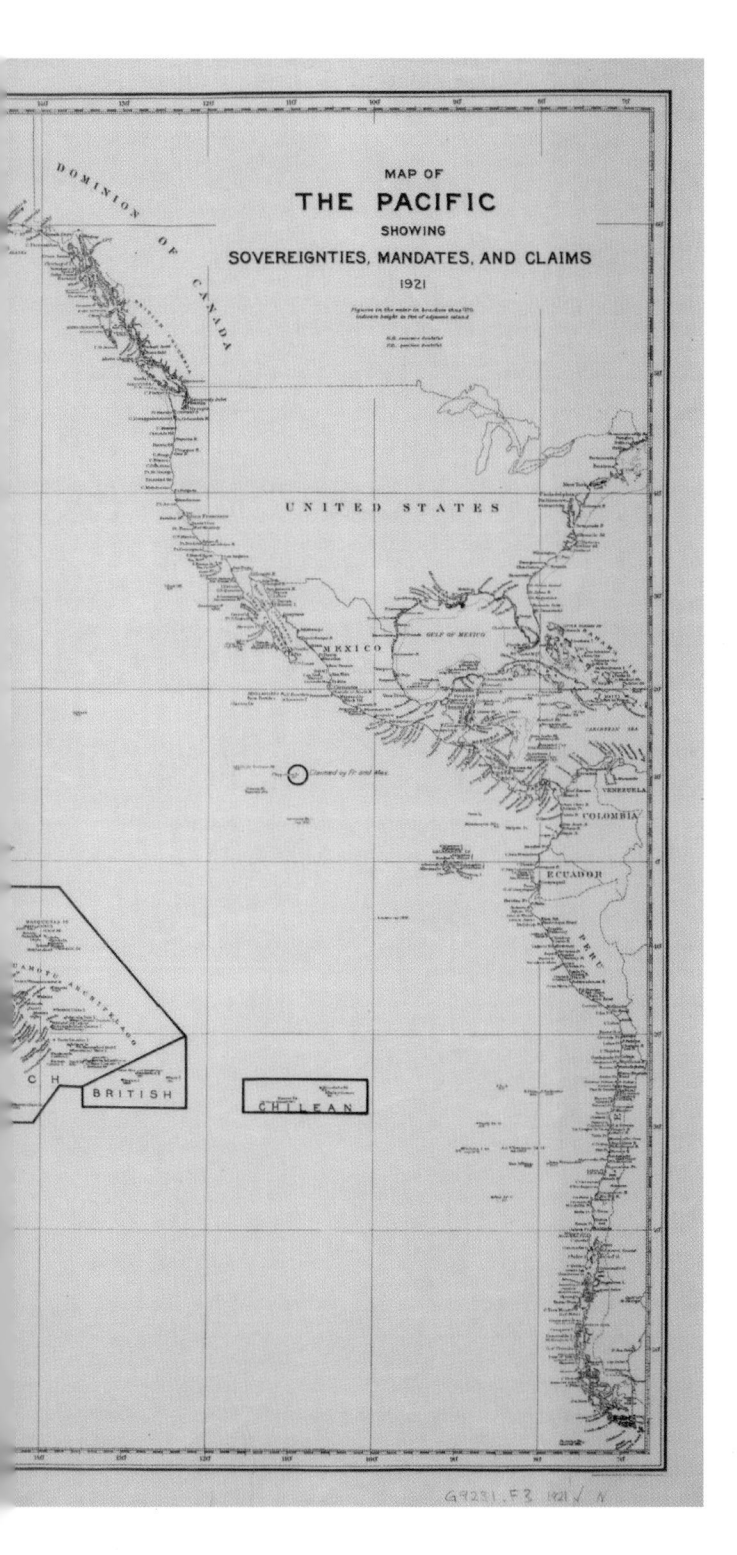

23 *Map of the Pacific showing Sovereignties, Mandates and Claims, 1921.* This map shows the administrative and political dissection of the Pacific after World War One. There was some expectation that Australia would be granted control of the islands to the north of New Guinea. Instead, they became Japanese territories in recognition of that country's allegiance to Britain during World War One.

National Library of Australia

24 Sarah Chinnery was the wife of Ernest Chinnery, the New Guinea territory anthropologist from 1924 to 1932 and director of district services until 1939. Sarah took dozens of photographs of Rabaul and surrounds including this rare colour image of their house staff around 1935.

National Library of Australia

25 Chinatown in Rabaul around 1929. Australian administrators and patrol officers came here to have their tropical whites made up by Chinese tailors. Photograph by Sarah Chinnery.

National Library of Australia

26 The Australian administration in mandated New Guinea inherited colonial infrastructure built by the Germans, such as this clocktower and building in Rabaul. The town was regarded as a model of imposed order and the Australians maintained distinct divisions between local people and 'whites'. Photograph by Sarah Chinnery c.1935.

National Library of Australia

27 Sir Hubert Murray, the lieutenant-governor of Australia's colony of Papua from 1908 to 1940.

National Library of Australia

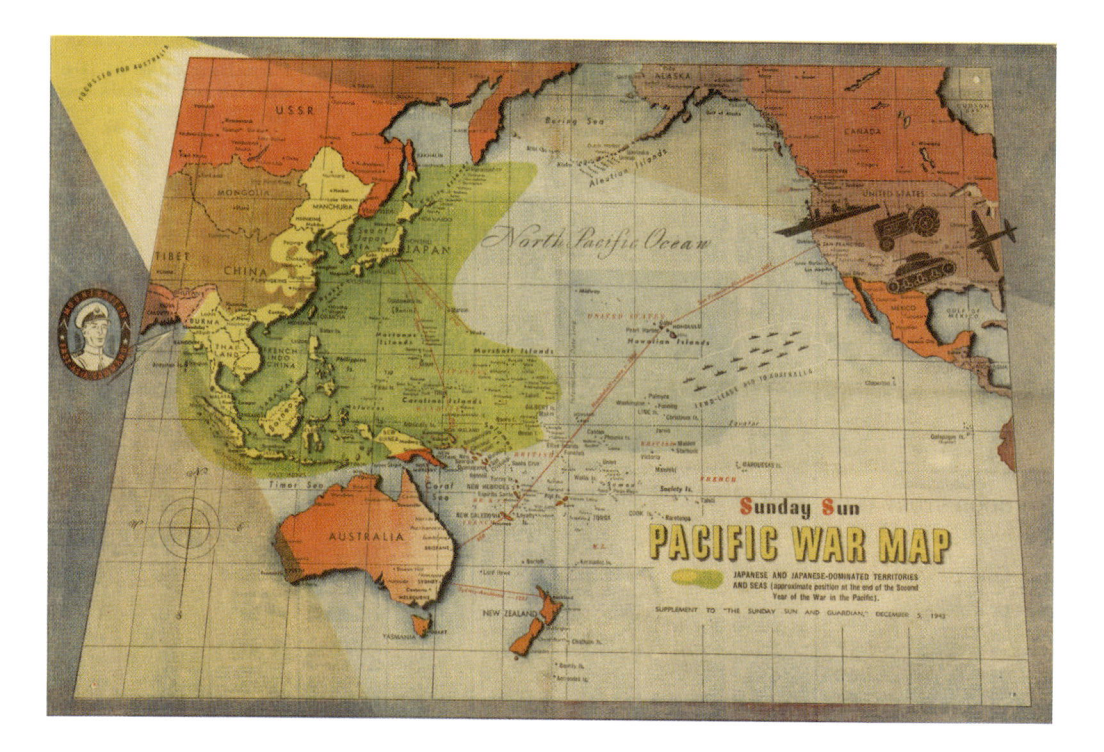

28 The *Sunday Sun* newspaper published this fold-out map detailing the geography of the Pacific War in 1943. American aid and the figure of British Far East **commander Louis** Mountbatten were reassuring references to Australia's two powerful friends. By this time the tide had turned against the Japanese.

National Library of Australia

29 Papuan man Raphael Oimbari helps Australian soldier Private George Whittington of the 2/10 Battalion near Dobodura in 1942. Initially censored by Australian authorities, George Silk's iconic photograph first appeared in the American *Life* magazine. It epitomises the image of the Papuans as 'angels'.

Australian War Memorial

30 Despite the brutality of the war in New Guinea there was recognition of the dignity of human life on the part of Australian soldiers. The Japanese warrior code elevated honour above all else. This photograph by George Silk shows Queenslander Private Haynes carrying a Japanese prisoner.

Australian War Memorial

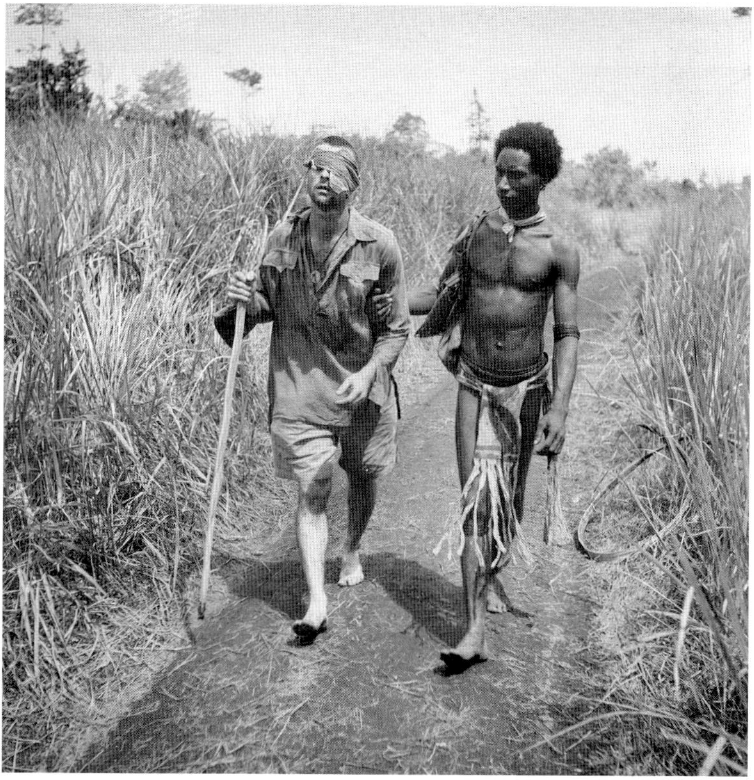

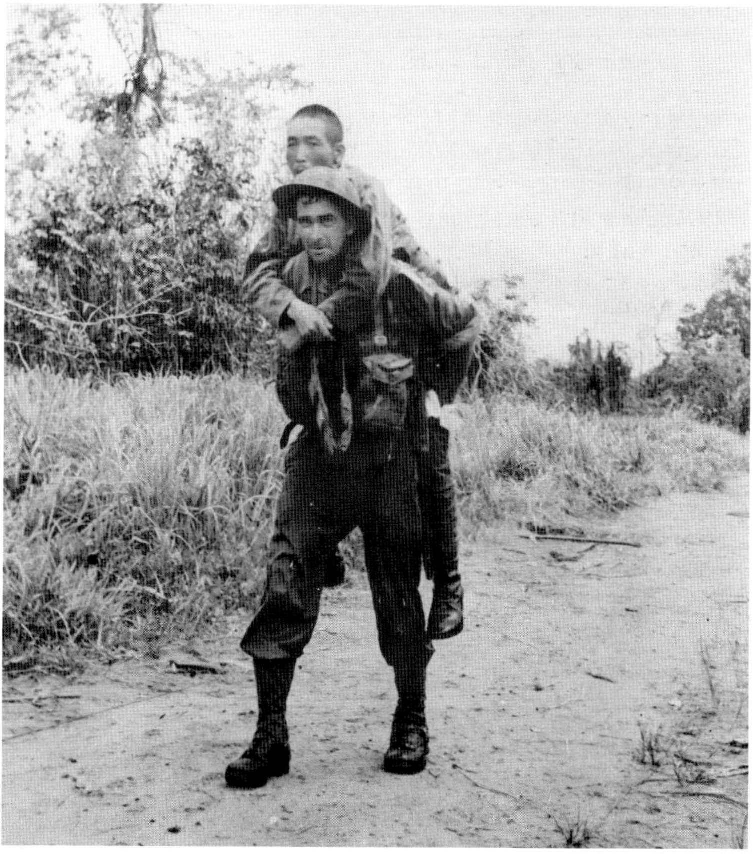

31 An Australian officer barters with Papuans for fresh fruit in November 1942. Local gardens were an important food source for Australian soldiers. The Japanese destroyed them in retreat. Photograph by George Silk.

Australian War Memorial

32 In Ivor Hele's 1944 oil painting *Stretcher Case awaiting bearers, Old Vickers Position*, Australian soldiers have become almost indistinguishable from the jungle.

Australian War Memorial

33 Australian soldier and photographer Alan Queale photographed a crowd of Japanese people observing the third anniversary of the first use of an atomic bomb in war in 1948. The building shown here was preserved as a memorial and became known as the Atomic Bomb Dome.

Australian War Memorial

Printed by the Commonwealth Government Printer, Canberra, A.C.T.

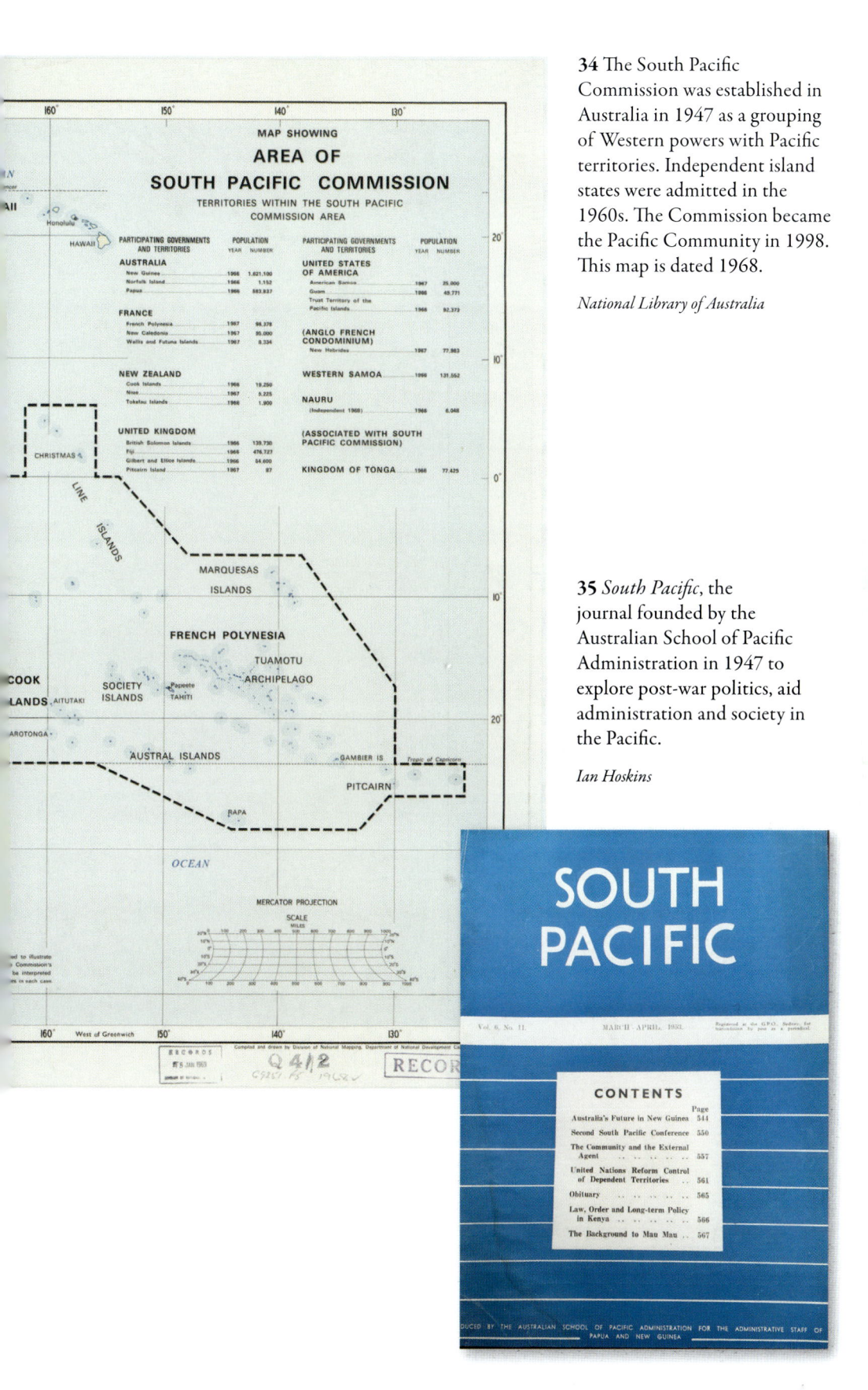

34 The South Pacific Commission was established in Australia in 1947 as a grouping of Western powers with Pacific territories. Independent island states were admitted in the 1960s. The Commission became the Pacific Community in 1998. This map is dated 1968.

National Library of Australia

35 *South Pacific*, the journal founded by the Australian School of Pacific Administration in 1947 to explore post-war politics, aid administration and society in the Pacific.

Ian Hoskins

36 The other Fijians. This photograph shows Indians on Fiji in 1941. Brought to work on sugar plantations by Australians among others, thousands of their descendants left for Australia after the rise of Fijian nativism in the 1980s. The man at the back is Arthur Tange, then working for the Bank of New South Wales in Fiji, part of the considerable Australian presence there. Colonial Sugar Refineries (CSR) was a major employer. Tange would become one of Australia's most powerful public servants.

National Library of Australia

37 Protest against French nuclear testing in the Pacific, Sydney, c.1985.

Courtesy SEARCH Foundation, Mitchell Library, State Library of New South Wales

38 *Canberra Times* cartoonist Geoff Pryor commented wryly on the newly conceived Pacific Solution in 2001.

National Library of Australia

39 Fijian–Australian Rugby League footballer, Petero Civoniceva. This was one of the portraits featured in the Body Pacifica calendar published in 2010. Photograph by Greg Semu.

Courtesy Greg Semu
Artefacts from Todd Barlin collection,
Stylist Niwhai Tupaea

40 A garden on Mer / Murray Island. The nature of horticulture on this small Torres Strait island would change Australia's foundation myth of *terra nullius* in 1992. This photograph was taken by the Anglican minister Dr Wilhelm Rechnitz in 1958.

State Library of Queensland

41 Australia's Pacific Islander communities were well represented at the major climate change rally in Sydney in 2015.

Ian Hoskins

Pacific. Tropical heat and the expense of refrigeration made canned food essential as economies once based upon self-sufficiency and the supply of freshly caught or harvested food gave way to market-based systems and the consequent need for stored provisions. Papua was a 'land of tins', wrote Kate Greig after she arrived to help run a plantation with her husband in 1929.[11] The Australian commando Stephen Murray-Smith had eaten Ox and Palm corned beef as he sat in the dank jungle awaiting contact with the Japanese. Recalling that occasion without enthusiasm in his unpublished journal, he remarked that the product's high proportion of offal was 'notorious' and a direct result of it being 'tinned for native consumption'.[12]

Australia's proximity to the islands and its status as a significant manufacturer and primary producer resulted in large trade imbalances. The value of exports to the south-west Pacific, excluding Papua New Guinea, increased from nearly $76 million in 1970 to well over $104 million in 1974. The worth of imports over this period also grew but from only $27 million in 1970 to barely $36 million in 1974. Nauruan phosphate comprised more than half the latter amount.

Fiji was one of Australia's major Pacific trading partners. Its exports were second in value only to Nauru's and it imported more Australian produce than any other island or group behind Papua New Guinea.[13] Although never a colony or territory of Australia, the archipelago's economy and society was profoundly affected by its wealthy neighbour, largely through the activities of the Colonial Sugar Refinery (CSR) firm, which had acquired land there in 1880 after establishing sugar mills in northern New South Wales. Sugar and CSR shaped the islands' economy and society. The sugar industry was the reason Indians went to Fiji as indentured labourers. They stayed on after their period of indenture. By 1956 Indians outnumbered Polynesian Fijians and had established themselves in trade and agriculture so successfully that some traditional landowners had begun to resent them. CSR left in 1973 following an industrial award in 1969 which favoured cane farmers over the monopolistic processor. The Australian company sold its assets to the Fijian government and consolidated its sugar-refining operations in Australia. Ratu Mara was annoyed at the role played by Australian labour unions in that negotiation. Labour rights were all well and good while a foreign firm was the antagonist. They were a nuisance when a new independent government was attempting economic reform.

Though well established, Australian trade with the south-west Pacific was small compared to that which had developed with the Pacific north-west in the 1960s. Japan's economy grew at an astonishing average of 10 per cent each year between 1955 and 1970. That phoenix-like recovery, fostered by a US keen on stabilising capitalism and its own influence in the western Pacific, both coincided with and stimulated the development of Australia's iron ore industry and the growth of its coal-mining sector. Japan also bought wool as the demand for that product of Australia's vast pastures declined elsewhere. Over this period exports to the former enemy surged from 11 per cent to 27 per cent of the national total. The significance of this transition was given dramatic emphasis by Great Britain's receding influence. For nearly 200 years that country had been a nurturing provider and buyer but, in 1973, it joined the European Economic Community, severing an historic relationship. In 1970 exports to Great Britain were just 11.26 per cent of the total. They would fall to half that within five years.[14] By then, Japan was Australia's largest trading partner, a position it would hold until 2007, when China assumed that mantle. In 1974, Australia became 'a dialogue partner' of the Association of South East Asian Nations (ASEAN), established in 1967. Writing in a major retrospective survey published by the Australian Institute of International Affairs, shortly after this shift, historian Geoffrey Bolton described 'the erosion of formal and informal links between Australia and Britain' in terms of epochal change.[15]

It was unprecedented and transformative on many levels, but constitutional connections remained unchanged. Britain's monarch was also Australia's. The Whitlam government was thereby removed from office by the queen's representative in Australia, the governor-general, after the parliamentary opposition refused to pass an Appropriations Bill and demanded an election. Whitlam's reform agenda and its quest for the international money to fund it had been all too enthusiastic for conservatives and possibly a little reckless even for moderates. That it coincided with a global financial crisis triggered by the devastating oil embargo Arab countries imposed in 1973 was just bad luck.

The 'Dismissal' remains the most controversial change of government in Australian history. In itself it evinced a reckless disregard for democratic process. The Coalition was returned to office after the three-year hiatus of Labor rule in a landslide win in December 1975. The divisiveness that resulted followed the schisms of the anti-conscription protests and moratorium marches, so that Australia seemed to be rocked by constant tumult. Added to the century-old battle between labour and capital were new contests based on gender, age and ethnicity, and to a lesser extent sexuality. Many believed the CIA had played a role in removing Whitlam, for he was not the enthusiastic ally to the US Holt and his successors had been. A renewal of the anti-Americanism that came with the war in Vietnam emerged. This questioning of the alliance would become louder as Cold War tensions between the US and the Soviet Union increased after the rapprochement with China.

Almost as soon as he assumed the prime ministership, Malcolm Fraser was faced with the problem of accommodating growing numbers of Vietnamese refugees fleeing the aftermath of war. His predecessor had been less than sympathetic to the plight of these people when the conflict came to a dramatic end in April 1975. Then and later, Whitlam described the asylum seekers as 'economic and ethnic' refugees moving about as a 'tide'. He used the term 'boat people' to describe those who fled in vessels in an attempt to get to Australia directly.

By 1979 Vietnamese refugees constituted the largest group of exiles in the region with some 300 000 people seeking a home elsewhere. In that year, Whitlam applauded the new communist government for allowing them to leave but questioned Australia's ability to absorb significant numbers of those seeking sanctuary. He had retired from parliament by then and was keeping busy as the visiting professor in Australian Studies at Harvard University. In that capacity he spoke at length about Australia's relationship to its 'Pacific Community'. 'It is foolish to assert that it is easier for the boat people to settle in Australia', he argued in response to perceptions that there was land enough for mass resettlement, for much of the country was 'uninhabitable'. In any case, the refugees were 'city dwellers', merchants avoiding relocation in the Vietnamese countryside. They would naturally move to Sydney and Melbourne, which were already crowded.[16] The implication was there was simply not enough space. Many were indeed traders, ethnic Chinese whose businesses in the south of the country had been taken from them or 'nationalised'.

The problem, as Whitlam correctly pointed out, was regional and international. In this regard it did not help that Australia was the only nation in South-East Asia to have signed up to the four UN conventions on refugees finalised since 1951. His government ratified the 1954 Convention relating to the Status of Stateless People, the 1967 Protocol relating to the Status of Refugees and the 1961 Convention on the Reduction of Statelessness. And yet Whitlam's reference to human 'tides' and 'boat people' echoed, however unintentionally, earlier concerns about Australia sitting vulnerable in an 'Asiatic sea'. But his objections related to ideology, not race. Those fleeing Vietnam were, by definition, anti-communist. In the context of the Cold War, when so much was assessed in terms of left and right wings, this was enough to disqualify them as worthy refugees in the minds of many in Labor and on the left.

The opposite was true of Coalition politicians, whose sympathies lay with those who had resisted communism. As both army minister and minister for defence, Malcolm Fraser's involvement in prosecuting the war had been particularly close. As prime minister in 1976 he committed to accepting 1350 refugees, albeit with a caveat that they must have existing family connections, a qualification which nearly halved the actual number who were initially resettled. Fraser and others also spoke of the moral imperative of assisting people for whom

Australia had fought for a decade, a less than compelling argument to those who opposed the war. Unauthorised boat arrivals began in April of that year. The first were accepted with the minimum of official agitation. But in the following year many more arrived, attracting both sympathetic and antagonistic publicity. There were suggestions that the 'boat people' were jumping the 'queues', a word which referred to the process of formal selection in the crowded refugee camps of Thailand and Malaysia. Nonetheless, Australia did not turn back boats as did other nations which were not signatories to the refugee conventions. Rather, in response, the Fraser government increased the humanitarian intake. The boat arrivals dwindled. Some 150 000 Vietnamese were resettled in Australia in the 1970s and 1980s. Fewer than 2100 came in unauthorised boat arrivals.[17]

Dealing with the fleeing Indo-Chinese was Australia's first refugee crisis. After 120 years of antipathy towards Asian people there were, unsurprisingly, many expressions of fear and outright racism in the still predominantly Anglo-Australian community. There were also expressions of empathy and humanity, as there had been throughout the previous century. The arrival of 'boat person' Hieu Van Le in Darwin Harbour in 1977 elicited one of those. He recalled his greeting by two men in a small metal dinghy, colloquially known as a 'tinnie', years later: 'Gradually emerging out of the morning mist, we saw a "tinnie" with two blokes with shorts and singlets in it ... one of them raised his stubby as if proposing a toast. "G'day mate', he shouted, "Welcome to Australia!"'[18] Hieu learned the vernacular Australian-English and made a way for himself and his family. Indeed, he became a model citizen and was sworn in as lieutenant-governor of South Australia in 2007.

The intake of Vietnamese, both 'boat people' and those who 'queued' in the camps, is widely remembered as exemplifying a humane refugee policy. It was a response of 'simple human decency', in the words of a later advocate for asylum seekers, Julian Burnside. But, as political scientist Katrina Stats has suggested, there is a degree of nostalgia in this remembering, prompted inadvertently or otherwise by comparison with later harsh government policies which equated boat arrivals with illegal immigration rather than legitimate asylum seeking. The possibility of temporary rather than permanent protection was first aired in the 1970s. The *Immigration (Unauthorised Arrivals) Act 1980* allowed for the detention of asylum seekers. 'The government's initial reluctance', Stats argues, '... then its careful selection of refugees from overseas camps, meant that it could appear to be exercising control over both the flow and the quality of migrants, who were selected according to their ability to contribute to, and integrate with, the nation, rather than simply their need for refuge and security'. Nonetheless, as Stats conceded, Fraser's 'genius' lay in his ability to combine national interest and humanitarian imperative.

There was one other aspect of the debate over Vietnamese asylum seekers which anticipated later responses. Sovereignty, it was posited, had primacy over humanitarianism and necessarily guided the interpretation of international commitments to refugees: 'Any sovereign nation has the right to determine how it will exercise its compassion and how it will increase its population'. That assertion came in 1977 from the president of the Labor Party and the man who would succeed Malcolm Fraser as prime minister, Bob Hawke.[19]

≈

'... unreasoning minds ...'

Hawke defeated Malcolm Fraser in 1983 and so began what would be Labor's longest term in office to date. By then, the refugee crisis was over. Hawke's government is remembered primarily for economic reforms which dismantled the previous hallmark Labor policy of protectionism, and promoted the benefits of international free trade. The imperial relationship with Britain was a receding memory.

Labor was also committed to regional arms control, in particular ending the testing and permanent presence of nuclear weapons in the south-west Pacific. The party's opposition to nuclear testing was well established. In 1973 Gough Whitlam had joined with the New Zealand government in challenging French atmospheric testing at Mururoa Atoll in the International Court of Justice.

The western Pacific had been the preferred testing 'ground' for the 'Free World' since the beginning of the Cold War. It was vast, with suitably isolated atolls and islands. With the defeat of Japan, the West dominated the region and could do as it pleased. But throughout three decades of detonations there was little consideration of the impact upon local people and the environment. Strategic interest dominated all else, morality included. That does not mean morality was not invoked. The Marshall Islands were among the most remote and their population tiny at only 167 in 1946. Most Marshallese were Christians and, in what journalist and author Simon Winchester has rightly characterised as a 'masterstroke' of persuasion, if not manipulation, the American Commodore Ben Wyatt convinced them to give up their home by casting the bomb as a tool of God's will and quoting from the Biblical story of Exodus.[20]

The US conducted 78 atmospheric tests between 1946 and 1962 on Bikini Atoll in the Marshall Islands, and elsewhere. Christmas and Line islands were the location of 25 British and American tests between 1957 and 1962. For its part, in the 1950s, Australia had dutifully allowed Britain to conduct tests on its own territory, the Montebello Islands and South Australia – well away from white communities and with as little regard for the Aboriginal people who lived around the Maralinga test site as for their Pacific counterparts.

The French used their island possessions to affirm the nation's status as a nuclear power just as Britain and the US ended their strategic Pacific tests. There were 41 atmospheric tests at Mururoa and Fangataufa atolls from 1966 to 1974 and a further 57 underground explosions between 1975 and 1983. The last of those was conducted at Mururoa Atoll in April 1983, one month after the Hawke government assumed power. The new administration responded by developing a position on securing a nuclear-free south-west Pacific. It presented its proposal to ban the acquisition, storage and deployment, as well as the testing, of nuclear weapons in the region at the South Pacific Forum in August that year. The member states largely supported the idea at the following forum.[21]

The year 1984 was significant in the story of the Cold War and the Pacific. It was the last year of Ronald Reagan's first term as president, a period marked by an aggressively messianic American nationalism. Less than a decade after the humiliation of 1975, the ghosts of Vietnam were being exorcised with chants of 'USA, USA!' at rallies and the Olympics, fortuitously held in Los Angeles that year. Reagan was a master of simplistic populist rhetoric. His talk of good versus evil appealed greatly to newly politicised evangelical Christians, who were obsessed with eschatology to the point of relishing an impending Armageddon. All the while, Reagan's administration supported murderous right-wing juntas and rebels in Central and South America, so that hypocrisy tainted the American claims to morality, perhaps even more than during the Democrat-led intervention in Vietnam, such was the religiosity of the neo-conservatives and the resurgent Republican Party. Reagan's domestic supremacy contrasted with the moribund instability of Soviet leadership following Leonid Brezhnev's death in 1982. Nuclear holocaust, thereby, seemed entirely possible, whether triggered by American hubris or a defensive Soviet decrepitude.

The 1984 Australian federal election, just 18 months after the poll which brought Labor to government, made clear the groundswell of antipathy towards nuclear weapons and nervousness about the course of American foreign policy. The newly formed Nuclear Disarmament Party (NDP) won a seat in the Australian Senate. The party launched the political career of Peter Garrett, the articulate and idealistic singer of the rock band Midnight Oil. His opposition to nuclear testing was accompanied by a call to remove US bases from Australia because of their 'integral' role in 'nuclear-war fighting capability'.[22] Groups in the Palm Sunday Peace Rally had already articulated those demands in

April 1984, when some 300 000 people turned out to protest against nuclear arms in the largest national rally in the nation's history.[23] For an increasingly secular society, it was a poignant expression of opinion on one of the most significant days in the Christian calendar.

A Labour government came to power in New Zealand in July that year, promising an end to visits by American ships carrying nuclear weapons. It followed up that position in 1985 by refusing entry to the USS *Buchanan* because the Americans would neither confirm nor deny the nature of its weaponry. The stand threatened the existence of ANZUS and set into relief the limits of Australia's opposition to nuclear arms in the Pacific. The Australian government had never sought to prohibit the passage of nuclear-armed vessels in the Pacific, and Bob Hawke firmly supported the American alliance. His attempt to mediate a resolution failed so that the US suspended its treaty commitment to New Zealand in 1986. Australia maintained independent defence relationships with each country but the ANZUS Treaty, thereafter, became an Australian–US agreement. Others in the Hawke government were more willing to criticise the nation's most important Pacific ally. Foreign Minister Bill Hayden spoke out against US support to Central American rebel groups. Hawke's parliamentary colleagues opposed his offer of assistance for American MX missile testing in the southern Pacific.

The French bombing of the Greenpeace protest vessel, *Rainbow Warrior*, in July 1985 added outrage to the anti-test impetus. The destruction of a vessel and the killing of a crew member in Auckland Harbour was an act of state-sponsored terror which mirrored clandestine American operations in Central America, and perhaps for that reason the US largely ignored it. The Australian government responded by fostering the South Pacific Nuclear Free Zone Treaty, signed by 13 states in August 1985; albeit without a clause excluding visiting warships. The agreement, also called the Treaty of Rarotonga, after the Cook Island where it was signed, was ratified by Australia in 1986.

In its first term the government appointed an Ambassador for

Disarmament and provided funding for a Peace Research Centre at the ANU, the first of its kind in Australia. The veteran professor of international relations at the same institution, TB Millar, questioned the reasoning of that decision in a lengthy commentary published in Melbourne's *Age* newspaper. It seemed based, he suggested with some bemusement, upon the moral assumption that 'those who study war are in favour of it whereas those who study peace are in favour of *that* ...' (italics in original).[24]

There was, indeed, a divide between the idealism of the thousands who marched on Palm Sundays throughout the 1980s and self-styled 'realists', who viewed the world in bleaker terms, usually men opining from the perspective of middle age. Whether they knew it or not, the former were the heirs of earlier peace and anti-nuclear activists such as Dymphna Cusack and novelist and Nobel Prize nominee Katharine Susannah Prichard, who remained a committed communist until her death in 1969. The 'realists' often characterised the activists as naïve at best and, at worst, one-eyed Soviet apologists. Max Harris, himself a former communist and ideological sparring partner with James McAuley, described the latter-day peace movement as one dominated by 'the unreasoning minds, the inadequates, the paranoids and the nutters'.[25] Some simply questioned the effectiveness of the rallies. At their height, they seemed to the cynical little more than a pleasant afternoon out for the morally righteous; the equivalent of Sydney's annual 'Fun Run'.[26]

Popular support for ANZUS remained strong throughout the heady days of the Palm Sunday marches, yet the Hawke government was aware of the shift in popular sentiment. The sudden appearance and electoral success of the NDP was received as a message from voters. Political scientist Stewart Firth has characterised Labor's interest in arms control in its first five years, at least, as 'a symbolic gesture to divert criticism from ANZUS'. Others have argued it was a genuine attempt to establish Australia as an effective regional 'middle power'.[27] In 1988 – a year in which the bicentenary of colonisation generated

The end of White Australia, refugees and reassessments

both self-congratulation and reflection – the task of navigating the course between idealism and realism, strategic dependence and greater regional influence, fell to a new foreign minister, Gareth Evans.

CHAPTER 18

Pacific solutions

*'to visibly prioritise our Asia-Pacific geography
over our Euro-Atlantic history'*

Gareth Evans had had a testy relationship with Bill Hayden as the minister assisting the foreign minister, and thereby an awkward introduction to foreign policy. He took over the portfolio when Hayden retired from parliament. The 'apprentice' greeted his elevation with relish. 'Bliss was it that dawn to be alive, but to be Foreign Minister was very heaven!' Evans recalled in his memoir. 'If ever there was a period in which it was possible to be optimistic about the state of the world, it was the late 1980s and the years that followed ...'[1]

The event which catalysed many others in this 'optimistic' time was the collapse of the Soviet Union and the consequent end of the Cold War, generally marked by the 'fall' of the Berlin Wall in November 1989. Paul Dibb, from the ANU's Strategic and Defence Studies Centre, had anticipated the demise of what he called 'the incomplete Superpower' in the mid-1980s. The Soviet Union was militarily strong but economically weak so there were dangerous times ahead as the leaders of the declining leviathan might act aggressively to preserve their own regime in the name of ideological necessity or provocation.[2] The end came rather more quickly than Dibb imagined.

Another writer, American political scientist Francis Fukuyama, felt confident enough to write of the triumph of 'liberal democracy' over monarchy, communism and fascism as early as mid-1989. His obscure article titled 'The End of History?' formed the core of a best-selling book called *The End of History and the Last Man* in 1992. The question mark had vanished from the later work because the Berlin

Wall had come down and all seemed settled. The world seemed to have arrived at the end point of the trajectory described by the 19th-century philosopher Georg Wilhelm Hegel. The story of humankind was a universal one in which people across cultures and time sought to realise what Christianity had posited in the first century, that all were equal in 'the sight of God'.[3] History had 'ended' in the sense that humanity had reached an ideological endpoint which accepted the right to equality and freedom. Fukuyama only referred to the Enlightenment once in his longer work but much of what he described had flowed from that prolonged overthrow of medievalism and its accompanying embrace of reason, science, discernible truths, individual dignity, empathy and a common humanity.

Fukuyama's message was welcome after a century of dreadful bloodshed in which empires wasted wealth and generations of their young men in a war of attrition, racial hatred had unleashed a genocidal Holocaust, and an ideological struggle between communism and capitalism threatened nuclear holocaust. The West had apparently triumphed, and had done so in the name of humanity. His thesis explained much: the gradual spread of suffrage to men and women regardless of wealth or colour; the UN's adoption of the Declaration of Human Rights, including the rights of children and of refugees; and the repudiation of race-based discrimination. That organisation no longer recognised 'race' as a biological category. Indigenous people were less likely to be called 'savages', and anthropologists more often regarded their subjects with respect and wonder rather than condescension, pity or disgust.

The promise of a Pax Americana was apparently confirmed by the response to Iraq's invasion of Kuwait and the decisive 'Desert Storm' campaign which defeated the dictator Saddam Hussein. Australia, under Bob Hawke's leadership, was an enthusiastic member of that UN-sanctioned coalition. However, the headiness did not last the first decade of the next century. The claim that humanity's collective desire had been settled became one of the most quoted and derided premature pronouncements of the era as tyrants remained and others emerged, right-wing populism flourished, 'ethnic cleansing' became a euphemism for genocide, and religious fundamentalisms rose to challenge reason. Fukuyama became a 'punching bag' in the words of Steven Pinker – the ever-optimistic defender of liberalism and Enlightenment values.[4]

Fukuyama's initial confidence had been firmed by Chinese student protests against their repressive government in Tiananmen Square in April 1989, an event which anticipated the breaching of Berlin's wall by six months and unfolded as the political scientist was completing his original article. The gathering of an idealistic new generation of China's youth followed Mao's death in 1976 and the end of the Cultural Revolution, in which young men and women had been zealous enforcers of conformity. Moves towards de-collectivisation and a market economy were underway. In fact, it was the death of the reformer Hu Yaobang which prompted the assembly in April. A replica of the Statue of Liberty erected in the square seemed both to symbolise democratic aspiration and reject the Chinese Communist Party's singular authority.

The protest was violently suppressed in early June. Footage of the carnage was broadcast internationally. Images of a single man standing defiant in front of a tank became iconic. For Fukuyama, the event delegitimised the Chinese state around the world. Gareth Evans described the 'brutal slaughter' as the 'most scarifying event' the Labor government confronted.[5] The emotional impact of the violence was on public display when Bob Hawke wept in parliament as he read out an account of tanks crushing bodies and students being machine-gunned. His instinctive humane reaction was to allow 20 000 Chinese students then studying in Australia to stay in the country regardless of their visa status. Australia granted permanent residency to many of that group in 1993.

The students' presence itself evidenced the thaw in the relationship between the two countries, something the Tiananmen Square killings might have interrupted. However, there was no lasting disruption to trade. Rather, it was the Americans who seriously considered ending Chinese access to markets in retaliation for the action. China acquiesced to that pressure and permitted an Australian delegation to visit and report upon the state of human rights in the country. It was the first deputation of its kind from a foreign nation and ran counter to the longstanding Chinese position that human rights were a matter of national, not international, interest. The visit was Gareth Evans' initiative; he was keen to elevate the profile of human rights, but it served Chinese interests too. 'China used Australia and Australia used China', in Stewart Firth's words.[6] The visit helped to forestall American sanctions. The Australians spent 10 days in the country in 1991 and again the following year and produced reports which condemned infringements of political and civil rights but did not, remarkably, result in such interactions ending.[7] Neither did it have much effect upon the regime.

Evans has described himself as a 'liberal internationalist' and, as such, a respectful heir to the work of HV Evatt and the Whitlam government. Advancing human rights was one part of this. He characterised his diplomacy with China and other states as follows: 'Always emphasise the universality of the rights in question, avoiding any hint that you are in the business of exporting your country's "Western values" ... so far as possible, make any such representations within a larger context of dialogue and engagement, so human rights and democracy do not come across as single-issue obsessions'.[8] It was a pragmatic approach that did not always satisfy cynics and non-governmental critics of human rights abuses, but was no less sincere for that. Within weeks of becoming foreign minister Evans attempted, in his words, to 'square the circle between realists and idealists'. He claimed credit for being the first to insert the term 'good international citizenship' as a third pillar into the framework of foreign policy and suggested that national reputation supported the other two standard foundational concerns: economic interest and security.[9]

Evans also prioritised improving 'the rather neglected' relationships with the South Pacific region. He had been influenced by Paul Dibb's 1986 assessment of Australian defence, written as the analyst was also recasting the Soviet Union as an 'incomplete superpower'. The Dibb Review called for greater defence and foreign policy independence, with a concomitant continental and regional focus. Unstable though the Soviet Union may have been, it did not constitute a direct threat to Australia. Accordingly, 'Forward Defence', such as had occurred in Vietnam, or indeed Gallipoli and Europe in World War One, was discounted; as was the need to court powerful allies.

Guided by the Dibb Review and a determination 'to visibly prioritise our Asia-Pacific geography over our Euro-Atlantic history', Evans travelled to the islands before visiting Britain or the US.[10] Within a month the minister had met leaders in Papua New Guinea, Nauru, the Solomon Islands, New Caledonia, Vanuatu, Western Samoa and New Zealand.

Fiji, too, was on the itinerary, although relations with that Pacific neighbour were strained in 1988. A military-led coup had undermined democracy in the archipelago nation the previous year, first deposing an elected government and then declaring a republic. That act exemplified the waxing and waning global fortunes of democracy and a belief in common humanity. It was evidence, too, of the limits of Australia's direct political influence. Pressure in the South Pacific Forum amounted to little. But neither did Fiji's partial suspension from the Commonwealth, the association of Britain and its former colonies which emerged with post-war independence movements in 1949.

The coup did, however, help Evans define Australia's regional role. His 'Ministerial Statement on Australia's Regional Security' of 1989 stressed 'self-reliance' and a multi-dimensional approach to problems. It allowed for the use of 'military force' in 'unusual and extreme circumstances' but 'explicitly' rejected 'any notion of Australia claiming the role of regional arbiter of political legitimacy or moral acceptability'.[11] Caution, responsibility and respect were the tenets. Balancing realism and idealism for the liberal internationalist became an actual policy challenge. And so rejecting or reinstating democracy was a matter for Fijians to resolve.

The issue was ethnic and religious and firmly grounded in the history of colonial-era population movements. Despite advantages granted them in the Constitution of 1970, many in the Indigenous Fijian population felt threatened by the numerically and economically dominant Indian Fijians. The communities were quite culturally distinct, a differentiation made clearer by faith. Indigenous Fijians were Christian, the legacy of the effectiveness of 19th-century missionary contact, while the Indian population retained their Hindu and Muslim beliefs. Many spoke Hindi. Such was the hostility and fear among Indigenous Fijians that Lieutenant-Colonel Sitiveni Rabuka took it upon himself to force the removal of Prime Minister Timoci Bavadra, who led a coalition of people with Indigenous and Indian heritage.

For many of Indian descent, the upset destroyed trust. A minidiaspora unfolded as descendants of those indentured sugar workers CSR had brought from the sub-continent and others left a country in which they felt unwelcome. A large number had been born on the islands but saw no future there. While ethnically defined national identity was potent enough to unseat their government, its power was dissipating in Australia. And so the Pacific-rim cities of the great southern continent became a haven for Fijians caught betwixt and between. An average of 1500 arrived annually between 1991 and 1996; a 300 per cent increase even over the decade which followed the end of the White Australia policy. Consequently, by the turn of the century, roughly 10 per cent of Fiji's Indian community were living in Australia, where they far outnumbered their Indigenous counterparts. In their new home Indian Fijians added another piece to a multicultural mosaic which was, remarkably enough, becoming a defining feature of the Australian identity just a generation after ethnicity had played that role almost exclusively. They joined an existing Indian community but remained connected to their island home through newspapers such as the Sydney-based *Fiji Times*.[12]

That Indians did not vacate the political field in Fiji was evidenced by yet another coup in 2000; one which removed Fiji's first prime minister of Indian descent, Mahendra Chaudhry. That resulted in a full suspension from the Commonwealth. There was a further coup in 2006, this one to undo the 'racist' and 'corrupt' government installed, then elected, after the previous deposition. Its leader, Commodore Josaia 'Frank' Bainimarama, assumed power as prime minister and justified his action before the UN General Assembly. Policies 'which promote racial supremacy, and further the interests of economic and social elites, must be removed once and for all', he argued. 'Racism, elitism and disrespect for the law are undemocratic' he continued.[13] Few would have argued with that in Australia but neither could the coup be endorsed. Therefore, despite the Commodore's laudable aim to end discrimination against Indian Fijians, Australia condemned the action. Process was as important as outcome. Limited sanctions were imposed to underline the disapproval without destabilising the country.

'every square metre of the apparent wilderness belonged to someone under customary land law'

Bainimarama's stated aim was to unite 'a fractured nation'. That was the difficult task of leaders throughout the Pacific islands where disparate groups, whose traditional loyalties might extend no further than kin, were implored to think in terms of nationhood. There was talk of a pan-Pacific identity by Michael Somare, PNG's first prime minister. In an act of neighbourliness, in 1980, that newly independent nation sent troops to help restore stability to Vanuatu – formerly the New Hebrides – on the eve of its independence after 74 years of divisive 'Condominium' government by the British and the French.

Even before Vanuatu came into being, separatist movements were springing up on its many islands. The most insistent of these emerged on Espiritu Santo, the island where Quiros planted a cross in 1606, thereby beginning the long age of disruptions that followed Europe's 'convergence on the Pacific'. There, in early 1980, the French-speaking island man Jimmy Stevens declared the Republic of Vemerana, rejecting the authority of the new Anglophone prime minister and Anglican priest, Father Walter Lini. Colonial legacies had created their own set of identities which militated against affiliation with Santo or Tanna or any of the other myriad islands. The Vemerana flag, sea-blue with a lone green star, remained aloft in Santo town until Stevens surrendered meekly to PNG forces on 1 September, having lost his son in a grenade explosion.[14]

In 1988 the PNG government itself confronted separatism on Bougainville, the large island east of New Britain. Named after a Frenchman and colonised by Germans before being taken by Australians, Bougainville had been transformed by the imposition of market-based agriculture. Large 'line villages' emerged where before there had been just small hamlets. The increased population assisted in creating a 'pan-Bougainville identity', which developed in opposition to the incipient nationalism associated with PNG independence. It was a distinction made even more apparent by skin colour. Bougainvilleans are much darker than those on islands to the west.[15] Physical appearance, and 'race' in particular, remained a powerful popular delineator despite official condemnation the world over. The various groups on Bougainville came together to assert their interest, separate to PNG, in what has been called an expression of 'micro-nationalism'.[16] By the late 1980s, a distinct separatist movement had formed. In 1989, a civil war broke out in which the Bougainville Revolutionary Army (BRA) battled the PNG military and local people who did not favour separation.

Gareth Evans described the crisis as 'the most difficult' he faced with PNG. It was in Australia's interest to prevent the country from fragmenting 'at the hands of a non-democratic, violent resistance movement'. Australia provided the helicopters and other equipment the PNG military used to engage the rebels – on many occasions with extreme brutality. The BRA fought effectively, and often viciously, on their home ground with captured and homemade weapons. The killing continued for nearly a decade, at the end of which a desperate PNG government enlisted the help of military contractors from an organisation called Sandline International in the hope of ending the protracted violence. That was 1997. When the Australian government voiced its opposition to the presence of mercenaries in the region, with the ensuing issues of military accountability, politicians in PNG responded by insisting the matter was one of national sovereignty. Advice from a former colonial master was unwelcome. The matter was ended when the PNG military intervened, alarmed by the prospect of being replaced by a foreign force. Ironically that action created the conditions for settling the wider crisis. New Zealand played a major role in negotiations, for it had no complicating colonial history in the territory to affect perceptions or influence interests. Australia funded much of Bougainville's reconstruction. Some 15 000 people had died.

The conflict was sparked by issues of royalties and land ownership arising from the mining activities of Bougainville Copper Limited (BCL), a company with a majority shareholding by Conzinc Rio Tinto Australia (CRA). At Panguna it ran one of the largest and most profitable copper and gold mines in the world. That operation, and its huge contemporary, the Ok Tedi gold and copper mine in the western highlands, spectacularly realised those dreams of vast mineral wealth and fortunes which had excited the armchair colonists of the late 19th century and motivated geologists and prospectors to scramble through tropical forests and rivers in search of lodes and alluvial deposits. The ore at Panguna was discovered in 1961 and the plant commissioned in 1972.

The PNG government received part of the profit which, by the time the fighting on Bougainville began, constituted as much as 20 per cent of national public revenue.[17] The government could scarcely afford to lose that money, yet the BRA and their supporters saw the resource as their own. They preferred to have the whole operation closed down rather than surrender control. In that, at least, they succeeded. The mine was closed in 1989. The vast plant was ransacked and vandalised so that 30 years later it still stood as an industrial ruin resembling a post-apocalyptic film set.

The national government, it should be noted, bore considerable responsibility for the breakdown in negotiations between themselves, BCL and Bougainville representatives. Yet land ownership and compensation were complex. As former CRA project manager Don Vernon recalled of his first visits to the jungle slopes in the mid-1960s, 'we were to learn that every square metre of the apparent wilderness belonged to someone under customary land law'.[18] Other problems arose after operations commenced. Some of them were the consequence of positive outcomes. By 1988, 80 per cent of the 3500 employees were Papua New Guineans. Improved infrastructure, wealth and education increased life expectancy and the local birth rate. Migration from other parts of PNG resulted from the job opportunities. All of that led to a land shortage and an exacerbation of the tensions that had followed the alienation of 13 000 hectares of land BCL leased for its operation.

No less significant was the mine's environmental legacy. The rock waste was such – 115 000 tonnes per day – that some 300 hectares of flat land was created out of natural valleys, destroying everything that existed there beforehand. The tailings, or sludge, created by mineral extraction was dumped into the nearby Kawerong River in the belief, or hope, that most of it would be carried out to sea. Instead it spread out beside the Kawerong and larger Jaba Rivers, badly affecting the riparian environment.[19] Such obvious impacts led to concerns about other unseen consequences. A range of misfortunes of varying probability were blamed on the mine. When a 1988 study found no evidence for major chemical contamination, scepticism and hostility grew. 'Who cares for a copper mine if it kills us?', was the response of Bougainvillean Paul Lapun, former minister for mines, who had previously supported the operation.[20]

AUSTRALIA & THE PACIFIC

'one of the more noble things ...'

The Bougainville crisis began during Labor's term in government and ended after the Coalition was returned to office in 1996. The cost of direct military involvement was assessed at the outset but deemed unacceptable. The experience of Vietnam loomed large in everyone's mind and influenced Evans' emphasis on cautious diplomacy.

That hesitation ended in September 1999 when Australian defence personnel landed in East Timor to lead a coalition of regional peacekeepers, the International Force in East Timor (INTERFET). The action was a response to the slaughter by Indonesian-backed militia of pro-independence Timorese after an overwhelming vote for independence in a Jakarta-sanctioned ballot. Australia acted after the passage of a supporting UN resolution. With up to 5000 men and women in Timor at one time, it was the largest commitment since Vietnam. Prime Minister John Howard described it as among his proudest achievements and 'one of the more noble things that Australia has done in many years'. 'Our nation', he continued, 'was directly responsible for the birth of a very small country whose people remain deeply grateful for what we did'.[21]

The intervention is significant for many reasons, not least its moral dimension. It set aside the 'realpolitik', in Howard's term, that had guided bipartisan policy towards Indonesia for decades. Australia had tacitly recognised that country's rule of Timor since it invaded the former Portuguese colony in 1975. Whitlam's acquiescence was followed by Fraser's. Neither party was willing to challenge such a populous, proud and near neighbour even after the Indonesian military murdered five Australian journalists in Balibo in 1975. Labor's 'realist' reluctance was driven also by its desire to engage with Asia after the experience in Vietnam, and its wariness of appearing to preach Western values to the developing world. Paul Keating became prime minister six weeks after the massacre of unarmed civilians in Dili in November

1991, yet he recalled candidly, 'I was not prepared to make the whole of our relationship with 201 million people [Indonesia] subject to this one issue'.[22]

John Howard's ability to act was facilitated by the forced resignation in 1998 of the longstanding dictator Suharto, who had permitted decades of abuse. But it was the post-election chaos that pressed the decision. The prime minister subsequently sought UN sanction for an Australian-led intervention on the basis of national responsibility: 'Australia would not only be expected to, but should, in my view, play a major role in that peacekeeping operation'.[23] The decision to act beyond cautious realpolitik was also made easier by public support. Indonesian soldiers and their allies had killed, tortured and raped with impunity in Timor since 1975. Many Australians were also aware of the murder of the journalists in Balibo. Howard described the popular sentiment in his memoir: 'To most [Australians], doing the right thing by the East Timorese was what really mattered' regardless of the consequences for relations with Indonesia. Strong foreign policy, as opposed to 'craven' diplomacy, needed to reflect national values.[24] Those values, he indicated on an earlier occasion, were grounded in 'European Western civilisation' and a relationship with the US.[25]

The East Timor intervention thereby stands in stark contrast to Australia's muted response to Indonesian repression in West Papua. Every administration, including that of John Howard, has maintained a public silence since the take-over of the province in 1963. Prior to that, the Dutch had defeated Indonesian incursions into their colonial possession, intending to establish West Papua as an independent Melanesian state. The Dutch masters even allowed the nationalist 'Morning Star' flag to be flown next to the Netherlands' national banner. Australia supported the Dutch until the US backed Indonesian claims, fearing appeals to the Soviets for support. Such was the gameplay of the Cold War. Britain remained neutral. The Dutch thereby relinquished their former colony in the face of the ongoing insurgency.

Australia, in turn, accepted Indonesia's position. Some commentators believed it to be the only sensible course. To do otherwise would have been to acquiesce to 'utopian thinking' and undermine its relationship with the rising populous neighbour at the outset.[26] The UN accepted a West Papuan 'Act of Free Choice', which the Indonesians staged in 1969 to validate their control, on the basis that other Dutch possessions in the East Indies had been incorporated into the archipelago 'Republik' in 1949.

Indonesia displayed more determination to hold on to its Melanesian province than it did in East Timor. West Papua is resource-rich where East Timor is not. Such is the prevalence of cronyism and corruption that much of the wealth from minerals and timber flows directly to army and private purses. The military thereby has a particular interest in maintaining control. Independence activists have consequently been murdered and terrorised for many years. The repression has been called a 'silent genocide', for an effective ban on reporting has minimised public awareness and concern in Australia and elsewhere.[27]

National honour, also, is at stake. Having lost a territory to Australia's intercession in 1997, Indonesia does not countenance expressions of foreign support for West Papuan independence lightly. When Australia granted 42 Papuan asylum seekers temporary protection visas in 2006 – an act of implicit criticism only – the Indonesian government responded by withdrawing its ambassador. Without a groundswell of domestic support for a stronger stand in West Papua, Australian governments have prioritised good relations over 'noble' action. It is perhaps ironic that the East Timor intervention makes any official support for West Papuan independence or even human rights less likely. The difference between 'craven' and 'realistic' foreign policy is usually context rather than the righteousness of the issue in question.

'a massive and disproportionate investment ... '

Australia's role in INTERFET established a precedent for its second intervention – the 2003 Regional Assistance Mission to Solomon Islands (RAMSI). As John Howard recalled, the decision to assist East Timor demonstrated Australia's 'capacity to play a larger role for good in our immediate region'. And with no contesting third power involved, the operation in the Solomon Islands was considerably less complex than that in East Timor.

As its name suggests, the state is a collection of islands and peoples, a demographic and geographic reality it shares with most Pacific nations. The Solomon Islands achieved independence in 1978 but 20 years later the effect of inter-island migration and urbanisation in response to economic change was creating rivalry between communities. Such post-colonial disruption was experienced throughout the region. Some on Guadalcanal, the 'main' island and home to the capital Honiara, resented the presence of others from nearby Malaita, such that they formed the Guadalcanal Revolutionary Army, subsequently called the Isatabu Freedom Movement. It attacked and killed Malaitans, who formed a rival militia in response. With support from the police, the Malaita Eagle Force essentially staged a coup by forcing the prime minister, Bartholomew Ulufa'alu, to resign. A parliamentary, rather than popular, vote elected Manasseh Sogavare to the leadership. Australia and New Zealand facilitated peace talks and the Townsville Peace Agreement was signed in the Queensland city of that name in October 2000. The fighting continued, however, and in mid-2003 Australia led the RAMSI to restore order, supported by the Pacific Islands Forum and a coalition of Pacific nations. The mission was given a name in pidgin, 'Operation Helpen Fren'.

Australian service personnel stayed for 10 years. The cost to Australia over that period was $2.6 billion, nearly one-quarter of the total aid budget to the Oceanic region. In the assessment of Australian Pacific policy expert Jenny Hayward-Jones, the operation 'restored law and order ... reconstituted a shattered economy ... [and] helped rebuild the broken machinery of government'. But for all that it also represented 'a massive and disproportionate investment given Australia's interests in Solomon Islands', leading her to question 'why development challenges in Solomon Islands were more deserving of Australian attention and resourcing than similar challenges in other neighbouring islands'.[28]

Consideration of context and Australia's shifting regional identity provides some answers. RAMSI's leadership was part of the so-called interventionist 'Howard Doctrine' which began with INTERFET. Howard himself has suggested that the altruism of the first enterprise was manifest in the second through promoting collective support among 'neighbours'. It also fulfilled a post-colonial responsibility to them. For though the Solomon Islands had been a British rather than Australian possession, Australia's 'Western' heritage gave it the ability to lead a coalition for good in material, organisational and ideological terms, just as it had in East Timor. RAMSI represented, in Howard's description, 'a paradigm shift' towards promoting good governance, 'better economic management' and 'improved criminal justice' in the Pacific.[29]

Be that as it may, RAMSI was only launched after successive Solomons prime ministers made earlier requests for support: Ulufa'alu in 2000 and Manasseh Sogavare in 2001. Both were rejected. The paradigm shifted after the attack on the Twin Towers in New York on 11 September 2001, the epoch-making event simply called '9/11', and the ensuing 'war on terror'. John Howard was in Washington when that emergency unfolded and therefore saw its impact first-hand. His response was to invoke the ANZUS Treaty and commit Australia to defending the US. That initiated Australia's first troop deployment in Afghanistan. The global manifestation of anti-Western terrorism that ensued became very real for Australians when 88 were killed while holidaying in Bali in 2002. In March 2003 John Howard further committed Australia to the war against Iraq alongside the US and Great Britain – the 'coalition of the willing' – on the basis of spurious evidence of that country's support of terrorism and possession of weapons of mass destruction. Consistency is the casualty of the ever-changing exigencies of diplomacy just as truth is the first victim of war. So, in a reversal of the situation which allowed intervention in East Timor, Australia joined a war that the UN did not sanction and which hundreds of thousands of its own citizens emphatically opposed. Intelligence officer Andrew Wilkie resigned from the Office of National Assessments and publicly criticised what he later described as 'an unjustified war [waged] on the basis of a preposterous lie'.[30]

By 2003 Australia, like the US, had come to regard any state instability or failure as an opportunity for terrorist activity. Whereas before 9/11, the chaos in the Solomon Islands was concerning but not compelling, by mid-2003 it constituted a real threat to Australian national security.[31] The Solomon Islands mission was, therefore, less a consequence of the 1999 'liberation of East Timor', to use John Howard's term, than it was an action in a new global war against terrorism. The intervention is better understood in the context of reviving 'Forward Defence' and re-engaging with US global strategy than simply regional altruism and guidance. It was clearly a departure from the independent Asia-Pacific focus which Dibb advocated and Evans supported. Indeed, Howard explicitly re-embraced the 'Euro-Atlantic history' which the erstwhile foreign minister had sought to supplant.

Both Evans and Howard were products of the Enlightenment. Both believed in the universal applicability of liberalism. The internationalist Evans thought human rights and liberal democracy were best advanced without a hint of hubris. For all his social conservativism John Howard was also an economic liberal who respected the rational individual's rights to make choices in the marketplace. Free enterprise created the modern Australia of which he was proud. That was as much a part of Australia's Western heritage as democracy and human rights. It gave the nation the wealth and responsibility to intervene when necessary. For Howard, Australia did not, and should not, have to 'choose between her geography and her history'. To demur from 'traditional' intimacies in unquestioning deference to neighbours' sensibilities was to deny one's identity – except, of course, in West Papua.[32] Australia was a Western nation in the Asia-Pacific region rather than simply an Asia-Pacific nation. And in the context of the 'End of History', supporting Pax-Americana made perfect strategic and moral sense.

≋

'Thus was born the Pacific Solution'

On 29 August 2001, barely two weeks before 9/11, the Norwegian cargo vessel MV *Tampa* entered Australian territorial waters, seeking sanctuary for the 433 asylum seekers onboard. The *Tampa*'s captain had rescued them on finding all adrift in fishing boats in the Indian Ocean, at the request of the Australian Maritime Safety Authority. Most were Hazara people from Afghanistan fleeing persecution at the hands of the Islamist Taliban. The ship was in Indonesia's search and rescue zone when the pick-up occurred but, fearing the consequences of travelling back to the fishing boat's port of departure near Jakarta with hundreds of desperate people aboard, Captain Arne Rinnan elected to steam 80 nautical miles to Christmas Island. In any case that Australian territory was closer than Jakarta. He was denied permission to enter the island's 12 nautical-mile zone, let alone disembark his unexpected passengers, and so waited outside overnight. Then, believing that the asylum seekers would jump overboard if entry was denied, Rinnan ignored the Australian authorities and approached the island.

The *Tampa* was quickly boarded by special forces, who removed the asylum seekers. John Howard introduced a new Border Protection Bill just hours later. It aimed to retrospectively validate the action he had approved that day, such were the legal implications of denying entry to a foreign vessel claiming 'distress', boarding it and detaining the asylum seekers within. The Labor Opposition debated and rejected the bill in the Senate. A version passed in late September. The action itself was contested and approved on appeal by the Commonwealth in the High Court.

The *Tampa*'s arrival was part of a spate of unauthorised boat arrivals which had escalated over the previous two years. Most of the 8000 or so people came from the Middle East, which was in even more turmoil than usual after the war against Saddam Hussein. Having survived 'Desert Storm', the dictator was repressing political opponents and members of the Kurdish minority as he clung to power. Two distinct sets of boat arrivals from South-East Asia had, in turn, preceded those asylum seekers – the so-called 'second' and 'third' waves which followed the first after the Vietnam War. Seven hundred and thirty-five Cambodians and ethnic Chinese came between 1989 and 1992, fleeing upheaval as Khmer Rouge rebels fought their last battles against the Vietnamese in one of the many cataclysms that followed the Vietnam War and accompanied the end of the Cold War.

The sympathy which marked earlier receptions and, indeed, the plight of Chinese students in the contemporaneous Tiananmen Square massacre was less evident with those ensuing waves of boat arrivals. A detention centre at Port Hedland in Western Australia, isolated and far removed from population centres, was established in the last months of Hawke's prime ministership. The Keating government introduced mandatory detention of asylum seekers in 1992 'to enhance ... control of people who wish to cross our borders'. Unauthorised boat arrivals, rather than those who overstayed visas, were the particular focus of the new legislation. Significantly, that was tabled by the immigration minister Gerry Hand, leader of the left faction within the Labor Party. Paul Keating recalled the Cabinet consensus and his own sanguinity. If it had received the imprimatur of 'the philosophical Left', then 'the human rights issues' would surely have been covered.[33] That, apparently, was that.

There was, then, some bipartisan precedence for Howard's stance, distilled in his now famous phrase spoken in October 2001: 'We will decide who comes to this country and the circumstances in which they come'. That was itself an echo, albeit jarring to some, of Bob Hawke's words in 1977: 'Any sovereign nation has the right to determine how it will exercise its compassion and how it will increase its population'.[34]

The difference was the introduction of 'offshore processing'. Howard was quick to conclude that mandatory detention in Australia, even in its remote reaches, was no longer effective. The prime minister wanted a 'deterrent' and processing asylum seekers anywhere on Australian territory was 'defeating the original purpose' of denying access to the *Tampa*. Negotiations with Nauru began as early as 31 August and a deal was concluded shortly after. 'Thus was born the Pacific Solution', in Howard's words.[35] He concluded an arrangement with PNG in October so that a naval base on Los Negros Island adjacent to Manus Island, which once accommodated Douglas MacArthur and excited Herbert Evatt with the possibility of a forward Australian Pacific naval presence, was turned over to housing asylum seekers and opened by 31 October 2001. Other host locations were also considered, East Timor, Kiribati and Fiji among them.

Fiji's prime minister, Mahendra Chaudhry, dismissed the overture to his nation bluntly as 'chequebook diplomacy'.[36] Nauru's prime minister, Rene Harris, probably felt he had fewer options. By 2001 the legacy of the royalties of phosphate mining had been frittered away on calamitous investments, so that the future for the world's smallest republic was very uncertain. There had been nine changes of government since 1996 and Harris's stewardship was widely regarded as corrupt and inept. Among other things Australia guaranteed the island's fuel supplies for generating power for eight months, committed to replace some of the generating equipment, paying up the million dollars Nauru owed to Australian hospitals and doubling the number of Australian educational scholarships. It provided a further $26.5 million worth of aid.[37]

No additional aid accompanied PNG's permission for establishing the 'Manus Island Centre'. There was a sense that this was more an agreement between equals than one between regional power and client, or at least pliant state – as was the case with Nauru. The Memorandum of Understanding referred to the mutual recognition of the need to combat 'people smuggling and illegal migration in the Asia-Pacific'. The Manus Island Centre would be 'a visible deterrent to people smugglers' and 'enable joint co-operation, including the development of enhanced capacity in Papua New Guinea, to address these issues'. Nonetheless, Manus Island would receive some additional benefits such as 'fast tracking' AusAID projects and infrastructure upgrades. It was envisioned that the centre would provide local employment. PNG expected to receive assistance with its own management of 'illegal' entries.[38]

One thousand six hundred and thirty-seven asylum seekers were detained on Nauru and Manus between 2001 and 2008. Seventy per cent of these, 1153 people, were determined to be genuine refugees. Around 700 of them were resettled in Australia.[39] Between 2001 and 2004 the number of boat arrivals decreased from over 4000 to just 118.[40] In 2007 the Refugee Council of Australia estimated that the 'Pacific Solution' had cost $1 billion.[41] The offshore centres were shut down the following year soon after the Rudd Labor Government was elected and upon its promise to do so. The new minister for immigration and citizenship, Chris Evans, called them a 'cynical, costly and ultimately unsuccessful exercise'.[42]

But between 2011 and 2012, there was a surge in unauthorised boat arrivals to just under 14 500 people – largely due to the civil war in Sri Lanka. Well over 600 people had died at sea in failed attempts to get to Australia since 2007.[43] Attempts to establish a processing centre in Malaysia came to nothing without support from the Coalition and, in 2012, Julia Gillard, who had taken over the prime ministership in a Labor caucus vote, revived the Pacific Solution. The Nauru and Manus centres were reopened. Gillard acted upon the recommendation of an 'Expert Panel on Asylum Seekers'. It was to be a 'circuit breaker' for the surge in boat arrivals. The issue of refugees joined that of climate change to destabilise Labor and give its conservative opposition no end of opportunity for criticism. In 2013 Kevin Rudd, reinstalled as prime minister, announced the 'PNG Solution', which ruled out resettlement in Australia for any refugee who had arrived by boat. Instead they would be given asylum in PNG. Labor lost the election that year. In 2016 the Supreme Court of PNG determined that detention on Manus Island had been illegal. The Manus Detention Centre was closed in 2017, the detainees moved elsewhere on the island then on to Port Moresby by the end of 2019. Around 900 asylum seekers remained on Nauru in 2020.

≋

'... because she's desperate'

Many Australians probably share John Howard's assessment of the East Timor intervention as a 'noble' action, at least among those who are aware of the event. A great many more would have some knowledge of offshore processing – the Pacific Solution. It has been a matter of constant controversy since its inception in 2001. At best it is considered necessary, at worst ignoble. For much of the 20th century Australia imported Nauru's rock to fertilise its own barren soils; from 2001 it exported its refugee problem to the nation which was now struggling in the twilight of the mining. Nauruan parliamentarian Anthony Audoa's initial assessment remains as blunt as any: 'I don't know what is behind the mentality of the Australian leaders but I don't think it is right. A country that is desperate with its economy, and you try to dangle a carrot in front of them, of course, just like a prostitute ... if you dangle money in front of her, you think she will not accept it. Of course she will, because she's desperate.'[44] The implication was clear. In circumstances of such uneven power, Australia's offer compelled Nauru to sell itself.

The origins of the term 'Pacific Solution' are unclear. It bore an unpleasant similarity with 'Final Solution', the Nazi label for their attempted Jewish genocide in concentration camps established for the purpose. Despite that, 'Pacific Solution' was in common use by the end of 2001. It appeared frequently and matter-of-factly in the 2002 Senate Select Committee report which investigated the policy and the circumstances surrounding related contentious unauthorised boat arrivals – the so-called 'Certain Maritime Incident' or 'Children Overboard Affair', during which the government claimed asylum seekers threw their children into the sea to ensure rescue. John Howard referred to 'the Pacific Solution' without qualification or embarrassment in his 2010 memoir.

Possibly the term acquired a currency independent of historical antecedents, such is the unpredictability of collective memory. Despite its ignobility in the minds of many Australians, a great many more seemingly approved of the need to 'enhance' the nation's border security by immediately transferring asylum seekers to far-flung islands. It is widely accepted that the *Tampa* affair and the accompanying birth of the Pacific Solution helped a flagging Coalition win the election of November 2001. As Howard proudly recalled, those actions 'shifted community perceptions'.[45]

So too did the 9/11 attacks two weeks later. Public fear and anxiety suited strong measures and it was not a good time to argue for the rights of uninvited foreigners. In fact, public sentiment had been turning against humanitarian largesse for some time. Pauline Hanson's One Nation Party gathered considerable support by arguing against multiculturalism. She won a seat in the Australian House of Representatives in 1996 and spoke about a nation 'swamped by Asians' in her maiden speech. The party did well in the Queensland state elections in 1998 but suffered a negative swing in both houses in 2001, possibly as a result of the bolstered support for the Coalition and its stand on asylum seekers.

The Pacific Solution divided Australia upon its inception. Millions of words have been written in condemnation and defence. The finding of the report on 'A Certain Maritime Incident' at the outset gives some insight into the contention that followed: 'Moving asylum seekers to a safe third country where refugee status processes are available is not, in the Committee's view, a formal breach of the obligations conferred by the Convention Relating to the Status of Refugees, although it is arguably contrary to its humanitarian spirit'.[46] Two decades later human rights lawyers Jane McAdam and Fiona Chong argued that a 'good faith reading of the Convention' required that 'countries with the capacity to process and protect refugees' should do so in their own territory unless protection can be guaranteed in offshore sites. The many reports detailing prolonged mental and physical suffering on Nauru and Manus written in the intervening decades showed that 'such protection guarantees simply do not exist in Nauru or PNG'.[47] Against these accusations, proponents point to the correlation between offshore detention in the Pacific and the decrease in boat arrivals and, with that, fatalities at sea. It is not the asylum seekers they wish to ruin, but the 'business model' of the people smugglers who exploit them.

Critics of the Pacific Solution typically come from the left-liberal side of politics which accord pre-eminence to human rights obligations and the 'spirit of humanitarianism' in matters of domestic and foreign policy. Others found that banishing asylum seekers ran counter to their religious faith. The Christian website 'Common Grace', for example, advocates compassion and reminds readers that 'God has always expected his people to "welcome the stranger" and "love their neighbour"'.[48] Respect for a common humanity is the moral link between these two groups. It is also the link between opposition to detention centres and treatment of Pacific Islanders in decades past at the hands of labour recruiters and unscrupulous colonisers.

The issue remained more difficult for the Labor Party than the Coalition to resolve for, since the time of Gough Whitlam, the party of the centre-left attempted to appeal both to its traditional working-class base and the more affluent, tertiary-educated voters who emerged after the 1960s. The Vietnam War and anti-nuclear protests were earlier manifestations of their presence and concerns. John Howard successfully courted those 'battlers' whom 'progressive' Labor had alienated. It has been easier to drive the political 'wedge' of border protection between Labor's constituencies than it has been to split the supposed 'broad church' of the Liberal Party. Many Labor voters were predictably outraged by their own representatives when offshore detention was revived in 2012.

It might be argued that the Pacific Solution echoed the White Australia policy that Whitlam ended. There is certainly a resonance between the forcible return of sugar cane workers to the islands at the turn of the 20th century and the more recent exiling of unwelcome asylum seekers to the Pacific. Both were perceived solutions to problems besetting an affluent nation when confronted by the presence of foreigners, however pitiable they may be. In Australia's bifurcated relationship with its region, the Pacific Solution represented the separatist rather than integrationist urge.

Writer Christos Tsiolkas explored the long shadow cast by race-based immigration over more recent attitudes towards refugees in 2013, shortly after Labor revived the Pacific Solution. He empathised with the founder of the Asylum Seeker Resource Centre, Kon Karapanagiotidis, who recalled his treatment as the son of Greek immigrants at the hands of those who instinctively asserted the racial difference and superiority which had bed-rocked White Australia in the post-war years, such that the slightest variation of skin tone inspired spite: 'Wog, wog, why don't you go back to your own country, dirty wog?' In 2013 the issue was not quite that simple for, as Tsiolkas conceded, once-vilified immigrants were also antagonistic towards 'boat people'. In the case of older Greeks they had brought their 'ingrained suspicion' of outsiders with them from their villages. Xenophobia and fear of 'the stranger at the gate' is not exclusively an Anglo-Australian phenomenon. The defensive parochialism of One Nation supporters from Australia's regional towns and suburbs bore similarity to the suspiciousness of transplanted Greek villagers. Kevin Rudd's announcement of the PNG Solution prompted Tsiolkas to condemn political leaders who wilfully ignored the reality that immigrants – whether delivered by plane or boat – were essential to the future of the 'underpopulated' and aging country.[49] Sending asylum seekers off to the Pacific Islands in the hope that no more would follow them was not just cruel, it was a lost opportunity.

The outsourcing of responsibility for dealing with refugees highlights the unique nature of Australia's place in the Pacific. It is a vast, sparsely populated, wealthy and stable nation where almost everywhere else is crowded or struggling with dwindling and contested resources. As such it is an attractive destination, at least for the minority who decide not to join the larger throngs heading to Europe. John Howard might argue that Australia's 'Western' heritage has built the wealth that others want to share but that he was strong enough to defend it with offshore detention. There was, and is, no alternative to the human and monetary cost of such deterrence. Others, such as Christos Tsiolkas, point to the exemplary hard work of immigrants in creating that wealth. Aboriginal people talk of stolen bounty. The Pacific Solution has confronted contemporary Australia with difficult questions about its sense of self, its regional responsibilities and interests. The politicisation of the dilemma keeps alive the spectre of long-held racial anxieties about the vulnerability of an island continent and the exceptionalism of its inhabitants. Border security wins elections. In his 2018 Budget speech then treasurer Scott Morrison – former immigration minister – declared with a well-honed hectoring confidence that 'The Liberal and National parties can always be trusted to keep Australians safe'. This was done in the first instance by 'stopping the boats and keeping them stopped'.[50]

Six months later Morrison referred to the south-west Pacific as 'our region ... our neighbourhood ... our home'. The people there were 'family'. By then he was prime minister, for the right wing of his party had recently toppled the former leader Malcolm Turnbull for being too liberal on social issues and that other defining problem, climate change. Morrison was at the Lavarack Army Barracks in Townsville, announcing 'a new chapter' in the nation's relationship with the region. It was Australia's soft and hard power response to the growing influence of China in the region – otherwise know as the 'Pacific Step-up'.[51]

In between those two discordant reminders about their place in the Pacific, Australians were given the opportunity to read a verse addressed to a bird by Kurdish asylum seeker Behrouz Boochani, detained on Manus Island since 2013. It was at once a poetic message from one confined migrant to another flying free, and a more literal insight into the human cost of Australia's border security in the region its leaders called 'home':

> ... Inside a cage,
> the man loves you,
> inside the cage located between the vastest ocean and the greenest
>   forests.
> Forgive me, my love.
> Forgive me, my love, as I am only able to love you from a remote
>   island,
> inside the cage,
> from the corner of this small room.
> Forgive me, please, as the only portion of the world that belongs
>   to me is these pieces.[52]

CHAPTER 19

Pacific Islanders in Australia

'... giving thanks and glory to the father'

The Pacific is Australia's home, yet in 2016 less than 1 per cent of the population claimed Pacific island ancestry. Even that modest figure represents a doubling in a decade. By contrast, in 2013, Islanders numbered nearly 7 per cent of New Zealand's population. That figure did not include Māori.[1] Western Sydney and the outer suburbs of Brisbane and Melbourne are population centres in Australia but, as I write, it is not uncommon to see Tongans in their woven mat ta'ovalas outside a small stone Gothic church in Sydney's multicultural inner west; specifically Marrickville, where Vietnamese and Arabic migrants followed the Greeks who came in the 1950s and 1960s.

Were he looking on, the missionary minister John Paton would probably approve of the Tongan gathering, for it is evidence of the long legacy of Christian preaching – although these members of the Hepisipa Parish belong to that merging of Protestant denominations that comprise the Uniting rather than Paton's Anglican Church. There is music and some dancing but no hint of the papist idolatry which the missionary despised. Australia's first prime minister, who was still playing cricket for Sydney University when the beautiful church was begun in 1871, might be surprised. The permanent and peaceful presence of Islanders in the city of Edmund Barton's birth contradicts the views on 'racial' purity and separation which he promulgated in 1901 and which led to the banishment of sugar cane workers.

Football has given Pacific Islanders a profession and public profile out of proportion to their numbers in the community. The strength, speed and aerial abilities of young Polynesians has helped to change the way that Rugby League and Rugby Union are played in Australia, just as Māori men have kept New Zealand at the top of the world Rugby rankings for decades. Sydney and Brisbane are 'League' towns and so the impact of players of Samoan, Fijian and Tongan heritage is pronounced in that football code. Since Fijian-born Apisai Toga began playing in the Sydney competition in 1967, the number of Pacific Islanders has grown so that they constituted at least 45 per cent of the National Rugby League (NRL) competition in 2019.

The growth is such that there has been concern expressed at the 'pillage of the Pacific' as scouted players are contracted to play in Australia and elsewhere, to the detriment of the national teams in the islands.[2] Some of those who play in Australia were born in the country, the children of migrants. Many others have migrated. That most are Polynesian rather than Melanesian reflects the role New Zealand has played as an interim destination, a conduit. Migration from there is easier than from New Guinea, where Rugby League is the national sport and, of course, where Australia had much closer ties. Football did become something of a replacement for tribal fighting, as Lieutenant Governor Hubert Murray hoped it might. Rugby League was a transformative offering to PNG in the mid-20th century, just as surf bathing had been the Pacific gift that remade Australia in the first decades of that epoch.

Given the history between the two countries, the absence of players from PNG in Australia was a matter of regret for Sean Dorney, the veteran ABC reporter on Pacific matters, when he remarked upon the paradox in 2016. Dorney lived for many years in PNG, played football there, and retained an abiding affection for the place after returning to Australia. He has commented regularly upon the country's diminished media profile, along with the rest of the Pacific, within the shadow of the Pacific Solution and funding cuts to the ABC. Writing of the power of football in the former colony he suggested ruefully that a 'sports aid' program 'might do far more to improve Australia's relations with PNG than many of our other aid projects, and certainly it is a better option than expecting PNG to solve Australia's asylum seeker problem'.[3]

Pacific Islanders, and the footballers who have emerged from those communities, have remained connected to their heritage. In 2010 the NRL's Pacifica Players Advisory Group joined with the Western Sydney art institution, the Casula Powerhouse, in an extraordinary cultural project whereby Samoan-born photographer Greg Semu photographed 13 players with upper bodies bared but wearing variations of the ta'ovala, traditional accoutrements and ornaments (published as the Body Pacifica calendar in the same year). The result was a series of images that reinterpreted 19th-century ethnographic portraiture so the subjects confronted the viewer, confident in their physicality and identity, just as their ancestors might have faced colonists and missionaries. They were presented on their own terms: warriors, athletes and representatives of their people.

Strong as pre-contact tradition can be so, too, is the legacy of colonisation. Many 'Pacifica' players are devout Christians. In 2016 Suaia Matagi, of Samoan heritage, was part of a Bible and prayer group with other Islander members of the Penrith Panthers, based in far western Sydney. 'It's just helping us stay grounded and humble', he told an Australian media always interested in sporting stories, 'really focused on what's ahead but giving thanks and glory to the father'.[4] They prayed before and after games and some attended church together.

Isileli 'Israel' Folau was born in the outer western Sydney suburb of Minto in a large extended family of 10, the child of Tongan immigrants. The area is one of the more socially disadvantaged in Australia. Football and religion were two means of coping with that reality. The Folaus were Mormons, as were one-third of Tonga's population in the 1990s – the highest percentage of membership in any country. The Church of the Latter-Day Saints took their idiosyncratic brand of Christianity to the Pacific relatively late but the ground had been well prepared by earlier missionaries. The Folaus later changed their allegiance to the evangelical Assemblies of God, a Pentecostal church, after questioning polygamy and other Mormon teachings. In the interim the family moved to Brisbane, where Israel maintained his love of Rugby League. He was signed to the Melbourne Storm team in 2007 when he was just 17 years old. Within two years he had accepted a $600 000-a-year contract with the Brisbane Broncos. Folau bought his parents a house with his first year's earnings. He represented Australia in Rugby League, then switched to Rugby Union and did the same. By 2018 Rugby Australia was offering the star a seven-figure salary over four years, which would have made him the highest paid sporting figure in Australia.

Like other Polynesian footballers Folau had his body tattooed to express his Pacific heritage. Ink curls from his right pectoral up to his shoulder and arm, showing fish swimming beneath waves and the woven pattern of a ta'ovala. Soaring above are tropic or frigate birds. A media profile in 2015 emphasised the man's humility, his religiosity and his related belief that God 'intervenes directly in his life on a daily basis' – and so was the main reason for his success. So devout and abstemious was the young man that journalist Tim Elliott could write: 'In a footballing milieu where bad behaviour is commonplace, Folau remains resolutely uncontroversial'.[5]

Two years later he was the most controversial footballer in the country. The change followed a social media response to a question asked by a follower in April 2018 regarding Folau's views on 'God's plan' for homosexuals. The footballer answered in accord with his religious belief: that they would go to Hell 'unless they repented of their sins'. It essentially paraphrased the Biblical words of St Paul. There ensued a heated and hostile debate on social media and television, and in the newspapers, about the definition of so-called 'hate speech', free speech and where cultural power resided in the country. Folau's employer Rugby Australia instructed him to keep his opinions to himself. Another of his posts, on 10 April 2019, responded to Tasmania's passage of legislation allowing gender to be changed or left off birth certificates with the observation that 'the Devil has blindsided so many people in this world'.[6] He published yet another emphatic denunciation of homosexuality shortly after. Folau's contract was terminated on 17 May 2019.

In the year between the first and second pair of incendiary posts, Australia held a postal referendum on same-sex marriage. More than 60 per cent of the voluntary participants voted to support changes to marriage laws allowing women to marry women and men to marry men. A sizable minority did not. The consequent passage of enabling legislation overturned a law the Howard government introduced with the agreement of the Labor Party in 2004 which explicitly defined marriage as a compact between a man and a woman. Gay people had been beaten and murdered in Australia as a direct result of their sexuality for decades. The violence reached a height in the 1970s and 1980s after homosexual men began to assert their identity in public. Police themselves often carried out the attacks and the homophobia largely went unchallenged by political and religious leaders. It was not a mainstream issue despite the obvious immorality of the violence. The outcome of the 2017 referendum, therefore, represented a remarkable shift in public sentiment and highlighted the degree to which the views and caution of politicians could lag behind popular opinion.

It also indicated the ever-widening application of human rights and the associated claims to divergent identities in Australia. Class and race had long defined one's place in society, often without empathy or sympathy for those whose categorisation was imposed upon them with accompanying disadvantage. The discrimination which underpinned White Australia is a case in point. Gender entered the mix in the 1960s and 1970s and sexuality followed in the 1980s. Psychiatry, psychology and sociology gave academic, even scientific, credibility to the validity of the categories. The social structure of human binaries, most obviously represented by the simple division of the world into men and women, was being dismantled. Strong identification with any one or all of these categories of 'self' has become a way of acknowledging one's innate individualism and rejecting the strictures imposed by dominant groups. That the letters LGBTQI, meaning Lesbian, Gay, Bisexual, Transgender, Queer and Intersex, have entered the vernacular so quickly is evidence of the profundity of that multiplication of identities.

The psychologist Steven Pinker has explained the sudden support for, or at least tolerance of, same-sex marriage by referring to the general adoption of utilitarian moral codes. These stress the benefits of accepting practices with which one may not personally agree but that do not, in reality, cause hurt or injury. Those benefits include fewer conflicts, a decrease in mental illness and suicide, and an increase in social cohesion. The simple effectiveness of utilitarianism is itself a product of the humanism and reason which has spread throughout the Western world, at least, since the Enlightenment. An 'historical memory of centuries of religious carnage', Pinker argues, brought about that epochal shift in moral thinking which still 'privileges the well-being of individual men, women and children over the glory of the tribe, race, nation, or religion'.[7] He talks also of the significance of sympathy, hard-wired in the human psyche but given licence to flourish by the Enlightenment. What Pinker refers to as sympathy, historian Lynn Hunt calls empathy. The spread of that ability was, as I indicated at the beginning of this study, assisted by the reading of novels and travelogues, the literal broadening of horizons of which Pacific exploration was an important part. The practices of headhunting and cannibalism, thereby encountered, challenged the Europeans' ability to sympathise or empathise in the 18th and 19th centuries just as their historical existence bring into question Pinker's belief in the innateness of sympathy/empathy. Nonetheless, whether learned or 'endowed', or both, the ability to see oneself in the other and practise forbearance, if not total acceptance, is an essential part of the pluralism which defines modern Australian democracy.

The exchanges that followed Israel Folau's publicised views on homosexuality and gender identity exposed a series of fault lines in that pluralism. There is, perhaps, irony in the fact that it was a man of Islander descent who instigated the controversy, however unintentionally. He was speaking with the religious conviction that had been sown by missionaries and found acceptance in traditional societies willing to both set aside some practices for the new God and incorporate Christian doctrine into well-established beliefs about supra-natural power. Folau felt he was simply doing his duty as a Christian to warn others of the consequences of their 'sinning'. He was supported by other Islander players. Tongan Australian footballer, Billy Vunipola, 'liked' Folau's post and added that 'Man was made for woman to procreate that was the goal no?'[8]

The issue divided those on the liberal left along several lines, not least the boundaries of diversity in a democracy and the profound conservativism of many migrant communities. The populist right saw an opportunity to condemn the apparent dominance and hypocrisy of that 'progressive' side of Australian politics. Talkback radio hosts who maintain their ratings and incomes by fanning outrage and the Murdoch-owned media decried the 'elites' who purportedly ran the country. Folau was their victim. In this formulation a young lesbian waiting tables on the minimum wage to pay off a higher education debt somehow possessed more cultural power than a sports star on a seven-figure salary. But Folau was an everyman, a 'suburban boy'. He represented the 'quiet Australians', as Murdoch journalist Andrew Sammut wrote in evocation of Prime Minister Scott Morrison's recent election-night victory speech. These were hardworking common-sense people abandoned by a Labor Party which had lost its way after Whitlam, and a corporate Australia bent on 'virtue signalling' – all because of the influence the LGBTQI community had improbably gained in such a short time and after so long being confined to society's margins.[9]

In 1964 Donald Horne described the uncomprehending detachment with which Australian intellectuals regarded suburban dwellers, while himself partaking in that condescension; *The Lucky Country* was no love letter to the nation. The 'strong philosophy' of the suburbanite, he suggested, revolved simply around home ownership, raising a family and passing property to one's children. 'To ordinary Australians life has its seasons', he wrote bluntly, 'there are propagation and replacement'.[10] Half a century later the inner city and its subcultures symbolised smugness for the commentators of the right. Israel Folau became the unlikely authentic Australian delivering a message of conviction to out-of-touch politicians and high-flying company heads from the heartland of authenticity. Consequently, a young Tongan-Australian found himself at the centre of a cultural storm. The footballer was articulating binary beliefs, the legacy of 150 years of missionary work in the Pacific, in a society that had moved on – where the majority no longer held to such certainties. Humanism, science – the still relevant ripples of the Enlightenment, as Pinker would have it – had fractured such stable definitions to create a mirrored mosaic.

≋

'We had a slave trade'

It is not clear how many of the more than 200 000 'Pacific Islanders' in Australia also call themselves 'Australian South Sea Islanders'. The distinction is important, for the latter is the preferred name of the descendants of the 'blackbirded' workers who avoided deportation in the early 1900s. There are as many as 60 000 people who claim that ancestry, according to Emelda Davis, who heads the Port Jackson chapter of Australian South Sea Islanders (ASSI), formed in 2007 to further their recognition as a distinct community. Australian South Sea Islanders were, in fact, officially recognised by the Commonwealth as an ethnic minority in 1994 a year after the Human Rights and Equal Opportunity Commission (HREOC) tabled a parliamentary report on the status of the community and the disadvantage they experienced. Titled *A Call for Recognition*, it acknowledged that South Sea Islanders fell outside the definition of Aboriginal or Torres Strait Islanders, and were therefore denied funding assistance and, just as importantly, validation of their experience and identity.

ASSI works to maintain a profile for its community. Emphasising origins is a large part of that but finding 'space' in a national historical narrative replete with well-established, if partially understood, stories such as the role of the Anzacs, the Eureka Stockade and 'Kokoda' is difficult. There are many groups trying to join or disrupt the canon. Competing for the public attention is both easier and harder in the age of digital information. Australia's South Sea Islanders see themselves explicitly – and uniquely – as the Australian offspring of slaves. 'We had a slave trade', Davis said in a 2019 article for the magazine *The Monthly*. She has made that point many times previously to politicians, in talks and on social media. The definition is sometimes disputed, albeit politely. Most agree that Australia's blackbirding did not entail the chattel slavery African-Americans experienced. The cane workers were not traded like the sugar they helped to grow. Many may have been 'unfree' as they were forced or tricked, but others participated willingly, especially in the last two decades with greater regulation and policing. They worked for periods of employment rather than a lifetime of servitude. Historian Clive Moore, who pioneered the study of colonial 'blackbirding', was quoted in the same article: 'Even from the 1860s, there were people going backwards and forwards between Queensland and the islands'. While coercion was used, particularly early on, the Islanders participated in the process. They were able to 'make the system work for them'. The Australian labour trade allowed for that in a way that American slavery did not.

More unequivocally reprehensible, for Moore, was the forced deportation that followed Federation. Many Islanders had made a home in Australia yet they were uprooted and sent back to traditional societies in which they no longer had a permanent place. Life was difficult, too, for the 2500 who managed to remain in Australia. They were the 'unwanted', but from them 60 000 descendants are now Australian South Sea Islanders. For her part, Emelda Davis points to the significance of family stories and self-understanding within the community: 'We're not sitting around, colluding and making things up'.[11]

Faith Bandler was in no doubt that her father had been enslaved when he was delivered as a boy from Ambrym, in present-day Vanuatu, to colonial Queensland. That was around 1880. In their slab timber house in northern New South Wales, Bandler implored the man she adored to repeat the story of 'how he was kidnapped and taken into the boat by slavers'.[12] At the end of that century she was a patron of ASSI and working towards furthering the recognition of the South Sea Islander community. Bandler participated in the first conference of the newly established but short-lived Australian South Sea Islanders Council in 1975. Twenty years later as Vice-President of the Evatt Foundation, the research and policy institution established to mark and further the work of HV Evatt, she instigated a report that led directly to the investigation by HREOC which, in turn, resulted in official recognition of Australian South Sea Islanders.

In that capacity also she wrote to North Sydney Council requesting that it rename Ben Boyd Road, the street which ran downhill to the site of Boyd's erstwhile property on the Neutral Bay waterfront, where the first Islanders to be recruited in the notorious labour trade stayed before, or after, heading down to the Monaro region. 'I am loathed to see a man responsible for the perpetration of these indignities being remembered by having a road named after him', she told the mayor.[13] Just what prompted the letter at that moment, 5 March 1992, is unclear. For one described by her biographer, the historian Marilyn Lake, as a 'gentle activist' the tone was decidedly angry. Reference to her father's experience suggested the personal nature of the offence.

Yet the description of Boyd's activities were historically inaccurate. He did not, as Bandler claimed, bring South Sea Islanders to Australia 'to sell in the slave trade for labour for the Queensland sugar plantations'. They came to work on his sheep runs well before Queensland was a colony and sugar was a cash crop. It was as if Ben Boyd had become the symbol for the whole sorry but complicated story of 'blackbirding', much as Captain Cook represented the entirety of colonisation in some Aboriginal narratives. The error added to the negative response of local residents and undermined the case for a name change. Having received several outraged protest letters, and one or two that were well informed, the council unsurprisingly declined to change the addresses of the several hundred people who lived along Ben Boyd Road, with all the serious ramifications that would follow. The installation of an explanatory plaque was considered instead.

The furore was localised, but still unfortunate. Bandler had, by the 1990s, established a national profile and great respect as the public face of the Federal Council for the Advancement of Aboriginals and Torres Strait Islanders (FCAATSI) and an organiser for the successful 1967 Referendum, in which Australians agreed overwhelmingly that Aboriginal and Torres Strait Islander people be counted in the census and their welfare become a Commonwealth rather than state responsibility. It was a landmark event in the protracted fight for Indigenous rights. Many Aboriginal people regard it as the moment in which they gained full citizenship, following the extension of voting rights in 1962.

However, in the early 1990s Bandler was torn between two communities, one for which she had fought because of an abiding sense of social justice, but of which she was not a member by birthright, and another in which she belonged by descent. It was a difficult wrench which explains the motivation for the Evatt Foundation Report, and possibly the hasty letter to North Sydney Council. The Indigenous Australians she had supported won further recognition and a political voice with the passage of the *Aboriginal and Torres Strait Islander Commission Act* in 1989. But Bandler was all too aware that the representation of ATSIC, the body created by the legislation, did not extend to descendants of South Sea Islanders. She was particularly distressed by the identification of many of her fellow Australian South Sea Islanders as Aboriginal or Torres Strait Islanders so that they could qualify for social benefits. She regarded that, in the words of Marilyn Lake, 'as a form of betrayal' albeit one forced by social marginalisation and invisibility.[14]

'No Eddie Mabo, no case'

Aboriginal people and Torres Strait Islanders themselves have historically had distinct identities. These were maintained even after large-scale post-war migration from the islands to the mainland. Saibai Islanders were among the first. They were relocated to Bamaga on Cape York at their own request after their low-lying island home, a short boat ride from PNG, was inundated by king tides in 1948.[15] Townsville became a popular destination for Torres Strait Islanders from the 1960s, following the collapse of the pearl shell industry – the result of the mass production of plastics, particularly for buttons. A young man called Eddie Koiki Mabo, born on Mer in 1936, was one of the first to move there in 1957 when work on the luggers dried up.[16] Interviewed in the 1980s, he recalled two things that distinguished Islanders from Aboriginal people: treatment by white officials and a sense of 'cultural' superiority on the Islanders' part. Aboriginal people had a name in Meriam, 'agai'; it was one which denoted otherness and carried a sense of opprobrium.[17]

But Mabo also remembered instances of integration. At Halifax to the north of Townsville, Islanders had built a settlement called 'The Gardens' which bore similarities to Torres Strait villages. There was intermarriage with Europeans, Aboriginal people and Torres Strait Islanders. At 'The Gardens' Mabo met his future wife Bonita, 'Netta', a young woman of South Sea Islander descent.[18]

Distinctions notwithstanding, there quickly grew a sense of shared interest as the two peoples interacted further. That was reflected most obviously in 1963 by the inclusion of Torres Strait Islanders in the Federal Council for Aboriginal Advancement and the consequent naming of FCAATSI – the organisation in which Faith Bandler would play such an important role. The Department of Native Affairs was also recast. A new Department of Aboriginal and Islander Affairs in 1965 was established with the *Aboriginal and Torres Strait Islanders'*

Affairs Act. That legislation repealed the *Torres Strait Islanders Act* of 1939, which had previously controlled the movement of Mabo and his fellow Islanders.

But identity remained important. Three decades after FCAATSI was born, Torres Strait Islanders adopted their own flag. Replete with symbolism, it was designed by Thursday Island man Bernard Namok. At the centre is the distinctive omega-shaped headdress, called a Dhari on the eastern islands around Mer. A five-pointed star within that form represents the five island groups. These sit in a blue band that is the sea of the Torres Strait. Above and below are smaller strips of green representing PNG and Australia. The flag was presented at the 6th Torres Strait Cultural Festival on 29 May 1992. It was displayed officially alongside the Aboriginal standard at ATSIC meetings shortly after and was recognised by the Commonwealth in 1995.

The year 1992 was a most important year for Torres Strait Islanders. Five days after the Islanders accepted Bernard Namok's flag design as their own, the High Court of Australia passed down its finding on native title, a decision which followed Eddie Mabo's long-running fight for the recognition of his claim to ownership of a piece of Mer. It was one of the most momentous judgments in Australian history, overturning the legal fiction that the continent had been an empty land, *terra nullius*, when James Cook took possession of the east coast for the British Crown from the vantage of the Torres Strait in 1770. That claim was acted upon, of course, in 1788 with Arthur Phillip's seizure of half the landmass from a bay that the local owners called Warrane and he renamed Sydney Cove. It was the year in which Torres Strait Islanders redefined the origins of modern Australia.

Eddie Mabo became politically active in Townsville. He was interested in organised labour and race politics. In the immediate aftermath of the 1967 Referendum, he organised a conference which brought Europeans, Islanders and Aboriginal people together to discuss the future of race relations. In that year also Mabo was employed as a gardener at James Cook University using skills he learned as a boy and young man on Mer. The job gave him access to the university library, which held the 19th-century writings of Alfred Haddon on Torres Strait culture. It was not the first time that the colonised would use the studies of the colonisers to recover and reinforce an understanding of pre-contact culture, and would not be the last. Work at the university also brought Mabo into regular contact with historian Henry Reynolds and postgraduate student Noel Loos, whom he had already met. Through them he learned that, as Loos recalled, 'he did not have legal title to his land on Murray [Mer] Island'.[19] His island home was Crown land.

The revelation catalysed Mabo and deepened his interest in his island heritage. In 1982 Mabo and four other Meriam people – David and Sam Passi, James Rice and Celuia Salee – took their claim to particular plots on Mer to the High Court of Australia. It was the beginning of a decade-long legal drama. Many, perhaps most, Australians have heard of 'Mabo', the court case. Less appreciated is the fact that that judgment came at the end of a three-part process in which the first set of personal claims by Mabo, Salee and the others was followed by two other High Court cases, sometimes referred to as Mabo 1 and Mabo 2. The latter debunked *terra nullius*.

A young Jesuit priest and lawyer called Frank Brennan had just been appointed Adviser to the Queensland Catholic Bishops on Aboriginal Affairs when the plaintiffs were starting their action. He recalled Mabo's energy and the ethnic specificity of his argument:

> At numerous conferences Eddie Mabo explained to lawyers and to anyone willing to listen that Torres Strait Islanders were different from Aborigines. Traditionally, Aborigines were hunters and gatherers having communal interests over vast areas of land, while Torres Strait Islanders were vegetable gardeners living in small villages, cultivating family plots, and able to identify the boundary lines of their market gardens to the nearest square-inch.[20]

That was not strictly the case for all Torres Strait Islanders. Fishing was the primary means of procuring food in the less fertile low-lying central islands. But on the volcanic mount of Mer, good soil had formed. There, gardening acquired great practical and spiritual significance. The Meriam believed that fertility was the gift of their first god Bomai and property rights were protected by the second sacred being, Malo. His rules, Malo's Law, forbad trespass and theft. The understanding of that tradition gave Eddie Mabo confidence that his case was different from the one presented by the Yolngu people of Arnhem Land in the 'Gove Land Rights Case' of 1971, when Justice Blackburn rejected the legal standing of the spiritual knowledge presented to him. 'I am not satisfied on the balance of probabilities', he concluded, 'that the plaintiff's predecessors had in 1788 the same links to the same areas of land as those which the plaintiffs now claim'.[21] That dismissal came despite the anthropological support of distinguished experts such as WEH Stanner, who was disappointed but unsurprised by the outcome, having encountered often 'the hostility and derision towards the work and opinions of anthropologists' from administrations and the courts.[22]

Mabo's convictions were shored by the research of the historian Henry Reynolds, which would coalesce into the remarkable analysis of the legal standing of Australia's colonisation, *The Law of the Land*. In that 1987 book Reynolds showed that *terra nullius* contradicted both contemporary international and British law. The process of colonisation had been launched on the spurious assumption advanced by Joseph Banks that the interior of the continent must be empty for there were so few inhabitants on its coast, and those people neither farmed the land nor built substantial dwellings. *Terra nullius* developed a momentum and necessity of its own, despite immediate and ample evidence of Aboriginal attachment to place. 'The theory of an uninhabited continent was just too convenient to surrender lightly', Reynolds argued, '... The law retreated farther from the real world and farther into injustice as the nineteenth century progressed'.[23] All that despite the view of the great 18th-century jurist William Blackstone, who questioned the right in 'nature', 'reason' and 'Christianity' to 'drive out' or kill a resident people simply because 'they differed from their invaders'.[24] Reynolds himself questioned the assumption that 'the Crown claimed both sovereignty ... and the actual ownership of the land' in 1788.[25] To insert a single sovereign where there was apparently none was one thing. To acquire ownership of everything in that instant was quite another. That distinction anticipated the native title judgment in 1992.

The Queensland state government was less than sympathetic to the Islanders' High Court challenge. It responded by introducing the 'Queensland Coastal Islands Declaratory Bill', which aimed to retrospectively end any claim to land in the Torres Strait. Native title, it maintained, had been extinguished in 1879, when the colony of Queensland acquired the islands. The longstanding premier, Sir Joh Bjelke-Petersen, was a conservative who had clung to power by rearranging electoral boundaries and pioneering the politics of populism which would serve the conservative cause so well in later decades. Queensland was still in many respects a frontier state with an economy based upon resource extraction and agriculture. Environmental protection, Indigenous land rights, organised labour and civil liberties were readily presented as impediments to stability and wealth creation. The 'hard-working' folk of rural and regional areas were defined against political 'troublemakers' – those in the south-east urban pocket of Brisbane, particularly, but also activists such as Eddie Mabo. The repressive use of a highly corrupt police force and the politicisation of the civil service was widespread. Mabo was convinced that the Queensland Department of Aboriginal and Islander Affairs impeded his travel back to Mer in 1974 to see his dying adoptive father, Benny Mabo, on the basis of his political activity.[26]

The passage of the *Queensland Coastal Islands Declaratory Act* in 1985 allowed Mabo and his four co-plaintiffs to change tack – in an action called a demurrer – and test the validity of the law on the basis that it contravened the *Racial Discrimination Act* passed by the Whitlam government in 1975 in accord with the UN Convention on the Elimination of All Forms of Racial Discrimination. The Queensland legislation applied only to Torres Strait Islanders. It extinguished only their property rights. In 1988 the High Court consequently disallowed the Act. This was Mabo 1. The decision attracted little public comment for there was drama enough elsewhere. Bjelke-Petersen had resigned the previous year amidst revelations about the corruption which had flourished during his long reign. And 1988 was the bicentenary of the 'birth' of modern Australia and the beginning of Indigenous dispossession. Attention was, therefore, focussed on expressions of national pride and Aboriginal protest against such insensitivity.

With Mabo 1 decided, the Supreme Court of Queensland returned to the initial claim for land title on Mer and began hearings 'to determine the facts'. The plaintiffs had already presented evidence of their respective titles. That process continued. Mabo gave oral evidence and tabled a map drafted from memory showing marked garden plots, his own included. But he faced two problems. An absence from Mer for more than 25 years had alienated him from some on the island. In his time away, the population had fallen to just 200, one-third of the number when he had left. Mabo thereby became an interloper in the minds of a few who had remained. That, and his adoption by the Mabo family, left open doubt about his title to inherited land. In 1990 Justice Moynihan of the Queensland Supreme Court rejected Mabo's personal claims but allowed some of those put forward by the remaining plaintiffs, David Passi and James Rice. Celuia Salee had died in 1985 and Sam Passi withdrew from the case the following year.

Legal counsel for David Passi and Rice advised them to put a claim for native title for the whole of the island to the High Court. It was that case, Mabo 2, which delivered the rejection of *terra nullius* in June 1992. The finding, which accepted the legal existence of native title in Australia, bore the name of Mabo although the man himself had largely withdrawn from the proceedings by that stage, and his personal claim to land on Mer had not been recognised. If there was some irony in that, there was tragic poignancy in Eddie Mabo's death from cancer on

21 January that year. He did not live to hear the judgment with which his name would be associated thereafter. On the day the High Court passed down its finding, swastikas were painted on Mabo's grave and his bust removed. The desecration was testimony to the bitterness he confronted in life and a dramatic anticipation of the acrimonious debate which followed. Eddie Mabo was reburied on Mer in September 1992. While acknowledging the crucial role of all the plaintiffs, his legal counsel Bryan Keon-Cohen placed the Meriam man at the centre of the drama: 'No Eddie Mabo, no case'.[27]

Mabo 2, the case most commonly called simply 'Mabo', highlighted the question of whether native title was extinguished immediately upon declaration of sovereignty, as Henry Reynolds had questioned in 1987. The finding that it was not applied both to Aboriginal people and Islanders irrespective of whether they were horticulturalists or hunters. It is nonetheless significant that the legal argument which ended in the High Court in 1992 began because Eddie Mabo believed in the demonstrable distinctiveness of his island traditions, the gardens of Mer and the protective certainty of Malo's Law. As a result, the creation stories from a tiny Pacific island helped to overturn Australia's great foundation myth – *terra nullius*.

CHAPTER 20

Climate change

'the great moral challenge of our time'

In 2018 I was one of a small group of Australians who gathered to hear another, quite different Pacific story. In a modest seminar room at the University of New South Wales, three I-Kiribati people spoke of the environmental catastrophe that was unfolding in their Micronesian nation. Kiribati was once a collection of disparate island homes, settled during that great peopling of the Pacific which began 5000–6000 years ago. A British protectorate over the so-called Gilbert group was declared from 1892. That became a colony in 1915. Independence for the Gilbert Islands and two other clusters came in 1979. Britain having vacated the Pacific, the new Republic of Kiribati adopted the currency of the nearest large nation, the Australian dollar. In terms of awareness it is a one-sided relationship. Most imports to Kiribati come from Australia. The speakers I heard, one man and two women, referred to my country alternatively as 'a big brother' and 'a big sister' to their nation. Few Australians, I suspect, know of Kiribati let alone how to pronounce its name – 'Kirri-bus'.

The republic is a sprinkling of coral islands and atolls spread over more than 4500 kilometres of ocean, west to east, with a total landmass of only 811 square kilometres. Consequently, its population of fewer than 100 000 is quite densely settled on those islands that are inhabitable. The capital is on Tarawa around which, in late 1943, America staged the first of its bloody amphibious assaults in its strategy of island-hopping to Japan.

A Latvian-born Australian mariner called Karl Tschaun helped the Americans navigate the islands en route to their invasion, with knowledge gleaned in service to the ubiquitous Burns Philp company. Therein lay Australia's main involvement with the erstwhile Gilberts: resource extraction and the supply of those mining outposts. Ocean Island, now Banaba, is only 200 kilometres from Nauru. Like that island, it provided Australian farmers with thousands of tonnes of phosphate from which to produce fertiliser. Australian-born Albert Ellis discovered those deposits in 1900, working for the Pacific Islands Company while based in Sydney. Before Nauru was taken from the Germans, Ocean Island was a more convenient source of phosphate than its neighbour. The mining that ensued produced a barren landscape not unlike Nauru. I-Kiribati historian Katerina Teaiwa described the place she saw in 1997 as follows: 'Banaba was a desiccated field of rocks and jagged limestone pinnacles jutting out of grey earth with patches of dark green foliage. Roofless concrete buildings, rusted machinery and corrugated iron warehouses litter the vista ...'[1]

It was not that legacy of destruction which the trio wanted to discuss at the Practical Justice Initiative, but rather the greater issue of sea-level rise, and the changing climate at the heart of that existential crisis. Kiribati is no higher than 3 metres above sea level, so its people are watching their land disappear as glaciers thousands of kilometres away melt and the water itself warms and expands.

The El-Niño South Oscillation (ENSO), which ranges across the Pacific and alters weather patterns around the globe, is also significant. An El-Niño event involves warmer water accumulating in the eastern Pacific, causing greater evaporation and storm activity in that region. Conversely, cooler water in the west creates less evaporation and rainfall. El-Niño weather patterns therefore typically coincide with droughts and severe bushfire seasons in Australia. Together with La-Niña events, which bring rain to the west and drought to the east, El-Niños have affected people's fortunes and movements for thousands of years. Two particularly intense events in 1976 and 1998 appear to have had a dramatic and lasting effect. Since 1976 the frequency, duration and severity of El-Niños have increased. After 1998, sea temperature readings of 30°C have not been uncommon. That is five to ten degrees warmer than recorded in the decade after World War Two.[2] The relationship between atmosphere and oceans is astonishingly complex. How these new plateaus correspond to the increase in atmospheric carbon and the scientifically undeniable phenomenon of global warming is still being considered. However, few scientists dispute that ENSO, in combination with rising global temperatures, will unleash more frequent and severe weather events.

In the western Pacific, significant periodic sea-level rises often precede El-Niño events. The resulting inundations are causing freshwater shortages on Kiribati. The Islanders draw their water from wells which tap underground reservoirs of rain water, hydrological lenses, which have been built up over centuries by precipitation. In the porous natural containers of coral or volcanic rock it is only the weight of the underlying sea water that separates the two types of H_2O. Fresh water sits on top of the heavier saline solution. As immersions occur the differential is lost and the reservoirs become permanently salty. Without groundwater the people depend far more upon the rain which El-Niño denies. It is a very vicious cycle.

The speakers presented the Australians in the audience – myself included – with a blunt truth: our way of life was directly destroying theirs. We are the world's highest per capita emitters of carbon dioxide. More directly, the coal we export is changing the climate. There followed a question: 'What do you care about?' And then a challenge: 'The answer is in your hands'. None of this was delivered with acrimony, just conviction and sadness. One of the speakers broke down in tears as she considered her granddaughter's future. It was genuine emotion. There seemed to be no future on Kiribati, yet leaving their home was unthinkable. At least one member of the audience, however, remained unmoved. He responded with his own truth, delivered with the wry smile of the 'realist'. Australia needs the wealth, power and jobs generated by coal. Effectively he was saying, 'It is you or us'.

Kiribati's longstanding president, Anote Tong, was one of the first to draw the world's attention to his nation's plight. He addressed the UN in 2008, the year that the Pacific Islands Forum made climate change its theme. In that year also he had appealed to Australia to allow I-Kiribati to settle permanently in Australia as climate change refugees. He spoke of 'Migration with dignity'. Fiji was another possible destination and Kiribati bought land there for the purpose. President Tong had accepted a truth the speakers I heard a decade later were still coming to terms with: 'Ultimately low-lying island countries like Kiribati will have to face up to the reality of their islands being unable to support life'. The problem of climate change was not of his people's making yet they faced its consequences. The science on the issue was 'irrefutable', he declared, yet the 'international community continues to point fingers at each other regarding responsibility for and leadership on this issue'.[3]

The Intergovernmental Panel on Climate Change (IPCC) had handed down its fourth report the year before Tong spoke at the UN. He referred to its prediction of a sea level rise of more than 0.4 metres before the end of the century, which would be disastrous for his nation. Where Tong spoke of the 'irrefutable' science on climate change, the report itself indicated a 'very high confidence that the global average net effect of human activities since 1750 has been one of warming'. It explained in its 'Summary for Policymakers' that 'very high confidence' equated to a probability of 90 per cent or more.[4]

The IPCC had been reporting on what many still referred to as 'the greenhouse effect' for two decades before Kiribati's president urged the world to act on the science in 2008. The Kyoto Protocol – adopted in 1997 and enabled by 2005 – committed developed nations to reducing their emission of six 'greenhouse gases', including carbon dioxide and methane, by 5.2 per cent compared to their 1990 output. This was to happen between 2008 and 2012. Neither Australia under John Howard nor the US under President George W Bush formally agreed to, or ratified, the protocol. Australian endorsement was the first official act of the newly elected Labor prime minister Kevin Rudd in 2007. That very obvious decision followed his description of climate change as 'the great moral challenge of our time' at the UN. It accorded with an apparent consensus in the Australian community that climate change was 'the most important external threat' to the nation.[5]

Reports and policy suggestions followed. In 2008 Ross Garnaut, an economics professor at the ANU's Research School of Pacific and Asian Studies, presented his detailed 'Climate Change Review' into the threats and opportunities confronting Australia, which six Labor state governments and Federal Labor commissioned while in opposition. That year the Australian Senate called for a report from its Foreign Affairs, Defence and Trade References Committee into the economic and security challenges 'facing Papua New Guinea and the island states of the southwest Pacific'. The study, tabled in 2009, ranged over many issues, including climate change. It noted Australia's commitment to spend $150 million over three years on climate change adaptation 'in vulnerable countries in the Pacific region' and various AusAID projects including the provision of 300 large rainwater tanks in Funafuti, the capital of Tuvalu. The committee considered the legal and social ramifications of resettling displaced Islanders; for they would be, in effect, refugees who did not fit the definition of the 1951 Refugee Convention. It recommended that the government begin addressing the issues on the basis that climate change migration be facilitated on the basis of 'merit and dignity'.[6]

Amidst the ongoing angst about the Pacific Solution and asylum seekers, the government response to the matter of resettlement was unsurprisingly indirect and non-committal. By that time, too, Labor was preoccupied with the passage of its Emissions Trading Scheme legislation, which was aimed at reducing greenhouse gases through market forces. Negotiations with the conservative opposition came to nothing when Tony Abbott narrowly defeated the more moderate and co-operative Malcolm Turnbull for the leadership of the Liberal Party on 1 December 2009. Shortly after, the new leader would famously describe the 'argument' underpinning climate change as 'absolute crap'.[7]

Abbott's narrowly won ascension pushed the Liberal Party

dramatically to the right. It adopted a 'win at all costs' form of politics similar to that practised by the American Republican Party in their wholesale opposition to the newly elected Democrat president Barack Obama. There followed years of campaigning against climate science and an emphasis on the cost of mitigating emissions. Climate change joined the Pacific Solution as an issue used to drive a 'wedge' between Labor and its traditional working-class base. Where the government wanted to 'tax' carbon, the Coalition wanted 'hardworking' Australians to keep their earnings. The popular consensus on climate change was steadily eroded and the political consensus within Labor fell apart. Rudd lost the leadership, won it again and then lost the 2013 federal election. The new Abbott government promptly abolished the Climate Commission, established in 2011 to disseminate 'independent and reliable' information about climate change.

The right-wing media supported Abbott's single-minded strategy to destabilise Labor. It had campaigned against the theory of climate change, and policies formulated to prevent it, since before the election of the Rudd government. Rupert Murdoch's conglomeration of Australian outlets included the capital city tabloids in Adelaide, Sydney, Brisbane and Melbourne, home of the country's best-selling newspaper, the *Herald Sun*. The content of Sky News was beamed into many clubs and pubs. All took their editorial lead from the News Limited flagship newspaper the *Australian*. For every opinion piece by a scientist supporting the theory of human-induced climate change it printed between 2004 and 2011, the *Australian* published ten commentaries by the handful who rejected it.[8] It regularly aired the critiques of Danish environmental economist Bjorn Lomborg, who variously dismissed the urgency of climate change, the viability of alternative energies and the benefits of taxing carbon. Typically, those appeared after a pessimistic pronouncement by the IPCC or a climate-related emergency.

The bias mirrored the coverage of the Murdoch-owned Fox News network in the US.[9] In both countries, too, 'think tanks' generated large amounts of information casting doubt on the theory of climate change. They exploited the inherent caution of scientific modelling which never presented certainties, only probabilities. The Institute of Public Affairs (IPA) in Australia was particularly effective and well financed by the mining sector. The consensus which had coalesced around the causes of climate change was characterised as a controlling, almost conspiratorial, orthodoxy. Scientists thereby joined the ranks of that ill-defined class generally called the 'elite', while climate change 'sceptics' – tabloid columnists and broadcasters among them – were cast as rational critical thinkers speaking truth to power and defending 'ordinary Australians' against big government and vested interests. For the IPA this was simply democratic debate at its best. The people and their elected representatives, not scientists or academics, should decide policy.

As the polemical response to science unfolded in the mainstream media, and became febrile across the internet and new social media platforms, two critical events unfolded. The Global Financial Crisis undermined the willingness of business to consider the long-term risks of climate change, and Australia experienced its so-called 'mining boom'. The latter helped Australia financially withstand the former and also fuelled the campaign against action on climate change. Growth in the export of iron ore and coal in the decade to 2010 remade the Australian economy. Much of that was directly related to China's emergence as an economic superpower with its insatiable demand for steel's basic ingredient and the power to transform it. Since the Tiananmen Square killings in 1989, the Chinese Communist Party had enabled astonishing economic growth by embracing free markets as a way to ensure the social control it prioritised. Where many in the West had assumed that democracy would be welcomed with China's door finally opened to capitalism, it turned out that affluence could also encourage acquiescence.

In 2009 the nation became Australia's biggest trading partner, buying 27 per cent of exports. Within two years mining was contributing 60 per cent of overall exports. As writer Malcolm Knox remarked shortly after, 'Only once before, in the gold rushes, has Australian exporting been so minerals-dependent'.[10] Iron ore was by far the largest commodity. Coal was second. Australia exported more than $56 billion worth of that mineral in 2011.

Since the 19th century the success of the Australian economy, along with the relative equality and well-being which that has made possible, has been built upon the availability of vast amounts of accessible coal. It was the lucky bounty of Australia's Gondwanan past. Sydney was blessed by proximity to two large fields, one north and one south. Those fuelled the city's industry, trains and steamers, as well as generating electrical power for much of the state through the 20th century. Driven by the post-war revival of that first Asia-Pacific industrial power, Japan, coal production for export and steel-making doubled every 10 years between 1960 and 1980. Thereafter, local steel manufacturing declined with tariff cuts the Hawke government introduced, and coal mining for export increased. The rise of Chinese manufacturing from 2000 added another huge market for Australian coal. The demand throughout spurred prospecting in Queensland's Bowen Basin. In 2010, that state's Labor government announced an intention to double its coal production over the next two decades to 340 million tonnes per year. The potential of deposits in the vast untapped Galilee Basin added to the Cooper and Bowen Basins made that possible.

Considerable though the returns to public revenue were through fees and taxes, Federal Labor proposed a super-profits tax on mining enterprises in 2010 on the basis that as much as 80 per cent of the industry was foreign-owned and not enough of the boom's benefits were staying in Australia. The debate which ensued gave the conservative Opposition another issue on which to argue its case for small government and reduced taxation. One of its 2013 election commitments was to repeal any mining tax. It was aided during Labor's term by the Minerals Council of Australia's (MCA) well-funded and successful media campaign which positioned the mining industry as the 'backbone of the country'.[11] Where once the visage of Australian mining was simply that of a unionised man covered in coal or red dust, the new faces of the industry were young and old, male and female, black and white, Caucasian and Asian. Mining workers joined that pantheon of Australians – farmers, Anzacs, suburban 'battlers' among them – who embodied the best national characteristics of unpretentious, hardworking honesty. It was an effective use of the progressive political mantra of diversity.

All of that made it much easier to overlook the reality of climate change. Coal is the single largest source of 'carbon pollution', human-created CO^2.[12] In its monumental 2012 study of the nation's geology, posted out free to public libraries and made available on the internet, the government agency Geoscience Australia was matter-of-fact: 'Australia is a world-class producer of greenhouse gases, with CO^2 being a major contributor'.[13]

Having explored the fluctuating perceptions of mineral resource extraction in Australia, Malcolm Knox concluded that 'Mining is like meat-eating, only more so. We may not like the idea of what happens in abattoirs, but few of us refuse to eat meat on those grounds. A great deal fewer will refuse to dirty their hands with the products of mining'.[14] A public reliance on cheap abundant power helps to explain the willingness to avoid the implications of climate change. A reliance on public revenue and the difficulty of justifying coal sector job losses also explains the political reluctance to act. The latter is a conundrum that has confounded Labor more than the conservative Coalition, for mine workers have historically been among that party's most ardent supporters – strongly unionised and therefore ready and willing to assist with political campaigning. Before the unprecedented bushfires of 2019–20, it may be that the vastness of Australia made it more difficult to draw a direct line between climate change and wider environmental changes. On tiny Kiribati it is hard to ignore such changes.

But there was an attachment to coal mining in Australia that went beyond economics, politics and even geography. The end of car manufacturing in Australia in 2017 resulted in as many as 30 000 job losses, but the Coalition government rationalised that tectonic social and economic shift on the basis of market forces.[15] The consequent demise of the Holden, the car born of post-war reconstruction to become a national icon, was explained away with regretful realism. There were approximately 50 000 jobs in the coal mining sector. Yet both major parties defended those tenaciously despite recent market and technological change which have made the precautionary transition from fossil fuels to alternative energies sensible in the modelling of Ross Garnaut and others.

Furthermore, the monies and jobs that have been promised with opening up Queensland's Galilee Basin were increasingly disputed. So much so that writer James Bradley used the word 'infatuation' to describe the commitment to coal in the face of its increasingly chimeric rewards.[16] The reality of 'wedge' politics notwithstanding, the belief in coal was deeply ingrained, on the conservative side of Australian politics particularly, but also by some in Labor who feared their party would remain in Opposition if it abandoned its working-class base to satisfy environmental zealots. The Coalition's wholehearted support for coal was matched by a concomitant dislike of alternative energies, indeed the very culture of environmentalism. In 2014, then Liberal treasurer Joe Hockey described wind turbines as an 'utterly offensive' blot on the landscape without commenting upon the visual impact of open-cut coal mines.[17] In the lead-up to the 2019 election, the Coalition's small and family business minister, Michaelia Cash, furiously suggested that Labor's support for electric vehicles would undermine family life and the business of much-venerated 'tradies' – self-employed plumbers, builders and others – by compulsorily replacing the behemoth-like utility vehicles that were then commonplace on Australian roads. The claim was Trump-like in its populist overstatement. In 2020 National Party politician and former resources minister, Matt Canavan, strangely equated renewable energies with welfare recipients: they were the 'dole bludgers' of the energy sector compared to hardworking coal.[18]

But perhaps the most remarkable instance of all was Scott

Morrison's carefully staged parliamentary performance as treasurer in February 2017 when he goaded the Labor Opposition on the other side of the chamber with a large piece of coal: 'This is coal, don't be afraid, don't be scared'.[19] It was as if climate change was the figment of paranoid imaginations. The MCA supplied the specimen and the following year their former deputy chief executive officer became the treasurer's chief of staff. John Kunkel stayed with Morrison when he became prime minister shortly after the party again ousted Malcolm Turnbull, who had since displaced the increasingly erratic Abbott. Such was the chaotic nature of Australian politics in the era of climate policy and the intimate links between the mining sector and government.

What was being defended was an 'Australian way of life' apparently threatened by everything that carbon abatement entailed. In many ways it was the culture of Donald Horne's *Lucky Country*, now thoroughly reified without a hint of his irony. This was a land of suburban families going about their business in sports utility vehicles (SUVs), of the tradies in their 'utes' who built the homes, of farmers working hard to put the meat on suburban stoves and barbecues, and of coal miners who unearthed the mineral that powered it all affordably. It was the national house that coal built. It was symbiotic, an ecosystem in its own right.

There were, of course, costs. The Great Barrier Reef, Australia's magnificent Pacific necklace, had experienced serious coral bleaching as a result of warming seas in 1998, 2002, 2016 and 2017. After that last bleaching event, Ove Hoegh-Guldberg, Professor of Marine Science at the University of Queensland, said, 'If we continue to have warm summers like we had in '16 and this year, the next one could wipe out the remaining coral'.[20] Two years later Australia experienced its hottest year on record. For those in the pro-coal Coalition government who conceded that there might be a link between fossil fuels and global warming, destruction of the reef was an acceptable, if unfortunate, cost if the Australian way of life was to be maintained. There was no such regret for those who remained unconvinced of the association.

'Perhaps Australia is more like a prodigal son'

In 1973, EF Schumacher, the German-born economist and one-time advisor to Britain's National Coal Board, published *Small Is Beautiful* – his classic critique of the economics of limitless production and perpetual growth which drove capitalism and communism alike. The problem, he maintained, arose from '*western* man's attitude to nature' (emphasis in original). That being, whom Schumacher also called 'modern man', did not 'experience himself as a part of nature but as an outside force destined to dominate and conquer it. He even talks of a battle with nature, forgetting that, if he won the battle, he would find himself on the losing side'.[21] It described well the ethos of those who colonised Australia, an event which coincided with the birth of the modern industrial age. Battling nature is what occurred for the next two centuries. The Norfolk Island Providence petrel, extinct by 1800, may not even have been the first victim of that war. The devastation of Australia's flora and fauna that followed was apocalyptic. Yet despite the profundity of Schumacher's words, and the millions more that followed from those concerned at ecological devastation, little had changed on the side of conservative politics in Australia by 2019. Despite their etymological links, the words 'conservation' and 'conservatism' generally reside at far ends of the political spectrum. Rivers, forests, minerals, oceans and animals were, and still are, resources to be used simply for the benefit of humans and that benefit is measured in short-term economic gain. Taming nature was, and is, virtuous.

The American writer Bill McKibben contributed significantly to the rising count of warning words which followed Schumacher's missive against materialism. His book *The End of Nature* was published in 1990 and is regarded as the first popular work to discuss the 'greenhouse effect'. It was also an early salvo in the ideological battle over climate science. Scientists had been aware of the association between carbon and climate since the 1960s. In 1988 respected climate modeller James

Hansen announced the irrefutability of human-caused global warming. The political and industry campaign to undermine his finding began the following year. The first report of the IPCC supporting Hansen's thesis was released in 1990.[22] That year McKibben wrote, 'We are changing the atmosphere and thus we are changing the weather'. With that, he argued, we are ending nature. He was describing what would later be called the Anthropocene, the geological epoch in which humans, rather than entirely natural forces, are altering the way the Earth works.

Australia was not mentioned in *The End of Nature*, but 25 years later the author was very aware of the nation's role in the politics and science of climate change. In November 2018 McKibben informed readers of the *New York Review of Books* that the 'prime minister of Australia, the world's biggest coal exporter, is now Scott Morrison, a man famous for bringing a chunk of anthracite into parliament and passing it around so everyone could marvel at its greatness'.[23] The article was a pessimistic review of the latest IPCC Special Report which, as McKibben noted, was begun in hope following the 2015 Paris Agreement to keep global warming to '1.5°C above pre-industrial levels'. The report was tabled, however, in an altogether different 'age' – after the 2016 election of Donald Trump, the interminable distraction of Brexit and the elevation of Scott Morrison in August 2018.

The new Australian prime minister personified the demographic around which much of the populist elements of the climate change debate swirled. Where previous national leaders had been drawn from the legal profession, business, the union movement and simply the professional or dynastic world of politics, he appeared as the archetypal 'dad', cap-wearing and football-loving. Political historian and commentator Judith Brett has called it an 'exuberant suburban public persona'.[24] That Morrison had been an advertising executive prior to becoming a politician undoubtedly helped with the canny promotion of that image. The prime minister's demonstrated belief in the harmlessness of the coal was the political stunt of a man with experience in selling messages.

But it might also have reflected conviction. Scott Morrison is a man of faith. He is a Pentecostal, like Israel Folau. His brand of Christianity holds that God intervenes directly in daily life and the Bible is to be understood literally. Many followers of that teaching believe that the Earth was created in six days and that 'man' is to have 'dominion' over every living creature. Devotion, too, will be rewarded with success and wealth. That so-called 'prosperity gospel' is preached at Morrison's local Horizon Church near the Pacific coast in Sydney's southern suburbs. Such Biblical literalism and the embrace of the material benefits of religiosity are at odds with Schumacher's economics of 'small' and, for that matter, the conservative Catholicism of James McAuley, who despised the modernity that contemporary Christian fundamentalism celebrates. Such faith makes the science of climate change simply irrelevant.

Morrison's belief in a coal-driven future for Australia was given a democratic mandate at the 2019 election. The poll was widely seen as a referendum on climate change and the result was a surprise, not least to Morrison himself. 'I have always believed in miracles', he declared with a grin but no sense of irony. It may have been an allusion to divine intervention and, therefore, his god's approval. The prime minister certainly acknowledged the role played by those Queensland voters who helped deliver the victory and made clear their desire to mine the Galilee Basin in the process. Morrison went on to thank the 'Quiet Australians' who supported him and made a commitment to ensure 'A fair go for those who have a go'. On the outside were the truculent, the lazy and the noisy – those unwilling to be part of the Lucky Country's dream.

In September of that year Morrison was feted by Donald Trump during the prime minister's state visit to Australia's great Pacific ally. It was a rare courtesy. Much was made of the friendship between the two countries, 100 years old when measured, as it was, from World War One; but a little older if the 1908 Great White Fleet visit is the start date. In Ohio Morrison was caught up in the exuberance and adulation at one of Trump's many rallies, typically attended by cap-wearing white nationalists, climate change deniers and Christians. 'The President and I are here because we believe in jobs', he shouted.[25]

At the same time a Swedish teenager called Greta Thunberg addressed a very different audience at the United Nations Climate Action Summit in New York: 'We are in the beginning of a mass extinction, and all you can talk about is money and fairy-tales of eternal economic growth'. It was a mix of EF Schumacher and Bill McKibben delivered with remarkable bravery, passion and eloquence. A great many young people in Australia saw her as a heroic role model and protested accordingly. The hard men in Murdoch's media responded with misogyny and patronising put-downs. Preferring 'Quiet Australians' to the outspoken Swede, Scott Morrison opined that 'We should let our kids be kids, teenagers be teenagers'.[26]

The following month the prime minister visited Tuvalu for the Pacific Islands Forum. Fortified by his election victory in May, Morrison was unapologetic about his refusal to commit to any moratorium on new coal mines. He was 'accountable to the Australian people', not those of the Pacific.[27] When climate change threatened the very existence of island nations, it was Australia first. Upon hearing that I thought of the man who remained unmoved by the sobbing woman from Kiribati.

I also recalled the very different message delivered when the prime minister announced a 'new chapter' in Australia's Pacific partnership in 2018. Then Australia was part of a 'Pacific family' and the unspoken threat which unified all was the rise of China and the extension of its Pacific influence.[28] The contradiction was criticised by island leaders and some in the Australian media. Perhaps the most excoriating comment came from the Fijian cleric Reverend James Bhagwan, the General Secretary of the Pacific Conference of Churches, who spoke in the language of faith. 'I love him [Scott Morrison] as a Christian brother', said Bhagwan, 'but he is not demonstrating the attitudes of the Christian life and, of course, of leadership as a Christian ... We have heard so much rhetoric about Australia being part of the Pacific family', the cleric continued, '… and yet the demonstration of this family is not as strong as it should be. Perhaps Australia is more like a prodigal son …'[29]

The Bible, however, provides many answers. While Reverend Bhagwan saw moral lessons in the face of pending climate catastrophe, there are others who find solace in its myriad messages of deliverance. As many as one-third of the population of tiny Tuvalu, where Prime Minister Morrison remained defiant about his country's need to dig and burn coal, do not even believe in climate change because of God's pledge to Noah that there would be no second flood.[30] Faith gives hope to the powerless.

In Australia, science poses questions and answers that many Australians find disturbing. It is sometimes dismissed as just another article of faith rather than a method for objective analysis. For the former prime minister Tony Abbott, himself a professed Christian, climate science is at once a 'post-Christian theology' and a manifestation of pre-Christian savagery. Its adherents, he announced in 2017, are like 'primitive people … killing goats to appease mountain gods'.[31]

In an age without objective truth, one person's science is another's superstition. Faith provides hope but it also permits excuses.

≋

'It's not something we have an appetite to talk about'

Tony Abbott's reference to sacrifices and mountain gods echoed the dismissiveness of European ethnographers and missionaries as they encountered Pacific cultures. It did not help make the case for membership of the Pacific family but was probably not intended to do so. At best, Australia was the estranged son or perhaps a distant and snobbish cousin.

Despite the former prime minister's insult, the I-Kiribati at the Practical Justice Initiative generously addressed me and the other

Australians as 'Big Brother' and 'Big Sister'. Australia has wealth in abundance compared to their nation. And it does share some of that with the region. The $4 billion spent to stabilise the Solomon Islands was just one example. The prime minister promised $500 million in aid at the 2018 Pacific Islands Forum. But that was for climate change adaptation. It was largesse that both admitted that environmental change existed and avoided responsibility for contributing to it.

History is a bit like biology, it is possible to find connections everywhere, in culture as in nature. It stands to reason, as there have been global systems of weather, continental shift, and ocean currents since well before modern humans evolved. Since the European arrival in the Pacific and the consequent colonisation of Australia, humans have moved themselves, other organisms, and goods across the Earth with increasing rapidity. Unprecedented material wealth has been created in the process of globalisation, though not necessarily for all. The societies which emerged in this era have burned so much fossil fuel to meet their demands that humans are now changing the global weather patterns.

Ideas have spread too. A belief in unlimited progress is one of those. A 'common humanity' is another. As John Gascoigne has shown, the Pacific was a crucible for testing this idea. It was explored as Enlightenment ideas of equality and dignity swirled around similar Christian views and both butted up against the science of race theory, which held to difference and hierarchies. As the homeland of a major European Pacific society, Australia was often at the centre of those debates. For much of its existence, Australia's white residents have held themselves apart from those around, although that distinction did not rule out the urge to occupy the islands as traders, scientists, soldiers and colonists themselves.

The movement of people, of course, preceded the arrival of Europeans. The Pacific was the stage of the last great migration, a remarkable feat of navigation and determination on the part of the Austronesians who became Melanesians, Micronesians and Polynesians. Australia, as I have suggested, lay in the slipstream of this diaspora. Having been occupied for more than 60 000 years it remained the preserve of Aboriginal people whose cultures only clearly showed the influence of Pacific people at its northernmost boundary and then as a series of dovetailed adaptations, dugout and outrigger canoes among them. Asian people touched that top end but the interaction apparently stopped there. Aboriginal people traded but never engaged in the commerce which drove Asian cultures. That is not to agree with Herbert Basedow that Aboriginal people existed in primitive isolation. Rather it acknowledges that Australia's first people developed and maintained a unique and astonishingly resilient world view. The cultures which emerged on the vast continent were necessarily different from those which developed on smaller islands. Australia was a land of rainbow serpents whose pathways created long rivers, and songlines which connected the creation stories of people spread over thousands of kilometres. On the islands the sea is all defining. In mountainous New Guinea, terrain enforced a parochialism breached only by the arrival of Europeans.

Australia has changed its region but the Pacific has changed Australia. It provided the fertiliser needed to boost crop production on ancient soils. Pacific Islanders helped establish the continent's sugar industry. The Pacific and its people helped to define White Australia. Conversely, when white Australians finally accepted that excluding their 'coloured' neighbours was racist and counterproductive, it changed Australia. One man who arrived before the White Australia bans, Tommy Tanna, seeded the modern beach culture which is now a pillar of national identity. Many others who came afterwards have become national sporting heroes. The religious fundamentalism of one of them, Israel Folau, fuelled a debate about tolerance and free speech. The Pacific has shaped the lives of countless thousands of Australian families connected to the region through play, work and war. The well-tended military cemeteries at Port Moresby, Rabaul and Lae are testament to the enduring connection of the latter. The struggle of a Torres Strait man called Eddie Mabo reset our understanding of the nation's foundation. The exiled detention of asylum seekers on Pacific islands has led to an agonised and unresolved discussion about Australia's collective morality.

As I noted in the introduction, the later stages of this book were completed as half of Australia was on fire in the spring and summer of 2019–2020. After the 2019 federal election at which half the nation endorsed coal mining, implicitly or explicitly, the extent of the inferno reignited the debate over climate change. It seemed to 'change the narrative' so that the fundamental social change entailed in a low-carbon future was thinkable by more than an easily dismissed minority. However, it is not the first time there have been such thoughts. The 'world caught fire' in 1997–1998, in the words of the World Wide Fund for Nature, as a result of the weather effects of El-Niño Southern Oscillation. New South Wales, Victoria and Western Australia burned along with it but little changed in our consumption patterns, our agricultural methods and our production of coal. Israel Folau framed the recent fires as punishment for allowing same-sex marriage: 'God is speaking to you guys, Australia, you need to repent'.[32] Enlightenment-inspired pluralism had gone too far. Conservative politicians and commentators who may have shared Folau's social views were reluctant to endorse his stark eschatology. Rather they blamed forest management, government incompetence and arson for the inferno; anything but the complex ramifications of a changing climate. When asked about her community's attitude to climate change in 2020, the mayor of the coal-mining region of Singleton in New South Wales answered: 'It's not something we talk about. It's not something we have an appetite to talk about'.[33] Without good leadership, it can seem all too hard.

The departure of Australia from ancient Gondwana 80 to 100 million years ago shaped the Earth's climate and helped precipitate a glaciation which altered sea levels. Today, the extraction of Australia's ancient fossil fuel reserves is having the opposite effect. Until the nation accepts and deals with the unpalatable relationship between carbon, climate and an ever-rising, ever-warming sea, Australia will remain the

Pacific's 'prodigal son'. But regardless of the choices that are made in the short or even medium terms, climate change has been set in train and will unfold over many decades. Because the Pacific Ocean influences global climate, the complexity of consequence is profound. Australia may also be seen as a 'prodigal son' among its wealthy democratic peers. There is, in my mind, an unnerving resonance between the urgings of scientists and one of the Biblical warnings quoted by that young Australian of Pacific heritage:

> The earth is defiled by its people; they have disobeyed the laws, violated the statutes and broken the everlasting covenant. Therefore a curse consumes the earth; its people must bear their guilt.[34]

AFTERWORD
Mammon or millennial Eden?

'A virgin helpmate Ocean at your knees'

I began this history in one park and will end it another. It is a clear Sunday morning in early November 2020 and I am cycling around Sydney's Centennial Park trying to recoup the fitness lost to nine months of Covid-19 lockdowns and the sedentary life of writing without the forced discipline of my close-quarters boxing classes. Other middle-aged men in lycra whip past, pursuing personal bests or trying to turn back time.

The news just in is that the US election has been called for Joe Biden after a week of vote-counting in swing states and a premature claim of victory by Donald Trump. The tragic farce of his presidency is finally over, almost. There has been the expected recalcitrance and unfounded accusations of widespread fraud. Trump would rather fan the flames of distrust and division than admit defeat. It is a strategy of scorched earth. It is predicted that hundreds of thousands of Americans will die in a viral pandemic the president saw only as a political opportunity. That will be just one of the terrible legacies of a regime which began ironically with Trump decrying the 'American Carnage' he was supposedly inheriting. Another will be the damage to the very notion of truth. Trump's childish catch-cry 'fake news' has spread to infect debate in other democracies, Australia included.

The new president will reverse Trump's foreign policy of 'America First'. That will lead to a different form of engagement with a rising and aggressive China. The new administration is unlikely to acquiesce meekly to the challenge from a second superpower, but the tenor and substance of the response will not rest on racist taunts delivered to mass

Afterword: Mammon or millennial Eden?

rallies of white supporters. The return of respect for allies, absent during the Trump administration will be welcome in Australia, which has felt the effects of China's willingness to use trade as a tool of foreign policy. Scott Morrison's not unreasonable call for an enquiry into the origins of the Covid-19 virus was answered in Beijing with bans on Australian products.

And then there is conjecture about climate policy. Climate change was 'fake news' for Trump but Biden recognises the urgency of global warming. With Trump's departure, Australia's own tepid response to climate science – what Tony Abbott dismissed as a primitive religion and Prime Minister Morrison implied was paranoia – will seem even more anomalous internationally.

I know Centennial Park quite well, having written a doctoral thesis about this and Sydney's other green spaces 30 years ago. I feel my career as an historian began here. It is a complex landscape that embodies many of the themes of the nation's broader history. Most obviously the park is an emerald-like jewel in Sydney's suburban acres of black roads and red roofs – an example of enlightened government and democratic sentiment. In 1888 it was declared 'the people's park'. Yet this place was once part of a system of springs, streams and marshes which flowed south-east to the Pacific Ocean not far away. It was surely a haven for avian migrants from across the Pacific such as the Japanese snipe. The wetland here supplied Aboriginal people with waterfowl and eggs; and the colonists who replaced them with fresh town water. The newcomers polluted that water supply, found another and proceeded to turn what they then regarded as a swamp into a park to commemorate one hundred years since British civilisation arrived in Australia. Grand stands of water-loving paperbarks and a ring of spreading figs now replace the original sedges and shrubs. Introduced Greylag geese waddle where once native waterbirds flourished. One type of ecosystem has been swapped for another; beautiful but less diverse.

Centennial Park also exemplifies the spaciousness which distinguishes Australia from its Oceanic neighbours. It covers 189 hectares, more than three-quarters the size of Funafuti, the largest and most populous atoll in the Pacific nation of Tuvalu. While the park fills and empties each day, Tuvalu's capital is the permanent home to more than 6000 people.

Centennial Park sits within the federal electorate of Wentworth. That was Malcolm Turnbull's seat before Scott Morrison replaced him as prime minister in 2018. Turnbull's consequent resignation from parliament prompted a by-election and a win by Kerryn Phelps, an Independent candidate who supported action on climate change and same-sex marriage. The park borders Oxford Street, the unofficial main street of Sydney's gay community, which may explain that dalliance with progressive politics. In 2019, the Liberal Party regained the seat in the 'miracle' federal election, which returned the conservative Coalition to power despite, or perhaps because of, the prominence of climate change during the campaign.

The electors of Wentworth are among Australia's most affluent, and Centennial Park is a local reserve for many of them. Those who visit it represent a sample of Australian suburbia, albeit a wealthy one. On my morning cycle, large SUVs outnumber sedans and station wagons, such are the expanding needs of the modern family. Schumacher's argument for the beauty of 'small' is long lost, or so it seems. All the vehicles are squeezed between trees which line the circle drive originally designed for horse-drawn carriages. Many, possibly most, are expensive European and North American models. There are a few large utilities. One, emblazoned with the word 'Raptor', looks for all the world like a super-sized toy rather than a work vehicle. These 'utes' and SUVs are the automobiles the Coalition defended so aggressively against the uptake of electric vehicles during the 2019 election campaign. By contrast, the government of oil-exporting Norway promotes electric cars so effectively that they will soon outnumber diesel and petrol vehicles in that country.

I also pedal past the stark sandstone pavilion which stands on the site of the florid dome around which thousands gathered in January

Afterword: Mammon or millennial Eden?

1901 to celebrate the creation of the Commonwealth of Australia. The nation then was defiantly white. The 'colour-blind' hopes of critics like Bernard O'Dowd did eventually come to pass in policy if not always in practice. Australia is now multicultural. It is O'Dowd's words, from his poem 'Australia', that grace the new pavilion as something of a question to challenge contemporary park goers: 'Mammon or Millennial Eden'.

Thinking of that subtle inscription, I am reminded of the shrinking atolls of Tuvalu and of the question posed by the man from Kiribati as he pleaded for greater action on carbon emission reduction, not far from here at the University of New South Wales: 'What do you care about? ... The answer is in your hands'. Wealth brings options whether one chooses to exercise them or not. Australia's climate change policy has been debated without consideration for the devastating impact upon the people who live around us. That is surely a profound dereliction of regional responsibility. But the effects of mining and burning fossil fuels will adversely affect all Australians, some much more than others. And so the refusal to plan for change, to properly consider those with fewer options and to help progress the international transition to alternative energies, has also been a terrible failure of national leadership. The Australia First policy of the conservative Coalition, in particular, reflects the tragic triumph of populist nationalism over the interests of a common humanity. The issue of climate change perfectly embodies Australia's historical relationship to its Pacific region – one which is distinct and separate on the one hand and interconnected on the other.

Already two decades into the new millennium, we have almost certainly missed the opportunity to protect the 'Eden' referred to by O'Dowd. But the questions posed by the poet are still relevant for a lucky country born of Western ideas with their beneficial and 'fatal' consequences:

AUSTRALIA & THE PACIFIC

Australia

Last sea-thing dredged by sailor Time from Space,
Are you a drift Sargasso, where the West
In halcyon calm rebuilds her fatal nest?
Or Delos of a coming Sun-god's race?
Are you for Light, and trimmed, with oil in place,
Or but a Will o' Wisp on marshy quest?
A new demesne for Mammon to infest?
Or lurks millennial Eden 'neath your face?

The cenotaphs of species dead elsewhere
That in your limits leap and swim and fly,
Or trail uncanny harp-strings from your trees,
Mix omens with the auguries that dare
To plant the Cross upon your forehead sky,
A virgin helpmate Ocean at your knees.[1]

Acknowledgments

Many people have helped me with this book. The following have been particularly generous. Thank you to Phillipa McGuinness for both the support and many suggestions. Your encouragement was invaluable. The editing of Jocelyn Hungerford was patient, clear-eyed and always kind – thank you. The comments from Iain McCalman were most helpful and encouraging. Alison Wishart went above and beyond with her close read, thank you. Brett Evans, too, had a forensic eye for military detail – thank you. Val Attenbrow, David Mitchell and Phil Colman made many helpful suggestions for the early chapters, saving me some embarrassment. Thank you so much.

I owe a great deal to the State Library of New South Wales for awarding me the CH Currey Fellowship in 2019 to explore their remarkable Pacific collection. Thank you to Rachel Franks, Shari Amery and all the librarians who were so helpful with my exploration. Imelda Miller assisted me at the State Library of Queensland.

The State Library of New South Wales, the National Library of Australia and the Macleay Museum were very generous in allowing me to reproduce images from their collections. Thank you Greg Semu and Brent Kerehona for permission to use the photographs of Petero Civoniceva and Hongi Hika respectively. And thanks to Jude Philps for assisting.

I have met many helpful and knowledgeable people on my various Pacific travels but I owe local historian Albert Koni a great deal for his guidance around Rabaul. Two days of tunnels and tracks were perfectly timed to take in a Rugby League match between the Rabaul Gurias and a visiting team of highlanders. Blood was spilled but all came together at the end in religious song.

Papua New Guinea is not the easiest place to travel around. Thank you to Shane McLeod and Sean Dorney for tips.

Thank you to Robert from Arawa, Bougainville. The conch made it home safe and sound.

My employer North Sydney Council was supportive as always with my extra-curricular writing but the opinions given are my own. As are any errors that may have been made.

Thank you to Paul O'Beirne, Elspeth Menzies, Josephine Pajor-Markus and others at NewSouth for their forbearance.

Bibliography

Newspapers and magazines
Adelaide News
Advertiser (Adelaide)
Age (Melbourne)
Argus (Melbourne)
Australian
Bell's Life in Sydney and Sporting Reviewer
Bulletin
Canberra Times
Catholic Press
Colonist (Sydney)
Courier Mail (Brisbane)
Daily Herald (Sydney)
Daily Telegraph (Sydney)
Darling Downs Gazette
Dubbo Liberal and Macquarie Advocate
Empire
Freeman's Journal (Sydney)
Guardian (UK)
Guardian (Australia)
Herald
Illustrated Australian News for Home Readers (Melbourne)
Illustrated Sydney News
Johnstone River Advocate
Kalgoorlie Miner
Mail (Adelaide)
Maitland Daily Mercury
Maitland Mercury and Hunter River General Advertiser
Maryborough Chronicle
Mercury (Hobart)
Morning Bulletin (Rockhampton)
Nambucca and Bellingen News
Observer (Adelaide)
People's Advocate and New South Wales Vindicator
Saturday Paper
Shipping Gazette and Sydney General Trade List (Sydney)
Spectator (London)
Sun (Sydney)
Sydney Chronicle
Sydney Gazette and New South Wales Advertiser
Sydney Herald

AUSTRALIA & THE PACIFIC

Sydney Mail and New South Wales Advertiser
Sydney Morning Herald
Town and Country Journal (Sydney)
West Australian
Wikepin Argus
Worker

Documents, unpublished manuscripts, sources and collections

'Australia's Military Commitment to Vietnam', report tabled in Commonwealth House of Representatives, 13 May 1975

Calov, W, 'Untitled memoir', original and transcription undated, courtesy of Michael Bell

Collection of Mainly Queensland Parliamentary Reports and Papers on the Proposed Annexation of New Guinea, and Covering Aspects of Australia's Official Involvement in the Administration of British New Guinea, Mitchell Library, HQ 2013/4632

'Commission to Inquire into the Circumstances Under Which Labourers Have been Introduced into Queensland from New Guinea and Other Islands etc', 1885, *Journals of the Legislative Council*, Vol. 35, Pt 1, 1885

'Tabling Statement by Senator Gareth Evans, Minister for Foreign Affairs and Trade, Ministerial Statement on Australia's Regional Security', The Senate, 6 December 1989, <www.gevans.org/speeches/old/1989/061289_fm_regionalsecurity.pdf>

William and Kate Greig diaries and miscellaneous papers, 1870–1962, MLMSS 3014, Mitchell Library, State Library of New South Wales

Historical Records of Australia

Historical Records of New South Wales

'By the Commissioners for executing the office of Lord High Admiral of Great Britain & ca. Additional Instructions for Lt James Cook, Appointed to Command His Majesty's Bark the Endeavour', 30 July 1768, transcript <www.foundingdocs.gov.au/resources/transcripts/nsw1_doc_1768.pdf>

Lloyd, RJ, *Fathoming the Reef: A history of European perspectives on the Great Barrier Reef from Cook to GBRMPA*, PhD College of Arts, Society and Education, James Cook University, 2006

The Papers of James McAuley, ML MSS 7920, Mitchell Library, State Library of New South Wales

Jock MacLean New Guinea Diary, Dec 1941 – June 1942, ML MSS1250, Mitchell Library, State Library of New South Wales

Lord Morton, 'Hints to the consideration of Captain Cooke, Mr Bankes, Doctor Solander, and the other Gentlemen who go upon the expedition on Board the *Endeavour*', 1769, NLA MS9/113

New South Wales Parliamentary Debates, Session 1887–1888

North Sydney Heritage Centre collection

'The *Pandora* Story', Museum of Tropical Queensland exhibition notes, no date

Parliament of Australia Hansard Report of the Senate Select Committee on a Certain Maritime Incident, Commonwealth of Australia, 2002

Sir John Hubert Plunkett Murray papers 1886–1936 A3138-3141 and *Further papers 1935–1939* A3142 Mitchell Library, State Library of New South Wales

Royal Geographical Society of Australasia, *New South Wales Branch records, 1883–1906*, MLMSS853, Mitchell Library, State Library of New South Wales

Bibliography

The Papers of Bernard Smith, MLMSS 5202, Mitchell Library, State Library of New South Wales

Thomas, K, *Sepik region patrol reports and other papers, 1927–1934*, PMB 1197, Mitchell Library, State Library of New South Wales

Tinney, J, *Diary 1892–1902*, PMB 633, Mitchell Library, State Library of New South Wales

Broadcasts, films, speeches, lectures and interviews

'Address by the Prime Minister of Australia', 8 November 2018, Prime Minister of Australia website, <www.pm.gov.au/media/address-australia-and-pacific-new-chapter>

'Address by Commodore Josaia V Bainimarama Prime Minister and Commander of the Military Forces of the Republic of the Fiji Islands', 62nd Session of the General Assembly, New York, Friday 28 September 2007, *Official Records*, p. 30, <undocs.org/en/A/62/PV.10>

'Budget Speech 2018–19 Delivered in 8 May on the Second Reading of the Appropriation Bill (no.1) by the Honourable Scott Morrison MP, Treasurer of the Commonwealth of Australia', <archive.budget.gov.au/2018-19/speech/speech.pdf>

First Contact, directed by Robin Anderson and Bob Connolly, Arundel Productions, 1983

Yuval Harari in Conversation with Dan Ariely, 'Future Think – From Sapiens to Homo Deus', 92nd Street Y, 21 February 2017, <youtube.com/watch?v=5BqD5klZsQE>

'Hot Mess', Radio National, 3 May 2020

Jacques, M, 'What China will be like as a great power', 32nd Annual Camden Conference, 22–24 February, 2019, <www.martinjacques.com/uncategorised/32nd-annual-camden-conference-is-this-chinas-century/>

Keating, P, 'Speech by the Prime Minister, the Hon PJ Keating, MP, Anzac Day, Ela Beach, Port Moresby, 25 April 1992', <www.keating.org.au/shop/item/anzac-day---25-april-1992>

The Hon Scott Morrison, 'Australia and the Pacific: a New Chapter', 8 November 2018, <www.pm.gov.au/media/address-australia-and-pacific-new-chapter>

'Religion and Ethics Report', ABC Radio National, 11 December 2019

'Statement by His Excellency Anote Tong, President of the Republic of Kiribati', *The General Debate of the 63rd Session of the United Nations Assembly*, 25 September 2008

Books and articles

Ackland, M, '"A cold coming we had of it": The reception of literary Modernism and Tradition in the work of James McAuley and the Sydney Modernists', *Literature and Aesthetics*, 18 (1), June 2008, pp. 112–121

Adamson, G, 'The Rise of the Mass Anti-Nuclear Movement', *Green Left*, Issue 360, 12 May 1999, <www.greenleft.org.au/content/rise-mass-anti-nuclear-movement>

Allen, DW, 'The British Navy Rules: Monitoring and Incompatible Incentives in the Age of Fighting Sail', *Explorations in Economic History*, 39, 2002, pp. 204–231

Anderson, A and White, P, 'Prehistoric settlement on Norfolk Island and its oceanic context', *Records of the Australian Museum*, Supplement 27, 2001

Anderson, F and Trembath, R, *Witnesses to War: The History of Australian Conflict Reporting*, Melbourne University Press, Melbourne, 2011

Anderson, W, 'Liberal intellectuals as Pacific supercargo: White Australian masculinity and racial thought on the boarder-lands [sic]', *Australian Historical Studies*, Vol. 46, Issue 3, September 2015, pp. 425–439

AUSTRALIA & THE PACIFIC

Aplin, G (ed.), *A Difficult Infant: Sydney before Macquarie*, New South Wales University Press, Kensington, 1988

Askew, J, *A Voyage to Australia and New Zealand, Including a Visit to Adelaide, Melbourne, Sydney, Hunter's River, Newcastle, Maitland and Auckland*, Simpkin, Marshall and Company, Cockermouth, 1857

Atkinson, A, *The Europeans in Australia: A History Vol. 1*, Oxford University Press, Melbourne, 1997

Attenbrow, V, 'Aboriginal fishing in Port Jackson, and the introduction of shell fish-hooks to coastal New South Wales, Australia', in Lunney, D et al (eds), *The Natural History of Sydney*, Royal Zoological Society of NSW, Sydney, 2010

Australian National University News, 'Indigenous banana cultivation dates back over 2,000 years', 12 August 2020, <anu.edu.au/news/all-news/indigenous-banana-cultivation-dates-back-over-2000-years>

Bach, J, 'The Royal Navy in the Pacific Islands', *Journal of Pacific History*, Vol. 3, 1969, pp. 3–20

Bach, J, 'The Royal Navy in the South West Pacific: The Australia Station 1859–1913', *Great Circle*, Vol. 5, No. 2, 1983, pp. 116–132

Baker, R, *Land Is Life, from Bush to Town: The story of the Yanyuwa people*, Allen & Unwin, St Leonards, 1999

Ball, D (ed.), *The Anzac Connection*, George Allen & Unwin, Sydney, 1985

Bamforth, T, *The Rising Tide: Among the Islands and Atolls of the Pacific Ocean*, Hardie Grant, Melbourne, 2019

Banivanua-Mar, T, *Decolonisation and the Pacific: Indigenous Globalisation and the Ends of Empire*, Cambridge University Press, Cambridge, 2016

Banivanua-Mar, T, 'Shadowing Imperial Networks: Indigenous Mobility and Australia's Pacific Past', *Australian Historical Studies*, Vol. 46, Issue 3, September 2015, pp. 374–391

Banivanua-Mar, T, *Violence and Colonial Dialogue: The Australian-Pacific Indentured Labour Trade*, University of Hawaii Press, Honolulu, 2006

Basedow, H, *The Australian Aboriginal* [1925], David Welch, Virginia, 2012

Bateson, C, *Gold Fleet for California: Forty-Niners from Australia and New Zealand*, Ure Smith, Sydney, 1963

Batley, J, 'What does the 2016 Census reveal about Pacific Island communities in Australia?', 28 September 2017, <devpolicy.org/2016-census-reveal-about-pacific-islands-communities-in-australia-20170928/>

Battlecruiser HMAS Australia (1) *(1910–1924): Wreck Inspection Report*, Office of Environment and Heritage, Maritime Heritage Unit, Parramatta, 2011

Beaglehole, JC (ed.), *The Endeavour Journal of Joseph Banks, 1768–1771*, Vols 1 and 2, Angus and Robertson, Sydney, 1962

Beaglehole, JC, *The Exploration of the Pacific*, Stanford University Press, Stanford, 1966

Beaglehole, JC (ed.), *The Journals of Captain James Cook Vols 1–3*, Cambridge University Press, Cambridge, 1968

Beaglehole, JC, *The Life of Captain James Cook*, Adam and Charles Black, London, 1974

Beaumont, J (ed.), *Australia's War, 1939–45*, Allen & Unwin, Sydney, 1996

Beaumont, J, *Broken Nation: Australians in the Great War*, Allen & Unwin, Sydney, 2014

Becke, L, *The Ebbing of the Tide*, T Fisher Unwin, London, 1895

Beckett, J, *Torres Strait Islanders: Custom and Colonisation*, Cambridge University Press, Melbourne, 1987

Bedford, R, *Australia My Beloved Land: A National Song*, Allans, Melbourne, 1909

Beilharz, P, *Imagining the Antipodes: Culture, Theory and the Visual in the Work of Bernard Smith*, Cambridge University Press, Melbourne, 1997

Bibliography

Bell, C, *Dependent Ally: A Study in Australian Foreign Policy*, Oxford University Press, Melbourne, 1988

Bell, JH, 'Some Demographic and Cultural Characteristics of the La Perouse Aborigines', *Mankind*, Vol. 5, No. 10, June 1961, pp. 425–438

Berry, A, *Reminiscences of Alexander Berry*, Angus and Robertson, Sydney, 1912

Birch, A and Macmillan, DS (eds), *The Sydney Scene 1788–1960*, Melbourne University Press, Carlton, 1962

Blainey, G, *The Rush that Never Ended: A history of Australian mining*, Melbourne University Press, Melbourne, 1969

Blainey, G, *The Tyranny of Distance*, Sun Books, Melbourne, 1966

Blewett, R (ed.), *Shaping a Nation: A geology of Australia*, Australian National University E Press, Canberra, 2012

Board, P, 'History and Australian History', *Journal of the Australian Historical Society*, 1916, pp. 290–293

Bolton, AT (ed.), *Walkabout's Australia*, Ure Smith, Sydney, 1964

Bolton, GC, *A Thousand Miles Away: A History of North Queensland to 1920*, Australian National University Press, Canberra, 1970

Bonyhady, T, *The Colonial Earth*, Miegunyah Press, Melbourne, 2000

Boochani, B, 'Manus Island Poem', the *Saturday Paper*, 16–22 June 2018, p. 28

Booth, D, *Mountains, Gold and Cannibals*, Cornstalk, Sydney, 1929

Bourke, L, 'Joe Hockey says wind turbines "utterly offensive", flags budget cuts to clean energy schemes', ABC News, 2 May 2014, <www.abc.net.au/news/2014-05-02/joe-hockey-wind-turbines-utterly-offensive/5425804?nw=0>

Bradley, J, 'Holding on to the Madness: How an infatuation is keeping Adani's mine alive', *The Monthly*, April, 2019, pp. 19–38

Breen, B, *Struggling for Self Reliance: Four Case Studies of Australian Regional Force Projection in the Late 1980s and 1990s*, Australian National University E Press, Canberra, 2008

Brennan, F, *One land, one nation: Mabo – towards 2001*, University of Queensland Press, Brisbane, 1995

Brett, J, 'Howard's Heir: On Scott Morrison and his suburban aspirations', *The Monthly*, September 2019, pp. 23–31

Briskman, L, Latham, S and Goddard, C, *Human Rights Overboard: Seeking Asylum in Australia*, Scribe Publications, Melbourne, 2008

Broinowski, A (ed.), *Double Vision: Asian Accounts of Australia*, Pandanus Books, Canberra, 2004

Broughton, Bishop WG, *Sermons on the Church of England; Its Constitution, Mission, and Trials*, Bell and Daldy, London, 1857

Brune, P, *A Bastard of a Place: The Australians in Papua, Kokoda, Milne Bay, Gona, Buna, Sanananda*, Allen & Unwin, Sydney, 2004

Buckley, K and Klugman, K, *The History of Burns Philp: The Australian Company in the South Pacific*, Burns Philp and Co. Ltd, Sydney, 1981

Buden, DW, 'The birds of Nauru', *Notornis*, Vol. 55, 2008, pp. 10–16

Calaby, John (ed.), *The Hunter Sketchbook: Birds & Flowers of New South Wales Drawn on the Spot in 1788, 89 & 90, By Captain John Hunter RN of the First Fleet*, National Library of Australia, Canberra, 1989

Cameron, Captain JS, *Ten Months in a German Raider: A Prisoner of War Aboard the Wolf*, George H Doran, New York, 1918

Campbell, IC, *Worlds Apart: A History of the Pacific Islands*, Canterbury University Press, Christchurch, 2003

AUSTRALIA & THE PACIFIC

Campbell, J, *The Ghost Mountain Boys: Their Epic March and the Terrifying Battle for New Guinea – the Forgotten War of the South Pacific*, Crown Publishers, New York, 2007

Carson, R, *The Sea Around Us*, Penguin, London, 1956

Cathcart, M, *The Water Dreamers: The Remarkable History of Our Dry Continent*, Text Publishing, Melbourne, 2010

Chalmers, J, 'Notes on the Natives of the Kiwai Island, Fly River, British New Guinea', *Journal of the Anthropological Institute of Great Britain and Ireland*, Vol. XXXIII, 1903, pp. 117–124

Chalmers, J and Gill, W, *Work and Adventure in New Guinea*, The Religious Tract Society, London, 1885

Christian, D, *Origin Story: A big history of everything*, Allen Lane, London, 2018

Clark, CMH, *A History of Australia*, Vols 1–6, Melbourne University Press, Melbourne, 1979

Clark, CMH (ed.), *Select Documents in Australian History, 1788–1850*, Angus and Robertson, Sydney, 1966

Climate Change 2007: The Physical Science Basis, Working Group 1 Contribution to the Fourth Assessment of the Intergovernmental Panel on Climate Change, Cambridge University Press, Cambridge, 2007

Cochrane, P, *Australians at War*, ABC Books, Sydney, 2001

Codrington, RH, *The Melanesian: Studies in Their Anthropology and Folklore*, Oxford at the Clarendon Press, Oxford, 1891

Coghlan, TA, *Labour and Industry in Australia*, Vol. II [1918], Macmillan of Australia, 1969

Collingridge, G, *The Discovery of Australia* [1895], Golden Press, Sydney, 1989

Collins, D, *An Account of the English Colony in New South Wales, Vol. 1* (1798), AH and AW Reed, Sydney, 1975

Conrad, P, *Islands: A trip through time and space*, Thames and Hudson, London, 2009

Cooke, R, 'Democracy's Greatest Threat: Denialism, nihilism and the Murdoch propaganda machine', *The Monthly*, May 2019, pp. 23–31

Coulthard-Clark, C, *Action Stations Coral Sea: The Australian Commander's Story*, Allen & Unwin, Sydney, 1991

Coyne, P, '*Phorium tenax* (New Zealand Flax) – Norfolk Island Native?', *Cunninghamia*, 2009, 11(2), pp. 167–170

Crowley, FK (ed.), *Modern Australia in Documents, 1939–1970*, Vol. 2, Wren Publishing Pty Ltd, Melbourne, 1973

Cruises to the Pacific Islands and Papua, Burns Philp and Co. Ltd, Sydney, 1913–1914

Cumings, B, *The Korean War: A History*, Modern Library, New York, 2011

Cuneen, C, 'Jersey, seventh Earl of (1845–1915)', *Australian Dictionary of Biography*

Curran, J and Ward, S (eds), *Australia and the Wider World: Selected Essays of Neville Meaney*, Sydney University Press, Sydney, 2013

Currey, J (ed.), *A Voyage to the Great South Sea Completed: How England Learned of Cook's Return in 1771*, The Banks Society, Malvern [2012]

Cushman, G, *Guano and the Opening of the Pacific World*, Cambridge University Press, Cambridge, 2013

Dalton, D, 'Cargo Cults and Discursive Madness', *Oceania*, Vol. 70, No. 4, June 2000, pp. 345–361

Dalziel, A, *Evatt the Enigma*, Lansdowne Press, Melbourne, 1967

Dampier, W, *A Voyage to New Holland: The English voyage of discovery to the South Seas in 1699*, James Spencer (ed.), Alan Sutton, Gloucester, 1981

Darwin, C, *The Descent of Man and Selection in Relation to Sex*, D Appleton and Co., New York, 1889

Bibliography

Darwin C, *On the Structure and Distribution of Coral Reefs; also Geological Observations on the Volcanic Islands and Parts of South America* [1842], Ward, Lock and Bowden Ltd, London, [1891]

Darwin, F (ed.), *The Life and Letters of Charles Darwin: Including an autobiographical chapter*, Vol. II, Charles Murray, London, 1888

Davis, R (ed.), *Woven Histories Dancing Lives: Torres Strait Island identity, culture and history*, Aboriginal Studies Press, Canberra, 2004

Defoe, D, *The Life and Surprising Adventures of Robinson Crusoe of York, Mariner...* [1719], J Limbird, London, 1833

Defoe, D, *Robinson Crusoe*, Penguin Books, Camberwell, 2010

Dening, G, *Mr Bligh's Bad Language: Passion, Power and Theatre on the* Bounty, Cambridge University Press, Cambridge, 1992

Denoon, D, Mein-Smith, P and Wyndham, M, *A History of Australia, New Zealand and the Pacific*, Blackwell Publishers, Malden, 2000

Denoon, D (ed.), *Emerging From Empire? Decolonisation in the Pacific, Proceedings of a Workshop at the Australian National University*, 1996, Research School of Pacific and Asian Studies, Canberra, 1997

Denoon, D, *A Trial Separation: Australia and the Decolonisation of Papua New Guinea*, Pandanus Books, Canberra, 2005

Devereux, A, *Australia and the Birth of the International Bill of Human Rights 1946–1966*, The Federation Press, Sydney, 2005

Dibb, P, *Review of Australia's Defence Capabilities: Report for the Minister of Defence*, Australian Government Printing Office, Canberra, 1986

Dibb, P, *The Soviet Union: The Incomplete Superpower*, Macmillan Press Ltd, Hampshire, 1986

Diderot, D, *This Is Not a Story and other Stories*, Oxford University Press, New York, 1993

Dixon, R, *Prosthetic Gods: Travel, representation and colonial governance*, University of Queensland Press, Brisbane, 2001

Dobrin, LM and Bashkow, I, '"The Truth in Anthropology Does Not Travel First Class": Reo Fortune's Fateful Encounter with Margaret Mead', *Histories of Anthropology Annual*, Vol. 6, 2010, pp. 66–218

Doddridge, P, *Practical Discourses on Regeneration. In Ten Sermons*, Ruben Sears, Ballston Spa, 1815

Dorney, S, *The Embarrassed Colonist*, Penguin Books, Ringwood, 2016

Dorney, S, 'Pacific Games', *Griffith Review*, 53, July 2016, <www.griffithreview.com/articles/pacific-games/>

Dorney, S, 'The Papua New Guinea awakening: Inside the forgotten colony', *Australian Foreign Affairs*, No. 6, July 2019, pp. 71–87

Du Cross, H, *Much More Than Stones and Bones: Australian Archaeology in the Late Twentieth Century*, Melbourne University Press, Melbourne, 2002

Dunmore, J, *Storms and Dreams, Louis de Bougainville: Soldier, explorer, statesman*, ABC Books, Sydney, 2005

Duyker E (ed.), *The Discovery of Tasmania: Journal extracts from the expeditions of Abel Janszoon Tasman and Marc-Joseph Marion Duefresne, 1642 and 1772*, St David's Park Publishing, Hobart, 1992

Erlandson, JM, 'A Deep History for the Pacific: Where Past, Present and Future Meet', *Journal of Pacific Archaeology*, Vol. 1, No. 2, 2010, pp. 11–114

Erskine, JE, *Journal of a Cruise Among the Islands of the Western Pacific*, John Murray, London, 1853

Evans, G, *Incorrigible Optimist: A Political Memoir*, Melbourne University Press, Melbourne, 2017
'Excisions from the Migration Zone – Policy and Practice', Parliamentary Library Research Note, No. 42, 1 March 2004
Feldt, E, *The Coastwatchers*, Oxford University Press, Melbourne, 1946
Fidlon, PG and and Ryan, PJ (eds), *The Journal and Letters of Lt. Ralph Clark 1787–1792*, Australian Documents Library, Sydney, 1981
Firth, S, *Australia in International Politics: An Introduction to Australian Foreign Policy*, Allen & Unwin, Sydney, 2004
FitzGerald, CP, 'Reflections on the Cultural Revolution in China', *Pacific Affairs*, Vol. 41, No. 1, 1968, pp. 51–59
Fitzgerald, R, *A History of Queensland from the Dreaming to 1915*, University of Queensland Press, St Lucia, 1986
FitzGerald, S, *Comrade Ambassador: Whitlam's Beijing Envoy*, Melbourne University Press, Carlton, 2015
Fitzhardinge, LF, *The Little Digger 1914–1952: William Morris Hughes, A Political Biography*, Vol. II, Angus and Robertson, Sydney, 1979
Flannery, T, *Atmosphere of Hope: Solutions to the Climate Crisis*, Penguin, London, 2015
Flannery, T, *The Weather Makers: The History and Future Impact of Climate Change*, Text Publishing, Melbourne, 2005
Fletcher, CB, 'Australia and the Pacific 1788–1885', *Journal of the Royal Australian Historical Society*, Vol. XXVIII, Pt. 3, 1943, pp. 157–184
Flinders, M, *Journal on HMS Investigator*, Vol. II, 1802–1803, Mitchell Library, State Library of New South Wales
Forbes, C, *The Korean War: Australia in the Giants' Playground*, Pan Macmillan, Sydney, 2010
Fortune, K (ed.), *Malaguna Road: The Papua and New Guinea Diaries of Sarah Chinnery*, National Library of Australia, Canberra, 1998
Franklin, J, *Corrupting the Youth: A History of Philosophy in Australia*, Macleay Press, Paddington, 2003
Frost, A, *The Global Reach of Empire: Britain's maritime expansion in the Indian and Pacific Oceans 1764–1815*, Miegunyah Press, Carlton, 2003
Frost, A, *The Precarious Life of James Mario Matra: Voyager with Cook, American Loyalist, Servant of Empire*, Miegunyah Press, Melbourne, 1995
Fukuyama, F, *The End of History and the Last Man*, Penguin Books, London, 2012
Fulton, T, *No Turning Back: A memoir*, Pandanus Books, Canberra, 2005
Gale, SJ, 'The mined-out phosphate lands of Nauru, equatorial western Pacific', *Australian Journal of Earth Sciences*, Vol. 63, No. 3, 2016, pp. 333–347
Gammage, B, *The Sky Travellers: Journeys in New Guinea, 1938–1939*, Melbourne University Press, Melbourne, 1998
Ganter, R, *The Pearl-Shellers of Torres Strait: Resource Use, Development and Decline, 1860s–1960s*, Melbourne University Press, Melbourne, 1994
Gascoigne, J, *Encountering the Pacific in the Age of the Enlightenment*, Cambridge University Press, Melbourne, 2014
Gaskell, T, 'Did the Moon Come out of the Pacific?', *New Scientist*, No. 363, 31 October 1963, pp. 251–253
Gelber, HG, *The Dragon and the Foreign Devils: China and the world, 1100 BC to the present*, Bloomsbury, London, 2007
Gleeson, M, *Offshore: Behind the wire on Manus and Nauru*, NewSouth Books, Sydney, 2016

Bibliography

Gohau, G, *A History of Geology*, Rutgers University Press, New Brunswick (USA), 1990

Gomme, B, *A Gunner's Eye View: A Wartime Diary of Active Service in New Guinea*, Brian Gomme, Nambucca Heads, 1997

Goodenough, J, *Journal of Commodore Goodenough, RN, CB, CMG, During His Last Command as Senior Officer on the Australian Station, 1873–1875, Edited with a Memoir by his Widow*, Henry S King and Co. London, 1876

Goodman, D, *Gold Seeking: Victoria and California in the 1850s*, Allen & Unwin, Sydney, 1994

Gordon, A, *A Modern History of Japan: From Tokugawa Times to the Present*, Oxford University Press, New York, 2003

Grattan, M, 'Malcolm Turnbull condemns Scott Morrison's "gas gas gas" song as "a fantasy"', *The Conversation*, 22 September 2020, <theconversation.com/malcolm-turnbull-condemns-scott-morrisons-gas-gas-gas-song-as-a-fantasy-146705>

Gray, G, '"Being Honest to My Science": Reo Fortune and JHP Murray, 1927–1930', *Australian Journal of Anthropology*, 1999, 10:1, pp. 56–76

Gray, G, *A Cautious Silence: The politics of Australian anthropology*, Aboriginal Studies Press, Canberra, 2007

Grayson, BL (ed.), *The American Image of China*, Frederick Ungar Publishing, New York, 1979

Greenwood, G and Harper, N (eds), *Australia in World Affairs 1961–1965*, FW Cheshire, Melbourne, 1968

Groves, M, 'Sacred Past and Profane Present in Papua', *Quadrant*, Vol. 1, 3 June 1957, pp. 37–48

Gunson, N, 'Pomare II and Polynesian Imperialism', *Journal of Pacific History*, Vol. 4, 1969, pp. 65–82

Hainsworth, DR, *The Sydney Traders: Simeon Lord and His Contemporaries 1788–1821*, Melbourne University Press, Melbourne, 1981

Hall, RA, *Fighters from the Fringe: Aborigines and Torres Strait Islanders Recall the Second World War*, Aboriginal Studies Press, Canberra, 1995

Harari, YN, *Sapiens: A Brief History of Humankind*, Vintage, London, 2015

Hasluck, P, *The Government and the People*, Australian War Memorial, Canberra, 1970

Hastings, P, *New Guinea: Problems and Prospects*, Cheshire, Melbourne, 1973

Hayward-Jones, J, 'Australia's costly investment in Solomon Islands: The Lessons of RAMSI', *Lowy Institute Analysis*, May 2014, <www.lowyinstitute.org/publications/australias-costly-investment-solomon-islands-lessons-ramsi>

Hilliard, D, *God's Gentlemen: A History of the Melanesian Mission, 1849–1942*, University of Queensland Press, Brisbane, 1978

Hilliard, D, 'The South Sea Evangelical Mission in the Solomon Islands: The Foundation Years', *Journal of Pacific History*, Vol. 4, 1969, pp. 41–64

Hogan, A, *Moving in the Open Daylight: Doc Evatt, an Australian at the United Nations*, Sydney University Press, Sydney, 2008

Hogbin, HI, *Transformation Scene* [1951], Routledge, Abingdon, 2007

Hollinshed, J, *Innocence to Independence: Life in the Papua New Guinea Highlands, 1956–1980*, Pandanus Books, Canberra, 2004

Horne, D, *The Lucky Country: Australia in the Sixties*, Penguin Books, Ringwood, 1968

Horner, D, *Inside the War Cabinet: Directing Australia's War Effort, 1939–1945*, Allen & Unwin, Sydney, 1996

Hoskins, I, *Coast: A History of the New South Wales Edge*, NewSouth Books, Sydney, 2014

AUSTRALIA & THE PACIFIC

Howard, J, *Lazarus Rising: A Personal and Political Autobiography*, HarperCollins, Sydney, 2010

Hudson, WJ (ed.), *Australia in World Affairs, 1971–1975*, George Allen & Unwin, Sydney, 1980

Hudson, WJ, *Billy Hughes in Paris: The Birth of Australian Diplomacy*, Nelson and the Australian Institute of International Affairs, West Melbourne, 1978

Hughes, P, Denhem, T and Golson, J, 'Kuk Swamp', in J Golson et al (eds), *Ten Thousand Years of Cultivation at Kuk Swamp in the Highlands of New Guinea, Terra Australis 46*, Australian National University Press, Canberra, 2020

Hughes, R, *The Fatal Shore: A history of the transportation of convicts to Australia, 1787–1868*, Collins Harvill, London, 1987

Hughes, WM, *The Price of Peace*, Defence of Australia League, Sydney, 1934

Hume, JP, *Extinct Birds*, Bloomsbury, London, 2017

Hunt, L, *Inventing Humans Rights: A history*, WW Norton and Co., New York, 2007

Hunter, J, *An Historical Journal of the Transactions at Port Jackson and Norfolk Island*, Library Board of South Australia, Adelaide, 1968

Hutchinson, G (ed.), *Eyewitness: Australians Write from the Frontline*, Black Inc, Melbourne, 2005

Inglis, Rev. J, *In the New Hebrides: Reminiscences of Missionary Life and Work, Especially on the Island of Aneityum*, T Nelson and Sons, London, 1887

Inglis, KS, *This Is the ABC: The Australian Broadcasting Commission 1932–1983*, Melbourne University Press, Melbourne, 1983

Ishay, MR, *The History of Human Rights from Ancient Times to the Globalization Era*, University of California Press, Berkeley, 2004

Jinks, B, Biskup, P and Nelson H (eds), *Readings in New Guinea History*, Angus and Robertson, Sydney, 1973

Johnson, D, *The Geology of Australia*, Cambridge University Press, Melbourne, 2004

Johnston, G, *New Guinea Diary*, Angus and Robertson, Sydney, 1943

Jupp, J (ed.), *The Australian People: An Encyclopedia of the Nation, Its People and Their Origins*, Cambridge University Press, Cambridge, 2001

Kabutaulaka, T, 'Australian Foreign Policy and the RAMSI Intervention in Solomon Islands', *Contemporary Pacific*, 17:2, 2005, pp. 283–308

Keating, P, *Engagement: Australia Faces the Asia-Pacific*, Pan Macmillan, Sydney, 2000

Kelly, D and Reid, A (eds), *Asian Freedoms: The Idea of Freedom in East and Southeast Asia*, Cambridge University Press, Cambridge, 1998

Kelly, S, 'Leave No Trace: The story of Scott Morrison', *The Monthly*, November 2018, pp. 22–33

Keon-Cohen, B, *A Mabo Memoir: Islan Kustom to Native Title*, Zemvic Press, Melbourne, 2013

King, J and King, J, *Philip Gidley King: A biography of the third governor of New South Wales*, Methuen, Sydney, 1981

Kingston, B, *A History of New South Wales*, Cambridge University Press, Melbourne, 2006

Kinnane, G, *George Johnston: A Biography*, Melbourne University Press, Melbourne, 1996

Kirk, RW, *Paradise Past: The Transformation of the South Pacific, 1520–1920*, McFarland and Co., Jefferson, 2012

Klein, N, *This Changes Everything: Capitalism vs the Climate*, Allen Lane, London, 2014

Knox, M, *Boom: The Underground History of Australia from Gold Rush to GFC*, Viking, Melbourne, 2013

Bibliography

Knox, M, 'Hell Raiser: How Israel Folau lit a fire under the culture wars', the *Monthly*, August 2019, pp. 19–27

Kociumbas, J, *The Oxford History of Australia, Vol. 2, 1770–1860*, Oxford University Press, Melbourne, 1992

La Meslée, EM, *Past Explorations of New Guinea and a Scheme for the Scientific Exploration of the Great Island*, JL Holmes, Sydney, 1883

La Meslée, EM, *Past Explorations of New Guinea and a Scheme for the Scientific Exploration of the Great Island*, Paper Read before the Royal Geographic Society of Australasia, Sydney, 1883

Lake, M, *Faith Bandler: Gentle Activist*, Allen & Unwin, Sydney, 2002

Lake, M and Reynolds, H, *Drawing the Global Colour Line: White Men's Countries and the Question of Racial Equality*, Melbourne University Press, Melbourne, 2008

Laseron, CF, *The Face of Australia: The shaping of a continent*, Angus and Robertson, Sydney, 1957

Lett, L, *Sir Hubert Murray of Papua*, Collins, London, 1949

Levi-Strauss, C, *Structural Anthropology 2*, Peregrine Books, Harmondsworth, 1978

Lindsay, P, *The Essence of Kokoda*, Hardie Grant Books, Melbourne, 2005

Löfgren, L, *Ocean Birds: Their Breeding, Biology and Behaviour*, Croom Helm, Beckenham, 1984

Lomb, N, *The Transit of Venus: 1631 to the present*, NewSouth and Powerhouse Publishing, Sydney, 2001

Loos, N, and Mabo, K, *Edward Koiki Mabo: His life and struggle for land rights*, University of Queensland Press, Brisbane, 1996

Lourandos, H, *Continent of Hunter Gatherers: New perspectives in Australian prehistory*, Cambridge University Press, Cambridge, 1997

Low, T, *Where Song Began: Australia's birds and how they changed the world*, Viking, Melbourne, 2014

McAdam, J and Chong, F, *Refugee Rights and Policy Wrongs*, NewSouth Publishing, Sydney, 2019

McAuley, J, *Under Aldebaran*, Melbourne University Press, Melbourne, 1946
— 'In Defence of Native Art', *South Pacific*, Vol. 5, No. 6, 1951, pp. 99–100
— 'The Traditional View of Art', *Australian Quarterly*, Vol. 5, No. 12, 1952, pp. 57–66
— 'Anthropologists and Administrators', *South Pacific*, Vol. 6, No. 10, 1953, pp. 518–522
— 'Australia's Future in New Guinea', *South Pacific*, March–April 1953, pp. 544–556
— 'Editorial', *Quadrant*, Vol. 1, No. 1, 1955, p. 3
— 'Liberalism Today', *Quadrant*, Vol.1, No. 4, 1957, pp. 3–4
— *The End of Modernity: Essays on Literature, Art and Culture*, Angus and Robertson, Sydney, 1959
— 'On Being an Intellectual', *Quadrant*, Vol. IV, 13, Summer 1959–60, pp. 23–31
— 'We Are Men – What Are You?', *Quadrant*, 15 Winter, 1960, pp. 73–79
— 'My New Guinea', *Quadrant*, Vol.5, No. 3, 1961, pp. 15–27
— *Captain Quiros*, Angus and Robertson, Sydney, 1964
— *Collected Poems 1936–1970*, Angus and Robertson, Sydney, 1971
— (ed.) *A Map of Australian Verse: The Twentieth Century*, Oxford University Press, Melbourne, 1975

McCalman, I, *The Reef: A Passionate History*, Penguin, Sydney, 2014

McCamish, T, *Our Man Elsewhere: In Search of Alan Moorehead*, Black Inc., Carlton, 2016

McCarthy, D, *The Battle of Maryang San, 1951*, Army History Unit, Canberra, 2018

McCarthy, FD, '"Trade" in Aboriginal Australia and "Trade" Relationships with Torres Strait, New Guinea and Malaya', *Oceania*, Vol. 9, No. 4, June 1939, pp. 405–438
— '"Trade" in Aboriginal Australia and "Trade" Relationships with Torres Strait, New Guinea and Malaya' (Pt 2), *Oceania* Vol. 10, No. 1, September 1939, pp. 80–104
— '"Trade" in Aboriginal Australia and "Trade" Relationships with Torres Strait, New Guinea and Malaya' (Pt 3), *Oceania*, Vol. 10, No. 2, December 1939, pp. 171–195
McCarthy, JK, 'The Rabaul Strike', *Quadrant*, 10 Autumn, 1959, pp. 55–65
MacClancy, J, *To Kill A Bird with Two Stones: A Short History of Vanuatu*, Vanuatu Cultural Centre, Port Vila, 2002
McConnel, Ursula, 'The Wik-Munkun Tribe of Cape York Peninsula, Part 1', *Oceania*, Vol. 1, January 1930, pp. 97–104
McCoy, A, *The Politics of Heroin in Southeast Asia*, Harper Torchbooks, New York, 1972
McDonald, N, *Kokoda: Damien Parer's War*, Lothian Books, Melbourne, 2004
McFarland, A, *Mutiny in the "Bounty!" and Story of the Pitcairn Islanders*, JJ Moore, Sydney, 1884
McFarlane, Rev. S, *Among the Cannibals of New Guinea, being the story of the New Guinea Mission of the London Missionary Society*, Presbyterian Board of Publication, Philadelphia [1888]
McGibbon, R, *Pitfalls of Papua: Understanding the Conflict and Its Place in Australia-Indonesia Relations*, Lowy Institute for International Policy, 2006
MacGillivray, J, *Narrative of the Voyage of the HMS Rattlesnake*, Vol 2, T&W Boone, London, 1852
McKinnon, A, 'Blackbirds: Australia had a slave trade?', *The Monthly*, July 2019, pp. 44–55
McNiven, IJ, 'Colonial diffusionism and archaeology of external influences on Aboriginal culture', in David, B, Barker, B, & McNiven, IJ (eds.), *The Social Archaeology of Australian Indigenous Societies*, Aboriginal Studies Press, Canberra, 2006, pp. 85–106
Macintyre, S, *A Concise History of Australia*, Cambridge University Press, Melbourne, 2004
McKelvey, VE, 'Phosphate Deposits', *Geological Survey Bulletin*, 1252-D, United States Government Printing Office, Washington DC, 1967, pp. D1–17
Mackenzie, D and Parker, R, 'The North Pacific: An Example of Tectonics on a Sphere', *Nature*, Vol. 216, December 30, 1967, pp. 1276–1280
Mackenzie, SS, *The Official History of Australia in the War of 1914–1918, Vol. 10: The Australians at Rabaul*, Angus and Robertson, Sydney, 1939
McKibben, B, *The End of Nature*, Penguin Books, New York, 1989
McKibben, B, 'A Very Grim Forecast', *New York Review of Books*, Vol. LXV, No. 18, 22 November – 5 December 2018, pp. 4–8
Macleod, R and Rehbock, PF, 'Developing a Sense of the Pacific: The 1923 Pan-Pacific Science Congress in Australia', *Pacific Science*, Vol. 54, July 2000, pp. 209–225
Mair, L, *Australia in New Guinea*, Melbourne University Press, Melbourne, [1948], 1970
Major, T, 'North Queensland green power options ignored by Federal Government, Industry Claims', ABC News, 11 February 2020, <www.abc.net.au/news/2020-02-11/north-queensland-renewable-energy-ignored-by-federal-government/11951042>
Malaspinas, AS; Westaway, M; Muller, C et al, 'A genomic history of Aboriginal Australia', *Nature*, Vol. 538, 2016, pp. 207–214
Malinowski, B, *Argonauts of the Western Pacific: An Account of Native Enterprise and Adventure in the Archipelagoes of Melanesian New Guinea*, EP Dutton and Company, New York, [1922], 1960
Manchester, W, *American Caesar: Douglas MacArthur, 1880–1964*, Little, Brown, Boston, 1978

Bibliography

Mapping Our World: Terra Incognita to Australia, National Library of Australia, Canberra, 2014

Marcus, A, *Fear and Hatred: Purifying Australia and California, 1850–1901*, Hale and Iremonger, Sydney, 1979

Markham, AH, *The Cruise of the 'Rosario' Amongst the New Hebrides and Santa Cruz Islands, Exposing the Recent Atrocities Connected with the Kidnapping of Natives in the South Seas*, Sampson Low, Marston, Low and Searle, London, 1873

Masefield, J, *Gallipoli*, The Macmillian Company, New York, 1916

Matsuda, MK, *Pacific Worlds: A history of seas, peoples, and cultures*, Cambridge University Press, New York, 2012

Mead, M, *Growing Up in New Guinea: A Comparative Study of Primitive Education*, George Routledge and Sons, London, 1931

Meaney, N, *Towards a New Vision: Australia and Japan Through 100 Years*, Kangaroo Press, Sydney, 1999

Memmott, P, *Gunyah, Goondie and Wurley: The Aboriginal architecture of Australia*, University of Queensland Press, Brisbane, 2007

Mercer, PM and Moore, CR, 'Melanesians in North Queensland: The Retention of Indigenous Religious and Magical Practices', *Journal of Pacific History*, Vol. 11, No. 1, Labour Trade Pt 1, 1976, pp. 66–88

Meredith, Mrs C, *Notes and Sketches of New South Wales*, Penguin Books, Melbourne, 1973

Millar, TB, *Australia in Peace and War*, Australian National University Press, Canberra, 1978

Moon, P, *Encounters: The Creation of New Zealand: A History*, Penguin, Auckland, 2013

Moore, C (ed.), *The Forgotten People: A History of the Australian South Sea Island Community*, Australian Broadcasting Commission, Sydney, 1978

Moore, C, *Kanaka: A History of Melanesian Mackay*, Institute of Papua New Guinea Studies, Port Moresby, 1985

Moorehead, A, *Fatal Impact: The Invasion of the South Pacific 1767–1840* [1966], Mead and Beckett, Sydney, 1987

Morrell, WP, *Britain in the Pacific Islands*, Oxford at the Clarendon Press, London, 1960

Murray, AW, *The Bible in the Pacific*, James Nisbet and Co., London, 1888

Murray, JHP, *Anthropology and the Government of Subject Races*, Government Printer, Port Moresby [1930]

Murray JHP, *Native Administration in Papua*, Acting Government Printer, Port Moresby, 1929

Murray JHP, *The Response of Natives of Papua to Western Civilisation*, Government Printer, Port Moresby, 1929

Murray, JHP, *Review of the Australian Administration in Papua from 1907–1920*, Port Moresby, 1920

Neall, VE and Trewick, SA, 'The age and origin of the Pacific Islands: A geological overview', *Philosophical Transactions of the Royal Society*, Vol. 363, No. 1508, 2008, pp. 3293–3308

Nelson, H, *Taim Bilong Masta: The Australian Involvement in Papua New Guinea*, Australian Broadcasting Commission, Sydney, 1982

Neville, P, *The Tasman: Biography of an Ocean*, Penguin, New Zealand, 2010

Nicholas, JL, *Narrative of a Voyage to New Zealand*, Vol. II, James Black and Son London 1817

Nobbs, R, *George Hunn Nobbs 1799–1884: Reverend on Pitcairn and Norfolk Island*, The Pitcairn Descendants Society, Norfolk Island, 1984

Nunn, P, *Vanished Islands and Hidden Continents of the Pacific*, University of Hawaii Press, Honolulu, 2009

Nunn, P and Reid, NJ, 'Aboriginal Memories of Inundation of the Australian Coast Dating More than 7000 Years Ago', *Australian Geographer*, 47:1, 2016, pp. 11–47

O'Brien, K, *Keating*, Allen & Unwin, Sydney, 2016

O'Collins, M, *An Uneasy Relationship: Norfolk Island and the Commonwealth of Australia*, Australian National University E Press, 2010

O'Connor, M, *The Great Forest*, Hale and Iremonger, Sydney, 1989

O'Neill, A, 'Australia and the South Pacific nuclear free zone treaty: A reinterpretation', *Australian Journal of Political Science*, Vol. 39, No. 3, 2004, pp. 567–583

Oliver A, 2018 Lowy Institute Poll, Lowy Institute website, <www.lowyinstitute.org/publications/2018-lowy-institute-poll>

Oliver, P (ed.), *Encyclopedia of Vernacular Architecture of the World*, Vol. 2, Cambridge University Press, Cambridge, 1997

Oreskes, N and Conway, EM, *Merchants of Doubt: How a Handful of Scientists Obscured the Truth on Issues from Tobacco to Global Warming*, Bloomsbury Press, New York, 2020

Osmond, G, 'The Nimble Savage: Press Constructions of Pacific Islander Swimmers in Early Twentieth Century Australia', *Media International Australia, Incorporating Culture & Policy*, pp. 133–143

Osmond, G, 'The Surfing Tommy Tanna: Performing Race at the Australian Beach', *Journal of Pacific History*, Vol. 46, No. 2, September 2011, pp. 177–195

Painter, J, *Climate Change in the Media: Reporting Risk and Uncertainty*, IB Taurus, London, 2013

Palmer, S, *Hegel's Owl: The Life of Bernard Smith*, Power Publications, [Sydney], 2016

Parnaby, OW, *Britain and the Labor Traffic in the Southwest Pacific*, Duke University Press, Durham, 1964

Pascoe, B, *Dark Emu: Aboriginal Australia and the Birth of Agriculture*, Magabala Books, Broome, 2018

Pascoe, B, *Dark Emu: Black Seeds: Agriculture or accident*, Magabala Books, Broome, 2014

Paterson, TG (ed.), *Major Problems in American Foreign Policy, Vol. II, Since 1914*, DC Heath and Co., Lexington, 1989

Paterson, TG, Clifford, JG and Hagan, KJ, *American Foreign Policy: A History*, DC Heath and Co., Lexington, 1977

Paton, JG, *Missionary to the New Hebrides: An Autobiography*, Hodder and Stoughton, London [1889], 1911

Pearson, CH, *National Life and Character*, Macmillan and Co., London, 1893

Pearson, M, *Great Southern Land: The Maritime Exploration of Terra Australis*, Department of Environment and Heritage, Canberra, 2005

Perry, TM, *The Discovery of Australia: The Charts and Maps of the Navigators and Explorers*, Nelson, Melbourne, 1982

Phillips, J, 'The "Pacific Solution" revisited: A statistical guide to the asylum seeker caseloads on Nauru and Manus Islands', Parliamentary Library Background Note, 4 September, 2012

Phillips, J and Spinks, H, 'Immigration Detention in Australia', Parliamentary Library Background Note, 20 March 2013

Pinker, S, *Enlightenment Now: The Case for Reason, Science, Humanism and Progress*, Allen Lane, London, 2018

Pirie, AA, *Commando – Double Black: An Historical Narrative of the 2/5 Australian Independent Company Later the 2/5th Cavalry Commando Squadron*, 2/5 Commando Trust, Sydney, 1993

Plate, C, *Restless Spirits*, Picador, Sydney 2005

Bibliography

Pompallier, Rt Rev. JBF, *Early History of the Catholic Church of Oceania*, H Brett, Auckland, 1888

Pryke, J, 'Pacific Islanders in Australia: Where are the Melanesians?', DevPolicyBlog, 8 August 2014, <file:///C:/Users/user/Downloads/pacific-islanders-in-australia-where-are-the-melanesians-20140828.pdf>

Pulsford, E, *Special Record of the Proceedings of the Geographical Society of Australasia in Fitting out the Exploratory Expedition to New Guinea*, F. Cunninghame and Co., Sydney, 1885

Purnell, C, 'Invisible Threads: How Migratory Shorebirds Are Connecting Countries, Cultures and Communities', *Birdlife Australia*, December 2017, pp. 38–43

Pybus, C, *The Devil and James McAuley*, University of Queensland Press, Brisbane, 1999

Pyne, SJ, *Burning Bush: A Fire History of Australia*, University of Washington Press, Seattle, 1991

Quijano, JD, *Turning Their Weapons Against Them: Captured Spanish Ships and Their Influence on the British Royal Navy in the 18th Century*, MA Thesis, University of Bristol, 2013

Quilty, PG and Banks, MR, 'Samuel Warren Carey 1911–2002', Australian Academy of Science, 2003, <science.org.au/fellowship/fellows/biographical-memoirs/samuel-warren-carey-1911-2002#6>

Radcliffe-Brown, 'Editorial', *Oceania*, No. 1, Vol. 1, April 1930, pp. 2–3

Regan, AJ and Griffin, HM (eds), *Bougainville Before the Conflict*, Pandanus Books, Canberra, 2005

Rennie, N, *Treasure Neverland: Real and Imaginary Pirates*, Oxford University Press, Oxford, 2013

Renouf, A, *Let Justice Be Done: The Foreign Policy of Dr HV Evatt*, University of Queensland Press, Brisbane, 1983

Reynolds, H, *The Law of the Land*, Penguin Books, Melbourne, 1987

Rice, GW (ed.), *The Oxford History of New Zealand*, Oxford University Press, Oxford, 1995

Richards, R, 'Pacific Whaling 1820 to 1840: Port Visits, "Shipping Arrivals and Departures" Comparisons and Sources', *Great Circle*, Vol. 24, No. 1, 2002, pp. 25–39

Riseman, N, 'Australian [Mis]treatment of Indigenous Labour in World War II Papua and New Guinea', *Labour History*, No. 98, May 2010, pp. 163–182

Robertson, E, 'Norman Lindsay and the "Asianisation" of the German Soldier in Australia During the First World War', *The Round Table: The Commonwealth Journal of International Affairs*, Vol. 103, No. 2, 2014, pp. 211–231

Robertson, J and McCarthy, J (eds), *Australian War Strategy 1939–1945: A Documentary History*, University of Queensland Press, Brisbane, 1985

Rolls, E, *Green Mosaic: Memories of New Guinea*, Thomas Nelson, Melbourne, 1977

Rolls, E, *Sojourners: The epic story of China's centuries-old relationship with Australia*, University of Queensland Press, Brisbane, 1992

Romilly, HH, *The Western Pacific and New Guinea*, John Murray, London, 1887

Rowley, CDE, *The New Guinea Villager: A Retrospect from 1964*, FW Cheshire, Melbourne, 1968

Said, E, *Culture and Imperialism*, Chatto and Windus, London, 1993

Said, E, *Orientalism*, Routledge and Kegan Paul Ltd, London, 1980

Salmond, A, *Aphrodite's Island: The European Discovery of Tahiti*, University of California Press, Berkeley, 2009

Salmond, A, *The Trial of the Cannibal Dog: Captain Cook in the South Seas*, Allen Lane, London, 2003

Sambrook, J, *The Eighteenth Century: The Intellectual and Cultural Context of English Literature, 1700–1789*, Longman Harlow, 1986

Scarr, D, 'Authentic Identities – False Colours – False Steps in Politics', *Journal of Pacific History*, Vol. 25, No. 2, 1995, pp. 204–232

Scarr, D, *The History of the Pacific Islands: Kingdoms of the Reefs*, MacMillan, Melbourne, 1990

Schacht, T, *My War on Bougainville: War under the Southern Cross*, Australian Military History Publications, Loftus, 1999

Schop, J. William, et al, 'SIMS analyses of the oldest known assemblages of microfossils document theor taxon-correlated carbon isotope compositions', PNAS, 2 January 2018, 115, pp. 53–58.

Schumacher, EF, *Small Is Beautiful: A study of economics as if people mattered* [1973], Blond and Briggs, London, 1980

Searle, G, 'John Curtin (1885–1945)', *Australian Dictionary of Biography*

Searle, P (ed.), *An Australasian Anthology: Australian and New Zealand Poems*, Collins Bros and Co. Ltd, Sydney, 1946

Semmler, C (ed.), *The War Despatches of Kenneth Slessor*, University of Queensland Press, Brisbane, 1987

Severin, T, *Seeking Robinson Crusoe*, Macmillan, London, 2002

Shakespeare, W, *The Norton Shakespeare*, WW Norton and Co., New York, 1997

Sharp, N, *Stars of Tagai: The Torres Strait Islanders*, Aboriginal Studies Press, Canberra, 1993

Shineberg, D, *They Came for Sandalwood: A Study of the Sandalwood Trade in the South-West Pacific 1830–1865*, Melbourne University Press, Melbourne, 1967

Shineberg, D, 'Towns, Robert (1794–1873)', *Australian Dictionary of Biography*

Simmonds, AP, 'Cross-cultural Friendship and Legal Pluralities in the Early Pacific Salt-Pork Trade', *Journal of World History*, Vol. 28, No. 2, June 2017, p. 236–242

Simonelli, D, 'West Papuan Independence: Why Australia Should Take a Stronger Stance', *Australian Foreign Affairs*, <www.australianforeignaffairs.com/articles/next-voices/2019/09/west-papuan-independence/dominic-simonelli>

Singe, J, *The Torres Strait: People and History*, University of Queensland Press, Brisbane, 1979

Smith, B, *European Vision and the South Pacific*, Oxford University Press, Melbourne, 1989

Smith, B, *Imagining the Pacific: In the wake of the Cook voyages*, Melbourne University Press, Melbourne, 1992

Smith, B, 'Vision and the South Pacific', *Journal of the Warburg and Courtauld Institutes*, Vol. 13, No. 1/2, 1950, pp. 65–100

Sohmer, Sara H, 'Christianity Without Civilization: Anglican sources for an alternative nineteenth-century mission methodology', *The Journal of Religious History*, Vol. 18, No. 2, December 1994, pp. 174–197

Souter, G, *Acts of Parliament: A narrative history of the Senate and House of Representatives, Commonwealth of Australia*, Melbourne University Press, Melbourne, 1988

Souter, G, *New Guinea: The Last Unknown*, Angus and Robertson, Sydney, 1970

Stats, K, 'We Will Decide: Refugee and Asylum Policy during the Howard Era before Tampa', *Australian Studies*, Vol. 7, 2015, pp. 1–25

Stats, K, 'Welcome to Australia? A reappraisal of the Fraser government's approach to refugees, 1975–83', *Australian Journal of International Affairs*, Vol. 69, No. 1, 2015, pp. 69–87

Steffensen, V, *Fire Country: How Indigenous Fire Management Could Help Save Australia*, Hardie Grant Travel, Melbourne, 2020

Bibliography

Stephen, A (ed.), *Pirating the Pacific: Images of Travel, Trade and Tourism*, Powerhouse Publishing, Sydney, 1993

Stocking Jr, GW, *Victorian Anthropology*, The Free Press, New York, 1983

Stoddart, DR, 'Darwin, Lyell and the Geological Significance of Coral Reefs', *British Journal for the History of Science*, Vol. 9, No. 2, July 1976, pp. 199–218

Storr, C, '"Imperium in Imperio": Sub-Imperialism and the Formation of Australia as a Subject of International Law', *Melbourne Journal of International Law*, 11 (2018) 19(1)

Strauss, J, (ed.), *The Collected Verse of Mary Gilmore: Volume 2: 1930–1962*, University of Queensland Press, St Lucia, 2007.

Swift, J, *Gulliver's Travels*, Penguin Books, Harmondsworth, 1967

Tabucanon, GM and Opeskin, B, 'The Resettlement of Nauruans in Australia and Early Case of Failed Environmental Migration', *Journal of Pacific History*, Vol. 46, No. 3 (Dec 2011) pp. 337–356

Tavan, G, *The Long, Slow Death of White Australia*, Scribe Publications, Melbourne, 2005

Teaiwa, Katerina, 'Ruining Pacific Islands: Australia's Phosphate Imperialism', *Australian Historical Studies*, Vol. 46, Issue 3, September 2015, pp. 374–391.

Tennant, K, *Evatt: Policies and Justice*, Angus and Robertson, Sydney, 1970

Tent, J and Geraghty, P, 'Where in the World Is Ulimaroa? Or How a Pacific Island Became the Australian Continent', *Journal of Pacific History*, Vol. 47, No. 1, March 2012, pp. 1–20

Thomas, M, *The Many Worlds of RH Mathews: In search of an Australian anthropologist*, Allen & Unwin, Sydney, 2011

Thomas, N, *In Oceania: Visions, Artifacts, Histories*, Duke University Press, Durham, 1997

Thompson, P, *Pacific Fury: How Australia and Her Allies Defeated the Japanese Scourge*, William Heinemann, Sydney, 2008

Thompson, RC, 'Making a Mandate: The Formation of Australia's New Guinea Policies, 1919–1925', *Journal of Pacific History*, Vol. 25, No. 1, June 1990, pp. 68–84

Thorne, A and Raymond, R, *Man on the Rim: The peopling of the Pacific*, Angus and Robertson, Sydney, 1989

Townsend, I, *Line of Fire*, 4th Estate, Sydney, 2017.

Trembath, R, *A Different Sort of War: Australians in Korea 1950–53*, Australian Scholarly Publishing, Melbourne, 2005

Tsiolkas, C, 'Strangers at the Gate', *The Monthly*, September 2013, p. 22–31

Tucker, Rev HW, *Memoir of the Life and Episcopate of George Augustus Selwyn DD, Bishop of New Zealand, 1841–1869; Bishop of Lichfield, 1867–1878*, Vol. II, William Wells Gardner, London, 1879

Tudor, J, *Many a Green Isle*, Pacific Publications, Sydney, 1966

Turnbull, M, *A Bigger Picture*, Hardie Grant, Sydney, 2020

Turner, B (ed.), *The Stateman's Yearbook 2010*, Palgrave Macmillan, Basingstoke, 2009

Turner, M, *Papua New Guinea: The Challenge of Independence*, Penguin Books, Melbourne, 1990

Viviani, N, *Nauru: Phosphate and Political Progress*, ANU Press, Canberra, 1970

Walker, D and Sobocinska, A (eds), *Australia's Asia: From Yellow Peril to Asian Century*, University of Western Australia Press, Crawley, 2012

Ward, R, *The Australian Legend*, Oxford University Press, Melbourne, 1960

Ward, R, *A Nation for a Continent: The History of Australia 1901–1975*, Heinemann Educational, Richmond, 1983

Waterhouse, M, *Not a Poor Man's Field: The New Guinea goldfields to 1942 – an Australian history*, Halstead Press, Braddon, 2010

Watson, Capt. JH, 'James Mario Matra – The Father of Australia', *Journal of the Royal Australian Historical Society*, Vol. X, Pt III, 1925, pp. 152–168

Wawn, WT, *The South Sea Islanders and the Queensland Labour Trade: A Record of Voyages and Experiences in the Western Pacific, from 1875 to 1891*, Swan Sonnenschein, London 1893

Wedgwood, CH, 'Obituary, Alfred Cort Haddon, 1885–1940', *Oceania*, Vol. 10, No. 4, June 1940, pp. 463–464

Westad, OA, *Restless Empire: China and the World since 1750*, The Bodley Head, London, 2012

White, H, 'Without America: Australia in the new Asia', *Quarterly Essay*, No. 68, 2017

White, ME, *After the Greening: The browning of Australia*, Kangaroo Press, Sydney, 1994

White, O, *Green Armour*, Penguin Books, Melbourne, 1992

Whitlam, EG, *A Pacific Community*, The Australian Studies Endowment, Cambridge [Mass.], 1981

Whittaker, AM, *Joseph Fouveaux: Power and Patronage in Early New South Wales*, University of New South Wales Press, Sydney, 2000

Wildey, WB, *Australasia and the Oceanic Region*, George Robertson, Melbourne, 1876

Wilkins, L and Mattei, T, *Ivor Hele: The Heroic Figure*, Australian War Memorial, undated, Canberra

Williams, FE, *Papuans of the Trans-Fly*, Oxford at the Clarendon Press, Oxford, 1936

Williams, FE, *The Valaila Madness and the Destruction of Native Ceremonies in the Gulf Division*, Territory of Papua Anthropology Report No. 4, Port Moresby, 1923

Williams, G, '"Far more happier than we Europeans": Reactions to the Australian Aborigines on Cook's voyage', *Australian Historical Studies*, Vol. 19, No. 77, October, 1981, pp. 499–512

Winchester, S, *Pacific: The Ocean of the Future*, William Collins, London, 2015

Wood, R, 'Wangga: The Linguistic and Typological Evidence for the Sources of the Outrigger Canoes of Torres Strait and Cape York Peninsula', *Oceania*, Vol. 88, Issue 2, 2018, pp. 202–231

Wormworth, J & Şekercioğlu, ÇH, *Winged Sentinels: Birds and climate change*, Cambridge University Press, Melbourne, 2012

Yarwood, AT, *Samuel Marsden: The Great Survivor*, Melbourne University Press, Melbourne, 1977

Yearbook of the United Nations 1946–47, Department of Public Information, United Nations, New York, 1947

You and the Native: Notes for the Guidance of Members of the Forces in Their Relations with New Guinea Natives, Allied Geographical Section, Southwest Pacific Area, 1943

Young, MW, 'Francis Edgar Williams', *Australian Dictionary of Biography*, <adb.anu.edu.au/biography/williams-francis-edgar-9109>

Young, RJC, *Colonial Desire: Hybridity in theory, culture and race*, Routledge, London, 1995

Notes

Introduction

1. *Town and Country Journal*, 28 August 1875.
2. *Sydney Mail and New South Wales Advertiser*, 28 August 1875.
3. See my *Coast: A history of the New South Wales Edge*, NewSouth Publishing, Sydney, 2014.
4. Warwick Anderson, 'Liberal intellectuals as Pacific supercargo: White Australian masculinity and racial thought on the boarder-lands [sic]', *Australian Historical Studies*, Vol. 46, Issue 3, September 2015, p. 437.
5. Paul Keating, *Engagement: Australia Faces the Asia-Pacific*, Pan Macmillan, Sydney, 2000, p. 300.
6. Robert JC Young, *Colonial Desire: Hybridity in theory, culture and race*, Routledge, London, 1995, p. 4.
7. Young, p. 4.
8. Hugh White, 'Without America: Australia in the new Asia', *Quarterly Essay*, Issue 68, 2017, p. 30.
9. *Australian*, 28–29 September 2019, p. 15; *Australian*, 16–17 November, p. 24.
10. Malcolm Turnbull, *A Bigger Picture*, Hardie Grant, Richmond, 2020, p. 482.
11. Alex Oliver, 2018 Lowy Institute Poll, Lowy Institute website, <www.lowyinstitute.org/publications/2018-lowy-institute-poll>.
12. *Guardian* (UK), 13 January 2021.
13. *Guardian*, 18 November 2019.
14. Martin Jacques, 'What China will be like as a great power', 32nd Annual Camden Conference, 22–24 February, 2019.
15. Sean Dorney, 'The Papua New Guinea awakening: Inside the forgotten colony', *Australian Foreign Affairs*, Issue 6, July 2019, p. 77.
16. *Australian*, 22–23 July 2019.
17. 'Future Think – From Sapiens to Homo Deus', Yuval Harari in conversation with Dan Ariely: 92nd Street Y, 21 February 2017.
18. James McAuley, 'My New Guinea', *Quadrant*, Vol. 5, No. 3, 1961, p. 27.

1 Shifting continents

1. *Sydney Morning Herald*, 29 July 2015.
2. A palaeolatitude calculator for palaeoclimate studies website, <www.palaeolatitude.org/>.
3. Vincent E Neall and Steven A Trewick, 'The age and origin of the Pacific islands: A geological overview', *Philosophical Transactions of the Royal Society*, Vol. 363, No. 1508, 2008, p. 3294.
4. Richard Blewett (ed.), *Shaping a Nation: A geology of Australia*, ANU Press, Canberra 2012, p. 106.
5. David Johnson, *The Geology of Australia*, Cambridge University Press, Melbourne, 2004, p. 152.
6. Johnson, pp. 79–80.
7. Blewett (ed.), p. 205.

8 *Sydney Morning Herald*, 24 November 1912.
9 *Sydney Morning Herald*, 30 March 1912.
10 Quoted in Gabriel Gohau, *A History of Geology*, Rutgers University Press, New Brunswick, 1990, p. 191.
11 Gohau, p. 187.
12 *Wikepin Argus*, 9 July 1925.
13 Gohau, p. 197.
14 Charles F Laseron, *The Face of Australia: The shaping of a continent*, Angus and Robertson, Sydney, 1957, pp. 5, 87, 170.
15 Rachel Carson, *The Sea Around Us*, Penguin, Harmondsworth, 1956, pp. 12–13.
16 Dr Tom Gaskell, 'Did the Moon come out of the Pacific?', *New Scientist*, No. 363, 31 October 1963, pp. 251–253.
17 *Nature*, Vol. 216, 30 December 1967, p. 1276 (pp. 1276–1280).
18 'Samuel Warren Carey 1911–2002', <www.science.org.au/fellowship/fellows/biographical-memoirs/samuel-warren-carey-1911-2002#6>.
19 Patrick Nunn, *Vanished Islands and Hidden Continents of the Pacific*, University of Hawaii Press, Honolulu, 2009, p. 10.
20 Vincent E Neall and Steven A Trewick, 'The age and origin of the Pacific islands: A geological overview', *Philosophical Transactions of the Royal Society*, 2008, p. 3299.
21 Neville Peat, *The Tasman: Biography of an ocean*, Penguin, Rosedale, p. 24
22 J. William Schopf et al, 'SIMS analyses of the oldest known assemblages of microfossils document their taxon-correlated carbon isotope compositions', PNAS, 2 January 2018, 115, p. 53.
23 Nunn, p. 33.
24 SJ Gale, 'The mined-out phosphate lands of Nauru, equatorial western Pacific', *Australian Journal of Earth Sciences*, Vol. 63, No. 3, 2016, p. 334.
25 Donald W Buden, 'The birds of Nauru', *Notornis*, Vol. 55, 2008, pp. 10–16.
26 *Sydney Morning Herald*, 6 April 1929.
27 Janice Wormworth and Çağan H Şekercioğlu, *Winged Sentinels: Birds and climate change*, Cambridge University Press, Melbourne, 2012, pp. 33–35.
28 'The Godwit' (1930), in Jennifer Strauss (ed.), *The Collected Verse of Mary Gilmore: Volume 2: 1930–1962*, University of Queensland Press, St Lucia, 2007, p. 21.
29 Allen Keast, 'Over the sea and far away', in AT Bolton (ed.), *Walkabout's Australia*, Ure Smith, Sydney, 1964, pp. 149–157.
30 *Guardian*, 24 November 2019.
31 Neville Peat, *The Tasman: Biography of an ocean*, Penguin, Rosedale, 2010, p. 57.
32 Tim Low, *Where Song Began: Australia's birds and how they changed the world*, Viking, Melbourne, 2014, pp. 200–203.
33 See Low, pp. 174–176.
34 Low, pp. 88–95, 181–182; see also Mary E White, *After the Greening: The browning of Australia*, Kangaroo Press, Kenthurst, 1994, p. 131.
35 From 'The fruit salad jungle' in Mark O'Connor, *The Great Forest*, Hale and Iremonger, Sydney, 1989, p. 19.
36 Iain McCalman, *The Reef: A Passionate History*, Penguin, Melbourne, 2014, p. 58.
37 Charles Darwin, *On the Structure and Distribution of Coral Reefs; also Geological Observations on the Volcanic Islands and Parts of South America* [1842], Ward, Lock and Bowden Ltd, London [1891], pp. 12–13.
38 Charles Darwin to JD Hooker, 17 June 1865 and Charles Darwin to C Lyell, 25 June

1856 in Francis Darwin (ed.), *The Life and Letters of Charles Darwin: Including an autobiographical chapter*, Vol. II, Charles Murray, London, 1888, pp. 73–74. See also DR Stoddart, 'Darwin, Lyell and the geological significance of coral reefs', *British Journal for the History of Science*, Vol. 9, No. 2, July 1976, pp. 211–213.
39 McCalman, 247–248.

2   First peoples

1. David Lawrence and Helen Reeves Lawrence, 'Torres Strait: The region and its people', in Richard Davis (ed.), *Woven Histories Dancing Lives: Torres Strait Island identity, culture and history*, Aboriginal Studies Press, Canberra, 2004, p. 18.
2. Entry for 30 October 1802, Matthew Flinders, *Journal on HMS* Investigator, Vol. II, 1802–1803, Mitchell Library, State Library of New South Wales, Safe 1/25.
3. Claude Levi-Strauss, *Cultural Anthropology 2*, Peregrine Books, Harmondsworth, 1978, p. 6.
4. Nonie Sharp, *Stars of Tagai: The Torres Strait Islanders*, Aboriginal Studies Press, Canberra, 1993, p. 43.
5. Sharp, pp. 29–30, 49–51.
6. Sharp, pp. 60, 52.
7. Sharp, pp. 32–33.
8. CMH Clark, *A History of Australia Vol.1: From the Earliest Times to the Age of Macquarie*, Melbourne University Press, Melbourne, (1962) 1979, p. 3.
9. Alan Thorne and Robert Raymond, *Man on the Rim: The peopling of the Pacific*, Angus and Robertson, Sydney, 1989, pp. 45–46.
10. Anna Sapfo Malaspinas et al, 'A genomic history of Aboriginal Australia', *Nature*, Vol. 538, 13 October 2016, p. 208.
11. Malaspinas et al, p. 209.
12. Phillip Hughes, Tim Denhem and Jack Golson, 'Kuk swamp', in Jack Golson et al (eds), *Ten Thousand Years of Cultivation at Kuk Swamp in the Highlands of New Guinea, Terra Australis 46*, Australian National University Press, Canberra, 2020, pp. 87–116.
13. Thorne and Raymond, p. 134.
14. Matt K Matsuda, *Pacific Worlds: A history of seas, peoples, and cultures*, Cambridge University Press, New York, 2012, p. 20.
15. Rev. James Chalmers, 'Notes on the natives of the Kiwai Island, Fly River, British New Guinea', *Journal of the Anthropological Institute of Great Britain and Ireland*, Vol. XXXIII, Jan–June 1903, pp. 117–124.
16. John MacGillivray, *Narrative of the Voyage of the HMS* Rattlesnake, T&W Boone, London, 1852, Vol 2, p. 22.
17. Paul Oliver (ed.), *Encyclopedia of Vernacular Architecture of the World*, Vol. 2, Cambridge University Press, Cambridge, 1997, pp.1074–1075, 1149–1190, 1210–1226.
18. MacGillivray, pp. 25–26.
19. Chalmers, pp. 117–124.
20. FE Williams, *Papuan of the Trans-Fly*, Oxford at the Clarendon Press, Oxford, 1936, p. 17.
21. Ursula McConnel, 'The Wik-Munkun Tribe of Cape York Peninsula, Part 1', *Oceania*, Vol. 1, January 1930, p. 102.
22. 'Indigenous banana cultivation dates back over 2,000 years', Australian National University News, <www.anu.edu.au/news/all-news/indigenous-banana-cultivation-dates-back-over-2000-years>, 12 August 2020.

23 Paul Memmott, *Gunyah, Goondie and Wurley: The Aboriginal architecture of Australia*, University of Queensland Press, Brisbane, 2007, p. 10.
24 Bruce Pascoe, *Dark Emu: Black Seeds: Agriculture or accident*, Magabala Books, Broome, 2014, p. 11 and *Dark Emu: Aboriginal Australia and the Birth of Agriculture*, Magabala Books, Broome, 2018, p. 2.
25 Harry Lourandos, *Continent of Hunter Gatherers: New perspectives in Australian prehistory*, Cambridge University Press, Cambridge, 1997.
26 David Christian, *Origin Story: A big history of everything*, Allen Lane, London, 2018, p. 199.
27 Frank Brennan, *One land, one nation: Mabo – towards 2001*, University of Queensland Press, Brisbane, 1995, p. 9.
28 Richard Baker, *Land Is Life, from Bush to Town: The story of the Yanyuwa people*, Allen & Unwin, Sydney, 1999, p. 69.
29 Sharp, p. 30.
30 Paul Moon, *Encounters: The creation of New Zealand: A history*, Penguin, Auckland, 2013, p. 30.
31 Geoffrey, Irwin, *The Prehistoric Exploration and Colonisation of the Pacific*, Cambridge University Press, Cambridge, 1992, p. 209.
32 Val Attenbrow, 'Aboriginal fishing in Port Jackson, and the introduction of shell fishhooks to coastal New South Wales, Australia', in Daniel Lunney et al (eds), *The Natural History of Sydney*, Royal Zoological Society of NSW, Mosman, 2010, pp. 25–29; Atholl Anderson and Peter White, 'Prehistoric settlement on Norfolk Island and its oceanic context', *Records of the Australian Museum*, Supplement 27, 2001, p. 136.
33 RH Mathews, 'Folklore of the Australian Aborigines', 1898, quoted in Martin Thomas, *The Many Worlds of RH Mathews: In search of an Australian anthropologist*, Allen & Unwin, Sydney, 2011, pp. 225–227.
34 William Briscoe quoted in John Gascoigne, *Encountering the Pacific in the Age of the Enlightenment*, Cambridge University Press, Melbourne, 2014, p. 462.
35 JH Bell, 'Some demographic and cultural characteristics of the La Perouse Aborigines', *Mankind*, Vol. 5, No. 10, June 1961, p. 437.
36 Malaspinas et al, p. 209.
37 *Kalgoorlie Miner*, 22 April 1907; see also Michael Cathcart, *The Water Dreamers: The Remarkable History of Our Dry Continent*, Text Publishing, Melbourne, 2010, pp. 179–184.
38 Ian J McNiven, 'Colonial diffusionism and archaeology of external influences on Aboriginal culture', in Bruno David et al (eds), *The Social Archaeology of Australian Indigenous Societies*, Aboriginal Studies Press, Canberra, 2006, pp. 105–106.
39 *Daily Herald*, 23 July 1914.
40 John Gascoigne, p. 462.

3 Converging on Australia

1 Quoted in Adrian Mitchell, *Plein Airs and Graces: The life and times of George Collingridge*, Wakefield Press, Kent Town, 2012, p. 170. Wood's 1917 lecture was reiterated in his 1922 work, *The Discovery of Australia*.
2 OHK Spate, 'Terra Australis-Cognita?', *Australian Historical Studies*, Vol. 8, No. 29, 1957, pp. 18, 19.
3 OHK Spate, *The Spanish Lake: The Pacific since Magellan*, Vol. 1 [1979], ANU E Press, 2004, p. 289.

4 *Sydney Morning Herald*, 16 January 2014.
5 WP Morrell, *Britain in the Pacific Islands*, Oxford at the Clarendon Press, London, 1960, p. 239; Peter Hastings, *New Guinea: Prolbems and Prospects*, Cheshire Publishing, Melbourne, 1973, p. 32.
6 Susannah Helman, 'Rethinking the southern continent', *Mapping Our World: Terra Incognita to Australia*, National Library of Australia, Canberra, 2014, p. 92.
7 Spate, 2004, p. 139.
8 Spate, 2004, p. 118.
9 Laurence Bergreen, *Over the Edge of the World: Magellan's terrifying circumnavigation of the globe*, HarperCollins, London, 2003, pp. 163–167. The man was one of two taken captive. The other was on the ship *San Antonio*, which abandoned the expedition before Magellan reached the Pacific.
10 The encounter is described in Bergreen, pp. 206–208.
11 In John Gascoigne, *Encountering the Pacific in the Age of the Enlightenment*, Cambridge University Press, Melbourne, 2014, p. 66.
12 Alan Frost, *The Global Reach of Empire: Britain's maritime expansion in the Indian and Pacific oceans 1764–1815*, Miegunyah Press, Carlton, 2003, p. 18.
13 Martin Woods, '"Terre Australe", east of New Holland', in *Mapping Our World: Terra Incognita to Australia*, National Library of Australia, Canberra, 2014, p. 143.
14 Raymond Lister, *Antique Maps and their Cartographers*, G Bell and Sons, London, 1970, pp. 48–49.
15 Lincoln Paine, *The Sea and Civilisation: A Maritime History of the World*, Atlantic Books, London, 2014, pp. 188–189.
16 Andrew Gordon, *A Modern History of Japan from Tokugawa Times to the Present*, Oxford University Press, New York, 2003, pp. 16–19; Leonard Y Andaya, 'Interactions with the Outside World and Adaptation in Southeast Asian Society, 1500–1800', in Nicholas Tarling (ed.), *Cambridge History of South East Asia, Vol. 1: From Early Times to c.1800*, Cambridge University Press, Cambridge, 1992, p. 351.
17 Paine, p. 305.
18 Paine, p. 367.
19 Harry G Gelber, *The Dragon and the Foreign Devils: China and the world, 1100 BC to the present*, Bloomsbury, London, 2007, p. 89.
20 Gavin Menzies, *1421: The year China discovered the world*, Bantam Books, pp. 197–233; for a good summary of the reaction to Menzies' work see the transcript of 'Junk History', *Four Corners*, ABC TV, 21 July 2006, <www.abc.net.au/4corners/junk-history/8953466>.
21 Quoted in Anthony Reid, 'Economic and Social Change, c. 1400–1800', in Tarling (ed.), p. 496.
22 Gelber, *The Dragon and the Foreign Devils*, p. 90; Gascoigne, p. 29.

4 In the wake of Spain

1 Quoted in John Gascoigne, *Encountering the Pacific in the Age of the Enlightenment*, Cambridge University Press, Melbourne, 2014, p. 43.
2 Introduction to William Dampier, *A Voyage to New Holland: The English voyage of discovery to the South Seas in 1699*, James Spencer (ed.), Alan Sutton, Gloucester, 1981, pp. 16–17.
3 Dampier, pp. 39–40.
4 Dampier, p. 148.

5 Dampier, p. 125.
6 Dampier, p. 224.
7 Neil Rennie, *Treasure Neverland: Real and Imaginary Pirates*, Oxford University Press, Oxford, 2013, pp. 34–35.
8 Tim Severin, *Seeking Robinson Crusoe*, Macmillan, London, 2002, pp. 3–23, 40–45.
9 Gunn was subsequently clothed in 'old ship's canvas and old sea-cloth' in the novel *Treasure Island* at the insistence of Stevenson's father. Rennie, pp. 180–181.
10 Gascoigne, p. 48.
11 Gascoigne, p. 82.
12 Lynn Hunt, *Inventing Humans Rights: A history*, WW Norton and Co., New York, 2007, p. 40.
13 William Shakespeare, 'The Tempest', in *The Norton Shakespeare*, WW Norton and Co., New York, 1997, p. 3065.
14 Stephen Greenblatt, 'The Tempest', in *The Norton Shakespeare*, WW Norton and Co., New York, 1997, p. 3052.
15 Stuart Macintyre, *A Concise History of Australia*, Cambridge University Press, Melbourne, 2004, p. 24.
16 Jonathan Swift, *Gulliver's Travels*, Penguin Books, Harmondsworth, 1967, pp. 343–344.
17 Quoted in the Introduction, Jonathon Swift, *Gulliver's Travels*, p.12.
18 John Dunmore, *Storms and Dreams, Louis de Bougainville: Soldier, explorer, statesman*, ABC Books, Sydney, 2005, p. 197.
19 Quoted in Dunmore, p. 198.
20 Quoted in Dunmore, p. 148.
21 Denis Diderot, 'Supplement to Bougainville's *Voyage*' [1771–1796], in *This Is Not a Story and other Stories*, Oxford University Press, New York, 1993, pp. 67–68.
22 Nick Lomb, *The Transit of Venus: 1631 to the present*, NewSouth Publishing, Sydney, 2011, pp. 18–19.
23 JC Beaglehole (ed.), *The* Endeavour *Journal of Joseph Banks, 1768–1771*, Vol. 1, pp. 258, 274.
24 Beaglehole, p. 312.
25 'By the Commissioners for executing the office of Lord High Admiral of Great Britain & ca. Additional Instructions for Lt James Cook, Appointed to Command His Majesty's Bark the Endeavour' 30 July 1768, transcript <www.foundingdocs.gov.au/resources/transcripts/nsw1_doc_1768.pdf>.
26 Beaglehole, pp. 54, 93.
27 James Cook, *Journal of the HMS* Endeavour, *1768–1771*, p. 125.
28 Daniel Defoe, *Robinson Crusoe* [1719], Penguin Books, Camberwell, 2010, p. 129.
29 See Glyndwr Williams, '"Far more happier than we Europeans": Reactions to the Australian Aborigines on Cook's voyage', *Australian Historical Studies*, Vol. 19, No. 77, October, 1981, p. 499.
30 Bernard Smith, *Imagining the Pacific: In the wake of the Cook voyages*, Melbourne University Press, Melbourne, 1992, p. 208.
31 Lord Morton, 'Hints to the consideration of Captain Cooke, Mr Bankes, Doctor Solander, and the other Gentlemen who go upon the expedition on Board the *Endeavour*', 1769, NLA MS9/113.
32 *Captain Cook's Journal During the First Voyage Round the World*, Project Gutenberg ebook, May 2005.

5   A Pacific colony

1. 'Lieutenant Cook to Secretary Stephens, *Endeavour* bark, 12 July 1771', in John Currey (ed.), *A Voyage to the Great South Sea Completed: How England Learned of Cook's Return in 1771*, The Banks Society, Malvern [2012], pp. 18–19.
2. Quoted in JC Beaglehole, *The Life of Captain James Cook*, Adam and Charles Black, London, 1974, p. 250.
3. Lieutenant Le Dez in Edward Duyker (ed.), *The Discovery of Tasmania: Journal extracts from the expeditions of Abel Janszoon Tasman and Marc-Joseph Marion Dufresne, 1642 and 1772*, St David's Park Publishing, Hobart, 1992, pp. 32–33.
4. John Gascoigne, *Encountering the Pacific in the Age of the Enlightenment*, Cambridge University Press, Melbourne, 2014, p. 156.
5. JC Beaglehole (ed.), *The Journals of Captain James Cook*, Cambridge University Press, Cambridge, 1968, 566–567.
6. Alan Frost, *The Precarious Life of James Mario Matra: Voyager with Cook, American Loyalist, Servant of Empire*, Miegunyah Press, Melbourne, 1995, p. 104.
7. 'A Proposal for Establishing a Settlement in New South Wales', 23 August 1783, *Historical Records of New South Wales*, Vol. 1 Part 2 – Phillip, 1783–1792, Lansdown Slattery and Company, Sydney, 1978, p. 1.
8. Daniel Defoe, *The Life and Surprising Adventures of Robinson Crusoe of York, Mariner … [1719]*, J Limbird, London, 1833, p. 89; see also James Sambrook, *The Eighteenth Century: The Intellectual and Cultural Context of English Literature, 1700–1789*, Longman Harlow, 1986, p. 71.
9. 'A Proposal for Establishing a Settlement in New South Wales', 23 August 1783, *Historical Records of New South Wales*, Vol. 1 Part 2 – Phillip, 1783–1792, Lansdown Slattery and Company, Sydney, 1978, pp. 2–6.
10. 'A Proposal for Establishing a Settlement in New South Wales' 23 August 1783, *Historical Records of New South Wales*, Vol. 1 Part 2 – Phillip, 1783–1792, Lansdown Slattery and Company, Sydney, 1978, p. 9.
11. 'Lord Sydney to the Lords Commissioners of the Treasury' 18 August 1786, *HRNSW* Vol. 1, Part 2, *Historical Records of New South Wales*, Vol. 1 Part 2 – Phillip, 1783–1792, Lansdown Slattery and Company, Sydney, 1978, pp. 14–20.
12. Captain JH Watson, 'James Mario Matra – The Father of Australia', *Journal of the Royal Australian Historical Society*, Vol. X Pt III, 1925, pp. 152–168.
13. Robert Hughes, *The Fatal Shore: A history of the transportation of convicts to Australia, 1787–1868*, Collins Harvill, London, 1987, p. 2.
14. Geoffrey Blainey, *The Tyranny of Distance*, Sun Books, Melbourne, 1966, p. 33.
15. Blainey, p. 37.
16. See Alan Frost, *The Global Reach of Empire*, Miegunyah Press, Melbourne, 2003, pp. 182–184.
17. Jan Kociumbas, *The Oxford History of Australia, Vol. 2, 1770–1860*, Oxford University Press, Melbourne, 1992, p. 36.
18. Defoe, p. 166.
19. 'Instructions for our trusty and well-beloved Arthur Phillip Esp …', 25 April 1787, *Historical Records of New South Wales*, Vol. 1 Part 2 – Phillip, 1783–1792, Lansdown Slattery and Company, Sydney, 1978, p. 90.
20. Alan Atkinson, *The Europeans in Australia: A history, Vol. I*, Oxford University Press, Melbourne, 1997, p. 58.

Notes to pages 101–111

21 David Collins, *An Account of the English Colony in New South Wales, Vol.1* (1798), AH and AW Reed, Sydney, 1975, pp. 11, 63.
22 WW Grenville to Arthur Phillip, 19 June 1789 in John Cobley (ed.), *Sydney Cove, 1789–1790*, Angus and Robertson, Sydney, 1963, p. 205.
23 Helen Proudfoot, 'Fixing the settlement upon a savage shore: Planning and building', in Graeme Aplin (ed.), *A Difficult Infant: Sydney before Macquarie*, New South Wales University Press, Kensington, 1988, p. 62.
24 Collins, p. 81.
25 Collins, p. 423.
26 John Hunter, *An Historical Journal of the Transactions at Port Jackson and Norfolk Island*, Library Board of South Australia, Adelaide, 1968, p. 259.
27 Peter Coyne, '*Phorium tenax* (New Zealand Flax) – Norfolk Island Native?', *Cunninghamia*, 2009, 11(2), pp. 167–170.
28 Julian P Hume, *Extinct Birds*, Bloomsbury, London, 2017, p. 68.
29 Lars Löfgren, *Ocean Birds: Their breeding, biology and behaviour*, Croom Helm, Beckenham, 1984, p. 73.
30 Hunter, p. 260.
31 Tim Bonyhady, *The Colonial Earth*, Miegunyah Press, Melbourne, 2000, p. 38; Joseph M Forshaw, *Parrots of the World*, Lansdowne Press, Melbourne, 1973, pp. 140–142.
32 Keith Thomas, *Man and the Natural World: Changing Attitudes in England 1500–1800*, Penguin Books, Harmondsworth, 1987, p. 148.
33 Bonyhady, p. 32.
34 Atkinson, p. 72.
35 Paul G Fidlon and PJ Ryan (eds), *The Journal and Letters of Lt. Ralph Clark 1787–1792*, Australian Documents Library, Sydney, 1981, p. 96.
36 Atkinson, p. 75.
37 Robert Ross quoted in Atkinson, p. 74.
38 Atkinson, pp. 232, 236.
39 Atkinson, p. 230.
40 Jonathan and John King, *Philip Gidley King: A biography of the third governor of New South Wales*, Methuen, Sydney, 1981, p. 50.
41 In Collins, p. 440.
42 Governor King to Earl Camden, 30 April 1805, *Historical Records of New South Wales Vol. 5, 1803–1805*, Lansdown Slattery and Company, Sydney, 1978, p. 601.
43 Governor Hunter to the Duke of Portland, 10 January 1798, *Historical Records of New South Wales Vol. 3 Hunter, 1796–1799*, Lansdown Slattery and Company, Sydney, 1978, p. 349.
44 CMH Clark (ed.), *Select Documents in Australian History, 1788–1850*, Angus and Robertson, Sydney, 1966, p. 406.
45 Governor Hunter to the Duke of Portland, 10 January 1798, *Historical Records of New South Wales*, p. 348.
46 Governor King to Lord Hobart, 7 June 1803, *Historical Records of New South Wales*, p. 153.
47 Governor King to Lord Hobart, 1 March 1804, *Historical Records of Australia*, Series 1, Vol. IV, p. 553; Hunter, *Journal*, p. 266.
48 Governor King to Joseph Banks, 14 August 1804, *Historical Records of New South Wales Vol.5, King 1803–1805*, Lansdown Slattery and Company, Sydney, 1978, p. 447.
49 Atkinson, p. 311.

50 Peter Conrad, *Islands: A trip through time and space*, Thames and Hudson, London, 2009, p. 6.
51 Letter from Richard Hay and Edward O'Hara to John Piper, 22 February 1805, in M Barnard Eldershaw, *The Life and Times of Captain John Piper*, Ure Smith, Sydney, 1973, p. 69.
52 Governor Macquarie to Viscount Castlereagh, 30 April 1810, *Historical Records of New South Wales, Vol.7, Bligh and Macquarie, 1809–1811*, Lansdown Slattery and Company, Sydney, 1978, p. 345.
53 Quoted in Hughes, p. 461.
54 Quoted in Hughes, p. 463.

6   An ocean of opportunity

1 DR Hainsworth, *The Sydney Traders: Simeon Lord and His Contemporaries 1788–1821*, Melbourne University Press, Melbourne, 1981, p. 71.
2 Graeme Aplin and George Parsons, 'Maritime trade: Shipping and the early colonial economy', in Aplin (ed.), *A Difficult Infant: Sydney before Macquarie*, University of New South Wales Press, Kensington, 1988, p. 156.
3 Hainsworth, pp. 119, 126, 151.
4 Hainsworth, pp. 67–70.
5 Quoted in Atkinson, p. 291.
6 Hainsworth, p. 172.
7 Letter from John Macarthur to Elizabeth Macarthur, 3 May 1810, *Historical Records of New South Wales, Vol.7 Bligh and Macquarie, 1809–1811*, Lansdown Slattery and Co., Mona Vale, 1979, p. 368.
8 Hainsworth, p. 178.
9 'Contract with messers. Bass and Bishop for the Importation of Pork', 9 October 1801, *Historical Records of Australia*, Series 1, Vol. III (HRA), p. 337.
10 Hainsworth, pp. 158–164.
11 King Pomare to Acting-Governor King, 10 August 1801, *Historical Records of Australia*, Series 1, Vol. III, p. 333.
12 Anne Salmond, *Aphrodite's Island: The European Discovery of Tahiti*, University of California Press, Berkeley 2009, pp. 26–37, 455, 460–463.
13 Alecia Pru Simmonds, 'Cross-Cultural Friendship and Legal Pluralities in the Early Pacific Salt-Pork Trade', *Journal of World History*, Vol. 28, No. 2, June 2017, pp. 236–242.
14 Alexander Berry, *Reminiscences of Alexander Berry*, Angus and Robertson, Sydney, 1912, p. 87.
15 Berry, p. 104.
16 *Sydney Gazette and New South Wales Advertiser*, 1 September 1810.
17 Governor Macquarie to Viscount Castlereagh, 30 April 1810, *Historical Records of New South Wales, 1809–1811*, Vol. 7, p. 348.
18 Governor Macquarie to Viscount Castlereagh, 30 April 1810, *Historical Records of New South Wales, 1809–1811*, Vol. 7, p. 348.
19 AW Murray, *The Bible in the Pacific*, James Nisbet and Co., London, 1888, pp. 4–7; AT Yarwood, *Samuel Marsden: The Great Survivor*, Melbourne University Press, Melbourne, 1977, p. 162.
20 Tracey Banivanua-Mar, *Decolonisation and the Pacific: Indigenous Globalisation and the Ends of Empire*, Cambridge University Press, Cambridge, 2016, p. 52.

21 Letter from Governor Macquarie to Earl Bathurst, 17 January 1814, *Historical Records of Australia*, Series I, Vol. VIII, 1813–15, p. 96.
22 'Proclamation', 17 January 1814, *Historical Records of Australia*, Series I, Vol. III, pp. 98–100.
23 Robert Hughes, *The Fatal Shore*, Collins Harvill, London, 1987, p. 187.
24 Yarwood, p. 79.
25 Quoted in Yarwood, p. 169.
26 Governor Macquarie to Earl Bathurst, 17 January 1814, *Historical Records of Australia*, Library Committee of the Commonwealth Parliament, Sydney 1916, 1813–15, p. 96.
27 Governor Macquarie to Viscount Castlereagh, 12 March 1810, *Historical Records of New South Wales, Vol. 7 Bligh and Macquarie 1809–1811*, pp. 312–313.
28 *The Statutes of the United Kingdom of Great Britain and Ireland*, Vol. 7, London, 1819, p. 94; Yarwood, p. 192.
29 JMR Owens, 'New Zealand before Annexation', in Geoffrey W Rice (ed.), *The Oxford History of New Zealand*, Oxford University Press, Oxford, 1995, pp. 31–32.
30 Owens in Rice, pp. 32–33.
31 Rhys Richards, 'Pacific Whaling 1820 to 1840: Port Visits, "Shipping Arrivals and Departures" Comparisons and Sources', *Great Circle*, Vol. 24, No. 1, 2002, p. 28.
32 Mrs Charles Meredith, *Notes and Sketches of New South Wales*, Penguin Books, Melbourne, 1973, p. 36.
33 In Alan Birch and David S Macmillan (eds), *The Sydney Scene 1788–1960*, Melbourne University Press, Melbourne, 1962, p. 27.
34 Quoted in Yarwood, p. 106.
35 In Murray, p. 110.
36 Yarwood, pp. 177–178.
37 John Liddiard Nicholas, *Narrative of a Voyage to New Zealand*, Vol. II, James Black and Son, London, 1817, p. 222.
38 Nicholas, pp. 264–266.
39 In Paul Moon, *Encounters: The Creation of New Zealand: A History*, Penguin Books, Rosedale, 2013, p. 113.
40 Donald Denoon, Philippa Mein-Smith and Marivic Wyndham, *A History of Australia, New Zealand and the Pacific*, Blackwell, Malden, 2000, pp. 104–105.
41 *Sydney Gazette and New South Wales Advertiser*, 12 May 1836.
42 Owens in Rice, p. 41.
43 Quoted in Yarwood, p. 275.
44 Denoon, Mein-Smith and Wyndham, p. 109.
45 Quoted in Denoon et al, p. 109.
46 Henry Reynolds, *The Law of the Land*, Penguin Books, Melbourne, 1987, pp. 122–123.
47 Quoted in WP Morrell, *Britain in the Pacific Islands*, Oxford at the Clarendon Press, London, 1960, pp. 72–73.
48 John Askew, *A Voyage to Australia and New Zealand, Including a Visit to Adelaide, Melbourne, Sydney, Hunter's River, Newcastle, Maitland and Auckland*, Simpkin, Marshall and Company, Cockermouth, 1857, p. 2.
49 Askew, p. 291.
50 Askew, pp. 340–341.

7 Miners and mutineers

1 Charles Bateson, *Gold Fleet for California: Forty-Niners from Australia and New Zealand*, Ure Smith, Sydney, 1963, p. 19.

Notes to pages 141–155

2 *Shipping Gazette and Sydney General Trade List*, 19 June 1852.
3 Quoted in Bateson, p. 133.
4 Bateson, p. 135.
5 Alan Atkinson, *The Europeans in Australia: A history, Vol. II*, Oxford University Press, South Melbourne, 2004, p. 230.
6 Geoffrey Blainey, *The Rush That Never Ended: A history of Australian mining*, Melbourne University Press, Melbourne, 1969, pp. 13–27.
7 David Goodman, *Gold Seeking: Victoria and California in the 1850s*, Allen & Unwin, Sydney, 1994, p. 221.
8 Eric Rolls, *Sojourners: The epic story of China's centuries-old relationship with Australia*, University of Queensland Press, Brisbane, 1992, p. 86.
9 Quoted in Goodman, p. xxiii.
10 Russel Ward, *The Australian Legend*, Oxford University Press, Melbourne, 1960, p. 112.
11 Ward, pp. 124–125.
12 John Elphinstone Erskine, *Journal of a Cruise Among the Islands of the Western Pacific*, John Murray, London, 1853, p. 465.
13 Harry G Gelber, *The Dragon and the Foreign Devils: China and the World, 1100 BC to the Present*, Bloomsbury, London, 2007, pp. 157–203.
14 *Sydney Gazette and New South Wales Advertiser*, 19 September 1840.
15 'Speech to the Massachusetts Historical Society, December 1841', in Benson Lee Grayson (ed.), *The American Image of China*, Frederick Ungar Publishing Co., New York, 1979, p. 85.
16 George F Seward despatch to to State Department 22 April 1870 in Grayson (ed.), *The American Image of China*, p. 107.
17 Rolls, p. 58.
18 Rolls, p. 199.
19 Andrew Marcus, *Fear and Hatred: Purifying Australia and California, 1850–1901*, Hale and Iremonger, Sydney, 1979, p. 18.
20 *Empire*, 1857, quoted in Marcus, p. 20.
21 Quoted in Markus, p. 8.
22 *Empire*, 26 June 1858.
23 Quoted in Alfred McFarland, *Mutiny in the "Bounty!" and Story of the Pitcairn Islanders*, JJ Moore, Sydney, 1884, p. 190.
24 Greg Dening, *Mr Bligh's Bad Language: Passion, Power and Theatre on the* Bounty, Cambridge University Press, Cambridge, 1992, pp. 145, 59, 55–87.
25 Quoted in 'The *Pandora* Story', Museum of Tropical Queensland exhibition notes, no date.
26 Dening, p. 309.
27 'Sermons on Regeneration, Sermon I, Of the Character of the Unregenerate', in Philip Dodderidge, *Practical Discourses on Regeneration. In Ten Sermons*, Ruben Sears, Ballston Spa, 1815, p. 25.
28 The description comes from Raymond Nobbs. See his *George Hunn Nobbs 1799–1884: Reverend on Pitcairn and Norfolk Island*, The Pitcairn Descendants Society, Norfolk Island, 1984, p. 26. This book gives a good account of convoluted power plays on Pitcairn.
29 Quoted in McFarland, p. 190.
30 Quoted in Nobbs, p. 37.
31 Quoted in Nobbs, p. 44.

32 Quoted in McFarland, p. 209.
33 Robert W Kirk, *Paradise Past: The Transformation of the South Pacific, 1520–1920*, McFarland and Co., Jefferson, 2012, p. 65.
34 William Denison letter to GW Gregorie, 1856, quoted in Maeve O'Collins, *An Uneasy Relationship: Norfolk Island and the Commonwealth of Australia*, Australian National University E Press, 2010, p. 5.
35 Quoted in O'Collins, p. 7.
36 John C Patteson in McFarland, p. 30.
37 McFarland, p. 229.
38 Sir Henry Parkes in response to a question from Edward O'Sullivan, 5 July 1888, *New South Wales Parliamentary Debates, Session 1887–1888*, p. 6121.
39 O'Collins, pp. 12–13.
40 *Daily Telegraph*, 2 July 1914.
41 *Guardian* (Australia), 21 May 2015.

8 Saving souls and taking slaves

1 David Hilliard, *God's Gentlemen: A History of the Melanesian Mission, 1849–1942*, University of Queensland Press, Brisbane, 1978, p. 5.
2 'Letter to Rev. Ernest Hawkins 27 February 1857', in Rev HW Tucker, *Memoir of the Life and Episcopate of George Augustus Selwyn DD, Bishop of New Zealand, 1841–1869; Bishop of Lichfield, 1867–1878*, Vol. II, William Wells Gardner, London, 1879, p. 70.
3 Quoted in Hilliard, p. 1.
4 Patteson quoted in Raymond Nobbs, *George Hunn Nobbs 1799–1884: Reverend on Pitcairn and Norfolk Island*, The Pitcairn Descendants Society, Norfolk Island, 1984, p. 85.
5 Quoted in Nobbs, p. 86.
6 Arthur Innes Hopkins quoted in Sara H Sohmer, 'Christianity Without Civilization: Anglican sources for an alternative nineteenth-century mission methodology', *The Journal of Religious History*, Vol. 18, No. 2, December 1994, pp. 177–178.
7 Sohmer, p. 178.
8 RH Codrington, *The Melanesian: Studies in Their Anthropology and Folklore*, Oxford at the Clarendon Press, Oxford, 1891, pp. v, vii, 12.
9 John G Paton, *Missionary to the New Hebrides: An autobiography*, Hodder and Stoughton, London, [1889], 1911, pp. 72, 288.
10 Paton, p. 80.
11 'Sermon XVII "The Sanctified Use of God's Creatures" at Christ Church 23 March 1851', in Bishop William Grant Broughton, *Sermons on the Church of England; Its Constitution, Mission, and Trials*, Bell and Daldy, London, 1857, p. 240.
12 Paton, p. 293.
13 Rt Rev. Jean Baptiste Francois Pompallier, *Early History of the Catholic Church of Oceania*, H Brett, Auckland, 1888, p. 36.
14 Paton, p. 295.
15 Jane Tinney, *Diary 1892–1902*, PMB 633, Mitchell Library, State Library of New South Wales, p. 6.
16 Rev. Samuel McFarlane, *Among the Cannibals of New Guinea, being the story of the New Guinea Mission of the London Missionary Society*, Presbyterian Board of Publication, Philadelphia [1888].
17 Tinney, p. 2.

18   Chris Cuneen, 'Jersey, seventh Earl of (1845–1915)', *Australian Dictionary of Biography*.
19   Tinney, p. 5.
20   Tinney, p. 22.
21   Tinney, pp. 31–33.
22   Tinney, p. 100.
23   Tinney, p. 10.
24   Tinney, p. 81.
25   Tinney, p. 15.
26   Tinney, p. 96.
27   *Sydney Gazette*, 26 March 1826.
28   Dorothy Shineberg, *They Came for Sandalwood: A Study of the Sandalwood Trade in the South-West Pacific 1830–1865*, Melbourne University Press, Melbourne, 1967, p. 27.
29   Shineberg, p. 30.
30   Figures extracted from table in Shineberg, Appendix One.
31   Reverend John Inglis, *In the New Hebrides: Reminiscences of Missionary Life and Work, especially on the Island of Aneityum*, T Nelson and Sons, London, 1887, p. 306.
32   *The Colonist*, 4 December 1839.
33   *Sydney Herald*, 25 May 1842.
34   Shineberg, p. 108.
35   Shineberg, p. 245.
36   *Sydney Chronicle*, 28 April 1847.
37   *Sydney Morning Herald*, 7 November 1847.
38   *Maitland Mercury and Hunter River General Advertiser*, 6 November 1847.
39   *Maitland Mercury and Hunter River General Advertiser*, 30 November 1850.
40   *Bell's Life in Sydney and Sporting Reviewer*, 29 November 1851.
41   *The People's Advocate and New South Wales Vindicator*, 27 December 1851.
42   *Freeman's Journal*, 4 December 1851.
43   Dorothy Shineberg, 'Towns, Robert (1794–1873)' in the *Australian Dictionary of Biography*, <adb.anu.edu.au/biography/towns-robert-4741>.
44   TA Coghlan, *Labour and Industry in Australia*, Vol. II [1918], Macmillan of Australia, 1969, p. 981.
45   Coghlan, p. 901.
46   GC Bolton, *A Thousand Miles Away: A History of North Queensland to 1920*, Australian National University Press, Canberra, 1970, p. 78.
47   *Illustrated Australian News for Home Readers*, 7 August 1869.
48   Quoted in PM Mercer and CR Moore, 'Melanesians in North Queensland: The Retention of Indigenous Religious and Magical Practices', *Journal of Pacific History*, Vol. 11, No. 1, Labour Trade Pt 1, 1976, p. 84.
49   Coghlan, p. 901.
50   Quoted in OW Parnaby, *Britain and the Labor Traffic in the Southwest Pacific*, Duke University Press, Durham, 1964, p. 55.
51   Paton, p. 131.
52   *Argus*, 20 September 1873.
53   In Parnaby, p. 85.
54   Albert Hastings Markham, *The Cruise of the 'Rosario' Amongst the New Hebrides and Santa Cruz Islands, Exposing the Recent Atrocities Connected with the Kidnapping of Natives in the South Seas*, Sampson Low, Marston, Low and Searle, London, 1873, pp. 111, 117.

55 Parnaby, p. 18.
56 Markham, p. 118.
57 Tracey Banivanua-Mar, *Violence and Colonial Dialogue: The Australian-Pacific Indentured Labour Trade*, University of Hawaii Press, Honolulu, 2006, pp. 37–38.
58 James Goodenough, *Journal of Commodore Goodenough, RN, CB, CMG, During His Last Command as Senior Officer on the Australian Station, 1873–1875, Edited with a Memoir by his Widow*, Henry S King and Co. London, 1876, pp. 153–154, 345–349.
59 *Argus*, 30 August 1875.
60 Quoted in John Bach, 'The Royal Navy in the Pacific Islands', *Journal of Pacific History*, Vol. 3, 1969, p. 8.
61 Hugh Hastings Romilly, *The Western Pacific and New Guinea*, John Murray, London, 1887, p. 192.
62 *Journal of Commodore Goodenough*, p.117.
63 *Spectator*, 25 July 1874, p. 7.

9 Australia's Pacific

1 Regina Ganter, *The Pearl-Shellers of Torres Strait: Resource Use, Development and Decline, 1860s–1960s*, Melbourne University Press, Melbourne, 1994, p. 17.
2 GC Bolton, *A Thousand Miles Away: A History of North Queensland to 1920*, Australian National University Press, Canberra, 1970, p. 76; Ganter, pp. 2, 23.
3 Quoted in Jeremy Beckett, *Torres Strait Islanders: Custom and Colonisation*, Cambridge University Press, Melbourne, 1987, pp. 47–48.
4 Beckett, *Torres Strait Islanders*, p. 45.
5 Quoted in B Jinks, P Biskup and H Nelson (eds), *Readings in New Guinea History*, Angus and Robertson, Sydney, 1973, pp. 32–33.
6 'The Right Hon. The Earl of Derby to the Officer Administering the Government of Queensland', 11 July 1883 in the *Collection of Mainly Queensland Parliamentary Reports and Papers on the Proposed Annexation of New Guinea, and Covering Aspects of Australia's Official Involvement in the Administration of British New Guinea*, Mitchell Library, HQ 2013/4632.
7 J Chalmers and W Wyatt Gill, *Work and Adventure in New Guinea*, The Religious Tract Society, London, 1885, p. 17.
8 William Brackley Wildey, *Australasia and the Oceanic Region*, George Robertson, Melbourne, 1876, p. 170.
9 Memorandum for his Excellency the Governor from James Service, 20 December 1884, in *Collection of Mainly Queensland Parliamentary Reports and Papers on the Proposed Annexation of New Guinea, and Covering Aspects of Australia's Official Involvement in the Administration of British New Guinea*, Mitchell Library, HQ 2013/4632.
10 Cait Storr, '"Imperium in Imperio": Sub-Imperialism and the Formation of Australia as a Subject of International Law', *Melbourne Journal of International Law*, 11 (2018) 19(1), pp. 8–9.
11 John Paton to James Service, Enclosure No. 4 in *Collection of Mainly Queensland Parliamentary Reports and Papers on the Proposed Annexation of New Guinea, and Covering Aspects of Australia's Official Involvement in the Administration of British New Guinea*, Mitchell Library, HQ 2013/4632.
12 Edmond Marin La Meslée, *Past Explorations of New Guinea and a Scheme for the Scientific Exploration of the Great Island*, JL Holmes, Sydney, 1883, pp. 1, 20–21.
13 Derby's response via John Bramston to Agents General 'Colonial Office to the

Agents General for NSW, NZ, Qld and Vic, 31 August 1883', in *Collection of Mainly Queensland Parliamentary Reports and Papers on the Proposed Annexation of New Guinea, and Covering Aspects of Australia's Official Involvement in the Administration of British New Guinea*, Mitchell Library, HQ 2013/4632.

14. Neville Meaney, '"In History's Page": Myth and Identity', in James Curran and Stuart Ward (eds), *Australia and the Wider World: Selected Essays of Neville Meaney*, Sydney University Press, Sydney, 2013, p. 55.
15. James Elphinstone Erskine, 'Proclamation', 6 November 1884, in B Jinks, P Biskup, H Nelson (eds), *Readings in New Guinea History*, Angus and Robertson, Sydney, 1973, pp. 38–39.
16. OW Parnaby, *Britain and the Labor Traffic in the Southwest Pacific*, Duke University Press, Durham, 1964, pp. 129–120.
17. K Buckley and K Klugman, *The History of Burns Philp: The Australian Company in the South Pacific*, Burns Philp and Co. Ltd, Sydney, 1981, p. 24.
18. In Parnaby.
19. 'Commission to Inquire into the Circumstances Under Which Labourers Have been Introduced into Queensland from New Guinea and Other Islands etc', 1885, *Journals of the Legislative Council*, Vol. 35, Pt 1, 1885, pp. 1342, 1359, 1360.
20. William T Wawn, *The South Sea Islanders and the Queensland Labour Trade: A Record of Voyages and Experiences in the Western Pacific, from 1875 to 1891*, Swan Sonnenschein, London 1893.
21. Wawn, pp. 16–20.
22. Quoted in Clive Moore (ed.), *The Forgotten People: A History of the Australian South Sea Island Community*, Australian Broadcasting Commission, Sydney, 1978, p. 7.
23. Sid Ober interviewed c. 1970, quoted in Moore (ed.), p. 27.
24. Commission, p. 1359.
25. Commission, p. 1358.
26. Commission, p. 1385.
27. Quoted in GC Bolton, p. 251.
28. Quoted in Marilyn Lake and Henry Reynolds, *Drawing the Global Colour Line: White Men's Countries and the Question of Racial Equality*, Melbourne University Press, Melbourne, 2008, p. 151.
29. Quoted in Meaney, 'The End of White Australia and Australia's Changing Perceptions of Asia, 1945–1990', Curran and Ward (eds), p. 103.
30. Noel Fatnowna quoted in Moore (ed.), p. 68.
31. *Johnstone River Advocate*, 20 December 1906.
32. David Hilliard, 'The South Sea Evangelical Mission in the Solomon Islands: The Foundation Years', *Journal of Pacific History*, Vol. 4, 1969, p. 48.
33. *Darling Downs Gazette*, 9 January 1907.

10 A White Australia

1. Russel Ward, *A Nation for a Continent: The History of Australia 1901–1975*, Heinemann Educational, Richmond, 1983, p. 12.
2. *Bulletin*, 5 January 1901.
3. *Sydney Morning Herald*, 26 May 1888.
4. CH Pearson, *National Life and Character*, Macmillan and Co., London, 1893, pp. 50, 85, 344.

5 Charles Darwin, *The Descent of Man and Selection in Relation to Sex*, D Appleton and Co., New York, 1889, p. 182.
6 Thomas G Paterson, J Garry Clifford and Kenneth J Hagan, *American Foreign Policy: A History*, DC Heath and Co., Lexington, 1977, p. 240.
7 In Regina Ganter, *The Pearl-Shellers of Torres Strait: Resource Use, Development and Decline, 1860s–1960s*, Melbourne University Press, Melbourne, 1994, p. 104.
8 David Walker, 'Rising Suns', in David Walker and Agnieszka Sobocinska (eds), *Australia's Asia: From Yellow Peril to Asian Century*, University of Western Australia Press, Crawley, 2012, p. 80.
9 Quoted in Manning Clark, *A History of Australia: The People Make Laws, 1888–1915*, Vol. 5, Melbourne University Press, Melbourne, 1979, p. 191.
10 Quoted in John Bach, 'The Royal Navy in the South West Pacific: the Australia Station 1859–1913', *Great Circle*, Vol. 5, No. 2, 1983, p. 119.
11 *The Herald*, 12 June 1905; See also Stuart Ward, 'Security: Defending Australia's Empire', in Deryck M Schreuder and Stuart Ward, *Australia's Empire*, Oxford University Press, Oxford, 2008, p. 242.
12 In Meaney, *The Search for Security in the Pacific*, Sydney University Press, Sydney, 2009, p. 158
13 *Catholic Press*, 18 June 1908.
14 WE Vincent, 'Au Revoir: The Great White Fleet', *Dubbo Liberal and Macquarie Advocate*, 5 September 1908.
15 *Sydney Morning Herald*, 6 October 1913.
16 Randolph Bedford, *Australia My Beloved Land: A National Song*, Allans, Melbourne, 1909; *Sydney Morning Herald*, 6 October 1913.

11 World War One and its aftermath

1 Stuart Ward, 'Security: Defending Australia's Empire', in Deryck M Schreuder and Stuart Ward (eds), *Australia's Security*, Oxford University Press, Oxford, 2008, p. 243.
2 John Masefield, *Gallipoli*, The Macmillian Company, New York, 1916, p. 26.
3 SS Mackenzie, *The Official History of Australia in the War of 1914–1918, Vol. 10: The Australians at Rabaul*, Angus and Robertson, Sydney, 1939, p. 31.
4 Quoted in Joan Beaumont, *Broken Nation: Australians in the Great War*, Allen & Unwin, Sydney, 2014, p. 29.
5 Quoted in Mackenzie, p. 156.
6 Quoted in Mackenzie, pp. 157–158.
7 Captain John Stanley Cameron, *Ten Months in a German Raider: A Prisoner of War Aboard the* Wolf, George H Doran, New York, 1918.
8 Quoted in Emily Robertson, 'Norman Lindsay and the "Asianisation" of the German Soldier in Australia During the First World War', *The Round Table: The Commonwealth Journal of International Affairs*, Vol. 103, No. 2, 2014, p. 221.
9 Margaret MacMillan, *Peacemakers: Six Months that Changed the World*, John Murray, London, 2003, p. 21.
10 Quoted in Thomas G Paterson (ed.), *Major Problems in American Foreign Policy, Vol. II Since 1914*, DC Heath and Company, Lexington, 1989, p. 52.
11 Quoted in LF Fitzhardinge, *The Little Digger 1914–1952: William Morris Hughes, A Political Biography*, Vol. II, Angus and Robertson, Sydney, 1979, p. 484.

12   WM Hughes to Rt Hon. The Viscount Milner, 3 May 1919, in WJ Hudson, *Billy Hughes in Paris: The Birth of Australian Diplomacy*, Nelson and the Australian Institute of International Affairs, West Melbourne, 1978, p. 101.
13   'Territory of New Guinea', *Report to the League of Nations on Administration of the Territory of New Guinea, from September 1914 to 30th July 1921* in B Jinks, B Biskup and H Nelson (eds), *Readings in New Guinea History*, Angus and Robertson, Sydney, 1973, p. 228.
14   Quoted in Fitzhardinge, p. 396.
15   Quoted in Hudson, pp. 126–127.
16   *Maitland Daily Mercury*, 14 August 1922.
17   Neville Meaney, 'Australia and Japan: A Comparative History', in James Curran and Stuart Ward (eds), *Australia and the Wider World: Selected Essays of Neville Meaney*, Sydney University Press, Sydney, 2013, pp. 144–145.
18   Andrew Gordon, *A Modern History of Japan: From Tokugawa Times to the Present*, Oxford University Press, New York, 2003, p. 154.
19   Quoted in Meaney, 'Australia and Japan: A Comparative History' in Curran and Ward (eds), pp. 136–37 and Neville Meaney, *Towards a New Vision: Australia and Japan Through 100 Years*, Kangaroo Press, Sydney, 1999, p. 73.
20   Gordon, pp. 189, 195, 199.

12   World War Two

1   *Sydney Morning Herald*, 6 October 1913.
2   William Morris Hughes, *The Price of Peace*, Defence of Australia League, Sydney, 1934, p. 78.
3   '*Advertiser* 6/2/1924', in *Battlecruiser HMAS Australia (1) (1910–1924): Wreck Inspection Report*, Office of Environment and Heritage, Maritime Heritage Unit, Parramatta, 2011, p. 32.
4   *Sydney Morning Herald*, 19 July 1923.
5   Quoted in Gavin Souter, *Acts of Parliament: A narrative history of the Senate and House of Representatives, Commonwealth of Australia*, Melbourne University Press, Melbourne, 1988, pp. 302–303.
6   Note by Stanley Bruce, 20 November 1939 in John Robertson and John McCarthy (eds), *Australian War Strategy 1939–1945: A Documentary History*, University of Queensland Press, Brisbane, 1985, p. 143.
7   *Sydney Morning Herald*, 27 April 1939.
8   Peter Cochrane, *Australians at War*, ABC Books, Sydney, 2001, p. 96.
9   *Herald*, 4 September 1939.
10   'Curtin Cablegram 12', 25/11/1942 in Robertson and McCarthy, (eds), p. 205.
11   Joan Beaumont, 'Australia's war: Asia and the Pacific', in Joan Beaumont (ed.), *Australia's War, 1939–45*, Allen & Unwin, Sydney, 1996, p. 29.
12   In FK Crowley, *Modern Australia in Documents, 1939–1970*, Vol. 2, Wren Publishing Pty Ltd, Melbourne, 1973, pp. 50–51.
13   Cablegram from Curtin to Churchill, 23 February 1942 in Robertson and McCarthy (eds), p. 238.
14   Cablegram from HV Evatt to Richard Casey, 13 December 1941, quoted in McCarthy, pp. 216–217.
15   From *Allied Translator and Interpreter Section Bulletin* 60, quoted in Lex McAulay, *Blood and Iron: The Battle for Kokoda*, 1942, Hutchinson, Sydney, 1991, p. 19.

Notes to pages 236–250

16   'Treatment of Prisoners of War by Japanese', 28 April 1942, in Robertson and McCarthy (eds), *Australian War Strategy*, p. 222.
17   'Entries for 22 and 23 December 1941', *Jock MacLean New Guinea Diary, Dec 1941 – June 1942*, ML MSS 1250.
18   Quoted in Chris Coulthard-Clark, *Action Stations Coral Sea: The Australian Commander's Story*, Allen & Unwin, Sydney, 1991, p. 54.
19   Peter Thompson, *Pacific Fury: How Australia and Her Allies Defeated the Japanese Scourge*, William Heinemann, Sydney, 2008, pp. 328, 515.
20   War correspondent Seizo Okada quoted in Peter Brune, *A Bastard of a Place: The Australians in Papua, Kokoda, Milne Bay, Gona, Buna, Sanananda*, Allen & Unwin, Sydney, 2004, p. 242.
21   Brune, p. 420.
22   Kenneth Slessor, 'Cleaning up after the Japanese', in Clement Semmler (ed.), *The War Despatches of Kenneth Slessor*, University of Queensland Press, Brisbane, 1987, p. 381.
23   Hank Nelson, 'Bougainville in World War II', in Anthony J Regan and Helga M Griffin (eds), *Bougainville Before the Conflict*, Pandanus Books, Canberra, 2005, p. 194.
24   Kenneth Slessor, 'The Jungle', in Semmler (ed.), pp. 413–414.
25   *Argus*, 12 January 1944.
26   Garry Kinnane, *George Johnston: A Biography*, Melbourne University Press, Melbourne, 1996, p. 39.
27   George Johnston, *New Guinea Diary*, Angus and Robertson, Sydney, 1943, p. 182.
28   Johnston, pp. 165–169.
29   Quoted in Kinnane, p. 53.
30   *Courier Mail*, 12 September 1942.
31   Osmar White, *Green Armour*, Penguin Books, Melbourne, 1992, p. 204.
32   White, p. 222.
33   Unidentified interviewee quoted in Patrick Lindsay, *The Essence of Kokoda*, Hardie Grant Books, Melbourne, 2005, p. 119.
34   White, p. 205.
35   For an account of the production of the newsreel see Neil McDonald, *Kokoda: Damien Parer's War*, Lothian Books, Melbourne, 2004, pp. 236–239.
36   KS Inglis, *This Is the ABC: The Australian Broadcasting Commission 1932–1983*, Melbourne University Press, Melbourne, 1983, p. 96; Blamey quoted in Johnston, p. 253.
37   Quoted in AA Pirie, *Commando – Double Black: An Historical Narrative of the 2/5 Australian Independent Company Later the 2/5th Cavalry Commando Squadron*, 2/5 Commando Trust, Sydney, 1993, p. 99.
38   Lola Wilkins and Tina Mattei, *Ivor Hele: The Heroic Figure*, Australian War Memorial, undated, Canberra, p. 11; *Adelaide News*, 9 August 1945.
39   Eric Rolls, *Green Mosaic: Memories of New Guinea*, Thomas Nelson, Melbourne, 1977, p. 32.
40   Eric Rolls, 'Signal Station – Shaggy Ridge', in *Green Mosaic*.
41   Quoted in Robert A Hall, *Fighters from the Fringe: Aborigines and Torres Strait Islanders Recall the Second World War*, Aboriginal Studies Press, Canberra, 1995 p. 118.
42   Hall, pp. 173–174, 182.
43   Brian Gomme, *A Gunner's Eye View: A Wartime Diary of Active Service in New Guinea*, Brian Gomme, Nambucca Heads, 1997, pp. 4, 12, 27–28.
44   Ted Fulton, *No Turning Back: A memoir*, Pandanus Books, Canberra, 2005, p. 55.

45 Brune, p. 421.
46 I am referring here to the nation of Australia cognisant of the invasion of Aboriginal territory in the 18th and 19th centuries.
47 Eric Feldt, *The Coastwatchers*, Oxford University Press, Melbourne, 1946, p. 320.
48 Tod Schacht, *My War on Bougainville: War under the Southern Cross*, Australian Military History Publications, Loftus, 1999, p. 127.
49 Quoted in Noah Riseman, 'Australian [Mis]treatment of Indigenous Labour in World War II Papua and New Guinea', *Labour History*, No. 98, May 2010, p. 173.
50 *Jock MacLean New Guinea Diary, Dec 1941 – June 1942*, ML MSS1250, Mitchell Library, State Library of New South Wales, p. 4.
51 'Speech by the Prime Minister, the Hon PJ Keating, MP, Anzac Day, Ela Beach, Port Moresby, 25 April 1992', <www.keating.org.au/shop/item/anzac-day---25-april-1992>.
52 'Declaration by United Nations', Yearbook of the United Nations 1946–47, Department of Public Information, United Nations, New York, 1947, p. 1.
53 Quoted in Lindsay, p. 119.
54 Letter from Curtin to MacArthur 15 April 1942, in Robertson and McCarthy (eds), p. 299.
55 McAulay, p. 13
56 David Horner, *Inside the War Cabinet: Directing Australia's War Effort, 1939–1945*, Allen & Unwin, Sydney, 1996, p. 122.
57 Horner, p. 122.
58 *Canberra Times*, 27 March 1942.
59 William Manchester, *American Caesar: Douglas MacArthur, 1880–1964*, Little, Brown, Boston, 1978, p. 360.
60 Brune, p. 253.
61 Horner, pp. 188–193.
62 Blamey to Chifley, in Robertson and McCarthy, p. 407.
63 Paul Hasluck, *The Government and the People*, Australian War Memorial, Canberra, 1970, p. 624.
64 Schacht, p. 131.
65 James Campbell, *The Ghost Mountain Boys: Their Epic March and the Terrifying Battle for New Guinea – the Forgotten War of the South Pacific*, Crown Publishers, New York, 2007.
66 Hasluck, p. 624.
67 Personal correspondence with family, *Sydney Morning Herald*, 23 April 2018.

13 Governing Papua and New Guinea

1 Geoffrey Searle, 'John Curtin (1885–1945)', *Australian Dictionary of Biography*, <adb.anu.edu.au/biography/curtin-john-9885>.
2 Ben Chifley's national broadcast, 15 August 1945 in FK Crowley (ed.), *Modern Australia in Documents, 1939–1970*, Vol. 2, Wren Publishing, Melbourne, 1973, p. 129.
3 Quoted in Kylie Tennant, *Evatt: Policies and Justice*, Angus and Robertson, Sydney, 1970, p. 182.
4 *Daily Telegraph*, 6 September 1945.
5 Meaney, *Towards a New Vision: Australia and Japan through 100 years*, Kangaroo Press, Sydney, 1999, pp. 106–107.
6 Stuart Ward, 'Security: Defending Australia's Empire', in Deryck M. Schreuder and Stuart Ward (ed.), *Australia's Empire*, Oxford University Press, Oxford, 2008, p. 250.

7 Quoted in Ashley Hogan, *Moving in the Open Daylight: Doc Evatt, an Australian at the United Nations*, Sydney University Press, Sydney, 2008, p. 28.
8 Quoted in Annemarie Devereux, *Australia and the Birth of the International Bill of Human Rights 1946–1966*, The Federation Press, Sydney, 2005, pp. 253–257.
9 Micheline R Ishay, *The History of Human Rights from Ancient Times to the Globalization Era*, University of California Press, Berkeley, 2004, p. 223.
10 *Commonwealth Parliamentary Debates*, 22 November 1946 and 2 August 1945, quoted in Crowley (ed.), p. 126.
11 EH Burgmann, *A White Australia*, 1947, in Crowley, pp. 137–138.
12 Quoted in Meaney, *Towards a New Vision*, p. 107.
13 *Adelaide News*, 3 December 1947.
14 *Sun*, 12 March 1947.
15 *Sydney Morning Herald*, 8 July 1954.
16 Quoted in Marilyn Lake and Henry Reynolds, *Drawing the Global Colour Line: White Men's Countries and the Question of Racial Equality*, Melbourne University Press, Melbourne, 2008, p. 351.
17 Robert JC Young, *Colonial Desire: Hybridity in Theory, Culture and Race*, Routledge, London, 1996, p. 11.
18 Quoted in Young, *Colonial Desire*, pp. 9, 184.
19 Quoted in Young, *Colonial Desire*, p. 7.
20 George W Stocking Jr, *Victorian Anthropology*, The Free Press, New York, 1983, p. 283.
21 *Telegraph*, 22 December 1931 and *Nambucca and Bellingen News*, 16 September 1932.
22 Edmond Marin La Meslée, *Past Explorations of New Guinea and a Scheme for the Scientific Exploration of the Great Island*, Paper Read before the Royal Geographic Society of Australasia, Sydney, 1883.
23 *British New Guinea Annual Report for 1888–89*, in B Jinks, P Biskup and H Nelson (eds), *Readings in New Guinea History*, Angus and Robertson, Sydney, 1973, p. 56.
24 Quoted in Jinks, Biskup and Nelson (eds), p. 101.
25 In Jinks, Biskup and Nelson (eds), p. 99.
26 Lucy Mair, *Australia in New Guinea*, Melbourne University Press, Melbourne, [1948], 1970, p. 171.
27 Russel Ward, *A Nation for a Continent: The History of Australia 1901–1975*, Heinemann Educational Australia, Richmond, 1983, pp. 32, 36.
28 JHP Murray, *Anthropology and the Government of Subject Races*, Government Printer, Port Moresby, [1930], p. 3. Murray had come around to this view much earlier.
29 JHP Murray, *Review of the Australian Administration in Papua from 1907–1920*, Government Printer, Port Moresby, 1920, pp. 32–36.
30 In Jinks, Biskup and Nelson (eds), p. 143.
31 Lucy Mair, p. 142.
32 JK McCarthy, 'The Rabaul Strike', *Quadrant*, 10 Autumn, 1959, p. 65.
33 Kate Fortune (ed.), *Malaguna Road: The Papua and New Guinea Diaries of Sarah Chinnery*, National Library of Australia, Canberra, 1998, p. 31.
34 Judy Tudor, *Many a Green Isle*, Pacific Publications, Sydney, 1966, p. 66.
35 H Ian Hogbin, *Transformation Scene* [1951], Routledge, Abingdon, 2007, p. 276.
36 Papua Annual Report for 1937/38, in Jinks, Biskup and Nelson (eds), p. 135.
37 Hubert Murray, *Native Administration in Papua*, Government Printer, Port Moresby, 1929, p. 22.
38 Quoted in Lewis Lett, *Sir Hubert Murray of Papua*, Collins, London, 1949, p. 305.

39 Peter Hastings, *New Guinea: Problems and Prospects*, Cheshire, Melbourne, 1973, p. 47.

14 Learning from the Pacific

1 Bronislaw Malinowski, *Argonauts of the Western Pacific: An Account of Native Enterprise and Adventure in the Archipelagoes of Melanesian New Guinea*, EP Dutton and Company, New York, [1922], 1960, p. xvi.
2 James McAuley, 'We Are Men – What Are You?', *Quadrant*, 15 Winter, 1960, p. 74.
3 Camilla H Wedgwood, 'Obituary, Alfred Cort Haddon, 1885–1940', *Oceania*, Vol. 10, No. 4, June 1940, p. 463.
4 Roy Macleod and Philip F Rehbock, 'Developing a Sense of the Pacific: The 1923 Pan-Pacific Science Congress in Australia', *Pacific Science*, Vol. 54, July 2000, p. 218.
5 Quoted in Geoffrey Gray, *A Cautious Silence: The politics of Australian anthropology*, Aboriginal Studies Press, Canberra, 2007, p. 7.
6 Gray, p. 13.
7 Kenneth Thomas, 'Lecture notes 20/3/29', in *Sepik Region patrol reports and other papers, 1927–1934*, PMB 1197/Reel 1, Mitchell Library/State Library of New South Wales.
8 'Editorial', *Oceania*, No. 1, Vol. 1, April 1930, pp. 2–3.
9 Quoted in Michael W Young, 'Francis Edgar Williams', *Australian Dictionary of Biography*, <adb.anu.edu.au/biography/williams-francis-edgar-9109>.
10 Doug Dalton, 'Cargo Cults and Discursive Madness', *Oceania*, Vol. 70, No. 4, June 2000, p. 346.
11 Fortune to Murray, 22 April, in Geoffrey Gray, '"Being Honest to My Science": Reo Fortune and JHP Murray, 1927–1930', *Australian Journal of Anthropology*, 1999, 10:1, p. 66.
12 Radcliffe-Brown to Murray, 12 June 1928, quoted in Gray, 'Being Honest to My Science', p. 70.
13 Gray, 'Being Honest to My Science', p. 70.
14 *You and the Native: Notes for the Guidance of Members of the Forces in Their Relations with New Guinea Natives*, Allied Geographical Section, South West Pacific Area, 1943, pp. 1, 2, 8, 17.
15 Quoted in Bill Gammage, *The Sky Travellers: Journeys in New Guinea, 1938–1939*, Melbourne University Press, Melbourne, 1998, p. 10.
16 Gammage, pp. 20–21.
17 Gammage, p. 3.
18 Gammage, p. 3.
19 Lucy Mair, *Australia in New Guinea*, Melbourne University Press, Melbourne, 1970, p. 126.
20 Dan Leahy interviewed in *First Contact*, directed by Robin Anderson and Bob Connolly, Arundel Productions, 1983.
21 Territory of New Guinea *Annual Report* 1933–1934, in B Jinks, P Biskup and H Nelson (eds), *Readings in New Guinea History*, Angus and Robertson, Sydney, 1973, pp. 266–270.
22 Territory of New Guinea, *Annual Report*, 1938–39 in Jinks, Biskup and Nelson, p. 275.
23 *Observer*, 10 August 1929.
24 Margaret Mead, *Growing Up in New Guinea: A Comparative Study of Primitive Education*, George Routledge and Sons, London, 1931, pp. 10–11.
25 Mead, p. 19.

26 Mead, p. 206.
27 Doris Booth, *Mountains, Gold and Cannibals*, Cornstalk, Sydney, 1929.
28 Walter Calov, 'Untitled memoir', original and transcription undated, p. 37. Courtesy of Michael Bell.
29 *Argus*, 1 November 1910.
30 *Cruises to the Pacific Islands and Papua*, Burns Philp and Co. Ltd, Sydney, 1913–1914, pp. 2–13.
31 *Annual Report*, 1912 quoted in K Buckley and K Klugman, *The History of Burns Philp: The Australian Company in the South Pacific*, Burns Philp and Co. Ltd, 1981, p. 269.
32 Kenneth Thomas, *Sepik region patrol reports and other papers, 1927–1934*, PMB 1197, Reel 2, p. 2.
33 Nicholas Thomas, 'The beautiful and the damned', in Ann Stephen (ed.), *Pirating the Pacific: Images of Travel, Trade and Tourism*, Powerhouse Publishing, Sydney, 1993, p. 56.
34 Louis Becke, *The Ebbing of the Tide*, T Fisher Unwin, London, 1895.
35 Gary Osmond, 'The Surfing Tommy Tanna: Performing Race at the Australian Beach', *Journal of Pacific History*, Vol. 46, No. 2, September 2011, pp. 186–187.
36 Gary Osmond, 'Myth-making in Australian Sport History: Re-evaluating Duke Kahanamoku's Contribution to Surfing', in *Australian Historical Studies*, Vol. 42, Issue 2, June 2011, pp. 263–266.
37 *Sun*, 21 January 1913.
38 Gary Osmond, 'The Nimble Savage: Press Constructions of Pacific Islander Swimmers in Early Twentieth Century Australia', *Media International Australia, Incorporating Culture & Policy*, p. 157.
39 Quoted in Warwick Anderson, 'Liberal Intellectuals as Pacific Supercargo: White Australian Masculinity and Racial Thought on the Boarder-Lands [sic]', *Australian Historical Studies*, Vol. 46, Issue 3, September 2015, p. 432.
40 Quoted in Anderson, p. 433.
41 Quoted in Anderson, p. 436.
42 The institution became the Art Gallery of New South Wales in 1958.
43 Bernard Smith to Lucy Hutchinson, 6 December 1957. MLMSS 5202 add-on 1895 2(9).
44 Bernard Smith, *European Vision and the South Pacific*, Oxford University Press, Melbourne, 1989, p. 7.
45 Bernard Smith to Max Harris, 1 July 1960 MLMSS 5202 add-on 1895 2(9).
46 Quoted in Thornton McCamish, *Our Man Elsewhere: In Search of Alan Moorehead*, Black Inc., Carlton, 2016, pp. 254, 262.
47 Edward Said, *Orientalism*, Routledge and Kegan Paul Ltd, London, 1980, p. 12.
48 Edward Said, *Culture and Imperialism*, Chatto and Windus, London, 1993, p. 119.
49 Smith, p. 193.
50 Peter Beilharz, *Imagining the Antipodes: Culture, Theory and the Visual in the Work of Bernard Smith*, Cambridge University Press, Melbourne, 1997, p. 72.
51 Nicholas Thomas, *In Oceania: Visions, Artifacts, Histories*, Duke University Press, Durham, 1997, pp. 44–45.
52 Smith, p. 6.

15 Post-war Australia meets the Cold War Pacific

1 James McAuley, 'The Inception of the Poem', in *Collected Poems, 1936–1970*, Angus and Robertson, Sydney, 1971.

2   James McAuley, 'The True Discovery of Australia', in *Under Aldebaran*, Melbourne University Press, Melbourne, 1946, pp. 66–73.
3   James McAuley, *A Map of Australian Verse: The Twentieth Century*, Oxford University Press, Melbourne, 1975, p. 203.
4   See Michael Ackland, '"A cold coming we had of it": The reception of literary Modernism and Tradition in the work of James McAuley and the Sydney Modernists', *Literature and Aesthetics*, 18 (1), June 2008, pp. 112–121.
5   James McAuley, *Captain Quiros*, Angus and Robertson, Sydney, 1964, p. 15.
6   McAuley, *Captain Quiros*, p. 37.
7   McAuley, *Captain Quiros*, p. 79.
8   McAuley, *Captain Quiros*, p. 82.
9   McAuley, *Captain Quiros*, p. 83.
10 Donald Horne, *The Lucky Country: Australia in the Sixties*, Penguin Books, Ringwood, 1968, p. 29.
11 James McAuley, *The End of Modernity: Essays on Literature, Art and Culture*, Angus and Roberston, Sydney, 1959, pp. 4, 6.
12 Robert Dixon, *Prosthetic Gods: Travel, representation and colonial governance*, University of Queensland Press, Brisbane, 2001, p. 164.
13 Horne, p. 43.
14 Quoted in Cassandra Pybus, *The Devil and James McAuley*, University of Queensland Press, Brisbane, 1999, pp. 123–124.
15 Pybus, pp. 155–157.
16 Quoted in Allan Dalziel, *Evatt the Enigma*, Lansdowne Press, Melbourne, 1967, pp. 2–3.
17 Cameron Forbes, *The Korean War: Australia in the Giants' Playground*, Pan Macmillan, Sydney, 2010, pp. 27–28.
18 Quoted in Richard Trembath, *A Different Sort of War: Australians in Korea 1950–53*, Australian Scholarly Publishing, Melbourne, 2005, p. 96.
19 *Morning Bulletin* (Rockhampton), 2 August 1950.
20 Bruce Cumings, *The Korean War: A History*, Modern Library, New York, 2011, p. 13.
21 Trembath, pp. 2–7.
22 NSC 68 and Dean Acheson quoted in Thomas G Paterson (ed.), *Major Problems in American Foreign Policy, Vol. II, Since 1914*, DC Heath and Co, Lexington, 1984, pp. 311, 426.
23 Quoted in Cumings, p.15.
24 Quoted in Stewart Firth, *Australia in International Politics: An introduction to Australian foreign policy*, Allen & Unwin, Sydney, 2004, p. 35.
25 Quoted in Forbes, pp. 148–149.
26 Quoted in Peter Cochrane, *Australians at War*, ABC Books, Sydney, 2001, p. 200.
27 Cumings, p. 156.
28 In Paterson (ed.), pp. 410–412.
29 Dayton McCarthy, *The Battle of Maryang San, 1951*, Army History Unit, Canberra, 2018, pp. 23–25.
30 Forbes, p. 381.
31 Quoted in Forbes, p. 10.
32 Cumings, pp. 35, 243.
33 See Trembath, p. 180.

16 Confronting communism and decoupling a colony

1. James McAuley, Editorial, *Quadrant*, Vol. 1, No. 1, 1955, p. 3.
2. *(Melbourne) Herald*, 31 October 1950.
3. James McAuley, 'On Being an Intellectual', *Quadrant*, Vol. IV, 13, Summer 1959–60, p. 30.
4. Quoted in Thomas G Paterson (ed.), *Major Problems in American Foreign Policy, Vol. II, Since 1914*, DC Heath and Co. Lexington, 1984, p. 478.
5. Coral Bell, *Dependent Ally: A Study in Australian Foreign Policy*, Oxford University Press, Melbourne, 1988, p. 72.
6. Quoted in Paterson (ed.), p. 574.
7. 'Australia's Military Commitment to Vietnam', report tabled in Commonwealth House of Representatives, 13 May 1975, p. 9.
8. 'Australia's Military Commitment to Vietnam', *Prime Minister's Transcripts No. 3737*, 13 May 1975, p. 9.
9. Bell, p. 70.
10. Quoted in Alan Renouf, *Let Justice Be Done: The Foreign Policy of Dr HV Evatt*, University of Queensland Press, Brisbane, 1983, p. 264.
11. Stephen FitzGerald, *Comrade Ambassador: Whitlam's Beijing Envoy*, Melbourne University Press, Melbourne, 2015, pp. 6, 8.
12. Peter Cochrane, *Australians at War*, ABC Books, Sydney, 2001, pp. 217–218.
13. Quoted in James Franklin, *Corrupting the Youth: A History of Philosophy in Australia*, Macleay Press, Paddington, 2003, pp. 290–291.
14. Alfred McCoy, *The Politics of Heroin in Southeast Asia*, Harper Torchbooks, New York, 1972, pp. 166–170.
15. *Sydney Morning Herald*, 19 March 1966.
16. Quoted in Cassandra Pybus, *The Devil and James McAuley*, University of Queensland Press, Brisbane, 1999, p. 221.
17. Pybus, p. 237.
18. Stephen FitzGerald, *Comrade Ambassador*, p. 95; CP FitzGerald, 'Reflections on the Cultural Revolution in China', *Pacific Affairs*, Vol. 41, No. 1, 1968, p. 59.
19. Quoted in Odd Arne Westad, *Restless Empire: China and the World since 1750*, The Bodley Head, London, 2012, p. 341.
20. E Gough Whitlam, *A Pacific Community*, The Australian Studies Endowment, Cambridge [Mass.], 1981, p. 61.
21. 'Report of the 1962 United Nations Visiting Mission to the Trust Territory of New Guinea', in B Jinks, P Biskup and H Nelson (eds), *Readings in New Guinea History*, Angus and Robertson, Sydney, 1973, p. 382.
22. Quoted in Jinks, Biskup and Nelson (eds), p. 405.
23. Quoted in Jinks, Biskup and Nelson (eds), p. 386.
24. Donald Denoon, *A Trial Separation: Australia and the Decolonisation of Papua New Guinea*, Pandanus Books, Canberra, 2005, pp. 21–24.
25. Donald Horne, *The Lucky Country*, Penguin Books, Ringwood, 1968, p. 120.
26. CDE Rowley, *The New Guinea Villager: A Retrospect from 1964*, FW Cheshire, Melbourne, 1968, p. 11.
27. Horne, p. 137.
28. Rowley, p. 31.
29. Rowley, p. 35.
30. Murray Groves, 'Sacred Past and Profane Present in Papua', *Quadrant*, Vol.1, 3 June 1957, pp. 37–48.

31 James McAuley, 'Australia's Future in New Guinea', *South Pacific*, March–April 1953, pp. 544–556.
32 *New Guinea Diary*, in *The Papers of James McAuley*, 15 July – 5 September 1951, ML MSS 7920 1 (21), p. 30.
33 James McAuley, 'The Clash of Cultures', Address given at First Christian Social Week, 22 May 1956, p. 4 (MLMSS 7920 3 (21).
34 James McAuley, 'My New Guinea', *Quadrant*, Vol. 5, No. 3, 1961, pp. 24–27.
35 James Griffin, 'Papua New Guinea', in WJ Hudson (ed.), *Australia in World Affairs, 1971–1975*, George Allen & Unwin, Sydney, 1980, p. 348.
36 Quoted in Griffin, p. 347.
37 Judith Hollinshed, *Innocence to Independence: Life in the Papua New Guinea Highlands, 1956–1980*, Pandanus Books, Canberra, 2004, pp. 164, 156, 1–5.

17 The end of White Australia, refugees and reassessments

1 James Jupp (ed.), *The Australian People: An Encyclopedia of the Nation, Its People and Their Origins*, Cambridge University Press, Cambridge, 2001, p. 617.
2 PJ Boyce and RA Herr, 'South-West Pacific', in WJ Hudson (ed.), *Australia in World Affairs, 1971–1975*, George Allen & Unwin, Sydney, 1980, pp. 344, 333.
3 Gwenda Tavan, *The Long, Slow Death of White Australia*, Scribe Publications, Melbourne, 2005, p. 200.
4 Quoted in Nancy Viviani, *Nauru: Phosphate and Political Progress*, ANU Press, Canberra, 1970, p. 95.
5 'Phosphate Bounty Bill', Second Reading, *Parliament of Australia Hansard*, 1963.
6 Viviani, pp. 95, 128, 129.
7 Barry Turner (ed.), *The Stateman's Yearbook 2010*, Palgrave Macmillan, Basingstoke, 2009, p. 902.
8 Quoted in WD Forsyth, 'The South Pacific Commission', in Gordon Greenwood and Norman Harper (eds), *Australia in World Affairs 1961–1965*, FW Cheshire, Melbourne, 1968, p. 481.
9 Forsyth, in Greenwood and Harper, p. 493.
10 This is probably Australian dollars. Figures from PJ Boyce and RA Herr, 'South-West Pacific' in Hudson (ed.), pp. 342–343.
11 Kate Greig diary entry 20 March 1929 in *William and Kate Greig diaries and miscellaneous papers, 1870–1962*, MLMSS 3014.
12 Stephen Murray-Smith, quoted in Pirie, p. 62.
13 PJ Boyce and RA Herr, 'South-West Pacific', in Hudson (ed.), p. 341.
14 DCS Sissons, 'Japan' in Hudson (ed.), p. 234 and GC Bolton, 'The United Kingdom', in Hudson (ed.), p. 215.
15 GC Bolton, 'The United Kingdom', in Hudson (ed.), p. 209.
16 Gough Whitlam, *A Pacific Community*, Australian Studies Endowment, Cambridge, [Mass.], 1981, pp. 69–72.
17 Katrina Stats, 'Welcome to Australia? A reappraisal of the Fraser government's approach to refugees, 1975–83', *Australian Journal of International Affairs*, Vol. 69, No. 1, 2015, pp. 70–71.
18 Quoted in Stats, p. 70.
19 Quoted in Stats, pp. 71, 78, 82, 84.
20 Simon Winchester, *Pacific: The Ocean of the Future*, William Collins, London, 2015, pp. 50–51.

21. See Greg Fry, 'Australia, New Zealand and Arms Control in the Pacific Region', in Desmond Ball (ed.), *The Anzac Connection*, George Allen & Unwin, Sydney, 1985, pp. 92, 94, 99, 100, 117.
22. 'Letter to the Editor', *Sydney Morning Herald*, 18 December 1984.
23. Greg Adamson, 'The Rise of the Mass Anti-Nuclear Movement', *Green Left*, Issue 360, 12 May 1999.
24. *Age*, 15 July 1983.
25. *Australian*, 6 December 1986.
26. 'Letter to the Editor', *Sydney Morning Herald*, 27 March 1986.
27. Firth, *Australia in International Politics*, p. 65, Andrew O'Neill, 'Australia and the South Pacific nuclear free zone treaty: A reinterpretation', *Australian Journal of Political Science*, Vol. 39, No. 3, 2004.

18 Pacific solutions

1. Gareth Evans, *Incorrigible Optimist: A Political Memoir*, Melbourne University Press, Melbourne, 2017, p. 99.
2. Paul Dibb, *The Soviet Union: The Incomplete Superpower*, Macmillan Press Ltd, Hampshire, 1986, p. 276.
3. Francis Fukuyama, *The End of History and the Last Man*, Penguin Books, London, 2012, p. 56.
4. Steven Pinker, *Enlightenment Now: The Case for Reason, Science, Humanism and Progress*, Allen Lane, London, 2018, p. 201.
5. Evans, p. 172.
6. Stewart Firth, *Australia in International Politics: An Introduction to Australian Foreign Policy*, Allen & Unwin, Sydney, 1999, p. 263.
7. Evans, p. 129; Firth, pp. 260–262.
8. Evans, p. 129.
9. Evans, p. 108.
10. Evans, p. 122.
11. 'Tabling Statement by Senator Gareth Evans, Minister for Foreign Affairs and Trade, Ministerial Statement on Australia's Regional Security', The Senate, 6 December 1989, <www.gevans.org/speeches/old/1989/061289_fm_regionalsecurity.pdf>.
12. Brij V Lal, 'Fiji Indians', in James Jupp (ed.), *The Australian People: An Encyclopedia of the Nation, its People and Their Origins*, Cambridge University Press, Cambridge, 2001, pp. 438–439.
13. 'Address by Commodore Josaia V Bainimarama Prime Minister and Commander of the Military Forces of the Republic of the Fiji Islands', 62nd Session of the General Assembly, New York, Friday 28 September 2007, *Official Records*, p. 30, <undocs.org/en/A/62/PV.10>.
14. Jeremy MacClancy, *To Kill A Bird with Two Stones: A Short History of Vanuatu*, Vanuatu Cultural Centre, Port Vila, 2002, pp. 153–158.
15. Anthony J Regan, 'Identities Among Bougainvilleans', in Anthony J Regan and Helga M Griffin (eds), *Bougainville Before the Conflict*, Pandanus Books, Canberra, 2005, pp. 418–446.
16. Mark Turner, *Papua New Guinea: The Challenge of Independence*, Penguin Books, Melbourne, 1990, p. 124.
17. Donald Denoon, *A Trial Separation: Australia and the Decolonisation of Papua New Guinea*, Pandanus Books, Canberra, 2005, p. 135.
18. Don Vernon, 'The Panguna Mine', in Regan and Green (eds), p. 260.
19. Hugh L Davies, 'The Geology of Bougainville' in Regan and Green (eds), pp. 27–28.

20 Quoted in Denoon, *A Trial Separation*, p. 135.
21 John Howard, *Lazarus Rising: A Personal and Political Autobiography*, HarperCollins, Sydney, 2010, p. 336.
22 Paul Keating, *Engagement: Australia Faces the Asia-Pacific*, Macmillan, Sydney, 2000, p. 130.
23 Howard, p. 344.
24 Howard, p. 350.
25 Quoted in Tarcisius Kabutaulaka, 'Australian Foreign Policy and the RAMSI Intervention in Solomon Islands', *Contemporary Pacific*, 17:2, 2005, pp. 289–290.
26 Rodd McGibbon, *Pitfalls of Papua: Understanding the Conflict and Its Place in Australia-Indonesia Relations*, Lowy Institute for International Policy, 2006, pp. vii, 6.
27 See Dominic Simonelli, 'West Papuan Independence: Why Australia Should Take a Stronger Stance', *Australian Foreign Affairs*, <www.australianforeignaffairs.com/articles/next-voices/2019/09/west-papuan-independence/dominic-simonelli>.
28 Jenny Hayward-Jones, 'Australia's costly investment in Solomon Islands: The Lessons of RAMSI', *Lowy Institute Analysis*, May 2014, pp. 1, 8.
29 Howard, p. 526.
30 *Sydney Morning Herald*, 19 June 2004.
31 See Kabutaulaka, pp. 283–308.
32 Howard, p. 513.
33 Quoted in Kerry O'Brien, *Keating*, Allen & Unwin, Sydney, 2016, p. 758
34 Quoted in Katrina Stats, 'Welcome to Australia? A reappraisal of the Fraser government's approach to refugees, 1975–83', *Australian Journal of International Affairs*, Vol. 69, No. 1, 2015, p. 78
35 Howard, p. 402.
36 *Report of the Senate Select Committee on a Certain Maritime Incident*, Commonwealth of Australia, 2002, pp. 294–295.
37 *Report of the Senate Select Committee on a Certain Maritime Incident*, pp. 296–299.
38 *Report of the Senate Select Committee on a Certain Maritime Incident*, pp. 299–302.
39 Janet Phillips and Harriet Spinks, 'Immigration Detention in Australia', Parliamentary Library Background Note, 20 March 2013, p. 10.
40 'Excisions from the Migration Zone – Policy and Practice', Parliamentary Library Research Note, No. 42, 1 March 2004, p. 1.
41 Janet Phillips, 'The "Pacific Solution" revisited: A statistical guide to the asylum seeker caseloads on Nauru and Manus Islands', Parliamentary Library Background Note, 4 September, 2012, p. 7.
42 Quoted in Madeline Gleeson, *Offshore: Behind the wire on Manus and Nauru*, NewSouth Publishing, Sydney, 2016, p. 12.
43 Phillips and Spinks, p. 41; Gleeson, p. 12.
44 *Report of the Senate Select Committee on a Certain Maritime Incident*, p. 299.
45 Howard, p. 410
46 *Report of the Senate Select Committee on a Certain Maritime Incident*, pp. xliii–xliv.
47 Jane McAdam and Fiona Chong, *Refugee Rights and Policy Wrongs*, NewSouth Publishing, Sydney, 2019, p. 134.
48 'A Biblical Response', Common Grace website, <www.commongrace.org.au/the_bible_on_asylum_seekers>.
49 Christos Tsiolkas, 'Strangers at the Gate', *The Monthly*, September 2013, p. 22–31.
50 'Budget Speech 2018–19 Delivered in 8 May on the Second Reading of the Appropriation Bill (no.1) by the Honourable Scott Morrison MP, Treasurer of the Commonwealth of Australia', <archive.budget.gov.au/2018-19/speech/speech.pdf>.

51 The Hon Scott Morrison, 'Australia and the Pacific: a New Chapter', 8 November 2018, <www.pm.gov.au/media/address-australia-and-pacific-new-chapter>.
52 Behrouz Boochani, 'Manus Island Poem', *Saturday Paper*, 16–22 June 2018, p. 28.

19 Pacific Islanders in Australia

1 James Batley, DevPolicyBlog, 'What does the 2016 Census reveal about Pacific Island communities in Australia?', 28 September 2017, <devpolicy.org/2016-census-reveal-about-pacific-islands-communities-in-australia-20170928/>; Jonathon Pryke, 'Pacific Islanders in Australia: Where are the Melanesians?', DevPolicyBlog, 8 August 2014, <file:///C:/Users/user/Downloads/pacific-islanders-in-australia-where-are-the-melanesians-20140828.pdf>.
2 *Sydney Morning Herald*, 17 September 2019.
3 Sean Dorney, 'Pacific Games', *Griffith Review*, 53, July 2016, <www.griffithreview.com/articles/pacific-games/>.
4 *Sydney Morning Herald*, 15 September 2015.
5 Tim Elliott, 'The Game Plan', *Good Weekend*, 4 September 2015, p. 8.
6 Quoted in Malcolm Knox, 'Hell Raiser: How Israel Folau lit a fire under the culture wars', *The Monthly*, August 2019, p. 22.
7 Steven Pinker, *Enlightenment Now: The Case for Reason, Science, Humanism and Progress*, Allen Lane, London, 2018, pp. 10, 417–418.
8 Knox, p. 25.
9 *Australian*, 22–23 July 2019.
10 Donald Horne, *The Lucky Country*, Penguin Books, Ringwood, 1968, p. 30
11 Alex McKinnon, 'Blackbirds: Australia had a slave trade?', *The Monthly*, July 2019, pp. 46, 53.
12 Quoted in Marilyn Lake, *Faith Bandler: Gentle Activist*, Allen & Unwin, Sydney, 2002.
13 Letter from Faith Bandler to Mayor Gerry Nolan, 5 March 1992, North Sydney Heritage Centre collection, Stanton Library.
14 Lake, p. 186.
15 See John Singe, *The Torres Strait: People and History*, University of Queensland Press, Brisbane, 1979 p. 216.
16 Eddie Mabo is also referred to as Koiki Mabo.
17 Noel Loos and Koiki Mabo, *Edward Koiki Mabo: His life and struggle for land rights*, University of Queensland Press, Brisbane, 1996, p. 100.
18 Loos and Mabo, p. 118.
19 Loos and Mabo, p. 11.
20 Frank Brennan, *One land, One nation*, University of Queensland Press, Brisbane, 1995, p. 9.
21 Quoted in Brennan, p. 5.
22 Quoted in Brennan, p. 5.
23 Henry Reynolds, *The Law of the Land*, Penguin Books, Melbourne, 1987, p. 32.
24 Quoted in Reynolds, p. 34.
25 Reynolds, p. 41.
26 Loos and Mabo, p. 15.
27 Bryan Keon-Cohen, *A Mabo Memoir: Islan Kustom to Native Title*, Zemvic Press, Melbourne, 2013, p. 3.

20 Climate change

1. Katerina Teaiwa, 'Ruining Pacific Islands: Australia's Phosphate Imperialism', *Australian Historical Studies*, Vol. 46, Issue 3, September 2015, p. 382.
2. Tim Flannery, *The Weather Makers: The History and Future Impact of Climate Change*, Text Publishing, Melbourne, 2005, pp. 84–86.
3. 'Statement by His Excellency Anote Tong, President of the Republic of Kiribati', *The General Debate of the 63rd Session of the United Nations Assembly*, 25 September 2008.
4. *Climate Change 2007: The Physical Science Basis, Working Group 1 Contribution to the Fourth Assessment of the Intergovernmental Panel on Climate Change*, Cambridge University Press, Cambridge, 2007, p. 3.
5. Lynn McGaurr and Libby Lester, 'Australia' in James Painter, *Climate Change in the Media: Reporting Risk and Uncertainty*, IB Taurus, London, 2013, p. 79.
6. 'Australia's assistance – sustainable development', Parliament of Australia website, <www.aph.gov.au/Parliamentary_Business/Committees/Senate/Foreign_Affairs_Defence_and_Trade/Completed_inquiries/2008-10/swpacific/report/c06#c06f90>.
7. *Australian*, 12 December 2009.
8. In Painter, p. 82.
9. *Guardian*, 16 December 2019
10. Malcolm Knox, *Boom: The Underground History of Australia from Gold Rush to GFC*, Viking, Melbourne, 2013, p. 337.
11. Knox, *Boom*, p. xiii.
12. Tim Flannery, *Atmosphere of Hope: Solutions to the Climate Crisis*, Penguin, London, 2015, p. 90.
13. Richard Blewett (ed.), *Shaping a Nation: A geology of Australia,* Australian National University E Press, Canberra, 2012, p. 487.
14. Knox, p. 360.
15. *New York Times*, 20 October 2017.
16. James Bradley, 'Holding on to the Madness: How an infatuation is keeping Adani's mine alive', *The Monthly*, April, 2019, pp. 19–38.
17. Latika Bourke, 'Joe Hockey says wind turbines "utterly offensive", flags budget cuts to clean energy schemes', ABC News, 2 May 2014, <www.abc.net.au/news/2014-05-02/joe-hockey-wind-turbines-utterly-offensive/5425804?nw=0>.
18. Tom Major, 'North Queensland green power options ignored by Federal Government, industry claims', ABC News, 11 February 2020, <www.abc.net.au/news/2020-02-11/north-queensland-renewable-energy-ignored-by-federal-government/11951042>.
19. *Guardian*, 9 February 2017.
20. *The Saturday Paper*, 16–22 September 2017, p. 9.
21. EF Schumacher, *Small Is Beautiful: A study of economics as if people mattered* [1973], Blond and Briggs, London, 1980, p. 11.
22. Cf Naomi Oreskes and Erik M Conway, *Merchants of Doubt: How a Handful of Scientists Obscured the Truth on Issues from Tobacco to Global Warming*, Bloomsbury Press, New York, 2020, pp. 183–215.
23. Bill McKibben, 'A Very Grim Forecast', *New York Review of Books*, Vol. LXV, No. 18, 22 November – 5 December 2018, p. 4.
24. Judith Brett, 'Howard's Heir: On Scott Morrison and his suburban aspirations', *The Monthly*, September 2019, p. 30.
25. *Sydney Morning Herald*, 23 September 2019.

26 Quoted in *The Saturday Paper*, 28 September – 4 October 2019, pp. 1, 10, 15.
27 *Guardian*, 16 August 2019.
28 'Address by the Prime Minister of Australia', 8 November 2018, Prime Minister of Australia website, <www.pm.gov.au/media/address-australia-and-pacific-new-chapter>.
29 'Religion and Ethics Report', ABC Radio National, 11 December 2019.
30 *Sydney Morning Herald*, 27 November 2010.
31 *Guardian*, 10 October 2017.
32 *Sydney Morning Herald*, 17 November 2019.
33 Interviewed by Richard Aide, 'Hot Mess', Radio National, 3 May 2020.
34 *Guardian*, 18 November 2019.

Afterword: Mammon or millennial Eden?
1 Bernard O'Dowd, 'Australia', in Percival Searle (ed.), *An Australasian Anthology: Australian and New Zealand Poems*, Collins Bros and Co. Ltd, Sydney, 1946, p. 135.

Index

Illustrations from the photo sections are indicated by *.ill*

Abbott, Tony 16, 406–407, 412, 417, 423
Aboriginal Australians 1, 6, 45–50, 52–55, 56, 60, 66, 73, 85–87, 99–100, 117, 131–33, 135–36, 138, 181, 188, 190–92, 194, 225, 249, 267, 269–70, 282, 304, 317, 334, 353, 382, 391, 393–401, 418–19, 423, *ill.* 6
Aborigines Protection Act of 1897 48, 190
Aborigines Protection Society 181, 188
Acheson, Dean 318–19
Adams, John Quincy 147, 154, 155, 156
Admiralty Islands 291
Agassiz, Alexander 39–40
Agassiz, Louis 40
American Expeditionary Forces 219–20
anthropology 9, 45–46, 47, 48, 51, 52, 54, 55, 63, 76, 86, 130, 132, 162–63, 166, 190, 268–70, 275, 276, 280–97, 301, 305–306, 309–10, 313–14, 337–39, 359, 398
anti-Americanism 331–32, 349
anti-communism 315–19, 333, 341, 349, 350
anti-war movement *see also* peace movement 331–33
Anzac Day 3, 252, 254
ANZAC Pact 261–62, 345
ANZACs 216, 219–220, 320, 329, 391–92, 410
ANZUS Treaty 319, 326, 345, 355, 356, 372
Aotourou 89
Applethwaite, John 139
Applethwaite, Lucy 139
Arere, Asi 251
Arnhem Land 44, 78–79, 398
Ashbolt, Allan 313
Askew, John 138, 139–40, 268, 295

asylum seekers 345, 349–52, 374–83, 406, 419–20
atomic bomb *see also* nuclear testing 257, 262, 321, *ill.* 33
Audoa, Anthony 378
Australasian Association for the Advancement of Science 281
Australia Station 2, 5–6, 151, 183, 184, 185–87, 189, 196, 210, 212, 213
Australian Broadcasting Corporation 11, 16, 243, 245–46, 385
Australian Imperial Force 215–16, 219–220, 225, 230, 233, 239, 240
Australian Labor Party 201, 252, 254, 315–16, 330–31; 349, 352–53; 354, 356, 360, 368, 374, 375, 377–78, 380–81, 388, 405–407, 409, 410, 411–12
Australian Military Force 239, 240, 250
Australian National Research Council 281–82, 285
Australian National University 302, 303, 325, 338, 339, 355–56, 358
Australian New Guinea Administrative Unit 250, 251
Australian School of Pacific Administration 338, 339, *ill.* 35
Australian South Sea Islanders 391–94
Australian War Memorial 247
Austronesians 45–46, 50–51, 68, 418
Avery, Richard 74

Bainimarama, Josaia 'Frank' 364
Balboa, Vasco de 62–63
Banaba Island *see* Ocean Island
Bandler, Faith 392–94, 395
Banks, Joseph 53, 82–85, 86, 91–92, 93, 110, 120, 172, 301, 303, 398
Barton, Edmund 201, 204, 211, 384
Basedow, Herbert 54–55, 270, 419
Bass, George 109, 120
Batchelor, FS 156

Bathurst, Earl 127
Bavadra, Timoci 363
Bay of Islands 108, 123, 131, 133, 134, 135
Beaglehole, JC 85–86, 302, 304
Bean, CEW 248
Becke, Louis 298–99, 301
Bedford, Randolph 212, 214
Bell, JH 52–53
Berry, Alexander 121–23, 124, 158, 185, 294
Bhagwan, James 416–17
Biden, Joe 14, 422–23
Bikini Atoll 325, 353
birds 30–36, 42, 44, 103–106, 109–10, 413, *ill.* 8, *ill.* 9
Bjelke-Petersen, Joh 399, 400
blackbirding 2, 8, 10, 178–82, 189–202, 267, 347, 363, 391–94, *ill.* 13, *ill.* 14, *ill.* 15
Blackburn, Richard 398
Blackstone, William 398–99
Blackwood, Beatrice 283–84
Blamey, Thomas 245, 246, 256–57, 259
Bligh, William 41, 42, 111, 115–116, 117–118, 121, 122, 124, 151–53, 158
Blumenbach, Johann 138, 158, 268
Boas, Franz 291, 304
Bonwick, James 269
Boochani, Behrouz 383
Booth, Doris 293
Bougainville 29, 89, 240–41, 248, 250, 251, 257–58, 312, 365, 366–68
Bougainville Revolutionary Army 365–66
Bougainville, Louis 79–80, 81, 132–33, 172, 301, 312
Bounty mutiny 41, 42, 121, 151–53, 158
Boyd massacre 122–23, 127, 171
Boyd, Ben 174–77, 393–94
Bramble Cay 37, 41
Brennan, Frank 397–98
Brisbane, Thomas 112
British Commonwealth Occupation Force 262
British New Guinea 271–72, *ill.* 16
Broughton, Betsey 123
Broughton, William 163
Bruce, Stanley Melbourne 232
Brune, Peter 240, 250, 257

Buffet, John 154, 156
Buna 236, 238, 240, 245, 257, 258
Bungaree 132, 133
Burchett, Wilfred 262
Burgmann, Rev Ernest 266, 301–302, 325
Burns Philp 197, 218–19, 236, 273–74, 283, 295–97, 298, 346, 402–403, *ill.* 16
Burns, James 197
Burnside, Julian 351
Busby, James 134–35
Bush, George W 405

Cakobau 187
California 72, 141–45, 149, 176
Call, Sir John 93–94, 96
Calov, Walter 293
Calwell, Arthur 265, 266, 267, 331, 332
Camden, Earl 108
Cameron, John 219
Cameron, Mamie 219
Campbell, Robert 114, 116
Campbell, Rosa Praed 208–209
Canavan, Matt 411
cannibalism 129, 131, 132, 163, 168, 170–71, 172, 240, 277, 297, 389
Cape York 78, 97–97, 190, 198, 208
Carey, Sam 27
cargo cults 284–85, 314
Carteret, Philip 153
cartography *see* mapping
Casey, RG 254
Cash, Michaelia 411
Castlereagh, Lord 122–23
Catholicism 58–59, 60, 61, 66, 125, 137, 164–65, 176, 315, 317, 322, 331, 332, 397, 415
Cebu Island 64, 68
Centennial Park, Sydney 57, 203–204, 422, 423–25
Chalmers, James 46, 192
Chamberlain, Joseph 159
Champion, Alexander 115
Changi Prison 234, 253
Chase, Peter 115
Chaudhry, Mahendra 363–64, 376
Chifley, Ben 261, 316
China 7, 14–16, 29, 45, 68–71, 72, 92, 97, 98, 100, 114–17, 118, 132, 146–49, 170,

Index

189, 196, 206–207, 229–30, 239, 242–43, 301, 317, 318, 319–22, 324–25, 328–29, 331, 333–34, 348, 349, 360–61, 375, 382, 408–409, 416, 422–23
Chinese communities
    in Australia 7, 14, 15, 93, 94, 145–46, 148–50, 189, 205–206, 212, *ill.* 12, *ill.* 19
    in Nauru 217
    in Papua 274–75, *ill.* 25
    in the Philippines 70–71
    in Vietnam 350, 375
Chinese government, protests against 360, 375, 408, *ill.* 2
Chinnery, EWP 288, 291
Chinnery, Sarah 275, *ill.* 24–26
Chisholm, Alec 34
Christian, Fletcher 152, 153, 158
Christianity *see also* Catholicism 9–10, 17, 38, 63–64, 69, 75, 124–25, 130, 132, 133–34, 135, 138, 146, 155, 160–65, 171–72, 178–79, 180, 184–85, 202, 209, 212, 220, 221, 261, 264–65, 268, 284, 317, 336, 340, 353, 354–55, 359, 363, 380, 384, 386, 389–90, 398–99, 415–17
Christmas Island 344, 353, 374
Church Missionary Society 181
Churchill, Winston 232, 234, 235, 252, 255
Clark, CMH (Manning) 45, 325
Clark, Ralph 104, 106
climate change 14, 17–18, 22, 377, 382, 402–21, 423–25 *ill.* 3, *ill.* 41
coal 10, 14, 17–18, 23, 29–30, 141, 203–204, 316, 322, 348, 404, 408–20
Codrington, Robert 162–63
Collingridge, George 56–59, 60, 65, 68, 70, 78, 95, 226
Collins, David 101, 102
Colonial Sugar Refinery 347–48, 363
Columbus, Christopher 62, 63
communism *see also* anti-communism 6, 311, 315–19, 322, 324–28, 350, 358, 359, 413
Congress of the British Association for the Advancement of Science 281
Conlon, Alf 338
conscription 219, 220, 239, 317, 329, 331, 349

continental drift 24–29, 32, 282, 418
convicts 7–8, 29–30, 91, 93–94, 96–97, 99–102, 106–115, 118, 119, 122, 126, 127, 132, 135, 144, 156–57, 160, 175, 303
Cook Islands 153, 343
Cook, James 1, 6, 37–38, 57, 59, 61, 67, 72–73, 82, 83–84, 85–87, 88, 89, 90, 92, 95, 96, 98, 103, 120–21, 127, 133, 136, 153, 303, 312, 396
    statues of 57, 60, 185
copra 289, 338
cotton industry 177, 179–80
Crace, John 237
Craik, George Lillie 129
Cunningham, Peter 130
Curtin, John 231–32, 234–35, 252, 253–55, 256–57, 261
Cusack, Dymphna 325, 356
Cuthbert, Allan 262, 312
Cuthbert, John 186

Dalton, Doug 285
Daly, Reginald 40
Dampier, William 72–75, 77, 78, 79, 89–90, 216–17
Darwin, Charles 9, 25, 26, 30, 38–40, 53, 103, 138, 207, 268, 304
Darwin, George 26
Dauar Island 41, 43, 44
Davidson, JW 302, 303, 325
Davis, Emelda 391, 392
De Groot, Francis 226
Deakin, Alfred 211–12, 234–35
decolonisation 278, 326, 335–36, 341, 343, 344, 345–46, 364, 365, 368, 370, 371, 402
Defoe, Daniel *see also* 'Robinson Crusoe' 74–76, 77, 81, 92, 154
Democratic Labor Party 315–16
Denison, William 157–58, 161
Derby, Lord 192, 194–95, 197
Dibb, Paul 358, 361–62, 373
Diderot, Denis 81, 82, 85, 86–87, 194, 303
Dilke, Charles 195
Dillon, Peter 169, 173–74
Dobu Island 165, 166–69, 281, 285, 291
Doddridge, Philip 153–54
Dorney, Sean 16, 385
Douglas, James *see* Morton, Lord

Douglas, John 190–91
Drake, Sir Francis 72, 73, 116
Du Toit, Alexander 25
Dufresne, Marc-Joseph Marion 89
Dulles, John Foster 325, 326
Dutch imperialism 57, 58, 60, 66–67, 69, 77, 78–79, 92, 98, 234, 290, 369–70

Earle, Augustus 132, 133
East India Company 97, 98, 109, 115, 117, 119, 145, 146, 148, 170
East Indies 58, 92, 148, 233, 271, 286, 370
East Timor 368–73, 376, 378
Edgeworth David, TW 40
Edwards, Edward 41, 152
Eggleston, FW 215, 301, 302
Eisenhower, Dwight D 326
El-Niño South Oscillation 403–404, 420
Eliot, TS 309–10
Elkin, AP 301–302
Ellice Islands *see also* Tuvalu 40, 299
Elliott, Tim 387
Ellis, Albert 403
Enderby, Samuel 115
Eromanga, New Hebrides 169, 171
Erskine, James 196
Espiritu Santo 58, 61–62, 79, 80, 85, 311, 364–65
Evans, Chris 377
Evans, Gareth 357, 358, 360, 361–62, 365, 368, 373
Evatt Foundation 393, 394
Evatt, Herbert 'Doc' 261–64, 266–68, 301–302, 316, 318, 319, 330–31, 345, 361, 376, 393

Farrelly, Midget 314
Federal Council for the Advancement of Aboriginals and Torres Strait Islanders 394, 395, 396
Federation of Australia 54, 193, 195–96, 200, 203–205, 272, 392, 424–25, *ill.* 19
Feldt, Eric 250–51, 252
Fennell, Thomas 176
Fiji 2, 7–8, 46, 50–51, 98, 105, 115, 117, 118, 122, 166, 168, 181, 182, 187–88, 192, 193, 209, 238, 343, 347–48, 362–64, 376, 385, 405, 416, *ill.* 36

Fine, Oronce 65
Firth, Raymond 283, 313–14
Fisher, Andrew 213
fishing 34, 54, 92, 100, 101, 109–10, 131, 154, 189–90, 345, 374, 398
FitzGerald, CP 325–26, 334
FitzGerald, Stephen 329, 333, 334
flax industry 90, 92, 94, 96, 100–102, 103, 108, 110, 127–28, 128–29, 131, 134
Flinders, Matthew 30, 37–38, 42, 43, 67, 109, 132
flogging 112, 126, 127, 274, 293
Fly River 37, 46, 47
Folau, Isileli 'Israel' 17, 386–87, 389–91, 415, 419, 420
football *see* rugby
Forbes, Cameron 317
Fort Denison, NSW 151
Fortune, Reo 166, 285–86, 291
Foveaux, Joseph 111
Fox, Charles 91
Foxall, Edward 171–72, 182
Fraser, Malcolm 349, 350–52, 368
Frayne, Laurence 112
Frazer, James 309–10
Freehill, Norman Randolph 325
French imperialism 8, 66, 67, 79–82, 89–90, 97, 110–11, 136–37, 164–65, 169, 172, 173, 194, 308, 310, 324, 325–26, 329, 353, 364, 365
Fukuyama, Francis 358–60
Fulton, Ted 250, 254
Furneaux, Tobias 89, 90

Gallipoli 3, 5, 219, 225, 242, 250, 254, 362
Garden Island, NSW 185–86, 213
Garnaut, Ross 406, 411
Garrard, Jacob 294
Garrett, Peter 354
Gaskell, Tom 26
Gauss, Clarence 254
German New Guinea 8, 164, 196, 204, 216–17, 222, 223, 237, 271, 273–75, 281, 289, 365, *ill.* 24
Gilbert Islands 402
Gill, William Wyatt 192
Gillard, Julia 377
Gilmore, Dame Mary 33, 34

Index

gold rush 7, 140–46, 148–51, 176, 205, 209, 289, 293
Gombrich, EH 304
Gomme, Brian 249–50
Gondwana 1, 21–25, 27, 28, 29, 35, 36, 53, 54, 409, 420, *ill.* 4
Goodenough, James 2–4, 5–6, 8, 10, 184–85, 186, 188, *ill.* 1
Gordon, Arthur 192
Gordon, Harry 317
Gould, John 104–105
Gove Land Rights Case 398
Great Barrier Reef 30, 37–38, 39–40, 43, 50, 52, 79, 152, 412
Greig, Kate 347
Grenville, William 102
Grey, George 160
Griffin, James 341
Griffith, Samuel 197–98
Groves, Murray 339
Guise, John 341–42

Haddon, AC 190, 281, 397
Hall, Bob 249
Hall, Ken G 244–45
Hand, Gerry 375
Hansen, James 413–14
Hanson, Pauline 379
Hargraves, Edward 142–43
Harris, Max 304–305, 356
Harris, Rene 376
Hart, Jack 259–60
Hartog, Dirk 79
Harvey, Ted 237
Hasluck, Paul 257–58, 259, 335
Hastings, Peter 278
Hawaii 30, 51, 178, 185, 212, 233, 282, 300, 301, 306
Hawke, Bob 352–53, 355, 356, 359, 360, 375–76
Hawkesworth, John 153
Hayden, Bill 355, 358
Hayes, Bully 298
Haylen, Leslie 325
Hayman, May 239
Hele, Ivor 246–47, *ill.* 32
Henry, William 125, 127
Hess, Harry 26

Hideki, Tōjō 229
Hill, Joshua 154
Hiroshima 262, 312, *ill.* 33
HMS *Endeavour* 1, 53, 82–84, 88, 91
HMS *Rattlesnake* 3, 46
Hockey, Joe 411
Hoegh-Guldberg, Ove 412
Hogbin, H Ian 276, 283, 310
Hollinshed, Judith 342
Holt, Harold 267–68, 330, 331, 343, 349
Hong Kong 15, 146, 147, 149, 189, *ill.* 2
Hongi Hika 130–31, 133, 134, *ill.* 11
Hope, AD 309
Hopetoun, Earl of 203
Horn Island 249
Horne, Donald 312–13, 314, 323, 336–37, 344, 390, 412
Howard, John 4, 10, 368–69, 371, 372–76, 378, 379, 380, 382, 388, 405
Hughes, Robert 95, 99, 106, 112, 126
Hughes, William 'Billy' 15, 220, 221–25, 228, 230, 233, 259, 261, 263–64, 265, 273–74, 282, 329
Humabon, Rajah 64
Human Rights and Equal Opportunity Commission 391, 393
Hunga Tonga-Hunga Ha'apai 20–21, 28–29, 30
Hungerford, TAG 262
Hunt, Atlee 273–74
Hunter, John 104, 108–10, 114

immigration, Australian policies *see also* White Australia policy, asylum seekers 4, 149–50, 195, 201, 209, 211, 265–67, 272, 337, 343, 345, 351–52
indentured labour *see* blackbirding
Indo-Australian Plate 21–22, 28
Indonesia 50, 327, 368–70, 374
Institute of Pacific Relations 301
Institute of Public Affairs 408
Intergovernmental Panel on Climate Change 405, 407, 414
International Force in East Timor 368, 371, 372
Isle of Pines 170, 171
Iwo Jima Island 258

Janssen, Willem 57, 58, 61, 66, 78
Japan 6, 68–70, 207–208, 211, 215, 227–29, 230–31, 232, 233–34, 235–38, 239, 242–45, 253, 257, 261–62, 282, 317, 322–23, 348, *ill.* 23
Japanese 208, 239–42, 245–48, 262–63, 266, *ill.* 17
Java 57, 58, 59
Jenkins, Thomas Aloysius 226
Jersey, Earl of 166
Johnson, Lyndon 327, 328, 330, 331
Johnson, Richard 127
Johnston, George 242–43, 244, 250, 251
Juan Fernandez Island 74–75

Kahanamoku, Duke Paoa 300–301, 314, *ill.* 21
Kanaka indentured labourers *see* blackbirding
Karapanagiotidis, Kon 381
Katue, Sergeant 242
Kawashita, Hirokichi 259–60
Keast, Allen 34
Keating, Paul 4, 15, 18, 252, 254, 368–69, 375
Keon-Cohen, Bryan 401
Kermadec Islands 103
Kerry, Charles 294
Kimberley, Lord 187, 188
King, Philip Gidley 101, 102, 107–108, 110, 111, 115, 117, 119, 120, 121, 123, 186
King, Phillip Parker 38
Kingsford Smith, Charles 233–34
Kiribati 5, 344, 345, 376, 402–405, 410, 416, 417–18, 425
Kivell, Rex Nan 303
Kiwai Island 46, 47
Knibbs, SGC 291
Knox, Malcolm 408–409, 410
Kokoda 239–40, 242, 245–46, 250
Kokoda Trail 5, 242, 243–45, 247–52, 256–57, 390–91, *ill.* 29
Korea *see also* Korean War 68–69, 227–28, 324
Korean War 316–23, 327, 329
Kunkel, John 412
Ky, Nguyen Cao 332–33

Lae 237, 240, 247, 248, 276, 339, 419

Lane, William 309
Lang, Jack 226
Lapun, Paul 367
Laseron, Charles 25, 27
Lawes, William 191–92, 294
Lawrence, Peter 285
Le, Hieu Van 351
Leahy, Dan 289
Leahy, James 289
Leahy, Mick 289–90
Lewin, Ross 180, 182
Liberal Party of Australia 380–81, 406–407, 424
Lindsay, Norman 219, 245
Line Island 353
Lomborg, Bjorn 407
London Missionary Society 124–25, 128, 165, 171, 181, 191, 192
Lord Howe Island 28, 104
Lord, Simeon 114, 115, 116–17, 127–28
Los Negros Island 376
Lourandos, Harry 49
Lovejoy, Arthur O 304
Low, Tim 35, 36
Lowah, Tom 249
Loyalty Islands 170, 175
Lucas, Walter 273–74
Lyell, Charles 39

Mabo (High Court case) 397, 400, 401
Mabo, Benny 399
Mabo, Bonita 'Netta' 395
Mabo, Eddie 6, 49, 395–401, 419
Mabuiag Island 190
MacArthur, Douglas 253–57, 258, 320–21, 330, 376
Macarthur, John 117–118, 120, 131
MacGillivray, John 46, 47
MacGregor, William 168, 196, 271
Mackay, Qld 177, 179
Maclaren, Charles 40
MacLean, Jock 236, 251–52
Maconochie, Alexander 112–13
Macquarie, Lachlan 112, 114, 123–24, 125–26, 127–28
Magellan, Ferdinand 62–66, 67, 68, 76, 79, 308
Mahan, Alfred T 211–12

Index

Mai (Omai) 90
Makoto, Saitō 228
Malaita Eagle Force 371
Malaita Island 202, 371
Malaya 233–234, 235, 324, 329
Malinowski, Bronislaw 9, 166, 280, 281, 285
Manila 61, 66, 70, 80, 88, 92, 148, 212
Manly, NSW 299, 300, 314
Mannix, Daniel 315
Manson, Dickie 237
Manson, Marjorie 237
Manus Island 261, 291–92, 376–78, 380, 383
Māori 35, 52, 53, 84, 108, 122–23, 127, 128–37, 138–39, 158, 268–69, 294–95, 343, 384–85
Māori Village (1910 exhibition) 294–95, *ill.* 20
mapping 24, 57, 58, 59, 60, 61, 65–67, 73, 77, 78–79, 82, 286, 289, 400
Mara, Ratu 343, 345, 348
Maré Island 171
Marin La Meslée, Edmond 194, 270–71
Markham, Albert 183–84, 186
Marsden, Samuel 126–27, 128, 130–33, 135, 136, 140, 169, 171
Marshall Islands 218, 223, 353
Marshall, George C 255
Masefield, John 216
Masson, Elsie 281
Masson, Orme 281
Matagi, Suaia 386
Mathews, RH 52
Matra, James Mario 91–96, 99, 101
Mayor, Alfred 40
McArthur, William 188
McAuley, James 19, 308–12, 313–14, 315, 316, 324–25, 332–33, 334, 339–41, 342, 356, 415
McCarthy, Dudley 248
McConnel, Ursula 283–84
McCoy, Alfred 332
McFarland, Alfred 158
McFarlane, Samuel 165
McIlwraith, Thomas 191, 192–93, 194, 195–96, 197
McKenzie Dan 27
McKibben, Bill 413–14, 416

McNiven, Ian 54
Mead, Margaret 291–93
Medlin, Brian 332
Melanesia *see also* Melanesians, New Guinea, Papua, Papua New Guinea 6, 54, 169, 170, 190, 313–14
Melanesian Mission, Norfolk Island 160, 161–62, 177–78, 182–83, *ill.* 18
Melanesians *see also* blackbirding, New Guinea, Papua, Papua New Guinea 46–47, 50, 52, 160–62, 172, 174–78, 270, 304, 337, 385, 418
Melville, Herman 129
Mendaña, Alvaro de 61, 62, 125, 308, 310–11
Menzies, Robert 230, 232–33, 252, 316–17, 319–20, 326–27, 328, 330, 344
Mer Island 6, 40–44, 49, 50, 191, 281, 395, 396–98, 399, 400–401, *ill.* 5, *ill.* 40
Mercator, Gerard 65–66
Meredith, Louisa Anne 130
Micronesia 6, 47, 64, 286, 402, 418
Midnight Oil 354
Miklouho-Maclay, Nikolai 280–81, 284
Millar, TB 356
Milner, Lord Alfred 222–23
Minerals Council of Australia 409–410, 412
mining 10, 14, 17–18, 30, 31, 217, 272, 313, 344–45, 348, 366–67, 376, 378, 403, 408–11, 412, 420, 425
missionaries 2, 5, 17, 46, 124–25, 128, 133–34, 135, 136, 151, 155, 161–68, 169, 170–71, 172, 173, 179–80, 190, 191, 192, 193, 199, 200, 223, 239, 271, 286, 293, 297, 298, 310, 363, 384, 386, 389, 391, 417
Mitchell, Charles 302–303
Monash, Gen. John 219
Moorehead, Alan 305, 306–307
Moran, Patrick 58, 59, 61, 212
Moresby, Fortescue 154
Moresby, John 151, 154, 155, 189
Morgan, Henry 74
Morgan, W Jason 27
Morisette, James 112
Morrison, Scott 10, 14, 17–18, 382, 390, 411–12, 414–18, 423, 424
Morton, Lord 86, 127

Mosman, Archibald 129
Munro, Peter 20
Murdoch, James 228
Murray Island *see* Mer Island
Murray-Smith, Stephen 247, 347
Murray, Hubert 271–73, 276–79, 280, 284, 285–86, 287, 385, *ill.* 27
Murray, James 181–82
Murray, Sybil 276
Musgrave, Anthony 197

Namok, Bernard 396
native title 6, 49, 136, 396–400
Nauru 31–32, 33, 217, 222–23, 238, 343–47, 362, 376–78, 380, 403
New Albion 72, 73–74
New Britain *see also* Nova Britannia 73–74, 78, 148, 165, 194–95, 216–17, 218–19, 224, 236, 239, 242, 250, 258, 259, 271, 286
New Caledonia 28, 29, 39, 45–46, 50–51, 90, 170, 171, 173, 177–78, 362
New Guinea 5, 8, 9, 12, 19, 22, 28–29, 36–37, 41, 42, 44, 45–47, 50–51, 60–61, 63, 67, 72, 73, 74, 78, 88, 98, 162, 164–65, 166, 168, 170, 177–78, 190–98, 204, 216, 217, 222, 225, 237, 241, 242, 243, 244, 246, 248, 250–52, 254, 256, 257, 259, 261, 263, 270–72, 273–276, 280–83, 286, 287–89 290–93, 297, 310, 313, 329, 335–42, 345, 385, 419, *ill.* 5, *ill.* 10
New Hebrides *see also* Vanuatu 98, 163, 169, 170, 175, 183, 193, 199, 284, 286, 297, 364, *ill.* 13
New Holland 66–67, 72–74, 78–80, 84, 88–90, 91, 92, 98, 137
New South Wales *see also* Sydney, NSW 2, 22, 28, 29–30, 52, 57, 67–68, 88–89, 90–95, 97–99, 117, 120, 122–25, 127–28, 131, 132, 134–36, 137–38, 142, 145, 148–50, 155, 156–57, 158–59, 161, 164, 166, 174–75, 186, 187, 188, 195–96, 205–206, 266, 268, 347, 392–93, 420
New Spain 65–66
New Zealand *see also* Māori 1, 5, 6, 24, 28–29, 34–36, 46, 47, 51, 53, 66–67, 79, 84, 88, 90, 92, 93–94, 96, 98, 103, 104, 108, 114, 122–23, 126, 127–40, 141, 159, 160–61, 186, 187, 201, 210, 215–16, 223, 253–54, 258, 261–62, 268–69, 294–95, 319, 320, 326, 329, 343, 344, 345, 346, 354, 362, 366, 371, 384, 385
Newcastle, NSW 30, 112, 138, 141, 268
Nicholas, John 131–32
Nimitz, Chester W 255
Nixon, Richard 333
Nobbs, Charles 159
Nobbs, George Fletcher 159
Nobbs, George Hunn 154–55, 156, 161
Nobbs, Raymond 161
noble savage, idea of the 85–86, 123, 133, 172, 296, 301, 303
Noonuccal, Oodgeroo 249
Norfolk Island 6, 28, 52, 90–91, 93–94, 96–97, 98, 101–13, 114–15, 116, 119–20, 122, 134, 156–59, 160–63, 187, 253–53, 413, *ill.* 8, *ill.* 9, *ill.* 18
Norfolk Island Pine 90–91, 96, 103, 108–109, 119
North, Lord 91
Nova Britannia *see also* New Britain 73–74, 216–17
Nuclear Disarmament Party 354, 356
nuclear testing *see also* atomic bomb 26–27, 325, 352–53
nuclear testing, protests against 331, 353–55, *ill.* 37
Nuyts, Pieter 77

O'Brien, Denis 316–17, 321–22
O'Connor, Mark 36
O'Dowd, Bernard 209, 425–26
Ocean Island 344, 403
Oceania 283, 285
Ogut, Kup 336
Oimbari, Raphael 251, *ill.* 29
Omai 90
One Nation Party 379, 381
Ortelius, Abraham 65, 66
Ova, Ahuia 278

Pacific Islands Company 403
Pacific Islands Forum *see also* South Pacific Forum 405, 416, 418
Pacific Phosphate Company 217
Pacific Plate 28–29, 30, 36

Index

Pacific Solution 345, 374–82, 385, 406, 407, *ill.* 38
Pacific Station, Valparaiso 151, 186, 188
Pacifica Players Advisory Group 386
Paddon, James 173–74, 189
Palm Sunday Peace Rally 354–55, 356
Palmer, Arthur 181
Palmer, George 182
Palmerston, Viscount 137, 147, 148, 155
Pan-Pacific Science Congress 281–82
Pangaea 21, 23
Papakura, Makereti (Maggie) 294–95
Papua *see also* Papua New Guinea 5, 8, 60, 165, 168, 216, 222, 236, 239, 240, 241, 242, 250–52, 254, 256, 271–79, 280, 285, 286–87, 288, 289, 293, 296, 310, 313, 335–36, 337–39, 347, *ill.* 27, *ill.* 29, *ill.* 30, *ill.* 31
Papua New Guinea 3, 5, 8, 39, 251, 252, 286–90, 292–93, 313, 335, 336, 339, 341–43, 345–46, 347, 362, 364–67, 376–78, 380, 381, 385, 395, 396, 406, *ill.* 29
Papuan Infantry Battalion 239, 242
Parer, Damien 244–45, 246, 251
Parker, Robert 27
Parkes, Sir Henry 57, 159, 195–96, 203, 205–206, 209, 225, 265, 319
Parkinson, Mavis 239
Parkinson, Sydney 84
Pascoe, Bruce 48–49
Passi, David 397, 400
Passi, Sam 397, 400
Patagonia 63, 64, 76
Paterson, AB 'Banjo' 191
Paterson, Charles 300
Patey, George 217
Paton, John Gibson 163–65, 166, 172–73, 180, 193–94, 199, 201, 384
Paton, Maggie 164, 165
Paton, Mary 163, 173
Patteson, John Coleridge 161, 162, 182–83
peace movement *see also* anti-war movement 333, 354–56
Pearce, George 217–18
Pearl Harbour, bombing of 229, 233
pearl shell trade 50, 121, 189–90, 395, *ill.* 17
Pearson, CH 206–208, 209

Pere Island 292
Pethebridge, Sir Samuel 217–18
Phelps, Kerryn 424
Philippines 45, 62, 64, 68, 69, 70–71, 72, 114, 212, 255, 258, 286, 319, 326
Phillip, Arthur 57, 67, 94–95, 96–100, 101–102, 106, 107, 108, 109, 127, 159, 396
Philp, Robert 197
phosphate 31, 217, 222–23, 344–45, 347, 376, 403
Pickles, Edwina 20
Piesse, EL 228
Pigafetta, Antonio 63, 76
Pinker, Steven 360, 388–89, 391
Piper, John 111
pirates 72, 73–74, 77–78
Pita, Simogen 336
Pitcairn Island 151, 153–55
Pitcairn Islanders 151, 154–61, 300
Pockley, Brian Antill 217
Polehampton, Arthur 144
Polynesia 6, 8, 47, 86, 125–26, 131, 149, 164, 165–66, 172, 178, 301, 346
Polynesia Company 187
Polynesians 6, 51–52, 83, 84, 90, 103, 119–20, 127, 131, 152, 153–55, 165–66, 177, 180, 301, 304, 314, 346, 347, 384–85, 387, 418
Pomare I 120–21, 169
Pomare II 124–26, 137
Pomare V 137
Pomare, Queen 137
Portuguese imperialism 57–60, 64, 65, 66, 68, 70, 78, 95, 308, 368
Potts, Arnold 257
Practical Justice Initiative 402, 403, 404, 405, 417–18
Prichard, Katharine Susannah 356
primitivism, theories of 48, 49, 132–33, 157–58, 172, 244, 269, 276, 277, 280, 282, 288, 291–92, 296, 301, 304, 309–10
prisoners of war
  Australian 235–37, 239, 244, 247–48, 259, 318, 322
  Chinese 237
  Japanese *ill.* 30

485

Queale, Alan 262, 312, *ill.* 33
Queensland 8, 41, 46–47, 48, 57, 58–59, 137–38, 148, 152, 177–82, 187, 190–94, 196–200, 201–202, 208, 266–67, 275, 293–94, 336, 337, 340, 371, 379, 392–93, 397, 398–400, 409, 411, 412, 415
Queensland Kanaka Mission 202
Quintal, Edward 154, 156
Quiros, Pedro de 58–59, 61–62, 63, 66, 79–80, 125, 308, 364–65

Rabaul 217, 233, 235–38, 239, 240, 255, 258, 274–76, 283, 291, 292, 419 *ill.* 24, *ill.* 25, *ill.* 26
Rabuka, Sitiveni 363
racial discrimination *see also* White Australia policy 7, 9, 10, 131–32, 138, 149–150, 153, 161, 195, 200–201, 203, 209, 224–25, 227, 228, 243, 251, 253, 266–67, 269–70, 275–76, 282, 301–302, 343, 364, 381, 384, 399–400, 419, 422–23
Radcliffe-Brown, Alfred 282–83, 286
Rawlings, William 225
Reagan, Ronald 354
Reeves, Edward 297
refugees *see also* asylum seekers 124, 243, 349–52, 359, 360, 377, 380, 381, 382, 405, 406
Reibey, Mary 114
Reibey, Thomas 169
Research School of Pacific Studies 59, 302, 406
Retes, Iñigo Ortíz de 60
Reynolds, Henry 136, 397, 398–99, 401
Rice, James 397, 400
Ridgway, Matthew 321
Rivett, Rohan 248
Robinson, Hercules 188
'Robinson Crusoe' *see also* Defoe, Daniel 74–76, 85, 92, 99, 107, 111
Rodinia 21, 23
Rogers, Woodes 74–75
Rolls, Eric 143, 248
Roosevelt, Eleanor 265
Roosevelt, Franklin 221, 255, 256
Rosenthal, Joe 258
Ross, Robert 102, 105–107, 111
Rowell, Sydney 257

Rowley, CD 338
Ruatara 133
Rudd, Kevin 13, 377–78, 381, 405–406, 407
rugby 278, 384–87, *ill.* 39
Ruhen, Olaf 34
Ruska, Kathleen 249
Ryūkyū Islands 69

Sahul 22–23, 37, 41, 44, 45
Said, Edward 306
Salamaua 237, 247
Salee, Celuia 397, 400
same-sex marriage, referendum on 16, 387–89, 420, 424
Sammut, Andrew 390
Samoa 45–46, 50–51, 75, 165, 166, 194, 238, 291, 300, 343, 362, 385, 386
San Francisco 40, 141–42, 144, 145, 219, 263
sandalwood trade 7–8, 105, 115, 117–19, 121–22, 148, 169–71, 173–74, 189
Santa Anna 116–17
Santa Cruz Islands 2, 61–62, 183, 184, 194
Santamaria, BA 315, 332
Sarawia, George 162
Saunders, Reg 317
Schacht, Tod 250, 251, 254, 258
Schöner, Johannes 64, 65
Schumacher, EF 413, 415, 416, 424
Scott, Edmund 71
Scott, Monty 208
Scott, Sir Walter 78
sealing 7, 105, 116, 117, 119, 129, 145, 148
Searle, Geoffrey 261, 305
Seebohm, Henry 32
Seeley, Sir John 195
Selborne, Earl of 210–11
Selkirk, Alexander 74–75
Selwyn, George Augustus 160–61, 178
Semu, Greg 386, *ill.* 39
September 11, 2001 372, 373, 374, 379
Serong, Francis 'Ted' 327
Serventy, Dominic 34
Service, James 193
Seuss, Eduard 23–24, 25, 53
Seward, William 147
Sharland, Michael 32, 34, 35

Index

Sheridan, Greg 13
Silk, George 245, 251, *ill.* 29, *ill.* 30, *ill.* 31
Singapore 148, 231–32, 233–35, 244, 252, 324
Sir Edward Pellew Islands 50
slavery 2, 3, 9–10, 127, 133–34, 149, 180–82, 193, 198, 199, 223, 256, 265, 318, 391–94
Slessor, Kenneth 240, 241–42, 244, 245, 246
Smith, Bernard 8–9, 86, 132, 172, 302–308, 310, 325
Society Islands 28
Sogavare, Manasseh 371, 372
Solomon Islands 2, 29, 8, 61–62, 125, 166, 176, 183, 193, 194–95, 199, 201–202, 238, 286, 293, 296, 297, 300, 310–11, 362, 371–73, 418
Somare, Michael 341, 364
South Australia 77, 107, 136, 137, 150, 156, 351, 353
South East Asian Treaty Organization 326, 327–28
South Pacific Commission 345, *ill.* 34
South Pacific Forum *see also* Pacific Islands Forum 345–46, 362
Spanish imperialism 58, 60–72, 74, 78, 80, 88, 116, 141, 146, 185, 211–12, 308
Spate, OHK (Oskar) 59–60, 62, 66, 302
Spencer, Herbert 207, 268
Spender, Percy 319, 327
St Thomas's Anglican Church Cemetery 2, 3, 185, *ill.* 1
Staniforth Smith, Miles 272, 273
Stanley, Owen 3, 5–6
Stanner, WEH 55, 281, 310, 398
Stephens, Philip 88
Stettinius, Edward 264
Stevens, Jimmy 365
Stevenson, Robert Louis 75
Stewart, Douglas 309
Stirling, Frederick 183
Strack, Mary 142
Strehlow, Ted 55
Sturdee, Vernon 236, 255
Suess, Eduard 23–24, 39, 53
sugar industry 8, 92, 177, 179, 181, 187, 192, 197, 198–200, 202, 322, 347–48,
363, 381, 384, 392, 393, 419, *ill.* 21
Suharto 369
surfing 155, 299–300, 301, 314–15, 385, *ill.* 21
Swift, Jonathan 24, 77–78, 79, 81, 154
Sydney, NSW 1–3, 6, 11, 20, 22, 29–30, 38, 46, 52–53, 56–58, 75, 94–95, 100–103, 104–105, 106, 109, 110, 111, 112, 114–19, 120, 121–24, 125, 129–34, 138, 139, 142, 144, 151, 158, 163, 164, 165–66, 169–71, 173–76, 180, 182, 184–86, 193, 194, 203–206, 210, 212, 213, 216, 225, 226, 228, 230–31, 238–39, 280, 281–82, 292, 294–95, 298, 299–300, 330, 338, 343, 350, 384–85, 386, 393, 396, 403, 407, 409, 415, 422, 423–24, *ill.* 1, *ill.* 2, *ill.* 41
Sydney, Lord 93–94, 95, 99–100, 101, 109, 112, 118

Tabua, Robert 336
Tahiti 1, 7–8, 38, 50–51, 53, 80–87, 89, 90, 98, 103, 119–21, 124–28, 130, 132–33, 136–37, 151, 153, 154, 156, 159, 169, 186, 216, 312
Tampa 374–75, 376, 379
Tanna, Tommy 299, 314, 419
Taonui 136
Tarawa Island 245, 258, 285, 286, 402
Tasman, Abel 66–67, 79, 89
Tasmania *see also* Van Diemen's Land 22, 24, 25, 27, 34, 44, 89–90, 110, 111–12, 119, 122, 141, 142, 160, 164, 269, 329, 332, 333, 339, 341, 387
Taylor, Jim 288, 290–91
Teach, Edward 74
Terra Australis 58, 65, 72, 73, 79, 84, 308–309
terra nullius 49, 136, 396–401, *ill.* 40
Thévenot, Melchisédech 66–67, 73
Thom, Margaret 294–95
Thomas, Kenneth 282–83, 288, 297
Thomson, Basil 297
Thorpe, Harry 225
Thunberg, Greta 416
Thursday Island 40, 190, 191, 208, 216, 249, 281, 396
Thurston, Kathleen 250

487

Tinney, Jane 165–68, 172, 281, 283–84, 286
Toga, Apisai 385
Tong, Anote 404–405
Tonga 20, 46, 86, 145, 194, 343, 384, 385, 386, 390, 391
Torres Strait 6, 36, 37, 41, 42, 47, 61, 67, 88, 148, 189, 249
Torres Strait Islanders 6, 46, 48, 49, 168, 190–91, 249, 281, 391, 394–98, 400, 419, *ill.* 6
Torres Strait Islands 3, 8, 190–91, *ill.* 5
Torres, Luis Vaez de 59, 61, 63, 67, 78, 80
Towns, Robert 148, 173–74, 176–77, 179–80, 189, 199
Townshend, Thomas *see* Sydney, Lord
Townsville, Qld 177, 189–190, 191, 197, 371, 382, 395, 396
Trobriand Islands 9
Truman, Harry S 319, 320, 320, 328
Trump, Donald 12–14, 16, 319, 321, 414, 415–16, 422–23
Tschaun, Karl 402–403
Tsiolkas, Christos 381–82
Tsuyoshi, Inukai 228
Tudor, Judy 275–76
Tupaia 83, 84
Turnbull, Malcolm 13, 382, 406, 412, 424
Tuvalu *see also* Ellice Islands 40, 299, 345, 406, 416, 417, 423–24, 425

Ulufa'alu, Bartholomew 371, 372
Uluru Statement from the Heart 53
Underwood, James 114, 115
United Nations 12, 253, 263–65, 266, 267, 335, 343, 344, 345, 364, 398–99, 416
United States 6, 12–13, 14, 15, 18, 40, 58, 70–71, 115, 141, 144–45, 177, 180, 189–90, 203, 204, 206, 207, 211–12, 213, 221, 227, 229, 234–35, 238, 240–41, 242–43, 245, 249, 252, 253–59, 261–62, 263, 264, 265, 267, 275, 281, 282, 286, 287, 301, 317–20, 322, 325, 326–32, 333, 336, 341, 345, 348, 349, 353–55, 360–61, 362, 369, 372–73, 402–403, 405, 407, 422
University of Sydney 59, 228, 282, 283, 288
USSR 259, 261, 263, 264, 315, 317, 324, 349, 358, 361–62

Van Diemen's Land *see also* Tasmania 66–67, 77, 78–79, 89–90, 97–98, 110, 134, 137–38, 156–57, 160
Vanuatu *see also* New Hebrides 5, 8, 28, 46, 163, 284, 362, 364–65, 392
Vaugondy, Didier Robert de 79
Veale, Lionel 249, 250
Vernon, Don 367
Vietnam War 317, 321, 323, 325, 327–34, 341, 349–50, 351, 368, 375, 380
Vietnam, refugees from 349–352
Villalobos, Ruy López de 60–61, 62
Vunipola, Billy 390

Waier Island 41, 43, 44
Waitara, NSW 294
Waitz, Theodor 268, 269
Walker, Kath 249
Walker, Richard L 325
Walker, Tommy 300
Wallace Line 36
Wallis, Samuel 81–82, 153
Warburg, Aby 303
Ward, Eddie 338
Warner, Denis 324
Watlin, Thomas 303
Watson, John Christian 201, 269
Wavell, Archibald 234
Wawn, William 198–201
Wedgwood, Camilla 283–84, 310
Wegener, Alfred 24–25, 26, 53, 282
West Papua 369–70, 373–74
West, Claude 300
Westall, William 306
Western Samoa 343, 362
whaling 108, 114–15, 119, 129, 145, 169, 173, 174–75
White Australia policy 11, 15, 150, 224–25, 262–63, 265–68, 275, 301–302, 331, 340, 343, 363, 381, 419, *ill.* 19
White, Osmar 243–44, 245
Whitlam, Gough 15, 333–35, 341–42, 343, 345–46, 348–50, 353, 361, 368, 380, 381, 390, 399–400
Whittington, George 251, *ill.* 29
Wickham, Alick 300–301
Wilberforce, William 127, 149, 181
Wilkie, Andrew 373

Index

William Hyde 138–39
Williams, FE 47, 284, 286–87
Williams, Freddie 299
Williams, John 171
Wilmot, Chester 243, 244, 245
Wilson, Woodrow 220–22, 223, 256, 263
Wood, George Arnold 59, 70
Woodford, CM 297
Woof, Ada 225–26
Woof, William 225
wool industry 117, 131, 134, 203–204, 313, 320, 322, 348
Worgan, George 99–100
World War One 3, 8, 204, 215–29, 329, 344, 362, 415

World War Two *see also* Kokoda Trail 5, 230–60, 286, 317, 320, 321, 328–29, *ill.* 28, *ill.* 29, *ill.* 30, *ill.* 31, *ill.* 32, *ill.* 33
Wright, Judith 34, 309
Wyatt, Ben 353

Yaobang, Hu 360
Yates, Arthur 294
Young, George 93
Young, John 161

Zheng He 70